# STUDIES IN
# WORD-ASSOCIATION

EXPERIMENTS IN THE DIAGNOSIS OF
PSYCHOPATHOLOGICAL CONDITIONS
CARRIED OUT AT THE PSYCHIATRIC
CLINIC OF THE UNIVERSITY OF ZURICH

UNDER THE DIRECTION OF
## C. G. JUNG, M.D., LL.D.
(FORMERLY OF THE UNIVERSITY OF ZURICH)

AUTHORIZED TRANSLATION BY
### DR. M. D. EDER

I0085301

ISBN: 978-1-63923-792-0

Printed: March 2023

Published and Distributed By:
Lushena Books
607 Country Club Drive, Unit E
Bensenville, IL 60106
www.lushenabks.com

ISBN: 978-1-63923-792-0

# TRANSLATOR'S PREFACE

THIS book is a translation of a series of papers on the results of the association method applied to normal and abnormal persons, which appeared in the *Journal für Psychologie und Neurologie* (vols. iii–xvi) and were afterwards collected into two volumes.

The experiments were carried out at the instance and under the guidance of Dr. Jung. The work which Drs. Jung and Riklin published in 1904 gave an entirely new direction to association experiments. The principle of mental association is, of course, of reputable antiquity : " Do you not know, then, that lovers when they see a lyre, or a garment, or anything else which their favourite is accustomed to use, are thus affected ; they both recognize the lyre and receive in their minds the form of the person to whom the lyre belonged." [1]

Its experimental phase begins with Galton's work in 1879 and Wundt's in 1880.

The new departure which we owe to Dr. Jung is the application of the association method to *unconscious* mental processes ; the theory of unconscious complexes was developed by these experiments ; the results obtained by Freud's psycho-analytic technique were confirmed by the use of a very different method.

This confirmation by experimental methods compelled many who had hitherto looked askance at the psycho-analytic theory of the unconscious to investigate the phenomena for themselves. These studies in word-association have now acquired a permanent place in the historical development of this theory. Every serious student of psychology, every educationist, every one who wishes to engage in the study or treatment of morbid mental processes, will find in these " Studies " a storehouse of facts which will serve not only as a solid basis for his own studies but also as a starting-point for further research.

It was a most arduous and delicate task to establish objective criteria by which unconscious complexes could be recognized. Much thought and great ingenuity went to the discovery of these

[1] The *Phædo*.

" complex indicators " as they are called, and the resulting theses as elaborated in this work by Dr. Jung and his collaborators have all been found to be reliable.

Since the beginning of this work in 1904 it has been extremely productive in many different directions and is still reaping a rich harvest. Its application to education has been made quite recently ; here we may hope to establish some standard tests for normal and abnormal children, which will be complementary to the intellectual tests standardized by Binet.

In the investigation of nervous and mental disorders the association method is still opening up new paths, as seen, for instance, in the remarkable investigations by Dr. Josef Lang on familial associations in cases of schizophrenia.

I cannot refrain from pointing out that the germ of some of the views recently developed by Dr. Jung can be found in these early studies.

The work on association among normals had led to the establishment of psychological types. There are certain obvious relationships between the " objective " type here described in chapter ii and his later " introversion " type, and again there are certain resemblances between the " egocentric " type of the experiments and the " extraversion " type of the later view.

Indeed, in Dr. Jung's most recently published work (" Psychology of the Unconscious Processes," in *Analytical Psychology*, 1917), a foot-note (p. 405) indicates that psychology is not limited to two types : " other possibilities are known to us " ; this is perhaps a return to the position of these experiments where six principal types are described.

The extraverted and introverted types are, of course, not strictly comparable with the earlier types described in this work, but there are certain fundamental common qualities.

Again, Dr. Jung's introduction of an energic view-point into the psychology of the unconscious (paper given before the Thirteenth International Medical Congress in London, 1913) is foreshadowed in chapter vii, " On Psycho-Analysis and Association Experiments," written in 1906, in which Jung ascribes a patient's obsessional ideas to the locking up of energy, whilst the strengthening of the will, transferring this energy to new channels, is regarded as the chief therapeutic aim.

The results of the experiments on familial associations must, one imagines, have contributed to the formulation of Jung's conception of the composition of the *persona* and the composition of the collective psyche.

I have endeavoured in the translation to give the ideas of the different contributors as clearly and literally as possible. In a number of illustrative examples of word-associations, when clang-associations, assonances, alliterations, or rhymes occur impossible of literal translation, I have substituted reactions from my own experiments or constructed reactions on the lines of the original model. This nowhere impairs the interpretation or understanding of the text, and it has not been considered necessary to note these substitutions. In a few cases the German has been retained, a translation of the word being also given.

As the series of words used in Zurich does not altogether suit English requirements, I subjoin a list of words modified from Dr. Jung's list, of which I have made considerable use.

| | | | |
|---|---|---|---|
| 1. head | 26. blue | 51. frog | 76. wait |
| 2. green | 27. lamp | 52. try | 77. cow |
| 3. water | 28. carry | 53. hunger | 78. name |
| 4. sing | 29. bread | 54. white | 79. luck |
| 5. dead | 30. rich | 55. child | 80. say |
| 6. long | 31. tree | 56. speak | 81. table |
| 7. ship | 32. jump | 57. pencil | 82. naughty |
| 8. make | 33. pity | 58. sad | 83. brother |
| 9. woman | 34. yellow | 59. plum | 84. afraid |
| 10. friendly | 35. street | 60. marry | 85. love |
| 11. bake | 36. bury | 61. home | 86. chair |
| 12. ask | 37. salt | 62. nasty | 87. worry |
| 13. cold | 38. new | 63. glass | 88. kiss |
| 14. stalk | 39. habit | 64. fight | 89. bride |
| 15. dance | 40. pray | 65. wool | 90. clean |
| 16. village | 41. money | 66. big | 91. bag |
| 17. pond | 42. silly | 67. carrot | 92. choice |
| 18. sick | 43. book | 68. give | 93. bed |
| 19. pride | 44. despise | 69. doctor | 94. pleased |
| 20. bring | 45. finger | 70. frosty | 95. happy |
| 21. ink | 46. jolly | 71. flower | 96. shut |
| 22. angry | 47. bird | 72. beat | 97. wound |
| 23. needle | 48. walk | 73. box | 98. evil |
| 24. swim | 49. paper | 74. old | 99. door |
| 25. go | 50. wicked | 75. family | 100. insult. |

Finally, the grateful thanks of all students of psychology are due to Mrs. Harold F. McCormick, whose generosity has enabled this translation to be produced.

M. D. EDER

# CONTENTS

# UPON THE SIGNIFICANCE OF ASSOCIATION EXPERIMENTS

## By PROFESSOR BLEULER

EVERY psychical activity rests upon the interchange of the material derived from sensation and from memory traces, upon *associations* ; apart from the somewhat questionable capacity to perceive pain and pleasure which is perhaps inherent in the smallest organism, even in the atom, any psychical activity without association is unthinkable. The investigation of association activity is, therefore, of fundamental importance for psychology in general, and peculiarly so for psychopathology in particular.

The sensations chiefly studied up till now [1] vary but little from individual to individual ; even in psychopathology, apart from gross analgesic disturbances, hallucinations, and illusions, they are of slight importance.

Variations in emotions are, on the contrary, so great that there can be no agreement about what is normal. Is it not still debated whether the absence of moral feeling is to be regarded as a disease or not ?

Memory, so far as concerns the building up and the maintenance of its dynamic traces, is still entirely unapproachable, and the accessible part of the function, the capacity for recollection, rests chiefly upon the activity of association ; thus an understanding of the anomalies of recollection can only be arrived at when the function of association is accurately known.

The will, despite all attempts, seems almost to elude psychological investigation. A man's psyche can be fully described without making use of this vague concept. Psychopathology frequently ignores the will altogether. The facts, which lie behind the abstraction termed the will, can be traced back to the centrifugal tendencies which dwell within the elemental and complex psychical structures ; according to this very plausible conception the resultant of all these tendencies is the will.

[1] I omit naturally the many mere speculations about will, emotion. etc., which prove nothing.

It has indeed been maintained that the will cannot possibly be the resultant of strivings supporting and opposing one another ; for the resultant of the desire to skate and the desire to write an article is a something inconceivable, at any rate a something which could never lead to a choice.  If I have one wish to go east and another to go south, I do not go south-east but walk east or south.

This conception of a psychical resultant is quite absurd.  It is not a question of the resultant of diverse directions of the desires, but of the resultant of the desires themselves.  As an illustration :  a railway train comes to a station where many lines intercross, and thus its further course will be determined by the points.  Suppose there are various persons whose interests would send it in different directions ; it is to the interest of any one person to have his points open and all the others closed ; the strongest achieves his aim.  When the points are fixed the train moves in the desired direction ; the wishes of the other persons have become ineffective unless they make them good at a subsequent station.  There can be no question of a resultant of these different directions.  The resultant can only express itself positively, not negatively, in the choice of points ; the opening of the points is analogous to the decision of the will.

A compromise between the different strivings is only thinkable as resulting from some reciprocal influence, acting directly, or in such a way that both act upon a third (e.g. upon the ego-complex), i.e. they associate with it.  The " will " can be likewise explained by the activity of association ; at any rate, at the moment of our investigation association offers the most adequate explanation.

In our observations on the psyche we come upon the process of association again and again.  Everything else in these investigations is found to be subordinate to association.

It is self-evident that a number of other mechanisms condition the play of our psyche.  *Dynamic* differences in the individual presentations must play a great part.  If the train in our illustration is very heavy or very rapid it will be more difficult to turn it aside from its direction.  The strength of the desires themselves can be conceived as dynamic qualities, but we are not compelled to make such an assumption.  The *number* of factors which control the points (i.e. the number of associated individual presentations which form the presentation complex) can be just as well the determining condition as the dynamic relationship of the presentations.  Thus the entire psychic mechanism could be conceivably explained solely in terms of association.  On the other hand, we have at present no fixed point from which to determine the relative strength of a presentation. What we usually regard as such is decomposed into the number of the associative elements, and the " strength " of the accompanying feelings ; the strength of the feelings themselves can only be recognized by their effects, inhibitory and stimulating, upon the associations.

The function of attention has usually received a dynamic explanation, but this is never convincing ; what we really observe in alterations of attention are alterations in the number and direction of the associations.

Association is a fundamental phenomenon of psychical activity. Perception, thinking, doing, cease as soon as association is impeded. This process may be conceived physiologically quite as well as psychologically, and, in both, closely unites the psychical with the (other) neurophysiological functions.

The passage of a sensory stimulus to the motor part of the reflex arc is, in principle, the same process as we must assume occurs in the physiological processes that run parallel with the psychical events. The analogy becomes much stronger if the effects of several (simultaneous) stimuli upon the reflex process are considered. Simultaneous stimuli can, it is known, evoke reflexes which take their course quite independently of one another ; these stimuli do not associate with one another. Others, even when they arrive at remote parts of the spinal cord, can produce a (simultaneous) reflex process inhibiting or affecting the path. Here the stimuli must in some way flow together or act upon one another by a process comparable with induction ; they form inter-associations.

In psychical associations current processes generally link up with memory-traces, which are revivified by the association process. But there is no difference in principle from the reflex associations, for even here the after-effects of previous experiences are demonstrable and may be compared with the function of memory.

It is self-evident that associations lie at the foundation of sensation (so far as it is conscious), i.e. the connexion of the inflowing nerve stimulus with processes which represent the psyche. If this connexion is inhibited, whether reflexly in the lower centres or in the higher regions by distraction of the attention or by any kind of psychical anæsthesia, no sensation occurs.

Perception is always understood as association of the new sensation with memory-traces of earlier experiences. At the sight of a man, of a house, we have colour sensations in definite relationships and forms ; we have had similar sensations in connexion with a great number of other houses and men which make up the concept man or house. These other elements are aroused by the new sensation, and so we interpret the sensation as the image—of a man—of a house ; we " perceive " the men, the house.

That our laws of thought are but rules of association processes is strangely enough still contested. And yet law of thought and law of association must seem almost identical once it is realized that the law of association is not so simple as to be exhausted by a few shibboleths (association by similarity, contrast, simultaneity, relationship). *Every association in real thinking is accompanied by an almost endless number of more or less distinct presentations ;* at first those of the whole personality with its inner and outer past so far as this can come into consideration ; next a hierarchy of purposeful presentations insufficiently worked up for thought. First of all comes the general aim of our endeavour, then the aim of our thought in the particular case, then all the aims which give the special direction of our thinking and doing, right down to the aim of the thought expressed or the movement undertaken at the moment. Earlier experiences also have their effect in the measure in which they were recently real for our psyche and, *ceteris paribus*, can be more easily associated than others. This factor is termed a constellation. Of great importance also are the moods which supply adequate, or inhibit contrary associations, and much else which it would be too lengthy and tedious to enumerate. When, e.g., I am writing about associations there is at work in the background first of all that portion of my personality interested in scientific research, then my whole scientific and especially my psychiatric past ; in addition, the special call to this piece of work must always be present in condensed form. I must have before me not only the general aim of writing about associations, but at every moment some survey of all that preceded and all that is yet to come. It is self-evident that a mass of detail can be determined by the accidental experience of the immediate past ; in the same way it is equally clear that I am most inclined to think (and to say) those things which are coloured in any way by some affect (some special interest, some polemic, etc.). Physical feelings, fatigue, feeling fit, etc., also enter into this, since these induce me now to shorten, now to expand, and so on.

The affects and physical feelings exert much greater influence upon the associations in all that concerns decision and action.

*Thus in the activity of association there is mirrored the whole psychical essence of the past and of the present, with all their expe-*

*riences and desires. It thus becomes an index of all the psychical processes which we have but to decipher in order to understand the complete man.*[1]

The evaluation of the associations becomes, however, extremely difficult amid the ordinary complicated relationships. Although we are often able to make the diagnosis of a specific mental disease from a letter, from the repetition of a story, and even place certain types among normals by such tests—yet for a methodological experimental study such complicated series of associations are for the present but ill adapted.

The simplest associations readily accessible for our study are to be found in *perceptions,* i.e. the union of a sensation with those memory-images which render possible the interpretation of a sense-impression.

But, like the sensations, the perceptions can have no marked degree of variation if the relationship to the outer world is not to be seriously damaged. They only occur in a few combinations—does the same sensation ever condition the same perception ?—and by constant practice become so fixed that more marked deviations seldom occur within the normal (e.g. when the stimulus is too faint or too brief, or the affect too pronounced) ; even in a series of severe mental disorders the process of perception is but little disturbed as judged by our present methods of observation. In the present state of our knowledge we must not expect the ripest harvest, even although Kräpelin's experiments on perception have shown that much valuable knowledge is to be gained about the intoxications.

Most is gained, as previous experiments have shown us, when the association is quite free, and directed thought is, as far as possible, excluded. A definite sensation of shades of red with a distinct form is always changed by association into the perception of a rose. The paths are here given. But if the completed percept (rose), all purpose being excluded, is given, the associations are pretty free and the choice of the path of the association is, in the main, dependent upon relatively few factors ; these can be determined by their effects.

When a series of associations is demanded and the subject is requested to produce all his associations without stopping, the intrusion of more or less conscious purposes cannot, as a

---

[1] In a certain sense every psychical event, every movement, is only possible to that particular man with his particular past, in one definite way. Each single action represents the whole man : the endeavour to deduce the whole man from his handwriting, physiognomy, shape of the hand, his style, even the way he wears his shoes, is not altogether folly. More especially there should be a future for graphology.

rule, be prevented. A mass of valueless co-ordinations and coexistences occur. It is, therefore, well to demand only *one* association to the given percept, and at the same time to exclude the introduction of any directed thought by requesting as quick a reaction as possible.

The most convenient way to bring up an idea to the subject is to call out a word to him, and so far this method has proved so fruitful that we have limited our experiments to it.

We employ therefore a method which has already been introduced by Wundt and his pupils in psychology, and which has been successfully transferred by the Kräpelin school (especially by Aschaffenburg) to psychopathology.

The uttering of the first word which " occurs " to the subject after hearing the stimulus-word forms the reaction. It is self-evident that this word represents only a very small part of the complicated association complex that is set free ; this will be further discussed by Dr. Jung.

This method has proved most valuable. Under the direction of Dr. Jung material was brought together, which could be compared when large numbers were dealt with. This material serves not only for the presentation of psychological types among normal people, but also for the diagnosis and symptomatological understanding of a whole range of psychoses.

From the associations we are now in a position in many cases to diagnose dementia præcox, epilepsy, various forms of imbecility, certain forms of hysteria, not to speak of manic-depression with its well-known flight of ideas. By the help of associations we have also well-grounded hopes of classifying and grouping in a natural way diseases hitherto insusceptible of classification, like some paranoid forms, or those "diseases" vaguely grouped or differentiated under the names of hysteria, neurasthenia, psychasthenia.

But this does not exhaust the results. By ingenious interpretations, which can be readily proved correct, Jung and Riklin have shown that the unconscious mechanisms are accessible to this method far more extensively than we dared hope.

The word-associations not only give us information about the course of psychic processes in the exposed layer of our conscious thinking ; they also furnish us with selections of the unconscious working of the mind which throw an astonishing light upon normal and pathological phenomena.

Perhaps the most important result of all is that by the help of association experiments the mechanism of the stereotypes and vagaries of dementia præcox are laid bare in a way that we could formerly have scarcely dared expect.

We hope that the work, to which these words are introductory, will open up to us new regions in psychology and psycho-pathology. The results reached in the course of the last two years deserve the greatest attention, and we have good grounds for the definite hope that intelligent and cautious investigations along the same paths will give us much further insight into the depth of the human pysche.

# THE ASSOCIATIONS OF NORMAL SUBJECTS

### By Dr. C. G. JUNG and Dr. F. RIKLIN

FOR some time past great attention has been paid in this clinic to the study of association. To obtain material scientifically comparable my honoured chief, Professor Bleuler, arranged a schedule of 156 stimulus-words and made use of them in experiments upon psychoses of all kinds. A serious difficulty, however, soon arose. There was no means of differentiating with statistical precision the associations of the abnormal from the normal. There was no material from which to ascertain the variations in normal persons, or to express as definite laws the purely haphazard nature, as it seemed, of the associations. To remedy this want to some extent, thus paving the way for the investigation of pathological associations, I arranged to collect a considerable number of normal associations, studying at the same time their main determinants. I have carried out this work conjointly with my esteemed colleague Dr. Riklin.

The general outline of our experiment is as follows : In the first place we collected the associations of a large number of normal persons in order to ascertain, first, whether any kind of law was to be deduced, and, secondly, if any individual laws were present, i.e. if certain types of reactions could be discovered. With this investigation we united another of a general psychological nature.

The association process is an extremely transient and variable psychological process ; it is influenced by innumerable psychical events which evade objective control. Among the psychical facts having a supreme influence upon the association process, *attention* is cardinal. It is attention which primarily directs and modifies the association process, and at the same time it is the psychical factor which most readily submits to experiment. Attention is also a delicate affective apparatus which immediately reacts to abnormal physical and mental conditions and thus modifies the work of association.

Attention is that endlessly complicated mechanism which the association process by innumerable threads binds to all the other phenomena of psychical and physical origin represented in consciousness. If we knew the effects of attention upon the process of association then we should know, at least in broad outline, the corresponding effects of every psychical event which is able to influence attention.

These considerations induced us to investigate experimentally the influence of attention upon the association process, hoping thus to clear up the following questions in particular with some measure of certainty :

(1) What are the laws of the variations of attention within the limit of the normal ?

(2) What are the direct effects of attention upon the association process ? More especially, does the specific nature of the association decrease as the field of consciousness grows more distant ?

Our experiments have disclosed a series of facts which not only encourage us to pursue the quest into the pathological domain, but, we believe, also enable us to do so.

C. G. JUNG

## PART I

### I. General Plan of the Experiments

THE experiments were carried out alternately by the two authors ; each one carried out alone the whole series of experiments upon the subject. Altogether 38 persons took part in the experiments : 9 of the men and 14 of the women were highly educated persons ; 7 of the men and 8 of the women were ill-educated—their ages ranged from twenty to fifty years. Care was taken to select, as far as possible, quite normal individuals for the experiments ; this, however, especially among the well-educated, gave rise to unexpected difficulties, for it is just at this level that the discrimination of what is an average normal becomes an extremely nice question. All we can hope is that in the selection of the individuals we have not departed very far from the normal. We give the figures in detail, occasionally adding a very brief character-sketch of the person which will facilitate the understanding of a few anomalies. Naturally the two authors have carried out the experiments on one another. The associations in every case were obtained by calling out the stimulus-word. Altogether we made use of 400 different stimulus-words. Grammatically they were composed of the following :

| | |
|---|---:|
| Nouns . . . . . . | 231 |
| Adjectives . . . . . . | 69 |
| Verbs . . . . . . | 82 |
| Adverbs and numerals . . . . | 18 |

No attention was paid to the number of syllables (the stimulus-words were one to three syllables), nor were the stimulus-words arranged in definite categories as in Sommer's experiments. On the other hand, so far as possible, care was taken that stimulus-words similar in form or sense did not follow one another, so as to prevent the subject settling down after two or three reactions to one circumscribed domain. By an unfortunate accident it happened that among the first hundred stimulus-words there were about thirty to which there were ready associations in temporal and spatial coexistence, whilst in the second hundred there were only about twenty, thus making a notable difference in the coexistence associations between the first and second hundred. The want of stimulus-words of that particular kind is made good by verbs. Stress was placed on excluding difficult and rare words in order to prevent mistakes or prolonged reactions through want of knowledge on the part of the subjects. The stimulus-words were as far as possible taken from words in daily use.

This consideration was the more essential for us because in most of our experiments we laboured under abnormal conditions as to language. In German Switzerland the German-Swiss dialect, or rather dialects, not only differ considerably from literary German, but contain also no slight differences among themselves, especially differences in sound. The child learns literary German at school almost as a foreign language. Later on the educated acquire a fairly complete knowledge of, and practice in, the German tongue. The uneducated, however, unless he has lived for some time in Germany, retains at the most those German phrases which he has learnt at school, later adding little or nothing thereto. Literary German is not the less familiar to him in its written and printed form, and he understands it when spoken without being able himself to speak a fluent and faultless literary German. We, therefore, repeatedly tried to call out the stimulus-words in their dialect form, but we soon noticed that the ill-educated did not understand the dialect words as well as the literary German, and that they generally took pains to react in literary German. This somewhat paradoxical occurrence is due to the fact that Swiss-German is purely an acoustic-motor speech which is very rarely read or written. The Swiss is, therefore, not accustomed to sense his words as single items, but knows them only in acoustic-motor association along with other words. If he has to say one word by itself without the article he generally chooses the literary German form. We therefore gave up dialect stimulus-words entirely in our experiments. In the great majority of cases the reaction was the correct literary German ; likely reactions in Swiss dialect were accepted as valid. The reactions were written down as they were given. Persons who had never taken part in such an experiment were first of all informed as to its meaning and given practical demonstrations by examples as to how they had to react. Not a few amongst the uneducated believed it was a kind of Question and Answer game in which the object was to find an appropriate completion of the stimulus-word, e.g. *house— house-fly, wild—wild cat.* The experiments were only begun when it was quite clear that the nature of the experiment was understood. A case of non-understanding, we would emphasize, never occurred ; lack of intelligence is far less disturbing than affect, namely, an emotional stupidity which was not infrequent. A certain significance attaches to the kind of schoolroom attitude in which many of the uneducated approached the work, putting on a somewhat formal and stiff air.

We arranged our experiments in the following way : *First, 200 reactions were made without further conditions.* The reactions were timed by a one-fifth-second stop-watch, the stop-hand being released when the test-word was uttered and stopped when the reaction-word was spoken.[1]

Naturally we do not imagine that we have measured any intricate psychological times by this simple procedure. We only wanted to obtain a general idea of the average and approximate reaction-times, important in many cases, and more especially valuable in the classification of the associations. After 200 reactions the reactions were as far as possible forthwith classified with the help of subject. In the educated persons this was always done ; in the uneducated, who most rarely had any kind of capacity for introspection, this was, of course, not possible. It was there necessary to limit oneself to obtaining an explanation of the threads in the most striking associations. The result of the experiment was divided into a first and a second hundred and written down separately. During the experiment the psychical state was controlled objectively and subjectively as

---

[1] A report will be made later on about the time measurements. The time was not measured in all the persons experimented upon.

far as possible.  If for any reason there was any physiological fatigue the experiment with the second hundred was deferred till the next day.  Among the educated, one may say such fatigue never occurred, so that in most cases the second series could be concluded forthwith.

The second series consisted of 100 reactions which were carried out during a condition of inner distraction.  The subjects were requested to concentrate their attention so far as possible upon what is called the " A-Phenomenon " (Cordes),[1] and at the same time to react as quickly as possible, that is to say, as promptly as in the first experiment.  By the A-Phenomenon we understand with Cordes the sum of those psychological phenomena which are directly evoked by the perception of the acoustic stimulus.  To control the compliance of the A-Phenomenon by the subjects, they had to describe directly after each reaction what they noted during the reaction.  A further classification was made at the end of the experiment.  Naturally only educated persons could be used in these experiments, and these unfortunately required selecting, for a certain amount of psychological aptitude is required for the attentive consideration of one's own psychical phenomena.

The third experimental series was only carried out on the second day.  It consisted of 100 reactions carried out during a condition of outer distraction.  The distraction in these experiments was arranged as follows : To the beat of a metronome the subject had to make pencil strokes about 1 cm. in length.  The beats for the first 50 reactions were 60 per minute, for the second 50 reactions 100 per minute.  The results of the first 50 reactions and of the second 50 were written down separately, and for easier comparison were calculated to 100.  In some few of the subjects the metronome was accelerated after each 25 reactions in order to exclude habit being too rapidly formed.  The beats, in these cases, were increased from 60 to 72, and from 100 to 108 per minute.

Even so, the factor of habit unfortunately plays a great part in these experiments, as might be a priori expected.  Many persons become very quickly accustomed to the purely mechanical activity which in the second phase of the experiment only alters the beat.  It is not easy to devise other distraction stimuli of similar continuity and regularity and without the additional factor of a verbal image.  This is especially so in the case of the uneducated upon whose intelligence and will-power too great demands must not be made.

In seeking for some appropriate distraction stimulus we were

[1] Wundt's *Phil. Studien*, Bd. XVII, p. 30.

above all careful to exclude everything which could in any way arouse verbal presentations. In the arrangement of our experiments we believe that we have excluded this kind of influence.

With these experiments 300 to 400 associations were, on the average, carried out with each person. We also tried to complete our material in some other directions so as to obtain a kind of addendum to Aschaffenburg's results ; with this object we also carried out experiments with some of our subjects when in a state of obvious fatigue. We were able to do reactions of this kind with six persons. In one individual, associations were also carried out in a state of morning drowsiness after a good night's sleep, thus excluding the factor of fatigue. In one person associations were carried out in a state of severe depression (irritation) without fatigue.

In this way we obtained in round figures 12,400 associations.

## II. Classification

### 1. GENERAL

Every one who does practical work in association has found the classification of the results the hardest and most tedious part. We are in general agreement with Cordes [1] when he says that in the earlier experiments the erroneous assumption was made that the psychical phenomenon of departure corresponded to the stimulus-word, and that the connexion of stimulus-words and reaction was an " association."

This conception, somewhat too simple, is at the same time somewhat too pretentious, for it maintains that the psychical connexion (the association) is given in the connexion of the two verbal signs. We need not say that we do not accept this view, for we regard the stimulus-word merely as the stimulus, and the reaction merely as a symptom of psychical processes concerning whose nature we abstain from any immediate judgment. We do not, therefore, claim that the reactions which we describe are associations in the strict sense ; we would indeed ask if it were not better to drop the word " association " altogether and to speak rather of *verbal reaction*. For the external connexion between stimulus-word and reaction is much too coarse to give any absolutely exact picture of the extraordinary intricate psychical processes, i.e. of the real associations. Stimulus-word and reaction only convey the psychical relationship in the most

[1] " Experimentelle Untersuchungen über Assoziationen," Wundt's *Phil. Studien*, Bd. **XVII**, p. 33.

remote and incomplete manner. When we describe and classify the relationship expressed in speech we do not classify all the real associations but only their objective symptoms from which the psychical relationships must be reconstructed with due caution. It is only in psychologically trained persons that the reaction is what it really should be—the reproduction of the first idea that occurs. In all others it is clearly only an attempt to construct something out of the reaction ; in many cases it ends by being the product of deliberation, hence of a whole series of associations. In our association experiment we tend to produce an exclusive excitation of the speech organism. The more exclusive this excitation is the more strongly will verbal relations occur in the reaction. As we shall see, this is chiefly the case among the well-educated, among whom one may a priori expect the psychical mechanisms to be more finely differentiated, therefore with greater capacity for their isolated use. This must not lead to the sophism that the educated are generally prone to more outer combinations of ideas than the uneducated.[1] The difference is a more psychological one, for among the uneducated there is greater participation by the other psychical regions than among the educated. In the second part of this work we shall return to this difference.

Whilst we know so little about the connexions between mental experiences we must give up all claim to evolve, from the inner psychical data, the principles for a classification of their external appearances. For these reasons we have contented ourselves with a simple classification, based upon logical principles ; it was in our view safer thus to limit ourselves until we are in a position to deduce empirical laws from the mental associations.[2]

The logical principles of classification must also be adapted to the special conditions of the experiment—that is, to verbal reaction. In the classification of the associations regard must, therefore, be paid not merely to the logical quality, but when possible also to those outer factors which obtain by reason of the particular arrangement of the experiment.

The employment of the speech-hearing cerebral mechanism is naturally not without influence upon the associations. The purely intrapsychical association cannot become the object of

[1] Ranschburg states that among the uneducated inner associations predominate. *Allegmeine Zeitschrift für Psychiatrie*, Bd. LVII, p. 689.

[2] Aschaffenburg also expresses himself cautiously in this respect and limits himself entirely to the relation between stimulus and reaction as reflected in speech. He considers it important to adhere to this, since the verbal association by no means always accords with the simultaneous inner associations. Kräpelin, *Psychologische Arbeiten*, Bd. I, p. 220.

another's consciousness without translation into the current symbolism of speech. Thus there intervenes quite a new factor in the pure association, which exercises an indefinably great influence upon it. The main determination that occurs in the direction of verbal facility, that is to say, James Mill's generally valid " Law of Frequency," affects the reaction with a more marked power of selection in the direction of the accustomed. One of the fundamental principles of our classification will, therefore, be that of verbal facility.[1]

We have given the preference on the whole to the classification of the associations by the Kräpelin-Aschaffenburg scheme. We have preferred this system to others because, from our subjective view, it is heuristically the most valuable. Ziehen describes this classification as " a failure," an expression much too strong. Nobody will pretend that Aschaffenburg's classification is exhaustive ; Ziehen would not say that of his own classification.

Ziehen's classification has certainly opened up extremely valuable points of view, but completely satisfactory it is not. The differentiation between " leaping associations " and " judgment associations " is most unsafe if this refers entirely to the absence or the presence of the copula ; Claparède also criticizes this adversely.[2] The complete failure of the Aschaffenburg scheme should, surely, be first proved ; as a matter of fact that has not been done, on the contrary, the results obtained by this classification are most encouraging. We may for some time to come work profitably on these lines, not oblivious, however, of a certain one-sidedness, common in some form or other to this and all other classifications. There is no justification for the reproach that Aschaffenburg's scheme is purely logical, for it sufficiently considers not only the logical but also the visual or other sensual interconnexion and contiguity of things as well as the verbal factor. In dealing with reactions in the form of sentences the scheme is certainly inefficient ; in regard to this it is to be remembered that sentences seldom occur with normal persons. It is of great practical importance to remember that Aschaffenburg's scheme has been tried on a great mass of material, partly pathological, and has proved itself workable. Its *conditio sine qua non* is that the subject is not subsequently questioned

---

[1] Trautscholdt says : " In that relation use or custom holds the chief and dominant place, makes certain reactions so easy that finally they are completed mechanically, and causes others by comparison not to come into question at all." " Experimentelle Untersuchungen über die Assoziation der Vorstellungen," Wundt's *Phil. Studien*, Bd. I, p. 221.

[2] Claparède, *L'Association des Idées* (Paris, 1903), p. 218.

about the reaction phenomenon as in the schemes of Ziehen, Mayer and Orth, and Claparède ; it therefore permits an approximately correct classification without the co-operation of the subject, and this is of especial value in psychopathological investigations.

As we regarded our work as preparatory solely to psycho-pathological investigations we did not hesitate to give the preference to Aschaffenburg's scheme. The schemes of Münsterberg and Bourdon seem to us too exclusively logical ; Ziehen's objection does hold true of these that they are unpsychological in that they pay no heed to the content. Claparède's [1] very subtle and ingenious proposition certainly demands careful consideration, but its practical utility must be first tested on a greater mass of material.

It should never be forgotten that in classification experiments or acoustic-verbal associations, *presentations* are not investigated, only their verbal symbols. The investigation of associations is, therefore, peculiarly liable to indirect and fertile errors conditioned by the very complexity of the process itself.

In our experiment we investigate the resultants of a whole series of psychical processes—Perception, Apperception, Intra-psychic Association, Verbal Apprehension, and Motor Expression. Each of these processes leaves traces in the reaction. By virtue of the great psychical importance of motility, especially in the speech function, a chief part in the formation of a reaction must be granted to speech and practice in speaking. This is, therefore, a factor which will receive due consideration in the classification. It may be objected that this principle of classification introduces an extremely variable and indefinite quantum into the reckoning. We must grant that practice in speaking is a highly variable quantum, that in individual cases it makes for difficulties, and that even the logical character of the classification suffers no small loss. Something arbitrary thus enters into the classification with which we would certainly prefer to dispense. But, *faute de mieux* and on the grounds already stated, we selected this classification, taking as a guide certain empirical rules which we will discuss .

With these limitations, and with all possible consideration for the subject's individuality, we hope to have practically avoided all that seems arbitrary in the employment of this principle.

In the nomenclature subsequently employed (flight of ideas, association, etc.) it must always be borne in mind that we are dealing with speech phenomena ; it is from these that we deduce

[1] Claparède, *L'Association des Idées*, p. 226.

the conclusions as to the psychical experiences. We are fully aware that we are merely investigating a narrowly circumscribed psychical region, to wit, associations, chiefly displayed in the mechanism of speech. If we speak of *flight of ideas* we understand by this the verbal phenomenon, that is, outer representatives of inner processes. As a matter of fact the psychical occurrence need not be reacted *in toto* in the form of word-associations, but is only expressed by these verbal signs when it affects the speech-mechanism. The true thoughts in a state of *flight of ideas* would naturally present a very different picture if they could be directly objectivated. For instance, the *flight of ideas* where the presentations are more predominantly visual is a quite peculiar sphere which can hardly be satisfactorily made objective through speech ; hence it is almost inadequately inaccessible to external investigation. Again, as a rule, in maniacal patients the verbal excitement that is present precludes investigation.

## 2. SPECIAL CLASSIFICATION

### (A) *Inner Association* [1]

*a. Co-ordination.*—Under this heading we classify all associations which are in any way united by coadjunction, subordination, supraordination, or contrast. The association experiments require the following special classification of co-ordinations :

α. *Coadjunction.*—The two terms are united by an essential similarity, that is to say, they are formulated upon some more general concept in which both are included. Examples :

| *Word* | *Reaction* | *General concept* |
|---|---|---|
| Lake | sea | mass of water |
| Cherry | apple | fruit |
| Long | small | measurement |
| Unjust | faithlessness | wrong or vicious |

The association by coadjunction need not always be a mere shifting of an obvious, common supraconcept, but can also

---

[1] Ziehen (*Leitfaden der phys. Psychologie*, p. 141), in a polemic against " inner association," quotes the following examples : " Lust—Brust, Herz—Schmerz " (English equivalents would be Pain—Brain, Heart—Part. TRANSLATOR), remarking that the so-called inner association is purely outer and limited almost entirely to auditory presentations of similar sounding words. It is very easy to grant Ziehen this, for nobody would designate these as examples of inner association. For the rest, with Wundt, we conceive the associative *affinity* as the principle of inner, and *practice* as the principle of outer, associations (or similarity = inner association, contiguity = outer association).

result from a more or less vague similarity. The similarity can be so close as to be scarcely differentiated from identity as, e.g. :

| Indulgence | forbearance | Friendly | amiable | Hair | thrèad |

But the similarity can be very remote, so that what is common to the two presentations is not something essential, but a more or less accidental attribute of the stimulus presentation. In such cases the reaction seems very loosely linked to the stimulus-word, and is thus differentiated from the other coadjuncts. The distance of the association is to some extent a greater one. These coadjuncts can thus be separated to a certain degree from those already alluded to. Two categories can be differentiated amongst these loosely linked coadjuncts :

(1) The stimulus presentation is linked to the reaction by means of an important, but accidental, attribute, e.g. :

| | |
|---|---|
| Father (anxiety about) | sorrow |
| Play (of the child ?) | youth |
| War (League of Peace) | Bertha v. Suttner |
| Murderer (hang) | gallows |
| Sentence (contains something) | content |
| Star (romantic : night ?) | romantic poetry |

(2) The stimulus presentation is linked to the reaction by an unessential, external, quasi-coexistent attribute, e.g. :

| Pencil (long) | length | Lake (deep) | depth |
|---|---|---|---|
| Heaven (blue) | colour | Table (peculiar form) | style |

These two modes of coadjunction can be termed " Coadjunction by inner or outer relationship." The first category includes far more important coadjuncts than the second, justifying to some extent the terms " inner " and " outer." The coexistence of the attributes in the second category points to the origin of these coadjuncts from outer associations.

As a final group of co-ordinations we propose " coadjuncts used as examples." This category contains reactions which present in essence nothing but the reverse of the two modes just described ·

| | |
|---|---|
| Sorrow | father (viz. of the father, for example) |
| Contents | sentence (viz. of the sentence, for example) |
| Colour | heaven (viz. of heaven, for example) |
| Trouble | old woman (for example, an old woman has trouble) |

There is a series of reactions to adjectives and verbs which do not stand grammatically in a co-ordinate relationship to the stimulus-word, but are perhaps best included in the group of coadjuncts, more especially in that of "coadjuncts as example."

| To surrender | peaceable | Strange | emigrant |
| To pay attention | wiser | To pray | piety |
| To despise | wickedness | To help | goodness |

These associations can be regarded, if the expression be allowed, as "analytical"; they are concepts which are already quasi-implied in the stimulus-word, to which they thus stand in a kind of relationship of sub- or supra-ordination. As it is, however, difficult, if not impossible, to determine this relationship in concrete cases with absolute certainty, and as, moreover, the concept of whole and part is inadmissible in the case of adjectives and verbs, we include these reactions also under the "coadjuncts as example." Certain typical reactions will always occur among the possible substantives. The reactions are here extremely general and internally independent of the stimulus-word.

The special classification of the coadjuncts would thus be as follows :

(1) By common supraconcept.
(2) By similarity.
(3) By inner relationship.
(4) By outer relationship.
(5) As example.

| Examples of | (1) Father | uncle | (4) Father | our house |
| | (2) Father | God | (5) To pay attention | wiser |
| | (3) Father | sorrow | | |

It is to be specially noted that this classification by no means exhausts the copious differences in the coadjuncts. In individuals who associate very largely by subjective constellations there are possibilities of a series of co-ordinations which do not easily lend themselves to classification. In such cases impotence must be frankly admitted, and one must rest content with the classification "co-ordination." Consolation must be found in the fact that individual possibilities are incalculable, that no one scheme will ever be discovered by which all associations will be able to be classified typically and without a residue. But there are a number of coadjuncts which could without any extreme pressure be classified under different headings, i.e. they have no very distinctive character ; the classification can here be left in suspense or the reaction be finally placed under that type with which it has relatively most similarity. The designations set out are not to be regarded as absolutely compulsory categories, but merely as names for empirically discovered types which can on occasion merge into one another without sharp demarcation. More is not to be expected in the present stage of the theory of association.

β. *Subordination.*—The reaction is thought of as a part' or subconcept of the stimulus-word, e.g. :

Tree    beech-tree

Here we include also all those reactions which specify the stimulus-word, i.e. which demonstrate special cases of the universal stimulus presentations, e.g. :

| | | | |
|---|---|---|---|
| House | the house in X Street | Station | Derby |
| Horse | Mr. X's horse | | |

In some cases doubt may exist whether the association is to be taken as subordination or as predicate, e.g. :

Food    to-day's (*sc.* food)

γ. *Supraordination.*—The reaction is thought of as the whole or as the generalized concept of the stimulus-word, e.g. :

Oven    town         Cat    animal

Here, likewise, the separation from predicate is often difficult, e.g. "thirteen—unlucky number." Is "unlucky number" in this case a general concept, and is "thirteen" as such included in other unlucky numbers ?   According to our view it is in this case a question of a predicate ; on the other hand, we should classify Aschaffenburg's association "Baptism—obsolete custom" among the supraordinations ; "obsolete custom" is a general concept which includes many other subconcepts.

δ. *Contrast.*—The idea of contrast is intelligible without further explanation. Disproportionately difficult, on the other hand, is the classification and valuation of contrast. As a rule contrasts are not only closely connected presentations conceptually, but they are also connected visually, and above all verbally. There are indeed languages in which there only exists one and the same word for typical contrasts.   In the beginning of speech and conscious thinking it was no inconsiderable effort to separate contrasts verbally and conceptually.   At the present day, however, this effort of thought is ready made for us in speech ; it is imparted to us in our earliest youth with the first ideas of speech, with the first songs and reading lessons.   We possess extreme verbal facility for these closely connected concepts, often strengthened by reminiscences of quotations and rhymes, e.g. :

| Sorrow | joy | Bitter | sweet |
| Pain | pleasure | Light | dark |
| Good | bad | | |

"Bittersweet" is even a colloquialism. For these reasons we have classified a large number of these usual contrasts among the outer associations. We include among contrasts only those associations habitually linked together verbally :

| Friendly | angry | Intelligence | stupidity |
| Good | vicious | Revenge | forgive |
| Animal | plant | | |

Despite this detailed classification of the co-ordinations there are associations of this kind which cannot be classified in any subgroup. For these there remains simply the universal term "co-ordination," e.g. the association "short — silk." The stimulus-word "short" has been taken in the sense of a proper name, the bearer of this name has a silk business, hence the reaction "silk." This cannot be simple coexistence, rather the reaction is composed from a specific and a spatial coexistence, and hence is a somewhat complicated formation. As a last resource it might be brought under the heading "coadjunction by external relationship," but without much justification. The more prudent way for the present is simply to regard such co-ordinations as incapable of any further explanation.

The foregoing may be recapitulated in the following scheme :

α. *Coadjunction.*
{
1. By a common supraconcept.
2. By similarity.
3. By inner relationship.
4. By outer relationship.
}

β. *Subordination.*
{
1. True subordination.
2. Specific.
}

γ. *Supraordination.*

δ. *Contrast.*

ε. *Co-ordination of undetermined quality.*

*b. Predicate.*—With Aschaffenburg, we here include all judgments, attributes and activities which in any way refer to the stimulus presentation as subject or object. (Summarized by Kräpelin under the term "predicate relationships." [1])

The first judgments which pertain here, may, following Kant, be divided into analytic and synthetic.[2]

[1] Cp. *Psychologische Arbeiten*, Bd. I, p. 222.

[2] "In an analytic judgment I do not go beyond the given conception, in order to arrive at some decision respecting it. If the judgment is affirmative I

This logical principle of classification is only of value for us in so far as in the analytic judgment a part of a concept, i.e. a predicate, is produced which was already necessarily represented in the concept. It, therefore, gives only that which was implicitly already present. In the synthetic judgment something is added to the concept which was not already necessarily included in the concept. In relation to associative work, therefore, synthetic judgment, if such an expression be allowed, stands above analytic judgment. Approaching the question practically we find (in so far as this mode of classification can be used at all in practice) that in simple judgment reactions the analytic judgment consists chiefly in the pointing out of a co-existent attribute perceptually evident, whilst the synthetic judgment is generally a judgment as to value, with more or less marked reference to the ego. We see here a relationship analogous to that of "coadjunction by outer relationship" to that of "coadjunction by inner relationship." In the association *pencil—length*, "length" is necessarily included in the idea, that is, it is co-existent. Whilst in *father—sorrow* the concept "sorrow" adds something new, and thus effects a displacement of the concept. We should at once accept the classification of judgment-reactions into analytic and synthetic were it not for a difficulty of practical importance. We do not know in individual cases whether the analytic predicate is or is not something necessarily included in the idea. The solution of this question can be only attempted when we are able to distinguish in individual cases between a concrete and a universal image. Ziehen opines that he is able to do this, by direct questioning, even in children. We regard this method not only as extremely unsafe, but also, so far as the differentiation between a concrete and universal presentation is concerned, as extraordinarily difficult. What I name an inner presentation consists of condensations of many memory presentations ; whether their manner of appearance is more concrete than universal or vice versa depends upon minimal differences in perceptual vividness. In many cases, even psychologically educated persons would be at a loss if they were obliged to distinguish whether by *house— roof* they had imaged a particular or a universal roof. Naturally we are far from denying the existence of general images ; but in concrete cases of acoustic-verbal experiments we cannot

predicate of the conception only that which was already cogitated in it ; if negative I merely exclude from the conception its contrary. But in synthetical judgments I must go beyond the given conception, in order to cogitate, in relation with it, something quite different from that which was cogitated in it," etc. Kant's *Critique of Pure Reason*, Meiklejohn's translation, p. 117.

refrain from the suspicion that the so-called " universal images "
are merely words. They only escape the individual content
because they are as a rule much less universal concepts than
verbal-motor pictures where the other senses participate with
very slight intensity.

To answer the question whether a judgment is analytic or
synthetic we should require exact information as to whether the
idea was universal or concrete. For example, *snake — green*
is objectively entirely synthetic ; for green is not a necessity of
thought in regard to a snake ; but when a particular snake is
thought of, green must be already implicitly present, when it
would then be an analytic judgment. Apart from these considerations there are other practical difficulties which prevent
this mode of classification.

In order to obtain a special classification of the predicates
we must realize their different possibilities :

(1) The stimulus-word is a noun, the reaction an adjective.

(2) The stimulus-word is an adjective, the reaction a noun.

We have no grounds for separating these two cases or the
other forms of predicative relationship :

(1) The stimulus-word is subject, the reaction its active or
passive functioning.

(2) The stimulus-word is the active or passive functioning
of the reaction ; or

(3) The stimulus-word is object, the reaction the activity
relating thereto.

(4) The stimulus-word is an activity, the reaction the object
thereof.

Consider the first forms—the predicative connexion of noun
and adjective. Two main possibilities may be differentiated :

α. The adjective denotes an essential attribute of the stimulus-
image of inner import. This kind of predicate may be termed
" inner." Without any particular forcing these predicates can
be divided into two groups :

(1) *Judgment of Fact*, e.g. :

| | | | |
|---|---|---|---|
| Snake | green | War | bloody |
| Glass | brittle | Grandmother | old |
| Mild | spring | Winter | raw |
| Thirst | violent | | |

These predicates denote certain essential and important

elements of the stimulus-image. Their purely objective emphasis differentiates them from the second group :

(2) *Judgment of Value*, e.g. :

| Father | good | Pupil | good |
|---|---|---|---|
| Smell | unpleasant | Soldier | brave |
| Ride | dangerous | Wood | useful |
| Mountain | beautiful | Murderer | common |
| Book | interesting | Water | refreshing |

In these reactions the personal element stands out more or less strongly. But where the reference to the ego stands out clearly in the shape of a wish or a defence in an entirely subjective form we can speak directly of " egocentric predicates." We should, however, prefer not to separate these reactions, as an independent group, from judgments of value, for reasons which we shall give later. We include among judgments of value reactions like :

| Iron | useful metal | Scoundrel | disgrace |
|---|---|---|---|
| Water | one of the most interesting of chemical bodies | | |

Judgments of value which express themselves in the form of an activity, e.g. :

| Smoke | smells | Apple | tastes good |
|---|---|---|---|

are best included among the predicates.

Reactions where a value is not expressed but is required are also included among judgments of value. Example :

| Good | one should be | Threaten | one should not |
|---|---|---|---|
| Industrious | the pupil should be | | |

These reactions are not very frequent among normals ; we add them merely for the sake of completeness.

β. The adjective denotes an outer but slightly important attribute of the stimulus-image, one coexistent and sensually evident.

We prefer to designate this kind of predicate " outer " :

| Tooth | protruding | Tree | brown |
|---|---|---|---|
| Salt | granular | Water | surging |
| Shirt | blue | | etc. |

We estimate the predicate relationship between the adjective as stimulus-word and the substantive as reaction according to the principles just illustrated. That is, we judge " green — field " and " field — green " to be practically equivalent in the classification.

The *interjections* which Aschaffenburg classifies with some reason among the predicates we have placed elsewhere (see below).

A further subgroup of predicates is composed of the " relations between noun and verb."

α. *The Subject Relation.*—The noun as stimulus-word or reaction is the subject of a definite activity :

| Resin | sticks | | To cook | mother |
| Hunter | shoots | | | |

β. *The Object Relation* :

| Doors | open | | To recruit | soldiers |
| Throat | to stitch up | | To polish | brass |

If the attribute is a stimulus-word the predicates hitherto considered are often not easily to be separated from the previously mentioned " coadjuncts as example." As decisive of the latter we regard the obvious endeavour of the subject to find a reaction word or noun as far as possible suitable to the stimulus-word and of universal validity, as in :

| To pray | pious | | Despise | wickedness |
| To indulge | peaceable | | | |

We adjudge " polish — brass " to the object relation, but " polish — bright metals " to the " coadjuncts as example."

Associations denoting place, time, means, and purpose stand in somewhat close connexion with the group of predicates. (Ranschburg's " Association Denoting Purpose." [1])

| Place : to go — into town | Means : to hit    — with the stick |
| Time : eat    — noon | Purpose : wood — for burning |

Occasionally doubt arises in these reactions as to whether they are perhaps to be conceived as specific, and belonging, therefore, to the subordination group. The differentiation is easy in the great majority of cases and no gross error will arise. Definitions or explanations of the stimulus-word, which on the whole occur very seldom, have a certain connexion with the above groups ; we have, therefore, included them among the predicative relationships. Examples :

| Doors | noun | Blue | adjective | Star | heavenly constellation |

---

[1] Ranschburg and Balint," Ueber quantitative und qualitative Veränderungen geistiger Vorgänge im hohen Greisenalter," *Allgemeine Zeitschrift für Psychiatrie,* Bd. LVII, p. 715.

Predicate relationships may be thus grouped as follows :

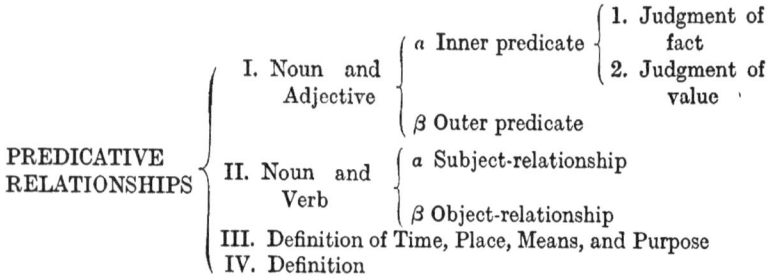

$$
\text{PREDICATIVE RELATIONSHIPS}
\begin{cases}
\text{I. Noun and Adjective}
\begin{cases}
a \text{ Inner predicate}
\begin{cases}
\text{1. Judgment of fact} \\
\text{2. Judgment of value}
\end{cases} \\
\beta \text{ Outer predicate}
\end{cases} \\
\text{II. Noun and Verb}
\begin{cases}
a \text{ Subject-relationship} \\
\beta \text{ Object-relationship}
\end{cases} \\
\text{III. Definition of Time, Place, Means, and Purpose} \\
\text{IV. Definition}
\end{cases}
$$

*c. Causal Dependence* (Münsterberg).

Stimulus-word and reaction are linked by a causal connexion. Examples :

| | | | | |
|---|---|---|---|---|
| Pain | tears | | To cut | pain |

## (B) *Outer Associations*

*a.* COEXISTENCE.—The connexion of the coexistence is one of contiguity or simultaneity, that is to say, the union of the two images is not solely effected by similarity or relationship, but by a union in time or immediate succession. Coexistence in space is included in contiguity in time, for spatial coexistence proceeds from successive sense impressions. Examples :

| | | | |
|---|---|---|---|
| Ink | penholder | Table | chair |
| Copy-book | knife | Mother | child |
| Pipe | tobacco | Handle | knife |
| Hospital | nurse | Lamp | family |
| Pupil | teacher | Sunday | church |

Reactions like

| | | | |
|---|---|---|---|
| Ride | horse | Ride | saddle |
| Eye | to see | Ear | to hear |

$$
\left.
\begin{array}{l}
\text{Pencil} \\
\text{Paper} \\
\text{Copy-book} \\
\text{Sing} \\
\text{Add}
\end{array}
\right\} \text{ to write}
$$

we likewise include here ; the associations with " write " are school memory-complexes, their connexion being essentially conditioned by simultaneity ; the remaining examples refer to reaction presentations which are linked to the stimulus-idea by essential coexistence.

*b.* IDENTITY.—The reaction implies no alteration or further development of the meaning, but is a more or less synonymous expression for the stimulus-word.

α. The synonymous expression arises from the same language as the stimulus-word.   Examples :

| | | | |
|---|---|---|---|
| Splendid | magnificent | Take care | look out |
| Quarrel | dispute | | |

β. The synonymous expression arises from a language other than the stimulus-word—it is a translation, e.g. :

| | | | |
|---|---|---|---|
| Postage-stamp | timbre | Sunday | dimanche |

*c.* VERBAL-MOTOR FORMS.—Ziehen, " Current Word-couplings and Associative Word-complements " [1] ; Kräpelin–Aschaffenburg, " Verbal Reminiscences " [2] ; Trautschold, " Word-Association." [3] In this subgroup of outer associations are included all those connected presentations which have become more or less mechanical through constant association in speech, although they perhaps have logically and historically another significance, and for that reason might be grouped under one of the above types.   In the " contrasts " we have already mentioned a series of reactions which we regard as due to such verbal usage, i.e. as being mechanical.

*α. Relationship by Verbal Usage.*

(1) Simple contrast.   Examples :

| | | | |
|---|---|---|---|
| Light | dark | White | black |
| Bitter | sweet | Like | unlike |

(2) Current phrases.   Examples :

| | | | |
|---|---|---|---|
| Hunger | suffer | Right | to be |
| Of age | to come | Come | go |
| Bat | shuttlecock | Time | space |
| Thanks | to give | Assault | battery |
| Knight | gentle | Bread | our daily |
| Grief | sorrow | Poor | and needy |
| Water | blue | Bed | board |
| Swim | to be able to | Walk | to go |
| Train | alight | Fear | never |
| Cat | mouse | | |

---

[1] Ziehen, *Die Ideenassoziation des Kindes*, p. 29.   *Sammlung von Abhandlungen aus dem Gebiete der pädagogischen Psychologie*, Bd. I, p. 6.

[2] *Psychologische Arbeiten*, Bd. I, p. 223.

[3] Wundt's *Phil. Studien*, Bd. I, p. 213.

β. *Proverbs and Quotations.*—Examples

| Hammer | tongs | Eye | tooth |
|---|---|---|---|
| Liberty | equality | Solid | flesh |
| World | flesh, devil | Fish | fowl |
| House | glass | Throw | stones |
| Peace | and war | | |

γ. *Word-complements.*—(1) The reaction-word extends the stimulus-word into another complete word.

| Book | -binder | Fish | -monger |
|---|---|---|---|
| Tooth | -ache | Needle | -holder |
| Tram | -way | Pin | -pricks |
| Table | -cloth | Purse | -string |
| Clear | -headed | Ear | -ring |

The reaction can also be in the following form where the stimulus-word is repeated in the reaction :

| Tear | tearfully | Glaze | glazier |
|---|---|---|---|
| Foot | football | See | seer |
| Horse | horse-dealer | Praise | bepraise |

(2) The reaction is essentially only a syntactic alteration of the stimulus-word (Wreschner : " Association resembling an inflexion " [1]). Examples :

| Die | dead | Find | found |
|---|---|---|---|
| Good | goodness | Drive | driven |
| Hero | heroic | Murderer | murderess |
| School | scholar | Fond | fondness |

δ. We mention a small group of reactions which can be denoted as premature, e.g. :

| Dark red | bright | Grand | small |
|---|---|---|---|
| Slow | short | | |

ε. We have placed the infrequently occurring *interjections* under " verbal-motor connexions," although they really denote a predicate as Aschaffenburg maintains. We justify our view by the verbal incompleteness of the reaction, which moreover contains a very strong motor element. Examples :

| Grand | ah ! | Love | oh ! |
|---|---|---|---|
| Shame | fie ! | | |

### (C) Clang-reactions

The content of this group corresponds to Aschaffenburg's group of " stimulus-words that only produce effects by their sound."

---

[1] Wreschner : " Eine experimentelle Studie über die Assoziation in einem Falle von Idiotie," *Allgemeine Zeitschrift für Psychiatrie*, Bd. LVII, p. 241.

*a.* WORD-COMPLETIONS.—We regard these words as Aschaffen-burg does, including here only those reactions which complete the stimulus-word by a word which cannot be split up.   Examples :

| | | | | |
|---|---|---|---|---|
| Wonder | - ful | | Modest | - y |
| Heart | - y | | Friend | - ly |

The completion of the stimulus-word to a name we also regard as a word-completion.   Examples :

| | | | | |
|---|---|---|---|---|
| Liver | - pool | | Dub | - lin |

*b.* CLANG.—The reaction is determined exclusively by the clang of the whole stimulus-word or its beginning.   Examples :

| | | | | |
|---|---|---|---|---|
| Pipe | pip | | Window | winter |
| Fate | fat | | Object | obtain |
| Green | greed | | | |

*c.* RHYME.   Examples :

| | | | | |
|---|---|---|---|---|
| Dream | scream | | Heart | part |
| Plate | great | | Moses | noses |
| Make | shake | | | |

A further classification of clang and rhymes into " meaningful and meaningless," following Aschaffenburg, is not worth making by reason of the great scarcity of the " meaningless " group. We have therefore refrained from so doing.

### (D) *Residual Group*

We have placed together in this not very numerous group a few modes of reaction which do not fit into the rest of the scheme and have but a very slight connexion with each other.

*a.* INDIRECT ASSOCIATION.—Aschaffenburg opposes the indi-rect mode of reaction to all other reactions known as the " direct." We have rejected this as lacking in quantitative proportion, for it can never be known, especially among uneducated persons, how many different ideas stand between stimulus-word and reaction.   We ourselves are often unable to state exactly how many conscious, semi-, or un-conscious constellations interweave in our reaction.   We do not here enter into the academic con-troversy about the indirect association (as to whether the middle term is conscious or unconscious), but limit ourselves to estimate within the limits of our cases the phenomenon of " indirect association."   *We call " indirect association " that mode of reaction which is only understandable by the assumption of a middle term different from the stimulus- and the reaction-word.* We distinguish five forms :

α. *Connexion by a Common Middle Term.* Examples :

| White | broad | | Dozen | 144 |
|---|---|---|---|---|
| Field of snow | | | Heap | |
| False | fair | | Turbid | shallow |
| Miss X. is false and fair | | | Water | |
| Remorse | black | | Red | fragrance |
| Mourning | | | Flower | |
| Lock | round | | Bike | round |
| Turn | | | Wheel | |
| Sick | odourless | | Walk | pears |
| Smell | | | 'Mid pear-trees | |
| Quick | whistle | | Revolve | earth |
| Locomotive | | | Turn | |
| Hay | green | | Rich | gold |
| Grass | | | Australia | |

It is to be observed that in these associations the middle term is sometimes clearly known. This kind of reaction is, on the whole, very scarce, and occurs almost exclusively in individuals of marked visual type.

β. *Centrifugal Clang-displacement* (" paraphasic indirect asso-ciation " of Aschaffenburg).—At first there is inwardly a more or less clear and sensible reaction, but this is replaced during the process of reproduction into speech by a clang-like association. We therefore call this group of indirect associations the centrifugal clang-displacement. Examples :

| Resolution | salve | | Dress | goat |
|---|---|---|---|---|
| (Resolve) | | | (Overcoat) | |
| Grief | fish | | Club | commit |
| (Selfish) | | | (Committee) | |
| Quarrel | spout | | Earth | van |
| (Dispute) | | | (Heaven) | |
| Hair | blue | | Clothes | fash |
| (Blonde) | | | (Fashion) | |
| Love | gate | | Ear | ground |
| (Hate) | | | (Sound) | |
| Pair | true | | Book | heaven |
| (Shoe) | | | (Heavy) | |

Cordes would exclude these from the indirect reactions—with a show of right from his point of view. The direct inner association seems to be correct, i.e. no clang-association. A completely adequate and direct intention is present, which, however, at the moment of utterance is displaced, at the expense of the sense, by a clang-similarity. Such displacements can only occur when the inner picture about to be expressed does not attract to itself intensity of attention sufficient to ensure the special speech mechanism. Aberrations and divergencies only occur when what is to be expressed has too weak an emphasis. We therefore hold that the middle term, despite correct intention, has been left abnormally stranded, which agrees perfectly with the accounts given by those who have been able to observe themselves. Some simply felt that they had not said the correct thing, but were at first unable to give the middle term.

Whether the displacement to clang-similarity when the association term is but vaguely conscious occurs at the place of utterance or inception seems to us entirely unessential as regards the valuation of the reaction.

γ. *Centripetal Clang-displacement.*—The stimulus-word is inwardly replaced by a clang-word which in its turn conditions the reaction. The middle term is usually semi-conscious or unconscious. It should be noted that in all these cases the stimulus-word is correctly understood, so that there is no question of a mere misunderstanding. Examples :

| Ride | wrong | | Malt | vinegar |
|---|---|---|---|---|
| (Right) | | | (Salt) | |
| Wallow | bird | | Mast | servant |
| (Swallow) | | | (Master) | |
| Glass | first | | String | beat |
| (Last) | | | (Strict) | |
| Police | yearly | | Misery | obstinate |
| (Lease) | | | (Surly) | |
| Map | sane | | Paper | cut |
| (Mad) | | | (Poor) | |
| Green | star | | Sling | tall |
| (E'en) | | | (Slight) | |
| Feat | mutton | | Brute | hen |
| (Meat) | | | (Brood) | |
| Fate | pudding | | Straight | stranger |
| (Ate) | | | (Strange) | |

In our experience clang accounts for the large majority of indirect displacements of association. What we have said in the previous paragraph in reference to the consciousness of the middle term holds here also. The occurrence of clang-associations denotes a lack of feeling-tone or attention about the stimulus-word. The reaction to the clang middle term is likewise a result of the insufficient feeling-tone of the stimulus-word. The clang-association in this case is in our experience just as obscure as the stimulus-word, and at the first moment the individual is even uncertain as to the nature of the stimulus-word. The reaction is innervated before the act of apperception is complete.[1]

δ. *Centrifugal and Centripetal Displacement by Word-completion or Verbal-motor Association.*

Examples :

| Normal | filter | | Hook | shepherd |
|---|---|---|---|---|
| (Solution) | | | (Crook) | |
| False | fickleness | | Miser | age |
| (Fickle) | | | (Old) | |
| Rat | poisonous | | Foot | gained |
| (Poison) | | | (-ing) | |
| Train | ground | | Milk | rosy |
| (-ing) | | | (-maid) | |
| Clean | fly | | Dog | astronomy |
| (Dirty) | | | (-star) | |
| Stock | mountains | | Chronic | pain |
| (Alpenstock) | | | (Disease) | |
| Brave | dark | | Slip | motor |
| (Fair) | | | (Side-) | |
| Sea | spade | | Stir | breakfast |
| (-side) | | | (-about) | |

ε. *Displacement by Several Middle Terms.*—The middle terms may be mechanical but nevertheless highly important associations. The associations of this class are very scanty and usually of abnormal origin. Under these reactions naturally all the types above can mingle. Examples :

| Ink | acid | | Revenge | white |
|---|---|---|---|---|
| (Red | litmus) | | (Sweet | sugar) |
| Bird | horror | | Book | differ |
| (Cage | prison) | | (Read | difficult) |
| Slow | weather | | Severe | dead |
| (Sure | uncertain) | | (Father | mother) |

---

[1] Münsterberg is of opinion that the outer excitation does not awaken association at the moment when it is transposed into a conscious process, but that there lies between external stimulus and conscious central excitation a non-conscious intermediate stage ; here an association activity occurs which is not illuminated by consciousness (*Beiträge zur Experimentelle Psychologie*, Heft 4, p. 7). But Münsterberg imprudently denies the occurrence of indirect associations by unconscious intermediate terms (Heft 4, p. 9).

We shall not here deal more particularly with a theory of indirect associations in acoustic-verbal experiment. For the present we may say that it is closely connected with alterations in attention.

*b.* MEANINGLESS REACTIONS.—In moments of emotion or of confusion reactions are occasionally given which are neither words nor associations. Among those which are merely sounds we naturally separate assonances as clang-associations. Among the words not associated there are, so to say, no words whose origin would be inexplicable. They are chiefly names of objects of the environment or of accidental presentations having no connexion with the stimulus-word. Some few meaningless reactions are perseverations of type *b* (see below).

*c.* FAULT.—We denote the omission of a reaction as a fault. The cause of the omission is usually emotional.

*d.* REPETITION OF THE STIMULUS-WORD.[1]—Quantitatively a very weak group which could really just as well be included among the faults. Still, there are normal individuals who cannot refrain from quickly repeating the stimulus-word before they really react. This is a phenomenon which, apart from experiment, can be observed in ordinary conversation. This latter mode of reaction would not, of course, come under this heading. The repetition of the stimulus-word is an emotional phenomenon. (This is also Wreschner's view.[2])

### (E) *The Egocentric Reaction*

Certain individuals betray an obvious tendency during the experiment to form egocentric relationships, to express extremely subjective judgments which are obviously conditioned by *desire* or *fear*. Reactions of this kind have something of temperamental individuality and are characteristic for certain personalities.

*a.* DIRECT REFERENCE TO THE EGO.    Examples :

| | | | |
|---|---|---|---|
| Grandmother | me | Praise | of me |
| Dancing | I don't like | Count | I can't |
| Wrong | I was not | | |

*b.* SUBJECTIVE CRITICAL VALUATIONS.    Examples :

| | | | |
|---|---|---|---|
| Idle | pleasant | Blood | horrible |
| Piano | horrid | Love | stupid |
| Arithmetic | troublesome | | |

[1] Meaningless reactions, faults, and repetition of the stimulus-words are sometimes grouped by English writers as False Associations, *e.g.* C. S. Myers' *Experimental Psychology*, Part I, 2nd edition, p. 143.—TRANSLATOR.

[2] *Allgemeine Zeitschrift für Psychiatrie*, Bd. LVII.

### (F) *Perseveration*

### (Aschaffenburg's " association to previous words ")

Under perseveration we understand a phenomenon of persis-tence [1] which consists in the previous association conditioning the reaction following. In this we have chiefly considered the effect upon the reaction that immediately follows. We leave aside, therefore, the effect upon an uninfluenced reaction, for we prefer to include influence of this nature under the general concept of constellation. We wish in no way to prejudge any-thing regarding the nature of the phenomenon of perseveration. We therefore again direct attention to the fact that persevera-tion can be conditioned just as well by current unknown psycho-physical causes as by peculiar constellations of feeling. There are two cases of perseveration to be distinguished in practice.

*a.* THE CONDITIONED REACTION IS AN ASSOCIATION to the stimulus-word to which it belongs. Examples :

| Winter | skating | To smelt | hot | Water | fall |
|--------|---------|----------|-----|-------|------|
| Lake | ice | Slow | fire | Dance | falling |

*b.* THE CONDITIONED REACTION IS NO ASSOCIATION to the stimulus-word to which it belongs. Examples :

Lid — box
Rat — basket

Softly — she comes hither
Gallant — up the steps

If a marked affect-toned complex dominates consciousness at the moment of the experiment, lengthy sequences of heterogeneous stimulus-words will be absorbed into the complex, since every reaction is conditioned by stimulus-word + complex constella-tion. The more powerful the complex constellation is, the more does the stimulus-image succumb to the phenomenon of assimi-lation (Wundt) ; that is to say, it will not be conceived in its true

---

[1] We employ the term perseveration in the sense of the investigations of Müller and Pilzecker, and denote thereby merely the continuance of the previous image so far as it is manifest in the nature of the reaction following. The term is purely formal and is not meant to explain anything. We leave aside the question of whether the " perseveration " is a cortical or cellular process (Gross), or the result of some special associative constellation. We should nevertheless like to state emphatically that our concept has no relation-ship to " perseveration " in organic cerebral processes, and just as little to the hypothetical " Secondary function of the cerebral cells " which is supposed to explain the psychological after-effect of the image's direction.

and usual meaning, but in some special meaning fitting in with the complex.

### (G) *Repetitions*

In each experiment the same number of reactions were made ; the first and second hundred of the associations were, in normal conditions, counted off separately. We could, if necessary, distinguish between repetition of the content and of the particular form. As in normals, however, stereotyped reactions constructed with auxiliary words very seldom occur, we abandoned counting the repetition of the form.

### (H) *Verbal Linking*

It is a striking fact that associations are not only connected by their meaning in accordance with the fundamental laws of association, contiguity, and similarity, but also in accordance with certain purely external motor-acoustic principles. So far as we know, Bourdon was the first to experiment on this question. In his valuable work, " Recherches sur la succession des phénomènes psychologiques," [1] he records investigations on phonetic linking in association. In certain selected books Bourdon took the first noun, adjective, or verb at the top of each page. In this way he compared 500 pairs of words. The total of phonetic similarities was 312 pairs, from which he argues a phonetic similarity when the words have one or several phonetic elements in common. It must certainly be admitted that Bourdon has somewhat unduly strained this similarity, e.g. *toi* and *jouer* on account of the W sound (!). Bourdon particularly investigated the *Ressemblance phonétique, graphique* (one or more letters in common), and *syllabique* (a common syllable). He found the following figures :

|  |  |  |  |  |  |
|---|---|---|---|---|---|
| *Ressemblance phonétique* | . | . | . | 0,629 |
| ,, | *graphique* | . | . | . | 0,888 |
| ,, | *syllabique* | . | . | . | 0,063 |

Bourdon writes : " Il reste néanmoins vrai, que les mots s'associent entre eux plutôt par leur signification que par leur ressemblance phonétique."

In accordance with these investigations we have formed a group which contains outer verbal factors.

*a.* SAME GRAMMATICAL FORM.—We simply counted how often the word-form of stimulus-word and reaction was the same, how often noun–noun, adjective–adjective occurred. We came to the

[1] *Rev. phil.*, T. 35, p. 225.

consideration of this problem from observing that very great individual differences exist.

*b.* SAME NUMBER OF SYLLABLES.—We counted how often the stimulus-word and reaction had the same number of syllables with the view of perhaps learning something about the influence of rhythm.

*c.* PHONETIC AGREEMENT. (1) Consonance.—We counted how often the first syllable of stimulus-word and reaction agreed as to vowels.

(2) Alliteration.—We counted how often there was alliteration in stimulus-word or reaction in initial vowels or consonants.

(3) Same ending.—Here the phonetic influence of the stimulus-word-ending upon the reaction-ending or upon the tendency to rhyme was investigated. Only the agreement in the end syllable was counted.

## Recapitulation

### (A) *Inner Association*

*a.* Co-ordination.

| | |
|---|---|
| α. Coadjunction. | 1. By common supraconcept. |
| | 2. By similarity. |
| | 3. By inner relationship |
| | 4. By outer relationship. |
| | 5. As example. |
| β. Subordination. | 1. True subordination. |
| | 2. Specific. |

γ. Supraordination.

δ. Contrast.

ε. Co-ordination of doubtful quality.

*b.* Predicate relationship.

I. Noun and adjective.

| | |
|---|---|
| α. Inner predicate. | 1. Judgment of fact. |
| | 2. Judgment of value. |

β. Outer predicate.

II. Noun and verb.

α. Subject-relationship.

β. Object-relationship.

III. Definition of time, place, means, and purpose.

IV. Definition or explanation.

*c.* Causal dependence.

### (B) *Outer Association*

*a.* Coexistence.

*b.* Identity.

c. Verbal-motor forms.
    α. Relationship by verbal usage.
        1. Simple Contrast.
        2. Current phrases.
    β. Proverbs and quotations.
    γ. Word-complement and -change.
    δ. Premature reaction.
    ε. Interjection.

### (C) *Clang-reaction*

a. Word-completion.
b. Clang.
c. Rhyme.

### (D) *Residual Group*

a. Indirect association.
    α. Connexion by common middle term.
    β. Centrifugal clang-displacement.
    γ. Centripetal clang-displacement.
    δ. Displacement by word-completion or verbal-motor form.
    ε. Displacement by several middle terms.
b. Meaningless reactions.
c. Faults.
d. Repetition of the stimulus-word.

### (E) *Egocentric Reaction*

a. Direct reference to the ego.
b. Subjective critical valuations.

### (F) *Perseveration*

a. Connexion with the stimulus-word.
b. No connexion with the stimulus-word.

### (G) *Repetition of the Reaction*

### (H) *Verbal Linking*

a. Same grammatical form.
b. Same number of syllables.
c. Phonetic agreement.
    1. Consonance.
    2. Alliteration.
    3. Same ending.

We have classified our material according to the principles laid down in this scheme. In order not to complicate the presentation of the results unnecessarily by a heaping up of figures, the tables published in the second part give the figures of the chief groups only ; the voluminous material can be thus more distinctly grouped than by the detailed rendering of the figures for the subgroups. We have been very scrupulous in rendering an exact account of the nature of the considerations which decided us to a classification in this or that chief group. Besides, it seemed of general interest to present the various empirical possibilities of the associations so far as they are known to us.

Our figures therefore refer only to the following chief groups of the scheme :

I. *Inner Association.*
1. Co-ordination.
2. Predicate relationship.
3. Causal dependence.

II. *Outer Association.*
1. Coexistence.
2. Identity.
3. Verbal-motor forms.

III. *Clang-reaction.*
1. Word-completion.
2. Clang.
3. Rhyme.

IV. *Residual Group.*
1. Indirect reactions.
2. Meaningless reactions.
3. Faults.
4. Repetition of stimulus-word.

(A) *Egocentric Reaction.*

(B) *Perseveration.*

(C) *Repetition.*

(D) *Verbal Linking.*
1. Same grammatical form.
2. Same number of syllables.
3. Alliteration.
4. Consonance.
5. Same ending.

## PART II

## Results of the Experiments

### A. ON INDIVIDUALS

THE subjects have reacted very diversely to disturbing stimuli. As already remarked, the experiment in inner distraction was the most difficult. It was not always successful among all the educated subjects. Outer distraction by beats of the metronome succeeded somewhat better. Nevertheless, there were also here great differences between the individuals experimented upon. Consequently we feel called upon to communicate the figures for each individual *in extenso* ; the multiplicity of tables thus occasioned cannot, unfortunately, be avoided. The figures indicate percentages.

As a whole, the character of these associations (see Table, p. 40) is a very objective one, almost entirely uninfluenced by subjective constellations. In the normal state the outer associations exceed the inner. Between the first and second hundred of the normal reactions there is a distinct difference, for there occurs an increase of 9 per cent. in the clang group. We attribute this change to the occurrence of a certain " weariness " when the second hundred words were given, which psychologically means nothing but a relaxation of attention.[1] There can be scarcely any question in this case of physiological fatigue, which, as Aschaffenburg has shown, similarly increases the clang-associations. The preceding psychical work was much too little for this. On the other hand, this relaxation of interest agrees well with " weariness " in Kräpelin's sense.[2]

The columns after the " normal state " display the change of association under the influence of an artificially disturbed attention.

In a purely dynamic conception, we could almost say the

[1] Aschaffenburg says : " Our attention is so extremely labile, the alterations of our psychical life—which we cannot control and cannot avoid—so great, that we are scarcely justified in deducing results from a small series of experiments. On the other hand, it must not be forgotten that during the course of longer experiments phenomena of fatigue occur ; it is not, for instance, right to compare the first twenty-five associations of a series of two hundred reactions with the last twenty-five without regard to this factor " (*Psych. Arbeiten*, Bd. I, p. 217). Aschaffenburg has therefore observed the same phenomenon but has not, in our opinion, correctly interpreted it.

[2] *Psych. Arbeiten*, Bd. I, p. 53. Kräpelin distinguishes between " weariness " (Müdigkeit) and " fatigue " (Ermüdung). " Weariness " he regards as a kind of warning sign, a subjective feeling which usually, but not invariably, develops into true fatigue.

## 1. EDUCATED WOMEN

*Fourteen subjects with* 4046 *reactions*

No. 1. *Subject aged 22, very intelligent*

| ASSOCIATIONS | NORMAL | | DISTRACTION | | |
| --- | --- | --- | --- | --- | --- |
| | 1st hundred | 2nd hundred | Inner | Outer | |
| | | | | 60 metro. | 100 metro. |
| Co-ordination . . . . . | 26 | 21 | 16 | 4 | 12 |
| Predicate relationship . . . . | 14 | 14 | 2 | 4 | 2 |
| Causal dependence . . . . | 2 | 1 | — | — | 2 |
| Coexistence . . . . . | 20 | 10 | 10 | 2 | — |
| Identity . . . . . . | 1 | 7 | 4 | 8 | — |
| Verbal-motor forms . . . . | 36 | 36 | 54 | 20 | 38 |
| Word-completion . . . . | 1 | 1 | 6 | 8 | 2 |
| Clang. . . . . . . | — | 8 | 6 | 34 | 38 |
| Rhyme . . . . . . | — | 1 | — | 6 | — |
| Indirect . . . . . . | — | — | — | 4 | — |
| Meaningless . . . . . | — | — | 2 | 4 | 6 |
| Faults . . . . . | — | — | — | — | — |
| Repetition of stimulus-word . . | — | — | — | 6 | — |
| Egocentric reaction . . . . | 1 | — | — | — | — |
| Perseveration . . . . . | 1 | — | 2 | 6 | 4 |
| Repetition . . . . . . | 5 | 8 | 2 | 0 | 6 |
| Same grammatical form . . . | 67 | 58 | 64 | 56 | 54 |
| Same number of syllables . . | 43 | 41 | 56 | 60 | 42 |
| Alliteration . . . . . | 10 | 12 | 12 | 42 | 48 |
| Consonance . . . . . | 12 | 15 | 16 | 52 | 52 |
| Same ending . . . . . | 10 | 6 | 10 | 14 | 6 |
| Inner associations . . . . | 42 | 36 | 18 | 8 | 16 |
| Outer associations . . . . | 57 | 53 | 68 | 30 | 38 |
| Clang-reactions . . . . . | 1 | 10 | 12 | 48 | 40 |
| Number of associations . . . | 100 | 100 | 50 | 50 | 50 |

"associative energy" (Ranschburg)[1] has been conducted to a definitely new region, so that only a fraction of it is available for the formation of reaction. It follows that a proportionately easier or lighter association—that is, one for which the way is well prepared—is reacted, because to excite prepared and habitual cerebral mechanisms demands a less amount of energy than to make a track for relatively new and unusual connexions. The increase in the verbal-motor forms to 18 per cent. in inner distraction is readily understood from this point of view.[2] On the other hand, it is more difficult to understand the origin of the numerous clang-reactions in outer distraction. Aschaffenburg thinks that the motor excitation which exists in mania, exhaustion,[3] and alcoholic intoxication can be made responsible for the occurrence of clang-reactions.[4]

It has been demonstrated that flight of ideas, or modes of association similar to flights of ideas, can also occur without motor excitation, e.g. in epilepsy (Heilbronner),[5] catatonia and maniacal stupor.[6] In our experiment motor excitation is practically excluded. (The movements of writing which could be interpreted as "motor excitation" are excluded in inner distraction, and the results agree with those of outer distraction.) Therefore, the clang-reactions are not in any demonstrable connexion with motor excitation; rather we perceive the cause of their appearance in the decline of attention. Distraction chiefly inhibits inner ("higher") association and favours the production of outer, i.e. more mechanical, forms of association— hence predominantly of the clang-reaction. In the further course of our work we shall have ample opportunity to demonstrate the shifting of the association form towards the outer, that is, towards the mechanical association.

It is a striking fact that this obvious tendency to mechanical reactions distinctly favours clang-association. But according to

---

[1] Ranschburg and Hajós, *Psychologie des hysterischen Geisteszustandes*, 1897.

[2] Aschaffenburg, *Psych. Arbeit.*, Bd. I, p. 239. At the moment of origin of the outer association verbal habit predominates, whilst later, on reflection, the tendency to co-ordinatism is often added secondarily.

[3] The term "exhaustion" should be reserved for a higher degree of damage to our physical and mental elasticity (Aschaffenburg, *Psych. Arbeit.*, Bd. II, p. 47).

[4] "As the most essential factor in the origin of a number of clang-reactions exceeding the norm, the relief from the releasing of motor-impulses must be considered" (Aschaffenburg, *Psych. Arbeit.*, Bd. II, p. 69). Cp. also the works of Smith, Fürer, and Rüdin on the effects of alcohol, in Kräpelin's *Psych. Arbeiten.*

[5] Heilbronner, "Ueber epileptische Manie nebst Bemerkungen über die Ideenflucht," *Monatsschrift für Psychiatrie u. Neurologie*, Bd. XIII, 1903.

[6] There are, moreover, maniacs who still show flight of ideas, especially in the stage of subsidence, when they are no longer otherwise restless.

previous experience clang-associations are not mechanical; apparently they are not habitual associations.

In our conception clang-associations are the most primitive of similarity associations, standing very little above mere repetition. After earliest childhood they are no longer habitual but are always easily excited in the act of speech, and force themselves to the front as soon as any disturbance removes the next higher stage of association (slip in speech, mishearing). On account of their purposelessness they are constantly suppressed in normal thinking, and usually exist outside consciousness.

We call the increase in verbal-motor forms and clang-reactions the *superficial reaction type*. The attentive association, which occurs at the flash-point of consciousness, is no clang-association (unless such a one is deliberately sought); but should we succeed in directing attention to another activity—pushing the psychical reaction away from consciousness—all those associations arise which were suppressed in the fully conscious act of reaction. We shall return later to a full consideration of the importance of this hypothesis in the pathology of association.

With weak attention the stimulus-image does not rise to its full height of clearness, or, in other words, it remains in a peripheral region of the field of consciousness and is merely apprehended by means of its external, clang-like manifestation. The cause of this want of apprehension lies in the weakness of the affective tone, which is, for its part, again dependent upon the disturbance of attention. Every apperceptive process of an acoustic stimulus begins at the stage of clang-like apprehension. At each of these stages associations can be expressed through speech centres which are ready for discharge at the moment. That this does not occur normally depends upon the inhibition exercised by the direction of the attention, i.e. by the raising of the threshold of the stimulus for all inferior and non-directed forms of association.

This case is remarkable for the large number of meaningless reactions—up to 6 per cent. in outer distraction. They are partly dependent upon strong perseveration, e.g. :

Intention— out of tune (" one notices the intention," etc.)

Save — art (*sc.* art of poetry)

Strong — powerful

Hate — splendid

partly upon distraction due to the unaccustomed noise of the metronome, e.g. :

Appearance    rhythm.

These reactions show in some measure how strongly the disturbance of the stimulus affected the subject. This extreme lowering of attention explains also the unusually large number of clang-reactions. The gradual predominance of the acoustic-verbal factors is also illustrated by the distinct rise of the figures in alliteration and consonance ; agreement in number of syllables shows also a distinct increase. The increase of perseveration in distraction is not easy to explain ; perhaps it is to be referred to the failure in association caused by the distraction. It is worth mentioning that the outer distraction in this case is progressive. We make use of the clangs to demonstrate this progression. We divide each experiment in outer distraction into three parts and reckon up the clang-associations in each part.

The progression is as follows :

     I. Experiment : 5, 5, 7.
     II. Experiment : 5, 6, 8.

No. 2. The general character of the association is objective (p. 44). The outer associations predominate but very little over the inner. Inner distraction seems to have worked most intensively. After the first hundred, clang-reactions steadily increased. The group of verbal linkage shows, in comparison with the previous case, certain differences in the distraction. Agreement in grammatical form shows a distinct increase, which is also seen in agreement in the number of syllables. But consonance and alliteration somewhat decrease. The individual causes of these divergencies are naturally not within our knowledge.

The relatively numerous faults are striking, the maximum being reached in the first hundred. Of the four faults in the first hundred, three occurred in stimulus-words toned with emotion. In the second hundred there is only one fault, but numerous predicates now occur, namely, judgments as to value. This fact appears to point to the fault being essentially an emotional phenomenon, a kind of inhibition of emotion, which disappears in the second hundred with the greater ease and more assured occurrence of subjective judgments. Perseveration shows, as in the previous case, distinct increase. We draw attention to the fact that in this case the maximum of indirect associations occurs with the minimum of clang-reactions, and, inversely, the maximum of clang-reactions with the minimum of indirect reactions.

The nature of the inner distraction here, which on the whole succeeded better than in the previous case, deserves a little discussion. We purposely directed the subject's attention to visual images chiefly, for in our experience these are the sense-phenomena that most frequently accompany the association

No. 2.  *Subject about 24, intelligent, well-read*

| ASSOCIATIONS | NORMAL | | DISTRACTION | | |
|---|---|---|---|---|---|
| | 1st hundred | 2nd hundred | Inner | Outer | |
| | | | | 60 metro. | 100 metro. |
| Co-ordination  .  .  .  .  . | 27 | 14 | 10 | 16 | 16 |
| Predicate relationship .  .  .  . | 18 | 26 | 18 | 18 | 20 |
| Causal dependence  .  .  .  . | 1 | 3 | — | 2 | — |
| Coexistence  .  .  .  .  . | 24 | 16 | 11 | 22 | 8 |
| Identity  .  .  .  .  .  . | 2 | 1 | 4 | 18 | 12 |
| Verbal-motor forms  .  .  .  . | 21 | 36 | 50 | 16 | 36 |
| Word-completion  .  .  .  . | — | 1 | 2 | 2 | 6 |
| Clang.  .  .  .  .  .  . | — | 1 | 1 | — | 2 |
| Rhyme  .  .  .  .  .  . | — | — | — | 2 | — |
| Indirect  .  .  .  .  .  . | 3 | 1 | 2 | 2 | — |
| Meaningless  .  .  .  .  . | — | — | — | — | — |
| Faults  .  .  .  .  .  . | 4 | 1 | 1 | 2 | — |
| Repetition of stimulus-word  .  . | — | — | 1 | — | — |
| Egocentric reaction  .  .  .  . | 1 | 1 | — | — | — |
| Perseveration  .  .  .  .  . | 1 | 1 | 2 | 2 | 4 |
| Repetition .  .  .  .  .  . | — | 4 | — | 2 | — |
| Same grammatical form  .  .  . | 55 | 47 | 63 | 76 | 64 |
| Same number of syllables  .  .  . | 31 | 24 | 29 | 36 | 40 |
| Alliteration  .  .  .  .  . | 12 | 15 | 10 | 2 | 6 |
| Consonance  .  .  .  .  . | 12 | 17 | 17 | 8 | 12 |
| Same ending  .  .  .  .  . | 4 | 9 | 14 | 6 | 8 |
| Inner associations  .  .  .  . | 46 | 43 | 28 | 36 | 36 |
| Outer associations  .  .  .  . | 47 | 53 | 65 | 56 | 56 |
| Clang-reactions .  .  .  .  . | — | 2 | 3 | 4 | 8 |
| Number of associations  .  .  . | 100 | 100 | 100 | 50 | 50 |

experiment, and in most of our subjects were also, relatively, the most vivid.  On the other hand, the capacity to observe and to report these phenomena correctly is much rarer.  Subject No. 1, for instance, gave rather unsatisfactory information in this respect ; No. 2, on the other hand, was usually a very keen observer and was able to give accurate information.

The experiment is best illustrated by some examples :

Singing     professional singing.

The subject sees directly after the apprehension of the stimulus-word a scene from *Tannhäuser* on a particular stage.

Fireplace     fire,

sees a definite memory-picture of a fireplace-scene in London.

Tile     roof,

sees red tiles.

Journey     projected journey,

sees a travelling Englishman.

Apple     -tree

sees a picture : Eve with the apple.

Honour (*Ehre*) feeling,

sees a memory-picture from a scene in Sudermann's *Honour (Ehre)*, lately witnessed.

Sail     -cloth,

sees a sailing ship.

Deportment     rule,

sees the memory-picture of her younger brother in the dancing and deportment lesson (a recent memory).

Modest     -y,

sees the image of a certain young girl.

Vegetable     kingdom,

sees a particular picture-book with illustrations of flowers.

Sign     -post,

sees a cross-road.

Placid     placid peace,

sees a particular little kitten.

Music     enjoyment,

sees the interior of a particular concert-room (recent memory-image).

These examples show that the reactions are very simple, mostly verbal-motor forms. The inner images stand in a certain associative connexion with the reaction. According to the subject's account they all arise, if not before the reaction, then just with it. In our view the reactions are for the most part mechanical by-associations which have been aroused, as it were, at a halt on the way to a higher reaction. The stimulus-image did not reach full clearness, for it lacked the energy necessary to ascend ; or, not to use Herbartian language, it remained stationary in the peripheral field of consciousness on account of the inhibition proceeding from the clear visual picture. The following examples show still more distinctly the halt of the reaction when the visual picture is very clear :

>Praise     the singer's praise,

she sees a particular teacher who praises her.

>Custom     good custom,

sees the picture of a Swiss village, of an old " custom."

>Like     like unto like,[1]

sees the written sign $2 \times 2 = 4$.

>Stretch (*Strecken*)     Cat-stretcher (*Katzenstrecher*),

sees a stretched rubber band (*Katzenstrecher* is a popular nickname for the Lucernese).

>Narrow     narrow-minded,

sees a narrow lead pipe.

>Stone     chat,

sees a collection of minerals.

>Change     time,

sees a bill of exchange.

>Fashion     fashionable lady,

sees an elegant youth.

>Hazy     eye,

sees a hazy, rainy landscape (constellation of the day of the experiment).

>Glass     smooth,

sees the display of a particular glass warehouse.

>*Vorwärts* [2]     march,

sees a number of the newspaper *Vorwärts*.

>Low     to butcher,

sees a low tabouret in a particular drawing-room.

In these reactions the connexion between reaction and inner picture is, it may be asserted, completely detached. The reaction proceeds as a rule quite mechanically from a lower stage of the process of apprehension, whilst the inner picture represents quite another conception of the stimulus-word.

---

[1] *Gleich und gleichgesellt sich gern.*  Proverb = " Birds of a feather flock together."—TRANSLATOR.

[2] *Vorwärts* = Forward ! march ; also the name of a well-known German Socialist daily paper.—TRANSLATOR.

Conversely, the visual picture can be excited by a lower stage of apprehension, as the following instances show :

Number    number, crowd,

sees a numb finger.

Would    you must,

sees a wooden hammer.

No. 3.   *Subject about 21 years old, intelligent, well-read*

| ASSOCIATIONS | NORMAL | | DISTRACTION | | | FATIGUE |
| | 1st hundred | 2nd hundred | Inner | Outer | | |
| | | | | 60 metro. | 100 metro. | |
|---|---|---|---|---|---|---|
| Co-ordination . . . . | 8 | 9 | 19 | 14 | 14 | 4 |
| Predicate relationship. . . | 16 | 22 | 13 | 22 | 4 | 1 |
| Causal dependence . . . | — | — | 2 | — | — | — |
| Coexistence . . . . | 22 | 7 | 4 | — | 2 | 10 |
| Identity . . . . . | 3 | 12 | 6 | 10 | 6 | 2 |
| Verbal-motor forms . . . | 46 | 44 | 26 | 32 | 54 | 40 |
| Word-completion . . . | 1 | 2 | 5 | 10 | 10 | — |
| Clang . . . . . | — | — | 15 | 6 | 6 | 1 |
| Rhyme . . . . . | 3 | 1 | 9 | — | — | 25 |
| Indirect . . . . | 1 | 3 | 1 | — | 2 | 3 |
| Meaningless . . . . | — | 1 | — | 6 | 2 | 12 |
| Faults . . . . | — | — | — | — | — | — |
| Repetition of stimulus-word . | — | — | — | — | — | — |
| Egocentric reaction . . . | — | 1 | — | — | — | — |
| Perseveration . . . . | 1 | 2 | 1 | 2 | — | — |
| Repetition . . . . | 7 | 12 | 6 | 8 | 8 | 8 |
| Same grammatical form . . | 63 | 50 | 62 | 52 | 54 | 70 |
| Same number of syllables . . | 52 | 46 | 60 | 44 | 50 | 73 |
| Alliteration . . . . | 6 | 4 | 16 | 14 | 12 | 18 |
| Consonance . . . . | 24 | 7 | 35 | 18 | 30 | 47 |
| Same ending . . . . | 13 | 20 | 22 | 20 | 16 | 44 |
| Inner associations . . . | 24 | 31 | 34 | 36 | 18 | 5 |
| Outer associations . . . | 71 | 63 | 36 | 42 | 62 | 52 |
| Clang-reactions . . . . | 4 | 3 | 29 | 16 | 16 | 26 |
| Number of associations . . | 100 | 100 | 100 | 50 | 50 | 100 |

The character of the associations is objective. The outer associations, namely, the verbal-motor forms, predominate. Both distraction experiments were very successful, especially inner distraction, which gave rise to 29 per cent. clang-reactions. A few reactions in inner distraction are of interest :

| | |
|---|---|
| Lid | fid (meaningless rhyme), |

sees a beer-jug with lid.

| | |
|---|---|
| Hall | hale, |

sees a particular hall.

| | |
|---|---|
| Fall | staff, |

sees a waterfall.

| | |
|---|---|
| Stein | fine, |

sees the picture of the little town of Stein on the Rhine.

The reason why the number of inner associations remained, nevertheless, above the normal level in inner distraction and the first half of outer distraction is due to the fact that the artificial lowering of attention was not uniform and permanent, but relaxed from time to time when the reactions became normal. The reactions which were registered by the same person in a state of severe physical and mental fatigue furnish a uniform picture of associative superficiality. According to this evidence, the state of fatigue, so far as the experiment is concerned, effects nothing but a uniform lowering of attention. Its retroaction upon the association does not differ in any way from the results of distraction experiments. Moreover, in the finer shades of individual associations which could not be counted and measured there is no perceptible difference, save in some few reactions whose content was conditioned by the particular constellation of the fatigue. From further observations on this point, and from Aschaffenburg's investigations, we conclude that no specific alteration can be demonstrated in fatigue except the superficiality. This superficiality of the reaction-type in fatigue can readily be explained by the lowering of attention. We have every reason for the statement that the superficiality of the reaction-type in alcoholic intoxication and maniacal excitement as demonstrated by Kräpelin's school is nothing but a symptom of disturbance of attention. The connexion with motor excitation assumed by Aschaffenburg is in our opinion only indirect. Motor excitation lowers the intensity of attention, and thus affects the superficiality of the associations. The disturbance of attention by motor excitation is a fact long known in the conditions described as " Distraction." Since attention as an affective state is linked with certain somatic processes, the lowering or the decrease of its stability by motor excitation is readily understood. Aschaffenburg is therefore incorrect in ascribing directly to motor excitation the superficiality of reaction, for motor excitation is absent in a whole series of abnormal superficial types of reaction. All these conditions have in common a disturbance of attention which is probably always the proximate cause of all types of association that resemble flight of ideas.[1]

The origin of the disturbance of attention is naturally very diverse—if not specific for each individual process. It may depend upon motor excitation or upon a decline or lessening of kinæsthetic sensations or upon a raising of the muscular stimulus-threshold or upon psychological dissociation, as in our experiments.

The extreme variability of the intensity of attention involves great and almost incalculable error in all association experiments with alcohol and fatigue. It is quite impossible with our present knowledge to say anything positive about the range of association disturbance from alcohol, etc. To judge from the percentage relationships of the above experiment in fatigue, the subject was in a distinctly psychotic condition. According to Aschaffen-burg's theory a person with only 5 per cent. inner associations and 27 per cent. clang-associations corresponds to a person in a state of severe intoxication, severe mania, or quite abnormal exhaustion. This extreme superficiality is readily explained by the fact that evident drowsiness accompanied the strong, normal fatigue. The lowering of attention with systematic increase of the outer stimulus-thresholds, peculiar to this condition, is to be regarded (by analogy with the distraction experiments) as one of the chief causes of the superficiality.[2] The intensity of the drowsiness is an immeasurable factor : how much drowsiness was there mingled with the fatigue conditions investigated by Aschaffenburg ?

Drowsiness is not merely a somatic-physiological, but to a certain extent a psychological phenomenon also, which might be almost given the name of " autohypnosis." In the first place, it is a psychological process occurring in the sphere of atten-tion ; this process is aroused chiefly by common sensation, but it can also be produced purely by suggestion. Exactly the same holds true of the effect of alcohol. The effects of alcohol must be largely purely suggestive, especially at the beginning of the narcosis ; to this must be referred the fact that the effects of alcohol can be very different under different conditions. In alcohol experiments can the suggestive effects

---

[1] Aschaffenburg is mistaken in supposing that Nordau's descriptions refer to hypomania : they refer rather to the far more general group of individuals who are unable to concentrate, and who have a superficial association type.

[2] Cp. the experiment on drowsiness in No. 1 of Educated Men, p. 65.

of alcohol be excluded or computed ? In our opinion it is not possible. Psychological experiments on the effects of alcohol demand, therefore, great caution. The disturbance of attention in fatigue and alcohol experiments need not always have its root in motor excitation, but can be quite as well derived from suggestive causes.

To return to our experiment. The marked preponderance of outer associations can be referred to a momentary lowering of attention. But the cause of the superficial reaction type may possibly lie deeper. It is not inconceivable that there are individuals who from congenital or acquired anomalies possess a more superficial mode of reaction than others ; this anomaly may ultimately lie in the region of attention, so that weariness occurs in them much more quickly than in others. From this point of view the figures of the sister and the mother of subject No. 3 are interesting as a familial-psychological observation. (See Tables on following page.)

No. 4, aged about 20, is the sister of No. 3. The associations are on the whole objective in character ; the outer predominate largely, more especially the verbal-motor forms. The clang-reactions are also correspondingly numerous, so that the type of the normal condition looks like the result of an experiment in distraction. In the experiment on inner distraction there was found an unexpected increase of the inner associations together with a distinct increase of the clang-reactions. The superficiality of the normal experiment is, in our experience, abnormal ; we must therefore assume some disturbance of attention in this condition. She is a pronounced " type moteur." The result of further psychological experiments with this subject shows that motor presentations predominate largely over those of the other senses.[1] The motor disposition shows itself also externally in a greater vivacity of movement and a highly developed capacity for motor expression.

It should be stated emphatically that the active mobility considerably oversteps the limits of conscious innervation, expressing itself in motor automatisms which are innervated by unconscious psychological complexes. Among the reactions in the normal state there are two verbal automatisms which in all probability refer to an unconscious complex. This complex stands in close connexion with the effect of a betrothal, which was just at that time a momentous question.

---

[1] Which does not imply that some kind of motor excitation was responsible for the superficial reaction type. In individuals of a motor type the motor parts of the word-picture combination perhaps play in this respect a separate rôle, producing a somewhat more facile disposition for speech.

Nos. 4 AND 5.  *Subjects: Sister and Mother of No. 3*

| ASSOCIATIONS | SUBJECT 4 | | | SUBJECT 5 | |
| --- | --- | --- | --- | --- | --- |
| | NORMAL | | DISTRACTION | NORMAL | |
| | 1st hundred | 2nd hundred | Inner | 1st hundred | 2nd hundred |
| Co-ordination . . . . . | 3 | 8 | 16 | 24 | 17 |
| Predicate relationship . . . . | 7 | 8 | 8 | 10 | 7 |
| Causal dependence . . . . | — | — | 1 | 1 | 0 |
| Coexistence . . . . . | 8 | 6 | 3 | 8 | 8 |
| Identity . . . . . . | 2 | 4 | 1 | 6 | 13 |
| Verbal-motor forms . . . . | 67 | 56 | 39 | 46 | 45 |
| Word-completion . . . . | 4 | 8 | 14 | 3 | 4 |
| Clang . . . . . . | 3 | 5 | 9 | — | 3 |
| Rhyme . . . . . . | 2 | 1 | 2 | — | — |
| Indirect . . . . . . | 2 | 3 | 5 | 1 | 2 |
| Meaningless . . . . . | 1 | — | 1 | 1 | 1 |
| Faults . . . . . . | 1 | — | — | — | — |
| Repetition of stimulus-word . . | — | 1 | 1 | — | — |
| Egocentric reaction . . . . | — | — | — | — | — |
| Perseveration . . . . . | 1 | — | 2 | 1 | 2 |
| Repetition . . . . . . | 9 | 7 | 4 | 9 | 5 |
| Same grammatical form . . . | 61 | 51 | 53 | 82 | 66 |
| Same number of syllables . . . | 48 | 47 | 35 | 51 | 38 |
| Alliteration . . . . . | 13 | 11 | 13 | 5 | 12 |
| Consonance . . . . . | 14 | 19 | 24 | 16 | 17 |
| Same ending . . . . . | 11 | 14 | 7 | 18 | 10 |
| Inner associations . . . . | 10 | 16 | 25 | 35 | 24 |
| Outer associations . . . . | 77 | 66 | 43 | 60 | 66 |
| Clang-reactions . . . . . | 9 | 14 | 25 | 3 | 7 |
| Number of associations . . . | 100 | 100 | 100 | 100 | 100 |

We have thus two probable grounds for the strikingly superficial type of reaction : the strong and abnormally independent
motor disposition, and an affect partly repressed into the unconscious.  To the latter must be ascribed the chief importance in

this superficiality. (It would take us too far to enter more minutely into the individual psychology of this case.)

The increase of the inner associations in the experiment on distraction is a phenomenon which we shall again find in another person of different character, who in the normal state likewise shows a superficial type.[1] For the improvement in the type of reaction in the previous case we know no better explanation than that the attention, normally linked to the affective complex, was set free by the conditions of the experiment, and was therefore available for use. Still, there were great variations in attention, as shown by the great number of clang-reactions compared with the relatively numerous inner associations.[2]

A peculiarity of this individual was the occasional occurrence of strong synæsthesias (*audition colorée*) influencing the reactions.

Examples from the normal condition :

| | |
|---|---|
| Küssen (Kiss) | yellow, |

ü is yellow for her.

| | |
|---|---|
| elend (miserable) | something red, |

e is red.

| | |
|---|---|
| Träge (lazy) | blue, |

ä is blue.

Examples during distraction :

| | |
|---|---|
| Orgy | orgy, |

sees a yellow mass.

| | |
|---|---|
| Pious | blessed, |

sees something yellow.

Remarkably enough, the subject who has the same reaction type as No. 4 is likewise a pronounced moteur and has likewise very vivid synæsthesias, which, however, as it happens, do not appear in the reactions.

The following phenomena in the distraction experiment are worth mentioning :

| | |
|---|---|
| Stork | -'s leg, |

sees a church tower.

| | |
|---|---|
| Ham | -let (Hamlet), |

sees Hampden (village).

| | |
|---|---|
| Fall | -chion (falchion), |

sees a high wall from which one could tumble down.

| | |
|---|---|
| Red | wine, |

sees a red ball.

| | |
|---|---|
| Carp | -et, |

sees a particular pond.

---

[1] Cp. No. 2 of Educated Men, p. 68.
[2] Cp. in this respect Nos. 1 and 2 of Educated Men, pp. 65 and 68.

According to the subject's account, the visual picture fills consciousness fully and exclusively ; the verbal reaction flows off almost involuntarily, touching consciousness but quite superficially. The above examples show distinctly the purely mechanical character of the verbal reaction.

Subject No. 5 is the mother of subjects 3 and 4. In its quantitative relationships her reaction type has great similarity with those of Nos. 3 and 4. The qualitative similarity so far as concerns the objective character of the reactions is also very great. The verbal-motor forms are particularly well marked in these three persons.

Characteristic of their familial type is the occurrence of clang-reactions in the normal state, which distinguishes this type from others. For ready comparison we repeat the chief figures of these subjects in the normal state :

|  | Inner Asssciations | Outer Associations | Clang-reactions |
|---|---|---|---|
| Mother  .    .    . | 29·5 per cent. | 62 per cent. | 5·0 per cent. |
| Elder daughter   . | 2·75 per cent. | 67 per cent. | 3·5 per cent. |
| Younger daughter  . | 13·0 per cent. | 71·5 per cent. | 11·5 per cent. |

The increasing degree of superficiality as we proceed towards the younger daughter should be noticed. If the figures were derived from the same individual one might believe it was an experiment in distraction. This behaviour is possibly accidental but possibly it has also its deeper psychological reasons. We refer below to a similar observation. Ranchsburg [1] found among his old men 11·8 per cent. more inner associations than among young people.

In subject No. 6 (see Table on p. 54) the outer associations predominate in the normal state. The second hundred shows a slight increase in outer associations, and a definite addition to the clang-reactions. The quality of the associations diverges significantly from the objective types hitherto considered, for in this individual some reactions of a strongly subjective character occur, some as vivid and emphatic critical valuations, e.g. :

| Pupil | boring | School | beautiful |
|---|---|---|---|
| Father | good | Frog | pretty |
| Book | interesting | Piano | atrocious |

They are partly predicates which denote more or less percep-

---

[1] Ranschburg and Balint, *Allgemeine Zeitschrift für Psych.*, Bd. LVII, p. 689.

No. 6. *Subject about 35, intelligent, very well-read, with poetical gifts*

| ASSOCIATIONS | NORMAL | | DISTRACTION | | |
| --- | --- | --- | --- | --- | --- |
| | 1st hundred | 2nd hundred | Inner | Outer | |
| | | | | 60 metro. | 100 metro. |
| Co-ordination | 9 | 14 | 8 | 8 | 6 |
| Predicate relationship | 32 | 14 | 30 | 24 | 36 |
| Causal dependence | 1 | — | — | — | — |
| Coexistence | 12 | 18 | 14 | 16 | 10 |
| Identity | 2 | 6 | 2 | 6 | 2 |
| Verbal-motor forms | 39 | 39 | 40 | 34 | 42 |
| Word-completion | — | 1 | — | 2 | — |
| Clang | — | 4 | — | 4 | 2 |
| Rhyme | 4 | 2 | — | 2 | 2 |
| Indirect | 1 | 2 | 2 | 2 | — |
| Meaningless | — | — | — | — | — |
| Faults | — | — | 2 | — | — |
| Repetition of stimulus-word | — | — | 2 | — | — |
| Egocentric reaction | 10 | 4 | 6 | 8 | 4 |
| Perseveration | — | — | — | 2 | 4 |
| Repetition | 15 | 5 | 4 | 4 | 4 |
| Same grammatical form | 43 | 52 | 48 | 46 | 40 |
| Same number of syllables | 50 | 33 | 36 | 42 | 42 |
| Alliteration | 11 | 13 | 6 | 8 | 2 |
| Consonance | 26 | 28 | 12 | 12 | 10 |
| Same ending | 8 | 10 | 6 | 2 | 8 |
| Inner associations | 42 | 28 | 38 | 32 | 42 |
| Outer associations | 53 | 63 | 56 | 56 | 54 |
| Clang-reactions | 4 | 7 | — | 8 | 4 |
| Number of associations | 100 | 100 | 50 | 50 | 50 |

tually evident qualities of the things. In the second hundred there is an increase of the co-ordinates from 9 to 14 and a decrease of the predicative references from 32 to 14. The quality of the reactions is correspondingly changed in so far as they take on a decidedly objective character with a tendency to indifferent

No. 7.   *Subject, aged over 50, highly educated, is the mother of No. 6*

| Associations | Normal 1st hundred | Associations | Normal 1st hundred |
|---|---|---|---|
| Co-ordination . . . | 9 | Same grammatical form . | 45 |
| Predicate . . . . | 61 | Same number of syllables . | 22 |
| Causal dependence . . | 8 | Alliteration . . . | — |
|  |  | Consonance . . . | 9 |
| Coexistence . . . | 12 | Same ending . . . | — |
| Identity . . . . | 3 |  |  |
| Verbal-motor forms . . | 4 |  |  |
| Word-completion . . | — | Inner associations . . | 78 |
| Clang . . . . | — |  |  |
| Rhyme . . . . | — | Outer associations . . | 19 |
| Indirect . . . . | — | Clang-reactions . . | — |
| Meaningless . . . | 1 |  |  |
| Faults . . . . | — | Number of associations . | 76 |
| Repetition of stimulus-word | — |  |  |
| Egocentric reaction . . | 40 |  |  |
| Perseveration . . . | 3 |  |  |
| Repetition . . . . | 25 |  |  |

combinations, often clichés. The decrease of the predicate relationships is to be referred to a subsidence of the subjective valuations, so that the finer quality of the reactions also shows a marked subsidence of interest. The lax attention is very clearly marked by the increase of egocentric reactions from 10 to 4. The distraction experiments must thus be regarded as a failure. This was also shown objectively by the subject's being unable to follow the metronome beats and to react at the same time ; either the writing movement stopped at the moment of the reaction or the reaction-time was prolonged to one of the succeeding intervals of the beats, when reaction occurred with concentrated attention. The disturbing influence made itself felt in the perseveration phenomena which, remarkably enough, first occurred during outer distraction. The almost unweakened personal interest at the time of outer distraction is well illustrated by the relatively great number of egocentric reactions. How far the relatively strong verbal connexion by consonance in the normal state is conditioned by the constellation of literary activity we will not judge. Many reactions of this subject betray a strongly visual disposition.  According to her own account every stimulus-idea at once presents itself to her as a quite definite picture.

The completely individual character of the reactions distinguishes this subject from others, and differentiates her from those hitherto considered.  It would be interesting to learn whether this type was more or less accidental or whether it was a familial condition.  We are, fortunately, in a position to be able to answer this question partially.

In subject No. 7 (Table on p. 55) the number of inner associations predominates considerably over the outer.  The number of predicate relations is extremely large.  Most of these are due to subjective valuations, some with strong marks of feeling, as ·

| Cook | laborious | Ride | dangerous |
| Water | delightful | Prison | horrible |
| Star | gorgeous | | |

Some 40 per cent. of the reactions are egocentric in character, directly betraying a wish or a defence.

No. 8.  *Subject, about* 38 *years old, cultured, is the elder sister of No.* 6

| Associations | NORMAL 1st hundred | Associations | NORMAL 1st hundred |
|---|---|---|---|
| Co-ordination   .   .   . | 6 | Same grammatical form  . | 29 |
| Predicate   .   .   .   . | 49 | Same number of syllables . | 33 |
| Causal dependence   .   . | 1 | Alliteration   .   .   . | 10 |
| | | Consonance   .   .   . | 10 |
| Coexistence   .   .   . | 18 | Same ending   .   .   . | 1 |
| Identity   .   .   .   . | 1 | | |
| Verbal-motor forms   .   . | 20 | | |
| Word-completion   .   . | — | Inner associations   .   . | 56 |
| Clang.   .   .   .   . | — | | |
| Rhyme   .   .   .   . | 1 | Outer associations   .   . | 39 |
| Indirect   .   .   .   . | 1 | Clang-reactions   .   . | 1 |
| Meaningless   .   .   . | 1 | | |
| Faults   .   .   .   . | — | Number of associations   . | 78 |
| Repetition of stimulus-word . | — | | |
| Egocentric reaction   .   . | 15 | | |
| Perseveration   .   .   . | — | | |
| Repetitions   .   .   . | 14 | | |

In No. 8, the inner associations are more numerous than the

outer. This individual also shows a very subjective reaction type, particularly noticed in the large number of predicate relations, and especially in the numerous subjective valuations. The number of egocentric reactions is also somewhat high.

From these figures and from the individual quality of the reactions there emerges a distinct familial relationship. We can, therefore, conclude with great probability that the subjective reaction type of No. 6 rests, not upon accident, but upon a familial condition. It becomes interesting to ascertain how the relations as to quantity hold within this family : whether the superficial phenomenon, demonstrated in subjects 3, 4, and 5 of this family and progressing towards the youngest member of the family, presents anything analogous. For this purpose we reproduce the chief figures of our subjects in the normal state.

|  | Inner Associations | Outer Associations | Clang-reaction | Egocentric Reaction |
|---|---|---|---|---|
| Mother    .    . | 70 per cent. | 19 per cent. | 0 per cent. | 40 per cent. |
| Elder daughter .    . | 56 per cent. | 39 per cent. | 1 per cent. | 15 per cent. |
| Younger daughter    . | 35 per cent. | 58 per cent. | 5·5 per cent. | 7 per cent. |

These figures show complete analogy with the condition demonstrated in subjects 3, 4, and 5. The picture as a whole looks like an experiment in distraction which has extended so far as to reverse the relationships between the inner and outer associations. The increase of the clang-reactions gives a similar picture, as does the decrease in egocentric reactions, which, as subject No. 6 showed, expresses to a certain extent the measure of the personal interests. Thus this remarkable analogy between the two family types seems to be something more than mere accident. Unfortunately, our material is not sufficient to explain the observations. The complete proof and explanation of these apparent facts must await an investigation from material specially collected for this purpose.

The reaction type of the last three subjects is one very characteristic and widespread. What distinguishes it from other, less marked types is the presence of numerous predicates, including a good many subjective valuations. We call this the Predicate Type. The three subjects Nos. 9, 10, and 11 are examples of this type (see Tables on pp. 58, 59, and 60). In No. 9, the preponderance of predicate relations is distinct in all phases of the experiment. Inner distraction could not be carried

## No. 9. *Subject about 20, well-read, fairly intelligent*

| ASSOCIATIONS | NORMAL | | DISTRACTION | |
|---|---|---|---|---|
| | 1st hundred | 2nd hundred | Outer | |
| | | | 60 metro. | 100 metro. |
| Co-ordination | 4 | 19 | 18 | 22 |
| Predicate | 37 | 37 | 38 | 34 |
| Causal dependence | 5 | 2 | 2 | — |
| Coexistence | 26 | 14 | 14 | 14 |
| Identity | 1 | 3 | 4 | 12 |
| Verbal-motor forms | 25 | 23 | 20 | 18 |
| Word-completion | — | — | 2 | — |
| Clang. | — | — | — | — |
| Rhyme | — | — | — | — |
| Indirect | — | — | — | — |
| Meaningless | — | — | — | — |
| Faults | 2 | 2 | 2 | — |
| Repetition of stimulus-word | — | — | — | — |
| Egocentric reaction | 3 | 4 | — | — |
| Perseveration | 2 | 1 | — | — |
| Repetitions | 13 | 10 | 6 | 4 |
| Same grammatical form | 29 | 33 | 20 | 46 |
| Same number of syllables | 38 | 34 | 56 | 54 |
| Alliteration | 10 | 6 | 8 | 16 |
| Consonance | 15 | 12 | 10 | 20 |
| Same ending | 3 | 8 | 8 | 16 |
| Inner associations | 46 | 58 | 58 | 56 |
| Outer associations | 52 | 40 | 38 | 44 |
| Clang-reactions | — | — | 2 | |
| Number of associations | 100 | 100 | 50 | 50 |

out, as the subject was not able to dissociate her attention. The experiment in outer distraction was a complete failure because the subject, like No. 6, could not carry out two activities at the same time and behaved towards the experiment exactly like No. 6. The larger figures for verbal connexion by syllable

No. 10.   *Subject about 20 years, intelligent, very well-read*

| ASSOCIATIONS | NORMAL | | DISTRACTION | | FATIGUE |
| | 1st hundred | 2nd hundred | Outer | | |
| | | | 60 metro. | 100 metro. | |
|---|---|---|---|---|---|
| Co-ordination. . . . . | 8 | 16 | 6 | 10 | 12 |
| Predicate . . . . . . | 31 | 17 | 38 | 34 | 30 |
| Causal dependence . . . . . | 1 | — | — | — | — |
| Coexistence . . . . . . | 14 | 13 | 10 | 4 | 12 |
| Identity . . . . . . | 3 | 11 | 18 | 14 | 6 |
| Verbal-motor forms . . . . | 31 | 35 | 18 | 20 | 30 |
| Word-completion . . . . . | — | — | — | — | 1 |
| Clang . . . . . . . | 1 | — | — | 4 | — |
| Rhyme . . . . . . . | — | — | 2 | — | 1 |
| Indirect . . . . . . | 1 | 1 | — | — | 2 |
| Meaningless . . . . . . | — | — | — | 4 | 2 |
| Faults . . . . . . . | 8 | 6 | 6 | 10 | 3 |
| Repetition of stimulus-word . . . | — | — | 2 | — | 1 |
| Egocentric reaction . . . . | 9 | 2 | — | 4 | 3 |
| Perseveration. . . . . . | — | — | 4 | 2 | 2 |
| Repetitions . . . . . . | 16 | 5 | 18 | 14 | 18 |
| Same grammatical form . . . . | 48 | 51 | 44 | 42 | 48 |
| Same number of syllables . . . | 36 | 33 | 46 | 40 | 41 |
| Alliteration . . . . . . | 10 | 3 | 8 | 10 | 8 |
| Consonance . . . . . . | 7 | 9 | 14 | 12 | 13 |
| Same ending . . . . . . | 5 | 8 | 18 | 16 | 18 |
| Inner associations . . . . . | 40 | 33 | 44 | 44 | 42 |
| Outer associations . . . . . | 48 | 59 | 46 | 38 | 48 |
| Clang-reactions . . . . . | 1 | — | 2 | 4 | 2 |
| Number of associations . . . . | 100 | 100 | 50 | 50 | 100 |

numbers, alliteration, consonance, suggest perhaps a certain leaning of the reaction towards the mechanical side.

Three out of the four faults in the normal state occurred in emotionally toned stimulus-words (*wrong, rich, stupid*).

The predominance, on the average, of inner associations over

*No. 11 is the mother of the previous subject, very intelligent,
cultured, well-read, about 56 years of age*

| ASSOCIATIONS | NORMAL | | ASSOCIATIONS | NORMAL | |
|---|---|---|---|---|---|
| | 1st hundred | 2nd hundred | | 1st hundred | 2nd hundred |
| Co-ordination . | 5 | 4 | Same grammatical form. | 27 | 34 |
| Predicate | 56 | 35 | Same number of syllables | 37 | 41 |
| Causal dependence | 2 | — | Alliteration . | 11 | 3 |
| | | | Consonance . | 8 | 14 |
| Coexistence | 4 | 4 | Same ending | 1 | 10 |
| Identity . | — | 1 | | | |
| Verbal-motor forms . | 28 | 50 | | | |
| Word-completion | 3 | 4 | Inner associations | 63 | 39 |
| Clang | — | — | | | |
| Rhyme . | — | — | Outer associations | 32 | 55 |
| Indirect . | 1 | — | Clang-reactions | 3 | 4 |
| Meaningless | — | — | | | |
| Faults . | — | 1 | Number of associations . | 96 | 96 |
| Repetition of stimulus-word | — | — | | | |
| Egocentric reaction . | 6 | 5 | | | |
| Perseveration . | 1 | — | | | |
| Repetitions | 5 | 4 | | | |

outer is noticeable in an educated person. The reaction type is
a mixed one and does not show the same subjective character as
Nos. 6, 7, and 8.

In No. 10, predicate relations exceed on the average
the number of co-ordinates. With regard to the failure in
distraction, the same must be said as in the case of subjects
6 and 9. The reaction type, in the first hundred of the normal
state, is somewhat subjective, and this is expressed by the
9 per cent. egocentric reactions. Perseveration occurs exclusively in distraction. Like No. 9, there is an increase in the
number of syllables and consonance, which perhaps betokens
a slight dissociation. The great number of faults in all phases
of the experiment is striking. Of the fourteen faults in the
normal state ten occur in stimulus-words charged with emotion
(*must, wrong, violence, threaten, suffer*, etc.); in another two the
subjective emotional tone of the stimulus-word is only probable.
It must be stated that the subject is slightly hysterical in so far as

she has somnambulic dreams.   The proof of this hypothesis we shall present in a later chapter on the association anomalies of hysteria.[1]

No. 12.   *Subject about 40, very intelligent and well-read*

| ASSOCIATIONS | NORMAL | | DISTRACTION | | |
|---|---|---|---|---|---|
| | | | Inner | Outer | |
| | 1st hundred | 2nd hundred | | 60 metro. | 100 metro. |
| Co-ordination. . . . . | 23 | 12 | 15 | 12 | 2 |
| Predicate . . . . . . | 1 | 6 | 19 | 6 | 8 |
| Causal dependence . . . . . | 1 | 1 | — | — | — |
| Coexistence . . . . . . | 34 | 18 | 18 | 22 | 6 |
| Identity . . . . . . | 7 | 6 | 9 | 4 | 10 |
| Verbal-motor forms . . . | 34 | 56 | 34 | 52 | 70 |
| Word-completion . . . . . | — | — | — | — | — |
| Clang . . . . . . . | — | — | — | — | — |
| Rhyme . . . . . . . | — | 1 | 1 | 2 | 2 |
| Indirect . . . . . . | — | — | — | — | — |
| Meaningless . . . . . | — | — | — | — | — |
| Faults . . . . . . . | — | — | 4 | — | 2 |
| Repetition of stimulus-word . . . | — | — | — | — | — |
| Egocentric reaction. . . . . | — | — | — | — | — |
| Perseveration. . . . . . | 1 | — | — | 2 | — |
| Repetitions . . . . . . | 6 | 5 | 5 | — | 2 |
| Same grammatical form . . . . | 57 | 92 | 64 | 82 | 56 |
| Same number of syllables . . . | 50 | 52 | 57 | 56 | 38 |
| Alliteration . . . . . . | 5 | 4 | 10 | — | 4 |
| Consonance . . . . . . | 16 | 18 | 12 | 20 | 12 |
| Same ending . . . . . . | 25 | 16 | 12 | 18 | 20 |
| Inner associations . . . . . | 25 | 19 | 34 | 18 | 10 |
| Outer associations . . . . . | 75 | 80 | 61 | 78 | 86 |
| Clang-reactions . . . . . | — | 1 | 1 | 2 | 2 |
| Number of associations . . . . | 100 | 100 | 100 | 50 | 50 |

[1] Among his experiments on normals Aschaffenburg had only one case who had a remarkable number of faults ; it was that of a dreamy. meditative, literary young man (*Psych. Arbeit.*, Bd. IV, p. 243).

### No. 13. *Subject about 22 years, intelligent, all-round culture*

The subject felt much embarrassment, hence the great number of repetitions. Only distraction with the metronome at 100 succeeded, and that but slightly. The writing movements were accordingly imperfect.

| ASSOCIATIONS | NORMAL | | DISTRACTION | |
| --- | --- | --- | --- | --- |
| | | | Outer | |
| | 1st hundred | 2nd hundred | 60 metro. | 100 metro. |
| Co-ordination | 11 | 21 | 22 | 10 |
| Predicate | 18 | 19 | 20 | 14 |
| Causal dependence | 5 | 1 | 2 | — |
| Coexistence | 10 | 10 | 16 | 20 |
| Identity | 3 | 12 | 16 | 16 |
| Verbal-motor forms | 46 | 31 | 14 | 34 |
| Word-completion | — | 1 | — | — |
| Clang. | — | — | — | — |
| Rhyme | — | 1 | — | — |
| Indirect | — | — | — | — |
| Meaningless | — | — | — | — |
| Faults | 6 | — | 6 | — |
| Repetition of stimulus-word | — | 4 | 4 | 6 |
| Egocentric reaction | — | — | — | — |
| Perseveration | — | — | — | — |
| Repetitions | 9 | 11 | 4 | 2 |
| Same grammatical form | 61 | 60 | 56 | 68 |
| Same number of syllables | 43 | 43 | 42 | 42 |
| Alliteration | 8 | 3 | 8 | 6 |
| Consonance | 10 | 14 | 8 | 14 |
| Same ending | 11 | 12 | 18 | 16 |
| Inner associations | 34 | 41 | 44 | 24 |
| Outer associations | 59 | 53 | 46 | 70 |
| Clang-reactions | — | 2 | — | — |
| Number of associations | 100 | 100 | 50 | 50 |

No. 14.  *Subject about 22 years, of moderate intelligence, cultured*

We add the figures of this subject only for the sake of completeness. The reaction type is objective. Inner distraction succeeded but imperfectly. Its effect is uncertain, for owing to the absence of the second hundred of normal reactions, information is wanting as regards the deviations in the normal state. For external reasons the second hundred could not be carried out.

| ASSOCIATIONS | NORMAL 1st hundred | DIS-TRACTION Inner | ASSOCIATIONS | NORMAL 1st hundred | DIS-TRACTION Inner |
|---|---|---|---|---|---|
| Co-ordination . . . | 29 | 9 | Same grammatical form. | 95 | 69 |
| Predicate . . . | 1 | 10 | Same number of syllables | 59 | 40 |
| Causal dependence . . | — | 1 | Alliteration . . . | 10 | 9 |
| | | | Consonance . . . | 15 | 22 |
| Coexistence . . . | 31 | 12 | Same ending . . | 24 | 7 |
| Identity . . . . | 2 | 12 | | | |
| Verbal-motor forms . . | 34 | 51 | | | |
| Word-completion . . | — | 1 | Inner associations . | 30 | 20 |
| Clang . . . . | 2 | — | | | |
| Rhyme . . . . | 1 | 2 | Outer associations . | 67 | 75 |
| Indirect . . . . | — | — | Clang-reactions . . | 3 | 3 |
| Meaningless . . . | — | — | | | |
| Faults . . . . | — | 2 | Number of associations . | 100 | 100 |
| Repetition of stimulus-word | — | — | | | |
| Egocentric reaction . . | — | — | | | |
| Perseveration . . . | — | — | | | |
| Repetitions . . . | 14 | 1 | | | |

No. 11 (p. 60) is a pronounced predicate type with numerous subjective valuations. A marked relaxation is seen in the second hundred, to be attributed to distinct ennui which was also objectively demonstrated. Therefore the second hundred no longer corresponds with the normal state but is rather an experiment in distraction. If, despite this, we compare her reaction type with that of her daughter (No. 10), we notice the same phenomenon as before—namely, that the reaction type of the daughter is a more superficial one than that of the mother.

|  | Inner Associations | Outer Associations |
|---|---|---|
| Mother . . . . . | 51 per cent. | 43·5 per cent. |
| Daughter . . . . . | 36 per cent. | 53·5 per cent. |

We take this opportunity of repeating that, despite this agreement, the phenomenon may be purely accidental and is one that still requires proof.

The figures for three other subjects are on pp. 61–64. No. 12, about 40, very intelligent, well-read. The lady is a North German. The great number of current phrases is peculiarly striking. Inner distraction was a failure. Outer association shows a distinct disturbance of attention. The reaction type is objective.

### Summary of the Group of Educated Women

The material collected in this group is, unfortunately, somewhat unequal so far as concerns the quantitative relations. The speech conditions are, on the other hand, very uniform in so far as there is only one North German in the fourteen individuals; the others are all Swiss, with the dialect as their common colloquial speech. The degree of culture is, on the whole, a very high one. Two have had an academic training; six of them have command of one or two languages apart from their mother tongue; ten are relatively extremely well-read. Distraction experiments were carried out in ten subjects: in five both in inner and outer distraction, in two cases only in inner, and in three only in outer distraction. The outer distraction led to a positive result in four cases, the inner in three cases. There was a partial success in one case of inner and one of outer distraction.

Distraction failed in four cases, three of whom were pronounced predicate types. (The predicate types, as a group, who took any part in the distraction experiments showed a much slighter distraction phenomenon than the other subjects.) Of the six persons over thirty years old, three showed a preponderance, on the average, of inner associations over outer; of the eight persons under thirty, only one showed a predominance of inner associations over outer.

## 2. EDUCATED MEN

*Nine subjects with 3793 associations*

No. 1.   *Subject intelligent, highly cultured, 28 years*

| ASSOCIATIONS | NORMAL | | DISTRACTION | | | FATIGUE | DROWSINESS | |
|---|---|---|---|---|---|---|---|---|
| | | | | Outer | | | | |
| | 1st hundred | 2nd hundred | Inner | 1st part | 2nd part | | 1st part | 2nd part |
| Co-ordination | 9 | 13 | 4 | 10 | 12 | 10·2 | 2 | — |
| Predicate | 6 | 16 | 19 | 10 | 4 | 10·2 | 5 | 2 |
| Causal dependence | — | — | — | — | — | — | — | 1 |
| Coexistence | 18 | 5 | 6 | 8 | 4 | 14·1 | 14 | 6 |
| Identity | 6 | 8 | 5 | 10 | 2 | 2·5 | 5 | 2 |
| Verbal-motor form | 54 | 52 | 56 | 46 | 54 | 53·8 | 40 | 51 |
| Word-completion | 1 | — | 8 | 4 | 12 | 2·5 | 2 | 2 |
| Clang | — | — | 2 | 6 | 2 | — | 4 | 5 |
| Rhyme | 4 | 4 | 1 | 2 | 8 | 2·5 | 20 | 21 |
| Indirect | 2 | 2 | 1 | 2 | 4 | — | 2 | 2 |
| Meaningless | — | — | — | 2 | — | 3·8 | — | — |
| Faults | — | — | — | — | — | — | — | — |
| Repetition of stimulus-word | — | — | — | — | — | — | — | — |
| Egocentric reaction | 1 | — | 3 | — | — | — | — | — |
| Perseveration | — | — | 2 | 2 | — | 2 | 4 | — |
| Repetitions | 5 | 5 | 2 | 6 | 2 | 6 | 9 | 2 |
| Same grammatical form | 73 | 47 | 47 | 54 | 46 | 63 | 59 | 60 |
| Same number of syllables | 53 | 45 | 49 | 46 | 42 | 44 | 61 | 58 |
| Alliteration | 7 | 6 | 5 | 10 | 4 | 4 | 17 | 9 |
| Consonance | 15 | 23 | 16 | 24 | 20 | 5 | 32 | 36 |
| Same ending | 19 | 15 | 9 | 18 | 18 | 14 | 33 | 36 |
| Inner associations | 15 | 29 | 23 | 20 | 16 | 20·4 | 7 | 3 |
| Outer associations | 78 | 65 | 67 | 64 | 60 | 70·4 | 59 | 59 |
| Clang-reactions | 5 | 4 | 11 | 12 | 22 | 5 | 27 | 32 |
| Number of associations | 100 | 100 | 100 | 50 | 50 | 78 | 78 | 78 |

In this subject reactions were carried out in four different states of disturbed attention : in a state of inner and outer distraction, of fatigue, and of morning drowsiness after awaking.

The reaction type is very superficial, as is shown by the ratio of the inner to the outer associations, 15 : 78 and 29 : 65. The reactions are of an objective, almost a purely verbal, character. The distraction experiments do not change much as to the ratio of inner to outer associations ; as against this, the progression of the clang-reactions demonstrates the increasing disturbance of attention, which reaches its maximum in the second experiment in outer distraction. The fatigue, which was not very great in this case, shows no change of type. The drowsy state exhibits a disturbance of attention far exceeding the effect of the second outer distraction. This subject, after mental work at night, is very drowsy in the morning and it is difficult to arouse him fully. These reactions were carried out while he was in bed and had just been partially awakened. He had been previously informed that the experiment was to come off. The two experiments were carried out on two different days, at an interval of about a week. As the figures show, the type is an extremely superficial one. The clang-reactions are extremely numerous, especially the rhymes. The figures for verbal connexion are very high. The picture of this manner of reaction shows reaction almost completely reduced to the most primitive verbal mechanisms. In these experiments fatigue is quite excluded ; it is only a question of a lowering of active attention, corresponding with the associative termination of the state of sleep. It is known that during sleep attention is completely obliterated. Were we to succeed in producing reactions in a person sleeping (not somnambulic sleep), clang-reactions would certainly be the exclusive results. In our view an absolute, undistracted inner concentration of attention must have the same results. We are, fortunately, in a position to report on a case in point.

It is the case of an individual, N——, who was terribly upset by unusual emotions. Outwardly, the chief symptom was almost complete want of ability to concentrate. The cause of her emotions she kept secret. In the experiment, to which she submitted from scientific interest, she produced mainly clangs and rhymes, together with a few inexplicable (meaningless ?) reactions. We should like to compare this case with an inner distraction experiment which extended over several days. Attention was completely chained to the inner, affect-toned complex,[1] from which she could not set herself free for more or less indifferent events. For everything that does not touch the complex there is thus abnormally slight attention. To what extent this

[1] By " affect-toned complex " we understand the total number of presentations relating to a definite experience that is charged with emotion. In what follows we shall always use the term " complex " with this meaning.

barrier is more or less conscious is naturally not within our purview. According to her own account, certain vivid presentations belonging to the complex hovered before her at the beginning of the experiment ; these she constantly tried to repress, fearing lest they might be betrayed in the reaction. From the second third of the experiment onwards there remained only the emotional tone of the complex in consciousness without the clear presentations belonging thereto. What occurred to her were only clangs. The stimulus-words only reached her at all through clangs and never through their meaning.

These investigations prove most distinctly the dependence of clang-reactions, of the superficial reaction type in general, on disturbance of attention. But how is this abnormally superficial type to be explained ? We are dealing with a psychologically trained person who brought the greatest interest to the experiment. The superficial reaction type must be connected with the fact that many educated persons conceive the experiment entirely as a verbal one ; they endeavour, by maintaining a ready speech-excitation, to affix the first word that comes up, without entering more closely into the meaning of the stimulus-word, for they see at once that no special significance can rest within a stimulus-word standing apart by itself. This is how we explain the marked preponderance of verbal and clang combinations. All persons who allow themselves to be influenced rather by the sense than by the mere word tend to make inner associations. The conception as to the meaning of the stimulus-word is different in different persons. In our experience there are two chief types :

(1) The subject endeavours to do justice to the word as objectively as possible ; in the reaction he accordingly constructs any universal or particular connexion of objective significance ; the reaction is mostly a co-ordinate relation.

(2) The subject endeavours to characterize pertinently the object called up by the stimulus-word, which he images as distinctly as possible. He expresses something about the stimulus-word, using for this the predicate form. The reaction is hence mostly a predicate relation.

On this hypothesis the superficial reaction type of certain educated persons is not to be regarded as the result of a disturbance of attention but as a " phenomenon of adjustment " (Bleuler). By the concept " phenomenon of adjustment " we understand, with Bleuler, the occurrence of an apparently abnormal reaction type through the spontaneous preference of a definite mode of reaction. But it must be emphasized that this mode is not one accidentally selected, but one motivated by the psychological individuality of the subject. The more intense the adjustment to the clang-appearance of the stimulus-word, the more superficial must be the reaction type ; for the attention, having been specially directed thereto, will accentuate and make prominent the primitive associations suppressed in the normal act of speech. A quite paradoxical picture may thus arise in the statistical presentation of the results, one which, on the above hypothesis, we are now able to understand. The following case serves to illustrate this possibility.

No. 2. *Subject intelligent, highly educated, aged 47*

| ASSOCIATIONS | NORMAL | | DISTRACTION | | | FATIGUE |
| | 1st hundred | 2nd hundred | Inner | Outer | | |
| | | | | 1st part | 2nd part | |
| --- | --- | --- | --- | --- | --- | --- |
| Co-ordination . . . . | 16 | 15 | 12 | 20 | 20 | 10·2 |
| Predicate . . . . . | 6 | 5 | 6 | 12 | 2 | 8 |
| Causal dependence . . . | — | — | — | 4 | 2 | — |
| Coexistence . . . . | 4 | 6 | 8 | 14 | 8 | 5 |
| Identity . . . . . | 6 | 8 | 2 | 10 | 10 | 6 |
| Verbal-motor forms . . . | 51 | 45 | 38 | 28 | 58 | 38 |
| Word-completion . . . . | 2 | 1 | — | — | — | 2 |
| Clang . . . . . . | 8 | 10 | 24 | 6 | — | 24 |
| Rhyme . . . . . | 1 | 3 | — | — | — | 2 |
| Indirect . . . . . | 6 | 6 | 10 | 4 | — | 1 |
| Meaningless . . . . . | — | 1 | — | — | — | — |
| Faults . . . . . | — | — | — | — | — | — |
| Repetition of stimulus-word . . | — | — | — | 2 | — | — |
| Egocentric reaction . . . | — | — | — | — | — | 5 |
| Perseveration . . . . | 1 | 1 | — | — | — | — |
| Repetitions . . . . . | 3 | 13 | 8 | 4 | 6 | 10 |
| Same grammatical form. . . | 75 | 63 | 62 | 70 | 74 | 58 |
| Same number of syllables . . | 48 | 37 | 42 | 48 | 56 | 41 |
| Alliteration . . . . . | 25 | 22 | 38 | 16 | 6 | 28 |
| Consonance . . . . . | 25 | 23 | 38 | 24 | 16 | 23 |
| Same ending . . . . | 14 | 12 | 10 | 10 | 12 | 10 |
| Inner associations . . . | 22 | 20 | 18 | 36 | 24 | 18 |
| Outer associations . . . | 61 | 59 | 48 | 52 | 76 | 49 |
| Clang reactions . . . . | 11 | 14 | 24 | 6 | — | 28 |
| No. of associations . . . | 100 | 100 | 50 | 50 | 50 | 78 |

In this subject we again find a strikingly superficial reaction type in the normal state which is illustrated particularly by the high number of clang-reactions. The superficiality increases considerably in the experiment on inner distraction, whilst in the experiment on outer association there is a striking " improvement" in the reaction for the number of inner associations rises far above those of the normal experiment. The " improvement " is demonstrated in the clearest way by the recession and final disappearance of the clang-reactions.

This remarkable result, unique in our experiments, demands critical inquiry.   We have referred to this experiment in reviewing No. 4 of Educated Women (p. 52).  She presented a similar picture.  We there accepted a suppressed affect as the cause of the superficial reaction type.  We refer also to the interesting condition which we expounded in the critical remarks on subject No. 1 of Educated Men.  The recent very strong affect which completely controlled N—— at the time was the direct cause of the occurrence of preponderant clang-associations.  In that case the affect was suppressed, for it did not manifest itself directly in the reaction but only indirectly through the disso-ciation of attention.  A similar psychological situation must be accepted for subject No. 4 of the Educated Women as explaining the superficial type.  That subject No. 4 of the Educated Women and subject No. 2 of the Educated Men present the same type is probably an accidental coincidence.

Affect is perhaps entirely to be excluded in subject No. 2. We must therefore seek for another cause of the superficial type ; we find it in the phenomenon of adjustment.  He is thoroughly at home in psychology and has, moreover, an extraordinary capacity for concentration.  He at once directed attention to the clang-manifestation of the stimulus-word, and consequently always reproduced the first association that occurred.  These cannot be anything but primitive verbal connexions and clangs, if our hypothesis is at all correct as to the associations which first arise on perceiving the stimulus-word.  This explains, without any straining, the abnormally superficial type in the normal experiment.

The superficiality increases in the experiment in inner distrac-tion.  The subject executed this experiment in the most classical manner.  The concentration upon the A phenomenon was excellent, as was also the reporting.  We have, therefore, no reason in this case to accept any disturbance of attention ; the superficial type of this experiment must be ascribed to the lowering of attention ; it arises from a root other than that of the normal experiment, and is consequently no phenomenon of adjustment.

In most subjects outer distraction has a disturbing influence upon attention and thus causes superficiality; in the present instance the effect is apparently the reverse. The normal state in this case is characterized by the phenomenon of adjustment; attention is directed exclusively towards the verbal factor. This adjustment becoming disturbed by outer distraction, the subject enters into another relationship to the stimulus-word, i.e. exclusive observation of the clang-manifestation is interrupted, thus preventing the rising up of those primitive associations which lie closest at hand. If under normal conditions the suppressed associations always fall back into repression, the succeeding associations must be those determined by the sense of the stimulus-word, i.e. the number of clang-reactions must decrease, and the number of inner associations increase. That is the case here.

The figures for fatigue show remarkable agreement with those of inner distraction. From the external condition the diagnosis might be made of very severe fatigue. But this was not the fact. The fatigue was by no means extreme, but a relatively slight evening tiredness which, according to the subject's account, had not noticeably influenced the reaction. We are dealing again with a phenomenon of adjustment, and not with a disturbance of attention. That the adjustment in this state was apparently more intense is perhaps to be ascribed to the fact that the subject as a " moteur " is somewhat excited physically when in a slightly fatigued condition.

Verbal motility naturally takes part in the general motor excitation, so that the speech apparatus very readily responds to a corresponding stimulus. This circumstance must have fallen in with the specific adjustment in this case, resulting naturally in a greater number of purely mechanical combinations.

As would be at once expected from such a type, the personal and subjective kinds of reaction, with a few exceptions, disappear.

In No. 3 (p. 71) the reaction type is a rather superficial one. The predicates are especially well marked in the inner associations, and have almost without exception an objective character. As the number of egocentric reactions show, comparatively few subjective factors occur in the reactions. But as predicate types are never allowed to miss emotionally charged constellations, we find here also a small emotionally charged complex observable in the reactions. The experiment was carried out on a very hot day. Among the repetitions there were twice " snow " and twice " perspire." The following perseverations also occurred:

| | | | |
|---|---|---|---|
| 1. Stove | warm | 4. Water | bathe |
| 2. Walk | hot | 5. To dance | perspires |
| 3. ( — | — ) | | |

No. 3. *Subject intelligent, about* 26

| ASSOCIATIONS | NORMAL | | ASSOCIATIONS | NORMAL | |
|---|---|---|---|---|---|
| | 1st hundred | 2nd hundred | | 1st hundred | 2nd hundred |
| Co-ordination . . . | 9 | 9 | Same grammatical form . | 44 | 49 |
| Predicate . . . | 23 | 26 | Same number of syllables | 44 | 46 |
| Causal dependence . . | — | — | Alliteration . . . | 6 | 4 |
| | | | Consonance . . . | 14 | 9 |
| Coexistence . . . | 21 | 5 | Same ending . . | 2 | 13 |
| Identity . . . . | — | 10 | | | |
| Verbal-motor forms . . | 41 | 41 | | | |
| Word-completion . . | 2 | 4 | Inner associations . | 32 | 35 |
| Clang . . . . | — | — | | | |
| Rhyme . . . . | — | 2 | Outer associations . | 62 | 56 |
| Indirect . . . . | 2 | 2 | Clang-reactions . . | 2 | 6 |
| Meaningless . . . | — | — | | | |
| Faults . . . . | 2 | 1 | Number of associations . | 100 | 100 |
| Repetition of stimulus-word | — | — | | | |
| Egocentric reaction . . | 3 | 3 | | | |
| Perseveration . . . | 5 | — | | | |
| Repetitions . . . | 9 | 5 | | | |

No. 4 (p. 72) is a physician, 36 years old, who did not feel himself favourably disposed in the normal experiment. The experiment in outer distraction could not be executed on account of illness. The 100 associations carried out in "fatigue" were carried out after a disturbed, sleepless night.

*Inner distraction* and *fatigue* show striking agreement : decrease of inner associations, pronounced increase of the outer, and especially of the clang-associations and word-completions, increase of "same number of syllables," whilst the figures for "same grammatical form" remain more or less uninfluenced. In the first hundred of the normal experiment the inner associations predominate over the outer (47 : 43), in the second hundred the relation is reversed (30 : 59).

The continuously rising tide in the word-completions and clangs is beautifully seen in the experiment with inner distraction, if counted separately in each third of the 100 associations :

    1st third : 2 word-completions, 6 clangs
    2nd  ,,   5     ,,     7 ,,
    3rd  ,   9     ,,     9 ,.

No. 4.   *Subject 36 years old*

| ASSOCIATIONS | NORMAL | | INNER DISTRACTION | FATIGUE |
|---|---|---|---|---|
| | 1st hundred | 2nd hundred | | |
| Co-ordination | 24 | 14 | 7 | 4 |
| Predicate | 23 | 13 | 11 | — |
| Causal dependence | — | 3 | — | — |
| Coexistence | 15 | 12 | 5 | 9 |
| Identity | — | 8 | — | — |
| Verbal-motor forms | 28 | 39 | 31 | 20 |
| Word-completion | 1 | — | 16 | 16 |
| Clang | 2 | 4 | 20 | 27 |
| Rhyme | — | — | 2 | 8 |
| Indirect | 7 | 6 | 7 | 8 |
| Meaningless | — | 1 | 1 | 1 |
| Faults | — | — | — | — |
| Repetition of stimulus-words | — | — | — | — |
| Egocentric reaction | 1 | 1 | — | — |
| Perseveration | 3 | — | 1 | 2 |
| Repetitions | 2 | — | — | — |
| Same grammatical form | 42 | 57 | 45 | 47 |
| Same number of syllables | 33 | 30 | 47 | 53 |
| Alliteration | 15 | 22 | 32 | 26 |
| Consonance | 18 | 27 | 41 | 39 |
| Same ending | 6 | 11 | 6 | 21 |
| Inner associations | 47 | 30 | 18 | 4 |
| Outer associations | 43 | 59 | 36 | 29 |
| Clang-reactions | 3 | 4 | 38 | 58 |
| Number of associations | 100 | 100 | 100 | 100 |

The predicates begin to decrease in the second hundred of the normal experiment, decrease still more during inner distraction, and completely disappear in fatigue. Rhymes first appear in the fatigue experiment; in inner distraction there are only two, in the normal experiment none.

## CONSTELLATIONS AND COMPLEXES

In subject No. 4 we encounter a relatively large number of associations which are only explicable by personal events of recent date or of the present moment, e.g. *ring — part of garden* ; a golden ring had just been found in a garden of the asylum where the subject was working, whose owner it was necessary to discover.

Or, for example, *clothes — Stapfer* ; a patient Stapfer, of whom the physician had charge, gave him great trouble by ordering clothes to which he constantly took exception and which he refused to wear ; there were consequently many unpleasantnesses with the tailor and other tradespeople.

*Lead pencil — Koh-i-noor.* The subject had at the time of the experiment first learnt the delights of this kind of lead-pencil.

*Murder — Kaufmann.* This physician had at the time of the experiment to give an opinion on a man named Kaufmann who had committed a murder whilst drunk.

These kinds of associations are conditioned by distinct *constellations* (Ziehen), for they refer to recent subjective events charged with feeling.[1]

With many subjects (e.g. Nos. 2 and 4 of Uneducated Women, see pp. 98, 107) we find none, or but very few. Such individuals react quite objectively and betray nothing personal in their individual associations ; e.g. they associate *river — stream* ; *pupil — girl* ; *table — floor* ; *lamp — oil* ; *mountain — valley* ; *kiss — laugh* ; *plunder — catch* ; *hit — bite* ; *prison — punishment*, etc.

Other individuals certainly make objective associations, but here and there among them are found some which, despite their objective nature, do permit of some conclusion as to the individual, without betraying in the slightest degree the inner personality. From the following collected associations it was not difficult to detect the asylum attendant (No. 4 of Uneducated Men, p. 117) : *fetch — run* ; *smell — impure air* ; *inform — report* ; *prison — asylum* ; *ill — dejected* ; *gait — run* ; *freedom — recovery* ; *consciousness — drunk* or *sober*, etc.

Still the constellation plays a very indirect part in these associations.

Then there were individuals in whose associations it was not

[1] We know, of course, that no reaction is accidental, but that each, even the most objective, is conditioned by definite constellations. But there is a great difference if, for example, in *murder—Meyer* the murder is associated in the mind with a definite murder, from *murder—criminal*, where murder is a general concept. It is this distinction that we want to emphasize by the special term " constellation."

the momentary constellations, but the personal events, which stand out strongly (e.g. No. 5 of Educated Men) : *lake — Lake Lucerne* (he was now and then on Lake Lucerne) ; *father — grandfather* (his grandfather is still alive) ; *mountain — Glärnisch* (he was once there—not that the trip meant anything to him) ; *hair — hair-wash* (he prescribes now and then a hair-wash for patients) ; *Sweet — Sweeting* (the proper name of a person to whom the subject is quite indifferent) ; *potato — tobacco-plantations* (accidental reminiscence of the journey from Basle to Heidelberg) ; *coffee — Brazilian* (he has sometimes drunk Brazilian coffee). These are chiefly subjective reminiscences.

If we go a step further we come across *true constellations*, such as we first referred to in subject No. 4 of Educated Men. Individuals with many constellations have usually also many reminiscences (e.g. Nos. 4 and 5 of Educated Men).

A peculiar group of constellations occurs in many persons through the influence of the momentary surroundings in which the experiment is carried out. The reaction-words : *carpet, flowers, inkstand, calendar, books, penholder, landscape, telephone, curtains, tapestry, looking-glass, sofa,* etc., refer usually, even when quite appropriate associations to the stimulus-word, to these articles present in the room where the experiments are conducted. It is not necessary that the subject should always see them, he need only know generally that the particular articles are in the room (see No. 2 of Uneducated Women).

Pathologically, pronounced cases of this association type are known to us in normal, imbecile, hysterical stupidity.[1]

If the stimulus-word sets free a subjective, affect-toned image with the reaction, we have a special kind of constellation associations, the *egocentric* (see Part I). In subject No. 4 we meet only a few, e.g. *piano — atrocious* (the subject suffers a good deal from the strumming of neighbours who are not exactly first-class musicians) ; or, e.g. *to idle — delightful* ; the egocentricity of this reaction is obvious in an extremely busy man joyously awaiting the approach of his holidays.

In many cases the egocentric reaction can directly stand for a fault by the want of any reaction (see definition in Part I). A reaction certainly occurs, but through conscious or unconscious inhibition it does not attain utterance as a reaction word. Probably all faults have not this origin, but the majority certainly have.

Girls, for instance, make faults at reaction words which impinge on the sexual sphere, as to *kiss*, to *love*, to *caress*, *choose*,

[1] Cp. Jung, "Ueber Simulation von Geistesstörung," *Journal für Psych. u. Neur.*, Bd. II, 1903.

*faithful,* etc.   Often it does not reach " a fault," but the association *love — brother* requires a relatively long reaction-time, so
that the experimenter with a little practice discovers at once
what the innocent reaction *brother* conceals.

The associations *wedding — misfortune, kiss — never,* and
others in subject No. 5 of Educated Men, have an entirely analogous significance, for he was at that time in a condition of " fear
and trembling."

An emotionally charged image-complex can stand out so
prominently and act so intensively as to form a whole number of
constellations, faults, reactions with long reaction-time, all
referring to this image-complex.   Subjects Nos. 5, 6, 7, and 8 of
Educated Men will give us occasion to return to this special
kind of constellation, the *complex constellation.*   The majority
of complexes which have hitherto presented themselves in the
association experiments refer to direct or transposed sexuality.
In the work on the association of hysterics we shall return to
the complex effect.

In subject No. 4 of this group there are exhibited, together
with many reminiscences, fifteen constellations in the first hundred
of the normal experiment, four in the second hundred, one during
inner abstraction, and twelve during fatigue.   In the normal
experiment the names of definite persons frequently occur, e.g. of
patients whom the stimulus-word recalls, e.g. *clothes — Stapfer* ;
*attendant — Baum* (the name of one of the attendants) ; *Zahn —
Göschenen* (in Göschenen he had had a discussion about the
writer Zahn).

In subject No. 5 of this group the constellation is often expressed
through proper names.   During fatigue, where in No. 4 of this
group the constellations increase, these nearly always consist in
the reaction being a proper name linked merely by clang-similarity
with the stimulus-word.   The inner connexion of *clothes — Stapfer*
contrasts, e.g., with the purely clang *Steel — Stapfer.*

In No. 5 (p. 76) the condition at ten o'clock at night, after a
hard day's work, was taken to be one of fatigue.

The relation of inner to outer associations is not very positive
in the different experiments.   We find the maximum for outer
associations (61 per cent.) in fatigue, but it is very little greater
than the number in the first hundred in the normal experiment
(57 per cent.).   A minimum of clang-associations corresponds to
this maximum of outer associations.

Inner distraction is stronger than outer.   The first fifty
associations were carried out with the metronome at 60 beats,
the second fifty at 100 beats, and the last eighty-five associations
at 108 beats.

## No. 5.  *Subject, a Physician 28 years old*

| ASSOCIATIONS | NORMAL | | DISTRACTION | | | | FATIGUE |
|---|---|---|---|---|---|---|---|
| | 1st hundred | 2nd hundred | Inner | \_60 metronome | 100 | 108 beats | |
| Co-ordination     .    .    .    . | 19 | 27 | 11 | 20 | 20 | — | 20 |
| Predicate     .     .     .     .     . | 9 | 20 | 10 | 12 | 6 | 10 | 13 |
| Causal dependence     .     .     . | — | 1 | 2 | — | — | 2 | 1 |
| Coexistence     .    .    .    . | 11 | 13 | 8 | 2 | 2 | 6 | 5 |
| Identity     .     .     .     .     . | 5 | 10 | 7 | — | 2 | 12 | 6 |
| Verbal-motor forms     .     .     . | 41 | 17 | 30 | 34 | 32 | 40 | 50 |
| Word-completion .    .    .    . | 3 | — | — | — | 2 | 1 | 1 |
| Clang .     .     .     .     .     . | 6 | 6 | 27 | 20 | 14 | 5 | 1 |
| Rhyme     .     .     .     .     . | — | — | 1 | — | — | 1 | — |
| Indirect     .     .     .     .     . | 6 | 5 | 6 | 12 | 12 | 18 | — |
| Meaningless .     .     .     .     . | — | 1 | 1 | — | 10 | — | 1 |
| Faults     .     .     .     .     . | — | — | — | — | — | — | — |
| Repetition of stimulus-word  .     . | — | — | — | — | — | — | — |
| Egocentric reaction     .     .     . | — | — | 2 | 2 | 8 | — | — |
| Perseveration     .     .     .     . | — | 4 | — | 2 | 2 | — | 1 |
| Repetitions .     .     .     .     . | 3 | 2 | 3 | 4 | 8 | 21 | 8 |
| Same grammatical form.     .     . | 60 | 59 | 66 | 52 | 52 | 50 | 50 |
| Same number of syllables     .     . | 28 | 27 | 50 | 46 | 46 | 36 | 37 |
| Alliteration .     .     .     .     . | 14 | 14 | 38 | 36 | 18 | 15 | 8. |
| Consonance .     .     .     .     . | 30 | 23 | 43 | 28 | 30 | 20 | 20 |
| Same ending     .     .     .     . | 11 | 9 | 11 | 4 | 4 | 9 | 6 |
| Inner associations     .     .     . | 28 | 48 | 23 | 32 | 26 | 12 | 34 |
| Outer associations     .     .     . | 57 | 40 | 45 | 36 | 36 | 58 | 61 |
| Clang-reactions     .     .     .     . | 9 | 6 | 28 | 20 | 16 | 7 | 2 |
| Number of associations .     .     . | 100 | 100 | 100 | 50 | 50 | 85 | 78 |

Inner associations reach the maximum in the headings clang, same number of syllables, same grammatical form, alliteration, consonance.

The clang-associations progressively decrease in outer distraction, the indirect associations progressively increase—a relationship which we do not often meet in the experiments on distraction. In the last third of the experiment in inner distraction the subject became more indifferent, almost hypnoidal. The number and intensity of the visual images which emerged at the same time decreased, whilst the clang-associations increased as follows :

<pre>
1st third :   3 clang-associations
2nd    ,,      6          ,,
3rd    ,,     18          ,,
</pre>

The number of perseverations oscillates within normal limits. Examples :

<pre>
Faithful ⌐— perjured
Once      ⌐— fidel
</pre>

The origin of this perseveration is obvious : *fidel* is on one side a clang-association to *fidèle*, which is itself a translation of faithful.

<pre>
Stimulus-word, Fruit      Thurgau
       ,,       False      Falk
</pre>

The family orders its fruit from a place called Thurgau, from a certain Mr. Falk. Falk is a clang-association to the second stimulus-word and a coexistence to the first stimulus-word.

<pre>
Love ⌐ Stern
Son  ⌐ Isaac
</pre>

Stern is the name of a Jewish young lady. Isaac, the son of Abraham, if it is not quite a verbal association, is almost one from common usage. The association to Stern is an inner one.

<pre>
Alt (old)            Uchtspringe
Freiheit (freedom)   in Altman
</pre>

Dr. Alt is the well-known head of Uchtspringe. Freiheit is the name of a peak in the neighbourhood of Altmann; thus a perseveration of a purely external nature.

In inner abstraction we find in this subject an example of continuous perseveration of visual images appearing at the same time as the reaction. The reaction-words are only linked to the stimulus-words by clang :

<pre>
Malt        malster. Visually : a brewery.
Almighty    Halma. Visually : a cask with malt.
Well        the house at the well. Visually : at the place where a
            strong smell of malt was always perceptible he
            often saw malt-carts as a lad.
</pre>

After the first reaction, *malt — maltster*, the subject could not repeat his own reaction-word—he had forgotten it ; during the associations attention was directed much more to the visual associations than to the verbal ones. We find this forgetfulness of the stimulus- or reaction-word much more frequently in pathological cases of emotional stupidity and hysteria.

### COMPLEX PHENOMENA AND THE UNCONSCIOUS

On going through the associations of our subjects, the practised hand comes across complex phenomena which in normal persons are very important for comparison with pathological cases where the complexes play a great part. Unfortunately, the reaction-times were not measured in the material used in No. 5.

The material used here is not only that given in the experiments in the above table (p. 76), but was also derived from some earlier work with this subject. The following experiments were made :

| On 17/9/19— | 78 associations without fatigue (not used in the work) |
| 27/12/19— | 78 „ „ „ „ „ „ |
| 27/12/19— | 78 „ during „ (made use of) |
| 22/2 of ensuing year | 156 „ „ „ (not used) |
| 19/8/19— | 200 „ without „ (used) |
| 19/8/19— | 100 „ in inner distraction |
| 25/8/19— | 185 „ in outer „ |

During the period in which all these experiments took place the subject had his emotions roused by his interest in a young lady. In order to understand the experiments, it must be further mentioned that the young man had not yet entirely escaped from the period of internal conflict, and that his feelings towards a Jewish girl caused him, who had been brought up a strict Christian, great distress. We will call her Alice Stern, which satisfies the demands of truth in so far as is necessary for the experiment In the experiment on 17/9/19— we find the following complex constellations :

1. Marriage — misfortune
2. Come — O come with me (1)
3. Suffer — my God, yes !
4. Sorrow — who never nights of sorrow !
5. Kiss — never
6. Play — by many a gay sport shall thy time be beguiled (2)
7. Sofa — a certain couch (in boudoir of the lady in question)
8. Love — is useless
9. Troth — sweetheart
10. Wreath — Jungfernkranz (thought of with the appropriate tune) [1]
11. Hope — thou shouldst us whilst living (continuation : love and solace be giving)

[1] From *Der Freischütz*—the Bridal Wreath (*Jungfernkranz*) song.— TRANSLATOR.

Nos. 1, 5, and 8 are concealed wishes, although their form is negative.

Nos. 2, 4, 6, 10, and 11 are quotations or verses from songs No. 6 is the continuation of No. 2, a quotation from the *Erlkönig*.

It is very remarkable that among the seventy-eight associations there is only one other quotation : ·

Must    no man must must

and that quotations as a rule very seldom appear in the associations of this subject. The complex thus makes use here of a form of reaction which is otherwise unusual in this subject. It is characteristic that he—to his shame, be it said—has only remembered from the *Erlkönig* the little fragment : " O come and go with me ; by many a gay sport shall thy time be beguiled." [1]

He knows the tune of the *Jungfernkranz* perfectly, but only the fragment of the libretto " For thee we twine the bridal wreath."

In the working out of hysterical associations we shall return to the emergence of songs, tunes, and quotations, often mere fragments, which is frequently quite unconscious and automatic (cp. the corresponding manifestation in No. 3 of the group of Uneducated Women, p. 101).

In the first experiment on 27/12/19— among the associations were :

| | | |
|---|---|---|
| 1. It | it, it, it, and it. It is a hard decision | |
| 2. Thou | yes . . . I | |
| 3. Separate | it hurts | |
| 4. Stern | h'm ! | |
| 5. Play | merrymaking (with a long reaction-time) | |
| 6. Heart | (begs not to be obliged to utter the reaction-word ; it would have been " Stern ") | |

The associations 1, 2, 3, 4, and 6 explain themselves from what has been already said. The sudden long reaction-time in No. 5 is suspicious after what has gone before.

From the experiment on 27/12/19— during fatigue the following associations were taken :

| | | | | |
|---|---|---|---|---|
| 1. A kiss | yesterday (*gestern*) | | 4. Wonder | yesterday |
| 2. Love | yesterday | | 5. Pray | yesterday |
| 3. Already | yesterday [2] | | | |

The reaction-times were generally quite brief. He had the feeling as if the reaction slipped out unobserved. In the whole

---

[1] In the original the subject misquotes even this fragment.

[2] *Schon* (already)—*gestern* (the previous stimulus-word was *Tränen*). The subject then thought he heard *schön* (beautiful) instead of *schon* (already) ; possibly there was a perseveration of the umlaut.

experiment there was no repetition of any reaction, except twice *vegetable* (after *potato* and *sour*). In the remaining experiments repetitions are also few.

All these stimulus-words belong to those having close relationship to the complex " Stern." The stimulus-word *schon* (already) is apprehended as *schön* (beautiful) (see foot-note, p. 79).

It will be remembered that the examples 4 and 5 were reactions which then stood in the closest connexion with the complex (Religion !). *Kiss* and *yesterday* (gestern) is not to be regarded as a reminiscence ; that was not the kind of relationship. Whether the unconscious had allowed itself to make use of the second syllable (ge — stern) symbolically, or whether the word is connected with the fact that the experiment took place directly after the Christmas holidays, when the subject was made exceedingly happy by a little attention on the lady's part, cannot be ascertained. But the fact that this word, and only this one, is so often repeated in the experiment as the reaction to the complex stimulus-words is most striking. It stands for the quotations in the previous experiments. In this experiment there is not a single quotation.

The experiment on 22/2 of the following year took place during fatigue. The following associations are worth mentioning :

Song        Nora : a complex quotation (" Of all the girls," etc., " Nora most does please me." The vowel *o* comes in the two-syllabled real name of the lady in question. The two names are very similar in clang)

Sacrifice — dog (apparently meaningless)
Marriage — wether

A perseveration of the reaction. In the combination *sacrifice — wether — marriage* the complex certainly plays a part ; in connexion with this the perseveration in the experiment on 19/8 explains itself.

{ Love — stern
{ Son — Isaac

One association has no sense : *rich — yesterday* (gestern). Probably yesterday occurred as the stereotype in the transferred associations. It occurs again in the experiment *people — yesterday* : here again one can only guess. Perhaps the concept Jews is a middle term. The association *sport — parents* is indirect ; the middle term, unconscious in this case, is the quotation

" O come and go with me, loveliest child," etc.

the meaning of which we have learnt above.

There are also :

| Inn | star (he was here conscious of the complex) | | |
|---|---|---|---|
| Kiss | together | To eat | is painful |
| Love | roses | To caress | is painful |
| Parting | painful | To hit | is painful |
| | | To sing | is painful |

The first four associations belong to the complex, the remainder are but stereotyped repetitions of " parting is painful " ; the repetitions must be here regarded also as effects of the complex.

In the distraction experiments there were no distinct complex manifestations :

No. 6.   *Subject : Teacher of Natural History, 25 years old*

| ASSOCIATIONS | NORMAL | | ASSOCIATIONS | NORMAL | |
|---|---|---|---|---|---|
| | 1st hundred | 2nd hundred | | 1st hundred | 2nd hundred |
| Co-ordination . . . | 19 | 21 | Same grammatical form. | 46 | 26 |
| Predicate . . . | 28 | 32 | Same number of syllables | 28 | 15 |
| Causal dependence . . | 2 | 1 | Alliteration . . . | 5 | 6 |
| | | | Consonance . . . | 8 | 14 |
| Coexistence . . . | 15 | 2 | Same ending . . | 1 | — |
| Identity . . . . | — | — | | | |
| Verbal-motor forms . . | 20 | 19 | | | |
| Word-completion . . | 2 | 5 | Inner associations . | 49 | 54 |
| Clang . . . . | — | 1 | | | |
| Rhyme . . . . | — | — | Outer associations . | 35 | 21 |
| Indirect . . . . | — | — | Clang-reactions . . | 2 | 6 |
| Meaningless . . . | 1 | 5 | | | |
| Faults . . . . | 10 | 11 | Number of associations . | 78 | 78 |
| Repetition of stimulus-word | — | — | | | |
| Egocentric reaction . . | 14 | 27 | | | |
| Perseveration . . . | 6 | 8 | | | |
| Repetitions . . . | 6 | 15 | | | |

In the second half of the normal experiment the following increased :

(1) Inner associations from 49 to 54 per cent., while the outer decreased.

(2) Clang-associations from 2 to 6 per cent.

F

(3) Perseverations from 6 to 8 per cent.

(4) Egocentric reactions from 14 to 27 per cent.

.. (5) Constellations from 56 to 73 per cent.

(6) Repetitions from 6 to 15 per cent.

The following were well above the average :

    Inner associations.

    Perseverations.

    Egocentric reactions.

    Faults.

    Predicates (see section on Averages, p. 142).

The verbal-motor reactions remain about the same in both halves ; there are no indirect associations. The figures indicate that the individual's reaction is very subjective and that by analogy one may suspect some complex. In favour of this view is the high number of constellations (56 and 73 per cent.). On analysis they are found to refer overwhelmingly to *school* and to *bride*. The subject is an enthusiastic teacher. The complex bride, wedding, etc., plays a predominant part in the second half, where generally the subjective phenomena increase. In the first half :

26 per cent. of the reactions refer to the school—21 per cent. to the *bride* complex.

In the second half :

21 per cent. of the reactions refer to the school—24 per cent. to the *bride* complex.

In addition, it must be noted that in the first half two to three, and in the second half the majority, of the faults relate to the *bride* complex, e.g. the faults to the stimulus-words *caress, ill, suffer, kiss.* Otherwise the complex expresses itself much more openly than in the previous case. He is less repressed and has no use for quotations from songs like No. 5. School and fiancée, moreover, are closely connected in No. 6, as shown by a dream that they would be soon married and that his wife would hold an important position in the institute.

Among the thirteen repetitions in the first half, there occur four times the name of the institute, twice an important event in the school, three times the name of his fiancée. In the second half the fiancée's name occurs seven times in the reactions, twice the word *child*, when he was thinking of his future paternity. The other repetitions refer mostly to school affairs. Three times the subject was annoyed by the stimulus-words appearing to him nonsense, reacting each time angrily with "rubbish."

With two exceptions the perseverations refer to school and family affairs.

Finally, a few of these complex associations may be grouped :

| | |
|---|---|
| Grandmother | S. will be (S. is his fiancée's name) |
| Angry | myself as teacher according to S. |
| ⎧ Come | wrote S. |
| ⎨ Year | will marry (in two years) |
| ⎩ Sunday | S. is coming |
| ⎰ Kiss | (subject does not react) |
| ⎱ Naturally | (  ,,      ,,    ,.    ,,  ) |
| Love | S. |
| Tears | she cried (S.) |
| ⎰ Faithful | S. |
| ⎱ Once | S. |
| ⎰ Hope | we have to marry |
| ⎱ Small | child (!) |
| ⎛ Pray | I never will (presentation of a child praying) |
| ⎜ Love | child |
| ⎟ Where ? | in bed |
| ⎝ Old | S. |
| Ring | engagement |
| Caress | (at first no reaction) S. |
| Child | my future one |
| ⎛ Sweet | a box of chocolates from S. |
| ⎜ Ride | M., the home of his fiancée, who used to ride when at home |
| ⎜ Friendly | S.'s family |
| ⎝ Three | members of the family (there are three in S.'s family) |

The stimulus-words bracketed together directly followed one another in the experiment.

As during the course of the experiment the subjective affect increased, the critical evaluation of the individual reactions also increased ; this is shown by the figures.

Subject No. 7 (p. 84).  In the second hundred of the normal experiment we come across a maximum of co-ordinations, predicate relationships, inner associations in general, whilst the outer associations decrease markedly.  This maximum also extends to the perseveration and egocentric associations.  Compared with the averages in Educated Men, the predicates in the second hundred, the total number of inner associations in general, as well as the perseverations and egocentric reactions, were far above the average ; their ratios are :

Predicates, 42 : 19·17 ;

Inner associations on the whole, 62 : 36·7 ;

Perseverations, 40 : 2·4 ;

Egocentric reactions, 19 : 2·8 ;

whilst the remaining figures diverge but little from the average. With the fifteenth stimulus-word of the second hundred (*kiss*)

No. 7.[1]   *Subject: Doctor, 23 years old*

| ASSOCIATIONS | NORMAL | | DISTRACTION | | |
| --- | --- | --- | --- | --- | --- |
| | 1st hundred | 2nd hundred | Inner | Outer | |
| | | | | 60 metro. | 100 metro. |
| Coordination | 19 | 20 | 7 | 12 | 8 |
| Predicate | 16 | 42 | 26 | 20 | 14 |
| Causal dependence | — | — | 3 | 2 | — |
| Coexistence | 24 | 5 | 10 | 30 | 22 |
| Identity | 5 | 3 | 5 | 10 | 4 |
| Verbal-motor forms | 29 | 23 | 22 | 12 | 38 |
| Word-completion | — | — | — | — | — |
| Clang | 2 | 3 | 18 | 4 | 6 |
| Rhyme | — | 1 | — | — | — |
| Indirect | 2 | 1 | 3 | 2 | 6 |
| Meaningless | 3 | 2 | 6 | 8 | — |
| Faults | — | — | — | — | — |
| Repetition of stimulus-word | — | — | — | — | — |
| Egocentric reaction | 4 | 19 | 2 | — | 2 |
| Perseveration | 4 | 40 | 5 | 4 | 10 |
| Repetitions | 8 | 8 | 8 | 4 | 4 |
| Same grammatical form | 58 | 26 | 32 | 62 | 42 |
| Same number of syllables | 34 | 22 | 35 | 50 | 52 |
| Alliteration | 12 | 8 | 31 | 12 | 10 |
| Consonance | 18 | 13 | 33 | 16 | 8 |
| Same ending | 6 | 5 | 2 | — | — |
| Inner associations | 35 | 62 | 36 | 34 | 22 |
| Outer associations | 58 | 31 | 37 | 52 | 64 |
| Clang-reactions | 2 | 4 | 18 | 4 | 6 |
| Number of associations | 100 | 100 | 100 | 50 | 50 |

[1] The reactions of this subject are reproduced *in extenso* in the section on Averages under " Complex Constellation Type," p. 140.

the complex reactions begin, at first interrupted by other reactions ; then the complex persists through twenty-six associations, then again there are interruptions, and finally disappears
towards the end of the second hundred.  On the whole, we find
as a maximum fifty per cent. complex constellations in the second
hundred of the normal experiment ; in the first hundred, thirteen
per cent., in inner distraction five, in outer eight.  In No. 6 of Educated Men we also found a rising tide of complex reactions in the
second hundred of the normal experiment.  The occurrence of
the complex, in this case conjured up by an adequate stimulus-
word—*kiss*—likewise caused a marked increase of the inner associations, in consequence of the great stirring up of attention.
That an increase of inner associations corresponds with the
manifestation of a complex is a proof that our classification is
to some extent correct and natural.  The more affect the
stimulus-words have for the individual, the more the stimulus-
words claim attention, the more do the inner associations increase.
This phenomenon is exactly the reverse of the distraction phenomenon ; attention is better in consequence of the irruption of
an affective complex influencing the whole personality, because
attention is more directed towards the significance of the stimulus-
word.

If the attention is diverted from the experiment by an
emotionally toned complex instead of by outer distraction, as,
for example, in No. 4 (experiment after sleepless night), who was
under the influence of a strong affect, we see the opposite of the
phenomena which we have just described in subject No. 7 :
the inner associations decrease and the result is very similar to
that obtained from inner or outer distraction.

We have in the second hundred the occurrence and persistence
of a complex charged with emotion, so that, contrary to what
usually obtains in the second hundred, there is an increase instead
of a decrease of the inner associations, predicates, etc.

The fact that among the stimulus-words in the second hundred
there are rather more which arouse slight emotional presentations
has no special import in this case any more than in No. 6, for
the complex manifests itself in response to apparently quite
indifferent stimulus-words.

It is remarkable that in the complex constellations the reactions
readily occur in the form of a sentence, very seldom doing so in
the remaining associations.

In distraction the complex plays no rôle.  We find in inner
distraction a maximum of clang-reactions (eighteen), which is
slightly above the average for Educated Men.

In the first part of outer distraction we find in the reactions a maximum of "same grammatical forms" (sixty-two) and "same number of syllables" (fifty); in inner distraction, on the other hand, a maximum of alliterations (thirty-one) and consonances (thirty-three per cent.).

No. 8.  *Subject: Chemist, about 24 years old*

| ASSOCIATIONS | NORMAL | | DISTRACTION | |
| --- | --- | --- | --- | --- |
| | | | Outer | |
| | 1st hundred | 2nd hundred | 60 metro. | 100 metro. |
| Co-ordinations . . . . . | 21 | 18 | 24 | 16 |
| Predicate . . . . . . | 20 | 14 | 2 | 10 |
| Causal dependence . . . . | 2 | 2 | — | 2 |
| Coexistence . . . . . | 18 | 11 | 16 | 16 |
| Identity . . . . . . | 5 | 9 | 24 | 10 |
| Verbal-motor forms . . . . | 26 | 32 | 28 | 44 |
| Word-completion . . . . | — | — | 2 | — |
| Clang . . . . . . | 2 | 2 | 4 | — |
| Rhyme . . . . . . | 1 | — | — | — |
| Indirect . . . . . . | 2 | 1 | — | 2 |
| Meaningless . . . . . | 1 | 1 | — | — |
| Faults . . . . . . | 2 | 9 | — | — |
| Repetition of stimulus-word . . | — | 1 | — | — |
| Egocentric reaction . . . . | 3 | 5 | 2 | 2 |
| Perseveration . . . . . | 2 | 1 | — | 4 |
| Repetitions. . . . . . | 11 | 12 | 8 | 2 |
| Same grammatical form . . . | 37 | 54 | 86 | 70 |
| Same number of syllables . . . | 35 | 34 | 58 | 42 |
| Alliteration. . . . . . | 7 | 5 | 8 | 8 |
| Consonance . . . . . | 7 | 11 | 24 | 12 |
| Same ending . . . . . | 9 | 8 | 24 | 12 |
| Inner associations . . . . | 43 | 34 | 26 | 28 |
| Outer associations . . . . | 49 | 52 | 68 | 70 |
| Clang-reactions . . . . . | 3 | 2 | 6 | — |
| Number of associations . . . | 100 | 100 | 50 | 50 |

*Inner Associations.*—In the second hundred of the normal experiment a decrease, which is much greater in distraction.

*Outer Associations.*—Increase in the second hundred and in distraction. Predicates increase chiefly in the second hundred, also constellations.

*Verbal-motor Forms.*—Increase in the second hundred and in the second half of distraction, where we find the maximum.

*Repetitions* and *faults* are found mostly in the second hundred of the normal experiment, besides an increase of " same grammatical forms" " same number of syllables," " alliteration," " consonances," and " same ending " in distraction.

In the second part of distraction an improvement of the association occurs (perhaps by the subject's becoming accustomed to the distraction) ; slight increase of inner associations, predicates, faults, clangs, slight decrease of same grammatical forms, number of syllables, consonances, and same ending. Against this increase of verbal-motor forms, and those of outer associations, most of the perseverations likewise occur here.

The constellations are nearly all conditioned by love or the subject's profession    There occur :

In first hundred normal experiment .   44 per cent.
,, second  ,,     ,,       .,   . 20   ,,
,, first half of distraction .    .  . 6   ,,
,, second  ,,     ,,  .   .  . 14   ,,

The following perseverations conditioned by a complex are worth noting :

1. { Lady      of my heart
    Shoulder   blade
    Brace      embrace (pictures to himself some erotic situation)
2. { Square    town hall
    Grass     square (the perseveration is not accidental)

Connected with the town hall is a very definite erotic affair not without importance to the subject.

We find faults of two kinds in No. 8. Often the verbal reaction fails and in its place there emerges, for example, a vivid visual image or a vivid emotional image, which he subsequently describes.

In the other kind there are inhibitions because definite erotic reminiscences emerge.

In distraction no " faults " occur. The " egocentric " reactions predominate in the normal experiment and refer mainly to erotic matters.

Of reaction-words repeated, only *bright, good,* and *beautiful* occur more than once.

*The Complex.*—The erotic complex took a large number of reactions into its service ; thirty were demonstrable in the normal experiment and ten in the second half of distraction, i.e. fifteen per cent. in normal experiment and twenty per cent. in the second half of distraction. In the first half, where the distraction was more complete, we came across none. The complex is hardly repressed at all ; on the contrary, it is most manifest.

The progressive decrease of the clang-associations in the course of external distraction, and increase of indirect associations correspond to the rules we have suspected (see Averages).

No. 9 (p. 89). The figures show a very moderate distraction phenomenon. The relationship of inner to outer associations is very little altered in the distraction experiment, so that, e.g., the variation between the results of the two experiments in fatigue is greater than that between normal experiment and distraction. On the other hand, the clang-associations increase in distraction, as in No. 5 of this group ; in both cases there are fewer clang-associations in fatigue. The fatigue-associations were carried out with both persons under very similar conditions (normal fatigue after professional day's work, ten o'clock at night), whilst the fatigue-associations of No. 4 of this group were preceded by a sleepless night with the mind severely taxed from affect. We there found an increase of the clang-associations in fatigue.

The inconsiderable result of distraction in No. 9 is perhaps connected with the number of inner associations being pretty small even in normal experiment (24 to 26 per cent. instead of 36·7 per cent., the average for educated men) and the number of outer associations pretty large (72 to 69 per cent. instead of the average of 52·7 per cent.).

The number of inner associations in the normal experiment is about as great as the average numbers of inner associations in distraction (Educated Men).

The effect of fatigue is visible in the first experiment on fatigue, not in the second.

In distraction the figures for alliteration and consonance have distinctly increased, as with Nos. 4 and 8 of this group.

The number of *repetitions* is also above the average ; there are relatively many words which are repeated twice, but very few which are often repeated. In nearly all the experiments *pleasant, unpleasant, willingly, unwillingly, friendly,* and similar words are among the words repeated. We will not enter here into the individual repetitions and perseverations because they do not so readily suggest affect-toned thoughts as the earlier cases ; nevertheless this background is not absent.

No. 9.    *Subject : Doctor, 25 years old*

| ASSOCIATIONS | NORMAL | | DISTRACTION | | | FATIGUE | |
| --- | --- | --- | --- | --- | --- | --- | --- |
| | | | Inner | Outer | | 1st experiment | 2nd experiment |
| | 1st hundred | 2nd hundred | | 60 metro. | 100 metro. | | |
| Co-ordination | 9 | 9 | 11 | 12 | 8 | 13 | 13 |
| Predicate | 14 | 17 | 18 | 16 | 16 | 6 | 20 |
| Causal dependence | 1 | — | — | — | — | — | 1 |
| Coexistence | 24 | 7 | — | 8 | 14 | 7 | 12 |
| Identity | 5 | 19 | 8 | 2 | 10 | 9 | 5 |
| Verbal-motor forms | 43 | 43 | 55 | 56 | 42 | 61 | 49 |
| Word-completion | — | — | 2 | — | — | — | — |
| Clang | — | 3 | 4 | 6 | 2 | 1 | — |
| Rhyme | 1 | — | — | — | — | — | — |
| Indirect | 2 | 1 | — | — | 4 | 1 | — |
| Meaningless | 1 | — | 2 | — | 4 | 1 | — |
| Faults | — | — | — | — | — | — | — |
| Repetition of stimulus-words | — | — | — | — | — | — | — |
| Egocentric reaction | 3 | 3 | — | — | — | — | — |
| Perseveration | 5 | 1 | 2 | 2 | — | 1 | 4 |
| Repetitions | 16 | 15 | 22 | 12 | 10 | 18 | 18 |
| Same grammatical form | 57 | 51 | 47 | 42 | 50 | 67 | 59 |
| Same number of syllables | 42 | 42 | 45 | 32 | 28 | 45 | 48 |
| Alliteration | 8 | 6 | 20 | 22 | 28 | 20 | 11 |
| Consonance | 14 | 10 | 28 | 26 | 38 | 21 | 14 |
| Same ending | 12 | 10 | 12 | 10 | 14 | 12 | 10 |
| Inner associations | 24 | 26 | 29 | 28 | 24 | 19 | 34 |
| Outer associations | 72 | 69 | 63 | 66 | 66 | 77 | 66 |
| Clang-reactions | 1 | 3 | 6 | 6 | 2 | 1 | — |
| Number of associations | 100 | 100 | 100 | 50 | 50 | 156 | 156 |

The constellations are but scanty.  Here we also find a decrease of the clang-associations and an increase of the indirect associations in the second part of outer distraction.

### GENERAL REMARKS ON THE EXPERIMENTS ON THE
### GROUP OF EDUCATED MEN

There were at our disposal nine persons aged from 23 to 47 with 3793 associations. On five persons experiments were made in inner and outer distraction, on one in inner only, on one with outer only, on two there were no experiments in distraction. From five persons associations were taken during fatigue, one of them in a state of drowsiness. All the individuals in this group have had a university career. Six of them are doctors, one a medical student, one a high-school teacher, and one a chemist. They are all German-Swiss.

Only one belongs to the predicate type (No. 3). Unfortunately, distraction experiments could not be made in this case.

The inner distraction experiment was successful in four cases ; most characteristic is the great increase of clang-reactions ; the lessening of inner, with the increase of outer, associations was less noticeable. In one case (2) the success was other than might have been expected ; in one (9) there was no definite result, the subject having already had a maximum of outer associations in normal experiment.

Outer distraction succeeded distinctly in two cases ; in two cases success was but moderate ; in one case (9) there was again no distinct affect. On the whole inner abstraction acted rather more intensively than outer. The subjects in question were always better able to fulfil the experimental conditions of inner abstraction.

The associations arising in fatigue gave in three of the five cases a result similar to that in distraction. In one case (4) it was peculiarly clear ; it is possible, however, that the fatigue was not responsible or not entirely so, for the patient had had a peculiarly exciting experience in the sleepless night and was probably still very much distracted by this during the experiment.

The association experiment during drowsiness likewise gave a result similar to an experiment in distraction in subject No. 1.

In four persons (5, 6, 7, 8), in the course of the experiments, especially in the normal experiment, we came across extensive complex phenomena. In the first three (5, 6, 7) we saw how the inner associations increased in the second hundred of the normal experiment, whilst the outer decreased ; thus the opposite occurred of what one might expect ; simultaneously we find a rise in the complex constellations. In the distraction experiment the complex constellations usually decreased or disappeared.

The complex phenomena need not be conscious to the individual and often are not apparent till the association material is statistically worked out and classified.    In individuals without pronounced complex types slighter complex phenomena are often discovered, e.g. in No. 4 (see below for the full discussion of association types), or again in No. 2, where in making a curve of the reaction-times some emotionally toned clang-associations came to light, part of them of quite old standing.

Every prolongation of the reaction-time, even within quite normal limits, and not reaching consciousness at all, denotes, so far as we know at present, that the stimulus-word in question has encountered an emotional complex.    A later chapter deals with these investigations.

## 3. UNEDUCATED WOMEN

*Eight subjects with* 2400 *associations* [1]

No. 1 (Table on p. 92).    Some of the associations of this individual are given on pp. 94–96.

As among uneducated persons in general, we find more inner and fewer verbal-motor reactions than among educated persons. The increase of the inner associations, especially of the predicates in the second hundred of the normal experiment, may be again referred to the occurrence of greater personal participation after the subject had become accustomed to the experiment.    We have met this phenomenon repeatedly.

Distraction did succeed but was not a striking success.    The outer associations increased, clang and indirect associations occurred, whilst they were absent in the normal experiment. It is remarkable that the perseverations are also more numerous.

There are many grounds for the slight effect of distraction. The subject has relatively many predicate relations without quite belonging to the predicate type, a mark of which is a lessened distraction phenomenon.    It was often difficult for the subject to dissociate her attention and to react simultaneously with the metronome and to the reaction-word.    Secondly, the experiments with uneducated women left us the impression that the dissociation of attention causes them more difficulty than it does the educated.    They are for the most part fully occupied by the experiment and work with their attention highly concentrated. The more powerful the means of distraction, the more do they strain every nerve.    Thirdly, we know that in this case the experiment had a very strong mental effect upon the subject. The affect of a strong complex that had been just recently partly

[1] On grounds of technique the experiment in inner distraction could not be carried out with any of the uneducated persons.

No. 1.   *Subject : Asylum Nurse, aged* 18, *Swiss ; secondary school education*

| ASSOCIATIONS | NORMAL | | DISTRACTION | |
|---|---|---|---|---|
| | | | Outer | |
| | 1st hundred | 2nd hundred | 60 metro. | 100 metro. |
| Co-ordination | 23 | 20 | 16 | 14 |
| Predicate | 23 | 37 | 20 | 22 |
| Causal dependence | 2 | 1 | — | — |
| Coexistence | 28 | 14 | 38 | 30 |
| Identity | 1 | 5 | 2 | 2 |
| Verbal-motor forms | 23 | 23 | 14 | 30 |
| Word-completion | — | — | — | — |
| Clang | — | — | 6 | 2 |
| Rhyme | — | — | — | — |
| Indirect | — | — | 2 | 2 |
| Meaningless | — | — | — | — |
| Faults | — | — | — | — |
| Repetition of stimulus-word | — | — | — | — |
| Egocentric reaction | 3 | — | — | — |
| Perseveration | 1 | — | 4 | 4 |
| Repetitions. | 11 | 9 | 14 | 2 |
| Same grammatical form | 60 | 53 | 68 | 58 |
| Same number of syllables | 36 | 44 | 48 | 46 |
| Alliteration. | 16 | 7 | 4 | 12 |
| Consonance | 15 | 11 | 12 | 8 |
| Same ending | 5 | 6 | 10 | 8 |
| Inner associations | 48 | 58 | 36 | 36 |
| Outer associations | 52 | 42 | 54 | 62 |
| Clang-reactions | — | — | 6 | 2 |
| Number of associations | 100 | 100 | 50 | 50 |

assuaged came to the surface and this markedly influenced the reaction. The experiment was a resurrection of a complex which had already become somewhat dormant. It thus happens that even in the distraction experiment we encountered a large number of distinct complex reactions, which is very unusual.

The complex phenomena demand a brief explanatory anamnesis of the subject. She is of country origin and became an asylum nurse at the age of 17, after having brooded at home for over a year over the unhappy ending of a love affair. Her father, a violent-tempered man, would not countenance, in any way, her love affair, and on one occasion there was a scene, when he cursed her because she dared to contradict him. Shortly before the associations were carried out she had burnt her face, which gave her a great shock ; her convalescence was slow. Reflection during this period reawakened her mental pain. The association experiment itself was a further cause of exacerbating her gloomy memories ; its effect lasted some time, a proof of how intensely these experiments act as a reagent among the uneducated and with what strong affinity an emotionally toned complex can absorb and render real a fairly large mass of reaction-words or reaction-images. Now, six months after the experiment, she is objective towards the complex, whose influence is still noticeable. Whilst she then laid chief stress on her unhappiness because her father had cursed her, now she no longer hides the deeper erotic threads in attempting to elucidate the reactions. It is remarkable how acutely she still remembers some of the particular reactions of that time.

The number of complex constellations distinctly provable amount to :

|  | 1st Half | | 2nd Half |
|---|---|---|---|
| In normal experiment | 15 | .. | 21 |
| In distraction | 16 | .. | 14 |

As already stated, we seldom, as a rule, find complex constellations in distraction, and rarely to this extent. Naturally distraction was much prejudiced through this. As in other cases, we explain the maximum of the complex constellations in the second hundred of the normal experiment by a new adjustment, by a gain of confidence during the course of the experiment.

The complex expresses itself in such ready mintage, as quotations, snatches of songs, titles of stories, and so on ; this perhaps makes the complex less noticeable, or makes the tax on the emotions less. Quotations are frequently masks. In ordinary life we use them in this way also. Certain songs are sung in certain moods, often to avoid expressing the thoughts which are the source of this mood—hence a masking. Again, the song or the quotation is used to exaggerate a rudimentary feeling, in order to awaken a spark of this feeling by the very exaggeration itself ; think, for example, of patriotic songs, or of birthday verses or those composed for feasts or other celebrations.   Examples :

Come      to the fields.

The quotation is from the story of the idle schoolboy who wants to make the good boy play truant ; the idle boy becomes later a scamp, the persevering, industrious boy becomes a respected teacher.   The quotation has a very different background for the subject herself.   It is not without reason that *fields* occurs twice in the normal experiment.   In the orchard at home there is a beautiful tree with a grass-plot around (*at home = field*) ; here she often dreamed, and, watching the railway-lines near by with the trains coming and going, her imagination would weave travel plans.   After the unhappy ending of her love affair she had a wish-fulfilment dream : " She lay in the tree-garden in the grass close to her lover."   To this day the thought of this dream gives her joy.   To the stimulus-word *dream* she at once reacted *joy*, and her eyes sparkled at the memory of the wish  dream.

 Further quotations :

At home      it's lovely

refers to a song ; the meaning is clear.
Again :

Once      was I happy.

She had once heard a troublesome, demented catatonaic sing :

Once was I happy<br>
But now nevermore ;<br>
Cheated me has love, the witch, cheated me sore.

In the three subsequent associations she is still fixed to the complex :

| | |
|---|---|
| Once | was I happy |
| Wonder | love |
| Blood | sin (thinks of her father's curse) |
| Wreath | death. (For months she wished she could die. For several weeks she scarcely ate anything, in order to get ill, and she became in consequence very thin. After the experiment which had revivified the complex, and after a visit home which she paid soon after, she again, on her return to us, began to eat little and to get thin, until this was noticed and the folly of her behaviour brought home to her.) |

In other places she quotes the titles of stories whose contents refer to the complex, e.g. :

Seven      brothers.[1]

---

[1] After breaking off her relationship her brother is the only person in whom she can confide at all.

" The Seven Brothers ' is the title of a story where the self-sacrificing brother is rewarded.

The association immediately following was :

Ill    my brother

The quotations, six in all, only occur in normal experiment, just as in No. 5 of Educated Men, and all refer to the complex.

We have already quoted two instances where the complex causes fixation to one presentation.  Some others occur, e.g. the perseveration.

Friendly—⌐ friendship<br>
Three   —⌐ friends

She has an intense need of friendship ; but disappointments always arose : her best friend married another girl.

Another example from the experiment in distraction :

Meadow—⌐ the tree-garden<br>
Bring   —⌐ apples

It is not a question of direct perseveration of the reaction but of the presentation of the situation lying at its root.   In the course of this work we shall include these forms under the term perseveration.   The connexion between *meadow* and *tree-garden* is obvious from the preceding.   The *apples* naturally arise from the same tree-garden.

Of the four ( = 8 per cent.) perseverations in the distraction experiment there is only one probably that refers to the complex.

*Repetitions.*—In the normal experiment seven reaction-words occur several times (two to five times) ; at least thirteen of these seventeen words belong by their context to the complex.   In the distraction experiment (100 reactions) there were in all eight reaction-words which occur several times (two to three times). The percentage relationship is therefore about the same as in the normal experiment ($2 \times 8 = 16$).   Four of these .(8 per cent.) certainly refer to the complex.

The word *man* (human being) is repeated with striking frequency, eight times in 300 associations (normal experiment + distraction).   Seven of these reactions certainly belonged to the complex ; at times quite definite persons are intended by *man*, often the subject herself.

Similarly, we frequently find the reaction-word *person* as universal concept with a quite concrete meaning in the sense of the complex, e.g. :

Station    the person<br>
Bad        the person

A quite definite person is meant—a woman friend of the subject who plays an important part in the complex, and who is not irreproachable morally—has an illegitimate child and has done various things open to criticism. By the reaction *man* this same friend is again sometimes understood, who with her easy-going ways of life has more luck in love than our more serious subject.

| Lazy | man |
| Virtue | of man |

In this instance there was a perseveration of the reaction-word itself, from which it may be gathered how strong is the emotional tone of this presentation.

We frequently find the definite article used in the reaction in the same way as in the masking of the complex constellation. Thus our subject in normal experiment used the article twenty-six times in the reaction, seventeen of these reactions certainly referring to the complex. In distraction the relation is less striking.

We find this same phenomenon again in other subjects. In illustration of the complex reaction a few instances are here given :

| Proper | person (see above) |
| To attend to | the person |
| Bad | the person |
| Pray | the devout (referring to herself ; she prayed very much in her times of difficulty) |
| ⎧Wonder | of love (referring to herself ; also atonement) |
| ⎩Blood | of the atonement (she feels herself guilty in regard to her father. There is here a perseveration of the outer form of the reaction) |
| Omen | of punishment (with the same sense ; this reaction is grammatically meaningless here and is only explicable as probably the after-effect of the previous reaction forms. This reaction is separated from the above reactions by a few others) |
| Normal · | the man (a definite one) |
| Meadow | the tree-garden |
| Bring | the apples |

(see above for the elucidation of these associations)

| Mild | the father |
| Subtle | the serpents (quite definite persons) |
| ⎧Docile | the pupil (with both associations she thought of the friend of her youth) |
| ⎨ | |
| ⎩Order | the industrious one |
| Angry | the man (means her father) |

and so on.[1]

---

[1] The brackets to the left of the stimulus-word mean that these stimulus-words followed one another in the experiment.

In the distraction experiment there were many words she did not understand, viz. *hate, love, remorse, fall, pleasant*; and, further, *rattle, glass, hammer, entrance, ears, hinder.*

It was seen at once in the analysis that under the influence of the complex, half consciously, half unconsciously, she could not or would not understand the first series of these stimulus-words because, according to her account, all these stimulus-words intimately touched the complex which she was trying to repress.

The second series of these stimulus-words were really not understood on account of the acoustic disturbance caused by the metronome. The subject has thus found a further device for concealing her complex in an apparently innocent way. It is appropriate to the situation because, as proved by the second series of stimulus-words—those that do not touch the complex—it is easy, with the constant noise of the metronome, not to understand or to understand incorrectly the stimulus-words in the distraction experiments. (The non-understood stimulus-word was always replaced by another word.)

The not-wishing-to-understand corresponds to a more or less conscious repression of the complex; it is not different in principle from those cases (hysteria) where failure to react or incorrect reacting occurs involuntarily.

Among the complex reactions we have a large group, that of masked complex reactions. In our subject this masking extends to the following kinds, so far as we can differentiate them :

(1) By quotations (songs, titles of books, quotations from books).

(2) By the use of simple, general concepts in the particular sense of the complex.

(3) By the addition of the article. The reaction thus receives an apparently objective varnish ; it then looks like the habitual answer of the elementary-school child.

(4) By the misunderstanding of those stimulus-words which arouse the complex.

Finally, it must be stated that in the complex reactions abnormally long reaction-times frequently occurred ; unfortunately, no complete measurements were made with this subject so that we cannot work out the point any further in this case.

In No. 2 (p. 98) the abnormally high figures for co-ordination and coexistence, in normal experiment as well as in distraction, are striking. They are in part far above the mean values. On the other hand, the number of predicate and verbal-motor reactions is relatively small, below the mean, especially the predicates. The figures certainly find their explanation in the extremely objective

STUDIES IN WORD-ASSOCIATION

uniform nature of the reactions, apparently little troubled by complexes.

**No. 2.** *Subject : a Nurse, intelligent but not highly educated ; 22 years old ; South German*

| ASSOCIATIONS | NORMAL | | DISTRACTION | |
| --- | --- | --- | --- | --- |
| | | | Outer | |
| | 1st hundred | 2nd hundred | 60 metre. | 100 metre. |
| Co-ordination | 33 | 34 | 18 | 22 |
| Predicate | 3 | 9 | 2 | 4 |
| Causal dependence | — | 1 | 4 | 2 |
| Coexistence | 36 | 25 | 28 | 34 |
| Identity | 6 | 11 | 24 | 18 |
| Verbal-motor forms | 15 | 16 | 20 | 18 |
| Word-completion | — | — | — | — |
| Clang | — | 1 | 2 | — |
| Rhyme | — | 3 | 2 | 2 |
| Indirect | 4 | — | — | — |
| Meaningless | 3 | — | — | — |
| Faults | — | — | — | — |
| Repetition of stimulus-word | — | — | — | — |
| Egocentric reaction | — | 1 | — | — |
| Perseveration | — | — | — | — |
| Repetitions | 5 | 8 | — | — |
| Same grammatical form | 91 | 78 | 92 | 88 |
| Same number of syllables | 67 | 56 | 58 | 48 |
| Alliteration | 8 | 7 | 2 | 2 |
| Consonance | 7 | 18 | 22 | 14 |
| Same ending | 22 | 19 | 22 | 16 |
| Inner associations | 36 | 44 | 24 | 28 |
| Outer associations | 57 | 52 | 72 | 70 |
| Clang-reactions | — | 4 | 4 | 2 |
| Number of associations | 100 | 100 | 50 | 50 |

There were just a few reactions with a rather longer reaction-time.  In our experience reactions of over 5·0 seconds arouse a strong suspicion of emotionally toned constellations.

In this subject we found in normal experiment twelve associations with a reaction-time of over five seconds, in the distraction experiment only three.

In the following examples of delayed reaction-time the delay is presumably to be regarded as the effect of an erotic complex.

| | | | |
|---|---|---|---|
| Marriage | girl : | 6·8 seconds | |
| To kiss | laugh : | 6 | ,, |
| To love | willing : | 5·6 | ,, |
| Male nurse | cupboard : | 8 | ,, |
| Dream | basket : | 6·4 | ,, |
| Ripe | fruit : | 6·6 | ,, |
| To bless | to receive : | 5·8 | ,, [1] |

The subject usually reacted strongly at any hint of an erotic nature and blushed very easily.

She herself states that she felt awkward in replying to the first three stimulus-words.

To the stimulus-word *male nurse* she felt too embarrassed to say the word *female nurse* which first occurred to her, obviously because her thoughts at once took an erotic turn. She looked around her and named the first object she saw in the room—*cupboard.*

To the stimulus-word *dream* the erotic thoughts in the background prevent her reacting.  Instead of making a sensible reaction the subject again thrust herself into the external world, saw the paper-basket in the room, and said " Basket."  The meaningless reaction was thus a result of the complex action.

The reactions *ripe — fruit* and *bless — receive* are obvious instances of the same sexual *gêne.*

Distraction by objects in the surroundings is, as we know from the experiences of psychopathology, a phenomenon to be regarded as the effect of emotion.[2]

In the embarrassment or confusion which arises where the stimulus-word arouses emotionally toned presentations, which the subject consciously or unconsciously tries to repress, she allows herself to be entirely distracted by the external world and reacts verbally by simply naming some object at hand.  Among certain hysterics this is a very pronounced phenomenon.

Out of sixteen stimulus-words which are repeated in the normal experiment we call attention to : *industrious,* five times ; *good,* three times ; *fine,* twice ; *right,* twice ; the remaining are

---

[1] The medium normal reaction is somewhere between one and two seconds.

[2] Cp. " Emotionelle Stupidität."  Jung, " Ueber Simulation von Geistesstörung," *Journal f. Psychol. u. Neur.*, Bd. II, 1903.

distributed among many diverse images ; these show her good moral training. It is characteristic that these suggestions of subjectivity disappear in distraction.

In the classification it became difficult to draw a precise line between co-ordination and co-existence. On the whole, it can be said that she belongs to a very objective type, one slightly influenced by constellations—a type we shall meet again in No. 4 of this group.

The following reactions illustrate to some extent her general objective reaction type :

| Soft | hard | Rinse | wash | Star | moon |
|------|------|-------|------|------|------|
| Youth | old age | Building | wall | Faithful | obedience |
| Trouble | sorrow | Sleeve | dress | Plunder | catch |
| Window | glass | Park | garden | Freedom | isolation |
| False | true | Glass | iron | Repentance | anxiety |
| Sweet | sour | Soft | chair | Stork | pigeon |
| Wide | narrow | Paint | whitewash | Bicycle | cart |
| Honey | bees | | | | |

The unusually large number of reactions with " same grammatical form " is a parallel to the many co-ordinations and co-existences, and confirms what has just been said.

*Distraction* is very distinct ; decrease of the inner, increase of the outer associations. We have clang-reactions only in the second hundred of the normal experiment and in distraction, indirect associations only in the first hundred. The rule we have suspected of the reciprocity between indirect and clang-associations would again hold here.[1]

Incidentally, it must be mentioned that the subject carried out the experiments with great zeal, and by concentrating her whole attention in distraction also strained herself to the utmost to do justice to the increased demands.

No. 3.   This subject has a fairly marked tendency to make rhymes which increases in the distraction experiment, chiefly in the second hundred.

The usual distraction phenomenon did not occur, although she belongs to the predicate type. The beats were also executed very irregularly. The predicates increase in distraction ; outer associations, especially the verbal-motor reactions, decrease, the clang-reactions alone continuously increase.

*Constellations* are found mostly in the second hundred of the normal experiment and in the first half of the distraction experiment. The latter fact proves that the distraction experiment has been, anyway in part, well chosen, for, with the exception of No. 1 of this group, where the distraction experiment was

[1] See section on Averages, p. 130.

likewise a failure, during distraction the constellations almost entirely disappear in the other subjects.

No. 3.   *Subject : Nurse, 21 years old ; Swiss ; secondary education*

| ASSOCIATIONS | NORMAL | | DISTRACTION | |
| --- | --- | --- | --- | --- |
| | | | Outer | |
| | 1st hundred | 2nd hundred | 60 metro. | 100 metro. |
| Co-ordinations . . . . . | 20 | 16 | 22 | 8 |
| Predicate . . . . . . | 5 | 11 | 16 | 18 |
| Causal dependence . . . . | 1 | 1 | 2 | — |
| Coexistence . . . . . | 24 | 10 | 18 | 8 |
| Identity . . . . . . | 4 | 6 | 10 | 14 |
| Verbal-motor forms . . . . | 43 | 47 | 24 | 36 |
| Word-completion . . . . | 1 | 1 | — | 2 |
| Clang. . . . . . . | — | — | 2 | 2 |
| Rhyme . . . . . . | 1 | 2 | 2 | 8 |
| Indirect . . . . . . | — | 5 | 2 | 2 |
| Meaningless . . . . . | — | — | 2 | 2 |
| Faults . . . . . . | 1 | 1 | — | — |
| Repetition of stimulus-word . . | — | — | — | — |
| Egocentric reaction . . . . | 1 | — | — | 2 |
| Perseveration . . . . . | 2 | 2 | 2 | — |
| Repetitions . . . . . | 6 | 5 | 8 | 4 |
| Same grammatical form . . . | 75 | 50 | 76 | 60 |
| Same number of syllables . . . | 48 | 39 | 56 | 46 |
| Alliteration . . . . . | 9 | 8 | 6 | 2 |
| Consonance . . . . . | 13 | 9 | 18 | 16 |
| Same ending . . . . . | 13 | 12 | 12 | 20 |
| Inner associations . . . . | 26 | 28 | 40 | 26 |
| Outer associations . . . . | 71 | 63 | 52 | 58 |
| Clang-reactions . . . . . | 2 | 3 | 4 | 12 |
| Number of associations . . . | 100 | 100 | 50 | 50 |

Here are a few individual examples.   To the stimulus-word *lamp* she did not react till after twenty seconds with *oil-*

*lamp.* Shortly before, she had had a pleasant dream in which, instead of the nine-o'clock supper which she seldom took, she was to have a new lamp which she had much desired in her room.

*Window-glass,* ten seconds (in between, thought of *plate-glass* windows). She thought of a big shop with beautiful plate-glass windows. The subject was for some time the private nurse 'of the wife of the owner of a business of this kind, and remained very devoted to her former patient. One sees how apparently indifferent expressions are determined in every connexion by coincident thoughts.

Strike      6 o'clock : 2 seconds

The subject had been on night duty in an observation ward and had to get up at six o'clock every evening.

The reaction
Paint      peintre : 6·8 seconds

with its long reaction-time, refers to a sojourn of one year in French Switzerland. The subject, then quite a young girl, was adored by a painter, who was most insistent in his desire to paint her. In the reaction-word *peintre,* besides the masking of the constellation by a superficial association, there is a further constellation, since she here uses a French word with the reminiscence of an erotic event in French Switzerland. In the distraction experiment she again reacts

Painter      peintre : 13 seconds

with the same constellation. The characteristic long reaction-time at both places is worth noting. The following reactions quickly followed one another :

Wedding      to-morrow : 2·2 seconds
and
Come      to-morrow : 1·4  ,,

This repetition is not accidental. The day after the normal experiment she was to celebrate her birthday. She was glad, for she wanted to go out and had been invited to spend the day ; she looked forward to receiving good wishes from all and was also expecting a letter from her sweetheart.

We find also the reactions :

Rich      in love : 2 seconds
and, later,
Poor      in virtue : 2·2 seconds

The first is a quotation from Ernst Zahn's *Albin Indergand* referring to a love story, and has the force of a complex-quotation for the subject, such as we have reported in No. 5 of Educated Men and No. 1 of Uneducated Women. The second is an analogous but self-made form. She was thinking of another nurse with whom she had had a discussion on " love " the previous day ; the other had taken up a far less ideal point of view on this question. The stimulus-word *poor* had become associated to the earlier stimulus-word *rich,* and the affect-toned reaction connected with it ; she thus became conscious that her own ideal of love was contrary to that of the other nurse. By *poor—in virtue* is understood the other nurse.

The same thought gave rise to the following quotation :

> Despise      dost imagine : 2·2 seconds

The quotation runs :

> Dost imagine that I should
> Hate life for ever,
> [To the desert fly
> Because not all
> Budding dreams do ripen ?]—PROMETHEUS.

She only knows the two first verses of this quotation ; the part in brackets she has quite forgotten.

She here thought of the other nurse and her base views about " love." It will be seen how closely similarly related expressions and quotations associate to emotional complexes ; helping in this way in the construction of the infinitely large unconscious material of speech which subserves emotional complexes, making it possible for the poet, for instance, to compose endless variations on a single idea.

A further quotation—

> At last      endures not for ever : 5·6 seconds

again refers to her love complex. The reaction-time is strikingly long. She thought " of the brother of a woman friend," who suddenly appeared in the light of a sweetheart ; she was ardently waiting news as to whether or no he had accepted a position abroad, and wished all the time that he would not go.

To the stimulus-word *kiss* she reacted in a tone of surprise : *kiss — yes—I cannot tell you that ; we were speaking about something.* It was about the discussion with the other nurse, who said that kissing was disgusting. To the stimulus-word *time* she reacted :

> Time      proportionate : 2 seconds

The second reaction following was :

> To rule      proportionate : 3·8 seconds

At "to rule" an elderly nurse came into her mind who is placed in charge of a whole section. A little episode of the day made her think, " She rules over us in everything." The reaction-word *to rule* liberated these thoughts, which she could not utter; instead she gave the reaction-word *proportionate*, which she had just used; this had a meaning in relation to *time* but not to *rule*, or only a very remote one. The gap in the reaction thus conditioned by the affect is filled up by a reaction-word already present. We demonstrated a similar phenomenon in No. 5 of Educated Men, who in an experiment in fatigue invariably answered to a series of stimulus-words that aroused complexes by *yesterday*.

The reaction

Love      needed : 4 seconds

was accompanied by a sudden change in the expression of her face. This phenomenon had reference to her love complex, and is important for us because in the pathology of associations we find similar reaction phenomena (altered expression, sudden lowered voice) when important affective complexes arise.

In

Choose      advice : 3·2 seconds

the subject thought that one must be very careful in choosing a husband; she thought that one should get good advice as to whom to choose.

Hope      not abandoned : 1·8 second

The reaction is a quotation from a letter recently received from the painter (*le peintre*) in West Switzerland, and from which it was evident that he had not yet renounced hope of her.

In the reaction

Love      empty : 3 seconds

the reaction-word was strongly emphasized; it refers to her own love affair, and must be placed alongside the reaction mentioned,

Love      needed : 4 seconds

with its altered expression of face.

The reaction

Weary      why : 1·8 second

is again a quotation. The verse runs as follows :

The maiden to the spider grieving,<br>
Asking : " Why so late ?<br>
Three long hours I sit here weaving.<br>
Is spinning all my fate ? "

In the stimulus-word *weary* the context of the verses is summarized. Besides this the reaction is determined by the clang between the stimulus-words *late* and *fate*. There is an obvious condensation (Freud) of two factors—situation and visible resemblance in the word, *weary*; and this condensation took place in the unconscious. This is proved by the fact of the reaction-time being very short, thus excluding any conscious attempt at a quotation. One also sees that the sub- or un-consciousness often likes to associate quotations or complexes in such a way that chance snatches of songs or verse become linked to the complex, the subject not knowing how the rest runs at all.

In the present instance, for example, the subject does not know the verses correctly by heart. We can further prove that behind this quotation there remains an adequate emotional-toned idea.

The lines, taken from some school verses, correspond to an emotional situation which existed about this time. As has been said, the subject was on night duty for some time in an observation ward. By day she slept; in the morning she was relieved by a nurse who had day charge of the same ward, and latterly she had been annoyed on several occasions at being relieved late by this nurse. This feeling is expressed in the reaction.

Behind the apparently very general reaction

Something    important: 1·2 second

there is concealed the thought of the festivity on the following day.

To the stimulus-words *to woo* there is no reaction. The cause of this is again the conversation with the other nurse about love. The latter had said that she had amused herself by writing to some out-of-the-way matrimonial agency and had been recommended a widower as a good *parti*. This idea displeased our subject very much. To the stimulus-words *to do* she reacts *and leave* (first section). Beneath this superficial reaction there is again masked the dispute about love.

When a complex is hidden by quotations of this kind or by superficial reactions, the reaction-time is generally a short one. Here we find a division of attention, whilst in so-called " faults " the attention is entirely absorbed by the complex, which is repressed; that is to say, it is to be concealed either from one's own consciousness or from that of the experimenter. A part of the attention is used up in the verbal reaction, and this then bears a very superficial (verbal-motor, clang-like) character; the other part is claimed by the affect-toned image. This part is frequently repressed, and does not reach full consciousness. This view is confirmed by the perception that such quotations and superficial reactions, which the observer may know very well, refer to and are conditioned by a powerful emotional complex, are often reproduced with the most indifferent countenance in the world.

The chief part of an affect-toned complex is dissociated and repressed from consciousness. The chain of images which occurs consciously at the same time contains, perhaps, merely a quotation as the representative of the complex. This may occur after a very short reaction-time, demonstrating to the experienced that under this cover an important complex is developing its effects in the unconscious.

In another case where the affect is already expressed in the quality of the reaction (emphasis, expression), this dissociation does not take place, the reaction becomes difficult and the reaction-time is delayed (see, for an example, *love — need* 4·0 seconds, in this subject).

In the distraction experiment, we found in No. 3 of Uneducated Women among the few cases of reaction-words repeated (*bicycle ride, Zurich, clear, sad*) two where a complex is certainly responsible for the repetition.

In the reactions

|  |  |  |  |
|---|---|---|---|
| Bicycle | wheel | Tram | trip |

she explained that her sweetheart frequently bicycled, and this came into her mind at once on hearing the stimulus-words.

In the reactions

| Fire | Zurich |
|---|---|

and

| Railway-station | Zurich |
|---|---|

she remembered that in the course of the discussion about love she had defended the town of Zurich and its inhabitants.

The reactions

| Moves | sad |
|---|---|
| Mild | sad |

are connected with family affairs.

In the reactions

| Sin | world : | 0·8 second |
|---|---|---|
| Repentance | death : | 1·2 „ |

a recent accident hovered before her, when a patient tried to drink some lysol taken out of the instrument cupboard. There were no serious consequences, but the event took place in this subject's ward and left a very painful impression and a great feeling of responsibility, hence the perseveration in the above reactions.

Nos. 4 AND 5.  *Subjects : Two Nurses, 27 and 28 years old respectively*

| ASSOCIATIONS | SUBJECT 4 | | | | SUBJECT 5 | | | |
|---|---|---|---|---|---|---|---|---|
| | Normal | | Distraction | | Normal | | Distraction | |
| | 1st hundred | 2nd hundred | Outer | | 1st hundred | 2nd hundred | Outer | |
| | | | 1st half | 2nd half | | | 1st half | 2nd half |
| Co-ordination    –    .    . | 46 | 46 | 54 | 26 | 21 | 32 | 14 | 16 |
| Predicate  .    .    .    . | 4 | 2 | — | 6 | 9 | 8 | 4 | 6 |
| Causal dependence    .    . | 1 | 3 | — | — | 1 | 1 | — | — |
| Coexistence    .    .    . | 30 | 15 | 18 | 32 | 32 | 15 | 14 | 12 |
| Identity  .    .    .    . | 4 | 13 | 16 | 18 | 6 | 8 | 12 | 8 |
| Verbal-motor forms    .    . | 14 | 18 | 12 | 18 | 30 | 32 | 50 | 48 |
| Word-completion    .    . | — | — | — | — | — | — | — | — |
| Clang.    .    .    .    . | — | — | — | — | — | 2 | 2 | 8 |
| Rhyme    .    .    .    . | — | — | — | — | — | — | 2 | — |
| Indirect    .    .    .    . | 1 | 2 | — | — | — | — | — | 2 |
| Meaningless    .    .    . | — | 1 | — | — | — | 1 | — | — |
| Faults    .    .    .    . | — | — | — | — | 1 | 1 | 2 | — |
| Repetition of stimulus-word . | — | — | — | — | — | — | — | — |
| Egocentric reaction    .    . | — | — | — | — | — | — | — | — |
| Perseveration    .    .    . | — | 1 | — | — | — | — | — | 2 |
| Repetitions    .    .    . | 8 | 5 | 6 | 4 | 10 | 9 | 0 | 2 |
| Same grammatical form    . | 85 | 86 | 96 | 90 | 76 | 69 | 68 | 70 |
| Same number of syllables    . | 60 | 53 | 58 | 56 | 54 | 43 | 48 | 42 |
| Alliteration    .    .    . | 11 | 6 | 8 | 2 | 16 | 19 | 28 | 28 |
| Consonance    .    .    . | 15 | 7 | 10 | 8 | 14 | 21 | 30 | 36 |
| Same ending    .    .    . | 25 | 17 | 12 | 24 | 17 | 14 | 12 | 22 |
| Inner associations    .    . | 51 | 51 | 54 | 32 | 31 | 41 | 18 | 22 |
| Outer associations    .    . | 48 | 46 | 46 | 68 | 68 | 55 | 76 | 68 |
| Clang-reactions  .    .    . | — | — | — | — | — | 2 | 4 | 8 |
| Number of associations    . | 100 | 100 | 50 | 50 | 100 | 100 | 50 | 50 |

## No. 4

*Nurse, Swiss, 23 years old ; elementary-school education*

The results of the experiments resemble very closely No. 2 of this group. The distraction phenomenon is less well marked (in both experiments she exerted all attention), clang-reactions are absent altogether, and the number of verbal-motor forms is still lower than in No. 3. The coexistences reach a high figure. The predicates are few, egocentric reactions are absent—a fact which speaks in favour of a very objective apprehension of the words. The figures for same grammatical form are, as in No. 2 of this group, remarkably high. The subject belongs, therefore, to the same objective reaction type without demonstrable constellations. Many associations had delayed reaction-times for which we had no subsequent explanations. We are not in possession of any more searching analysis.

## No. 5

*Nurse, Swiss, about 28 years old ; elementary-school education*

The predicates are relatively much diminished (in the normal experiment, for example, only 8·5 per cent. instead of 20·4 per cent., the average for Uneducated Women). The co-ordinations in normal and distraction experiments are below the average—the verbal-motor forms, on the other hand, above the average—for Uneducated Women (the average is 24 per cent. in normal experiment and 28·8 per cent. in outer distraction). On the whole, we have a case with relatively few inner, but many outer associations.

Nevertheless—or rather, because the general reaction type seems somewhat superficial—the distraction experiment succeeded, whereas usually, among Uneducated Women with many predicates, distraction does not succeed so well. Although the outer associations in the second part of the distraction are not more numerous than in the first hundred of the normal experiment, still the inner associations do distinctly fall off, whilst the clang-reactions increase.

In the second hundred of the normal experiment we have an increase of the inner associations, and at the same time we find, as is fairly usual, an increase of the constellations, which we consider, as is so often the case, the cause of the alteration. (The fact that in the second hundred stimulus-words there are many more which arouse emotional images than in the first hundred may also have its influence.) In the first hundred of the normal experiment six constellations were noticed, ten in the second hundred, and two in the distraction experiment. They diminish in the distraction experiment. They are almost exclusively complex constellations.

The complex is bound up with a love affair with an unhappy ending ; after a long friendship she was jilted by her sweetheart.

The long reaction-times (mostly over five seconds) are almost entirely limited to these complex constellations. Examples :

| | | | |
|---|---|---|---|
| Attendant | male nurse : | 11·4 | seconds (her sweetheart was an attendant) |
| Heart | stomach : | 6·4 | ,, |
| Caress | love : | 5·6 | |
| Separate | go : | 5·6 | |
| Love | wicked : | 8·8 | ,, |
| Freedom | confined : | 6 | ,, |
| Despise | respected : | 18·4 | ,, |
| Tie | tear : | 5·2 | ,, |
| False | falseness : | 7·2 | ,, |

The subject was unwilling to give any exact account about a small remaining number of constellations and long reaction-times, which could not be set down to the complex as a matter of course ; they are, on that account, the more suspect. We have here another good instance of that special kind of complex expression—prolonged reaction-times (by this is not meant that these do not occur in other cases also, e.g. with rather difficult, unusual stimulus-words).

We have already met prolonged reaction-times as complex phenomena (subjects 3 and 4 of this group) ; here they are almost exclusively complex signs. They pass into the so-called " faults " when no verbal reaction follows at all.

The repetition of the reaction word is almost entirely limited to the normal experiment and concerns sixteen different words, the majority referring to things connected with the daily life of an asylum nurse.

## No. 6

*Nurse, Swiss, 18 years ; elementary-school education*

A glance at the proportion of predicates to co-ordinations teaches us that this subject must be accounted a predicate type. In accordance with the rule for this type, we find no distinct effect of distraction. Clang-reactions and indirect associations only occur in the first part of distraction. The egocentric reactions are pretty well represented and equally divided. The highest number of inner and the smallest number of outer associations again occur in the second hundred of the normal experiment.

Nos. 6 AND 7.    *Subjects : Two Swiss Nurses, 18 and 27 years respectively*

| ASSOCIATIONS | SUBJECT 6 | | | | SUBJECT 7 | | | |
|---|---|---|---|---|---|---|---|---|
| | Normal | | Distraction | | Normal | | Distraction | |
| | | | Outer | | | | Outer | |
| | 1st hundred | 2nd hundred | 1st half | 2nd half | 1st hundred | 2nd hundred | 1st half | 2nd half |
| Co-ordination . . . | 22 | 19 | 14 | 12 | 19 | 30 | 4 | 8 |
| Predicate . . . . | 27 | 45 | 50 | 48 | 32 | 32 | 36 | 16 |
| Causal dependence . . | 1 | 1 | — | — | 2 | 1 | — | — |
| Coexistence . . . | 31 | 14 | 6 | 12 | 26 | 12 | 10 | 6 |
| Identity . . . . | 2 | 3 | 6 | 10 | 2 | 4 | 6 | 2 |
| Verbal-motor forms . . | 16 | 11 | 18 | 18 | 18 | 18 | 36 | 36 |
| Word-completion . . | — | — | — | — | — | — | — | — |
| Clang. . . . . | — | — | 2 | — | — | — | — | 2 |
| Rhyme . . . . | — | — | — | — | — | — | — | — |
| Indirect . . . . | — | — | 4 | — | — | — | — | — |
| Meaningless . . . | — | — | — | — | — | — | 4 | — |
| Faults . . . . | 1 | 7 | — | — | 1 | 3 | — | — |
| Repetition of stimulus-word . | — | — | — | — | — | — | 4 | — |
| Egocentric reaction . . | 3 | 2 | 2 | 2 | — | — | — | — |
| Perseveration . . . | 7 | 1 | 2 | — | 2 | — | 8 | 14 |
| Repetitions . . . | 13 | 11 | 14 | 6 | 14 | 9 | 18 | 4 |
| Same grammatical form . | 50 | 29 | 28 | 32 | 31 | 35 | 38 | 60 |
| Same number of syllables . | 37 | 24 | 48 | 52 | 53 | 43 | 20 | 14 |
| Alliteration . . . | 6 | 3 | 6 | 6 | 13 | 9 | 28 | 30 |
| Consonance . . . | 9 | 5 | 12 | 6 | 15 | 12 | 34 | 30 |
| Same ending . . . | — | 2 | 2 | 4 | 6 | 11 | 20 | 28 |
| Inner associations . . | 50 | 65 | 64 | 60 | 53 | 63 | 40 | 24 |
| Outer associations . . | 49 | 28 | 30 | 40 | 46 | 34 | 52 | 74 |
| Clang-reactions . . . | — | — | 2 | — | — | — | — | 2 |
| Number of associations . | 100 | 100 | 50 | 50 | 100 | 100 | 50 | 50 |

We see there also a maximum of " faults " (seven), which are almost all evoked by a complex.

Unfortunately, the subject vouchsafed no real explanation, and her reserved character forbade persistence on this point. She merely stated that reminiscences of certain family affairs were concealed beneath the faults and long reaction-times. Unusual stimulus-words were responsible for a few of these.

## No. 7

*Nurse, Swiss, 27 years ; elementary-school education*

Distraction was a distinct success ; it was chiefly characterized by a diminution of co-ordinations and an increase of the verbal-motor forms, whilst the predicates, although pretty numerous, were more stable in quantity. Perseveration occurs mainly in distraction, especially in the second hundred of the distraction experiment.

There are no egocentric reactions.

From the nature of the reactions it is not evident whether constellations or complexes do or do not play a part in the associations. Some conclusions can be more readily drawn from the reaction-times, inasmuch as some of the strikingly long reaction-times occur in reaction to insidious stimulus-words ; e.g. :

| Kiss | morning kiss : | 8·4 seconds |
| Remember | letter : | 11   ,, |
| Bad | — | (fault) |
| Vagabond | without fortune : | 12·6 seconds |

Any accurate mental analysis, however, is absent in this case.

In the distraction experiment repetitions of the form of the reaction occur ; they are mostly reactions in the form of a simple sentence, e.g. :

| Sin | men sin |
| Repentance | men repent |
| Love | men love |
| Strong | men are strong |
| Hate | men hate, etc. |

But no strikingly long reaction-times occur. Whether this repetition of the word, especially the repetition of the word " men," denotes complex phenomena similar to those we found in No. 1 of this group cannot be elicited.

Looked at externally, the associations of this person make a very objective impression, without many subjective constella-tions. But the rather changing reaction-times, often remarkably long, suggest that behind the apparently objective reactions true

## No. 8.  Subject : a Swiss Servant, 27 years

|  | SUBJECT 8 | | | |
|---|---|---|---|---|
| ASSOCIATIONS | Normal | | Distraction | |
|  | | | Outer | |
|  | 1st hundred | 2nd hundred | 1st half | 2nd half |
| Co-ordination | 10 | 13 | 10 | 20 |
| Predicate | 48 | 32 | 37 | 32 |
| Causal dependence | — | — | — | 2 |
| Coexistence | 11 | 4 | 14 | 4 |
| Identity | 2 | 5 | 2 | 2 |
| Verbal-motor forms | 23 | 42 | 25 | 32 |
| Word-completion | — | 2 | 2 | 2 |
| Clang. | — | — | — | 2 |
| Rhyme | — | — | 2 | — |
| Indirect | — | — | 2 | — |
| Meaningless | — | — | — | — |
| Faults | 6 | 1 | 6 | 4 |
| Repetition of stimulus-word | — | — | — | — |
| Egocentric reaction | — | — | 2 | — |
| Perseveration | — | 1 | — | — |
| Repetitions | 15 | 15 | 8 | 2 |
| Same grammatical form | 38 | 38 | 34 | 40 |
| Same number of syllables | 42 | 36 | 44 | 54 |
| Alliteration | 3 | 11 | 6 | 8 |
| Consonance | 11 | 15 | 10 | 8 |
| Same ending | 6 | 8 | 4 | 6 |
| Inner associations | 58 | 45 | 47 | 54 |
| Outer associations | 36 | 51 | 41 | 38 |
| Clang-reactions | — | 2 | 4 | 4 |
| Number of associations | 100 | 100 | 50 | 50 |

complex constellations are probably to be found.   For practical reasons it was not feasible to carry out the mental analysis in all the subjects so exhaustively as it, fortunately, proved possible with a certain number of them.

The marked predominance of the predicates is a characteristic of the reaction ; these are mainly responsible for the high number of the inner associations. A definite tendency to critical valuations is present, but these have no pronounced subjective (egocentric) character. The reactions denote active participation in the experiment—as to the sense of the stimulus-words. Despite a certain reserve and bashfulness, the more intimate content of the images comes out pretty distinctly. The subject is a very excellent and practical servant, very religious, and was thinking of getting married. In the reactions of the normal state the following reactions are repeated :

| | |
|---|---|
| Practical, twice | Good, thrice |
| House, twice | Beautiful, four times |
| Room, twice | Splendid, thrice |
| Church, twice | Man, thrice |
| God, twice | Child, five times |

Shortly before carrying out the associations she happened to be attacked by a big dog, which frightened her very much.

The reaction *dog* was four times repeated. Once there was strong perseveration at the picture of the dog.

| | |
|---|---|
| Growl | dog |
| Lumps | lumps on the dog's paws |

The reaction *wolf* was twice repeated. To the stimulus-word *sly* she reacted with *wolf*, spontaneously announcing that really *fox* was the first to come to her mind. These reactions and repetitions distinctly point to emotional complexes and to an active participation of the personality in general.

The distraction experiment—which was, however, only carried out very incompletely—had no effect at all. Thus we see here the same characteristic behaviour as in the predicate types described above.

The numerous faults in this subject can be thus grouped :

Of the seven faults in the normal experiment, four occur with undoubted emotionally charged stimulus-words (such as *heart, manners, hypocrite, faithful, rich, revenge*, etc.) ; of the ten faults in distraction 8 per cent. (four) with emotionally charged stimulus-words ; a further proof that faults in the majority of cases are referable to emotional causes.

H

SUMMARY

In the group of Uneducated Women we have eight subjects aged from eighteen to twenty-eight years, with 2400 associations. We have 200 associations from each in normal experiment and 100 associations in outer distraction.

Most of the subjects are fairly intelligent. More than half had attended a secondary school after the elementary school. Seven habitually spoke the Swiss dialect ; only one spoke a South German dialect (which is nearer to High German). Seven were hospital nurses, one was a servant. Two reacted with a predicate type ; in neither was the distraction experiment successful. In a third with considerable predicates, but yet not exactly belonging to the predicate type, the distraction experiment likewise miscarried. This was partly because at many stimulus-words, not wishing her attention to be distracted, she failed to make the strokes to the beats of the metronome. The distraction experiment only half succeeded in one subject, with many co-ordinations and absence of constellations. In the distraction experiment she redoubled her efforts, in order to pay attention to the stimulus-words as well as to the metronome beats. In the other four subjects the distraction experiment succeeded, although these on the whole also put forth all their efforts in the distraction experiment and strained themselves considerably more than in the normal experiment, because it was more difficult for them than for educated persons to keep their attention divided. As a whole, the Uneducated Women are the least able of all the groups to divide their attention. Clang-associations play a much slighter part as distraction phenomena than in the groups of the educated. Two subjects belong to a purely objective type with few predicates, no constellations to speak of, and remarkably many reaction-words with the same number of syllables as the stimulus-words. In two others (Nos. 1 and 3) complex phenomena come to the fore in the most diverse forms. In three subjects there was, in the second hundred of the normal experiment, an increase of the inner and decrease of the outer associations. It was then generally noticed that the complex phenomena were more distinct in the second hundred of the normal experiment, whilst they diminished more and more in distraction. In the most pronounced cases, e.g. No. 1, the manifestation of the complex in the second hundred of the normal experiment is certainly not dependent upon the increase of emotionally charged stimulus-words. This manifestation occurred with stimulus-words which possess nothing of this quality for other people.

## 4.  UNEDUCATED MEN

In this group we give the tables of the first six cases in summary, the columns omitted having no special interest.  So far as the group of verbal-motor forms is especially concerned, we get the following averages, to which all six subjects adhere pretty closely : normal experiment : first hundred twenty-seven, second hundred thirty ;  outer  distraction : first  half  twenty-two, second  half thirty-four.  Distinct complex constellations are hardly to be demonstrated, and in nearly all cases a thorough analysis was wanting.

| ASSOCIATIONS | SUBJECT 1 (Male nurse, Swiss, aged 40) | | | | SUBJECT 2 (Male nurse, South German, aged 25) | | | | SUBJECT 3 (Male nurse, aged 54) | | | |
|---|---|---|---|---|---|---|---|---|---|---|---|---|
| | Normal | | Distraction Outer | | Normal | | Distraction Outer | | Normal | | Distraction Outer | |
| | 1st hundred | 2nd hundred | 1st half | 2nd half | 1st hundred | 2nd hundred | 1st half | 2nd half | 1st hundred | 2nd hundred | 1st half | 2nd half |
| Co-ordination. . . . | 34 | 12 | 16 | 16 | 32 | 37 | 24 | 20 | 5 | 22 | 10 | 12 |
| Predicate . . . . | 12 | 28 | 18 | 10 | 1 | 4 | 2 | 8 | 17 | 16 | 12 | 30 |
| Inner associations . . . | 49 | 41 | 34 | 26 | 33 | 42 | 26 | 28 | 23 | 38 | 22 | 42 |
| Outer association . . . | 50 | 51 | 62 | 60 | 64 | 53 | 64 | 66 | 75 | 59 | 56 | 48 |
| Clang-reactions . . . | — | — | — | — | 2 | 1 | 6 | — | — | 1 | 4 | 2 |
| Residual group . . . | 1 | 8 | 2 | 14 | 1 | 4 | 4 | 6 | 2 | 2 | 18 | 8 |
| Number of associations . . | 100 | 100 | 50 | 50 | 100 | 100 | 50 | 50 | 100 | 86 | 50 | 50 |

No. 1.  *Subject : Male Nurse, aged 40, Swiss ; elementary-school education, rather well-read*

The outer associations predominate over the inner, but not to the same extent as in the educated.  The effect of distraction is clear.  In the second hundred of the normal experiment we see the number of inner associations decrease, and the outer increase.

The figures for faults and egocentric reactions (four, eight, six, four) are remarkably high ;  they exceed the mean for these reaction forms.  In the absence of any exact analysis it is not possible to determine the significance of the faults in each association. There are no distinct constellation associations. The reaction-times, apart from the few faults, betray no complex constellations; they remain within small limits, 0·6 to 2·6 seconds.

No. 2.　*Subject: Male Nurse, about 25 years ; South German ; elementary-school education*

The outer associations predominate over the inner, as in the previous case. In the second hundred of the normal experiment there is an increase of the inner and decrease of the outer associations. When we met this phenomenon in the other groups we were able to ascribe it to the emotionally charged association complexes emerging more distinctly. Probably this is the case here also ; still, the constellation associations are not very distinct and we only possess a partial analysis. The sum of the reaction-times is greater in the second than in the first hundred ; longer reaction-times are more numerous. In the second hundred there is the reaction *family — alone*, 4·4 seconds, the longest reaction-time which occurred in this subject. The young man is engaged to a hospital nurse. A series of reactions with a rather long reaction-time is very probably conditioned by this complex.

We met the strongest distraction phenomena in the first part

| ASSOCIATIONS | SUBJECT 4 (Male nurse, aged 37) | | | | SUBJECT 5 (Male nurse, aged 30) | | | | SUBJECT 6 (Male nurse, aged 34) | | | |
|---|---|---|---|---|---|---|---|---|---|---|---|---|
| | Normal | | Distraction | | Normal | | Distraction | | Normal | | Distraction | |
| | | | Outer | | | | Outer | | | | Outer | |
| | 1st hundred | 2nd hundred | 1st half | 2nd half | 1st hundred | 2nd hundred | 1st half | 2nd half | 1st hundred | 2nd hundred | 1st half | 2nd half |
| Co-ordination. . . . | 15 | 15 | 22 | 10 | 32 | 16 | 18 | 12 | 46 | 27 | 30 | 22 |
| Predicate . . . . | 31 | 28 | 20 | 16 | 3 | 5 | — | 2 | 9 | 11 | 6 | 10 |
| Inner associations . . . | 49 | 46 | 44 | 26 | 35 | 21 | 18 | 14 | 56 | 40 | 38 | 32 |
| Outer associations . . . | 48 | 48 | 46 | 68 | 63 | 78 | 68 | 80 | 40 | 56 | 56 | 58 |
| Clang-reactions . . . | 1 | 1 | 4 | — | 1 | 1 | 8 | 4 | 1 | 1 | — | 2 |
| Residual group . . . | 2 | 5 | 6 | 6 | 1 | — | 6 | 2 | 3 | 3 | 6 | 8 |
| Number of associations . . | 100 | 100 | 50 | 50 | 100 | 100 | 50 | 50 | 100 | 100 | 50 | 50 |

of the distraction experiment, where we also found six clang-associations.

There are hints of constellations in some of the reactions, which refer to military service :

| | |
|---|---|
| Schoolboy | soldier |
| Faithful | soldier |
| Rank | file |

Others in all probability refer to his engagement and fiancée :

| | | |
|---|---|---|
| Love | trust : | 1·6 seconds |
| Hope | at last : | 1·6 ,, |
| Wreath | ripe : | 3·2 |
| Faithfulness | go a journey : | 2·4 ,, |
| Everywhere | alone : | ? |
| Family | alone : | 4·4 |
| Separate | meet : | 1·6 ,, |

The reaction-times, which are rather longer in proportion to the other associations, support this idea. There were no quotations or the like in this or the previous subject.

No. 3. *Subject : Male Nurse, 54 years ; secondary education, somewhat neurasthenic*

The distraction experiment did not succeed well ; it should be stated, however, that interest in associations which belong to the clang and residual group was stronger in the distraction experiments than in the normal experiments, whilst the egocentric reactions disappeared in distraction experiment—phenomena which may be regarded as more or less the effects of distraction. There were no manifest constellation or complex associations.

No. 4. *Subject : Male Nurse, 37 years ; elementary-school education*

He can also be counted among the *predicate* types. A certain distraction result can, however, be recorded. We notice that the inner associations visibly decrease ; we meet a distinct rise of the outer associations only in the second part of the distraction experiment ; on the other hand, we see in the first part of the distraction experiment a maximum of clang-reactions. Perseverations and egocentric reactions are quite absent. There are no distinct constellation associations. We have reviewed this case (one of the previous cases from this group would have done) in a discussion about constellations and complexes (see No. 4 of Educated Men) as an example of those cases where we meet the first constellations or subjective reminiscences (p. 73).

## No. 5. *Subject : Male Nurse, 30 years*

Inner associations diminish in this case as in the first two of this group. The predicates especially are very few in number. Obvious effects of distraction : The inner associations decrease considerably in the second hundred of the normal experiment as well as in the distraction experiment, especially in the second part. Clangs, rhymes, indirect and meaningless reactions increase in the distraction experiment, especially in the first part. In the second part they again diminish slightly, the decrease of inner and increase of outer associations being there most pronounced. The figures for " same grammatical form " are extremely high (eighty-six in first hundred of. normal experiment, forty-four in second hundred ; eighty-eight each in both halves of the distraction experiment). They are also high in the next case and in Nos. 2 and 4 of Uneducated Women. In accordance with this result, egocentric associations are absent, and the constellation associations diminish altogether and are not distinctly recognizable, just as in the other cases mentioned.

In the second part of the distraction experiment there are certain repetitions, probably from embarrassment, and as a phenomenon of distraction.

| No. 17.[1] | Door | castle |
|---|---|---|
| „ 55. | Hall | castle hall |
| „ 57. | Bridge | castle bridge |
| „ 69. | Banner | castle banner. |
| | Cellar | cellar door |
| | Corridor | door |

## No. 6. *Subject : Male Nurse, 36 years ; secondary education*

With fairly numerous inner associations co-ordinations are chiefly to be found, whilst the predicates are not particularly numerous. The verbal-motor forms are relatively scarce. A glance at the relation of inner to outer association shows at once that the distraction experiment was successful. In the second hundred of the normal experiment there is already an alteration of these figures in the sense of a distraction.

Our subject resembles No. 5 of this group and Nos. 4 and 2 of Uneducated Women by the marked occurrence of co-ordination, and of the figures for " same grammatical form," diminution of the predicate relations, and an almost entire absence of egocentric reactions and constellation associations. It is a case of strikingly objective, uniform reaction type.

[1] The numbers refer to the serial number of the stimulus-word in the scheme ; they only serve to show at what intervals these repetitions occur.

The present case differs from the others by the prominence of subordinations and definitions within the co-ordinations, whilst in the others, the three subjects referred to below, true coadjuncts are rather made.

| Stimulus-word | No. 2 Uneducated Women | No. 4 Uneducated Women | No. 5 Uneducated Men | No. 6 Uneducated Men |
|---|---|---|---|---|
| Sunday | Tuesday | Monday | Monday | Holiday |
| Schoolboy | girl | teacher | teacher | boy |
| Head | foot | arm | neck | part of the body |
| Ink | pen | pen | pencil | writing material |
| Bread | meat | cheese | meal | food-stuff |
| Lamp | oil | candle | light | object in a room |
| Tree | chair (?) | bush | bush | plant |
| Wood | charcoal | charcoal | charcoal | for lighting fires |
| Slate | pen | pen | slate-pencil | school furniture |
| Helmet | glove | sword | cuirassier | head-covering |

No. 7 (p. 120) may, perhaps, still be counted among the predicate type, although the predicates are not very predominant in the second hundred ; remarkably many co-existences ; no reactions in the clang group.  In the residual group the number of faults is noticeable ; the maximum (five) occurs in the second hundred of the normal experiment.  The sudden appearance of 6 per cent. repetitions of the stimulus-word in the second part of the distraction experiment is most surprising.  We found also 2 per cent. perseverations.  In the second part of normal experiment the figures for inner association rise and those of outer association fall, which, in conjunction with the occurrence of complex constellations we have already found several times.  Despite the predicate type the distraction experiment was successful. The number of inner associations continued to decrease and that of outer associations to increase.  The predicates, especially, diminish in the distraction experiment.

The exact number of recent constellations could not be subsequently ascertained, but a series of constellations were certainly present, among these being a great number of reminiscences from the courses in the intermediate school.  Some of the specific associations with very long reaction-times are striking, e.g. :

| Copy-book | squarish: | 7·4 seconds |
| Book | interesting: | 10·1 ,, |
| Insolent | the enemy: | 17·2 ,, |
| Caress | caresser:[1] | 6·4 |
| Evil | devil: | 10·4 |
| Angry | devil: | 28 ,, |
| Come | the yellow danger: 8·4 ,, |

[1] Reaction in French.

| Kiss | Oberon : | 6·8 seconds |
| Love | mother : | 13 ,, |
| To indulge | indulgent : | 9 |
| Dear | mother : | 9 |
| Strange | a poem : | 11 ,, |
| Nausea | dirty : | 6·8 |

No. 7. *Subject : Pupil at an Intermediate School, 17 years ; fairly intelligent, nervous*

| ASSOCIATIONS | Normal | | Distraction | |
|---|---|---|---|---|
| | 1st hundred | 2nd hundred | Outer | |
| | | | 60 metro. | 100 metro. |
| Co-ordination | 13 | 22 | 26 | 12 |
| Predicate . . | 35 | 26 | 12 | 14 |
| Causal dependence | — | 1 | — | — |
| Coexistence | 26 | 10 | 22 | 12 |
| Identity . | 3 | 2 | 14 | 8 |
| Verbal-motor forms | 22 | 34 | 22 | 44 |
| Word-completion | — | — | — | — |
| Clang. . | — | — | — | — |
| Rhyme | — | — | — | — |
| Indirect . | — | — | — | — |
| Meaningless | — | — | — | — |
| Faults . . . . | 1 | 5 | 4 | 4 |
| Repetition of stimulus-word | — | — | — | 6 |
| Egocentric reaction | 2 | — | — | — |
| Perseveration | — | — | — | 2 |
| Repetitions | 12 | 5 | — | — |
| Same grammatical form | 44 | 48 | 82 | 64 |
| Same number of syllables | 32 | 30 | 40 | 40 |
| Alliteration | 12 | 15 | 12 | 16 |
| Consonance | 17 | 18 | 26 | 22 |
| Same ending | 2 | 13 | 10 | 14 |
| Inner associations | 48 | 49 | 38 | 26 |
| Outer associations | 51 | 46 | 58 | 64 |
| Clang-reactions . | — | — | — | — |
| Number of associations | 100 | 100 | 50 | 50 |

In the distraction test the reactions with unusually long re-action-times are scarce.    Probably a more exact analysis would have found one or more complexes behind these reactions.    Eros, school, fear of a slight operation, were probably the reasons conditioning the prolongation of the reaction-times.

### Summary

In the group of Uneducated Men we have seven subjects with 2086 associations.    They are all fairly intelligent, but, with the exception of No. 6, who had had a secondary education, and of No 7, who attends a technical school, they had only at-tended the elementary schools.    Four of them are German-Swiss, speaking the current dialect; one is a South German, but long settled in Switzerland and quite adept in the Swiss dialect.    Only one speaks the Swabian dialect, which is rather more like High German.    The pupil at the technical school speaks High German at home.

Two of the subjects can be counted as belonging to the predicate type; as in most cases of this type, distraction did not succeed well in one case though it did in the other.    In another subject, who in normal experiment had relatively few inner and many outer associations, the distraction was not a great success. In all the rest of this group the effect of distraction—only external distraction is referred to in this group—was evident.

Clang-associations as signs of distraction never occur as they do among the educated.

Two subjects (5 and 6 of this group) belong to a type with very many co-ordinations, few predicates, and many reactions having the same grammatical form ; at the same time they are marked by the absence of egocentric reactions and constellations. We meet this type also in Uneducated Women (Nos. 2 and 4 of Uneducated Women).    For the rest, the entire group of Uneducated Men is distinguished by the great decrease of constellations and complexes in the associations, just an indication of these being occasionally found.    This does not exclude the variations in reaction-times, although within narrow limits, which denotes the action of complexes.    Quotations and similar reactions which make one suspect complexes were only found in one particular case in this group.    This exception was the youngest member of the group—the pupil at the technical school.    He reacted by a very great number of subjective reminiscences and constellations which might be regarded partly as complex constellations.

In subjects 2, 3, and 7 we found an increase of inner associa-tions in the second hundred of the normal experiment.    Whether this should always be regarded as the effect of a complex cannot be stated with certainty in all cases.

In our experiments the Uneducated Men differ from the Uneducated Women in that, subjective as they are, they exhibit their emotions much less than the latter. This difference hardly exists among the educated. Among the educated men we meet almost as many very subjective types whose reactions exhibit strong emotion as we do among women. The educated men in this respect have more feminine traits than the uneducated.

In conclusion, it is perhaps not superfluous again to call attention to the fact that the overwhelming number of complexes which we have discovered among our subjects are of an erotic nature. There is nothing very remarkable in this, seeing the great part love and sexuality play in human life.

## B. Group Statistics

### The Normal Experiment

Having now reviewed the subjects individually it remains for us to study the group behaviour of the reactions. The ratio of the figures among individuals is a very variable one, as a glance at the tables shows. A chief cause of these variations is, apart from specific individual causes, the intensity of attention, to the effects of which we have already referred several times. The fact that some individuals react preferably by inner association, others preferably by outer, is primarily a phenomenon of attention. Every person endowed with speech has at disposal all the different kinds of association ; the nature of the association produced depends chiefly upon the degree of attention bestowed upon the stimulus-word. Where our distraction experiment succeeded, i.e. where the conditions of the experiment were carried out so as to fulfil the intentions of the experimenter, the same phenomenon was manifest—the outer associations and the clang-reactions increased at the expense of the inner associations. A change took place in the direction of habit and routine, that is, of mechanically simple or verbal connexions. With increasing distraction the effect of the "law of frequency" increases, since things which are frequently together in time and space attain expression. With the decreasing stress of attention on the images the next layer (mostly verbal elements) attains a higher valency, i.e. a lower liminal value, and thus reaches reproduction.

We do not wish to discuss here the different psychological theories of attention. We conceive attention as a state leading up to association complexes, and in the last analysis characterized by muscular tensions ; a state which supplies the psycho-physical basis to the accentuated complex. The purpose of the physical echo seems to be to make stable the accentuated image in the field of consciousness. Through this somatic connexion the accentuated image is probably kept more fluid than all the others which are also at the summit of clearness, or under other conditions of the " feeling " which is its representative. It becomes " a tendency presentation " or a " tendency feeling." Two effects proceed from this :

(1) Acceleration of all associated presentations and especially of all those having the same " tendency."

(2) Inhibition of all non-associated presentations, especially to those not associated with that " tendency."

If the tone of attention is heightened for a non-associated presentation, the tendency presentation is correspondingly put out of focus, i.e. it loses in tone. The effects proceeding from it become proportionately lower in intensity, so that the difference in the liminal value of all the remaining associations decreases. The selection as regards the tendency becomes more difficult and becomes more subordinate to the influence of the law of frequency ; that is to say, that all those associations thrust themselves to the front which by use and practice form the most frequent content of consciousness, and thus possess the lowest liminal value. The law of frequency takes over the part which had formerly been played by the tendency presentation. Transferred to the practice of our experiments, it means that the presentations which are ready-made and mechanical in the language are substi-tuted for the endeavour to apprehend and work out the meaning of the stimulus-word.

In the act of apperception, and of the further working out of the stimulus-words, all these purely verbal connexions are re-pressed, so that a part of them chime softly and vaguely and a part remain completely unconscious. If the verbal connexions enter the field of consciousness, the higher associations are pushed into the shade ; some of them chime feebly, some pass away unconsciously (according to Wundt " unperceived "). (That they do not occur at all is possible, but that is difficult to prove.) But verbal mechanism is not the lowest level in the reaction process ; mere mimicry of speech or clang-reaction is repressed during mechanical verbal reaction. If by further lowering of attention we take away verbal mechanisms, which after all do possess in most cases some meaning, the clang-reactions rise ; these represent the lowest level of verbal reaction, and on that account remain in ordinary life constantly below the threshold of consciousness. In the infantile process of speech development clang-reactions, it is well known, play a pretty large part ; later they become more and more repressed, ending in a habitual unconsciousness from which in the normal state they can only be evoked by a certain degree of effort.

We have purposely only spoken about the effect of distraction on verbal functions. We must now observe that the law of frequency occurs also in the selection of the inner pictures. We were struck by the frequency with which, while the subject was in a state of inner distraction (N.B., much more frequently than in the normal state), old, childish reminiscences emerged, even with everyday objects.

In the individual descriptions we have referred to the similarity of the phenomenon of distraction to that of maniacal reaction. The reactions in the state of distraction are in no way to be differentiated from maniacal reactions, as Aschaffenburg discovered, and as we have ourselves observed in many maniacal associations.

Liepmann,[1] who explains " flight of ideas " as due to a disturbance of attention, has arrived at the same point of view as ourselves as a result of his own investigations. Considerations similar to Liepmann's have for some time past mainly inspired our experimental investigations. The results of our experiments confirm his views. As regards the psychological mechanisms of the flight of ideas, our views agree completely with Liepmann's ; we therefore refer the reader to his work.

Aschaffenburg has acquainted us with another reaction type similar to that of the maniacal—the fatigue type. Other workers, guided by Kräpelin's elaborate investigations, record analogous results from the effect of alcohol. Aschaffenburg makes motor excitation responsible for the occurrence of clang-reactions. But against this conception it is enough to point out that the conditions in question are characterized to a large extent by disturbance of attention. Our experiments have proved that clang-reactions are conditioned, it may be said exclusively, by disturbance of attention. Motor excitation is probably an unessential by-symptom, which at the most may be the cause of the disturbance of attention. This seems to be the case in fatigue and alcoholism. In maniacal flight of ideas another factor certainly enters as the cause of the disturbance of attention, the specific excitation, the psychological nature of which is at present quite obscure. The disturbance of attention due to motor excitation in fatigue and alcoholism we should conceive as

[1] Liepmann, Ueber Ideenflucht, Begriffsbestimmung und psychologische Analyse, Halle, 1904.

follows : The physical correlate of the phenomenon of attention, muscular tension, undergoes, under the influence of the motor excitation, a certain abbreviation in duration and a certain abnormal variability in its nature.   The psychophysical basis of the accentuated images thus become labile is psychically represented as the *Decline of the tendency images*.   From this decline of the tendency image there must result, following Liepmann's views, flight of ideas, which appear in the association experiment as clang-reactions, etc.   In acoustic verbal experiments there is a possibility that motor excitation, which is naturally communicated to the verbal-motor system also, encounters the mechanical reactions now set free ; but it is never the sole cause of these.

From these considerations we should expect in every case *of disturbance of attention a superficial reaction type, clang-reactions, or, inversely, where clang-reactions occur we should suspect a disturbance of attention.*

This fact seems to us to be of great diagnostic value ; moreover, it is an essential foundation for any general understanding of reactions.

With the relatively great variations in the individual figures a survey of our large number of statistics is difficult ; we have therefore prepared for easier comparison tables of certain groups giving the arithmetical mean in percentages.   We do not deny that any dealing with averages in such delicate quantitative relationships is a somewhat daring undertaking.   Even though the quantitative ratio of the individual groups towards one another must be somewhat variable, we are still convinced that the chief figures at least, namely, those of the inner and outer associations and of the clang-reactions, do give, nevertheless, a pertinent picture of the nature of the reaction.   The quantitative relationship of certain special groups to one another, e.g. the co-existences, is partly influenced by definite sources of error conditioned by the selection of the stimulus-words.   It is obvious that reactions with nouns only show different relationships from reactions with mixed stimulus-words.   Nevertheless our relative figures maintain their value, since all the subjects were examined by the same scheme of stimulus-words.

We have classified our material from different points of view ; we were, above all, interested in the question of the relationship of the educated to the uneducated.   Aschaffenburg found among his educated subjects a relatively strong preponderance of outer over inner associations.   On the other side, Ranschburg and Balint found a strong preponderance of the inner associations among the uneducated.

STUDIES IN WORD-ASSOCIATION

Here are the tables for the first and second hundred of normal associations :

UNEDUCATED

| | Women | | Men | |
|---|---|---|---|---|
| | 1st hundred | 2nd hundred | 1st hundred | 2nd hundred |
| Co-ordination. . . . | 24·2 ⎫ | 26·2 ⎫ | 25·2 ⎫ | 21·5 ⎫ |
| Predicate . . . . | 18·8 ⎬ 44·0 | 22·0 ⎬ 49·3 | 15·4 ⎬ 41·7 | 16·8 ⎬ 39·4 |
| Causal dependence . . . | 1·0 ⎭ | 1·1 ⎭ | 1·1 ⎭ | 1·1 ⎭ |
| Coexistence . . . . | 27·2 ⎫ | 13·6 ⎫ | 21·7 ⎫ | 13·0 ⎫ |
| Identity . . . . | 3·3 ⎬ 52·8 | 6·8 ⎬ 46·1 | 7·8 ⎬ 55·7 | 12·2 ⎬ 55·7 |
| Verbal-motor forms . . | 22·3 ⎭ | 25·7 ⎭ | 26·2 ⎭ | 30·5 ⎭ |
| Word-completion . . . | 0·2 ⎫ | 0·5 ⎫ | — ⎫ | — ⎫ |
| Clang . . . . | — ⎬ 0·3 | 0·3 ⎬ 1·4 | 0·7 ⎬ 0·7 | 0·5 ⎬ 0·6 |
| Rhyme . . . . . | 0·1 ⎭ | 0·6 ⎭ | — ⎭ | 0·1 ⎭ |
| Indirect . . . . | 0·6 ⎫ | 0·8 ⎫ | 0·5 ⎫ | 1·2 ⎫ |
| Meaningless . . . | 0·3 ⎬ 2·1 | 0·2 ⎬ 2·6 | 0·1 ⎬ 1·4 | 0·2 ⎬ 3·6 |
| Faults . . . . | 1·2 ⎭ | 1·6 ⎭ | 0·8 ⎭ | 2·2 ⎭ |
| Repetition of stimulus-word . | — | — | — | — |
| Egocentric reaction . . | 0·8 | 0·8 | 2·0 | 1·5 |
| Perseveration. . . . | 1·5 | 0·6 | 1·0 | 0·4 |
| Repetitions . . . . | 10·2 | 8·8 | 14·1 | 10·5 |
| Same grammatical form . . | 63·2 | 54·7 | 60·1 | 58·4 |
| Same number of syllables . | 49·9 | 42·2 | 41·1 | 37·0 |
| Alliteration . . . . | 10·2 | 8·7 | 9·0 | 9·0 |
| Consonance . . . . | 12·3 | 12·2 | 11·1 | 14·0 |
| Same ending . . . . | 11·7 | 11·0 | 16·4 | 16·2 |
| Total number of associations . | 800 | 800 | 700 | 700 |
| Total number of subjects . | 8 | | 7 | |

Our uneducated subjects were almost all male or female nurses in the asylum. We will agree that this selection of the uneducated was not a very fortunate one, for among the nursing staff there were a number of persons who were above the average level of education. The term half-educated would be, perhaps, better than uneducated. The level of culture and intelligence of the men is, on the whole, somewhat higher than that of the women.

The women exhibit a relatively high figure for inner associations ; remarkably enough, the number of inner associations does not rise considerably in the second half of the experiment, where the predicates show an increase. Moreover, in the second hundred there is an increase in the residual group and in the clang-reactions. With the increase of predicates and of verbal-motor forms must be connected the diminution of agreement in the grammatical forms. The figures for verbal linking are very high.

The men show, on the whole, a more superficial reaction type than the women. The second hundred does not perceptibly differ from the first, only the figures for indirect associations and consonance present a fairly striking increase.

EDUCATED

| | Women | | Men | |
|---|---|---|---|---|
| | 1st hundred | 2nd hundred | 1st hundred | 2nd hundred |
| Co-ordination. . . . | 13·4 ⎫ | 14 ⎫ | 16·1 ⎫ | 16·5 ⎫ |
| Predicate . . . . | 21·8 ⎬ 36·9 | 18·6 ⎬ 33·2 | 17·3 ⎬ 34 | 22·2 ⎬ 39·5 |
| Causal dependence . . . | 1·7 ⎭ | 0·6 ⎭ | 0·6 ⎭ | 0·8 ⎭ |
| Coexistence . . . . | 16·5 ⎫ | 11·2 ⎫ | 18·2 ⎫ | 7·5 ⎫ |
| Identity . . . . | 2·7 ⎬ 57·2 | 6·7 ⎬ 58·9 | 3·2 ⎬ 56·6 | 8·3 ⎬ 49 |
| Verbal-motor forms . . | 38 ⎭ | 41 ⎭ | 35·2 ⎭ | 33·2 ⎭ |
| Word-completion . . . | 1 ⎫ | 2 ⎫ | 1·1 ⎫ | 1·1 ⎫ |
| Clang . . . . . | 0·3 ⎬ 2·1 | 1·9 ⎬ 4·5 | 1·5 ⎬ 3·3 | 2·3 ⎬ 4 |
| Rhyme . . . . . | 0·8 ⎭ | 0·6 ⎭ | 0·7 ⎭ | 0·6 ⎭ |
| Indirect . . . . | 0·9 ⎫ | 1 ⎫ | 2·8 ⎫ | 2·2 ⎫ |
| Meaningless . . . . | 0·1 ⎬ 2·9 | 0·1 ⎬ 2·4 | 0·7 ⎬ 5·2 | 1·2 ⎬ 6·1 |
| Faults . . . . . | 1·9 ⎭ | 0·9 ⎭ | 1·7 ⎭ | 2·6 ⎭ |
| Repetition of stimulus-word . | — ⎭ | 0·4 ⎭ | — ⎭ | 0·1 ⎭ |
| Egocentric reaction . . | 2·7 | 1·5 | 3·6 | 2·6 |
| Perseveration. . . . | 0·8 | 0·5 | 3·1 | 1·8 |
| Repetition . . . . | 8·0 | 6·5 | 7·5 | 7·6 |
| Same grammatical form . . | 53·9 | 54 | 52·1 | 46·1 |
| Same number of syllables . | 43·9 | 39·2 | 37 | 32·6 |
| Alliteration . . . . | 9·0 | 7·8 | 9·2 | 8·8 |
| Consonance . . . . | 14·6 | 15·2 | 15·1 | 16·2 |
| Same ending . . . . | 9·8 | 11·3 | 8·2 | 8·8 |
| Total number of associations . | 1100 | 1100 | 800 | 800 |
| Total number of subjects . | 11 | | 8 | |

The increase of faults in the second hundred of both groups is perhaps attributable to the unfortunate accident that the number of stimulus-words with an emotional tone is rather larger in the second hundred than in the first. As we have seen, faults chiefly occur with such stimulus-words.

It is noticeable that the men present a greater number of egocentric reactions than the women, although they have a distinctly lesser number of predicates. The number of per-severations is partly connected with the egocentric reactions, i.e. with the inflow of personal wishes and valuations. In the women it is, indeed, somewhat higher than in the men ; it changes, however, in accordance with the retrogression of egocentric judgments—a fact that will be confirmed later. We relate this condition to the fact that reactions with accentuated feeling have a tendency to perseveration, as we have demon-strated several times in the individual statements.

In the table on p. 127 one is most of all struck by the generally superficial type of the reactions. The men are almost all highly educated persons, the women likewise, with few ex-ceptions, being highly cultivated.

The difference between the men and women is not considerable so far as the first three groups are concerned, with the exception of a slight preponderance of the inner associations among men over those among women, in which the co-ordinations especially participate. There are considerable differences in the residual group where the high figures in men for *indirect associations* are striking, more than double that of the women. The average of the clang-reactions is also somewhat higher in men than in women. The suspected inverse ratio between indirect associa-tions and clang-reactions is thus again suggested here :

| | Women | | Men | |
| --- | --- | --- | --- | --- |
| | 1st hundred | 2nd hundred | 1st hundred | 2nd hundred |
| Clang-reactions . | 2·9 | 2·4 | 5·2 | 6·1 |
| Indirect associations | 0·9 | 1·0 | 2·8 | 2·2 |

We shall discuss this phenomenon in our critique of the distraction averages.

The men exceed the women in the *egocentric reactions* also. The number of *perseverations* accords here, as among the unedu-cated, with those of the egocentric reactions, a further proof of the largely affective nature of the perseverations (*N.B.*, only in the normal experiment).

The differences which separate educated and uneducated are best illustrated by placing the average figures for the two groups in parallel tables.

| | Educated | Uneducated |
|---|---|---|
| Co-ordination.    .    .    .    . | 15 ⎫ | 24·2 ⎫ |
| Predicate    .    .    .    .    . | 19·3 ⎬ 35·8 | 18·2 ⎬ 43·4 |
| Causal dependence .    .    .    . | 0·9 ⎭ | 1· ⎭ |
| Coexistence  .    .    .    .    . | 13·3 ⎫ | 18·8 ⎫ |
| Identity    .    .    .    .    . | 5·2 ⎬ 55·3 | 7·7 ⎬ 52·4 |
| Verbal-motor forms    .    .    . | 36·8 ⎭ | 26·1 ⎭ |
| Word-completion  .    .    .    . | 1·3 ⎫ | 0·1 ⎫ |
| Clang  .  .    .    .    .    . | 1·5 ⎬ 3·4 | 0·3 ⎬ 0·5 |
| Rhyme .    .    .    .    .    . | 0·6 ⎭ | 0·1 ⎭ |
| Indirect    .    .    .    .    . | 1·7 ⎫ | 0·7 ⎫ |
| Meaningless  .    .    .    .    . | 0·5 ⎪ | 0·1 ⎪ |
| Faults  .    .    .    .    .    . | 1·7 ⎬ 4·0 | 1·4 ⎬ 2·2 |
| Repetition of stimulus-word   .    . | 0·1 ⎭ | — ⎭ |
| Egocentric reaction    .    .    . | 2·4 | 1·1 |
| Perseveration.    .    .    .    . | 1·5 | 0·8 |
| Repetitions  .    .    .    .    . | 7·3 | 10·9 |
| Same grammatical form .    .    . | 51·5 | 59·2 |
| Same number of syllables    .    . | 38·2 | 42·5 |
| Alliteration  .    .    .    .    . | 8·7 | 9·3 |
| Consonance  .    .    .    .    . | 10·2 | 12·3 |
| Same ending .    .    .    .    . | 9·5 | 13·8 |
| Total number of associations  .    . | 3800 | 3000 |
| Total number of subjects    .    . | 19 | 15 |

The educated show a distinctly shallower type than the uneducated. This difference can be graphically described by the statement : *The educated exhibit a distraction phenomenon as compared with the uneducated.*

Put the case thus : the figures for the uneducated being those of a subject in normal experiment, the figures of the educated behave like those obtained in a distraction experiment. The clang-reactions and the figures for the residual group are correspondingly increased just as we have found in the individual tables.

Whence comes this difference ? It cannot be assumed that the educated really think more superficially than the uneducated ; that would be nonsense. It can merely be assumed that so far as the experiments are concerned they think more superficially than the uneducated. That seems to be really the case, and this to us seems to be the explanation of the reaction type.   The following points must be considered in favour of this postulate :

(1) The agreement in grammatical forms and number of syllables between stimulus-word and reaction is decidedly greater among the uneducated.   This fact speaks for the uneducated adhering more closely to the stimulus-word—being more influenced by it—than the educated.

(2) The number of meaningless reactions is considerably smaller among the uneducated.   The latter controls himself more, i.e. he pays more attention to the reaction.

(3) The uneducated exceeds the educated in the number of co-existences, which are chiefly constructed from spatial perceptions ; i.e. the uneducated takes the trouble to image distinctly the object named by the stimulus-word, so that he must naturally associate what is co-existent with it.   The educated, on the other hand, has fewer co-existences because he contents himself with joining verbal forms to one another.

(5) The uneducated has about one-half fewer *egocentric reactions* than the educated.   This suggests that he lets himself go much less and allows fewer disguised subjective wishes and valuations to break through.   He strives after the utmost possible objective apprehension of the stimulus-word.

(6) One great point is that among the educated the clang-reactions are almost seven times as numerous.   Here the slackness is most distinctly evident.   The subject who takes most care makes no clang-reactions, as it were,[1] except for some specific adaptation.

On these grounds we regard it as proved that the difference between the educated and uneducated reaction types, so far as it is expressed in these figures, is entirely functional, and has only the significance of a phenomenon of attention.

If it be permissible to grade the degree of attention by the figures of the clang-reaction, of the residual group and of the verbal-motor forms, the uneducated women stand highest in the work of attention, educated men the lowest.   This fact is evident if we examine the groups according to sex from the above points of view.

Whence arises the difference of attention between educated and uneducated ?[2]

(1) The experiment is something foreign to the uneducated. Naturally it is for him something more unknown and more difficult than for the educated, who is in a position to survey the

---

[1] Naturally with the exception of any particular adjustment.

[2] By this must be understood a difference of attention in the quantitative sense only ; it is not any kind of qualitative dissimilarity.

range of the experiment, and who must feel at once more at ease in an intellectual activity than the uneducated. The excitation of the uneducated is thus greater and more general in the experiment, and he therefore reacts with greater strain.

(2) Words are called out to the subject without any sentence connecting them. Under ordinary circumstances, if something is called out to one in this way it is commonly a command or a question. The uneducated is, contrary to the educated, not used to being concerned with individual words apart from sentences, more especially if he has never learnt a foreign language out of books. The stimulus-word has thus something uncanny for the uneducated. Influenced by habit he instinctively apprehends it as a question, with the intensity of attention necessary for a proper answer. The stimulus-word to the uneducated is something to which he must frame for himself a connecting question, which he then answers.[1]

(3) The uneducated only knows words, as it were, in a connected sentence, especially when they occur as an acoustic phenomenon. Connected in a sentence the words always have a meaning ; the uneducated person knows the word less as a mere " word " or verbal sign than as something with a meaning. Hence single words are apprehended by the uneducated according to their meaning in some imaginary sentence ; to the educated the stimulus-word remains merely a word without any special meaning.[2]

Recapitulating, we may say that the uneducated person demonstrates, appropriately to his lower education, a narrower conception of the experiment, especially of the stimulus-words called out, than the educated, who approaches the question much more coldly and in a more businesslike fashion. In other words : the uneducated person shows a certain tendency to assimilate the stimulus-word in the sense of a question because usually verbal ejaculations denote a question. This relationship to the stimulus-word appears distinctly in certain pathological states, where the association experiment is nothing but a long conversation of 2 × 200 sentences on some emotionally charged theme. From these considerations it follows that

[1] It can be said generally that the more uneducated and unintelligent the subject is the more he will conceive the stimulus-word as a question. This is seen most clearly with idiots, who, with few exceptions, always conceive the stimulus-word as a question and thus give, in the reaction, a definition or explanation thereof.

[2] The educated person, however, proceeds in the same manner as the uneducated when it is a question of the words of a language he has never seen printed or written. If the stimulus-words are called out in dialect, the educated person has occasionally trouble in understanding them just because he is accustomed to these dialect words in connected sentences only.

the uneducated bestows greater attention, chiefly because the significance of the stimulus-word influences him more than it does the educated.

The difference between educated and uneducated is the different conception of the stimulus-word. This difference in principle might allow us to separate off two rather vague groups. This separation is, however, so general that it does not take into consideration other essential differences in the reaction types. We have, therefore, endeavoured to discover other and finer bases for a classification. We asked ourselves : Are there other universal factors, apart from the phenomena of attention, which visibly influence the reaction ?

One chief factor lies in the individual temperament. The difference in apprehension which we have just discussed is an intellectual or associative disposition which would be just the same in persons of the most diverse characters. But it is different with temperament. From our experiments two well-characterized types emerge :

(1) A type who in the reaction makes use of subjective experiences, often emotionally charged.

(2) A type who shows in the reaction an objective, impersonal habit of mind.

The first type is characterized by the occurrence of pictures of personal memories, which are often markedly emotional. The latter type preferably relates words to words or concepts to concepts, the personal element playing quite a subordinate rôle in the reaction. This may be termed the objective type.

The first type is conveniently divided into three groups :

α. *The stimulus-image evoked by the stimulus-word acts through its emotional tone.* Usually the emotional tone which the stimulus-image possesses at once excites a memory-complex which is completely equal to it. The reaction then follows under the constellation of this complex. In practice individuals of this type can be separated from others, at least in extreme cases. We term this type the *complex constellation type.*

β. *The image aroused by the stimulus-word is an individual reminiscence generally taken from daily life.* The reaction contains the image, or at least is markedly constellated by it. We term this the *simple constellation type.*[1]

[1] We again repeat that in this classification we merely wish to mark the quite distinct and obvious differences in the manner of reaction. We know very well that fundamentally every person belongs to the complex constellation type, for no reaction is accidental but is invariably conditioned by the psychological past of the individual. What we wish to elucidate by our classification is only the more or less of the subjective conditioning so far as it is clearly expressed in the reactions.

γ. *The image aroused by the stimulus-word acts through one or other of the attributes associated with it* (partly sensual portions of the presentation, partly emotional tones). Presumably in this type the stimulus presentation is primarily very plastic, so that first one, then another trait is thrust forward, by means of which the reaction is conditioned ; it thus generally contains a predicate of the object designated by the stimulus-word. We term this the *predicate type.*

What is common to types α, β, γ, as opposed to the objective type (2), is a strong accentuation of the individual, personal part of the reaction independent of the stimulus-word. We can therefore say that the difference between types (1) and (2) is the egocentricity of the adjustment.

These points of view elucidate the universal psychological laws which govern our experiment. This is far from disclosing all the roots of the complications in the reactions.

In the egocentric adaptation we have tacitly assumed that the reaction is a more or less distinct symbol of inner processes. So long as we know that the subject is expressing himself freely we can grant this postulate *cum grano salis.* But the picture of the reaction is altered when the egocentric adaptation leads to the raising of emotionally charged complexes which the subject will not reveal.[1] This is the case in the complex constellation type ; e.g. the stimulus-word raises the complex of an unhappy love affair hidden as far as possible. Were the subject now to react according to his inner pictures he would express in the reaction a piece of his complex, which he would thus reveal. The concealment of an affect is always characterized by a quite peculiar adjustment, a peculiar condition of feeling. Perhaps without the occurrence of any conscious critique, the complex as it emerges is immediately repressed again by the conscious emotional tendency of not wishing to reveal something—a tendency giving rise to discordant inhibitions.

Naturally this process of repression can be carried out much more consciously (or even more unconsciously, as in hysteria). In the place of the repressed complex presentation another association is substituted and expressed, one corresponding to the momentary feeling of the tendency. Thus the real inner association is concealed from the world and the secret preserved. For the experimenter who perhaps does not enjoy the subject's full confidence it may be extraordinarily difficult in some cases to

---

[1] We have convinced ourselves by numerous experiments that this "will not reveal" is by no means always a conscious not-willing, but very frequently an unconscious inhibition which in most cases causes a prolongation of the reaction-time also.

distinguish whether there is something concealed or not. The distinction may be impossible in some people who are able to exercise complete self-control. But in most cases the subject betrays himself after a little time. In accordance with the laws set forth above, certain phenomena occur which betray the repressed complex. Here we want to set aside the prolongation of the reaction-time, which is a regular occurrence.[1]

Repression is betrayed :

(1) By an unusual and suspicious setting of the reaction which the reaction-word by itself does not explain, but whose peculiar character must be constellated by an X. Occasionally this X can be read directly from the peculiarly forced nature of the reaction. Such reactions frequently appear in sentence form.

(2) By the phenomena of attention. A subject who is taking the stimulus-word altogether in the sense of a " question," and reproducing a series of superior associations, suddenly reacts by a clang or other strikingly superficial association, in the absence of any external disturbance. The occurrence is suspicious ; some inner disturbance, some inner distraction, must have taken place. The subject perhaps gives no information. The phenomenon is repeated at a similar stimulus-word. We are now fairly certain that there is something behind this. This suspicion has seldom led us astray. A complex has suddenly emerged, has drawn a certain intensity of attention to itself ; meanwhile the reaction takes place, and in consequence of the disturbance of attention the reaction can be only a superficial one.

(3) By fault. The emerging complex absorbs all the attention, so that the reaction is either forgotten or, in the absence of every association, cannot be expressed.

(4) By perseveration. In this case the critical reaction may be quite unnoticeable, but the succeeding one bears an abnormal character, so that the preceding reaction has undertaken the part of the constellating X. The perseverating factor is the affect excited by the preceding association.[2]

(5) By assimilation of the stimulus-word. For no obvious reason the stimulus-word is taken in a peculiarly rare sense,

---

[1] Chapter v deals with the question of the reaction-times.

[2] A subject whose mental life was influenced by an unpleasant financial transaction reacted with normal time to *ill — poor* and to the next reaction, *vain — tane*, with a prolonged reaction-time. Without obvious reason the association is a senseless rhyme. Clang associations and rhymes only occur in this subject in " critical " situations." *Poor* has a very special affective significance for him ; attention remains attached to the aroused complex, thus creating disturbance by inner distraction for the succeeding reaction.

or it is misunderstood in some remarkable way in accordance with the affective idea which fills up consciousness.[1]

These points are the chief criteria of a concealed complex.[2]

We have purposely devoted so much attention to the review of these finer psychological phenomena, for the affective processes whose traces we have followed with the utmost possible care in the normal reaction play the leading rôle in pathological reactions.  This we shall see subsequently in detail.  What may be, perhaps, put aside in the normal reaction as capriciousness is seen to be the most important factor in pathological reactions.  Provisionally, we place the greatest value upon the knowledge that the reactions are an extremely refined reagent for affective processes in particular, and for the individual outlook of the subjects in general.

In illustration of our arguments we append associations of the six chief types.

### 1. OBJECTIVE TYPE

The reactions of a subject whose adjustment is essentially objective.  The conception of the stimulus-word in the sense of a question is in the background.  There is a great tendency merely to group the words serially, partly according to the law of similarity, partly according to verbally current connexions (No. 1 of Educated Men).

| | | | |
|---|---|---|---|
| Christmas | Easter | Friendly | painful |
| Sunday | Monday | Cut | knife |
| Winter | spring | Crown | rich |
| Lake | sea | Saw | bone |
| Pupil | teacher | Prison | custody |
| Father | mother | Divorce | avoid |
| Table | leg | Ill | weak |
| Head | kerchief | Song | carol |
| Ink | pen | Potato | salt |
| Needle | holder | Easy | chair |
| Bread | earn | Coffee | drink |
| Lamp | shade | Sacrifice | bring |
| Dream | froth | Wedding | feast |
| Book | knife | Grandmother | father |

---

[1] The subject quoted in the previous foot-note reacts to *pity — poor* (*poor* is a special affect).  The succeeding association runs: *monkey — much.*  Again a perseveration of the financial complex, monkey being assimilated as money, although this individual has been well acquainted for some time with all the stimulus-words in our scheme.

[2] In some subjects *repetitions* have also a certain significance as the indirect expression of the complex (in the special sections we have drawn attention to this more than once).  Certain words are frequently repeated which are more or less closely associated with the complex, or represent it indirectly.

| | | | |
|---|---|---|---|
| Tree | beat | Angry | naughty |
| Mountain | green | Clap | hands |
| Paper | cutter | Year | month |
| Book | read | Threaten | fist |
| School | attend | Long | narrow |
| To sing | to write | Rich | poor |
| Ring | finger | Sorrow | joy |
| Tooth | tune | Eye | tooth |
| Window | pane | Youth | play |
| Frog | leg | Inn | Goat and Compasses |
| Sweet | sour | Family | scandal |
| Ride | drive | Trouble | sorrow |
| Pay attention | pay heed | Once | panic |
| ·Faust | Goethe | Wonder | beyond wonder |
| People | insurrection | Blood | revenge |
| Murderer | blood | Rose | campion |
| Everywhere | I am at home | Choose | choice |
| Reckon | measure | Justice | violence |
| Kiss | mouth | Must | no one must must |
| Bad | right | Hope | be not confounded |
| Bond | of love | Small | all |
| Ripe | fruit | Unjust | faithlessness |
| Giver | friend | Welt | Schmerz |
| Play | the bells | Strange | unknown |
| Way | to Canossa | Slate | write |
| Quarrel | strife | Growl | dog |
| Blue | red | Knob | stick |
| Flower | cabbage | Fruit | eat |
| Cherry | stone | Sly | fox |
| Asylum | keeper | Handle | ornament |
| Piano | play | Hay | straw |
| Oven | town | Clean | mean |
| Walk | go | Guess | W. (name of an acquaintance who has suggested a particular hypothesis). |
| Cook | eat | | |
| Water | drink | | |
| Dance | music | | |
| Cat | mouse | Chieftain | full of blood and ·wounds |
| Dozen | by the dozen | | |
| Dark | light | At home | it's good |
| Heart | part | Brown | thorn |
| Bird | nest | Idle | lazy |
| White | black | Vinegar | sour |
| Play | cards | Hot | cold |
| Kaiser | Wilhelm | Pit | fall |
| Moon | shine | Nausea | horrible |
| Beat | throw | Resin | rivet |
| Fire | house | Throat | sew up |
| Shooting | star | Steep | mountain |
| Stroke | cat | Swing | swinging |
| Grand | magnificent | Fetch | carry |
| Child | dog | Skull | formation |
| Sofa | lie | Use | can |
| Wild | animal | Stamp | timbre |
| Tears | flow | Faithful | German |

The subject is a doctor ; a few medical terms such as " needle-holder " and " skull-formation " point to this. We do not reckon the reactions constellated by the profession among the " constellations," using this term in the narrower sense. Reactions of that kind are not subjective, belonging not to the individual alone, but more or less to a whole class. The only subjective constellation is *guess — W.*

(b) The reactions of a person whose adjustment is objective and in whom the stimulus-word works much more by its meaning than in the foregoing. The tendency is to give the most correct reaction possible (No. 4 of Uneducated Women).

| | | | |
|---|---|---|---|
| Table | chair | Friendly | angry |
| Head | arm | File | hammer |
| Ink | pen | Crown | helmet |
| Needle | thread | Hit | bite |
| Bread | cheese | Star . | sun |
| Lamp | candle | Caress | beat |
| Tree | bush | Paint | oil |
| Mountain | valley | Thank | ask |
| Wood | coal | Rough | fine |
| Salt | meal | Smell | taste |
| Dream | sleep | Prison | jail |
| Paper | stuff | Divide | together |
| Book | newspaper | Potato | bread |
| School | church | Fall | catch |
| Ripe | ring | Nausea | taste |
| Tooth | mouth | Resin | pitch |
| Sing | shout | Lazy | work |
| Window | floor | Coffee | milk |
| Frog | stork | Sacrifice | saviour |
| Flower | grass | Wedding | funeral |
| Cherry | peach | Angry | contented |
| Asylum | school | Soldier | civilian |
| Piano | violin | Clap | sing |
| Fern | rose | Threaten | hit |
| Walk | jump | Behaviour | polite |
| Water | wine | Fall | level |
| Dance | sing | Suffer | healthy |
| Dozen | ten | Youth | age |
| Heart | warm | Inn | hotel |
| Bird | cat | Family | man |
| Swim | walk | Fist | hand |
| Play | sing | People | household (interpolate " family ") |
| Emperor | king | | |
| Moon | star | To pay attention | to listen |
| Haughty | gentle | Murderer | robber |
| Kindle | extinguish | Everywhere | here |
| Magnificent | wonderful | Kiss | flatter |
| Child | woman | Bad | good |
| Ride | drive | Ripe | bitter (interpolate " sweet ") |
| Hope | joy | | |

| Band | stuff | Pray | believe |
|------|-------|------|---------|
| Ground | floor | Freedom | caught |
| Gait | jump | World | people |
| Quarrel | contented | Strange | home |
| Sofa | chair | Growl | bite |
| Love | hate | Knot | cord |
| Wild | tame | False | faithful |
| Tears | laughter | Helmet | sword |
| Indulge | bitter | Plate | dish |
| Wonder | nature | Hay | grass |
| Blood | man | Clean | neat |
| Wreath | flowers | Suppose | doubt |
| Choose | meet | Head | arm |
| Justice | false | Home | away |
| Violence | willing | Vinegar | wine |
| Revenge | freedom | Swing | throw |

The subject is a nurse in our asylum. Subjective factors are entirely absent in the reactions. The tone is extraordinarily objective and quiet. In contrast with the previous case, one may notice that the meaning of the stimulus-word is here the exciting factor, as is seen by the many contrasts.

## 2. EGOCENTRIC ATTITUDE

### (a) Simple Constellation Type

The reactions of a person in whom numerous subjective experiences were made use of in the experiment. The attitude is egocentric in so far as the stimulus-word arouses preferably subjective memories (No. 4 of Educated Men).

| | | | |
|------|------|------|------|
| Father | anxious (he is the father of a child just born) | Tausend (Thousand) | Basle (a Basle student friend is called Tausig, which is the dialect form of Tausend (1000). |
| Walk | L. (name of a patient who walks a great deal) | | |
| Head | round | | The stimulus-word was, of course, called out in High German but assimilated in its dialect form) |
| Ink | acid (interpolate " red — litmus ") | | |
| Cook | cookery course | | |
| Water | supply | | |
| Needle | ear | Ring | A II-garden (a ring had been found in that garden) |
| Dance | concert hall (hall in which the dances of the asylum are held) | | |
| Bread | machine bakery | Zahn | Göschenen (Zahn, the writer, lives at Göschenen) |
| Lamp | smells | | |
| Tree | F. (name of a friend who is connected with a definite event) | Window | opening |
| | | Frog | tree-frog |
| | | Like | ball |
| Dark | room (he is an enthusiastic amateur photographer) | Flower | rose |
| | | Son | little one (he has just had a son) |

| | |
|---|---|
| Mountain | Ütli mountain |
| Heart | valvular disease |
| Hair | falling out |
| Bird | paw (interpolate " claw") |
| Salz | Rhine fields where there are salt-pits |
| Swim | L. (name of a patient who attended the swimming-bath frequently) |
| Dream | R. (name of a colleague who was at the time engaged in dream analysis) |
| Paper | fraud (papers in the sense of documents about a case of fraud) |
| White | malaria (a patient called White suffered from malaria) |
| Wood | ebony-wood |
| Game | Halma (much played at the time in the wards) |
| Book | -seller |
| Pencil | Koh-i-noor (he uses this kind of pencil) |
| Thirteen | shorthand (interpolate write; he is greatly taken up with shorthand) |
| School | S. (name of the place where he went to school) |
| Sing | Miss S. (name of a singer who was then in the asylum) |
| Strange | stranger |
| Growl | bulldog |
| Rude | East Swiss (memory of student days) |
| Coffee | Mocha |
| Fruit | steal |
| Sacrifice | L. (name of an ill painter who preferably painted sacrificial scenes) |
| False | trap |
| Helm | house (public building in Zurich) |
| Wedding | no alcohol (he is a total abstainer) |
| Misery | hunger |
| Hay | Hayward (name of a place) |
| Asylum | R. (an asylum for feeble-minded children) |

| | |
|---|---|
| Wild | dentist (" Wild " is the name of a dentist) |
| Warder | R. (name of a warder) |
| Tears | vale |
| Fern | tapeworm |
| War | rumour |
| Oven | nuisance |
| Faithful | doggy |
| Once | again shorthand (see above) |
| Wonder | Lourdes |
| Bloody | English (in England the word must not be used) |
| Must | Lessing (interpolate " well-known quotation from Lessing ") |
| Rights | and duties |
| Revenge | thirst |
| Hope | pregnancy (constellation intelligible from earlier statements) |
| Lock | and barrel |
| Small | warder (Small is the name of a warder) |
| Arm | W. (name of a patient who injured his arm) |
| Play | thing |
| Liberty | statue (he had been admiring the Statue of Liberty in New York) |
| Blue | grotto in Capri |
| Wrong | confine (constellation from daily intercourse with querulous patients) |
| Sorrow | sorrowful |
| Stern | C (Stern is the name of a patient who was in C block) |
| Take care | Association experiments (momentary constellation) |
| Stroke | kitten |
| Nature | R. (patient's name) |
| Grand | Grant (patient's name: a clang-association) |
| Folk | Wundt's *Folk-Psychology* (a work recently acquired by the asylum) |
| Sweet | banana (cp. the reaction " wood-ebony." He has recently given a lecture on journeys in Africa) |

| | | | |
|---|---|---|---|
| Grand-mother | dead | Family | family day |
| Angry | R. (name of a patient with moral deficiency) | Murderer | G. (name of a murderer who was just then under observation in the asylum) |
| Raspberry | garden (the raspberries in the asylum garden) | Friendly | H. (name of an acquaint-ance) |
| Need | B. (name of a colleague) | | |
| Year | and day | Everywhere | every man |
| Home | newspaper (*Home* is the name of a newspaper) | Hover | C. (name of a well-known aeroplanist) |
| Threaten | threatmonger (nickname of a patient who fre-quently utters threats) | Count | counterfeit |
| | | Rank | M. (name of a person who made a joke about the work rank) |
| Vinegar | home-made | | |
| Trap | mouse-trap | Skull | occiput |
| Sour | yeast | Row | A 1 (Row is the name of a patient in block A 1) |
| Throat | epiglottis | | |
| Youth | Munich (newspaper *Ju-gend* [youth], published in Munich) | | |
| | | Warn | warder |
| | | Analyse | sulphuric acid |
| Hit | name of a doctor who was hit by a patient) | Prison | police-station (in Zürich) |
| | | Ill | diabetes |

The characteristic of this type is the emergence of numerous subjective experiences, mostly of recent date, and belonging for the most part to the daily round. It is self-evident that despite the objective character of the constellations on the whole, some are intermingled belonging to an emotionally toned complex. But, compared with the others, these are relatively few and part of them certainly well concealed. The recently experienced joy of a father is seen in *father — anxious, hope — pregnancy, son — little one.* This emotional-toned diminutive seems to us to resound also in the reactions *caress — kitten, faithful — doggy.*

### (b) Complex Constellation Type

(1) Reactions of a patient in whom an emotional complex occurs undisguised in the reactions. The significance of the stimulus-word is made to relate to the complex (No. 7 of Educated Men).

| | | | |
|---|---|---|---|
| Wood | hit | To idle | delightful |
| Dream | studies (simple constella-tion) | Angry | I am not |
| | | Come | with us to theatre (defi-nite theatre) |
| Dance | F. (hotel where dancing goes on) | | |
| | | Year | 1904 |
| Copy-book | pen | Family | V. (subject's own family) |
| Paper | line | Take care | I should |
| Pencil | big | At last | it will end |
| School | bench | People | very worthy |
| Sing | choir | Murderer | in C (a certain criminal lunatic in section C) |
| Walk | long way | | |

| | |
|---|---|
| Dark | room |
| Heart | red |
| Bird | feathers |
| To set fire | S. (name of a pyromaniac) |
| Tooth | teeth |
| Window | frame |
| Flower | plant |
| Frog | hops |
| Asylum | big |
| Piano | I can't play |
| Warder | B. (name of a certain warder) |
| Oven | wood |
| Swell | fie ! |
| Magnificent | ah ! |
| Child | children |
| Dark red | again ah ! |
| Rough | table |
| Divorce | name of a certain mental patient who has been divorced |
| Potato | mashed |
| Son | father and son (on account of his love affair he has had unpleasant discussions with his family) |
| Wild | mother (wild == angry here) |
| Tears | she has now (i.e. the forsaken sweetheart) |
| Protection | I cannot offer her |
| War | if there were but |
| Faith | I have not held |
| Once | and never again |
| Miracle | must happen |
| Blood | she's anæmic |
| Wreath | on the coffin |
| Choose | another |
| Separate | I need not |
| Right | she is not |
| Must | I must not |
| Violence | I do none to her |
| Revenge | oh no ! |
| Hope | I know none |
| Small | not at all ! |
| Pray | perhaps— |
| Love | I did love her |
| Wool | a woman's dress |
| Old | perhaps— |
| Freedom | she could have |
| Wrong | I was not |

| | |
|---|---|
| Every-where | is K. (name of an active catatoniac) |
| Do accounts | I cannot |
| Kiss | always again |
| Natural | glorious |
| Bad | no |
| Time | not know |
| Ripe | I am for it |

} complex of a love affair which had recently come to an end

| | |
|---|---|
| Row | soldiers |
| Land | and houses |
| Game | child |
| Poor | as a beggar |
| Stern | Miss Stern (definite person) |
| Ride | track |
| Friendly | very nice |
| Crown | queen |
| Shrill | woe |
| Quarrel | bah ! |
| Sofa | soft seat |
| Love | ah ! |
| World | wide |
| Strange | she is now |
| Slate-pencil | she is a teacher |
| Growl | poodle |
| Knob | stick |
| False | fair (interpolate " a lady" who is false and fair) |
| Helmet | fire brigade |
| Clothes | a woman's dress |
| Softly | she comes |
| Gallant | up the steps |
| Plate | on the table |
| Misery | she cries |
| Hay | there's a peasant there |
| Raspberries | in the wood |
| Home | (in D., where the loved one lives) |
| Hedge | fence |
| Indolent | often (i.e. she is often indolent) |
| Woo | a woman |
| Hot | live |
| Conscious | yes, in supraconsciousness |
| Vinegar | sour |
| Trap | in |
| Nausea | so so |
| Row | not on that account |
| Resin | hair |
| Trim | beautiful and gay |
| Omen | bad |

Characteristic of these reactions is the strong emotionally toned complex. The stimulus-word is assimilated in the form of a conversation ; the experiment thus bears the stamp of an interrogatory in which the consciousness of the situation of the moment has, so far as the subject is concerned, receded slightly into the background. That explains the somewhat abnormal character of such a conversation. Reactions of this nature are due to extreme sensitiveness. The relatively numerous inter-jections and the egocentric relationships, even those unrelated to the complex, point to the same thing. The subject's egocen-tricity is very distinctly shown in everything. He is mentally quite healthy, and at another time would probably present a much more objective type. The abnormal character of the reaction is to be attributed entirely to the temporary, but ruling, affect. We may here remark that this abnormal state evoked by affect is the usual prototype of the hysterical anomalies in reaction.

(2) A good instance of a concealed emotional complex is No. 1 of Uneducated Women. We refer the reader to the associa-tions already recorded in the special part.

### (c) Predicate Type

Reactions of a person who evaluates the object denoted by the stimulus-word from the personal standpoint (No. 7 of Educated Women).

| | | | |
|---|---|---|---|
| Sea | beautiful nature | Fern | beautiful wood |
| Schoolboy | industrious | Stove | glorious in cold weather |
| Father | something majestic, good, sacred | Work | must sometimes |
| | | To cook | irksome |
| Needle | work | Water | glorious |
| Bread | best form of food | Dance | pleasant when one's |
| Lamp | work | | young |
| Tree | something beautiful | Cat | sneak |
| Mountain | terrible, climbing is nicer | Dozen | exact, order |
| | | Dark | horrible |
| Hair | head-dress | Heart | beating |
| Salt | strengthening food | Bird | glorious, fly |
| Wood | fire | Swim | glorious |
| Dream | many events | White | hard, shining |
| Copy-book | much work for the chil-dren | Game | pleasure |
| | | Thirteen | clumsy |
| Paper | blessed because we write upon it | Moon | beautiful |
| | | Hit | needless |
| Book | joy | Kindle | art, till one could |
| School | joy | Star | magnificent |
| Sing | beautiful | Grand | pompous |
| Ring | stupid thing | Child | God's gift |
| Tooth | glad that one has no more | Sweet | pleasant |
| | | Ride | dangerous |

| Frog | something unnecessary | Friendly | duty |
| Flower | joy | Crown | unnecessary |
| Cherry | good fruit | Raw | winter |
| Asylum | narrow | Smell | sometimes, slums |
| Piano | troublesome | Shining | hurts |
| Warder | great esteem | Ill | hurts |

The characteristic of this kind of reacting is an unusually marked emergence of what is personal, leading to a constant valuation of the object, mostly in reference to the self.

### 3. Sex Difference in the Normal Experiment

We have also considered the figures from the point of view of sex difference, and calculated the corresponding averages.

| | Men | Women |
|---|---|---|
| Co-ordination. . . . . | 19·8 ⎫ | 19·4 ⎫ |
| Predicate . . . . . | 17·9 ⎬ 38·6 | 20·3 ⎬ 40·7 |
| Causal dependence . . . . | 0·9 ⎭ | 1 ⎭ |
| Coexistence . . . . . | 15 ⎫ | 17·1 ⎫ |
| Identity . . . . . | 7·8 ⎬ 54 | 4·8 ⎬ 53·6 |
| Verbal-motor forms . . . | 31·2 ⎭ | 31·7 ⎭ |
| Word-completion . . . . | 0·5 ⎫ | 0·9 ⎫ |
| Clang . . . . . . | 1·2 ⎬ 2 | 0·6 ⎬ 2 |
| Rhyme . . . . . . | 0·3 ⎭ | 0·5 ⎭ |
| Indirect . . . . . | 1·6 ⎫ | 0·8 ⎫ |
| Meaningless . . . . . | 0·5 ⎬ 3·9 | 0·1 ⎬ 2·4 |
| Faults . . . . . . | 1·8 ⎭ | 1·4 ⎭ |
| Repetition of stimulus-word . . | | 0·1 |
| Egocentric reaction . . . | 2·2 | 1·3 |
| Perseveration. . . . . | 1·5 | 0·8 |
| Repetitions . . . . . | 9·9 | 8·2 |
| Same grammatical form . . . | 54·3 | 56·4 |
| Same number of syllables . . | 37 | 43·7 |
| Alliteration . . . . . | 9·1 | 8·9 |
| Consonance . . . . . | 14·0 | 13·5 |
| Same ending . . . . . | 12·4 | 10·9 |
| Total number of associations . . | 3000 associations | 3800 associations |

We are surprised when we glance at the figures to see the minimal difference between the two sexes. With few exceptions the figures are in substantial agreement; at any rate, there is an absence of the distinct difference which, e.g., separates the group of the educated from the uneducated. The type is somewhat more superficial in the men than in the women ; the men have rather more clang-associations, also more indirect associations—phenomena which can be directly connected with the more superficial type. The greater number of egocentric reactions and perseverations appears, from the considerations adduced, to be connected with the more unembarrassed behaviour of the men. The difference in the figures for agreement in grammatical form and number of syllables is analogous to the corresponding difference between the educated and the uneducated. This must be due to the fact that in our uneducated male subjects the level of culture is somewhat higher than in the corresponding female subjects. These figures in the normal experiment have disclosed nothing typical of the psychology of women, which must not, however, be regarded as evidence that no differences exist. Our method of investigation is obviously much too coarse a one to discover such fine differences.

#### 4. AVERAGES OF THE DISTRACTION EXPERIMENTS

We give here a recapitulation of the average figures from the distraction experiments. For easier comparison we retabulate the averages in the normal state (see Tables on pp. 145, 146, and 147).

The figures in the distraction experiment show a progressively more superficial type of reaction than in the normal state. The principle change is quite obvious : the inner associations recede during distraction in favour of the increasing outer associations or clang-reactions.

In surveying the figures for internal association we see that the women have higher figures in this group than the men. The lowest figures occur among the men. The objection that the women start with a higher number of inner associations in the normal state is only true of the uneducated women. Educated women have a rather more superficial type of reaction in the normal state than educated men. The fact that the number of inner associations in women does not fall so low as in men means that the women have responded less than the men to the aims of the experiment. The parallel columns of the minus differences for inner association show clearly that the experiment appealed less to the women.

The remaining differences cannot, unfortunately, be presented with equal evidence, for they are divided into three groups, the contents of which are of varying psychological value. Hence the figures for inner associations are the best test for the amount

UNEDUCATED

| | Women | | | Normal | 60 metro. | |
|---|---|---|---|---|---|---|
| | Normal | Outer distraction | | | | |
| | | 60 metro. | 100 metro. | | | |
| Co-ordination | 25·2 ⎫ | 19 ⎫ | 15·7 ⎫ | 23·2 ⎫ | 20·8 ⎫ | 4·8 |
| Predicate | 20·4 ⎬46·6 | 20·6 ⎬40·3 | 19 ⎬35·2 | 16·1 ⎬40·5 | 10 ⎬30·8 | 2·8 |
| Causal dependence | 1 ⎭ | 0·7 ⎭ | 0·5 ⎭ | 1·1 ⎭ | — ⎭ | — |
| Coexistence | 20·4 ⎫ | 18·2 ⎫ | 18·5 ⎫ | 17·3 ⎫ | 19·1 ⎫ | |
| Identity | 5 ⎬49·4 | 9·7 ⎬52·2 | 9·2 ⎬61 | 10 ⎬55·6 | 17·4 ⎬58·5 | |
| Verbal-motor forms | 24 ⎭ | 24·3 ⎭ | 33·3 ⎭ | 28·3 ⎭ | 22 ⎭ | |
| Word-completion | 0·3 ⎫ | 0·2 ⎫ | 0·5 ⎫ | — ⎫ | — ⎫ | — ⎫ |
| Clang | 0·1 ⎬0·7 | 1·7 ⎬2·9 | 2·0 ⎬3·7 | 0·6 ⎬0·6 | 1·4 ⎬3·1 | 0·8 ⎬1 |
| Rhyme | 0·3 ⎭ | 1 ⎭ | 1·2 ⎭ | — ⎭ | 1·7 ⎭ | 0·2 ⎭ |
| Indirect | 0·7 ⎫ | 1·2 ⎫ | 0·7 ⎫ | 0·8 ⎫ | 3·4 ⎫ | 1·4 ⎫ |
| Meaningless | 0·2 ⎪ | 0·7 ⎪ | 0·2 ⎪ | 0·1 ⎪ | 1·1 ⎪ | 2 ⎪ |
| Faults | 1·4 ⎬2·3 | 1·0 ⎬3·4 | 0·5 ⎬1·4 | 1·5 ⎬2·4 | 1·4 ⎬6·4 | 2·2 ⎬7 |
| Repetition of stimulus-word | — ⎭ | 0·5 ⎭ | — ⎭ | — ⎭ | 0·5 ⎭ | 2 ⎭ |
| Egocentric reaction | 0·5 | 0·5 | 0·5 | 1·7 | — | — |
| Perseveration | 1 | 2 | 2·5 | 0·7 | 0·5 | — |
| Repetitions | 9·5 | 8·5 | 3 | 12·3 | 5·1 | 4 |
| Same grammatical form | 58·9 | 62·5 | 62·2 | 59·5 | 67·7 | 64·5 |
| Same number of syllables | 46 | 47·5 | 44·7 | 39 | 45·7 | 48·2 |
| Alliteration | 8·4 | 11 | 11·2 | 9·2 | 8 | 12·4 |
| Consonance | 12·2 | 18·5 | 15·7 | 12·5 | 23·4 | 18·8 |
| Same ending | 11·3 | 11·7 | 16·0 | 16·3 | 14·3 | 18·2 |
| Total number of associations | 1600 | 400 | 400 | 1400 | 350 | 350 |
| Total number of subjects | 8 | 8 | 8 | 7 | 7 | 7 |

### EDUCATED

| | Women | | | |
|---|---|---|---|---|
| | Normal | Inner distraction | Outer distraction | |
| | | | 60 metro. | 100 metro. |
| Co-ordination . . . | 13·7 ⎫ | 14 ⎫ | 11·7 ⎫ | 11·5 ⎫ |
| Predicate . . . . | 20·2 ⎬ 35 | 15 ⎬ 29·5 | 21·2 ⎬ 33·6 | 19 ⎬ 30·7 |
| Causal dependence . . . | 1·1 ⎭ | 0·5 ⎭ | 0·7 ⎭ | 0·2 ⎭ |
| Coexistence . . . . | 13·8 ⎫ | 10 ⎫ | 12·7 ⎫ | 8 ⎫ |
| Identity . . . . | 4·7 ⎬ 58 | 4·3 ⎬ 44·8 | 10·5 ⎬ 48·9 | 9 ⎬ 56 |
| Verbal-motor forms . . | 39·5 ⎭ | 30·5 ⎭ | 25·7 ⎭ | 39 ⎭ |
| Word-completion . . . | 1·5 ⎫ | 4·5 ⎫ | 3 ⎫ | 2·2 ⎫ |
| Clang . . . . | 1·1 ⎬ 3·3 | 5·1 ⎬ 11·6 | 5·5 ⎬ 10·2 | 6·5 ⎬ 9·2 |
| Rhyme . . . . . | 0·7 ⎭ | 2 ⎭ | 1·7 ⎭ | 0·5 ⎭ |
| Indirect associations . . | 0·9 ⎫ | 1·6 ⎫ | 1 ⎫ | 0·2 ⎫ |
| Meaningless . . . | 0·1 ⎬ | 0·5 ⎬ | 1·2 ⎬ | 1·5 ⎬ |
| Faults . . . . | 1·4 ⎬ 2·6 | 1·1 ⎬ 3·8 | 2 ⎬ 5·7 | 1·5 ⎬ 3·9 |
| Repetition of stimulus-word . | 0·2 ⎭ | 0·6 ⎭ | 0·5 ⎭ | 0·7 ⎭ |
| Egocentric . . . | 2·1 | 1 | 1·2 | 1 |
| Perseveration. . . . | 0·6 | 1·0 | 2·2 | 1·7 |
| Repetitions . . . | 7·2 | 3·5 | 6·5 | 5 |
| Same grammatical form . . | 53·9 | 59 | 54 | 53 |
| Same number of syllables . | 41·5 | 45·5 | 47·7 | 43·5 |
| Alliteration . . . | 8·4 | 11·1 | 11·7 | 12·5 |
| Consonance . . . | 14·9 | 19·3 | 19 | 20·6 |
| Same ending . . . | 10·5 | 11·8 | 11·7 | 13 |
| Total number of associations . | 2200 | 500 | 400 | 400 |
| Total number of subjects . | 11 | 6 | 8 | 8 |

EDUCATED

| | Men | | | |
|---|---|---|---|---|
| | Normal | Inner distraction | Outer distraction | |
| | | | 60 metro. | 100 metro. |
| Co-ordination . . . | 16·3 ⎫ | 8·6 ⎫ | 15·6 ⎫ | 10·8 ⎫ |
| Predicate . . . . | 19·7 ⎬36·7 | 15 ⎬24·4 | 12 ⎬28 | 10·4 ⎬21·8 |
| Causal dependence . . . | 0·7 ⎭ | 0·8 ⎭ | 0·4 ⎭ | 0·6 ⎭ |
| Coexistence . . . . | 12·8 ⎫ | 6·1 ⎫ | 12·8 ⎫ | 12 ⎫ |
| Identity . . . . | 5·7 ⎬52·7 | 4·5 ⎬49·2 | 9·2 ⎬57·2 | 6·6 ⎬61·4 |
| Verbal-motor forms . . | 34·2 ⎭ | 38·6 ⎭ | 35·2 ⎭ | 42·8 ⎭ |
| Word-completion . . . | 1·1 ⎫ | 4·3 ⎫ | 1·2 ⎫ | 2·6 ⎫ |
| Clang . . . . . | 1·9 ⎬ 3·6 | 15·8 ⎬20·7 | 8 ⎬ 9·6 | 3·8 ⎬ 8·2 |
| Rhyme . . . . . | 0·6 ⎭ | 0·6 ⎭ | 0·4 ⎭ | 1·8 ⎭ |
| Indirect associations . . | 2·5 ⎫ | 4·5 ⎫ | 3·2 ⎫ | 6·2 ⎫ |
| Meaningless . . . . | 0·9 ⎮ | 1·6 ⎮ | 2 ⎮ | 1·8 ⎮ |
| Faults . . . . . | 2 ⎬ 5·5 | — ⎬ 6·1 | — ⎬ 5·2 | — ⎬ 8 |
| Repetition of stimulus-word . | — ⎭ | — ⎭ | — ⎭ | — ⎭ |
| Egocentric . . . . | 2·8 | 1·1 | 0·8 | 1·6 |
| Perseveration. . . . | 2·4 | 1·6 | 2 | 3 |
| Repetitions . . . . | 7·5 | 3·8 | 6·8 | 6·2 |
| Same grammatical form . . | 49·1 | 50·5 | 50·2 | 51·8 |
| Same number of syllables . | 35 | 44·6 | 46·4 | 41 |
| Alliteration . . . . | 9 | 27·3 | 17·6 | 13·2 |
| Consonance . . . . | 15·6 | 33·3 | 23·6 | 20·6 |
| Same ending . . . . | 8·5 | 8·3 | 11·2 | 10 |
| Total number of associations . | 1600 | 550 | 250 | 435 |
| Total number of subjects . | 8 | 6 | 5 | 5 |

of distraction. The differential figures show a certain agreement in the men, whilst the minus difference of the uneducated women is greater than in educated women, which would speak in favour of a better adjustment to the experiment on the part of the uneducated women.

| | Educated | | Uneducated |
|---|---|---|---|
| | Inner distraction | Outer distraction | Outer distraction |
| Men  .  .  .  . | − 5·5 | − 2·8 | − 8·8 |
| Women  .  .  .  . | − 12·3 | − 11·8 | − 11·3 |

Minus difference of inner associations

Certainly the plus differences in the group of clang-reactions again show a more important increase in the educated than in the uneducated women.

| | Uneducated women | Educated women |
|---|---|---|
| Plus difference of clang-reactions  .  . | 2·6 | 8·3 |
| | | sometimes 6·4 |

The reason for this contradiction must lie in the fact that the educated women behaved much more unequally towards the distraction experiment than the uneducated women. Both groups fulfilled the conditions of the experiment, writing the strokes and reacting at the same time, with rather more difficulty than the men. Comparing, e.g., the differences between educated men and women in the distraction experiment, one is struck at once by the more complete effect of distraction in men. The only essential difference in the two female groups appears to be that the educated women are able, at least for a time, to divide their attention.

It seems to us as if there were here a certain difference in the reacting of men and women—a difference which might be estimated quantitatively. As, however, from the paucity of the material, sources of error cannot be excluded, we shall reserve this for further discussion.

The figures in the individual groups of the scheme show certain variations which demand a critical inquiry.

Whilst the co-ordinations decrease fairly regularly with distraction, the predicates show in distraction a somewhat different behaviour in men and women.

| | Educated Outer distraction | Uneducated Outer distraction |
|---|---|---|
| Women  .  .  . | − 0·2 | − 0·6 |
| Men  .  .  . | − 8·5 | − 4·7 |

Minus difference of the predicates.

The table shows that in distraction the decrease of the predicates is less in women than in men.  Let us here recall the hypothesis put forward in our review of the predicate type that it is the primary sensual vividness of the stimulus-images which really evokes predicates.  This psychological peculiarity is naturally maintained also in the state of experimental dissociation of attention ; it will hinder the experiment, inasmuch as the primary vivid pictures, without the addition of active attention, engross the interest.  In this way the dissociation of attention, according to the regulations of the experiment, is hindered and made more difficult.  We shall see this phenomenon very clearly in the occurrence of distraction with the predicate type, to which we refer the reader.  Among the women there are, relatively, very many predicate types, which must be the cause of the apparently steadier maintenance of the predicates.

In contrast with the decrease of inner associations, there is a corresponding increase of outer associations, in so far as this is not influenced by a stronger increase in the clang-reactions.  In the increase of the outer associations all three groups do not take an equal part.  We shall see that the number of co-existences shows rather a tendency to diminish.  We again present the differences in a table.

| Uneducated | | Educated | |
|---|---|---|---|
| Women | Men | Women | Men |
| − 2 | − 1·5 | − 3·4 | − 0·4 |

Difference between normal experiment and distraction in respect to co-existences.

Contrary to expectation, they are entirely minus differences.  This shows that the co-existences do not participate in the increase of the outer association.  When we recall that co-existences frequently arise from an endeavour to represent distinctly the object of the stimulus-word, the decrease in the distraction experiment is to be understood.  Co-existence is to a certain extent a first step to inner association, and thus participates in the decrease of the latter.

The groups of identities and verbal-motor forms show, on the whole, an increase, which is, however, influenced by a strong increase of the clang-reactions, conditioning, e.g., in educated women, a decrease in both groups.  We explain this variation by the repeatedly proved irregularity of distraction.  The quantitatively lessened occurrence of word-completions is striking among the uneducated.  We think that want of verbal readiness is responsible for this, especially want of practice in literary German.  Experiments with uneducated Germans, notably North Germans, would perhaps disclose other figures.  Clang-associations are much more numerous among the educated than among the uneducated.

The indirect associations exhibit a peculiarity. We have already referred to an inverse relationship of their increase with that of clang-associations. In our averages we are at once struck by their independence of the degree of distraction.

|  | Uneducated | | Educated | |
|---|---|---|---|---|
|  | Women | Men | Women | Men |
| Normal experiment . . | 0·7 | 0·8 | 0·9 | 2·5 |
| Distraction . . . | 0·9 | 2·4 | 0·9 | 4·6 |

These figures show that the uneducated, in normal experiment, produce on the average fewer indirect associations than the educated and that the women produce fewer than the men. In distraction the disinclination of the women to indirect associations is still clearer. Whilst in the men there is a most distinct increase, the average remains the same for educated women as in normal experiment, and there is but an insignificant increase in the figures for uneducated women. In this respect there must be some distinctive difference between the sexes, the meaning of which is at present unknown to us. The nature of indirect associations previously discussed (clang-reactions preponderating as intermediaries) enables us to understand its dependence on distraction. We should therefore expect with the increase of clang-reactions an increase also of the indirect associations. We recapitulate the figures in question :

|  | Uneducated | | | | Educated | | | |
|---|---|---|---|---|---|---|---|---|
|  | Women | | Men | | Women | | Men | |
|  | Clang | In-direct | Clang | In-direct | Clang | In-direct | Clang | In-direct |
| Normal experiment . . | 0·7 | 0·7 | 0·6 | 0·8 | 3·3 | 0·9 | 3·6 | 2·5 |
| Outer distraction 1 . . | 2·9 | 1·2 | 3·1 | 3·4 | 10·2 | 1 | 9·6 | 3·2 |
| Outer distraction 2 . . | 3·7 | 0·7 | 1 | 1·4 | 9·2 | 0·2 | 8·2 | 6·2 |
| Inner distraction (among educated only) . . . | — | — | — | — | 11·6 | 1·6 | 20·7 | 4·5 |

Although these figures point in general to the expected simultaneous increase of clang-reactions and indirect associations in distraction, still the movement of the two groups is not alike in certain individual places. If there were really a common movement of the two groups one would expect that the maxima of indirect association would coincide with the maxima of clang-reactions. But that is by no means the case. If we look at the maxima of the indirect associations in the figures of the distraction experiment we see that only in two cases are the maxima coincident.  To the maxima of the clang-reactions there occur no corresponding increase of the indirect associations. There is therefore no simple and clear correlation in the sense of a direct ratio, nor do the figures give any obvious evidence of an inverse relationship.  Only in the group of educated men do we see the coincidence of a striking maximum of indirect associations with the minimum of clang-reactions, which is certainly a remarkable occurrence.  In the two female groups we notice that the increase in the indirect associations is strikingly less than in the clang-reactions.  In the educated men the great increase of the clang-reactions from 3·6 per cent. normal to 20·7 per cent. in distraction corresponds to a mere 2 per cent. increase of the indirect associations, whilst the maximum, as has been said, coincides with the minimum of clang-reactions.  This behaviour of the indirect associations seems to us to speak in favour of a certain dependent relationship of the two groups to one another.  We think that an increase of indirect associations chiefly prejudices the group of clang-reactions.  If the group of clang-associations is considered in its relation to indirect associations the following picture is obtained :

|  | Uneducated | | | | Educated | | | |
|  | Women | | Men | | Women | | Men | |
|  | Clang | In-direct | Clang | In-direct | Clang | In-direct | Clang | In-direct |
|---|---|---|---|---|---|---|---|---|
| Outer distraction 1 . . | 1·7 | 1·2 | 1·4 | 3·4 | 5·5 | 1 | 8 | 3·2 |
| Outer distraction 2 . . | 2 | 0·7 | 0·8 | 1·4 | 6·5 | 0·2 | 3·8 | 6·2 |

The behaviour of the pure clang-associations shows, with few exceptions, the inverse relationship of the two groups.  The choice of clang-associations for the purpose of demonstration is not an arbitrary one, for they are the chief part of the entire clang-group, and are at the same time those associations which are suppressed in the normal state—a fact that does not hold true of all rhymes.  It is just the fact that pure clang-associations are suppressed in the normal state which is of greatest importance for the explanation of the inverted relationship.  The unspoken, for the most part quite unconscious, intermediate terms of the indirect associations are preponderantly clang-associations.  In the normal state, clang-associations are constantly meeting inhibitions, for as a rule they are extraordinarily ill-adapted for the process of association and are thus cast out.

There will be always present a certain tendency to suppress clangs ; this will always be stronger the less the disturbance of attention, it will also be weaker the greater the distraction. With increasing distraction the reaction always becomes more inclined towards clangs, and finally nothing but a clang becomes associated. Between the inclination towards clangs and the clang-reaction there comes a point, however, where the clang-association cannot break down the inhibition opposing it, but nevertheless is able to control the sense of the reaction that follows, by breaking the connexion between stimulus-word and reaction. It is then a matter of indifference whether the sub-conscious clang-association arises centripetally or centrifugally.

This mediating clang-association, which almost reaches the threshold value of the reaction, leads to the formation of the indirect associations. It is self-evident that the intermediate terms need not always be clang-associations, they only require to attract to themselves just so much inhibition as to remain below the threshold value of the reaction. We, therefore, conceive the indirect association as a symptom of the repression of inferior associations which nearly reach the threshold value of the reaction.[1]

This conception allows us to understand readily the apparent inverse relationship of clang-associations and indirect associations. If the clang-associations gain the upper hand, it may be concluded that the inhibitions to clangs have been abolished ; hence the repressions also, and consequently the indirect associations, are stopped. But if the number of clang-associations decreases, it is a sign that the inhibitions increase, and this offers the conditions for the occurrence of indirect associations. The indirect associations are therefore a phenomenon of transition which reaches its optimum at a certain stage of distraction. This explains also the apparently proportional increase in the clang-reactions and the subsequent decrease in the inverted relationship when the critical point is passed.[2]

[1] We only claim for this view of the indirect associations at present the value of a working hypothesis. We willingly submit our figures and our conception to further discussion, in the hope that the combined work of different investigators may result in a satisfactory solution of this question.

[2] The occurrence of indirect associations under the influence of a distraction of attention has been long known. Picture-naming in alcoholic delirium (Bonhöffer), in epileptic mania (Heilbronner), in certain catatoniac and hysterical states, is nothing but indirect association. This does not arise, as in our experiment, by a change in clang similarity but by a change in picture similarity. It is in this case, therefore, a by-product to flight of ideas in the visual sphere, and corresponds in every point with the phenomena we have demonstrated in the acoustic-verbal sphere.

Claparède, who has worked at the question of indirect associations from another side, believes that they are the " résultat du concours de plusieurs associations intermédiaires chacun trop faible pour être consciente." [1]

We agree with this view entirely, in the sense of the results of our experiment. The tendency to form associations according to the sense which proceeds from the stimulus-image prevents the occurrence of the clang-reaction. They are both, however, too weak to attain a reaction. Should the clang-association, not linked by its sense to the stimulus-image, predominate, an indirect association arises ; in the contrary case a reaction arises which has sense, though strongly affected by clang.

Fiéron's [2] view, that the third term of the indirect association would have a greater interest for the individual than the middle term, does not coincide with the results of our experiment. Still, Fiéron's view has something to recommend it and holds good of all those cases where the outer stimulus is unconsciously assimilated in the sense of a strongly accentuated complex filling up the conscious. (We shall consider this further possibility of an indirect association in a later work.) Piéron's view does not fit the endless number of indirect associations that occur in daily life. Out of many instances we mention one very instructive observation in our own experience. One of the authors, who had a long railway journey in front of him, was smoking a cigar, when it suddenly occurred to him that he had no more matches on him, whilst he possessed another good Havana cigar to smoke *en route*. He concluded he would have to light the second cigar at the end of the one he was smoking. That satisfied him, and he dropped this chain of thought. He was looking out of the window for a minute, carefully considering the landscape ; he suddenly noticed that spontaneously and quite softly he was saying *Bunau - Varilla*. B.-V. is the name of the well-known Panama agitator in Paris. He had read the name a few days before in the *Matin*. As the name seemed to have no connexion at all with the content of consciousness he at once directed his attention to the name, taking note of what came up in his mind (Freud's Method of Free Association). There came to him at once " Varinas," then " Manila " ; almost at the same time " cigarillo," accompanied by a vague feeling of a South American *milieu* ; the next distinct term was the Havana cigar and the recollection that this cigar had formed the content of

---

[1] Cp. Claparède, *L'association des idées*, p. 140 ; and Claparède, " Association médiate dans l'évocation volontaire," *Archives de Psychologie*, Tome III, p. 201.

[2] H. Piéron, " L'association médiate," *Rev. phil.*, Août 1903, Tome XXVIII, p. 147.

the previous cycle of thought. The middle terms "Varinas" and "Manila" denote kinds of tobacco which have for the narrator something "Spanish" about them; "cigarillo" is the Spanish for a cigarette, and he had smoked cigarettes made from Manila tobacco in a Spanish colony, but not in South America. Nevertheless there clung to "cigarillo" a faint image of something "South-Americanish." Whilst he had been looking out of the window he had not had the slightest feeling of any such chain of thought, his attention being concentrated on the landscape. The unconscious chain of thought which led to the formation of *Bunau-Varilla* was fashioned in the following way : Havana cigar—"cigarillo" with Spanish South-American background—recollection of a journey with "Manila-cigarillo" —Spanish-American tobaccos "Varinas" — ("Varinas" and "Manila" condensed by dream-mechanism into) *Varilla =* *Bunau - Varilla.* The sufficient basis for the unconscious carrying on of the cigar idea was that the observer had resolved not to miss lighting the Havana cigar at the end of the one he was smoking.

According to Piéron, *Bunau-Varilla* must be the emotionally toned final term desired by the thinker. That clearly it is not, but merely a condensation product arising from the concurrence of several weak middle terms (in accordance with Claparède's view). The mechanism of its rise is a verbal-motor automatism not infrequent in normals (in certain hysterics incomparably more frequent). The unconscious chain of association is stirred by picture and clang similarities, as are all associations occurring in the unconscious—i.e. external to the stress of attention (with the exception of certain somnambulic processes).

Referring to Jerusalem's article,[1] Wundt calls the middle term "unperceived," in contradistinction to "unconscious," in which we can discover no essential criticism; it is but a mere logomachy. It will not astonish any one that Scripture obtained[2] doubtful results, Smith[3] and Münsterberg[4] none at all, for their experiments were at the outset ill devised to produce indirect associations. The best examples of indirect associations are

---

[1] Wundt, "Sind die Mittelglieder einer mittelbaren Assoziation bewust oder unbewust?" *Phil. Studien.*, Bd. X, p. 1326. Jerusalem, "Ein Beispiel V. Assoziation durch unbewuster Mittelglieder," *Phil. Stud.*, Bd. X, p. 323.

[2] Scripture, "Ueber den assoziativen Verlauf der Vorstellungen," *Phil. Stud.*, Bd. VII, p. 50.

[3] William Smith, *Zur Frage der mittelbaren Assoziation.* (Diss : Leipzig, 1894.)

[4] Münsterberg, *Beiträge zur experimentellen Psychologie*, Heft 4, p. 9. Münsterberg writes: "There are no indirect associations through unconscious middle terms." Certainly in his experiments there were none.

furnished by careful self-observation in daily life.[1] Indirect verbal associations arise, as our experiment shows, chiefly in distraction experiments.

Meaningless reactions show, as was to be expected, an increase in distraction.

Faults, whose general emotional nature we have insisted upon several times in the individual accounts, are, strangely enough, quite absent among educated men in distraction. Among the others they show a consistent behaviour. We shall return to this group in reviewing the averages of the predicate type.

Repetition of the stimulus-words shows a reaction similar to that of meaningless reaction ; it increases likewise with the distraction.

We joined together the last four groups in what we called the residual group. Our original idea was to collect in this group the abnormal by-occurrences of the association experiment. From the figures of this group we hoped to obtain a certain coefficient of emotion, the subject being replaced by the experiment. We included the indirect associations in this group on the supposition, not in itself improbable, that the indirect associations, by reason of their origin from clang alterations, were really faults. The meaningless reactions we likewise held to be faults, as well as the last two groups. This view was strengthened by some experiences in the pathological sphere, by the association phenomenon in emotional stupidity.[2]

As the results of our experiments show, our earlier suspicion as to the emotional nature of the indirect associations must be relinquished, but this does not apply to the other three groups. The nature of the emotion in these three groups must be more precisely determined.

According to our experience, meaningless reactions and repetition of stimulus-words arise as a rule from the confusion which is conditioned by the rules of the experiment, whilst faults rest mostly upon the emotion which is evoked by the arousal of strong emotionally toned complexes. Confusion due to the rules of the experiment can be here entirely excluded. The inclusion of faults in the residual group is thus open to question. The

---

[1] A few beautiful examples of indirect associations are found in Cordes, *Phil. Studien*, Bd. XVII, pp. 70, 71, 75. Cordes regards the supposition that the middle terms of indirect associations are unconscious phenomena as a " theoretical construction which can never be empirically proven, for unconscious psychical phenomena are outside experience." The author would surely make this sentence less absolute were he at all acquainted with the experiences of hypnotism.

[2] Cp. Jung, "Ueber Simulation von Geistesstörung," *Journal f. Psych. u. Neurologie*, Bd. II, p. 181.

earlier name, " Emotion Group," originally chosen for this group was therefore replaced by the indifferent term " Residual Group." The statistics of the figures in this group were arranged so as to have a synoptical table, which we were fully aware was merely provisional and inadequate.  Everybody who has done experimental work, especially with so intricate a material, knows that an apprenticeship must be served, and that one only knows afterwards what ought to have been known beforehand.

The egocentric reactions, which to a certain extent serve as an index of emotionally toned reactions, show a behaviour in distraction best demonstrated by a summary of the figures of the differences from normal experiment.

|  | Uneducated | | Educated | |
|---|---|---|---|---|
|  | Women | Men | Women | Men |
| Number of egocentric reactions in normal experiment . . | + 0·5 | + 1·7 | + 2·1 | + 2·8 |
| Difference in distraction . . | — | − 1·7 | − 1 | − 1·6 |

These figures show that according to our material the minus differences of the men are greater than those of the women. Although the women do not betray in normal experiment a stronger egocentricity than men, yet in distraction the women do exhibit it rather more strongly than men.

With reference to the perseverations, we have repeatedly proved a certain relationship dependent on strongly marked emotions.

We regarded the absence of association in distracted attention as the cause of its more frequent increase in distraction. Obviously, various complicated conditions are here intermingled which we cannot for the moment consider separately.  The following summary of the differences from the normal experiment shows the behaviour of perseveration in distraction.

| Uneducated | | Educated | |
|---|---|---|---|
| Women | Men | Women | Men |
| + 1·2 | − 0·4 | + 1·1 | − 0·2 |

From these figures it is clear that in distraction the perseverations decrease in men but increase in women.

The number of egocentric reactions give us a fair index of how many emotional ego-relationships occur in the reactions [1];

[1] In women the egocentric relationships are far from revealing themselves without protest—for the simple reason that the experimenters are males.

the number of the perseverations gives us somewhat similar help but in a less direct form.

As we have seen above, the women show a slighter effect of distraction upon the reaction. It may be concluded from this that female attention has proved itself less easily dissociable towards our experiment. With that must also be connected the slighter change in the number of egocentric reactions among the women. If the number of egocentric reactions evinces only a slight tendency to decrease, it is to be expected that the perseverations will show a similar behaviour ; but as a matter of fact they actually increase. Our explanation of this is that, owing to the lack of association artificially produced by the distraction, an emotional content of consciousness can be more easily persisted in than otherwise. But we do not know why the women to a greater degree than the men should have this tendency to perseverate more in distraction. Perhaps it is connected with more intensive feeling ?

The somewhat lesser tendency to dissociation of female attention has been based upon the following causes :

(1) We have already made it clear that different individuals (predicate types) have, it is to be presumed, primarily more vivid inner pictures than others. By more " vivid pictures " is meant such as have concentrated on themselves a greater intensity of attention, or, in other words, such as occur in company with many other associations. The greater an association complex, the more the " ego-complex " is drawn into sympathy. It is, therefore, understandable that with the vividness of the inner picture not only does the number of inner predicates grow but also, and chiefly, the number of subjective evaluations—that is, of egocentric reactions.

(2) The vividness of the inner picture is by no means always a primary, arbitrary phenomenon but can be also an artificial one. The attention can be voluntarily directed to it, or, in other words, innumerable new associations can be linked on to the picture that occurs with few by-associations. This activity is only aroused by the emerging picture, it is executed by another association complex which fills consciousness. The vividness of the inner picture is thus in one case primary and involuntary, in the other case secondary and desired. The latter form, then, stands under the influence of any other intellectual phenomenon which just happens to be present.

(3) If the inner pictures are primarily very vivid and plastic— that is, if they occur from the beginning with many by-associations—they must always possess a very definite effect upon attention ; varying with the degree of vividness, this will render

difficult or totally inhibit any dissociation of the same. This is, as we shall see, the case in the predicate type.

(4) If the inner pictures are either artificially vivid or plastic under the influence of an association complex already present, it depends only upon the stability of this complex whether the dissociation of attention becomes possible or not.

(5) We have no reason to assume that among women generally the inner pictures are primarily more vivid than among men (otherwise all women would probably belong to the predicate type). We have, however, a well-grounded supposition, as we have already demonstrated, that the reactions, relatively of high value among the uneducated, especially the uneducated women, rest upon a (quasi) intentional vividness of the stimulus-image. The association complex which executes this activity is the peculiar conception which the uneducated hold about the association experiment. Since they apprehend the stimulus-word from the point of view of its meaning, they are bound to direct greater attention to the stimulus presentation ; hence they surrender less to distraction, as our figures show.

Again, the fact that it is especially the uneducated women who submit least to distraction agrees with their being more strongly under the influence of this peculiar conception of the experiment. But that the educated women also show a lesser tendency to distraction than the men cannot rest merely upon this particular conception of the experiment. This must depend upon the condition already mentioned, that there were many predicate types among our educated women, and this type in general exhibits no distraction phenomenon.

We therefore classify the average figures of those educated women who are not predicate types in the table on page 159.

From the figures of the tables it is at once obvious that the women as such have no lesser capacity for dissociation than the men ; but it was the predicate type alone which so strongly affected the average of the educated women. Our figures show a distinct phenomenon of distraction not inferior in any way to that of men.

The *repetitions* of the same reactions decrease with distraction ; the reasons for this can be readily understood.

The figures for *verbal union* rise in distraction, so that the influence of the reaction becomes expressed quantitatively through more outer and mechanical determinants. It is noticeable among the uneducated that not only in normal experiment is there a quantitatively greater agreement in the *grammatical forms* than among the educated, but that the distraction experiment works

EDUCATED WOMEN, EXCLUDING THE PREDICATE TYPES

| | Normal | Outer distraction | |
|---|---|---|---|
| | | 60 metro. | 100 metro. |
| Co-ordination . . . . | 15·2 ⎫ | 13·5 ⎫ | 10·8 ⎫ |
| Predicate . . . . . | 14 ⎬ 30·2 | 14 ⎬ 28·3 | 9·6 ⎬ 20·8 |
| Causal dependence . . . | 1 ⎭ | 0·8 ⎭ | 0·4 ⎭ |
| Coexistence . . . . | 15·3 ⎫ | 12·4 ⎫ | 7·2 ⎫ |
| Identity . . . . . | 48 ⎬ 62·6 | 11·2 ⎬ 50·4 | 8·8 ⎬ 62·8 |
| Verbal-motor forms . . . | 42·5 ⎭ | 26·8 ⎭ | 46·8 ⎭ |
| Word-completion . . . . | 1·5 ⎫ | 4 ⎫ | 3·6 ⎫ |
| Clang . . . . . . | 1·4 ⎬ 3·7 | 8 ⎬ 14 | 9·2 ⎬ 13·2 |
| Rhyme . . . . . | 0·8 ⎭ | 2 ⎭ | 0·4 ⎭ |
| Indirect . . . . . | 1 ⎫ | 1·2 ⎫ | 1·6 ⎫ |
| Meaningless . . . . . | 0·1 ⎬ 2·4 | 2 ⎬ 5 | — ⎬ 3·2 |
| Faults . . . . . | 0·9 ⎭ | 1·6 ⎭ | 0·4 ⎭ |
| Repetition of stimulus-word . . | 0·4 | 0·2 | 1·2 |
| Egocentric reaction . . . | 0·3 | 0·4 | 1·6 |
| Perseveration . . . . | 0·7 | 2·4 | — |
| Repetitions . . . . . | 6·9 | 4·8 | 3·6 |
| Same grammatical form . . | 41·8 | 63·2 | 42·4 |
| Same number of syllables . . | 60·1 | 47·6 | 57·2 |
| Alliteration . . . . . | 8·5 | 13·2 | 15·2 |
| Consonance . . . . . | 14·7 | 21·2 | 24 |
| Same ending . . . . | 12·6 | 15·2 | 13·2 |
| Total number of associations . . | 1200 | 250 | 250 |
| Total number of subjects . . | 6 | 5 | 5 |

more powerfully and even more intensively than among the educated, although the uneducated show a slighter distraction phenomenon. The following differences demonstrate this clearly.

Differences between the number of same grammatical forms in normal experiment and the average figures of the experiment:

| | Women | Men |
|---|---|---|
| Uneducated . . . . | + 3·4 | + 6·6 |
| Educated . . . . . | + 1·4 | + 4·7 |

The figure for agreement in grammatical form thus begins among the uneducated not only at a higher level, but in distraction rises still higher than the corresponding figure among the educated. The reason for this probably lies in the fact that among the educated numerous smuggled-in phrases stand ready for completion at any moment.

The figures for agreement in *number of syllables, alliteration, consonance,* etc., show nothing requiring further commentary.

The almost general decrease of the figures for verbal union in the second part of distraction is correlated with the decrease in clang-reactions. This change must be referred to habit, through which the individual factors of extreme distraction gradually diminish.

### 5. AVERAGE OF THE PREDICATE TYPE IN NORMAL EXPERIMENT AND IN DISTRACTION

We summarize here the average figures of all those subjects whom we term " Predicate Types." We have reckoned as belonging to this type those persons in whom the inner associations prevail as against the group of verbal-motor forms, and where the number of predicates is on the average about double that of co-ordinations. Seven women and two men are dealt with in this statistical table [1] (see Table, p. 161).

For the sake of comparison we have placed by the side of the predicate type the average of all other types. The difference is striking. In distraction the predicate type shows no change worth mentioning. The predicate type does not dissociate its attention, whilst all other types prove themselves, to some extent at least, accessible to the disturbing stimulus. This fact is extremely remarkable.

As we have already suggested, the individuals who belong to the predicate type have, we assume, primary vivid inner pictures, upon which the attention is involuntarily fixed at the moment of the appearance (in contrast to a voluntary directed vividness). We have observed in our material that among the reactions of the predicate type, together with numerous evaluations, there are found remarkably many predicates which denote sensual qualities of the stimulus-object, all of which are visual. Some of the subjects stated at once that they obtained at times quite distinct plastic pictures.[2] It is upon this that we founded the theory of the predicate type.

[1] Of the three members of one predicate family only one has been included in the table.

[2] These plastic pictures correspond pretty nearly to Ziehen's individual presentations. In the experiment we purposely did not ask about this, in order to prevent attention being at once directed thereto by suggestion. In many persons only a slight effort of attention is required to produce at once plastic pictures. In this case only the word-pictures, in themselves blank and universal, become repressed ; this, under appropriate suggestion, can occur half

| | Normal | Outer distraction 60 metro. | Outer distraction 100 metro. | Normal | 60 metro. | |
|---|---|---|---|---|---|---|
| **Predicate type** | | | | | | |
| Co-ordination | 12·5 ⎫ | 14·8 ⎫ | 13·1 ⎫ | 21·5 ⎫ | 18·0 ⎫ | |
| Predicate | 32·1 ⎬45·7 | 31·2 ⎬46·5 | 30·5 ⎬43·8 | 13·5 ⎬36·0 | 11·3 ⎬29·9 | |
| Causal dependence | 1·1 ⎭ | 0·5 ⎭ | 0·2 ⎭ | 1·0 ⎭ | 0·6 ⎭ | |
| Coexistence | 13·5 ⎫ | 13·7 ⎫ | 11·7 ⎫ | 17·2 ⎫ | 16·0 ⎫ | |
| Identity | 4·1 ⎬48·6 | 8·0 ⎬44·9 | 8·5 ⎬49·3 | 7·3 ⎬58·2 | 13·2 ⎬57·2 | |
| Verbal-motor form | 31·0 ⎭ | 23·2 ⎭ | 29·1 ⎭ | 33·7 ⎭ | 28·0 ⎭ | |
| Word-completion | 0·8 ⎫ | 0·8 ⎫ | 0·2 ⎫ | 0·8 ⎫ | 1·3 ⎫ | |
| Clang | 0·3 ⎬1·5 | 1·4 ⎬3·0 | 1·1 ⎬1·5 | 1·1 ⎬2·5 | 4·7 ⎬7·5 | |
| Rhyme | 0·4 ⎭ | 0·8 ⎭ | 0·2 ⎭ | 0·6 ⎭ | 1·5 ⎭ | |
| Indirect | 0·8 ⎫ | 1·7 ⎫ | 0·2 ⎫ | 1·5 ⎫ | 2·2 ⎫ | |
| Meaningless | — ⎪ | 0·2 ⎪ | 1·1 ⎪ | 0·3 ⎪ | 1·2 ⎪ | |
| Faults | 2·4 ⎬3·2 | 2·5 ⎬4·6 | 2·5 ⎬4·6 | 1·0 ⎬2·9 | 0·8 ⎬5·1 | |
| Repetition of stimulus-word | — ⎭ | 0·2 ⎭ | 0·8 ⎭ | 0·1 ⎭ | 0·9 ⎭ | |
| Egocentric reaction | 3·6 | 1·7 | 1·4 | 1·0 | 0·6 | 0·7 |
| Perseveration | 0·8 | 1·1 | 1·1 | 0·9 | 1·8 | 1·9 |
| Repetitions | 9·9 | 8·0 | 4·8 | 8·5 | 6·5 | 4·0 |
| Same grammatical form | 40·7 | 43·1 | 45·4 | 62·1 | 66·9 | 63·8 |
| Same number of syllables | 37·3 | 44·0 | 47·4 | 42·9 | 47·3 | 43·5 |
| Alliteration | 7·9 | 8·8 | 10·8 | 9·4 | 12·4 | 14·1 |
| Consonance | 12·9 | 15·4 | 14·2 | 14·4 | 22·4 | 20·8 |
| Same ending | 6·7 | 7·7 | 11·1 | 14·0 | 15·4 | 16·6 |
| Total number of associations | 1792 | 350 | 350 | 4586 | 1000 | 1085 |
| Total number of subjects | 9 | 7 | 7 | 23 | 20 | 20 |

An inner picture is vivid when the associations directly connected with it accord with it in sound. The closest associations to the picture of something concrete are the organs of sense—the visual, acoustic, tactile, and motor senses. A vivid visual image finds itself in a state of attention.[1] The more vivid the

unconsciously, especially in inexperienced persons. We do not know whether this presumably special vividness of the pictures is a constant feature in this subject or whether it was merely present during the association experiment.

[1] I.e. it draws the attention to itself.

picture, the stronger are the inhibitions which react to every-thing not associated, and the slighter therefore will be the dissociation of the attention. The practical absence of the distraction phenomenon in the predicate type is a proof of the correctness of our conception. The predicate type is unable to dissociate his attention because his primary vivid inner pictures make such a demand upon his attention that inferior associations (which make up the distraction phenomenon) cannot arise.

All the peculiarities of the predicate type can be explained on this hypothesis :

(1) *The Higher Number of Predicates.*—The subjects point to some peculiarly striking quality of the inner picture, and naturally employ the predicate for that. The great number of inner associations is to be referred chiefly to the number of predicates. The relationship of the inner to the outer association recalls the relationship among the uneducated. But what is common is merely the intensity of the attention em-ployed. The predicates are also retained in distraction, and this we regard as a distinct proof of the spontaneity of the plastic nature of the picture.

(2) *The Great Number of Egocentric Reactions.*—The greater the vividness of the picture or the greater the association complex filling consciousness at the moment, the more must the complex arouse and attract associations, thus moulding the individual's consciousness, in order to remain conscious by means of this synthesis. In this way a whole series of personal traits reach the emerging association complex and become marked out and reacted to as peculiarly striking qualities of the picture. Thence proceed the egocentric reactions.

(3) *The Relatively Great Number of Faults.*—Faults are, as a rule, defective reactions, due to the arousal of a strong emotional complex which so chains the attention that no reaction is pos-sible. It is highly probable that, by reason of the greater vividness of the picture, more emotional pictures are aroused in the predicate type than in other types. It is a necessary sequence of our supposition that in distraction the faults show a tendency to increase. If the minimum of free attention which is still present, together with that bound to the picture, is claimed by some activity (writing to beats), no attention is left to carry out the reaction ; in any case no diminution in faults can then occur.

From the figures of the distraction experiment it can be stated that the predicate type is no merely accidental momentary attitude, but corresponds to an important psychological characteristic—one which is maintained amid altered conditions.[1]

## 6. THE INFLUENCE OF THE GRAMMATICAL FORM OF THE STIMULUS-WORD UPON THE REACTION

As may be readily understood, the choice of the stimulus-word, with all its diverse qualities, is not a matter of indifference. There is a whole series of stimulus-words which have selective reactions. There is, for instance, a whole number of terms for concrete objects to which regularly co-existent images are associated, quite apart from stimulus-words which arouse stereotyped word-connexions: e.g. *divorce—wicked*, or *divorce—averse*, *blood — red*, etc. For the quantitative relationships it is of consequence whether the stimulus-word is a noun, adjective, or verb. The frequency of the appropriate form of word will be here a chief factor. According to the statistics to be found in any reference work, it may be said that language uses nouns twice as often as adjectives and adverbs. According to the law of frequency, therefore, a noun as stimulus-word will be " answered " more easily than any other form of word. Inversely, the lessened frequency of verbs and adjectives causes greater difficulty in the reactions. This is quite apart from the fact that for most persons an adjective or verb in the infinitive, apart from the text, seems stranger than a noun. The latter probably will denote some concrete object or other, about which something can be said. We have carried out some comparative investigations on our material from this point of view and have found the following averages :

| | React to Verbs | | | | | | React to Adjectives | | | | | |
| | Nouns | Adjectives | Verbs | Associations Inner | Associations Outer | Clang | Nouns | Adjectives | Verbs | Associations Inner | Associations Outer | Clang |
|---|---|---|---|---|---|---|---|---|---|---|---|---|
| Educated men . . | 63·2 | 15·8 | 20·6 | 48·4 | 41·6 | 7·4 | 53·1 | 43·6 | 2·9 | 43·5 | 45 | 8·0 |
| Uneducated men . | 32·7 | 21·7 | 45·5 | 49·6 | 47·4 | 1·1 | 32·4 | 64·8 | 2·7 | 44·8 | 51·0 | 3·4 |
| Educated women | 45·7 | 19·4 | 34·7 | 55·5 | 39·2 | 4·5 | 39·1 | 52·6 | 7·4 | 43·3 | 45·4 | 3·1 |
| Uneducated women . | 52·8 | 14·4 | 32·6 | 69 | 29·6 | 0·3 | 49·4 | 47·3 | 3 | 60·8 | 37·3 | 1·1 |
| Predicate type . | 54·8 | 26·2 | 18·9 | 62·8 | 33·4 | 2·7 | 64 | 29·7 | 5·2 | 64·2 | 28·3 | 1·9 |
| Non-predicate type | 46·7 | 15 | 38·1 | 52·4 | 41·8 | 4·2 | 35·5 | 59·9 | 4·4 | 42·8 | 51·0 | 4·3 |

[1] By which we mean, of course, only our experimental conditions. Under the influence of fatigue and alcohol the predicates practically vanish ; this branch of the work, however, remains for investigation.

The figures which we invariably give for agreement in grammatical form in the tables show generally that the stimulus-word and reaction by no means always agree in grammatical form. The above table gives the averages in percentages for the most characteristic groups among our subjects. We have refrained from presenting the separate figures of each individual, to avoid heaping up immense series of figures. The average figures show clearly enough the characteristic variations, the matter of chief interest.

In the group of verbs we find that nouns are generally reacted to verbs, with the exception of one group, the uneducated men, who generally react by verbs to verbs. Educated men react with most nouns. Remarkably enough, the uneducated women most nearly approach them, whilst the educated women came nearest to the uneducated men. It is certain that the verbal law of frequency greatly influences the preference for this or that way of reaction. It is, therefore, quite easy to understand that the educated men, who have in any case a very superficial reaction, prefer the more colloquial noun to the rarer verb; but that the uneducated women should apparently behave in a similar way is not at first sight comprehensible and demands further investigation.

Whilst, according to our observations, the educated men mostly react current nouns to verbs, the uneducated men endeavour to do justice to the sense of the stimulus-word by reacting with a similar verb. Rather less clear is a similar endeavour in the educated women. This form of reaction, the psychology of which we have reviewed in detail, is determined by the endeavour to react according to the meaning of the stimulus-word. We have already seen that in this respect the uneducated women stand at the head. We should accordingly expect that the uneducated women would react with a still greater number of verbs than the uneducated men. But it must be remembered that the educational level of the uneducated women is lower, and that therefore their verbal facility and expression are weak; reaction to verbs will be therefore most difficult of all for this group, for to them verbs are even more difficult than they are to the other groups.[1] Consequently they are driven to nouns which can be most readily linked on to verbs. The endeavour of the uneducated women to give a reaction that makes sense determines the selection of the noun, which is not merely strung on to the verb, but wherever possible expresses something significant to the meaning of the verb.

[1] Note also that the subjects are chiefly Swiss and thus under burdensome speech conditions.

We therefore made a further investigation to confirm this view and to discover how large is the number of inner associations which are reacted to verbs. The figures obtained enable us to prove the above hypothesis. Together with the figures which give the preferred word forms, we have placed the figures which exhibit the kind of associations which are reactions to verbs. For the chief groups in question we recapitulate the figures in question, together with those of the normal experiment :

EDUCATED MEN

|  | Inner association | Outer association | Clang-reaction |
|---|---|---|---|
| Normal experiment  .  .  . | 36·7 | 52·7 | 3·6 |
| React to verbs  .  .  .  . | 48·4 | 41·6 | 7·4 |
| Plus difference  .  .  .  . | 11·4 | — | — |

This summary shows that the reaction type is considerably less superficial for verbs as stimulus-words than for our schedule of stimulus-words, which is preponderantly composed of nouns. The figures confirm the fact that, for educated men also, far fewer casual connexions exist between verb and verb than between noun and any of the three other forms of words. Comparing these figures with the corresponding figures of the uneducated women, we find our assertion confirmed that the nouns preferred by this group possess a higher quality :

UNEDUCATED WOMEN

|  | Inner association | Outer association | Clang-reaction |
|---|---|---|---|
| Normal experiment  .  .  . | 46·6 | 49·4 | 0·7 |
| React to verbs  .  .  .  . | 69 | 29·6 | 0·3 |
| Plus difference  .  .  .  . | 22·4 | — | — |

From these figures it is clear that by far the greater number of the associations which are reactions to verbs are of high value and correspond to the meaning of the stimulus-word. The behaviour of the clang-reactions in the two groups is also worth noting. The number, surpassing that of the normal experiment in educated men, shows how slight is the influence of the stimulus-word. Inversely, the decrease in the corresponding figures among the uneducated women is characteristic of the increased influence of the verbs. From these ratios the deduction may be made that the influence of the verbs upon attention, in consequence of their lesser frequency and the consequent greater difficulty in " answering," is greater than that of nouns.

The adjectives show, as a glance at the table teaches, a behaviour similar to that of verbs, having on the whole a somewhat lesser influence upon the reaction type. It may therefore be assumed that the reaction to adjectives encounters on the whole fewer difficulties.

The predicate type reacts to verbs preferably by nouns, whilst all the non-predicate types react by double as many verbs to verbs as the predicate type.[1]

We again investigate the quality of the associations reacted to the verbs by the predicate type.

|  | Predicate type | | | Non-predicate type | | |
|---|---|---|---|---|---|---|
|  | Inner association | Outer association | Clang-reaction | Inner association | Outer association | Clang-reaction |
| Normal experiment . . | 45·7 | 48·6 | 1·5 | 36·6 | 58·2 | 2·5 |
| Reaction to verbs . . | 62·8 | 33·4 | 2·7 | 52·4 | 41·8 | 4·2 |
| Plus difference . . . | 17·4 | — | — | 16·4 | — | — |

As the plus differences show, the influence of the verbs is about the same in both groups ; there is no plus difference of inner associations corresponding with the numerous nouns of the predicate type which surpasses that of the non-predicate type. We have, therefore, no ground to presume that in the predicate type the verb has a greater influence upon attention or greater difficulties for the reaction. The predicate type shows no difference of attention towards the verbs, but merely the difference which the educated have in general, namely, their preference for the noun because of its greater currency. This arises from the fact that among our predicate types the majority are educated.

The behaviour of the predicate type towards adjectives is in contrast to the earlier results. As the figures of the common tables show, in the reactions of the first four groups there occur more adjectives to adjectives than verbs to verbs. In the predicate type, who is characterized by his attributes in the form of adjectives, the difference only amounts to 10·8 per cent. There is strong preference for nouns (as compared with the non-predicate type), i.e. by 28·5 per cent. more. This preference for the noun arises from the endeavour of the predicate type to

[1] Note here that among the eleven predicate types there are only two uneducated persons, of whom one is a woman.

react chiefly by attributes.   Our figures show, not merely that a predicate is thus reacted, but also, inversely, a noun is given to the adjective when this is the stimulus-word.[1]   Let us now investigate the relationship of the figures in regard to the quality of the adjective reactions.

| | Predicate type | | | Non-predicate type | | |
|---|---|---|---|---|---|---|
| | Inner associa- tion | Outer associa- tion | Clang- reactions | Inner associa- tion | Outer associa- tion | Clang- reactions |
| Normal experiment . . | 45·7 | 48·6 | 1·5 | 36 | 58·2 | 2·5 |
| Reaction to adjectives . | 64·2 | 28·2 | 3·9 | 42·8 | 51 | 4·3 |
| Plus difference . . . | 18·5 | — | — | 6·8 | — | — |

As these figures show, the high figure for the nouns is combined with a corresponding increase of the inner associations in the predicate type.   This is not the case of a mere stringing together of current nouns, but of constructions adapted to the stimulus-word and executed with regard to the adjustment, although the stringing together of similar adjectives is much easier in itself, as witness the figures which agree herein for the remaining groups. This latter fact is clearly brought out by the lesser plus difference of the inner associations in the adjective reactions of the non-predicate type.

It is clear, also, from the figures of the adjective reactions that the predicate attitude is not accidental but corresponds to a definite psychological disposition, which is maintained even when other kinds of reaction would be much easier than the pre-dicate forms.

## RECAPITULATION

The associations vary, within the range of the normal, chiefly under the influence of :

(1) Attention.
(2) Education.
(3) The individual peculiarity of the subject.

a. Reduction of attention through any kind of inner or outer impulses makes the reaction type a more superficial one ; that is,

---

[1] This behaviour can be explained from the psychology of the predicate type.   The subjects of this type are distinguished by peculiarly vivid pictures. Therefore they see the adjective at once as the attribute of a particular object, which they denote in their reaction.

the inner or higher associations recede in favour of outer associations and clang-reactions.

*b.* The distraction of attention in our experiment effected, besides the change mentioned, an increase of the indirect associations. These must therefore be regarded as distraction phenomena derived from the concurrence of two weakly accentuated (or inferior) associations as the intermediate terms.

*c.* The educated have, on the average, a more superficial reaction type than the uneducated. The difference is essentially due to a difference in the apprehension of the stimulus-word.

*d.* As to the degree of the dissociation of attention effected by distraction, there are no essential differences between the educated and the uneducated.

*e.* The most important variations of association are conditioned by individual differences.

(1) As regards the influence of sex upon the reactions in normal experiment, no distinct differences result from the statistics of the averages. The peculiarities of the female subjects first appear in the distraction experiment : they have, on the average, a lesser capacity for dissociation of attention than the male subjects.

(2) The individual variations may be arranged in the following types :

I. OBJECTIVE TYPE.—The stimulus-word is apprehended objectively :

α. *Chiefly according to its Objective Meaning.* The reaction is appropriate, as far as possible, to the stimulus-word and linked by its meaning to the stimulus-word.

β. *Chiefly as Verbal Stimulus.* The reaction is partly a verbal adaptation and partly denotes a linking together of some prepared association ; any relationship to meaning falls considerably into the background.

II. EGOCENTRIC ADJUSTMENT.—The stimulus-word is taken in a subjective (egocentric) fashion.

α. *Constellation Type.* The personal elements used in the reaction belong to one or more emotionally toned complexes : two possibilities present themselves :

αα. The complex-constellation is expressed without disguise.

ββ. The complex-constellations occur in a disguised form in consequence of a repression which is not always conscious.[1]

β. *Predicate Type.* This type has presumably the psychological peculiarity of experiencing its inner pictures in a peculiarly vivid (plastic) way ; no special manner of reaction is to be

[1] We use the term " repression " in the sense of Breuer and Freud, to whose work, *Studies in Hysteria,* we are indebted for valuable stimulus in our investigations.

explained therefrom.  This type shows also an abnormally lesser capacity for dissociation of attention, and at times none at all ; this expresses itself in the distraction experiment on the whole by an almost complete absence of the phenomenon of shallowness.

We obtain this result, which for pathology is of universal import : that the superficial nature of the reaction type in fatigue, alcoholic intoxication, and mania is to be chiefly referred to a distraction of attention.  The observations on the affective side of associations (the effects of emotionally toned complexes) should be of importance in the experimental investigation of pathological changes in emotions and their consequences.

In conclusion, we would wish to express our thanks to our esteemed chief, Professor Bleuler, for much valuable stimulus. We are also much indebted to Mrs. Jung for her active co-operation in repeatedly working over the vast material.

### EXPLANATION OF THE FIGURES

The accompanying figures exhibit the arithmetical mean of the inner associations, outer associations, clang-reactions, and reactions of the residual group of the different groups.

*I*. signifies average of the total of inner associations.

*O*.          ,,                    ,,          outer          ,,

*C*.                                               clang          ,,

*R*.                                               reactions in the residual
                                                          group.

FIG. 1

a. Averages of the normal experiment among the educated of 23 subject with 3800 associations.

b. Averages of the normal experiment among the uneducated of 18 subjects with 3000 associations.

In the normal experiment the educated have fewer inner, more outer associations and more clang-reactions than the uneducated.

FIG. 2

AVERAGES OF THE EXPERIMENTS IN OUTER DISTRACTION AMONG THE EDUCATED

a. Normal experiment (= Fig. 1 a, 23 subjects, 3800 associations).

b. Distraction experiment with 60 metronome beats to the minute; 13 subjects, 650 associations.

c. Distraction experiment with 100 metronome beats; 13 subjects, 835 associations.

A distinct, regular decrease of the inner associations from a to c, i.e. corresponding to the intensity of the means of distraction, is seen. Secondly, the tables show an increase of the clang-reactions in both distraction experiments. The result of the distractions consists generally of the increase of the outer associations plus increase of clang-reactions. This sum (O and C) is shown by the column O being overtopped at times by a dotted column whose height is equal to the height of C. This column (O and C) increases regularly from a to c. The decrease of I and the increase of (O and C) in the distraction experiment illustrate clearly the effect of distraction. Cb and Cc are both greater than Ca. The reactions of the residual group increase from a to c.

Fig. 3

AVERAGES OF THE EXPERIMENTS IN OUTER DISTRACTION
AMONG THE UNEDUCATED

a. Normal experiment (like Fig. 1 b); 15 subjects, 3000 associations.
b. Distraction experiment; 60 metronome beats; 15 subjects, 750 associations.
c. Distraction experiment; 100 metronome beats; 15 subjects, 750 associations.

Apart from dissimilar origin, the picture is the same as in the distraction experiments among the educated.

Regular decrease of the inner associations from a to c.

Regular increase of the outer associations plus clang-reactions from a to c.  R increases in the distraction, C only slightly; the clang-reactions generally play a lesser part than among the uneducated.

Fig. 4 (p. 172).  Whilst among the educated the ratio of $1 : I = 2 : 3$ and among the uneducated $1 : I = 5 : 6$, here it amounts to about $1 : 1·1$.  C is less than among the educated, but greater than among the uneducated in normal experiment. In the group R the ratio is reversed.  In a remarkable way this ratio scarcely changes in distraction, quite contrary to the previous pictures.  There is but a minimal decrease of I and a very slight decrease of (O and C).  R has somewhat increased.

Fig. 5 (p. 172) offers a striking contrast to the picture in Fig. 4.  In the normal experiment the ratio is $I : (O + C) = 10 : 17$, approximately $2 : 3$; in the distraction experiment $10 : 24$, approximately $2 : 5$.  C increases substantially, R less so.

FIG. 4

AVERAGES OF THE EXPERIMENTS AMONG PERSONS OF THE PREDICATE
TYPE (EDUCATED AND UNEDUCATED)

a. Normal experiment; 9 subjects, 1792 associations.
b. Distraction experiments (outer distraction with 60 and 100
metronome beats); 7 subjects, 700 associations.

FIG. 5

AVERAGES OF ALL EXPERIMENTS IN THE REMAINING SUBJECTS
(NON-PREDICATE TYPE)

a. Normal experiment.     b. Distraction experiment.

# CHAPTER III

# THE ASSOCIATIONS OF IMBECILES AND IDIOTS

## By Dr. K. WEHRLIN

At the instance of Professor Bleuler and Dr. Jung, I have for some time carried out investigations on the associations of feeble-minded children and adults. Experiments on adults have given me material which warrants certain conclusions, whilst the investigations among children are so far inconclusive. I shall limit myself in the following essay to the material obtained from the experiments on the adult feeble-minded.

The technique of the association experiments is similar to that employed by Jung and Riklin, fully described in chapter ii, to which the reader is referred for further details.

As is well known, similar investigations among idiots have already been carried out by Sommer and Wreschner.

Wreschner [1] has made experiments on an idiot in time-reactions by Sommer's schedule. He came to the following conclusions :

The quality of the stimulus-word has a great influence upon the kind of association ; the more inferior the quality of the reaction the higher the quality of the stimulus-word. The store of images in Wreschner's subject, so far as it was expressed by association, was overwhelmingly composed of adjectives.

The inner associations require generally a longer reaction-time than the verbal ones.

The worse the quality of the association, and the more unaccustomed, therefore, the subject was to the stimulus-word, the longer the reaction-time ; this holds good for inner as well as for verbal reactions.

Practice shortens the reaction-time and improves the quality of the association. The verbal associations decrease in favour of the inner ones.

[1] "Eine experimentelle Studie über die Assoziation in einem Falle von Idiotie," *Allgemeine Zeitschrift für Psychiatrie*, 1900.

Sommer [1] reviews in his *Methods of Investigations* the associations in a case of imbecility.

He found great similarity and poverty in the store of images, with in places a total absence of associations. We quote a couple of his examples which in our experience are peculiarly characteristic of the feeble-minded :

| | |
|---|---|
| Doctor | who looks after the sick |
| Cleverness | who is not stupid |
| Memory | who remembers something |
| Law | who disobeys no order |

Fuhrmann [2] mentions that the idiot (in contradistinction to epileptics) is unable to form sub- and super-ordinated concepts in his reactions. As will be seen below, we have not been able to confirm this view in our experiments, for universal concepts were sometimes given.

As may be gathered from the investigations of Sommer and Wreschner, these experiments on the feeble-minded meet with peculiar difficulties, due to the pathological peculiarities of the subject examined.

### 1. DIFFICULTIES WHICH THE EXPERIMENT ENCOUNTERS FROM THE INTELLECTUAL SIDE

It is to be expected that the apprehension of the stimulus-word among imbeciles encounters greater difficulties than among normals, for it is in general characteristic of imbeciles to apprehend slowly and with difficulty ; certain words, especially abstracts, are understood with much more difficulty by the imbecile than by a normal uneducated person.

Concrete concepts are also more difficult for him to understand, as, in consequence of the poverty of his mental life, these always find fewer related concepts. This fact must be taken into consideration in the working out of the stimulus-image which he has received. In accordance with the rules of the experiment, the subject should put into one word (the reaction-word) the first thing that occurs to him.

The intention is to arouse a succession of presentations. Among normals a presentation is generally called up in accordance with the law of contiguity or of similarity. Among imbeciles, who, unlike normals, do not possess a great mass of material derived from experience, and among whom especially

---

[1] Sommer, *Lehrbuch der psychopathologischen Untersuchungsmethoden*, pp. 349–355.

[2] *Analyse des Vorstellungsmaterials bei epileptischem Schwachsinn*, p. 30 (Diss : 1902).

the higher associations, constructed chiefly by similarity, are not labile—there is great difficulty in drawing on the associated presentations.

Language is a factor of great importance for the association experiment among imbeciles.

Language, as a condensation product of innumerable associated processes, is an index of feeble-mindedness.

It is here that we must expect the greatest difficulties. The imbecile's poverty in imagery is reflected in the poverty and deficiencies of his language. The imbecile lacks not only an understanding of numerous rather complicated and rare things, but also the *words* which denote them. Stimulus-words which are somewhat rare are therefore very badly understood and arouse much fewer related images because they are hardly known to the imbecile. Even if he succeeds in evoking a related image, the further difficulty arises of discovering the appropriate verbal symbol. Here again deficient verbal education is a hindrance. The result is that numerous awkward and clumsy reactions are formed which betray, on the one hand, an imperfect understanding of the stimulus-word, and, on the other, a difficulty in verbal expression. A great number of results may therefore be expected which by their peculiarity not only characteristically distinguish imbecile reactions from all others, but also afford deep insight into the essence of the imbecile activity in association.

My subjects are Swiss. As Jung and Riklin have insisted, the peculiar verbal conditions of the German-Swiss must be seriously considered in the association experiment. Jung [1] says : " The uneducated, however, retains at the most those German phrases which he has learned at school, later adding little or nothing thereto. Literary German is not the less familiar to him in its written and printed form, and he understands it when spoken without being able himself to speak a fluent and faultless literary German." As Jung shows, Swiss-German is a purely acoustic-motor language which is very seldom read and written. The Swiss, therefore, knows his words only in connexion with what is spoken and heard. He has not a sense of words as " individual things," but only as different terms, not distinctly separated, in a continuous verbal chain. " If he has to say one word by itself without the article he generally chooses the literary German form." If among the uneducated there is a certain difficulty owing to deficiency in verbal habits, it is obvious that for the imbecile the difficulty is much greater. He will not only have greater difficulty, through his imperfect knowledge in apprehending the literary German stimulus-word, but has also

[1] Chapter ii, p. 10.

more strain in constructing the verbal form of his reaction. In my experiments the reaction was frequently rendered, not in literary German, but in the dialect form. Moreover, with the idiots it was often necessary to utter the stimulus-word in this dialect form, generally adding the article also, as that considerably increases the understanding of the dialect word.

The verbal difficulties coupled with the increased difficulty of apprehension are of great importance in the peculiar formation of the imbecile reaction.

As Jung and Riklin have exemplified, the uneducated react, on the average, with greater attention than the educated. They endeavour to do greater justice to the sense of the stimulus-word, the " word " as a sound receding to the background. The inferior verbal education of the uneducated makes a word, apart from its context, seem to him something strange, unaccustomed ; hence a hypothetical context is built up for the single stimulus-word. The uneducated, therefore, betray in their reactions a distinct tendency, from the constellation of habit, to apprehend the stimulus-word in the sense of a question, something like " What does —— mean ? " " What do you know about —— ? " The contrary of the stimulus-word is also much sought for or constructed. Consequently, in the reactions of the uneducated it is much less a question of the automatic direct impressions of the educated than of something sought for and thought about.

The tendency to form these kinds of reactions increases among the uneducated, in proportion to the decrease of culture and intelligence. And, as seems to follow from some hitherto unpublished investigations made in this clinic, certain normal individuals approximate in point of culture and intelligence to a reaction type resembling that of imbecility. The similarity consists in a limitation to the meaning of the stimulus-word, with an endeavour to show by the reaction that this meaning is understood.[1]

Hence the uneducated person's way of reacting is met again in imbecility ; and, proportionate to the deficient culture of the imbecile, it plays an immeasurably greater part. If one may regard the deficient culture which most markedly influences the reaction as an index of feeble-mindedness, the associations measure in some degree the intensity of the intellectual disturbance. On the whole, one is prepared to find an uninterrupted gradation of type leading up from idiots and imbecility to the intellectual plane of the normal.

It is, therefore, a priori probable that the signs of feeble-mindedness differ merely in strength and number from the signs of a low intelligence and education in the normal.

[1] See chapter x.

In any evaluation of the imbecile process of association another fact must be taken into account. The imbecile is not only intellectually undeveloped, but he is above all a degenerate, presenting as a rule, together with his weak-mindedness, other anomalies in the mental region. The most important anomalies are found, as in all psychopathic degenerates, in the *emotional functions*. The frequent anomalies of temper and the frequent moral defects are not markedly expressed in the associations, especially not the latter ; but, on the other hand, various hysterical traits, so common among imbeciles, will, as one can easily imagine, markedly influence the reaction.

I have found in my experiments that a certain quickly aroused confusion can considerably disturb the experiment, and render it difficult. Jung [1] has recently called attention, with experimental proof, to this trait of the imbecile. He reports on two imbeciles, under investigation and confinement in the asylum, who fell into a state of severe dementia, characterized by marked prolongation of the reaction-time, difficulty in remembering, and the occurrence of meaningless associations. These meaningless associations had reference chiefly to objects which were accidentally in the field of vision, but had no kind of relation to the stimulus-word ; they were simply liberated by the utterance of the stimulus-word. This state of obvious inhibition Jung terms " emotional stupidity."

To elucidate the nature of this disturbance I will cite a short series of associations from Jung's case :

| | | | |
|---|---|---|---|
| Christmas | tree | Schoolboy | tree |
| Easter | book | Father | pencil |
| | | Table | wall |
| Sunday | tree | Head | cloth |
| Winter | house | Ink | paper |
| Lake | school | Needle | window |

We take it for granted that imbecility includes numerous and diverse groups which again present relationships to all other possible forms of psychopathic deficiency. Thus cases seem to occur which are essentially marked out by incapacity for concentration—where the intellectual weakness expresses itself chiefly by its great associative superficiality. Individuals of this kind frequently show strong social instability with a tendency to pseudological scheming. Their manner of speaking and of

---

[1] Jung, " Ueber Simulation," op. cit., p. 181.

M

thinking has something extraordinarily confused and vague, often
recalling a slight flight of ideas. They are differentiated from manic-
depressive insanity [1] by the absence of symptoms of maniacal
excitement, exaltation of spirits and restlessness. These forms
are frequently really difficult to separate from pure imbecility,
more especially when they present structural defects similar to
imbecility—which, however, can finally be ascribed to their
unstable ways of life, their volatility and inattention. In cases
of otherwise undoubted imbecility this condition can also occur
as a by-product.

This kind of feeble-mindedness must present in its associations
a picture different from that of pure imbecility.


### 3. Arrangement of the Experiment

To survey the possibilities of imbecile reaction and thus
obtain a point of view of universal validity, I have collected
as wide a material as possible and submitted it to a qualitative
analysis. It was soon apparent that the Kräpelin-Aschaffenburg classification, which Jung and Riklin employed, was ill-
adapted to the associations of imbeciles ; that even where it
could be used it did not bring out what was of pathognomonic
importance.

I perceived that a classification adapted to the reality of the
situation must proceed from other points of view. My endeavour
was then to discover the points of view by which the material
could be classified. From the point of view of the associations
my twenty-seven patients are divisible into three groups, which
are, however, not sharply divided from each other :

(1) Imbeciles of a lethargic temperament.
(2) Imbeciles of a sanguine temperament.
(3) Higher imbeciles.

As will be seen, this classification agrees also with the clinical
and symptomatological one. Thirteen of the subjects certainly
show a lethargic temperament, and their associations likewise
show characteristic features differentiating them from the two
other groups. For this reason I chose this group as the starting-
point of my investigations.

This work is limited to the analysis of the associations of
thirteen idiots and imbeciles, aged from seventeen to sixty-nine
years, about whom clinically there is no doubt. By thus selecting

[1] Jung, "Ueber manische Verstimmung," *Allgemeine Zeitschrift für Psychiatrie*,
1903.

my experimental material it seemed to me most possible to discover certain laws which might serve as the starting-point for later and deeper investigations. For the solution of all those problems which occur in the second and third groups I neither had time nor the requisite number of subjects. The material upon which my work is founded consists in round numbers of 2000 single reactions. The reaction-time was measured in five persons, i.e. in 764 reactions. There are eleven men and two women.

Only in the more severe cases were the stimulus-words called out in their dialect form. The reaction was always put down exactly as it was given, therefore in a large number of my patients in dialect form. The test words which I reproduce I have translated as faithfully as possible into literary German.

At the beginning of the experiment an explanation was given, with examples as to how the person had to react ; the experiment was only begun when it was quite certain that the subject had grasped the matter.[1] In most cases some two hundred reactions could be carried out, sometimes with intervals varying from a couple of days up to several weeks. In the severer cases the experiment was so laborious and tedious that after the fifty-eighth reaction one patient was hopelessly bored of the matter.

The list of stimulus-words was that used by Jung and Riklin (see chapter ii). It sometimes happened in the severer cases that the stimulus-words were not understood because they were unknown to the individual, and had then to be struck out. In cases where the subject could not react he was asked whether he knew the stimulus-word ; when it was quite certain that the word was known the missing reaction was held to be a "fault." In the severer cases the stimulus-word had occasionally to be repeated several times. In these cases the time measurement was omitted. The time was only measured in those slighter cases where the experiment went smoothly.

### 4. Results of the Experiment

I have arranged my subjects clinically, according to their degree of feeble-mindedness ; first come the idiots, then the imbeciles. About thirty tests have been chosen from each

---

[1] I need scarcely add that those who could not understand the experiment were excluded from the investigation.

case—those which I regard as peculiarly characteristic and best adapted to demonstrate briefly the course of the experiment.

### No. 1.  *Total reactions* 72

| | | | |
|---|---|---|---|
| 1. Sunday | consists of—a day on which one does nothing | 18. Flower | a pot plant |
| | | 19. Cherry | a thing in the garden, on the trees |
| 2. Winter | consists of snow | 20. Piano | where there is music, upstairs |
| 3. Lake | consists of water | | |
| 4. Schoolboy | when he goes to school | 21. Oven | good for warmth |
| 5. Father | companion together with mother | 22. Walk | that is when you stretch your legs for a pint on Sundays |
| 6. Table | consists of wood | | |
| 7. Ink | something to write | 23. Cat | four-legged animal |
| 8. Bread | to eat | 24. Bird | also of the animal kingdom |
| 9. Tree | a part of—there are trees in the garden | 25. Swim | in the lake, in water |
| 10. Mountain | a high mountain | 26. White | the wine |
| 11. Hair | part of the head | 27. Game | there are lots of games |
| 12. Copy-book | consists of paper | 28. Stroke | you can stroke men and animals |
| 13. Paper | you write upon it | 29. Sweet | something sugary |
| 14. School | consists of schoolboys | 30. Friendly | when you are not angry |
| 15. Sing | consists of notes and song-books | 31. Crown | a kind of head-covering |
| 16. Ring | on the finger | 32. Ill | when you are not well |
| 17. Window | consists of wood and window-panes | 33. Star | part of the sky |

These tests give a clear view of this patient's way of reacting. As is at once evident, the tendency here is to explain or to define the stimulus-word in some way. The subject seeks to explain the stimulus-words by stating of what the thing denoted by the stimulus-word consists ; he denotes the material (reactions 3, 6, 12, 14, 17) ; the way in which this tendency runs off at a tangent in reaction 2 is characteristic of idiots :

Winter    consists of snow

The defective verbal education is here typical, as manifested in the quite inappropriate use of the phrase " consists of." This is a well-known phrase in school use, one but seldom used in later life, especially by an idiot. He is only half familiar with the limitations of its use and employs it where it does not really apply well. It is thoroughly typical of the idiot that the winter consists " of snow." He observes only the external phenomena, things that occur together or that follow one another, without making any kind of deductions as to the causal connexion. I have no doubt that to these patients also the cold and the short days are typical of the presentation " winter " ; but from their reactions it is very obvious that what is simply visual and external has greater importance than the less striking, but causally more important, collateral phenomena of the cold and short days.

The most illuminating example of the idiot's purely visual and external apprehension of things comes to light in the reaction

| Sing | consists of notes and song-books |
|------|----------------------------------|

Here it is distinctly seen how the external manifestation of the act, something really quite secondary, overcomes what is essential. Reactions of this kind are characteristic and suffice for the diagnosis of imbecility or idiocy, as against the so-called secondary states of feeble-mindedness.

In order to convince himself that he understands the meaning of the stimulus-word, our patient tries to characterize the object it denotes by naming the place where the thing occurs or is found (cp. reactions 9, 16, 20, 25). Or he names the purpose of the thing (7, 8, 21) in its use or the action which it executes (4, 13, 28) ; sometimes he designates the object by another expression, synonymous as a rule, which he perhaps accentuates by giving it some particularly typical attribute (*mountain — a high mountain ; flower — a pot plant*), or he tries a tautological elucidation by bringing the opposite with its negative into the reaction (e.g. *dark — not bright* : cp. also reactions 30, 32).

Universal concepts, taken too widely, which are supraordinated to the stimulus-word, form a characteristic group. These supra-ordinations are much too extensive to be able to fulfil their object of being explanatory. Occasionally the universal concept is so remote and indefinite that it really contains practically nothing relating to the stimulus-word, e.g. *tree — a part*. The disparity is here so great that the patient himself feels this gap, and therefore adds, " The garden has trees " : cp. 23 and 24. As this example shows, the patient tends to eliminate or limit the extension, and therefore the inappropriateness, of his supra-ordinated general concept by particularizing his concept in the actual object. This, again, he does in a way typical of feeble-mindedness. He particularizes his general concept by affixing some definite place to it ; this, by its naïve simplicity, often puts it in strange contrast with the unlimited universality of the concept (*particularized universal concept*). Almost classical are :

| Sky | part of heaven |
|-----|----------------|
| Father | a companion together with mother |
| Cherry | a thing in the garden (cp. also 11, 31) |

The favourite kind of explanation by means of an example is also used by our patient. Reactions of this kind are generally recognized by the form of sentence : "is, if you." The example can be *universal* (26, 28, 30, 32) or *particular*, when the subject, as a rule, takes an active part himself. In this connexion a typical reaction is *walk — that is when you stretch your legs for a pint on Sunday.*

The patient here uses the reminiscences of his Sunday excursions at the asylum. Here the great preponderance of the outer phenomenon over the meaning is very evident.

Looking at these reactions from the standpoint of Wundt's classification, we find here, as contrasted with normal persons, a marked preponderance of " inner associations " (if the use of this concept may be allowed at all in imbeciles). The number of inner associations far exceeds the average figures as given by Jung and Riklin for the uneducated, who were, however, not of the lowest grade of education.

The use here of the concept " inner association " is decidedly open to question. A calculation has shown that there are among the reactions seventy-seven per cent. of definitions, which are decidedly not the reproduction of the first impression, but rather the products of a lengthy process of reflection—that is, they are quite complicated mental structures. According to Jung's experiences with nearly twenty thousand associations in the uneducated, the intermixture of conscious reflection in the reaction begins high up in the region of the normal. The direct manner of reacting found among the educated, where practically the reaction-word is automatically linked on to the stimulus-word, is frequently neglected by the uneducated even of a relatively high grade. Conscious reflection as to the significance of the stimulus-word, with consequent tendency to explanation and to the formation of sentences, takes the place of the direct reaction ; there is almost habitually a suppression of the first words that do actually occur. As Jung and Riklin point out, the stimulus-word takes on more and more the character of a question the further we proceed from intelligence and education.

The inner associations of the uneducated are therefore not merely sudden ideas resting upon important relationships, but frequently a construction consciously sought out. This is pronouncedly the way in which imbeciles react. There is never a sharp demarcation from the normal ; they are only separated by certain differences in degree.

I have, therefore, no reason not to use the term "inner association," although there is really an essential difference between the imbecile " definition " and the " inner association " of the educated. I therefore use the word " association " rather in the sense of an intellectual reaction.

As the form of the reaction, especially the small number of outer associations, shows, the feeble-minded react with a great expenditure of attention. The association experiment means an important mental exercise to the imbecile. It seems strange that the subject should give himself such trouble instead of expressing himself, as most educated persons do, by simply giving one word for every stimulus-word. It cannot be maintained that the feeble-minded, who are able to define as our patient can, do not command a certain number of simple verbal connexions to the stimulus-word, taken from everyday language. Why do they not express themselves by these connexions, which are certainly present, in the reaction ? The stimulus-word, as Jung and Riklin show, is taken even by the uneducated normal as meaning something, by the side of which the merely verbal links fall into the background. The uneducated is not accustomed to deal with single words, but only knows them in connexions as symbols with a meaning ; under the influence of this habit constellation he is chiefly concerned with the meaning of the stimulus-word. All the reasons which hold good for this peculiar adjustment of the uneducated hold good also for the feeble-minded. His attention is fixed almost exclusively upon the meaning of the word, and, despite example and repeated admonition, can only by dint of great exertion, if at all, take up another mode of reaction. If we give any imbeciles time enough, and warn them constantly only to react with one single word appropriate to the stimulus-word, most of them will be able by training to produce a result which looks like the associations of a normal person. On the other hand, if we give the imbecile a free hand, only making clear at the beginning, by means of examples, that he has to say the first thing that occurs to him, he will force himself in the first reactions (as was frequently the case with my subject) into the mode recommended ; but he soon slips back into reacting by way of explanation, which suits him better.[1]

If the subject is constantly warned and requested to give a reaction in one single " appropriate " word, the experiment loses that freedom of its conditions by which what is specific can be brought out. A series of limited associations arise in which whatever is typical of the case cannot be recognized at all or at best with extreme difficulty. Our experiment is not designed to test the working capacity of the subject in any definite direction, but to create a method by which what

---

[1] There are, however, exceptions which we shall mention later.

is valuable for diagnosis may be brought out quickly and with certainty.

No. 2.    *An idiot*, 38 *years old*.    *Total reactions*, 66

| | | | |
|---|---|---|---|
| 1. Sunday | that is to-day | 17. Asylum | that is one |
| 2. Winter | that will come again | 18. Attendant | sick attendant |
| 3. Head | (points to his head) forehead | 19. Oven | cylinder oven |
| 4. Ink | ink-bottle | 20. Walk | we are doing that now with Andrew |
| 5. Bread | where we eat (i.e. what we eat) | 21. Cook | the women do |
| 6. Tree | a big and long (shows its size with his hands ) | 22. Dance | the others do that |
| | | 23. Cat | a kitten |
| | | 24. Dark | it is now (it is rather dark in the room) |
| 7. Mountain | that is far away | 25. Heart | there (points towards his heart) |
| 8. Salt | we want that for food | | |
| 9. Copy-book | where we write | 26. Bird | a vulture |
| | | 27. Moon | above in the sky |
| 10. Book | a little book | 28. Sleep | we do that at night |
| 11. Lead-pencil | of lead | 29. Dark red | quite red |
| | | 30. Sweet | quite sweet |
| 12. Sing | they sing upstairs | 31. Friendly | when we shake hands |
| 13. Ring | a large one (describes a circle in the air) | 32. Smell | we should stop smelling |
| 14. Frog | what hops about on the ground | 33. Prison | that is a kind of little window (describes a small square in the air) |
| 15. Flower | bunch | | |
| 16. Cherry | where we eat | | |

This test exhibits essentially the same thing as the previous case—a pronounced tendency to explanation. But the manner of explanation is in some degree different from the previous case. The designations of time and purpose are common to both (5, 7, 8, 9, 16), as are also the accounts of the material (11) or the accounts of the action which the thing executes, or of the thing which executes a definite activity (2, 12, 14, 20, 21, 22, 28). The tautologies, which are partly specified by a slight external change, are relatively numerous. The particularization often takes place (as in the previous case) by the addition of an attribute characteristic of the object, or one which denotes it more concretely. Among the reactions which especially exhibit this are : *tree — a big and long ; ring — a large one*. These attributes serve to elucidate the object better, and to show at the same time that the subject has fully understood the stimulus-word. The same explanation holds good of those reactions where the stimulus-word is simply translated into its diminutive form (10, 23). It must be remembered that the subject only reacts in dialect. In dialect the diminutive form has a more familiar air ; hence its use by the patient. He wants to show that he is at home with the idea of the stimulus-word, and that the thing is usually thus described. If the reaction were completed to a sentence, as it probably is at first in thought, the reaction runs :

Cat that is a kitten
Book that is a little book

The reaction *quite sweet* must be taken in a similar way.

The tendency to explanation is clear here ; but it is characteristic of this case that most of the associations are very brief and arid. The above-mentioned associations especially show the absence of further associations. To a certain extent the subject contents himself with apprehending the sense of the stimulus-word, and because he does not exactly know what to do with it, he confirms the stimulus-word by a similar expression. The great poverty in associations seems also to favour a mode of reaction which could not be proved in the previous case, i.e. the mere reference to the surroundings : *asylum — that is one ; dark — it is now.* These explanations again show clearly the poverty in associations. The subject does not go beyond the stimulus-word at all and contents himself by showing that he has understood it. Reaction 33 illustrates beautifully the imbecile manner of apprehension. To the patient the small square window-panes are the most important part of the presentation *prison*, because that is just the recognizable mark of it when seen from without.

There is in these reactions, as a whole, a cleaving to the concrete, to sensual perceptions. There is not much beyond that. In contrast to the previous case, we find no universal concepts here. The reaction is never far removed from the stimulus-word, and the explanations are distinguished by a quite special absence of any influx of associations. This absence, visible in the quality of the associations, was also shown in another way—by real faults, that is, experiments in which no reaction at all occurred ; although, as was proved by questioning him, the meaning of the stimulus-word was understood.

In my opinion a good deal of the striking poverty in associations is to be ascribed to this inhibition. As was stated in the introductory remarks, a state of emotional stupidity occurs relatively frequently among imbeciles, especially in the form of an " examination paralysis " during association experiments. As Jung has shown,[1] stupidity is chiefly characterized by an inhibition of associative activity, the stimulus-words arousing no associative processes. The subject reacts with very long

[1] Jung, " Ueber Simulation von Geistesstörung," loc. cit., p. 181.

times naming surrounding objects, which, however, are in no way connected with the stimulus-word. The subject thus makes up for his lack of associations. If the inhibition (or rather prohibition) is stronger, perhaps he does not react at all ; faults then arise.

There is every appearance of a disturbance of this kind being present here, but a degree slighter than in Jung's case. The relatively numerous faults and the striking insufficiency of the definitions point to this. The timing of the reactions would naturally be a valuable means for the accurate recording of the momentary psychical condition ; unfortunately, my experiments were carried out at a time when our knowledge of the processes of association was very incomplete and when the great importance of the reaction-time was still unknown to us.

It is of practical importance to pay attention to anomalies of the emotions conditioned by momentary constellations. Stupidity can temporarily increase so much in a feeble-minded person as to lead one to think that it is a case of severe dementia. In forensic cases this phenomenon requires serious consideration.

### No. 3.  *Idiot, 65 years old*

There are no pronounced signs of dementia senilis. Patient has trouble in understanding the experiment, and throughout has very long reaction-times.

*Total reactions, 58*

| | | | |
|---|---|---|---|
| 1. Schoolboy | schoolboy repeating | 16. Ring | white |
| 2. Father | once threw me down- | 17. Tooth | wisdom teeth |
|  | stairs | 18. Window | of glass |
| 3. Head | white | 19. Frog | black |
| 4. Ink | black | 20. Asylum | there where people |
| 5. Needle | where we sew with it | | are in |
| 6. Bread | white | 21. Cherry | black |
| 7. Tree | trees grow with | 22. Piano | people can play on it |
|  | quinces on them | 23. To cook | to cook potatoes |
| 8. Mountain | there is a tree where | 24. Water | cold |
|  | quinces grow on it | 25. To dance | on the floor |
| 9. Hair | white | 26. Cat | they are white |
| 10. Salt | white | 27. Resin | black |
| 11. Wood | black | 28. Bird | white |
| 12. Copy-book | white | 29. Swim | I can also |
| 13. Paper | white | 30. Ride | on a horse |
| 14. Book | has leaves | 31. Sweet | that is white—that is |
| 15. Lead- | has pictures on— | | sugar |
| pencil | pointed | | |

In this case we again find those traits of feeble-mindedness which we have repeatedly emphasized : statements of place, purpose, chief action or chief quality, etc. (5, 14, 15, 18, 20, 22, 25, 30). We find side by side with this the tendency to elucidation, to concrete understanding (1, 17, 23, 24). With this tendency there is connected also certain egocentric reactions in which distinct subjective reminiscences come to light, as in the characteristic reaction *father — once threw me downstairs* (cp. also 29).

A peculiarity of this case is the frequent repetition of the predicates *white* and *black*, which occur also in places where they are quite meaningless. *White* forces itself to the front, where it is only indirectly conditioned, as in 31. *White* perseverates also several times. Phenomena of this kind are occasionally found in marked stupidity, as, e.g., in the case mentioned before. In reaction 8 the subject does not hear the stimulus-word and in 15 only reacts to the stimulus-word subsequently. These phenomena require the same explanation as the abnormal perseverations of the previous case. Meaningless reactions likewise occur abundantly in emotional stupidity whenever this reaches a high degree, as Jung's case shows.

Some of the perseverations are certainly so marked that the suspicion of their being due to early cerebral atrophy cannot be put aside. As no definite observations of the effect of senile cerebral changes upon the mechanism of association have yet been made, I cannot decide how far the perseveration is conditioned entirely by emotional stupidity.

### No. 4. *Idiot of a mild degree, 38 years old*
### *Total reactions, 145*

| | | | | |
|---|---|---|---|---|
| 1. Christmas | that is Christ's birth-day | 17. Heart | the heart of a man | |
| 2. Sunday | for walks | 18. Bird | a beast of prey | |
| 3. Winter | when it's cold | 19. Swim | when we bathe in the Rhine | |
| 4. Father | when he has a son of his own | 20. Hit | when we clout some one | |
| 5. Bread | for eating | 21. Friendly | when we're jolly | |
| 6. Lamp | to make it light | 22. Caress | flatter | |
| 7. Tree | where there are shadows | 23. Grand | when they are proud | |
| 8. Mountain | when we go a journey | 24. Wedding | that is when people marry | |
| 9. Hair | when we cut it | 25. Sour | when it is sour | |
| 10. Sing | a song | 26. Eel | a fish | |
| 11. Ring | when you are engaged | 27. Eye | when we see | |
| 12. Cat | a beast of prey | 28. Faithful | when nothing is taken (i.e. stolen) | |
| 13. Tooth | for eating | | | |
| 14. Oven | for heating | 29. Blood | that is from oxen | |
| 15. Dark | when it is night | 30. Barn | at school | |
| 16. Dance | at holidays when music is heard | 31. Family | when there are many children | |

We see again in this case a pronounced tendency to definition. It looks as if the subject had been told to say what he understood by the stimulus-word. The task is carried out in the usual way ; we have again accounts of time, place, purpose, and tautological elucidations (10, 17) in the forefront. There are, besides, a few explanations by example of a more universal character (4, 11, 15, 21, 23, 24) that are frequently but slightly separated from tautological elucidation or from a more particular character (8, 9, 19, 28, 31). Instances of the latter are the reactions *mountain — when we go a journey* and *family — when there are many children* ; these are very characteristic of the psychology of feeble-mindedness, which adheres to concrete externality. The patient uses now and again the form of supraordination of a universal concept as a means of explanation (12, 16, 18). In 18 the general concept is not quite appropriate, but it is constellated by the previous reaction, 12 (*cat — beast of prey, bird — beast of prey*). Feeble-minded persons, especially those who are somewhat inhibited by emotion, willingly lend themselves to constellations from previous stimulus- or reaction-words. In consequence of the blank association to the reaction, they make use of the same words even when they are not quite appropriate to the stimulus-word. I am inclined to regard such supraordinates as *cat — beast of prey, eel — fish*, as signs of a rather higher grade of the feeble-minded. These are universal concepts of a kind absent in a severe idiot unless they have to some extent been drilled into him in some educational asylum. General concepts, in the ordinary sense, are entirely absent ; he has only certain words which designate something general and indefinite to him, as *fact, part, thing, means, tools*, then *animal, plant, food,* etc. He brings his concrete instances under these universal concepts, which he uses quite widely and indiscriminately, even promiscuously ; if he wants to do more he particularizes, as we have seen, by simply appending the designation of a place or the like to his universal concept. All variants in concept between the concrete and universal supraconcept are either unknown to him or are unfamiliar. The occurrence of appropriate and proximate supraordinations like *dog — a mammal, tree — wood, lamp — means of lighting*, speaks, on the whole, against the presence of severe congenital feeble-mindedness. Therefore in this milder form of idiocy the occurrence of a few appropriate supraordinates cannot be entirely accidental.

No. 5.   *A Peasant*, 40 *years old.   Severe form of imbecility*
Total reactions, 200

| | | | |
|---|---|---|---|
| 1. Sunday | day of rest | 24. Angry | when you are not |
| 2. Winter | cold | | satisfied |
| 3. Schoolboy | they must go to | 25. Proper | when he behaves |
| | school | | quietly |
| 4. Father | support of the house- | 26. Inn | that is a restaurant |
| | hold | 27. Family | four to five persons |
| 5. Table | furniture | 28. Fist | when you close the |
| 6. Head | part of a man | | fingers this way |
| 7. Ink | for writing | | (gesture) |
| 8. Bread | that is a food-thing | 29. People | many persons |
| 9. Lamp | that is a lighting | 30. Every- | when you are in many |
| 10. Carriage | a pleasure-thing | where | places |
| 11. Tree | for growing fruit | 31. Gait | E. (a patient who |
| 12. Wood | a thing for burning | | limps) has a gait |
| 13. Paper | for writing | | like that |
| 14. Book | for reading | 32. Ointment | when you have some- |
| 15. Sing | that is for enjoyment | | thing on the body |
| 16. Tooth | for biting things | 33. Child | that is a person |
| 17. Frog | an animal in water | 34. Star | that is a thing in the |
| 18. Oven | that is a thing in the | | sky |
| | room | 35. Roe | that is an animal |
| 19. Heart | thing of a man | 36. To thank | when you get some- |
| 20. Swim | that is a favourite | | thing from some- |
| | enjoyment | | body |
| 21. Marriage | that is for support | 37. Brush | when you have dirty |
| 22. Grand- | | | clothes |
| mother | that is a person | 38. Plumb | for instance, you make |
| 23. Hunter | he is in the wood | | a fence plumb |

The subject uses the definition form almost exclusively in the reaction.   The majority of the reactions are in the form of sentences.   Occasionally there is a slight tendency to abbreviation of the reaction, probably to be referred to the order given at starting to say the first word that occurred.   This is the case in the explanatory supraordinates.   Among these there are certain universal concepts which appropriately denote the stimulus-word (1, 5); but others are far too general and too broad to characterize the meaning of the stimulus-word satisfactorily (10, 20, 22, 33, 35).   The patient seeks to meet this difficulty, as we have frequently seen, by adding some simple definition to the general concept, e.g. *frog — an animal in water, star — that is a thing in the sky* (similarly 6, 7, 12, 18, 19).   These supraordinates frequently show a certain verbal awkwardness, as *lamp — that is a lighting* (similarly 11, 12).   As usual, designations of purpose and place occur.   Very characteristic of the imbecile's external apprehension is the purpose of marriage, which serves for *support*.   Similarly the explanation of the concept *family*, for which it is sufficient designation that it consists of *four to five persons* (similarly 25, 29).

The explanations by example show a very narrow and strongly individual view (24, 25, 28, 30, 36–38).

With the verbal awkwardness is linked a certain carelessness in the construction of new words, which are made *ad hoc.*

No. 6.   *Severe form of imbecility.*   *Peasant, 30 years old*
Total reactions, 278

| | | December 9 | December 15 |
|---|---|---|---|
| 1. | Sunday | —— (fault) | Sunday has gone |
| 2. | Winter | winter is here | winter is here |
| 3. | Lake | —— (fault) | comes from a spring |
| 4. | Schoolboy | the schoolboy is active | the schoolboy must be active |
| 5. | Father | the father | —— (fault) |
| 6. | Table | the table is household furniture | the table is household furniture |
| 7. | Tree | is a vegetable | apple-tree |
| *⎧ 8. | Mountain | the beautiful mountain | a beautiful mountain |
| ⎪ 9. | Hair | the beautiful hair | beautiful hair |
| ⎤10. | Salt | —— | is a food |
| ⎩11. | Wood | the beautiful wood | for burning |
| 12. | Sing | the beautiful song | beautiful song |
| 13. | Ring | is a beautiful | finger ring |
| ⎧14. | Tooth | the teeth | wisdom-tooth |
| ⎨15. | Window | the windows | house furniture |
| ⎩16. | Frog | the frogs | frog in water |
| 17. | Piano | the beautiful piano | is house furniture |
| 18. | Dance | the beautiful dancing | on holidays |
| 19. | Bird | the beautiful bird | canary-bird |
| 20. | Swim | the birds swim | man can swim |
| 21. | Walk | —— (fault) | on Sundays |
| 22. | To cook | —— (fault) | food |
| 23. | Flowers | in the garden | |
| 24. | Cherry | is a food | |
| 25. | Oven | belongs to the house | |
| 26. | Badger | is an animal | |
| 27. | Heart | in the chest | |
| 28. | Dark | moonshine | |
| 29. | Beat | church | |
| 30. | To kindle | fire | |
| 31. | To stroke | cat | |
| 32. | Amiable | the man is amiable | |
| 33. | Ride | dragoons | |
| 34. | Cut | cutler | |
| 35. | Thirst' | when you are thirsty | |
| 36. | Thumb | index finger | |
| 37. | Ill | the man is ill | |

\* The associations bracketed followed one another in the experiment.

*December* 9

| | |
|---|---|
| 38. Wedding | the wedding (dialect form) |
| 39. Grandmother | older mother |
| 40. Rich | when one is rich |
| 41. Angry | when one is angry |
| 42. Inn | the inn-house |
| 43. Family | when father and mother are together |
| 44. Hunger | when you are hungry |
| 45. Murderer | with a knife |
| 46. Pray | when you pray |
| 47. Wrong | when you are shut up |
| 48. Candle | a lighting up |
| 49. Reward | when you are rewarded |
| 50. School | day-school |

We have two series of experiments from this patient. For the sake of readier comparison we have placed them in parallel tables. By comparing these two series a distinct difference can be noticed between the way of reacting on December 9 and that of December 15.

In the first experiment a series of perseverations, which I have bracketed, is noticeable. Beside these there are (as other tests show) numerous repetitions. The quality of the reaction is limited chiefly to tautological elucidations which are, in many cases, combined with a particular form of predicate (*beautiful*), used as frequently as possible, and perseverating through many terms. Another peculiarity of the tautology is the translation of the stimulus-word into the plural form (*frog — the frogs*). On the whole, these reactions show nothing which tells against the tendency to definition. Explanation and sentence-formation remain, however, stationary in the more primitive tautologies; no wider association to the stimulus succeeds. These phenomena denote a certain blankness of association like that peculiar to emotional stupidity. It is simply that nothing new occurs to the patient; he is like the nervous student at an examination. Further confirmation of this view is shown by the presence of faults. The faults mostly occur when a stimulus-word comes along to which the reaction form hitherto used can be no longer employed. The subject then finds himself bereft of all help, and makes a fault.

What is peculiar to this case is the occurrence of marked phenomena of perseveration, which were not demonstrated in the previous cases; this approximates to Jung's case, where there were a great number of perseveration phenomena. As shown by the investigations of Jung and Riklin in associations in a state of distraction, the perseveration exhibits a distinct, although not large, increase in distraction. The blankness of association produced by this distraction seems to be the cause of this phenomenon. In the absence of a new association the subject takes that content of consciousness which has remained over from the previous reaction. It seems to me that this explanation is exactly true of this case of perseveration. The subject when possible accepts the previous form of reaction because nothing new occurs to him.

Now consider the second experiment of December 15. The tendency to definition is also very pronounced here. Among the first seven reactions, which show a stiff schoolboyish manner, there is one fault. Only after the eighth reaction do the reactions take on a somewhat freer appearance. The supposition that there was at first a certain emotional inhibition is thus to some extent justified. If we consider the other reactions we are struck by the relatively numerous tautological elucidations—a form of reaction which we first noticed to any considerable extent in patient No. 2, who was shown to have emotional stupidity. The tautologies of No. 6 show in part the quite primitive type of repetition of the stimulus-word in its dialect form, with the article frequently preceding the dialect word (38, 42). A further number of tautologies show a nearer determination by combination with a very near association, e.g. *school — day-school, tooth — wisdom-tooth* (similarly 8, 9, 12, 16, 19). Other tautologies occur, by way of example : " *is, if one,*" e.g. *thirsty — if one is thirsty* (also 40, 41, 44, 46, 49). As usual, designations of time, place, and purpose are present ; there are also found estimates of the quality or activity in relation to the subject or, inversely, estimates of the subject. The subject there prefers the word *man* (20, 32). There also occur a few more or less appropriate supraordinations (6, 10, 24, 26).

Amongst this material there are just a few reactions which exhibit a higher value, and cannot be fitted into the form of a definition. I mean the reactions *thumb — index finger, beat — church* (clock), *dark — moonshine, murderer — with a knife.* These reactions suggest an apparently creative imagination ; the patient fashions the inner picture of a situation of which he then names some part, without regard to the meaning of the stimulus-word. The reactions only contain, it is true, simple coexistent composite parts, but the fact that they occur at all in a free form proves that the patient is not entirely chained to the stimulus-word as a direct question. Reactions of this kind are traces of a mental activity which has been freed to some extent.

The personal basis of the explanations is shown in the concept *family—when father and mother are together* ; patient was an orphan brought up in a strange family. The reaction *cut — cutler* shows a certain superficiality and verbal-clang connexion which are not very usual among imbeciles, any more than they are among the lower grade uneducated. Reactions of this kind are found chiefly among the educated. This fact also seems to suggest that association and verbal capacity are not very deep-seated.

The very primitive tautologies which we have established in this case offer a certain contrast with these signs of rather higher intellectual gifts. Clumsy and primitive reactions of this kind point, as we have seen, to emotional inhibition of associations. If we cannot prove this influence in the later reactions with all the certainty we should like, still the discovery is a warning to be cautious, for emotional stupidity can be made to represent an imbecile as much more demented than he actually is. Great care is, therefore, necessary before accepting the rapid tests of intelligence occasionally used in statistical works, with results which frequently afford such delightful bizarreries. This factor deserves consideration also *in foro*.

No. 7. *Imbecile woman, 58 years of age*
*Total reactions, 59*

| | | | |
|---|---|---|---|
| 1. Christmas | a tree like where it has presents on it | 16. School | when you go to school |
| 2. Sunday | —— (fault) | 17. Sing | when you do the singing |
| 3. Schoolboy | goes to school | 18. Tooth | there in the mouth |
| 4. Father | a father | 19. Flower | it's in the garden |
| 5. Table | for writing | 20. Asylum | I am in an asylum |
| 6. Head | headache | 21. Piano | when you can play with it |
| 7. Bread | for eating | 22. Dark | when it is night |
| 8. Lamp | for hanging up | 23. Heart | —— (fault) |
| 9. Tree | what grows apples or pears | 24. Bird | when you have one in the cage there |
| 10. Mountain | up there on the mountain | 25. Game | when you can play with it |
| 11. Hair | up there on the head | 26. Sugar | when you get sugar |
| 12. Salt | when you have salt so that you can cook with it | 27. Ill | when you have to lie in bed |
| 13. Wood | when you have wood for cooking | | |
| 14. Copy-book | when you have a copy-book | | |
| 15. Lead-pencil | when you have a lead-pencil | | |

This reaction type is obviously the same as that of the preceding cases. We again find the designations of place and purpose, and explanations by example (1, 9, 24, 26, 27) which are sometimes very characteristic. The tautologies are remarkably frequent ; this, as in subjects 2 and 3, indicates a poor and primitive temperament (4, 10–17, 25). Subsequently the tautologies are partly linked to designations of purpose. Faults occur from time to time. (The reaction-times are extraordinarily long.) The phenomena of perseveration are noticeable, and, as usual, are particularly common when a series of convenient nouns occurs. Unless such perseverations are purposely required from the feeble-minded, care must be taken in drawing up the lists that nouns do not directly follow one another several times. In the list used in these experiments this, unfortunately, happens a few times, but not to such an extent as in Sommer's schedule.

From the relatively numerous primitive tautologies, the faults and the marked perseverations, it is justifiable to assume that here also a slight emotional stupidity complicates the picture.

### No. 8.  *An idiot woman of slight grade, aged* 24

This patient exhibits a series of hysterical symptoms, chiefly conditions of excitement, with a slight limitation of consciousness and sexual content. Her conduct is generally shy and reserved. It is strongly influenced by sympathies and antipathies. There is, on the whole, inhibition towards the doctors, whilst her behaviour towards her fellow-patients is distinctly freer.

*Number of reactions,* 186

| | | | |
|---|---|---|---|
| 1. Sunday | day after to-morrow | 19. Dance | you dance |
| 2. Lake | is big | 20. Dark | when it is night |
| 3. Father | is my father | 21. Heart | the heart, which one has |
| 4. Table | is brown | | |
| 5. Head | head with the face | 22. Swim | you can swim |
| 6. Ink | you write with it | 23. White | a thing, where it's white |
| 7. Bread | for eating | | |
| 8. Lamp | is lighted at night | 24. Coffee | coffee where it's drunk |
| 9. Carriage | for riding in | | |
| 10. Tree | is a tree | 25. Wedding | when there's a wedding |
| 11. Hair | you comb it | | |
| 12. Salt | you salt with it | 26. Angry | when one's angry |
| 13. Pencil | for writing | 27. Sour | vinegar is sour |
| 14. Sing | you sing | 28. Rich | when one's rich |
| 15. Ring | ring on the finger | 29. Eyes | the two eyes, which you have |
| 16. Window | for looking out of | | |
| 17. Frog | is a frog | 30. Plant | when one plants something |
| 18. Walk | when you go for a walk | | |

The tendency to definition in this case is obvious. The patient announces what is the use of the object, what is done with it, what she does, etc. Sometimes she explains by example (23, 27). Tautologies are most distinct, generally in the *when* form. Tautologies are particularly distinct when she adds anything to make the thing obvious (*head — head with the face ;* cp. also 21, 29). This tautology is sometimes limited to a quite primitive repetition of the stimulus-word (*tree — is a tree ;* cp. 17). In the original there was often marked perseveration in the reaction form, this could not be expressed in the tests given here.

Thus this case, too, follows the previous ones closely. Here again we find primitive tautologies and perseverations which are not to be explained by the feeble-mindedness alone, but which are complicated by slight inhibition of association based upon emotion.

The nature of the reactions agrees very well with the reserved and hampered behaviour of the patient.

### No. 9. *An imbecile of severe degree, aged* 32

In jail he was taken ill with prison psychosis, was brought to the asylum and fully recovered. During convalescence a hysterical syncope occurred.

#### *Number of reactions,* 290

| | | | |
|---|---|---|---|
| 1. Sunday | holiday | 17. Frog | legs for eating |
| 2. Lake | water | 18. Flowers | in the garden |
| 3. Table | for eating | 19. Asylum | to get better |
| 4. Head | men | 20. Walk | when one goes a walk |
| 5. Ink | writing | 21. To cook | is to cook food |
| 6. Needle | sewing | 22. Cat | good for mice |
| 7. Bread | eat | 23. Swim | when one's in the water |
| 8. Lamp | light | | |
| 9. Tree | fruit | 24. Beat | one hits |
| 10. Hair | on the head | 25. Star | stars |
| 11. Salt | eating | 26. Stroke | when you stroke |
| 12. Copy-book | for writing | 27. Moon | the moon (in dialect form) |
| 13. Book | for eating | | |
| 14. Sing | not well | 28. Ride | ride (in dialect form) |
| 15. Ring | on finger | 29. To watch | take care |
| 16. Tooth | in the mouth | 30. Arm | an arm |

One is struck by the fact that at first the reaction is in one word ; but if we look at the quality of the reactions more closely we notice that we have only to add the usual *for* and other forms to get the same picture as in other imbeciles. This is distinctly seen in reaction 11, *salt — eating,* where the imbecile *for* is omitted. The first reactions are obviously due to the order "to react with one word." In the later reactions the formation of sentences occurs increasingly, and thus we get the usual picture of the weak-minded (designations of purpose and place, tautologies, etc.). Tautological elucidations by translation into the dialect form occur frequently in this case (cp. Subject No. 2). The stimulus-word was given in literary German.

No. 10.   Imbecile (see below)
Number of reactions, 200

| Sunday | beautiful | Schoolboy | young |
|--------|-----------|-----------|-------|
| Winter | cold | Needle | pointed |
| Head | clever | Father | old |
| Lake | big | Bread | tasty |
| Ink | black | | |

These were the first reactions in the experiment; they all had a very long reaction-time, generally over twenty seconds as measured by the watch. It was then suggested to the patient that it was not necessary for him to give an adjective to everything but just to say what occurred to him at the moment. The patient then continued :

| Lamp | for burning | Salt | for eating |
|------|-------------|------|-----------|
| Tree | for bearing fruit | Wood | for burning |
| Hair | for protecting the head | Paper | for writing |

After the patient had continued in the for direction during six reactions it was again pointed out to him that it was not necessary that he should constantly react by for. The form of the reaction then became a little freer. Nevertheless, until the end of the experiment the patient repeated this sixty-seven times in the two hundred reactions. The extremely forced style of the reaction, as seen in these experiments, gradually disappeared towards the end of the experiment and gave room to another type of reaction which, apart from the occasional repetition of for, gave but a slight impression of imbecility. I give some reactions from the end of the second half of the experiment :

| 1. Slate-pencil | for writing | 13. Hot | summer |
|-----------------|-------------|---------|--------|
| 2. Growl | angry | 14. Scissors | cut |
| 3. Fruit | for cider | 15. Vinegar | acid |
| 4. False | faithless | 16. Trap | catch |
| 5. Soft | overheard | 17. Sick | bad |
| 6. Proud | haughty | 18. Resin | sticky |
| 7. Hay | dry | 19. Polish | clean |
| 8. Raspberry | sweet | 20. Candle | for lighting |
| 9. Mouth | for speaking | 21. Vertical | horizontal |
| 10. Home | for oneself | 22. Pastry | food |
| 11. Hedge | hedge (in dialect) | 23. Wages | work |
| 12. Cunning | sly | 24. Lungs | for living |

The *fors* which occur here are, it will be seen, in places which are less striking. The remaining reactions produce but a very slight impression of imbecility. The tendency towards explanation is, of course, not difficult to discover. The meaning of the stimulus-word is often confirmed by a synonym or the typical properties, or the actions of things are given. The meaning of the stimulus-word is reacted to with strict adhesion to its conceived meaning. This mode of reaction approximates very closely to that of many uneducated normals, and its differential diagnosis (apart from the frequent *for*) would be difficult to separate from mere want of education in a person with a rather low intellectual level. We will now compare these end reactions with a selection taken from the beginning and middle of the experiment.

| | | | |
|---|---|---|---|
| Sing | for pleasure | Joke | from love |
| Flowers | in the garden | Right | for keeping |
| Piano | for music | Hope | for comfort |
| Oven | for warmth | Choose | for choice |
| Cook | for hunger | Flag | for carrying |
| Bird | for flying | | |

These reactions produce a greater impression of feeble-mindedness than the final ones. The whole course of the experiment shows that the patient was at first uncertain as to how he ought to react. When he was freed from the predicates he fell into another form which he chose spontaneously ; in this he persisted until far on in the second half of the experiment, but with decreasing intensity. Finally he arrived at a mode of reaction not far removed from the normal uneducated type.

The first reactions in the predicate form are, in my opinion, laboured constructions. Freed from this, the patient falls into another form of explanation in which he again persists for a long time. He only loses this narrow view after over one hundred reactions, the reaction then acquiring a much more normal appearance.

This behaviour appears to be only a particular expression of emotional stupidity. Here it occurs in the form of embarrassment at not knowing exactly what he is expected to do with the stimulus-word. This embarrassment is marked by an inhibition of association. The subject never sees more than one possible way of reacting, and that is always the same one ; all other possibilities seem to him remote. The inhibition thus acts chiefly upon the outer form of the reaction, and much less upon its content.

As stated above, this is not a case of severe imbecility.

The patient first came to the asylum late in life, and not on account of any intellectual weakness but chiefly because of his temperamental eccentricities. He is perverse and "obstinate," mistrustful, will only give a proper answer after much persuasion, usually much confused when first addressed, silent and very reserved even with the other patients, troubled by numerous tics. A behaviour frequently presented by hysterical imbeciles is recognizable from these traits. It is in these individuals that we most frequently find emotional stupidity.

No. 11. *An imbecile of slight grade,* 40 *years old, who could support himself independently*
*Total reactions,* 100

| | | | |
|---|---|---|---|
| 1. Green | hope | 16. Lamp | the lamp is a room light |
| 2. Prick | smash | | |
| 3. Angel | little angel | 17. Yellow | gold is yellow |
| 4. Ship | sailing | 18. Manners | politeness is manners |
| 5. Friendly | practise friendship | 19. Despise | a criminal is despised |
| 6. Table | keep table ready | 20. Tooth | the tooth aches |
| 7. Bear | bear sorrows | 21. Frog | the frog swims in water |
| 8. Rod | Aaron's rod | | |
| 9. Dance | dance joyously | 22. Ring | a ring on the finger is a remembrance |
| 10. Lake | sailing in the lake | | |
| 11. Ill | have often been ill | 23. Lead- | the pencil is used for |
| 12. Swim | swim in the lake | pencil | writing |
| 13. Blue | the sky is blue | 24. Take care | the schoolboy must take care |
| 14. Bread | bread is a food | | |
| 15. Threaten | somebody is threatened | 25. Flower | is a garden-ornament |

It is easy to see in this case how the order given at the start to react with one word only is obeyed, how its effect gradually diminishes and soon gives place to explanation and formation of sentences. By the addition of the necessary parts of the sentence the reactions, at first given curtly, are easily turned into the customary type of sentence. The later reactions are correctly phrased school expressions. The subject is back in his schoolboy attitude and tries to find the most appropriate and best-worded sentence. He is obviously more at home in this position than in the one prescribed for him by the experimenter; when he apprehends the stimulus-word it is more difficult for him to answer in telegraphic style than by forming a sentence. The sentences of this subject are differentiated from most of the previous cases by their correctness and proper grammatical form. This by itself entitles one to assume a certain education and intelligence. All the same, formations occasionally occur of a markedly imbecile nature (e.g. *room-light; garden-ornament* is also somewhat suspicious).

The stimulus-word is explained in the usual way by designations of purpose and place, by a statement of the object and subject of the activity or a statement of the action of the thing, by example or by supraordination, etc.

Contrasted with the previous subject, it is to be noted that every reaction here is more adequate, somewhat more intelligent and correct. This impression may perhaps be confirmed by the absence of tautologies. No emotional inhibition can be observed here.

I will now give the reactions of two similar patients :

### No. 12. *An imbecile, 49 years of age*
#### *Number of reactions, 156*

| | | | |
|---|---|---|---|
| 1. Sunday | holiday | 18. Cat | is a domestic animal |
| 2. Lake | water | 19. Heart | blood flows from the heart |
| 3. Father | man | | |
| 4. Table | room-furniture | 20. Moon | shines at night |
| 5. Head | part of body | 21. Hit | the teacher hits the inattentive boy |
| 6. Bread | food | | |
| 7. Lamp | for lighting | 22. Caress | the girl caresses the cat |
| 8. Mountain | high | 23. Child | is cold in winter |
| 9. Wood | grows in forest | 24. Amiable | the man is amiable |
| 10. Book | for reading | 25. Cut | the reaper cuts the corn |
| 11. School | good for learning | 26. Ill | many people are ill in winter |
| 12. Tooth | white | | |
| 13. Frog | is an insect | 27. Star | is in the sky |
| 14. Flower | is a plant | 28. White | is a colour |
| 15. Cherry | is sweet | 29. Kindle | the baker kindles the wood |
| 16. Walking | it is nice to walk out in fine weather | | |
| 17. Dance | people dance at a ball | 30. Emperor | is a person |

### No. 13. *An imbecile, 17 years old*
#### *Total reactions, 200*

| | | | |
|---|---|---|---|
| 1. Sunday | church | 18. Cat | flesh, hair |
| 2. Lake | water | 19. Heart | flesh |
| 3. Father | man | 20. Moon | the moon is in the sky |
| 4. Table | wood | 21. Hit | the teacher hits the boy |
| 5. Head | flesh | 22. Caress | the mother caresses the cat |
| 6. Bread | flour and salt | | |
| 7. Mountain | stone and gravel | 23. Child | the father has children |
| 8. Lamp | petroleum | 24. Friendly | the father is friendly with the boy |
| 9. Wood | tree | | |
| 10. Book | paper | 25. Cut | I cut the bread |
| 11. School | schoolboy | 26. Ill | I have been ill |
| 12. Tooth | the teeth are in the jaw | 27. Stars | there are innumerable stars in the sky |
| 13. Frog | flesh | | |
| 14. Flower | blossom | 28. White | the sheet is white |
| 15. Cherry | stalk, flesh, and stone | 29. Kindle | the mother kindles the fire |
| 16. Walk | the people go for a walk | | |
| 17. Dance | the people dance | 30. Emperor | Germany has an emperor |

In these milder cases of imbecility there is a greater wealth of ideas and a greater verbal dexterity. We find here, on the whole, an entire limitation to the meaning of the stimulus-word, but the reactions do not imply merely that the patient has understood the stimulus-word (the absence of primitive tautologies shows this) but they can also form a sentence with the stimulus-word, such sentences being no longer exclusively explanations or definitions. The examples show that a sentence is formed much as in school, when the master says, " Make a sentence with the word . . ." The sentence as such thus becomes the purpose and the tendency towards explanation recedes into the background. The tendencies are so mixed in our examples that it is difficult to decide whether we have to do with a school-sentence or an explanation.

Dr. Jung informs me that such school-sentences occur in lower-grade normal uneducated and in educated hysterical persons. For a differential diagnosis a very large material is necessary—at least one hundred reactions, better two hundred, in which signs of imbecility must be looked for that differentiate it from simple want of education.

In our experiments the most striking feature is the course of the reactions. At first, obeying the injunctions, both patients answer in a single word, but they soon relinquish this inconvenient form and make sentences, which form they retain to the end. It becomes interesting to see how the two patients conceive their tasks. No. 12 constructs mainly supraordinated concepts, together with a few designations of purpose and predicates ; No. 13 endeavours to give whenever possible the substantial nature of the thing referred to by the stimulus-word (e.g. bread — flour and salt). This divergence in apprehension apparently conditions a deep difference between the two. But directly they discover their own appropriate sentence-formation the difference at once disappears and the reactions assume the same, often most surprisingly similar, character.

The one-sided apprehension at the beginning has something of the imbecile about it ; this comes to light distinctly when the chosen form of reaction encounters a stimulus-word where anything rather than that kind of reaction would be in place (e.g. 'frog —flesh ; cat — flesh, hair), or, again, where the supraordinated concept is even wrong (e.g. 'frog — is an insect). If reactions of this kind occur only once or are very exceptional the diagnosis of slight imbecility would be rather speculative, but if they occur frequently its probability is great.

So far as the sentence reactions are concerned, the discovery of imbecile traits becomes rather more difficult. Taken as a whole, the sentence form gives rise to a suspicion of slight imbecility, or at least of a very low grade of culture. Marked leaning to the meaning of the stimulus-word is a differential factor from the reactions of certain hysterics who also employ the sentence form ; but these use it with a school-like restriction often deliberate, and with great circumlocution as to that meaning of the stimulus-word which is of most importance to the patient.

As we have seen in every case, the tendency to definition is of the greatest importance in the reaction of the feeble-minded. The more striking this tendency in the reactions, the more probable, on the whole, is the imbecility of the patient. Special attention should be paid to tautologies, to awkward turns of the reaction, to examples which denote a very peculiar temperament (e.g. *friendly — the man is friendly; glaring — that is a glaring colour; sweet — the new cider is sweet; ill — I have been ill; child — the father has children; emperor — is a person*, etc.).

### 5. TIME MEASUREMENTS

As previously mentioned, 764 time measurements were taken in five subjects ; the measurement was recorded on a one-fifth second stop-watch, set when the stimulus-word was spoken and stopped at the utterance of the reaction. The time was measured in patients 6, 5, 8, 11, 13. The stimulus-words were divided into concrete, abstract, adjective, and verb. The mean numbers, which I give individually for each of these groups, are the probable mean in seconds.[1]

| | No. 6 | No. 5 | No. 8 | No. 11 | No. 13 | Average of uneducated normals [2] | Average of the subjects |
|---|---|---|---|---|---|---|---|
| Concretes | 4 | 4 | 4·8 | 3 | 1·4 | 1·8 | 3·4 |
| Abstracts | 4·4 | 4 | 5 | 3·4 | 2 | 2·3 | 3·7 |
| Adjectives | 3·2 | 4 | 5 | 3·4 | 2 | 1·9 | 3·5 |
| Verbs | 3·8 | 4 | 4 | 3·4 | 1·4 | 2·2 | 3·3 |
| Probable mean of all times | 3·8 | 4 | 5 | 3·4 | 1·6 | 2 | 3 |

Patient No. 6 is not so feeble-minded as she seems to be from her position in this series. She was only treated as among the most difficult cases because she has a certain similarity with these cases by reason of her emotional stupidity. By her intelli-

[1] The method of reckoning is the same as given by Aschaffenburg.

[2] I am indebted for these figures to Dr. Jung ; they are taken from 2200 time measurements. The average figures are the arithmetical mean of the individual subjects.

gence she belonged to about No. 9. Viewing the table with this correction, we notice that with the increasing degree of intelligence there is a shortening of the probable mean. No. 8 is the only one who affords any considerable exception to this. No. 8 is the idiot with the hysterical characteristics who in daily intercourse shows also much retardation and inhibition.

The average figures of our patients, which I have placed alongside those of the uneducated normals, show prolongation of the association times among imbeciles, although No. 13 is below the probable mean of the uneducated normals. As will be seen from the table, the longest times occur, on the average, with the abstract stimulus-words ; this is also the case among the uneducated normals. The shortest times, however, do not occur, as among normals, with concretes but with verbs ; the cause of this is not at once obvious.

The marked prolongation of the association times among imbeciles is chiefly due to the difficulty of intellectual effort. But that this is not the whole ground is shown by No. 6, in connexion with whom I possess two series of experiments. The first of the series was taken at the beginning of his detention in the asylum, after continuous and exhaustive examination ; the second about a week later. The probable mean of the first series is 8·6 seconds, that of the second 3·8.[1]

These figures show that, besides intellectual difficulty, emotional factors have also a considerable influence upon the reaction-time. A first set of experiments upon an imbecile therefore possesses only very relative value so far as reaction-time is concerned (and also quality).

## 6. RECAPITULATION

One of the most striking peculiarities of the imbecile reaction as contrasted with the normal consists in the fact that the feeble-minded seldom react with one word ; generally they employ several words or make whole sentences. In the introduction I quoted the view of Jung and Riklin, who say that the uneducated conceive the stimulus-word as a question, i.e. as standing in some fictitious connexion with a sentence. That is the explanation of the greater care bestowed upon the reaction by the uneducated, as shown by their reproducing on the average more inner associations than the educated. The imbeciles, who in every respect are linked to the lowest grade of the uneducated, show fundamentally the same phenomena. They apprehend the

---

[1] The stimulus-words of the first series were in part repeated at the second experiment, but this could have had but very slight effect on the great difference in the figures.

stimulus-word quite unmistakably as a question. That is the explanation of their preference for the sentence form in the reactions. As we have seen, school reminiscences play no small part ; as Cordes [1] pertinently remarks, it often seems as if the teacher's behest " to answer in a whole sentence " was still taking effect. The tendency to " answer " with a whole sentence is strongly marked in my patients ; when they were requested to give the reaction in one word and shown by example how to do so, the experiment was soon ruined by the limited apprehension, the verbal poverty, and the consequent formal method of expression.

The frequent sentence-formations render the classification of imbecile associations considerably more difficult. The Kräpelin-Aschaffenburg classification is only helpful in exceptional cases ; in the majority of cases this logical-verbal classification is out of the question ; its application to sentences is a forced one. For these cases we must use the points of view which follow from the analysis of my material.

We have found that the *tendency to definition* is the chief sign of the feeble-minded reaction. The feeble-minded tries by reason of his sluggish temperament to explain the stimulus-word, or at least to express something which is a characteristic of it. The association experiment thus loses something of the character it has acquired from experiments with the educated. The re-action does not follow directly ; it no longer arises automatically from the unconscious, but it is something sought for, it is a construction that follows a definite scheme. The reproduction of the first (verbal) thought that occurs, as demanded by the original experiment, thus completely fails ; this is replaced by the con-scious evoking of a series of associations in a definite direction. We thus find an " adjustment " which is exclusively directed to the meaning of the stimulus-word, the exact opposite of the adjustment which Jung and Riklin have demonstrated in highly cultured persons, whose reactions were chiefly determined by the uttered word. Between these two extremes lie all the remaining possibilities of reaction in the educated and the uneducated. The tendency to definition can, as we have seen, obtain expression in many forms. The primary form is :

### (A) *Tautological Elucidation*

This is a very simple form of explanation and is expressed rather in the form of the spoken word than in the words themselves, in so far as it is concerned with the most rudimentary form of

---

[1] Wundt's *Phil. Studien*, Bd. XVII.

the mere repetition of the stimulus-word (i.e. finally with the article and translation into dialect : *cat — the little cat*). The *when* form is not much higher : *quarrel — when you quarrel, angry — when you're angry.* Tautologies, to which any more or less indifferent predicate is added, belong here : *mountain — the high mountain ; hair — the beautiful hair.* Rising above these primitive forms there is a whole series of tautological elucidations, which approximate more or less to an analysis and thus cannot be sharply separated from this form of explanation.

### (B) *Analysis*

The meaning of the stimulus-word is formally defined by a sentence, as general as possible, with numerous factors conditioning it : *prison — consists of cells where useless people are locked up ; year — twelve months.*

### (C) *Supraordination*

/ The stimulus-word is supraordinated to some universal concept, always with a tendency to explanation. The following possibilities occur :

(1) The supraordination is an appropriate one, i.e. the stimulus-word is marked with sufficient sharpness by the supraordinated general concept (*cat — domestic animal ; table — furniture ; bread — food*).

(2) The supraordination is inappropriate ; the general concept is too wide and too indefinite to characterize sufficiently the stimulus-word (*head — part ; tree — thing ; father — a man ; son — human being*).

(3) The supraordination is too wide a general concept but it is limited by some particular by-concept—generally some designation of time or purpose (*cherry — a garden thing ; star — part of the sky ; wood — thing for burning*).

### (D) *Definition of Time, Place, Means, Purpose, Origin, etc.*

The stimulus-word is denoted by the addition of one of these designations (*book — for reading ; stove — for heating*).

### (E) *Statement of the principal Quality or Activity*

The meaning of the stimulus-word is explained or defined by giving the chief action or quality of the object in question (*bird — flies ; wood — burns*).

## (F) *Statement of the Subject of the Activity or Quality*

The stimulus-word is an adjective or verb. The reaction is a noun, whose chief activity or quality is given by the stimulus-word (*swim — fish swim ; blue — the sky*).

## (G) *Example*

The example, which is given to explain the stimulus-word, can be universal (e.g. *war — when two countries quarrel with one another*) or particular, i.e. of a subjective nature, e.g. :

| | |
|---|---|
| Ill | I have already been ill |
| Sorrow | when you have much work and can't do it |
| Wreath | there is one at a gymnasium festival |
| Wages | that is when you work in a factory |
| Father | he once threw me downstairs |

So far as my experience goes, these groups include pretty well most of the possibilities that occur. The overwhelming majority of imbecile reactions (the sluggish variety) betray the tendency to definition. As we have seen, however, in the slighter forms of imbecility, sentences occur which have no pronounced character, but are merely school-sentences which state something about the stimulus-word. These reactions, of course, remain outside our schedule.

CHAPTER IV

# ANALYSIS OF THE ASSOCIATIONS OF AN EPILEPTIC

By Dr. C. G. JUNG

Epilepsy is one of the few mental diseases whose symptomology is thoroughly known, and its limits defined, by a wealth of cases and of systematic studies. Psychiatry has proved that together with the epileptic fits mental degeneration is extremely common ; of the latter it may be asserted that it is specific and therefore of diagnostic value. We will merely mention the chief features of epileptic degeneracy as given in any good textbook :

(1) Intellectual : Feeble-mindedness, retardation of mental reactions, loquaciousness, limitation and poverty of the imagination, with a corresponding poverty and stereotypy of speech, frequently abnormalities of fantasy.

(2) Emotional : Irritability, waywardness, marked egocentricity, exaggeration of all intellectual feelings, especially of religiosity.

These qualities form the so-called epileptic character, which, once set up, must be regarded as a permanent structure. Temporary augmentations of one or other quality, which spring from an intercurrent fit, are probably present. Even without knowledge of the epileptic attacks the diagnosis can be made with sufficient certainty by the presence of the epileptic character, although cases of this kind seldom arise. When the attacks are rare it frequently happens that the epileptic character is only slightly developed. From a practical point of view it becomes therefore of some value to find an exact expression of epileptic degeneration.

Attempts have been repeatedly made of late to investigate the epileptic aberrations by experimental methods. Colucci [1] and Breukink [2] have experimented with the ergograph ; Sommer [3]

[1] Colucci, " L'Allenamento ergografico nei Normali e negli Epilettici," *Riforma medica*, Anno XVIII, No. 36, 1902.

[2] Breukink, " Ueber Ermüdungskurven bei Gesunden und bei einigen Neurosen und Psychosen," *Journal für Psych. u. Neur.*, Bd. IV, 1904.

[3] Sommer, *Lehrbuch der psychopath. Untersuchungsmethoden.*

and more especially his pupil Fuhrmann,[1] directed their attention to association in epileptics. We regard these latter investigations as peculiarly adapted for a more exact formulation of epileptic degeneration.

Fuhrmann gives an account of the investigation of the associations in two epileptics. The first case was that of a patient who had suffered since the age of ten. The author demonstrated in this case that the predicates were strongly marked and that the egocentric factor played an unusually large part. The reactions in this case could not all be regarded as " associations " ; there were also word-reactions whose content and form were in no inner connexion with the stimulus-word. Fuhrmann calls these reactions " unconscious." These reactions were found (according to his tables) at the beginning of the experiment. Series 1 began with the following reactions :

| 1. Light | belief | 5. Red | parents |
| 2. Dark | health | 6. Yellow | father |
| 3. White | arm | 7. Green | chair |
| 4. Black | blue | 8. Blue | arm |

Furhmann did not attempt any interpretation. Kräpelin[2] has accepted this observation in the new edition of his textbook, vol. ii, p. 626, where he makes the following remarks :

" It seems as if these images, which were liberated, but not produced, by the experiment, proceeded from permanent general tendencies of ideas. Their content was mostly related to the state of the disease, or, anyway, to the personal relationships of the patient. We must take it that the frequency of such associations, determined by inner conditions, not by outer excitation, are more peculiarly favoured by the sluggishness of the epileptic. It is this which, unlike the healthy person, prevents his finding quick and easy links to the stimulus-word."

In 1903 I showed in my work " Ueber Simulation von Geistesstörung " (loc. cit., p. 181) the disproportionate occurrence of similar meaningless associations in an imbecile during a state of emotional stupidity. Wehrlin[3] has proved this exhaustively with documentary evidence in his investigations on imbeciles and idiots. In our experience such meaningless reactions always occur when the subject is in a condition of emotional stupidity ; this may, of course, occur in every possible condition of mental aberration. There is, thus, nothing specific of epilepsy in these " unconscious " reactions.

[1] Fuhrmann, *Analyse des Vorstellungsmaterials bei epileptischem Schwachsinn* (Diss : Giessen, 1902).

[2] Kräpelin, *Lehrbuch*, VII. Auflage, 1904.
  See chapter iii.

To return to Fuhrmann's work : after about a month the experiment was repeated with the same stimulus-words in the first case.

The second case was that of a patient who had been ill since his seventeenth year. Four repetitions of the reactions were made here within eight months, demonstrating a considerable limitation of the " field of association," a marked monotony of the reactions. Upon the basis of the associations of two female idiots Fuhrmann holds it as a " delimitating " difference between epilepsy and idiocy that the latter knows no supraordinated concepts. But Wehrlin has shown that the idiot does recognize supraordinated concepts although they are extremely primitive. The distinction must therefore really be something much more subtle than Fuhrmann seems to suppose.

Riklin [1] in his valuable article on " Hebung epileptischer Amnesien durch Hypnose " (Occurrence of Epileptic Amnesia through Hypnosis) refers to some association experiments on epileptics. He enters more into the quality of the reactions and thus reaches various important conclusions.

He demonstrated *adherence to the content of the reaction, clinging to the same grammatical form, marked relation to the ego, personal constellations, frequent emotional accentuation of the content of the reaction, and poverty of the imagination.*

These peculiarities are for the most part nothing but reflections of the epileptic character. Riklin has proved the possibility of reading the signs of epileptic degeneration from a series of association experiments. In criticism of Riklin's observations it must, however, be stated that (1) perseveration of the grammatical form is not necessarily an epileptic symptom—Wehrlin has shown enormous perseveration of the form in imbeciles and idiots (chapter iii) ; (2) perseveration of the content occurs also in normals, as I have shown in my joint work with Riklin (chapter ii). Ego-relationships and personal constellations also occur among normals and feeble-minded, as does likewise the emotional accentuation of the content of the reaction. Poverty of the imagination is obviously not characteristic of epilepsy, but of the feeble-minded as a whole ; as it is also, in a certain sense, for emotional stupidity, where it acquires the peculiar form of " blank association."

In epilepsy, therefore, we have rather to do with a greater or lesser degree of the symptoms which have something of a specific character. My endeavour has been to clarify these conditions and to attempt to separate what is specific in epileptic associations from the different types of normal persons and

[1] Riklin, *Jour. für Psych. u. Neur.,* 1904.

from congenital feeble-mindedness. Work of this kind must obviously rest upon a large material. The Swiss Asylum for Epileptics in Zurich, with its large number of patients, afforded me an exceptionally favourable opportunity. The greater part of the material was collected by the superintendent of the asylum, Dr. Ulrich ; a small part was obtained in the Burghölzli Asylum for the Insane. The total number of persons examined was 158 ; the total number of associations, 18,277. This extensive basis permitted, to a certain degree, an estimate of the various possibilities in the associations of epileptics : Dr. Ulrich and myself therefore undertook a methodical working up of this field, which covers so much that is of great interest. In order to apprehend the essence of the alterations of associations in epileptics as closely as possible, I proposed the following division of the material :

First of all I separated those cases who were not born feeble-minded and who were attacked by epilepsy only after the completion of their development, or at least after puberty.

I was thus able to reject from among the epileptics those extremely numerous cases where congenital feeble-mindedness complicates the picture of the disease. As Wehrlin's work shows, the imbeciles, in so far as they are to any extent distinctly feeble-minded, appear to have a fairly characteristic type of association, marked chiefly by the tendency to " definition " of the stimulus-word. The first investigation of epileptics showed us association types which had, at first sight, great similarity with the imbecile type. The similarity was still greater in the case of epileptics congenitally imbecile or with marked deterioration in early youth. This separation was thus absolutely essential for the recognition of what is specifically epileptic.

For external reasons a further division of the work was made ; in the first instance I analysed the reactions of a typical case as exhaustively as possible, whilst Dr. Ulrich investigated the different possibilities of the epileptic reaction types.[1]

Before beginning the report on the observations I must make a few remarks on the technique of the procedure.

The preparation of the patient for the experiment is an absolutely necessary step. It must be remembered that these persons have, as a rule, no notion of what the experiment demands from them ; they thus become easily confused, and this, when at all pronounced, affects the result most distinctly, as I have repeatedly seen. Therefore we provide some kind of instruction before the experiment. The patient is told that some word will be called out to which he is to answer as quickly as possible—

[1] Dr. Ulrich's work is not included in this volume.

without thinking at all about it—with the very first word or the very first idea that occurs to him. Some examples are then given, the experimenter giving a pretty complete selection of the different associations. The subject is thus placed in a position freely to select the mode of reaction proper to him. If he is not prejudiced he will naturally choose the mode which is characteristic for him. We take care that the subject is not cramped by restricting himself to a reaction with a single word. Should this be the case the characteristic mode of reaction is quite effaced and the reaction-time considerably affected. With women it is not infrequently necessary to subdue impending emotion by a rather simple explanation. I usually do this by representing the experiment as a kind of game of thoughts.

A fresh list of stimulus-words was used in these experiments. It was composed of two hundred different words, of which seventy-five were concrete, twenty-five abstract, fifty adjectives, and fifty verbs. The serial order is noun–adjective, noun–verb. The intermixture was as complete as possible, so that related words did not follow one another. No notice was taken of the number of syllables. The stimulus-words were taken from quite different spheres of daily life, practically avoiding all rare words. A series of emotionally toned concepts such as love, kiss, luck, friendly, etc., were purposely interspersed, for a peculiar significance attaches to such words.

I select the following case from our material :

M. Joseph, machine-locksmith, born 1863, a widower, childless. Has been convicted nineteen times. Alleged to have no familial predisposition. Good at school ; served a three years' apprenticeship to a locksmith, good testimonials as to work. No illness of moment in his youth, no signs of epilepsy : was married in 1888. His wife became insane in 1893 and died in an asylum. Since his wife's illness the patient, till then settled and industrious, began a restless life, travelling nearly all over Europe. He soon ran away from any settled work, took to drink, travelling without any plan and wandering about in the forests. In this period he was often in the hands of the police, mostly for theft. Patient states that he has amnesia for the greater part of this period. During 1893–94 he was three times in an asylum for severe " mania transitoria." In 1896 patient fractured his skull. In 1896–98 he was again in various asylums with delirium. In 1898 tremors were observed confined to one side, occurring in paroxysms. At this time there was noticed a rather connected delirium with plastic and very stable visions, which were described by the patient with much emotion. At the end of 1904 patient wandered about aimlessly and half starved in the mountains. Then he wound up a drinking bout by stealing a bicycle. After this he again wandered about aimlessly, and was caught by the police. Placed in this asylum for observation, the following report was made :

" Feeble-minded, with epileptic character. There are frequent brief seizures of momentary unconsciousness with aura : Sees dark points, five to six in a row, which are always going up and down ; feels as if his head were pressed in or fastened together by screws ; his chest feels as if drops of water were trickling down; there is a buzzing in the ears; then anxiety and dread gets hold of him as if he had done something wrong, or he feels pains in his back which mount up to his head; he has the feeling as if he must tear everything, or he feels as if a locomotive were suddenly rushing towards him."

He becomes dizzy after this aura, everything turns round and he loses consciousness. These lapses of consciousness were also objectively observed during conversation, and especially whilst card-playing. Very marked intolerance for alcohol.

The associations of this case seem to me in many respects very typical for epilepsy, although all the characteristic symptoms were not present. Each case has its own peculiarities, for even here individual differences between the reaction types play a great part.

| | | |
|---|---|---|
| 1. Coal | pit coal : 7·2 seconds | |
| 2. Moderate | not eat much : 12 seconds. | |
| 3. Song | sing, to sing a song : 6·2 seconds | |
| 4. Suppose | I suppose, what do I suppose ? many things : 23·2 seconds | |
| 5. Pain | because I am ill : 4·2 seconds | |
| 6. Dirty | when an apple is dirty, a plant, everything can be dirty · 5·8 seconds. | |
| 7. Moon | that is the moon in the sky, the moon is there : 3·4 seconds | |
| 8. Laugh | people laugh : 4·2 seconds | |
| 9. Coffee | people drink it, people drink it every day : 4 seconds | |
| 10. Wide | that is the width of a distance (with explanatory gesture): 6·2 seconds | |
| 11. Air | that is the air, the air of nature, healthy or unhealthy, good air is good air : 2·2 seconds | |
| 12. Carry | I carry something, a burden or good clothes : 5 seconds | |

These first twelve reactions allow us to draw certain conclusions. The most striking thing is that the patient does not react merely by one single word but generally by a whole sentence. A certain significance attaches to this fact. In my experience, based upon an investigation of over thirty thousand normal associations, normal persons prefer, as a rule, the reactions in one word (*N.B.*, after preliminary instruction as described). There are exceptions where educated persons favour the sentence form ; Riklin and myself quoted an instance of this in our work on the associations of normals. This particular person belonged to the " complex constellation type," that is, to the reaction type whose associations at the time of the experiment were under the influence of a presentation complex marked by emotion.[1] In cases of that kind we recognize at once the peculiar constellation by the content of the associations. Among normals there is another type who prefers to express his reactions not exactly in the sentence form but in two or more words :

---
[1] See p. 140.

## The Predicate Type [1]

Persons of this type form judgments upon and evaluate the object designated by the stimulus-word. This naturally takes the form of a predicate, which sufficiently explains the use of several words. In any case these two types cannot be mistaken for the reactions with which we are now concerned.

The sentence form is, however, so frequent and widespread in the pathological sphere that it becomes difficult to regard it as pathognomonic. An observation worth mentioning—which I cannot, however, support by figures—is that uneducated mental patients seem to have a greater tendency to the sentence form than educated ones. Should this observation be confirmed, it could easily be brought into harmony with the fact that the uneducated attach much greater importance to the stimulus-word than the educated—a fact repeatedly brought out in the previous chapters. Extremely uneducated persons, whose aim is to give the most " appropriate answer " and to explain the stimulus-word as well as possible, require for this purpose many more words than the educated, who frequently just string the words together verbally. This tendency is seen most distinctly in idiots and imbeciles, where sentences are very frequently constructed.[2]

It would be difficult to understand the preference for the sentence form in our case without some such special supposition ; this preference entitles us to believe, with great probability, that there is some abnormality.

Before investigating the content of the reactions, we must pay some attention to the reaction-times. These are abnormally long. (The average reaction-time of the uneducated is two seconds.) No conclusions can for the moment be drawn from this, for there is no form of disease in which the reaction-times may not be prolonged. Aschaffenburg has found the reaction-times somewhat prolonged in maniacal excitement. It is not advisable to investigate the reaction-times in association experiments for themselves, apart from the analysis of the content of the association, for they are absolutely dependent upon the momentary content of consciousness.

Now consider the quality of the associations.

It is at once apparent that the patient gives himself up to the meaning of the stimulus-word, with a pronounced tendency

[1] See p. 142.
[2] In Bleuler's view another fact favours the occurrence of the sentence form in the feeble-minded. The feeble-minded not only grasp with great difficulty a word apart from its context in a sentence, but can hardly think of words apart from the context.

to elucidate and characterize the thing designated by the stimulus-word. Wehrlin has regarded this tendency as peculiarly characteristic of congenital feeble-mindedness. Our case is certainly not one of congenital feeble-mindedness. Perhaps this tendency to explanation arises in every high-grade feeble-minded person ; perhaps it should be assumed that the demented approximates to the congenital imbecile in certain points, even if the causes of the two conditions are quite different. In our case the tendency towards explanation is so distinct that we can readily confirm the forms found in Wehrlin's work on imbeciles.

As " tautological elucidation " consider, for instance :

| | |
|---|---|
| Suppose | I suppose, etc. |
| Carry | I carry something, etc. |
| Air | that is the air, etc. |

As explanation by " example " we have :

| | |
|---|---|
| Moderate | not eat much |
| Dirty | when an apple is dirty, etc. |
| Wide | that is the width of a distance (with explanatory gesture) |

As " statement of the principal quality or activity " we have :

| | |
|---|---|
| Laugh | people laugh |
| Coffee | people drink it |

In this respect we can demonstrate obvious agreement with the imbecile tendency to explanation. It can be even said that the patient endeavours not to be misunderstood in this respect. For instance, when there might be some possible doubt as to whether there is a superficial current verbal connexion, as *song — sing, coffee — people drink*, he adds something so as to confirm and complete the explanation :

| | |
|---|---|
| Song | sing, to sing a song |
| Coffee | people drink, people drink it every day. (Similarly 4, 11, 12) |

These instances show that the patient seems to need to emphasize this tendency to explanation.

Besides this tendency, three of the twelve reactions exhibit the word " I." Reactions of this kind are egocentric. Egocentric reactions occur also in normals, where they are found in persons with the " egocentric attitude." [1] This adjustment can be found in three different forms :

(1) The subject uses a series of personal reminiscences in his reactions.

(2) The subject is under the influence of an emotionally toned presentation complex. He refers nearly every stimulus-word to

[1] See p. 138.

himself (i.e. to the complex) and responds to it as if it were a question touching the complex.

(3) The subject belongs to the predicate type and evaluates the thing denoted by the stimulus-word from the personal standpoint.

In these three types the ego comes occasionally to the front. Besides this, egocentric reactions occur, on the average, more frequently in the educated than in the uneducated, and most frequently when the subject is unembarrassed. We found the average figures of egocentric reactions to be 1·7 per cent. in uneducated men, only 0·5 per cent. in uneducated women. This makes the marked occurrence of egocentricity all the more striking in this case. One might think the chief cause of it to be feeble-mindedness. Imbeciles use personal reminiscences relatively often, for their limited horizon provides no others.

Wehrlin has given some beautiful instances of this. Subsequent figures from our material on imbeciles have shown that the figures for egocentric reactions vary between 0 and 2·4 per cent. Among fifteen imbeciles there were in all only nine who exhibited egocentric reactions. But it should be stated that in Wehrlin's material there was an imbecile [1] who exhibited no less than 26·5 per cent. egocentric reactions. That is quite an exception, and has its own special basis. This imbecile is differentiated from the others by having no true tendency to explanation, but by forming whenever possible a school-sentence to each stimulus-word, which so frequently begins with "I".

| Fall | I fall down | Advice | I ask my father for advice |
| Run | I run quickly | Head | I have a head |
| Sick | I get sick with bad fish | Wages | I have earned the wages |

These examples show, as Wehrlin points out, that this imbecile endeavours above everything to form school-sentences, using *I* where other imbeciles would say *we* or *people*. The term " egocentric " should be, therefore, only used with caution for these reactions. This case is, as we have said, an exception, and does not alter the fact that imbeciles do as a rule avoid the reference to self. Egocentric reactions do not force themselves on the imbecile, who prefers, on the contrary, such expressions as *one, a person, people*, etc., in order to get round the " I " form. Hysteria also, with its innumerable references to the ego, prefers the use of the less incriminating *one*.

Our case, with its pronounced tendency to explanation, exhibits the occurrence of egocentric reactions in a way not

---

[1] No. 13 of Wehrlin's cases.

found among imbeciles with the same kind of tendency to explanation. It may be objected that the reaction

> To carry     I carry something, etc.

is a school-sentence. This objection cannot, however, be made to reaction 5 :

> Pain     because I am ill

If this egocentric factor tells somewhat against imbecility, still more so does the peculiar method of explanation adopted by the patient.

I have already drawn attention to the fact that the patient to a certain extent accentuates his tendency to explanation by repeating his reaction by way of confirmation, or by the addition of an attribute. But he goes still further ; he does not content himself with a simple reaction, but can obviously not go far enough to satisfy this need for the full completion of his explanation. In reaction 4 :

> Suppose     I suppose, what do I suppose ? many things

one sees by the form how he endeavours to add something characteristic. He passes into a really abnormal exuberance in reaction 11 :

> Air     that is the air, the air of nature, healthy or unhealthy, good air is
>          good air

The impulse towards completeness becomes a pleonasm in reaction 10 :

> Wide     that is the width of a distance

(with explanatory gesture) (cp. also reactions 6, 7, 12). In reactions 11

>             good air

and 12

>             good clothes

the predicates seem to express some quite special emphasis. The effort with which he reacts has something altogether inadequate, for this display of concepts exceeds for the most part anything that was really necessary to cover the stimulus-word. This behaviour at once gives the impression of an unnecessary and exaggerated exuberance. It is this factor which is absent in the imbecile, who contents himself with a fairly short reaction—one which appears to him more or less appropriate, but one which is frequently limited to the most primitive hints and to the most unfinished ideas. Our patient, on the contrary, has a strong tendency to heap up as much as possible and to exhaust the reaction, occasionally giving far beyond what is necessary.

The twelve reactions hitherto referred to give us grounds for the supposition of *intellectual feeble-mindedness*, specifically tinged by *a marked egocentric factor* and by *exaggerated exuberance*.

Now consider these further reactions of our patient

13. Plate        dinner-plate—dinner-plate—for dinner

The reaction is repeated for confirmation. But that is not sufficient, and another designation is added which is simply an unnecessary piling up. Constructed similarly but much more specific is reaction

14. Tired        I am tired—aye, tired—the body is tired : 3 seconds
15. Notion       I have a notion—to discover a machine—to draw—to place—to live properly : 13 seconds

This reaction is exaggerated in its completeness ; it contains two explanations through definite examples, one of which, a personal constellation (the patient is a machine locksmith), is thrice determined :

16. Fly          the bird flies : 4·8 seconds
17. Eye          the eye sees : 2·8 seconds
18. Strong       I am powerful, that is strong : 4·6 seconds

Again a blunt reference to the ego with a confirmatory but unnecessary addition.

19. Seed         that is a pip, a seed-pip

The tendency to confirmation and completion here leads to the formation of a neologism, *seed-pip* (see below concerning this reaction).

20. Producing    working industriously is called producing : 3·6 seconds

*Working* is endowed with an emotionally toned attribute.

21. Sail         a sail is a sailing ship on the water : 6·8 seconds

Note the frequent recurrence of the stimulus-word in the reactions. So far only three associations have occurred in which the stimulus-word does not recur in some form in the reaction.

22. Modest       indeed the man is modest who has learned something : 9 seconds

*Indeed* is an expression which represents an emotion, and is designed to objectivate self in presentations and words (cp. R. 14).

In all places where vivid emotions, either easily aroused or very intense, take part, *indeed, yes* and *no* frequently occur (as in hysteria and certain organic affections of the brain). The content of this association suggests a trend of thought which we are hardly likely to meet in congenital idiots.

| 23. Floor | floor of a room : 3·8 seconds |
| 24. Whistle | I whistle : 3·2 seconds |
| 25. Purpose | for what purpose ? for what purpose are you doing that ? for what purpose ? 5·6 seconds |

This reaction is peculiarly remarkable by reason of the extreme repetition of the stimulus-word. It will be seen that the patient conceives the stimulus-word as a question.[1]

| 26. Hot | it's too warm, too hot : 2 seconds |

Perhaps none of the previous reactions portray so well as this one the patient's tendency to confirm and to strengthen the reaction. It is as if he wanted to illuminate the meaning every time by additional impressiveness. This energetic emphasis is beautifully expressed in the ascending *too warm, too hot.*

| 27. Resin | resin from fir, resin grows on fir-trees, on pine-trees 3·8 seconds |
| 28. Awake | I awake my friend, he is asleep : 8·4 seconds |

Both reactions are marked by their completeness, especially the latter, where the patient adds *he is asleep.*

| 29. Apple | there's different apples : 6·6 seconds |

This reaction, exactly in the same form, is found with extraordinary frequency among imbeciles.

| 30. Bad | one says who is bad ? he's and he's—bad, that's a bad man : 6 seconds |
| 31. Case | letter-case : 3 seconds |
| 32. Drink | I drink lemonade : 3 seconds |
| 33. Bed | for sleeping—I have the bed : 3 seconds |
| 34. Worthy | the man is worthy, which the honour is due to him : 9·4 seconds |

This reaction has gone verbally wrong. Thus the epileptic feeble-minded seems to have, in common with the congenital feeble-minded, the defect of handling speech clumsily and arbitrarily. We find among imbeciles a number of faulty constructions and impossible neologisms. But verbal clumsiness should not be too easily assigned to the feeble-minded in association experiments, for the verbal expression may be due to some passing affective inhibition. We shall return to this later.

| 35. Danger | I am in danger, in danger of life : 4·2 seconds |
| 36. Visit | I visit a patient : 4·8 seconds |

This reaction must be another reference to the ego.

[1] Chapter ii, p. 131.

37. Locksmith    I'm a locksmith, artisan : 2·8 seconds
38. High         the church steeple is high usually : 4·8 seconds
39. Hatchet      the hatchet is an axe : 3·4 seconds
40. Meddle       don't meddle in other's affairs : 6·2 seconds

This reaction recalls a colloquial phrase ; it is the first of the kind in this case. Such reactions are, as we know, very frequent among normals.

41. Path         is a footpath, a field path : 3·2 seconds
42. Round        is a ball, otherwise it is not a ball, if it is not round : 3·8 seconds

A reaction very characteristic of this patient's pedantic exaggeration.[1]

43. Blood        has every man, every animal, but good or bad, that's the difference : 3·4 seconds

In these long-winded reactions we find the same estimates as in R. 11. There it was a question of *healthy or unhealthy air*, here *good or bad blood*. The constellation in common is obviously the question—important for the patient—of health. Reactions 5 and 16 also refer to this complex. Fuhrmann has also emphasized the marked occurrence of the disease complex in the associations of the epileptic.

44. Hire         I hire an apartment : 6 seconds
45. Prudent      Man be prudent : 4·8 seconds
46. Jolly        I'm jolly, I'm gay : 3·6 seconds

---

[1] Reactions of this kind are notably differentiated from certain reactions which may be exceptionally received from talkative imbeciles. Instances of this type are :

Sunday        consists of a day when you do nothing, when you go to church
Mountain      a high mountain, with houses or without houses
Salt          something to salt, bread is salted
Copy-book     consists of paper. A newspaper is made of it
Ring          on the finger, jewellery, chain
Attendant     who attends in hospitals, asylums, homes
Piano         when there is music, upstairs, where the organ is, near there. The young lady played it. (Tells another story about an organist)
Swim          in the lake, in the water, in the Rhine, you require swimming drawers
To cook       necessary for eating, soup, flour, meat, kitchen utensils, kettle
Star          part of the sky, planets, sun, moon, and stars

In these associations the insistence and the confirmation of the epileptic are absent, they do not so nicely strike the emotional factor ; they are more like stories suggesting rather a flight of ideas—the flow of thought goes on and does not stick doggedly to the stimulus-word.

47. Market     annual market, that is a market, there has just been the fair in Basle : 7 seconds
48. Forget     I have forgotten something : 5 seconds
49. Drum     the tummy is a drum : 3·2 seconds
50. Free     I am free—I am free, I am a free citizen, it would be fine if it were so : 4 seconds

In this reaction, besides the insistent emphasis on *free*, one is struck by the egocentric reference in the form of the valuation *fine.*

51. Cart     a cart, a team : 4·4 seconds
52. Eat     I eat, I eat a hash : 2·4 seconds
53. Impudence     if a man—there are men who are impudent, impudent in their talk, impudent manners : 6·8 seconds
54. Quick     quick—the machine runs : 3·8 seconds

A constellation from his daily occupation.

55. Fireside     chimney—a factory chimney : 2·4 seconds
56. Enjoy     I enjoy a talk in the evening, I enjoy the pleasures : 4 seconds
57. Clergyman     is a priest, a parson, he must be a good man : 2·2 seconds

To the reaction, quite enough by itself, there is added a valuation of feeling. This recalls 15 :

Notion     to live rightly

Are these, perhaps, hints of the moralizing tendencies of the epileptic ?

58. Easy     what is not easy is difficult : 5 seconds
59. Neck     this is the neck (points to his neck)—every man has a neck : 2·8 seconds
60. Wish     I wish you good luck for the New Year : 3 seconds
61. Stone     marble stone, there are different stones, stone is a naturality : 4·6 seconds

A tendency to the use of learned words is also found in imbeciles (e.g. substance, element, composition, etc.), which they frequently use in quite a grotesque way.

62. Eminent     the educated man is eminent : 6·2 seconds
63. Hose     India-rubber hose is a hose : 4 seconds
64. Love     I love my neighbours like myself

This reaction seems to me characteristic of the epileptic ; Biblical form, marked emphasis of feeling and egocentricity. For comparison I give the ten reactions to *love* of ten imbeciles selected at random :

1. Friendly
2. Angry
3. Bridegroom
4. When you love somebody
5. Pleasant
6. I love my father
7. When you love one another
8. When two persons like each other
9. When you like some one
10. When you love some one

With one exception (6) the imbeciles react quite impersonally and ever so much more colourlessly than the epileptic.

| 65. Tiles | there are grooved tiles in Basle |
| 66. Mild | it is mild weather, it's mild, it's warm : 2·8 seconds |

It is hardly necessary to add to these examples. The further associations of this case contain nothing new in principle.

A few general remarks will not be out of place. It is to be noted that the patient accompanied most reactions with a gesture (which has occasionally been noted in the above formula). Whenever possible the gesture expressed something of confirmation and completeness. In 30 per cent. of the reactions the stimulus-word was repeated. As will be shown in chapter v, the repetition of the stimulus-word in normals is not something accidental but has its deeper reasons, as may be said of all disturbances occurring in the experiment. Apart from those rare cases in normals where the stimulus-word, owing to some kind of embarrassment or other, is quickly and softly repeated, this disturbance mostly occurs in those places where an affect perseverates from a previous reaction and inhibits the association in the one following. Among hysterics I have also seen that the stimulus-word which is a " complex excitant " [1] causes a certain repetition of the stimulus-word in a tone of inquiry. These observations show us that, among normals, the places where repetitions of the stimulus-words occur are not indifferent places. But other mechanisms may be in question in epilepsy. In our case the first four stimulus-words were repeated, the fourth (*suppose*) three times. The next to be repeated was the 15th (*notion*).[2] A general embarrassment may be presupposed at first. In *suppose*, the " difficulty " of the word, perhaps, had something to do with it, as also with *notion*. Both had also very prolonged times (23·2 and 13 seconds), which far exceed the reaction-times to the words in close proximity. But perhaps the repetition of the stimulus-word *notion* is not entirely to be explained by the difficulty of the word, but may be conditioned by the perseveration of an emotional tone. The previous reaction runs :

I am tired, aye, tired, the body is tired : 3 seconds

the next reaction-time is 13 seconds.

---

[1] Certain stimulus-words can encounter a very personal, important, and markedly emotional presentation complex ; certain disturbances of the association result, which we term " complex signs." The chief of these are : abnormally long reaction-times, repetition of the stimulus-word, abnormal behaviour at the critical reaction or at the one following.

[2] " Notion " is a very insidious word for some people.

Apart from the context, the word *aye* points to the existence of some strong emotional tone. The next repetition of the stimulus-word is in R. 19 : *seed*. The previous reaction runs :

Am powerful, that is strong : 4·6 seconds (following R.T. 7 seconds)

21. *Sail* is repeated. Previous reaction :

Work industriously *is called* producing : 3·6 seconds (following R.T. 6·8 seconds)

22. *Modest* is repeated. Previous reaction :

A sail is a sailing-ship on the water : 6·8 seconds (following R.T. 9 seconds)

We have two repetitions of the stimulus-word following immediately upon one another, where the reaction-time rises in step-ladder fashion : 3·6–6·8–9 seconds.

The reaction to *sail* is a verbal slip. (In my investigations in reaction-times verbal slips proved to be complex signs.) At the foot of the ladder we have *work industriously*—an emotionally charged, probably egocentric reaction. The third reaction (22) runs :

Indeed the man is modest who has learnt something

It is not difficult to recognize a substantial relationship with *work industriously*. The supposition that the emotional tone of *work industriously* perseverates amid the verbally disturbed reaction and constellated reaction (22) is thus not improbable.

47. *Market* is repeated. Previous reaction :

I am joyful, I am jolly : 3·6 seconds (following R.T. 7 seconds)

51. *Cart* is repeated. Previous reaction :

I am free, I am a free citizen, it would be fine if it were really so : 4 seconds
(following R.T. 4·4 seconds)

With the exception of the first four reactions, most of the repetitions of the stimulus-words occur in reactions which immediately follow egocentric associations. The reaction-time is, as a rule, abnormally prolonged in these places ; not to dilate further upon this, I will not give more instances, but I can assure the reader that, with insignificant exceptions, all the other repetitions of the stimulus-words occur where the emotions are strongly aroused.

A certain verbal clumsiness occurred in some reactions. One is tempted to make epileptic feeble-mindedness, like that in imbecility, responsible for these faulty constructions. But we know another source for these verbal errors—the strong emotional complex aroused by the stimulus-word. In my article on the behaviour of the reaction-time in association experiments (chapter v) I shall bring forward a series of examples from which it will be seen that the reaction is influenced, in normals, by an emotional complex. Verbal slips, apparently quite accidental, which the subject scarcely notices himself, prove to be the purposeful, determined mixed product of two concurrent ideas.[1]

Before ascribing the verbally incorrect reactions to feeble-mindedness, it behoves us to investigate whether the mechanism which we have discovered among normals be not here also the cause of the faulty construction of sentences or words. There are three such verbal errors in the associations. I put these three associations together with the previous ones (the faulty construction is in italics).

| | | |
|---|---|---|
| 18. Strong | I'm powerful, that is, strong: 4·6 seconds | |
| 19. Seed | that is a pip—a *seed-pip*: 7 seconds (the stimulus-word is repeated) | |
| 20. Producing | working industriously is called producing | |
| 21. Sail | *a sail is a sailing-ship* on the water: 6·8 seconds (the stimulus-word is repeated) | |
| 33. Bed | for sleeping, I have the bed: 3 seconds | |
| 34. Worthy | the man is worthy, *which the honour is due to him*: 9·4 seconds (the stimulus-word is repeated) | |

These three faulty constructions have the following in common:

(1) The stimulus-word of the faulty association is invariably repeated.

(2) Each of the faulty associations has a reaction-time which is not only higher than that of the previous reaction but is delayed far beyond the average of the others.[2]

(3) Two of the faulty associations follow reactions having an emotional tone; in the third case this is at least probable from its content and by analogy with similar cases.

These observations entitle us to say that we are scarcely justified in ascribing the faulty construction to feeble-mindedness.

From this exposition it follows that no specific epileptic mechanism is to be found either in the frequent repetitions of the stimulus-word or in the faulty construction of sentences. There merely remains for discussion, therefore, the question of whether anything specifically epileptic may be found in the intensity of these otherwise normal processes. Perhaps the reaction-times can help us, as these are a valuable aid for judging emotional processes.

[1] Cp. also Freud's observations in *The Psychopathology of Everyday Life.* (English translation by Dr. A. A. Brill.)

[2] I have found in normals that those reactions which are constellated by a conscious or unconscious complex very often have an abnormally long reaction-time; the emotional tone can be carried on to the reaction following, when the reaction-time becomes likewise prolonged.

All the mean times, which I quote, are the probable mean.[1]

From the time-measurements made on this subject we obtain as the general probable mean 4·2 seconds (uneducated normals 2 seconds). The general reaction-time is thus more than double that of corresponding normal. But this mean is only " gross," it is composed of different non-comparable measures. As I shall show in the next chapter, reactions complicated by emotion are usually prolonged. Therefore, if there are many such reactions the general mean becomes, other things being equal, strongly affected. If we exclude all those reactions which, according to the criterion we have laid down, are marked by an emotional egocentric content, and also the reactions immediately following, we get as the probable mean for all presumably non-complicated reactions 3·8 seconds, whilst the probable mean for those discarded amounts to 4·8 seconds.

The emotional tone thus makes a difference of 1 second. This behaviour is not so very far removed from that of normals. We have given many instances to show that there is a considerable difference between the time of an emotional association and that of the reactions immediately succeeding. We have, therefore, investigated the times of these two groups apart. The mean of the reactions containing an emotional presentation is 3·6 seconds, a number which is 0·2 seconds lower than the mean of the non-emotionally toned associations ; but the mean of the associations immediately succeeding the foregoing is 5·8 seconds. This extremely high mean, which exceeds the non-complicated reactions by no less than 2 seconds, expresses the important fact that the emotional tone which inhibits association perseverates from the critical reaction and only reaches its full effect in the succeeding reaction. As a rule, therefore, the inhibitory effect of the emotional tone is not shown in the critical reaction itself, but only in the succeeding reaction. It must be, therefore, taken that in this case the emotional tone only sets in properly at the end of the critical reaction, swells very slowly, and then, gradually running down, influences the next reaction. This behaviour is the more remarkable when one takes into account that meanwhile the experimenter has to write down the reaction, to read the time, to call out the next stimulus-word ; the writing down of the reactions, often pretty lengthy, taking up most time. I have tried to investigate this on the associations of normals. I have taken the associations of a case of which I possess an extremely detailed analysis so that I was fully initiated into all the associations constellated by a complex.

[1] Cp. Aschaffenburg : Kräpelin's *Psych. Arbeiten*, Bd. I. (As regards the counting I must refer to chapter v on reaction-times.)

The probable mean of all associations not complicated by emotion amounted to 1·2 seconds. The mean of the emotionally toned associations was 1·6 seconds. The mean of the reactions immediately succeeding to those emotionally toned was 1·2 seconds; it is therefore equal to the mean of the non-complicated reactions. Consequently, if in mentally healthy subjects the " complex-excitant " stimulus-word is followed, on the average, by a reaction-time 0·4 seconds longer than the stimulus-word which immediately follows or which is indifferent; this means that in normal persons the emotional tone arises much more quickly and is obliterated incomparably more quickly than in an epileptic. Hence the reaction-time of the associations following is on the average not affected at all among healthy persons, whilst, as we have seen, in our epileptic an extraordinary prolongation of the time occurs in the association following the critical one.

This important and interesting peculiarity seems to be of a pathological nature ; how far it is typical of epilepsy will be learnt from the working out of our large material.

The phenomenon seems to have something characteristic for our case, for the existence of such an abnormal emotional process can be presumed also from the quality of the associations. I have repeatedly called attention to the fact that the subject frequently gives subsequent confirmation in an emphatic tone, often with expressions betraying an emotion (e.g. *hot — it's warm, too hot ; tired — I'm tired, aye tired, the body is tired*, etc.). This peculiar form of the reaction also seems to speak in favour of the emotional tone setting in slowly and gradually swelling up, thus liberating more associations with a similar tendency. The emotional tone has very probably a higher intensity among epileptics than among normals, which again must conduce to the prolongation of the tone. But it is difficult to say whether the epileptic emotional tone is not itself abnormally prolonged.[1]

In my analytical investigations on the reaction-times of normals I was able to demonstrate the existence of one or more presentation complexes charged with emotion which constellated a great number of the associations. I have already referred to the fact that a complex exists in our epileptic which constellates

---

[1] This conception would explain the epileptic fixation by the abnormality of the emotional tone. But it is not inconceivable that the epileptic presentation in this respect has something abnormal, that it lasts longer than in normals and thus produces a series of associations which cling to the original presentation. Under these conditions relatively numerous perseverations of the context would be expected. None was present, however, in our case.

a series of associations. It is the complex of disease. The following associations must be referred to this complex :

| Pain | because I am ill : 4·2 seconds (succeeding R.T. 5·8 seconds) |
|---|---|
| Tired | I'm tired, aye tired, the body's tired : 3 seconds ; S.R.T. 13 seconds[1] ; R.S.[2] |
| Strong | I'm powerful, that is strong : 4·6 seconds; S.R.T. 7 seconds ; R.S. |
| Blood | every man has—but good blood or bad blood, that's the difference : 3·4 seconds; S.R.T. 6 seconds ; R.S. |
| Joyous | I'm joyous, I'm jolly : 3·6 seconds ; S.R.T. 7 seconds ; R.S. |

A constellation somewhat more remote might be :

| Air | that is the air—healthy or unhealthy : 2·2 seconds ; S.R.T. 5 seconds |
|---|---|
| Visit | I visit a patient : 4·8 seconds |

The reaction following runs :

| Locksmith | I'm a locksmith : 2·8 seconds |
|---|---|

The patient is confined to an asylum in consequence of his disease and this has powerfully affected him. He was afraid that he would not get free again, not be able to work and earn money again. Home-sickness troubled him likewise. The following reactions perhaps refer to this side of the complex :

| Producing | work industriously means producing : 3·6 seconds. S.R.T. 6·8 seconds ; R.S. |
|---|---|
| Danger | I'm in danger, in danger of life : 4·2 seconds; S.R.T. 4·8 seconds. |
| Free | I'm free—it would be fine if it were so : 4 seconds ; S.R.T. 4·4 seconds ; R.S. |
| Wish | I wish you good luck for the New Year : 3 seconds ; S.R.T. 4·6 seconds ; R.S. |

About this last association it should be said that the tests were carried out just before Christmas, a period when sensitive patients find the confinement doubly difficult to bear.

These few instances should suffice to show that a whole series of associations are constellated by an emotionally toned complex. This behaviour is not in itself anything abnormal, for the associations of normals are constellated by the same kind of complexes.

### RECAPITULATION

(1) As in the associations of normals.

*a.* Patient adapts himself to the importance of the stimulus-word like uneducated persons. Consequently superficial word-associations are absent.

---

[1] S.R.T. = reaction-time of succeeding reaction.

[2] R.S. = repetition of the stimulus-word in succeeding reaction.

*b.* The associations are in part constellated by a disease complex.

(2) As in the associations of imbeciles.

*a.* The attitude towards the meaning of the stimulus-word is so intense that a large number of the associations must be apprehended as " explanations," in the sense used by Wehrlin in his work (chapter iii).

*b.* The associations have the sentence form.

*c.* The reaction-times are considerably prolonged as compared with normals.

*d.* The frequent repetition of the stimulus-word.

(3) Peculiarities as compared with normals and imbeciles.

*a.* The " explanations" have an awkward, circumlocutial character, particularly expressed by the confirmation and completeness of the reaction (*tendency towards full completion*). The stimulus-word is frequently repeated in the reaction.

*b.* The outer form of the reaction is not stereotyped or limited, with the exception of the egocentric form, which occurs with peculiar frequency (31 per cent.).

*c.* Frequent emotional references which are fairly obvious (religious, moralizing, etc.).

*d.* The reaction-times only display their greatest variations after the critical reaction. The abnormally long times do not occur in particularly difficult words, but in places which are determined by a perseveration of the emotional tone. From this it may be concluded that in this patient the emotional tone sets in later and lasts longer than in normals.

In conclusion, I would observe that my analysis is for the moment of value only for this case, and that I do not venture to draw any universal deduction. There are many different kinds of epilepsy which perhaps exhibit different psychological characteristics. Inasmuch as my case is complicated by fracture of the skull, it is perhaps exceptional.

CHAPTER V

# REACTION-TIME IN ASSOCIATION EXPERIMENTS

## By Dr. C. G. JUNG

THE present investigation deals with the behaviour of the time interval which occurs between the calling out of the stimulus-word and the utterance of the reaction-word. I term this interval simply " reaction-time," with the knowledge that it is made up of a composite series which can be deductively and empirically reduced into numerous components. I forbear venturing upon an analysis of that kind, for the results would be just like hypotheses which had to be supported by anatomical data to which they were not entitled. The components of our " reaction-time " are only known to us in part, and in an exhaustive critique would prove extremely complicated, as Claparède's summary shows [1]:

(1) Transference of the sound to the ear of the percipient.
(2) Nerve conduction to the acoustic centre.
(3) Recognition of the word (primary identification).
(4) Understanding of the word (secondary identification).
(5) Evoking of the induced presentation, i.e. the pure association.
(6) Naming of the presentation evoked.
(7) Excitation of the speech-motor apparatus or of the motor centre of the hand, if measured by means of the Morse communicator.
(8) Nerve conduction to the muscle.

A superficial consideration of these eight factors shows that we have only emphasized some of the most important factors. The innumerable possibilities of intracerebral processes have been in no wise exhausted.

So far as we know these components, they are of very short duration, the longest not exceeding $50 \sigma$. (Ziehen). Under normal

[1] Claparède, L'Association des Idées, p. 275. The scheme is based upon Ziehen, Die Ideenassoziation des Kindes, 2. Abhandlg., p. 14.

conditions some of these components, e.g. the time for nerve conduction, excitation of the centre, etc., have a fairly constant duration. In any case, variations here take place within relatively narrow boundaries. Variations in identification time are greater, and greatest of all are the true association time and the time for the verbal formation of the reaction. In the association experiment the last factors have therefore greatest importance.

Whoever has undertaken association experiments knows how wide are the limits of the reaction-times. In our experience times up to six seconds are not at all exceptional even among normal persons. This great difference of the times gives us a needful hint as to the methods of time measurement. So long as we have not sufficient knowledge of the causes of the variations, small differences in the times cannot tell us anything. We do not, therefore, require any complicated experimental conditions to measure times of one-thousandth of a second ; we may quietly ignore slight differences so long as the causes of the greater differences do not escape us. Apart from the fact that complicated methods of measuring the finer intervals disclose nothing more than measurements with the one-fifth second stop-watch, there are weighty considerations against the use of mouth-whistles, trumpet-calls, or dark chambers. If Mayer and Orth [1] regarded it as necessary to shut the eyes during the experiment to avoid all disturbing sense impressions, the apparatus mentioned certainly does nothing to simplify the experiment or prevent disturbing influences. In any case unpractised persons cannot be employed in these experiments if gross disturbances of attention are not to be risked. Finally, in mental patients the more exact time measurements are obviously excluded.

Measurement by the one-fifth second watch seems, therefore, not only quite sufficient but has stood the test in the investigations of several workers. Mayer and Orth [2] have worked with it, as have Thumb and Marbe,[3] Wreschner,[4] Sommer, and others. Claparède's view is that it suffices for all experiments in successive association.[5] Besides simplicity in handling, the stop-watch has the especial advantage of disturbing the experiment least, and this fact was important in the experiments with the uneducated, who are prone to emotion.

[1] *Zeitsch. f. Psychol.*, Bd. XXVI.
[2] Loc. cit.
[3] *Experimentelle Untersuchungen über die Grundlagen der sprachlichen Analogiebildung* (Leipzig, 1901).
[4] *Allgemeine Zeitschrift für Psychiatrie*, Bd. LVII.
[5] Loc. cit., p. 261.

With the great differences in time that have to be considered, it is of little consequence that the times measured are all somewhat too large. Any one who has worked with this stop-watch knows that the apparatus is only approximately correct in its working, for the stop arrangement does not always put the hand exactly at the place at which the stop is liberated. To this must be added certain variations in the personal equation which may influence the measurement. Although the uncontrollable disturbances are not minimal, one can, at least in my experience, take it that the measurements are correct to about one-fifth of a second = 200 $\sigma$. This slight disadvantage has hitherto done no real harm to our experiments.

The material upon which this investigation is based consists of the time measurements which were published by Riklin and myself [1] on the associations of normal persons. Of the thirty-eight persons whose associations are there reviewed, the reaction-time was measured in twenty-six persons. Approximately one-half were measured by Riklin. The difference of the personal equation in the measurements of the two experimenters is less than one-fifth of a second, as we have proved by control experiments ; it may therefore be left out of account.

The number and composition of the measurements are :

| | | | | |
|---|---|---|---|---|
| 1. In 7 uneducated women there were | 1201 | time measurements |
| 2. In 7 „ men „ | 1007 | „ „ |
| 3. In 6 educated women „ | 948 | „ „ |
| 4. In 6 „ men „ | 988 | „ „ |

Total 26 persons                    4144 time measurements

(A) *The Average Duration of an Association*

In his studies on association Aschaffenburg says [2] : " It is of the greatest importance that the duration of an association of a normal subject can differ by one-half from the average duration of the rest, which lies between 1200 and 1400 $\sigma$. It teaches us in the most striking way what little value should be ascribed to the absolute length of time."

Aschaffenburg bases this judgment on the observation that the reaction-time is subjected to great individual variations. In accordance with this fact, we find in the literature of the subject rather wide divergences as to the average length of associations. Féré [3] gives as the mean for men 700 $\sigma$, for women

---

[1] See chapter ii.
[2] Kräpelin's *Psychol. Arbeiten*, Bd. I, p. 272.
[3] *La Pathologie des émotions*.

830 $\sigma$.[1] Galton gives the average time as 1·3 second. Trautscholdt's [2] figures vary between 1154 and 896 $\sigma$.

These figures will suffice to show how little agreement there
is among investigators. The differences are probably referable
to the following points :

(1) The methods of measuring vary with the apparatus and
other conditions of the experiment.

(2) The amount of practice varies in the subjects.

(3) The methods of reckoning the mean figures are different.

Practically there are only two methods of reckoning the
mean figures :

*a.* The arithmetical mean.

*b.* The probable mean (Kräpelin).

In view of the fact that in association experiments excessively
long times frequently occur, the use of the arithmetical mean
does not seem advisable. In this method high values affect the
otherwise low average value in a very disturbing way and may
be quite misleading. This difficulty is overcome by the method
of the probable mean. In this method the figures are arranged
in a series according to their value, and then the nearest mean
figure is taken. This excludes the effect of excessively high
values. In the great majority of cases the probable mean is
lower than the arithmetical. For instance, three of my subjects
exhibit the following values :

> Probable mean　：　1·8, 2, 1·6.
> Arithmetical mean :　2·8, 3, 3·6.

As this instance shows, differences of this kind can influence
the general mean to a high degree. It is therefore not a matter
of indifference which method of reckoning has been used.
Ziehen's " representative value," which demands a pretty detailed
calculation, should not, for this reason, find much appreciation,
although it renders possible a very accurate review of the individual figures. The *composite value* is dependent upon external
accidents, and is only to be used under certain conditions.

These considerations seem to indicate that the probable mean
is the method most to be recommended for calculating the mean
figures more quickly from great numbers of figures.

(4) The number of subjects is generally too limited and the
selection too one-sided in the previous writers.

I have not endeavoured to find absolute mean figures but
only approximate probable figures which will give us to some
extent the heights to which the values tend in normal subjects of

---

[1] " Psychometric Experiments," *Brain*, 1879, vol. ii, p. 149.

[2] Wundt's *Phil. Studien*, Bd. I.

different social status. Believing that the association experiments used somewhat as they have been for some years in this clinic will play an important part in the future diagnosis of mental diseases, it seems to me of practical importance to discover universal normal mean values, which will afford a certain basis for judging pathological values.

The universal mean value for the duration of an association was found to be :

1·8 second

This was arrived at in the following way : First, the probable mean of each of the twenty-six subjects was calculated, and from the individual values so obtained the arithmetical mean was drawn. The latter method was then chosen because twenty-six persons are, after all, but a small number, and it was therefore unfair to exclude the individual values from the calculation by the use of the probable means.

This mean figure shows a pretty long duration of the association time. It exceeds by quite a good deal the values given in the literature of this subject. The causes of this prolongation are :

(1) The points already above mentioned (measurement by the second-watch, unpractised subjects, who in part come from the lower classes).

(2) The majority of the subjects are Swiss, a circumstance whose importance in acoustic-verbal experiments was discussed in chapter ii.

This summary of principles will clear up the way in which the significance of the values is conditioned. The variability of the mean figures is shown much more simply by grouping the subjects from certain simple points of view and comparing the individual groups with one another.

(B) Sex and Reaction-time

As already mentioned, Féré gave a longer association time for women than for men. We can confirm this by our figures :

Men . . . . . . 1·6 second
Women . . . . . 2 seconds

which show that the women reacted considerably more slowly in our association experiments. It should be mentioned, however, that the educated women are approximately at the same level of culture as the educated men, but, on the other hand, the uneducated women are somewhat below the level of the culture of the uneducated men. As Ranschburg's [1] and our

[1] *Allgemeine Zeitschrift für Psychiatrie*, 1900.

own previous investigations [1] have shown, uneducated persons, and especially women, exceed the educated in inner associations by a considerable percentage, whilst in purely verbal associations they are left far behind. According to Ziehen's [2] observations on children, their associations are marked by the inner references (relationship of significance) having longer reaction-times, whilst the verbal associations require the shortest time. These facts, emphasized by Ziehen, are, it is true, contested by Aschaffenburg,[3] who finds "there are no characteristic differences in the reaction-times of forms of association." The figures given by Aschaffenburg certainly allow no other interpretation, but they may perhaps be explained as the consequence of the one-sided selection of his subjects. Ziehen's [4] contention that "presentations having greater external relationship, as, e.g., rhymed verbal presentations," are reproduced more quickly is fully in accordance with everyday experience. This point should therefore be taken into consideration in the explanation of the longer association times of women. Whether this is the whole explanation we shall learn in our further inquiries. In any case, before discussing a difference of sex in the reaction-time we must investigate the influence of education.

### (C) *Educational Rank and Reaction-time*

|  | Educated |  | Uneducated |
|---|---|---|---|
| Men | . . . 1·3 second |  | 1·8 (1·6 [5]) second |
| Women | . . 1·7 „ |  | 2·2 seconds |
| Educated in general | 1·5 „ | Uneducated in general : | 2 (1·9) seconds |

Our earlier investigations invariably showed that the uneducated subjects produce more inner associations than the educated. The ratio of inner association to outer is among the uneducated 43 : 53 per cent., among the educated 36 : 59 per cent. One is tempted to connect the difference in the reaction-time with this relationship, and to maintain that the smaller number of inner associations among the educated corresponds with the shorter reaction-time, and, inversely, the greater number of inner associations among the uneducated corresponds with the longer reaction-time. However plausible this assumption (especially in view of

---

[1] Chapter ii, p. 144.

[2] *Die Ideenassoziation des Kindes.*

[3] *Psych. Arbeiten*, Bd. I.

[4] *Leitfaden der Physiol. Psychologie.*

[5] Among the uneducated male subjects there was a young man with slight hysterical disposition whose mental stability we have perhaps overestimated. His probable mean is no less than 3·4 seconds (i.e. an abnormally high value). If this suspicious case is excluded, the mean of the men is only 1·6 second.

Ziehen's results) might seem, a consideration of the figures for the two sexes shows us that the facts are not so simple. On a closer examination of the educational rank of the subjects, it must be stated absolutely that the difference in culture between the educated and the uneducated is incomparably greater than that between the educated men and women. It therefore remains quite inexplicable why the time difference of 0·4 is the same between the educated men and women as between the educated and the uneducated. Add to this that the reaction-time, 1·7 of the educated women as compared with 1·3 of the educated men, does not correspond at all with the percentage ratio of the inner and outer associations : that of the women is 38 : 61 per cent., whilst that of the men is only 36 : 56 per cent. Analogous to this, the time difference of ·4 (or ·6) between the uneducated men and women in no wise corresponds to the difference of culture between the sexes in the uneducated group. In both cases there remains a time difference to the debit of the women corresponding in no wise with the difference of culture. If we take the time difference of the men of the two groups by themselves and that of the women by themselves the difference in cultuie suffices for an explanation, and this is very nicely shown also in the ratio of the kinds of association to each other. This supposition is also supported by the observations of Wreschner [1] and Wehrlin,[2] who have dwelt upon the general prolongation of association activity in pathological absence of intelligence and culture (congenital feeble-minded). Wehrlin has shown that together with the prolonged reaction-time there goes an increase of inner associations.

Whilst the uneducated women exhibit slightly more inner associations than the men, the facts are reversed in educated men and women, for the educated women have fewer inner associations than the men ; nevertheless there is a time difference between the sexes which is in part greater than that between educated and uneducated. As we have seen, neither a higher number of inner associations nor the lesser difference of culture can be held responsible for this. There seems a new factor interposed—presumably a sex difference.

We shall consider the justification for this supposition later. Before discussing this theme it becomes necessary to investigate the influences which the individual stimulus-word exercises upon the reaction.

[1] *Allgemeine Zeitschrift für Psychiatrie*, Bd. LVII.
[2] Chapter iii.

(D) *The Influences of the Stimulus-word upon the Reaction-time*

The previous investigations on association times have been chiefly concerned to discover a connexion between the quality of the association (i.e. of the reaction) and its duration. Trautscholdt has already tried to establish certain relationships. He states that the verbal associations require the shortest time. We have already mentioned the observations of Ziehen and Aschaffenburg. We must now see if the two components of the association, stimulus-word and reaction, cannot be examined separately as to their influence upon the duration. Definite results can only be expected from an enormous material. I have already tried with Riklin to estimate the influence which the stimulus-word has upon the quality of the reaction. Certain laws were established :

(1) The grammatical form of the stimulus-word has a great influence upon the form of the reaction ; that is to say, the subject betrays a distinct tendency to give the reaction the grammatical form of the stimulus-word.[1]

The individual figures with this tendency show great variations. My stimulus-words, which consist of 60 per cent. nouns, 18 per cent. adjectives, and 21 per cent. verbs (mixing the different word forms so as to prevent perseveration of the reaction form), gave the following :

The individual figures for grammatical agreement vary between 26 and 95 per cent. The average figure for the educated amounts to 51 per cent., for the uneducated to 59 per cent. The uneducated thus show a rather more distinct tendency to be influenced by the form of the stimulus-word. (This holds good not only of the grammatical forms but also of the number of syllables and of alliteration.)

(2) The tendency to agreement in grammatical form is under the limiting influence of the law of frequency. In language, adjectives and verbs occur about one-half as often as nouns.[2] The noun has thus a higher frequency value, so that the probability of the reproduction of a noun is greater than that of an adjective or verb.

[1] Münsterburg, Kräpelin, and Aschaffenburg have to some extent dealt with this question. Kräpelin finds in reactions to nouns 90 per cent. agreement ; Aschaffenburg, among sixteen subjects, 81 per cent. It should be noted that "on principle" he only used nouns as stimulus-words. But this circumstance encourages to a great degree the favourite perseveration of the same form of reaction, and thus his figures have at most but conditional value. As grammatical forms I understand purely the form as noun, adjective, or verb.

[2] I have made adequate calculations from newspapers and dialogues of the feuilleton kind and have found approximately this ratio.

In our experiments noun stimulus-words were followed on the average by nouns in 73 per cent. (Aschaffenburg 81 per cent.). Since verbs and adjectives have a lesser frequency value, their influence upon the reaction form is correspondingly lower. Experience confirms this supposition : to verb stimulus-words there followed, on the average, 33 per cent. verbs. The number of nouns amounts to, on the average, 49 per cent., and has thus been reduced by the tendency to agreement in grammatical forms. Adjective stimulus-words have a rather stronger influence, being followed by 52 per cent. adjectives. The number of nouns is reduced by adjective stimulus-words to 44 per cent. on the average. We see from these facts that by the use of verb and adjective as stimulus-words the frequency of nouns can be lessened by about one-half on the average.

(3) Our previous investigations [1] have shown that the quality of the association is not inconsiderably influenced by the grammatical form of the stimulus-word. Whilst, for instance, among uneducated women the inner associations were to the outer as 1 : 1·06, the ratio of the associations to adjective stimulus-words was 1 : 0·62 and to verb stimulus-words 1 : 0·43. The number of inner associations to adjective and verb stimulus-words is quite considerably increased. We find the same phenomenon in the educated, only in a much weaker degree. The increase of inner associations seems to rest upon this—that in consequence of the lower frequency value of verbs and adjectives there are much fewer current word connexions with these than with nouns. The associations that follow verbs and adjectives are thus much less prepared and demand a greater stress of attention ; this naturally gives rise to significant relationships rather than to superficial and purely external connexions. We therefore see that more inner associations result with verbs and adjectives than with nouns.

From the observations of Ziehen, who has proved that higher figures occur when there are relationships of meaning, it is to be expected that verbs and adjectives will be, on the average, followed by higher figures than nouns. But as the nouns can themselves consist of presentations with different values, and as this can itself greatly influence the reaction-time, the nouns are classified into concrete and universal concepts, a further reason for this being that uneducated persons are also easily confused by many universal concepts.

The probable mean of all subjects is :

| For concrete concepts 1·67 second | For adjectives 1·70 second |
|---|---|
| „ universal „ 1·95 „ | „ verbs 1·90 „ |

[1] Chapter ii.

The figures agree with expectation; reactions to verbs and adjectives show a longer time than those to concrete stimulus-words. Reactions to universal concepts require the longest time, which also agrees with expectation.

*Probable Mean of the Reaction-times to Concrete and other Stimulus-words*

|  | Uneducated | | Educated | |
|---|---|---|---|---|
|  | Women | Men | Women | Men |
| Concrete concepts . . | 2 | 1·7 | 1·6 | 1·4 |
| Universal concepts . . | 2·8 | 1·9 | 1·8 | 1·3 |
| Adjectives . . . . | 2·2 | 1·7 | 1·7 | 1·2 |
| Verbs . . . . | 2·4 | 2 | 1·9 | 1·3 |

The table shows that the uneducated have higher reaction-times than the educated.[1] The longest time occurs among uneducated women when the stimulus-words are universal concepts, whilst these stimulus-words require among educated men a shorter time than the concretes. It is curious that, in contrast with all other subjects, the educated men have their longest times with concretes. This fact is important in so far as it shows that the influence of the stimulus-word upon the duration of the association does not consist merely in the factors just discussed. Comparing these figures with the values given by Aschaffenburg for similar subjects, it is seen that our figures taken with the second-watch are approximately the same as those obtained by him when using the whistle and chronoscope.[2]

(E) *The Influence of the Reaction-word upon the Reaction-time*

We have discussed the behaviour of the reaction-time when the stimulus-word is a noun, adjective, or verb. We have now to find out how the reaction-time behaves when the reaction-word is a noun, etc.

---

[1] The individual values upon which this table is based vary between 1 and 4·4 seconds.

[2] A whole series of questions could easily be opened up here. For instance: what is the reaction-time when verb is followed by verb or noun by noun, and how does this compare in the different subjects? But these would take us too far from the object of this investigation.

The probable means of all subjects are :

| | | | | |
|---|---|---|---|---|
| With concretes as reaction-words . | . | . | . | 1·81 second |
| „ universals „ „ | . | . | . | 1·98 „ |
| „ adjectives „ „ | . | . | . | 1·65 „ |
| „ verbs „ „ | . | . | . | 1·66 „ |

If these tables are compared with the previous one of the mean values for the correspondingly classified stimulus-word, it is seen that the universal concepts have in both cases the longest duration (1·95 and 1·98 second). When the reaction-word is a concrete it shows a longer duration than when caused by a concrete stimulus-word (stimulus-word 1·67, reaction-word 1·81 second). This difference must rest upon the fact that many more current word connexions exist to a noun, whilst noun to noun generally means an inner relationship, or at least an association by coexistence (which for the rest behaves among the uneducated as an inner association—see chapter ii). Under the heading "concretes as reaction-words" numerous inner association words have been grouped, which is probably the cause of the prolongation of the reaction-time. We find the contrary in verbs and adjectives as reaction-words. Their mean values are diminished as compared with those of the previous table (1·7, 1·9 : 1·65, 1·66 second) because in these classes, especially among the verbs, many current verbal connexions occur.

The probable mean values of the individual groups of the subjects are as follows :

*Probable Mean of Reaction-times for Concrete, etc., Reaction-words* [1]

| | Uneducated | | Educated | |
|---|---|---|---|---|
| | Women | Men | Women | Men |
| Concretes . . . . | 2·2 | 1·85 | 1·7 | 1·5 |
| Universals . . . . | 2·7 | 2 | 2 | 1·4 |
| Adjectives . . . . | 2 | 1·7 | 1·7 | 1·2 |
| Verbs . . . . | 1·9 | 1·7 | 1·8 | 1·3 |

The relatively low values above mentioned for adjectives and verbs are here present in all four groups. Here again the uneducated women present the highest figures. The relatively

[1] The individual figures upon which this table is based vary between 1 and 4 seconds.

high figures for the concretes are striking. The fact mentioned in the last section, that the educated men have their longest reaction-times with the concretes, is found here also. Perhaps the explanation of this may be sought in the fact that in this group there occur very many significant relationships and these prolong the duration.

### (F) *The Influence of the Quality of the Association upon the Reaction-time*

As we have seen, Aschaffenburg's investigations on the influence of the quality of the association upon the reaction-time led to no unequivocal result ; Ziehen's success, already alluded to, is therefore all the more encouraging. I have likewise investigated the influence of the quality of the association upon the time, limiting myself to the three groups of our former classification : inner and outer associations and clang-reactions. The average figures are as follows :

|  | Uneducated | | Educated | |
|---|---|---|---|---|
|  | Women | Men | Women | Men |
| Inner associations | 2·8 | 1·9 | 2·1 | 1·6 |
| Outer associations. | 1·9 | 1·7 | 1·8 | 1·3 |
| Clang-reactions | 2·6 | 2·4 | 2 | 1·3 |

There is a distinct difference between the time duration for inner and outer associations, the outer associations requiring a distinctly lesser time. The matter is different in clang-reactions, where we should, from all we know, have expected the shortest times, since these are the lowest and simplest associations and should arise in the shortest time. Obviously in practice the relations are not so simple as one might expert theoretically. I have frequently found that it is just the most superficial clang-reactions which are often very long. It is my experience that, as a rule, clang-reactions are abnormal reactions due to some kind of distracting disturbance. The following section shows us what is the usual nature of this disturbance.

### (G) *The Overlong Reaction-time*

To limit practically the concept " overlong " reaction-time, I shall call that time " overlong " which is above the probable mean of the subject in question. If, e.g., the probable mean amounts to 2·5 seconds, 3 seconds is an "overlong" reaction-time.

Let us first of all recapitulate what is so far known as to the causes which (we are naturally referring to our experiments only) prolong the reaction-time :

(1) Certain grammatical forms of stimulus- and reaction-words.

(2) A significant relation between stimulus- and reaction-word.

(3) The rarity or difficulty of the stimulus-word (universal concepts).

(4) Ziehen [1] has proved the remarkable fact that (as contrasted with reactions in common currency) individual associations prolong the reaction-time.

(5) Mayer and Orth [2] found in their experimental studies on association that the reaction-time was prolonged when conation interpolated itself between stimulus and reaction. If an emotional content of consciousness occurred at all between stimulus and reaction the reaction-time was considerably increased as compared with the rest of the associations. Painful emotions more especially prolonged the time.[3]

(6) In our previous investigations (chapter ii) we called attention to the fact that abnormally long reaction-times more especially occur when an emotionally accentuated complex was aroused by the stimulus-word. We were thus able not only to confirm the observations of Mayer and Orth, but could also prove in many cases—

(1) The complex is generally the cause of several, or indeed of very many long times, and

(2) What is the nature of the complex.

The fact that the overlong times can denote the presence of emotional complexes seems to us of great importance. That would perhaps give us the means by a short and simple examination to discover things of personal import, especially the complexes which characterize the psychology of the individual. Pathology would get much help also, for in this way we should get valuable sign-posts, say among hysterics, for the discovery of the complexes making for disease, of which the hysteric is himself not always aware.

[1] *Die Ideenassoziation des Kindes.*

[2] *Zeitschrift für Psychol.*, Bd. XXVI.

[3] Ziehen was the first to point out that in cases of prolonged reaction-time "a relatively strong emotional accentuation" had often arisen. Op. cit., p. 36.

To elucidate these questions further I have undertaken, with the co-operation of some educated subjects, who possessed good powers of introspection, the detailed analyses of the individual associations.

No. 1 is a married lady who placed herself in the readiest way at my disposal for the experiment and gave me every possible information. I report the experiment in as detailed a way as possible so that the reader may receive as complete a picture as possible.

The probable mean of the experiment amounts to 1 second.

| | | | |
|---|---|---|---|
| 1. Head | -cloth | : 1 | second |
| 2. Green | grass | : 0·8 | ,, |
| 3. Water | -fall | : 1 | ,, |
| 4. Prick | cut | : 0·8 | ,, |
| 5. Angel | -heart | : 0·8 | ,, |

These reactions followed without the slightest emotion, smoothly and indifferently. Reaction 5 is striking : subject cannot explain to herself how she comes to *heart*, which was used by her as a composite word. Then there suddenly occurred to her *Angelard*, a name formerly very familiar to her. It is, therefore, an indirect association following the known type of displacement by clang-similarity. The question now arises : What is the reason for this sudden appearance of an indirect association ? Our earlier investigations have shown (chapter ii) that, under certain conditions, the indirect associations are increased in states of disturbed attention. It must therefore be accepted that disturbance of attention can produce indirect associations. The subject rejects altogether any disturbance from without, nor can she disclose any internal disturbance. Although the conscious can render no data, it is possible that some unconscious stimulus has disturbed the reaction. The stimulus-word *angel* has no special emphasis for her. As we already know, emphasis from a previous association can resound, and can constellate the reaction unconsciously,[1] especially when there has been something of strong emotional interest in the previous associations. Reaction 4, *cut*, calls up a certain slight shade of anxiety, an image of blood,[2] etc. The subject is pregnant and has now and then feelings of anxious expectancy. Whether the presentation *blood* also determined the reaction *heart* I leave undecided.

The emotional tone of *cut* was, the subject stated, so slight and so secondary that the connexion did not occur to her. It was for this reason that the prolongation of the reaction-time, common at such places, was here absent.

| | | | |
|---|---|---|---|
| 6. Long | short | : 0·8 second | |
| 7. Ship | journey | : 0·8 | ,, |
| 8. Plough | field | : 1 | ,, |
| 9. Wool | silk | : 1 | ,, |
| 10. Friendly | amiable | : 1·2 | ,, |
| 11. Table | chair | : 1·2 | ,, |
| 12. Carry | lift | : 1·2 | ,, |
| 13. State | make | : 1·2 | ,, |
| 14. Haughty | naughty | : 1·2 | ,, |
| (*trotzig*) | (*protzig*) | | |

---

[1] Regarding perseveration, cp. Muller and Pilzecker, *Experim. Beiträge zur Lehre vom Gedächtnis* (Leipzig, 1900).

[2] Cp. later reaction 143, *blood*.

The rhyme is a constellation : the subject remembers having read it in one of my association lists.

| | | | |
|---|---|---|---|
| 15. Dance | jump | : 0·8 second | |
| 16. Lake | sea | : 0·8 | ,, |
| 17. Ill | well | : 1·2 | ,, |
| 18. Proud | fiery | : 1·2 | ,, |

The last two reactions have some emotional tone, though very weak.

| | | | |
|---|---|---|---|
| 19. To cook | to learn | : 0·8 second | |
| 20. Ink | black | : 1 | ,, |
| 21. Evil | good | : 0·8 | ,, |
| 22. Needle | cotton | : 1 | ,, |
| 23. To swim | to learn | : 0·8 | ,, |

Reaction 19 returns here with the same short reaction-time. The subject admits that she has not properly learnt either cookery or swimming.

| | | | |
|---|---|---|---|
| 24. Journey | Berlin | : 1·2 second | |

Constellation of a journey a few months back; the date, moreover, is about the same as that of the beginning of pregnancy.

| | | | |
|---|---|---|---|
| 25. Blue | sky | : 0·8 second | |
| 26. Bread | eat | : 1·2 | ,, |
| 27. Threaten | fist | : 1·2 | ,, |
| 28. Lamp | green | : 1·4 | ,, |

This is the first longish time. The subject scarcely noticed her hesitation and perceived no special emotional tone. But the previous stimulus-word *threaten*, is rather insidious. Recalling the feeling of anxious expectancy already mentioned, we have perhaps a point of departure for the explanation of this delayed time : it is another perseveration. It is not necessary for the emotional tone to arise at the previous reaction. Affective processes always arise somewhat more slowly and proceed somewhat more slowly than purely associative processes. The emotional tone follows a little later, as can be observed in certain hysterics.

The reaction *green* is a constellation derived from her home life (lamp-shades).

| | | | |
|---|---|---|---|
| 29. Rich | poor | : 1 second | |
| 30. Tree | green | : 0·8 | ,, |

Reaction 28 returns here with a very short time, a phenomenon which may rest on associative processes which have just emerged from consciousness, have a tendency to recur, or can be very readily reproduced.[1]

Our previous investigations (chapter ii) have also taught us that repetitions of the reaction frequently rest upon a peculiar emotional tone, for the words repeated are associated with an emotionally toned complex. The emotional tone resting upon such words is the mechanism which again pushes it forth at every opportunity.

| | | | |
|---|---|---|---|
| 31. Sing | can | : 2·4 seconds | |

A very superficial reaction, like *learn to cook and swim,* with a remarkably long reaction-time. The subject is very musical, but has always regretted that she could not sing, a deficiency which has occasioned her more pain than, for instance, her inability to swim.

| | | | |
|---|---|---|---|
| 32. Pity | have | : 1 second | |
| 33. Yellow | gold | : 1 | ,, |
| 34. Mountain | ascend | : 1 | ,, |
| 35. Play | children | : 1 | ,, |
| 36. Salt | salty | : 1·4 | ,, |

---

This is the first reaction where this subject found an inhibition; the previous ones had followed quite "smoothly." She states that at first she did not apprehend the meaning of the word *salt* at all and had to imagine it to herself by an effort of will. Despite the long reaction-time and the stress of attention a very superficial reaction followed, one largely determined by clang. She cannot explain this disturbance. We notice the previous reaction, *children*, that obviously belongs to the pregnancy complex; its tone has perseverated and produced the disturbance.

| | | | |
|---|---|---|---|
| 37. New | old | : 1 | second |
| 38. Manners | customs | : 1 | ,, |
| 39. Ride | drive | : 1 | ,, |
| 40. Wall | -maps | : 1 | ,, |
| 41. Stupid | clever | : 1 | ,, |
| 42. Copy-book | slate | : 1 | ,, |
| 43. Despise | mépriser | : 1·8 | ,, |

Again a long reaction-time, and moreover, oddly enough, the reaction is in French. The reaction is very superficial and adds nothing new to the presentation content of the stimulus-word.

*Despise* is accompanied by an unpleasant emotional tone. Immediately after the reaction it came to her that she had had a passing fear that her pregnancy might in different ways decrease her attractiveness in the eyes of her husband. She immediately afterwards thought of a married couple who were at first happy and then separated—the married couple in Zola's novel "Vérité." Hence the French form of the reaction.

It is scarcely necessary to add that these reminiscences were not conscious at the moment of the reaction.

| | | | |
|---|---|---|---|
| 44. Right | time | : 1 | second |
| 45. Tooth | false | : 1 | ,, |
| 46. People | faithful | : 1·4 | ,, |

Again a longish time with a slightly unpleasant tone; thinks it could refer to a song called "Faithful People," but has the feeling of something personally unpleasant.

The previous reaction, which is without any perceptible emotional tone, runs *false*; *faithful* is the opposite. This observation suffices for the subject to find the correct explanation. The reaction *false* excited the pregnancy complex, more especially the fear of losing her husband's affection.

| | | | |
|---|---|---|---|
| 47. Smell | scent | : 1 | second |
| 48. Book | read | : 1 | ,, |
| 49. Unjust | just | : 0·8 | ,, |
| 50. Frog | -leg | : 1·2 | ,, |
| 51. Separate | avoid | : 0·8 | ,, |
| 52. Hunger | thirst | : 0·8 | ,, |
| 53. White | black | : 1 | ,, |
| 54. Ring | finger | : 1 | ,, |
| 55. Take care | listen | : 1 | ,, |
| 56. Fir-tree | woods | : 1 | ,, |
| 57. Gloomy | jolly | : 1 | ,, |
| 58. Plum | pear | : 1 | ,, |
| 59. Meet | certain | : 1 | ,, |
| 60. Law | follow | : 1·2 | ,, |
| 61. Dear | husband | : 1·2 | ,, |
| 62. Glass | glad | : 1 | ,, |

The strong clang-like determination of the last reaction is probably likewise conditioned to some extent by the previous reaction.

| | | | |
|---|---|---|---|
| 63. Dispute | quarrel | : 1·2 second |
| 64. Goat | bleat | : 1·2 | ,, |
| 65. Big | little | : 0·8 | ,, |
| 66. Potato | field | : 1 | ,, |
| 67. Paint | painter | : 1 | ,, |
| 68. Part | piece | : 1 | ,, |
| 69. Old | young | : 1 | ,, |
| 70. Blossom | red | : 0·6 | ,, |

She explains this short reaction-time by saying that the first syllable of the stimulus-word *blo-ssom* brought up the presentation *blood*; cp. reactions 4 and 143. Here we have a kind of assimilation of the stimulus-word to the strongly accentuated pregnancy complex.

| | | | |
|---|---|---|---|
| 71. Hit | prick | : 1 | second |
| 72. Box | -bed | : 1 | ,, |
| 73. Bright | brighter | : 1·4 | ,, |
| 74. Family | father | : 1·4 | ,, |

These four reactions are of interest. It will be remembered that in the association *prick — cut* (R. 4) the pregnancy complex was first encountered. Without the subject's having had the slightest feeling of the significance of the reaction, the association *prick* is consequent on *blood* brought up by the word *blo-ssom*. Reaction 72, which followed, went quite smoothly without any tinge of emotion. But the reaction is curious. The subject has now and then paid a visit to our asylum and was alluding to the deep beds used there, the so-called " box-beds." But the explanation rather surprised her, for the term " box-bed " was not very familiar to her. This rather peculiar association was followed by a clang-association (73) with a relatively long time, a phenomenon which we have already had occasion to regard as suspicious. *Bright* is the name of an in- dividual who had a certain, though somewhat remote, significance for her. In any case there are no strong emotional reminiscences linked with the name. The subjective feeling present was merely that of slight hesitancy. The supposition that the clang-reaction is connected with the previous curious reaction does not, therefore, seem quite baseless. The reaction *bed* is repeated later on, with a distinct feeling of word-making, at the stimulus-word *mild — bed* (R. 199), a meaningless connexion quite inexplicable to her ; but assuming a clang-altera- tion at the suppressed pregnancy complex, the association becomes the very sensible *child — bed*. Accepting this hypothesis, the above series becomes quite clear ; it is again the pregnancy complex with *blood, operation, child-bed*. The emotional tone becomes more accentuated and disturbs the following reaction (perhaps *bright* cannot be assimilated to the complex), and finally comes *father*.

| | | | |
|---|---|---|---|
| 75. Washer | washerwoman | : 1 | second |
| 76. Cow | stupid | : 0·8 | ,, |
| 77. Odd | -ness | : 1 | |
| 78. Happy | -ly | : 0·6 | ,, |
| 79. Tell | mother | : 1·4 | ,, |
| 80. Angle | bi-right | : 2 | seconds |

Reaction 78 is very short, which is rather curious in a stimulus-word which might so easily have aroused the complex. So the next reaction requires a much longer time, 1·4 second, and this has hitherto always been a complex symptom. The reaction *mother* explains the long time. Reaction 80 is disturbed, which is not surprising since the complex has been so distinctly encountered.  The reaction *right* takes 2 seconds, having been preceded by the uttering of the syllable *bi*.  To the subject herself the emotional tone of *mother* is still present.  She cannot find any connexion between *angle* and *bi*.  She cannot think at all what word she thought of beginning with *bi*.  We are thus altogether thrown back on conjecture.  In reaction 79 the pregnancy complex again occurs.  We have already seen several times that it is chiefly marked by anxious expectancy.  We have also seen that the first syllable of the stimulus-word can be assimilated to the complex (*blossom — blood*); the first clang-syllable of *angle* = *ang*, assimilated as *anxiety* and then *bi* = *birth* ?  This suggestion was accepted by her immediately.  The construction may appear to many as an interpretation by omens ; I should not report it were it not that I have had numerous analogous phenomena both in healthy people and patients.

|       |       |       |       |
|-------|-------|-------|-------|
| 81. Narrow | -hearted | : | 0·6 second |
| 82. Brother | sister | : | 0·8   ,, |
| 83. Injure (*schaden*) | avoid | : | 1·2   ,, |

This recalls *separate — avoid*.  Possibly *schaden* (injure) is repressed as being emotionally unpleasant in view of the complex and has been assimilated as *scheiden* (to separate).  Such repressed assimilations are frequent among hysterics. The subject is not able to confirm this explanation.

|       |       |       |       |
|-------|-------|-------|-------|
| 84. Stork | bring | : | 3·4 seconds |

The causation of this abnormally long time by the complex is clear.[1]

|       |       |       |       |
|-------|-------|-------|-------|
| 85. False | cat | : | 1   second |
| 86. Anxiety | have | : | 1   ,, |
| 87. Kiss | me | : | 1·2   ,, |

The marked emphasis on the personal ego in reaction 87 is perhaps also determined by the critical reaction 86.

|       |       |       |       |
|-------|-------|-------|-------|
| 88. Burning | fire | : | 1·2 second |
| 89. Dirty | yellow | : | 1   ,, |
| 90. Door | shut | : | 0·8   ,, |
| 91. Choose | choice | : | 1·2   ,, |
| 92. Hay | grass | : | 1   ,, |
| 93. Quiet | peaceful | : | 0·8   ,, |
| 94. Scorn | ridicule | : | 1   ,, |
| 95. Sleep | wake | : | 1   ,, |
| 96. Month | May | : | 1   ,, |
| 97. Shade | blue | : | 1·2   ,, |
| 98. Dog | cat | : | 1   ,, |
| 99. Talk | speak | : | 1   ,, |
| 100. Coal | dust | : | 1   ,, |
| 101. Moderate | drink | : | 1   ,, |
| 102. Lid | eye | : | 1   ,, |
| 103. Suppose | believe | : | 1·2   ,, |
| 104. Smart | heart | : | 0·8   ,, |

She states that this rhyme, which has a relatively short time, was dragged in by her.

|       |       |       |       |
|-------|-------|-------|-------|
| 105. Lazy | idle | : | 1 second |
| 106. Moon | calf | : | 1   ,, |
| 107. Laugh | cry | : | 1   ,, |

[1] The popular explanation given to children in Switzerland (as in Germany) is that new babies are brought by storks.—TRANSLATOR.

| 108. Coffee | drink | : 1 second |
|---|---|---|
| 109. Broad | narrow | : 1 ,, |
| 110. Air | thick | : 1 ,, |
| 111. Carry | lift | : 1 ,, |
| 112. Plate | round | : 0·8 ,, |

Reaction 110 is rather curious; it looks as if the constellation *broad — narrow* had acted particularly strongly. Is it possibly still acting at reaction 112 ?

The succeeding reactions were entirely objective; neither the subject nor the observer found anything noticeable about them. We can therefore omit them.

| 143. Blood | red | : 0·6 second |
|---|---|---|
| 144. Award | award | : 1·2 ,, |
| | -avoid | : 2 seconds |
| 145. Foresight | forbear | : 1 second |

Reaction 143 followed with great promptness. It is the same reaction that occurred at *blossom* (70). It is followed by a longer time and the repetition of the stimulus-word—the only case in the whole experiment. Reaction 145 is likewise very superficial, not even making sense but simply linked by a motor-clang association.

The succeeding reactions I omit as unimportant.

| 162. Rank | noble | : 1·2 second |
|---|---|---|
| 163. Slide | sly | : 0·8 ,, |

The subject states that the emotional tone of *rank* was still there at the moment of the subsequent reaction. The lady was formerly in better financial circumstances and occasionally feels the change.

| 172. Turn | round | : 1·4 second |
|---|---|---|

The cause of the longer reaction-time is here obscure, unless *round* has the emotional tone suspected above. She can give no explanation.

| 175. Confidence | me | : 1·4 second |
|---|---|---|

Here again we have the fear bound up with the complex of the husband's estrangement.

| 190. Bring | something : 1·2 second |
|---|---|
| 191. Hotel | Stork |
| | (hotel) : 1 ,, |

What *something* means is seen by the reaction that followed.

| 195. Mirror | glitter | : 1·4 second |
|---|---|---|
| 198. Punish | prison | : 1·4 ,, |

The two long reaction-times cannot be satisfactorily explained. The subject states that at 195 at first the presentation of *glaze* rose up, but it became changed to *glitter*. It is difficult to say why *glaze* was repressed.

At 198 she could only say that she felt a slight hesitancy. Even though we cannot discover anything plausible, we may be sure from previous experience that some kind of emotionally toned complex is at the back of it. As a later instance will show, it need not be anything current but can be a reminiscence of something apparently long done with.

| 199. Mild | bed | : 1 second |
|---|---|---|

Cp. what was said about this reaction at reaction 72. Particularly interesting in this case was the complete absence of any suspicion in the subject herself as to the significance of this reaction.

Others are:

| | | | |
|---|---|---|---|
| 164. Love | faithful | : 1 | second |
| 167. Change | false | : 1 | ,, |
| 181. Duty | faithful | : 0·8 | ,, |
| 187. Serpent | false | : 0·8 | ,, |

In reaction 45, *false — tooth* 1 second, *faithful* 1·4 seconds. These words, for which she has obviously a predilection, seem to occur with gradually abbreviated reaction-time.[1] It is also interesting that words of this kind referring to the complex seem to have a tendency to become stereotyped in places where they do not quite make sense; it is not the case here, it is true, but we have demonstrated it in one case in an earlier investigation.

The analysis of the reactions of this subject has shown that the times exceeding 1·2 seconds, with the exception of the few reactions referred to, may be traced in two ways to the influence of an emotionally toned complex.

(1) The association has too long a reaction-time when the complex is aroused.

(2) The association directly following the one arousing the complex has a prolonged reaction-time in consequence of the maintenance of the emotional tone.

Besides the associations with prolonged reaction-time, numerous others contained complex constellations. On the whole, reactions with strong emotional tone and distinct reference to the complex have longer reaction-times. Her awareness of the significance of an association was only constant in the following respect : a very strong and differentiated emotional tone or a very marked style of the reaction alone awakened the consciousness of the complex. In the above reactions this was only once the case : in *stork — bring*. In all the other reactions the emotional tone or peculiar style of the reaction merely formed the indications for the subsequent recognition of the complex. At the moment itself there was only present to consciousness that portion more or less represented in the reaction. Here is evidence of how slight is the importance of the conscious for the activity of association.

Our whole thinking and doing, which seem to us so overwhelmingly conscious, are in reality composed of these small fragments which are determined to the minutest degree by the innumerable factors lying quite outside the conscious. To our conscious self the association process appears to be our own work, subordinate to our valuations, our free will, and our attention ; but in reality, as our experiment shows beautifully, the conscious self is merely the marionette dancing upon the stage to a hidden automatic impulse.[2]

---

[1] In cases of this kind a more exact measurement of the time would be desirable.

[2] Those, therefore, who maintain the mind = consciousness really take a part for the whole.

The analytic consideration of this experimental series shows the effect of a complex upon the association activity. Although, we are wont to say, the association is subject to a free valuation and the subject can say what he will, he really does not say what he will, but must disclose that which he believes is most secret. The reactions are not in any way free associations, but merely symptomatic acts (Freud) [1] conditioned by a psychical factor which behaves as an independent entity. The emotionally toned complex, momentarily separated from consciousness, is an activity constantly in successful rivalry with the intentions of the ego complex. Despite the distracting and repressing adaptation of the ego complex, this complex brings forth subjective reactions and associations of whose significance the ego complex has no suspicion. In our subject we find a series of intimate secrets given away by the associations ; not merely those of the moment, but all the presentation complexes of most import to the individual, all those which make up the content of her personality in joy and in sorrow. We find her strongest actual complex to be bound up with thoughts about her pregnancy, her rather anxious expectancy, and love for her husband with jealous fears. This is a complex of an erotic kind which has just become acute ; that is why it is so much to the front. No less than 18 per cent. of the associations can certainly be referred to it.[2] In addition there are a few other complexes of considerably less intensity : loss of her former position, a few deficiencies which she regards as unpleasant (*singing, swimming, cooking*), and finally an erotic complex which occurred many years back in her youth and which only shows itself in one association. (Out of regard for the subject of the experiment I must, unfortunately, omit a report on this.) The probable mean of this person amounts to 1 second, 30·5 per cent. of the times exceed this mean. 20·5 per cent. of the times have 1·2 second ; of these 32 per cent. can be definitely referred to the influence of complexes. Six per cent. of the times are 1·4 second, 75 per cent. of these being certainly determined by the complex. Three per cent. exceed 1·4 second, all of which are certainly due to the effect of a complex.

Subject No. 2 is a cultured gentleman of middle age. The reaction type is like that of No. 1, objective and superficial. I shall therefore confine myself to the critical reactions. He is a physician and often takes part in our experiments, which he follows with interest.

The probable mean of the series is 1·2 second.

---

[1] Cp. Freud, *The Psychopathology of Everyday Life.*

[2] Whilst only 4 per cent. can with certainty be referred to other complexes.

| 1. Head | part | : 1·21 second |
| 2. Green | blue | : 1   ,, |
| 3. Water | to clean | : 2·6 seconds |

The stimulus-word immediately aroused an unpleasant emotional tone recalling something sexual, with an accompanying feeling of inhibition. Directly after the reaction he clearly recognized that water had been apprehended in the sense of urine.

| 4. Prick | hit | : 1   second |
| 5. Angel | pure | : 1   ,, |
| 6. Long | big | : 1·2   ,, |
| 7. Ship | big | : 1   ,, |

Here there is a distinct perseveration. At *big* in reaction 6 there first occurred a distinctly sexual feeling, then followed the second reaction, and immediately afterwards there was clear knowledge of its cause. It is a reminiscence. He had heard from us that certain female patients frequently associate sexual suggestions to *long*.

| 8. Plough | plough up | : 1   second |
| 9. Wool | sheep | : 1·2   ,, |
| 10. Friendly | bude bud | : 1·2   ,, |
| 11. Table | gable | : 0·8   ,, |

Reaction 10 is clearly disturbed. A slip of the tongue occurred which the subject at once corrects to *bud*. A mildly unpleasant feeling of uneasiness is experienced which continues during the next reaction. Hence the aimless rhyme. *Friendly — bud* is curious; he cannot explain it. The slip of the tongue seems to him as if it should really have been *bad*. But this reaction would be equally unintelligible to him. (For the probable explanation see below, reaction 86.)

| 15. Stalk | long | : 1·2 second |
| 16. Dance | lance | : 1·8   ,, |
| 17. Lake | big | : 1·2   ,, |

In reaction 15 the sexual tone of *long* recurs and almost simultaneously the reminiscence already referred to. Reaction 16 is a clang-association with an abnormally long time. The sexual tone of reaction 15 kept up, mixed with vexation, and led again up to the former association, *long — big*.

| 18. Ill | poor | : 1·2 second |
| 19. Pride | dried | : 1·6   ,, |

*Poor* is accompanied by a slightly unpleasant tone of feeling, but there is no definite presentation. *Pride* is still more unpleasant, with a feeling of distraction and inhibition. The meaningless rhyme and the long time are doubly determined. He has an unpleasant money affair which has worried him for some time. He was frequently reproached, more especially formerly, with pride. This reproach affords a painful contrast with the money affair. The clear presentation of this connexion did not, of course, occur until after the reaction.

| 20. Cook | good | : 1   second |
| 22. Ink | come | : 1·4   ,, |

The association runs *come in the ink* and has a mixed unpleasant tinge referred by him to the money affair, but there immediately arises the reminiscence of an erotic complex, with strongly unpleasant tone, dating back several years.

| 24. Swim | good | : 1·2 second |
| 25. Travel | jolly | : 1·6   ,, |

Numerous indistinct reminiscences of travel of a predominantly pleasant tone.

26. Blue     lake     : 1·2 second
27. Bread     daily     : 2   seconds

*Bread* arouses a slightly unpleasant feeling; something like that at *poor* obtrudes itself with a feeling of inhibition. Afterwards a clear bearing upon the money affair.

28. Threaten     bad     : 1·2 second

Very unpleasant tone, subsequent recollection of the erotic complex which is bound up with feelings of guilt.

29. Lamp     shade     : 1·2 second
30. Rich     poor     : 1·4   „

*Poor* has again a painful tinge and again arouses subsequently the reminiscence of the money affair.

31. Root     shoot     : 1·2 second
32. Sing     jump     : 1·8   „

*Root* again arouses the sexual tone like *long* and for the same reason, then annoyance; the rhyme and long reaction-time are referable to this.

33. Pity     the poor     : 1·42 second
34. Goal     much     : 1·2   „

*The poor* again arouses the money complex, this time with distinct and adequate emotional tone. Goal is assimilated as gold, although the stimulus-word is correctly apprehended. The money complex overcomes the ego complex with its telltale *much*.

36. Play     ball     : 1·2 second
37. Salt     fault     : 1·4   „

The association *play — ball*, which is in itself quite innocent, at once took on an erotic emotional tone, the word *ball* changing its meaning to *evening dance*. The erotic complex again made its appearance; hence the rhyme with the long reaction-time in the following association. I need scarcely add that at the moment of the reaction the chain of thought here exposed did not exist in consciousness, but was only represented by passing feelings. The presentations belonging to these feelings arise as a rule only afterwards, when the attention is especially directed to the emotional tone.

38. New     old     : 1·2 second

The *o* in old was spoken with a curious drawling, as if *oo = (p)oor* were coming; but *old* came out. The money complex has lately reached a more acute stage.

39. Habit     bad habit : 1·8 second

Feeling of hesitation; in *bad habit* there is a slight shade of a feeling of guilt. The erotic complex again.

40. Ride     drive     : 1·4 second
41. Wall     place     : 1·8   „
42. Stupid     clumsy     : 2   seconds

No. 41 is quite inexplicable to the subject; a feeling as if it should be *no place in the sun*. In reaction 42 a very painful tone leads at once to the money complex, with the distinct knowledge that *drive* is determined by the complex, although the feeling tone peculiar to the complex did not distinctly arise till reaction 42. The reaction *place* thus belongs much more to the money complex than to *wall*. Reaction 42 has also something of the erotic complex attached to it.

43. Copy-book    book    : 1·4 second
44. Disesteem    esteem  : 1·4  „
45. Paint        money   : 1·4  „

*Esteem* seems to have hit the money complex very hard, for *paint* was assimilated as *pay*—hence *money*. The money complex here again overcame the ego complex.

46. Right    wrong   : 1·2 second
47. People   poor    : 1·8  „

Again the money complex with a long time.

60. Meet    defence  : 1·2 second
61. Law     lord     : 4·8 seconds

At reaction 61 an inexplicable feeling of inhibition, which for a long time would not permit any reaction to take place, then a very disturbed meaningless reaction accompanied by something like disgust. Afterwards a whole series of painful reminiscences about actions which did not correspond with the *laws of morality*, among these the erotic complex.

The following reaction:

62. Dear    good    : 2 seconds

is also entirely under the influence of these memories, of all his past iniquities.

69. Part    part of the
            body    : 1·8 second

We have again the sexual constellation of reactions 6 and 15.

76. Wash    filth   : 1·6 second

Slight feeling of guilt and repentance; afterwards erotic complex. As regards the blunt expression cp. reaction 90.

78. Strange    new hand : 2 seconds

At first a feeling as if *poor* should come, then a reaction which is determined by reaction 38—*new — old*. Naturally the reaction occurs without the slightest consciousness of this constellation. *Strange* again struck the money complex.

79. Luck    ill luck    1·4 second

Constellated by the previous reaction.

80. Tell       mother    1·2 second
81. Propriety  improper : 3·6 seconds
82. Narrow     narrow-
               hearted : 1·8 second

Reaction 80 occurred without any special emotional tone; but at *propriety* an immediate inhibition, with unpleasant feeling, which distinctly persisted during the next reaction; afterwards immediate recollection of various scenes of childhood which are distinctly constellated by *mother*. Instances are impressed upon him when his mother was really angry, and said that the boy behaved improperly and would always do so. One scene is very distinct, when as a hobbledehoy he behaved improperly and was rude to a lady. This reminiscence at once led back to the erotic complex, where a somewhat similar reproach must be made to himself. This is certainly the complex which is concealed behind this long reaction-time, and various *cover memories* (Freud).

86. False    bad    : 1·4 second

Here the reaction *bad* returns for the third time. (In the experimental series it recurred six times and *good* five times.) *Bad* carries the feeling of guilt with it proper to the erotic complex. It will be seen that this word, together with *good*, has a similar tendency to arise, as has *poor* for the money complex. (*Poor* occurs four times as a manifest reaction, and three times as a repressed one.) *Bad* occurred for the first time in reaction 10, but was obviously repressed there, since in his present emotional life there are strong inhibitions against the emotional complex.

89. Brand      poultice    : 1·8 second

The stimulus-word was correctly apprehended, but was at once changed into *bran*, to which *poultice* was associated with a rather long time. Thus *brand* was assimilated. The previous association contained no constellation for this assimilation. *Brand* has, however, an unpleasant tone and is forthwith associated with the idea of acute alcoholism, and therewith a reminiscence of that state on one occasion, which is accompanied by very painful feelings. This time the ego complex got the lead of the old, but still watchful reminiscence, and assimilated the stimulus-word in a most appropriate sense. The painful memory was thus disguised or concealed from himself. This mechanism (censure in Freud's sense) [1] plays a very prominent part in hysteria. It is not a case of a function of the conscious which must find expression, but of an automatic regulation thereof, which may or may not come into consciousness.

90. Dirty      filthy    : 1·4 second

The blunt style of this reaction is determined by moral repugnance, which is bound up with the erotic complex.

91. Door      to show    : 1·4 second

This reaction with its uninviting, repellant manner is determined by the same feeling.

92. Choose      mayor    : 2·2 seconds

Here a new complex is met. It is the hope of advancement, of a *mair* (more) from different points of view. It is at the same time the hope of a leading position, not of a subordinate one. The determination of *mayor* is therefore not merely a pure clang, but it is something conceivable—in a symbolic form, however. The correct reaction would be *superintendent*. But this word is associated with the secret wish, and therefore the inhibition which represses the whole desire extends to this word. Instead of the correct reaction we obtain a presentation associated with it which is externally determined by the word *mair* (more), this being again characteristic of the mood of the moment.

This process is very similar to the hysterical talking at random in the Ganser complex, [2] or perhaps even more with the associating at random of dementia præcox, where metaphors of this kind are especially employed. Similar phenomena are found relatively frequently in everyday life ; I mean in melody and word automatisms. A lady gave me the following delightful instance : she told me that for some days the word *dagon* was constantly on her lips, although she had no idea whence it came. I asked her for any recent affect towards events or suppressed wishes. After some delay and hesitation she told me that she had very much wanted a " morning-gown " but her husband had not seen his way to it. *Dagon = day-gon = day-gown = morning-gown* shows the partial relationship of sense and clang. The determination of the form *dagon* arose from the fact that about the same time she was reading about Dagon. [3] Similar combinations can be demonstrated in great number if the trouble is taken to

---

[1] Freud, *Interpretation of Dreams*.

[2] Riklin, " Zur Psychologie hysterischer Dämmerzustände und des Ganser-schen Symptoms," *Psych.-neur. Wochenschr.*, 1904, No. 22.

[3] For a similar word automatism see chapter ii, p. 153.

go into the tunes one is humming oneself or that are being hummed by others. A colleague who on his round caught a glimpse of a nurse who was said to be pregnant presently caught himself softly humming, " Es waren zwei Königskinder, die hatten einander so lieb," etc. (" Fondly two royal children loved "). At the same time he was consciously occupied with a quite other matter. Another colleague betrayed to me through his automatic humming the ending of an unhappy love complex.

These instances give us some insight in what direction trains of thought move when conscious attention is absent. Every association occurring in consciousness arouses to a certain extent an echo of similarities and analogies which runs through all stages, from similarity of meaning through similarity of form to merest similarity of clang. The most beautiful instances of this are furnished by dreams.

| | | |
|---|---|---|
| 95. Ridicule | derision | : 1·4 second |
| 96. Dead | dog | : 1·6 „ |

This association surprised the subject. He does not understand how he came to this unusual association. The somewhat prolonged time leads one to suspect an emotional tone which he first acknowledges as vague and then as painful. At the catchword " painful " a distinct recollection returns; it is now more than twenty years ago. He was obliged to shoot a favourite dog and the loss was " painful " to him for a long time.

102. Moderate    immoderate : 1·6 second

The somewhat longer time in this superficial reaction is explained by its relation to 89 (brand).

104. Suppose    believe    : 2 seconds

Suppose is an insidious word and there are very few persons who do not find themselves caught by it. The erotic complex was encountered here.

| | | |
|---|---|---|
| 105. Pain | derision | : 1·2 second |
| 108. Laugh | prate | : 2·8 seconds |

The p of prate was drawled out. At first, just for an instant, pain distinctly came up; hence the long time. But pain was involuntarily at once suppressed. The emotional tone has something amounting almost to nausea; he agrees that he has an almost morbid sensitiveness to ridicule. Reaction 95, ridicule — derision, 105, pain — derision, 108, laugh — pain (prate), are now seen to be intimately connected. The determination of prate is on one side an alliteration, on the other a significant relationship, " prating about people."

120. Create    work    : 2 seconds

The professional complex is the cause of the prolongation of the reaction.

127. Hart    deer    : 2 seconds

The first feeling was as if the association was hard — poor, and the word poor was almost uttered. Another assimilation to the money complex. The next reaction:

128. Waken    awaken    : 1·6 second

is on this account very superficial, with a relatively long time.

| | | |
|---|---|---|
| 130. Wicked | bad | : 0·8 second |
| 131. Portfolio | hold | : 0·8 „ |

Portfolio had the sense of pocket-case, where he used to hold his money. The reaction hold is quite meaningless and at first surprised the subject, who

REACTION-TIME IN ASSOCIATION EXPERIMENTS 253

then recalled the meaning he had given to *portfolio*. Another reference to the money complex.

| | | | |
|---|---|---|---|
| 148. Forget | -fulness | : 2 | seconds |
| 149. Drum | beat | : 1·2 | second |
| 150. Free | -dom | : 1·2 | ,, |
| 151. Wagon | -burg | : 3 | seconds |

Reaction 148 has a very unpleasant tone; nothing special was noticed at 149 and 150; there is a marked and inexplicable inhibition at 151.

*Forget* arouses an event of many years back—a breach with an unfaithful friend. Reaction 149 is " The Trusty Comrade " :

" The drums beat up to action
And he was by my side," etc.

Reaction 150 refers to the breach. Reaction 151, *wagon*, seems to have been only assimilated with great difficulty ; its completion, *burg*, is curious. It becomes clear when the subject explains that it was at Augsburg that his friend's falseness was first recognized. All these data were unconscious at the moment of the reaction. The complex was represented at reaction 148 only by an unpleasant feeling, which could not at first be more closely defined. The connexion between the reactions in this series was only recognized subsequently.

| | | | |
|---|---|---|---|
| 153. Impudence | accursed | : 2 | seconds |
| 154. Rapid | -ity | : 0·6 second | |

Reaction 153 belongs to the mood of the above reactions (the analysis was only taken up after the completion of the experiment). It is anger at the impudence of his false friend. The strong emotional tone seems to have extended even to reaction 154.

| | | | |
|---|---|---|---|
| 167. Change | of time | : 1·8 second | |

The stimulus-word again hit the money complex, hence the long time.

| | | | |
|---|---|---|---|
| 184. Deaf | neat | : 2·6 seconds | |

He assimilated *deaf* as *deft*, although he understood the stimulus-word. (He knows the list well and has even used it himself a few times in experiments.) The reaction-time is very long. *Deaf* causes a slight anxiety complex. He has several times had catarrh of his Eustachian tube, leaving the hearing in one ear slightly deficient. He has an exaggerated fear of becoming entirely deaf. *Deaf* has too unpleasant a tone and is therefore quickly suppressed.

| | | | |
|---|---|---|---|
| 190. Bring | money | : 1·2 second | |
| 191. Wording | fetch | : 2·2 seconds | |

The last reaction is meaningless, but it is explained by the money complex aroused by *bring*.

| | | | |
|---|---|---|---|
| 195. Mirror | mind | : 1·8 second | |
| 196. Full | filth | : 1·4 | ,, |
| 197. Reason | good | : 1·6 | ,, |
| 198. Punish | for evil | : 2·2 seconds | |
| 200. Beautiful | good | : 1·6 second | |

Reaction 195 is somewhat inhibited for an unknown reason. Perhaps the *mirror of the mind* had something of the ethical tone of the subsequent reactions. In *full* this is, of course, self-evident: *the mind is full of* . . . The strong expression expresses the disgust already demonstrated (reaction 90). The following *good* is loosely connected with the stimulus-word and is repeated at the earliest opportunity (200). It likewise refers to the erotic complex.

Reaction 198 is obviously constellated by the complex.

In contrast with the previous subject, there is here a whole series of emotionally toned complexes which have little or no connexion with each other. Whilst in the female subject No. 1 the sexual complex (pregnancy) with its offshoots (anxiety, jealousy) dominates the scene, in the male subject No. 2 the sexual complexes play a less important part. Out of personal consideration for the latter I cannot review the whole of the reactions. But it is easy to demonstrate :

(1) Sexual complexes.

An erotic complex belonging to the past and now closed, which expresses itself almost exclusively in ethical emotional constellations (disgust, repentance).

An erotic complex of the moment which is expressed merely by erotic emotional constellations (not reviewed).

There are at least three sexually toned presentations independent of each other.

(2) Money complex.

(3) Ambition, with at least four secondary memory complexes.

(4) Personal sensitiveness with at least three secondary memory complexes.

(5) Friendship.

(6) Two emotional-tinged reminiscences independent of one another (*dead dog, deafness*).

We thus have something like ten complexes which are, so to say, independent of one another. Subject No. 2 is a few years older than No. 1 ; in the latter 18 per cent. of the associations refer to the sexual complex, whilst only 4 per cent. occur with other emotionally toned constellations. In No. 2, on the other hand, 53 per cent. of the associations can be referred to the influence of a complex. This greater number of complex constellations does not merely mean that the analysis was driven further, or that No. 2 gave us better information than No. 1, but it can be objectively recognized that the emotion of No. 2 (at least at the time of the experiment) was greater. This is recognized by the frequent disturbed reactions, and by the curious assimilations and repressions.[1]

Of the 53 per cent. complex constellations 10 per cent. only are really sexual, i.e. refer to an erotic complex of the moment ; 11·5 per cent. refer to the money complex, 2·5 per cent. to ambition, 4·5 per cent. to personal sensitiveness, 3 per cent. to the breach of friendship, 9 per cent. to an erotic complex now closed and constellated by feelings of disgust and repentance ; 12·5 per cent. relate to about six small more or less separated complexes with emotional tones. The really sexual

---

[1] Cp. also "complex signs" in chapter ii.

complex falls into the background as compared with many of the other constellations (10 : 43).

This case shows us even better than the first how much of the individual element is contained in the associations. The experiment furnishes us with information of great importance about his mental content ; to a certain extent it gives us a cross-section of the present psychological personality.

No. 3 is a younger man of education. I limit myself entirely to the critical associations, and review the case chiefly to point out that we find here, in principle, the same thing as was found in the two previous cases. The probable mean of the subject is 1·6 second.

| | | | |
|---|---|---|---|
| 1. Head | neck | : 1·2 second | |
| 2. Green | mouse | : 0·8 | ,, |
| 3. Water | green | : 1 | ,, |

This series strikes one by the peculiar reaction *mouse*, and the perseveration of *green*. *Neck* is a reminiscence of the day before the experiment; he had seen a cinematograph scene of the death of Marie Antoinette.

He is not certain whence came *mouse*; he has rather the feeling that it was a slip of the tongue—supposes it was *house*.

| | | | |
|---|---|---|---|
| 4. Prick | fight | : 1·2 second | |
| 5. Angel | house | : 1·6 | ,, |

Here the conjectured reaction to No. 2—*house*—returns with a long reaction-time and the recollection comes up also. His grandfather was often in the habit of singing " Through all the lands an angel goes," etc ; but with equal frequency he used to sing " My house in the green field stands." Linked with these songs are a series of emotionally toned images, which are only partly pleasant. The perseveration *green* and the slip of the tongue—*mouse* for *house*— now become clear.

| | | |
|---|---|---|
| 13. State | church | : 1·8 second |

The reaction took place with hesitancy, for *church* stands for the great complex of a strong religiosity.

| | | |
|---|---|---|
| 16. Dance | not | : 1·8 second |

The reaction really is *I cannot dance*, with which is connected a very disagreeable feeling, for he has experienced a rebuff in love which a friend, who can dance well, has been spared.

| | | |
|---|---|---|
| 18. Ill | not | : 1·6 second |

This stimulus-word he again ascribes to himself ; in spite of the unfortunate result of the affair, he was yet not entirely without hope.

| | | | |
|---|---|---|---|
| 22. Wicked | friendly | : 1·8 second | |
| 23. Needle | need | : 1·2 | ,, |

*Wicked* arouses the feeling of jealous animosity which he manifests towards a certain rival. The clang-association following is conditioned by perseveration of the emotional tone.

| | | |
|---|---|---|
| 30. Rich | fairly | : 2·8 seconds |
| 31. Tree | gnarled | : 1·6 second |

Reaction 30 belongs to the lost fiancée, hence the long reaction-time. The subsequent reaction is also somewhat long and has a rather affected and remote character; the tone seemed somewhat ironical, and this holds true also in the following reactions:

32. Sing        amiable    : 1·4 second
33. Pity        absolutely
                none       : 1·8  „

By which is meant that he really deserves no pity, for every one is master of his destiny.

44. Despise     fellows    : 5   seconds
47. People      religion   : 1·6 second
48. Smell       disgusting : 1   „
50. Unjust      abominable : 1·8 „

In reaction 44 by *fellows* are meant the Jews. The lady in question is a Jewess. *People* again arouses the presentation " Jews," but it is repressed. *Religion* takes its place because to the religiously disposed subject the religion of his sweetheart caused scruples. The subsequent predicates, strongly tinged with emotion, really refer to the complex and not to the stimulus-words that aroused them (as with No. 2, where the coarse form of the reaction likewise betrayed the affect).

54. White       snow       : 1·8 second

A feeling of " finished " or " death "; refers to the love complex.

61. Law         absolute   : 1·4 second

This is again the reaction 33 and expresses the same feeling: so the law says it, it must be so.

62. Dear        beautiful  : 1·2 second
66. Big         fine       : 1·2  „

Both reactions have an ironical tone and refer to the complex.

74. Wild        animal     : 1·8 second

*Wild* (which in dialect = *wicked*) the subject attributes to himself on account of the complex.

75. Family      house      : 1 second

The word *house* seems to be the representation of the complex of all family recollections (also *to cook — house*). It occurs here with a relatively short time.

79. Fortune     play       : 1·8 second

distinctly refers to the love complex.

80. Relate      talk       : 1·6 second

The reaction was given in English. We have already learned to view French reactions with suspicion; the reaction in English also refers to the complex. He at first wanted to relate the story of his disappointment to a brother who was living in America, but afterwards altered his intention. The English form is determined by this.

83. Brother     sister
                (in English): 2 seconds

Another reaction in English with a long reaction-time. *Brother* probably aroused again unconsciously the presentation of the former reaction. *Sister* comes because the sister of the subject was then about to go to a French boarding-school, just as the brother had shortly before gone to America. This analogy was condensed in the *sister*.

88. Kiss   absolutely : 1·6 second

Absolutely is a word standing for the love complex.

91. Door   mouse  : 1·6 second

The slip of the tongue to reaction 2 occurs again, probably to mask the complex *house*.

92. Choose  Kaposi

The word *caprice* was really the word that emerged for a moment, but was immediately inhibited and changed into *Kaposi*. The choice of the lady in question was a *caprice*. *Kaposi* is only a clang-similarity and constellated by a conversation which took place the day before, when *Kaposi* was mentioned.

105. Pain   kiss   : 1 second
106. Lazy   sow    : 1·4 ,,

The coarse expression of the last reaction rests upon the feeling of anger which perseverates from reaction 105.

115. Resolute  kiss   : 1·8 second

*Resolute* was assimilated as "absolute," the representative of the complex, and the reaction was in accordance with this meaning.

125. Purpose  absolutely
        none   : 1·2 second
126. Hit     yes    : 2·2 seconds
134. Worthy   purblind : 1 second
135. Danger   liking   : 1·4 ,,
136. High    no, low  : 2·8 seconds
140. Mix     blood   : 2  ,,
143. Blood    mix    : 1·4 second

These constellations are all more or less constellated by the love complex; the constellating factor was, of course, not a clear image at all but merely a kind of indefinable mood.

144. To let   family  : 1·6 second

For a moment *house* came up, but it was repressed and replaced by the rather curious *family*. This is association 75 suddenly taken up again to mask the word *house*, which stands for the complex.

145. Retribute resolute : 2 seconds

Again *absolute* at first forced its way up, but was inhibited and masked by *resolute*, by a clang-association in which perhaps reaction 115 had some effect also.

160. Wish   absolutely
       none   : 1·8 second

I will not accumulate further instances ; they do not show anything new in principle but merely confirm what has been already demonstrated in the previous subjects.

The love complex was well to the front in this case ; 52 per cent. of the associations certainly refer to it. The family complex can be demonstrated in 11 per cent. of the associations. Then there occurs, here and there, a complex of ambitious endeavour, provable in 7 per cent. Numerous single emotional reminiscences can be shown in 27 per cent. of the associations. The general probable mean of this case is 1·6 second : 31 per cent.

of the reaction-times exceed this mean; 17 per cent. amount to 1·8 second; of these 85 per cent. are constellated by the complex, whilst in 15 per cent. this influence is doubtful or not proven. 4·5 per cent. of the associations take 2 seconds; 89 per cent. of these can be referred certainly to the complex, whilst in 11 per cent. the influence is uncertain. Nine per cent. of the associations take over two seconds; they are all referable to the complex influence.

There is no object in multiplying instances, for it would be only a constant repetition. So far as my experience goes the complex phenomena are the same in all subjects. Naturally the nature of the complex varies with sex and education.[1]

The perseveration of the emotional tone deserves attention. Perseveration plays, as we know, a peculiarly large share in the pathology of the association process. Perhaps the investigations on normals have helped to elucidate the essential problem of morbid perseveration. In these experiments, the perseveration of the emotional tone occurred so often that it can be expressed to some extent statistically. For instance, No. 2 shows thirty-two reaction-times over 1·6 second, of which sixteen are likewise followed by prolonged reaction-times. The reaction-time following is prolonged on ten occasions, the two next reactions thrice, and once the third, fourth, and fifth reactions following. As this summary shows, a *quasi* step-ladder increase of the reaction-times is not infrequently observed. In certain cases of hysteria and dementia præcox I have seen the same increase, but much more distinctly, of the step-ladder pattern, and this usually in places where a complex was suspected.

To recapitulate :

(1) These figures demonstrate that almost without exception very long reaction-times are caused by the interpolation of a strong emotional tone.

---

[1] The concept *repression*, which I have so frequently used in my analyses, requires a brief exposition. With Freud the concept (as, moreover, the word suggests) has the character of an active doing, frequently indeed that of a function of the conscious. In hysteria there is certainly the impression that *repression* = willed forgetting. But when it comes to normal persons a more passive transference to the background is found; to say the least the repression here is something unconscious to which the idea of willed, or rather of *desired*, can only be indirectly attributed. If I still speak of " repressing " or " concealing," this use of the word may be regarded, if preferred, as a metaphor from the psychology of the conscious. Materially it is all the same, for objectively it is perfectly indifferent whether a mental process is conscious or unconscious. (Cp. Bleuler, " Versuch einer naturwissenschaftlichen Betrachtung der psychologischen Grundbegriffe," *Allgemeine Zeitschrift für Psychiatrie*, Bd. L.)

(2) Strong emotional tones belong, as a rule, to extensive and personally important presentation complexes.

(3) The reaction can belong to a complex of this kind and bear the emotional tone of the complex without the complex necessarily being present in consciousness. The constellation (Ziehen) of an association is mostly unconscious (or " not conscious ") ; the constellating complex then plays the part of a quasi-independent entity, of a " second personality."

(4) The emotional tone can also, unconsciously, influence the succeeding reactions, when diverse phenomena may be observed:

*a.* The reaction under the influence of the perseverating emotional tone has too long a reaction-time.

*b.* The reaction is an association which still belongs to the sphere of the presentation of the previous complex.

*c.* The reaction is abnormal : it can

    ($\alpha$) be disturbed by a slip of the tongue or repetition of the stimulus-word ;

    ($\beta$) be abnormally superficial (clang-reaction).

(5) The emotional tones in question are mostly of a disagreeable nature.

(6) The signs of an unconscious constellating complex are : long reaction-time, peculiar reaction, fault, perseveration, stereotyped repetition of a reaction-word (" representative of a complex "), translation into a foreign tongue, energetic expression, quotation, slip, assimilation of the stimulus-word (or misunderstanding of the stimulus-word).

(7) Erotic complexes seem to play a peculiarly important part.[1]

### (H) *On the Quantitative Behaviour of the Delayed Reaction-times in a Large Number of Subjects*

*a.* STIMULUS-WORD AND DELAYED REACTION-TIME.—It would be of interest to learn whether the laws deduced from the above analysis could be employed on a larger number of subjects about whom we possess but meagre information. Practical experience teaches us that there are very few people who can follow their own psychological processes to the minutest details. Subjective analysis has therefore very narrow limits. But it ought to be

---

[1] The analysis of the associations of an uneducated person would require to be differently formulated, and in a more complicated way. As Riklin and I have shown, the uneducated attaches chief importance to the meaning of the stimulus-word ; therefore he has a longer reaction-time, making it difficult to judge out how far this is conditioned by the emotions or by the difficulties of the adaptation.

possible, guided by the results obtained, to penetrate objectively into the complexes concealed in the associations, and at least to demonstrate the probability that the laws obtained by subjective analysis are universally true. On the same lines I have therefore investigated the kinds of stimulus-words that, as a rule, produce delayed reactions. The material was eleven persons, of whom nine were uneducated and two educated.

(1) Five subjects always reacted with long times to the following stimulus-words :

| | | |
|---|---|---|
| Needle | False | Hope |
| (Hair [1] | | Strange |
| (Salt | Fern | Resin |
| ((Tooth) three persons [2] | (Disgust | ((Disguise) seven persons [2] |
| (Window | (Increase | (Inn |
| Pyramid | Remember | Hit |
| Ripe | Threaten | Weave |

It is not surprising that stimulus-words like *fern, increase, resin, pyramid*, require a delayed reaction-time, for they are rather rare words to which the uneducated have not at their disposal an off-hand connexion. But this cannot be maintained of the words *needle, hair, hit*, etc. ; these are extremely common in colloquial speech. The reason for the delayed reaction-times for these words must be sought for on the basis of the above analyses. On the whole, these are words which usually evoke emotionally toned combinations, like *hope, false, hit threaten, remember, ripe*, etc, for they have in themselves a certain emotional value. For women *hair* must have a certain emotional value. The words *salt, window, increase, inn*, have, it is true, no emotional value which at once springs to the mind, but in the original they follow on stimulus-words that do excite emotion ; thus, as repeatedly demonstrated, they still come within the sphere of the perseverating emotional tone. *Hair* and *tooth* can, especially among women, cause long times, whilst *disgust* and *despise* universally excite emotion. *Needle* does not follow any stimulus-word exciting emotion, but here another factor comes into play. This word is in German *nadel*, and as pronounced, the nearest and only clang-association for those who speak the Swiss dialect is *nabel* (navel). Thus *nadel* (needle) for these persons almost invariably arouses the word *nabel* (navel). As we have seen, it is not at all necessary that this fact should come into consciousness, but it can nevertheless occasion an inhibition

---

[1] The stimulus-words bracketed together followed each other directly in the original.

[2] The word in parentheses was given because as a complex excitant it is more suspect than *window* or *inn*.

in the association. That this is no idle speculation is seen from the occurrence of the same phenomenon in other words where a similar tendency exists.[1]

(2) Six out of eleven subjects always reacted with a long time to the following :

| | | |
|---|---|---|
| Dream | Injure | Swing |
| Paper | Indulge | Omen |
| Book | Shocking | Smell |
| Frog | Soft | Forge |
| Attendant | {(Guess) eight persons | Caress |
| Right | {Of age | Family |

Words like *swing* and *omen* can be regarded as difficult words in which the rarity may overcome the emotional value. From the ubiquity of *paper* it is difficult to say what is in general the factor that arouses emotion. *Attendant* acts under the constellation that the uneducated persons were all male and female attendants in our asylum. The factor in *soft* was due to the German clang-similarity with another word, *leise = soft*, apprehended as *läuse = lice*. It is curious that to the word *frog* there was so frequent a prolonged time. Those in whom it occurred were, with a few exceptions, women. The male subject who reacted with a long time was able to give us an explanation ; *frog* had encountered the emotional complex arising from the recent birth of a son. Possibly for the woman's unconscious, *frog* has an emotional similarity with the small, naked, crawling infant ; thus encountering a sexual complex which is surely present in every woman, even if entirely unconscious.

The emotional value of the remaining stimulus-words is clear and requires no further discussion.

(3) Seven of the eleven reacted to the following stimulus-words with prolonged time :

| | |
|---|---|
| (Freedom | Sick |
| Unjust | Despise |
| World | Take care |
| Faithfulness | Kiss |
| Consciousness | |

The only " difficult " word is *consciousness*. It is not difficult to understand that the stimulus-words *freedom, unjust, take care,* cause a prolonged time-reaction among the asylum attendants. *World* seems to be within the sphere of influence of two stimulus-words that excite emotion.

[1] It is also seen in stimulus-words that have more than one meaning, especially when one meaning has a vulgar or obscene usage.—TRANSLATOR.

(4) Eight to ten of the eleven persons reacted with prolonged time to the following :

| Heart | Suppose |
|---|---|
| Violence | ((Kiss) seven persons |
| Wonder | ((Naturally) nine persons |

With *suppose* it was less the somewhat rare occurrence of the word than its effect upon the emotions. *Wonder* seems frequently to have aroused religious complexes attended by inhibitions. *Naturally* is erotically constellated by *kiss* immediately preceding it, and therefore a very "insidious" word for both sexes. *Violence* obtained the maximum of the delayed times. The fact that all the subjects are very closely connected with the asylum perhaps played an important part here.

We see from this critical analysis that the difficulty or rarity of a stimulus-word has no inconsiderable effect upon the duration of the reaction-time, but that in the overwhelming majority of cases the stimulus-words with delayed reactions are marked by a high emotional value.

I have tried to estimate the quantitative values of these four series in the following table :

Of the two hundred stimulus-words, forty-eight excited in five or more persons a delayed reaction-time.

In five subjects there were delayed times with seventeen words ; 76 per cent. took place with presentations of emotional value.

In six subjects there were delayed times with seventeen words ; 76 per cent. took place with presentations of emotional value.

In seven subjects there were delayed times with nine words ; 89 per cent. took place with presentations of emotional value.

In eight to ten subjects there were delayed times with five words ; 90 per cent. took place with presentations of emotional value.

Thus, on the average, 83 per cent. of the stimulus-words with a prolonged time had an emotional value, whilst only 17 per cent. of the prolongations were due to difficulty of the words. Of the stimulus-words arousing emotion at least 28 per cent. had an emotional value, chiefly erotic.

*b.* OCCURRENCE OF DELAYED REACTION-TIME AMONG INDIVIDUALS.—We can conclude that abnormally long reaction-times are mainly due to emotional processes. Daily experience tells us that it is just in the world of the emotions that the greatest individual differences exist. It is, therefore, worth while to investigate the behaviour of the abnormally long times in the different subjects. In this investigation I have used the material supplied by twenty-six persons (uneducated—seven women, seven men ; educated—six women, six men), with a total of four thousand individual measurements.

As already mentioned, all reactions which exceeded the individual probable mean were regarded as delayed. In that way a series of reactions was encountered which showed neither long duration nor distinct influence of complex. But, on the other hand, if the upper individual limit for normal times is raised, one is thrown on to the arithmetical mean, in which the delayed times are included. But this limit is far too high for individuals and the method brings out no characteristic figures. I therefore resolved to choose the individual probable mean as the upper limit: first, because the abnormally long times are not considered therein (the probable mean is, as a rule, lower than the arithmetical); and secondly, because about one-third of those times (see analysis of No. 1) which exceed the probable mean by merely 0·2 seconds is constellated by emotional complexes, whilst the very long times are all due to complexes. In this way we deal pretty well with all the times delayed by emotion. As many of the examples show, there exists a certain ratio between the intensity of the emotion and the length of the reaction-time. From very long reaction-times one may deduce, *cum grano salis*, very intense emotion. On calculating the average by the arithmetical mean the delayed times become too abundant. In the following table I present the figures of the probable and the arithmetical mean for the four groups as well as the percentage figures of the delayed times, in addition to the difference between probable and arithmetical mean.

| | | Prob. mean | Arith. mean | Difference | Delayed times in per cent. |
|---|---|---|---|---|---|
| UNEDUCATED . | Women . | 2·2 | 2·9 | 0·7 | 49·2 |
| | Men . | 1·8 | 2·4 | 0·6 | 40·9 |
| EDUCATED . . | Women . | 1·7 | 2·2 | 0·5 | 42·4 |
| | Men . | 1·3 | 1·7 | 0·4 | 41·8 |

All the columns of this table express in different ways pretty much the same thing ; the uneducated women have the highest probable mean and the greatest number of delayed reaction-times. The differences between probable and arithmetical mean are instructive : the group of educated men have a lesser difference than the other three groups. This fact says that the long reaction-times of this group are, on the average, shorter than that of the other groups ; that the emotional inhibition (for that is the chief import, and not differences of culture) in all the other subjects, even if they do not always occur absolutely more frequently, are more fundamental and excessive than those of the Educated Men. In this I see the expression of the fact that the experimenter, who in every respect stands at the level of the group of Educated Men, is for the remaining groups a person of the opposite sex or a person placed over them. This seems to me to be a sufficient reason for the universally stronger occurrence of emotional inhibitions in the remaining groups.

With the demonstration of the emotional influences upon the duration of reaction-time I have opened up a territory which is so complicated and subject to such great individual variations that for the present there would be no advantage in communicating the individual figures which form the bases of the above tables.

## GENERAL RECAPITULATION

(A) The average reaction-time of the measurements taken with the second stop-watch among the educated and uneducated is 1·8 second.

(B) The times for the male subjects (1·6 second) are, on the average, shorter than those of the female subjects (2·9 seconds).

(C) Likewise the times of the educated (1·5 second) are, on the average, shorter than those of the uneducated (2 seconds).

(D) The quality of the stimulus-word exercises a definite influence upon the reaction-times. The shortest average times are responses to concretes (1·67 second), the longest to universal concepts and verbs (1·95 and 1·9 second). The educated men form an exception to this rule, for in their case the concretes are, on the average, followed by the longest reaction-times.

(E) The quality of the reaction-word also seems to have a distinct influence upon the duration of the reaction-time. The longest times occur with universal concepts (1·98 second). The shortest times occur with adjectives and verbs (1·65 and 1·66 second). The concretes (1·81 second) are in the middle. The educated men here again form an exception, for their longest time is again with concretes.

(F) The nature of the association has a distinct influence upon the reaction-time. Inner associations demand a longer reaction-time than outer ones. Clang-reactions show, generally, relatively long times because they are abnormal and their occurrence is due to certain disturbances from inner distraction.

(G) The reaction-times which exceed the probable mean are, in large part, caused by the occurrence of intense emotion which belongs to the presentation complexes significant to the individual. The reason for the prolongation is generally not conscious at the moment. The delayed reactions can therefore serve as a means for the discovery of affect-toned (often unconscious) presentation complexes (of importance in hysteria).

(*H*) Certain stimulus-words are commonly followed by a delayed reaction. About 83 per cent. of these stimulus-words are chiefly characterized by their emotional value, whilst only about 17 per cent. have delayed times on account of the difficulty or rarity of the word.

The emotional tone often calms down slowly, extending to the subsequent reaction, which thus becomes disturbed (perseveration).

## CHAPTER VI

# CONSCIOUSNESS AND ASSOCIATION

### By PROFESSOR E. BLEULER

MENTION is often made in this volume of unconscious or sub-conscious mental functions, or of unconscious processes that influence mental functions.

Curiously enough, these things, which one meets with at every step in psychological investigation, are in Germany generally ignored, misunderstood, or attacked upon doctrinaire grounds. In France it would be unnecessary to make any special reference to the existence of unconscious mental phenomena ; both the Janets, for instance, imply this constantly in their experimental work, and Grasset has even formed a special theory (anatomical) for it.

In Germany the concept of the unconscious has become so twisted by Ed. v. Hartmann, among others, that it has become quite useless for scientific psychology. Others base their ideas on a theoretical standpoint, which to some extent is defensible enough : mental is conscious, the essence of the mental lies in its consciousness ; it is then, nonsense to speak of unconscious mental processes.[1]

But these professors forget, strange as it may sound, that observation is unable to draw any border-line between conscious and unconscious. Exactly the same functional formations and mechanisms which we find in the conscious are demonstrable outside it, and these are just as capable of determining our psyche as the analogous conscious processes. In this sense there are, then, unconscious sensations, perceptions, deductions, feelings, fears and hopes, simply and solely distinguishable from similarly named conscious phenomena by the absence of the conscious quality. Their separation is, therefore, entirely artificial, and can never be justified by observation ; whoever denies the existence of these functions renders the explanation of conscious processes impossible, for unconscious mechanisms are ever

---

[1] Ziehen, *Leitfaden der phys. Psychologie.* This limited view is to me as if some one were to describe the life of the amphibia as observed on land, whilst ignoring their life in water.

modifying or even determining the course of conscious processes.

It seems to me that Wundt's psychology is at present the chief hindrance to any impartial investigation of the facts. I do not wish to be misunderstood: Wundt has done more, very much more, for scientific psychology than any other psychologist, but his attitude towards the questions with which we are immediately concerned is not justified by the facts, although from many expressions one might conclude that he is aware of these facts and even subscribes to our theory.

Wundt says in his *Physiologische Psychologie* (5th edition, vol. iii, p. 521): " On the mental side an association of immediate events is that condition by which consciousness invariably appears in experience." This sentence is, of course, quite correct, but if nothing more is said many readers may forget, as perhaps the writer did himself, that it cannot become reversed. As we hope to show, there are numerous associations of presentations, following the same laws, where consciousness is absent. The ordered association of presentations is therefore only a condition of consciousness in the sense that without this probably no consciousness can exist; but not in the sense that whenever the association is present then there is consciousness. On p. 320 consciousness is said to be the condition of every experience. That may be in harmony with the theory of apperception, but it is a somewhat bold statement. A spider clearly gathers experience, a bee gathers manifold experiences. But is it so certain that these creatures have consciousness ? One may believe this or accept it, but not prove it.

In the *Psychologie* (1st edition, p. 238) consciousness itself is said to be the association of psychical images. But it is difficult to say what is to be made out of this idea. In other places the concept of consciousness is approximated to that of apperception, the latter being presented as a kind of personification at the back of the rest of the psyche. According to Wundt this feeling is the subjective reaction " of consciousness " or of " apperception " to an impression ; our consciousness criticizes the word and its course (*Physiologische Psychologie*, 3rd edition, vol. ii, p. 3).

With such lack of clearness it is not surprising that Wundt confuses things with one another which have nothing to do with one another, as, e.g., a latent memory-picture and unconscious psychical function. Is the " latent memory-picture " (the memory-trace) constantly reproduced in a feeble way, or is it only revivified at times by a new stimulus ? This question passes on to the related one whether the acquired presentations have a permanent existence (somewhat in Herbart's sense), or whether they arise afresh every time by some kind of functional act when they emerge into " consciousness " or become otherwise active.

This sets out from the view that there can be memory-traces (physical and psychical) which only become active at times. A memory-trace, a predisposition, would then be generally of no importance at all, something like the predisposition of a stationary pendulum to swing, or of a canal in which for the time being there was no water running. The trace would only take on function when the memory-picture played any kind of part in a new mental process. Whether it then became conscious or not does not come into the question ; although most people, implicitly or explicitly, generally consider *conscious* memory-pictures only.

Despite the similarity of names, unconscious actions, reflections, and presentations in our sense differ from these *toto cœlo*. We are here dealing with actual functions which are not conscious to the individual. Wundt amalgamates both latent memory-pictures and unconscious mental happenings, and even mixes up with these the question of inborn presentations.

In his *Physiologische Psychologie* (vol. iii, p. 748) the conception of a mental occurrence, resulting from the analogy of conscious motives, but which is at the same time not conscious, coincides completely with the concept of the life-forces of vitalism.

Such obscure concepts are useless in the practical psychology of the asylum, or in the investigation of normals. They have, moreover, the great disadvantage that they stand in the way of impartial observation and must be first of all pushed aside by those who wish to arrive at any kind of useful view.

There is no better testimony to the value of a psychological theory than its applicability in psychopathology. The philosophic psychology of the study must seem to be pure phantasy in the eyes of every physician because its theories are valueless in practical life. Psychiatry (one could almost say each individual psychiatrist) has to create for itself a psychology for home use.

However fruitful other sides of Wundt's "physiological" psychology have been in pathology, his theories have failed completely where we tried to unravel all that is denoted by "conscious, unconscious," "dissociated personality," etc. His theories have not even helped their originator to appreciate the significance of such relatively simple phenomena as occur in hypnotism.

It becomes our task to show briefly that there are unconscious mental phenomena, and to point out the diverse means by which these find expression.

Experience tells us, however, that this will not be enough. Even scientists, as a rule, only assimilate new ideas which harmonize with their previous content of presentations.

I shall, therefore, in conclusion, indicate briefly a theory of these unconscious phenomena which has enabled me for twenty-six years to "explain" all these observations. The whole psychology of the unconscious, all the phenomena of hypnotism, of dissociation of the personality, of hysterical conscious conditions, are brought into harmony with the rest of our knowledge, while the theory helps to remove the odium of the weird and inconceivable which so many people still attach to these phenomena.

Much of this I shall only suggest here. A psychology of the unconscious with any pretension to completeness would fill volumes.

### THE FACTS

Most people agree that there is no conscious quality in the actions of the works of a watch or of physical events in general. But the expression "unconscious" is not properly used in this connexion, but only of processes in our brains where consciousness is absent, although in all other respects equivalent to or obviously like conscious processes.

We deduce these processes from their effects, or are able to learn about them in individual instances from their memory-pictures becoming subsequently conscious.

I am walking in the street occupied with some problem, make way for other people, go the right way ; of all the sense-impressions not one-hundredth part becomes conscious to me, yet they guide my steps.

That these are not simple reflex processes may be deduced from the following facts, among others :

Embarking on and maintaining the direction in walking, making way, and so on is originally a mental act which has only become unconscious ("automatic") in many cases, and that quite gradually, without one being able to state exactly at what moment or during what action consciousness completely disappeared. The activity which has become automatic cannot be something different in principle from the action originally conscious ; at any moment it can become again more or less conscious.

Our whole pathology shows that in man, at least, such activities are governed by the cerebral cortex and become disordered in agreement with the corresponding conscious functions.

The purpose and choice of the road set out upon is generally consciously determined by the mind beforehand. A reflex process cannot thus be voluntarily managed ; a reflex is distinguished from psychical functions by being non- "plastic." Now and again the unconscious psyche (the "unconscious") commits the same kind of mistakes as the conscious psyche ; for instance, instead of taking the preselected but unusual path, another is taken to which one is more accustomed, or a side street which one intended to take is passed by if the buildings have undergone any alteration.

In such cases purposeful, unconscious changes are made in the original plan ; if a street for any cause is impassable I can choose another without reference to my consciousness. Such unconscious choice of action has analogies with conscious mental activity, but not with reflex activities.

Later on everything that my senses have perceived can emerge as memory-pictures identical with the memory-traces consciously grasped. It is relatively frequent for a spoken sentence, a word read in passing, the stroke of a clock, and the like to pass into consciousness after an interval, sometimes only after several minutes. Thus after a considerable time some passing incident, some dream or hypnotic suggestion, a memory-picture received unconsciously, may emerge into consciousness.

Here we have to do with the analogies to sensation and perception in the region of the unconscious. Again, it is unconscious sensation when, my attention being strongly fixed, a boot-nail sticks into my foot; I get up, feel worried. I notice this fact without recognizing the cause of my change of mood until for some reason or other my attention is turned towards the slight pain. All unconscious sensations and perceptions can suddenly pass into consciousness.

Among the passers-by, for whom I make room without taking notice of them, is a friend or a negro; there is some very strong smell; danger of some kind threatens me; I see fruit for sale when I am thirsty; some clumsy person pushes me aside—in all such cases consciousness is suddenly added to the unconscious process without our being able to notice any other change.

I am awaiting my fiancée and see her coming through the garden shrubbery; I am amazed at not feeling the usual pleasurable excitement. A minute later she comes out of the shrubbery—and it is not my fiancée at all; I have mistaken her for another girl, who wears dresses of the same colour. The same thing happens to me again: recalling the previous occurrence, I meant to be cautious, and nevertheless arrived at the same (false) conclusion, that the girl approaching must be my fiancée. A third time, in a mist, I get joyfully excited at the approach of a person whom I consciously did not recognize as my fiancée. The unconscious was right there also.

When reading I am accustomed to adopt various postures, which are more comfortable than elegant. Should some one knock at the door before whom I do not feel quite at my ease I sit up automatically. I have an old housekeeper from whom I do not hide my inelegant postures. Now it has happened to me to feel quite sure that the step and the knock belonged to another person—to my younger servant; and yet I could hardly make up my mind to sit up. Once, indeed, just before the expected servant entered I had time to reflect a little; I decided, in a way quite foreign to my usual thoughts and feelings, that I must accustom the girl also to see me on the sofa with my legs on the table. In all these cases, as in all similar incidents, my unconscious was right—it was the old housekeeper who was at the door.

These are cases of unconscious recognition in contrast with the conscious malcognition; add to this that the unconscious phenomena dominated the conscious feeling, the motor reaction, and even reflection.

When I was working in the physiological laboratory I frequently had to carry a lot of rabbits in a net an hour's walk. Naturally my hand got tired and I often had to change hands. I wanted to study the phenomenon of fatigue, and find out how long under conscious strain I could stop from changing hands. I did not once succeed in determining the moment of fatigue ; when I turned my attention to the rabbits, either I was not as yet tired or I had already changed hands. The sensations of fatigue had already, without appearing in consciousness, informed my brain and set an activity in motion which cannot possibly be apprehended as a mere reflex.

Just as every unconscious sense-image or its memory-picture may, from any kind of accident, become conscious, so conscious doings may become unconscious. You have only to think of the well-known instances of piano-playing, reading aloud whilst thinking of something else, or of any similarly complicated functions which have become automatic through practice ; at any moment they may become, in part or wholly, conscious and again unconscious.

But there are also unconscious analogies to reflections, to logical thinking. Carpenter in his *Mental Physiology* cites a number of instances which have become known to all since then, which prove that long series of reflections can be made in the unconscious, the result only appearing in consciousness.

Unconscious poetical productions have been made as well as discoveries ; long-sought-after mathematical problems have suddenly emerged into consciousness ready solved. Lord Mansfield certainly spoke from a ripe experience when he advised a young and newly appointed judge, " Never give reasons for your decisions : your judgments will very probably be right, but your reasons will almost certainly be wrong." [1]

By inferences which scarcely ever become conscious to us perceptions are formed from sensations. The size of an object we infer from the size of the retinal picture ; the convergence of the eyes and other sensations, again, enable us by unconscious inference to determine the distance. In the analysis of peripheral illusions of sense it is quite common to speak of such unconscious inferences (Helmholtz).

From " impressions " which we cannot analyse we often make far-reaching conclusions which we know only from the results. People who have no knowledge of graphology diagnose a rascal from the handwriting without knowing why ; a young and inexperienced girl gives an acute and poignant character of a new friend after a brief acquaintance ; a physician makes a

[1] Carpenter, *Mental Physiology*, p. 482.

correct diagnosis in difficult cases, the grounds of which he cannot properly give. A little girl from the outset distrusted a swindler who had introduced himself into a respectable family as one in great need, and who was liked by every one else.

Compare also the explanation of the cases published in the literature of so-called clairvoyance.

In unconscious reflections unconscious motives very frequently play their share. One cannot adequately explain on conscious grounds many of one's own decisions ; he who often conscientiously analyses himself will often find the decisive factor in a motive which was quite unconscious at the time of deliberation and decision. Try and find out the reasons for the doings of those dearest to you ; you get at nothing without the acceptance of unconscious motives. (For beautiful examples as to how opinions arise, see Forel, *Die Zukunft*, 1902–1903, p. 1.[1])

In this respect self-observation is very interesting when a quick action or response is demanded. The conscious self is quite unable in such cases to exercise exact reflection. The " feelings " are often derided. This word comprises, as a rule, two quite distinct things : real affects (fear, anger, etc.), then ill-considered intellectual motives and reflections. The latter must be thought out more thoroughly somewhere—" in the unconscious "—otherwise our actions would only be correct by accident ; they would become in every way equivalent to the doings of those weak-minded persons who never get beyond

[1] Those who know something about the alcohol question or wish to know something about it should study the arguments of the moderate drinkers for wonderful examples of the ignorance of motives. Teetotalism is opposed, e.g., by pointing out that people drank as much or even more in former days— in direct contradiction to the fact that the development of breweries and distilleries belongs to the last century, almost to the last decades. (In Switzerland the brewery was practically non-existent fifty years ago.) It is said that moderation strengthens the character—although millionfold observation has shown that alcohol weakens the character on the psychical side. In every other field care is taken to protect youth against corruption ; who, for example, would send his daughter into bad company so as to strengthen her character ? It is said in all seriousness that God has made wine so that man may drink of it. But we have long lost the habit of swallowing everything which God permits to grow. Moreover, God has at most let the grapes grow ; without man's additional effort there would be no wine. Such halting statements, such as otherwise one is only accustomed to get from imbeciles, one can hear on the drink question by the hundreds from the most intelligent people. They are easily shown to be false by the simplest person who here thinks objectively. The true motives can easily be discovered from any moderate drinker whom you know at all well. Most persons cannot be among wolves without joining in the howling, they cannot bear being regarded as peculiar. Others cannot give up their habits, their usual pleasures ; others feel embarrassed before their wives or neighbours or some relative who is a brewer or innkeeper, and so on.

such obscure concepts. But it is quite the contrary; the individual is often astonished, on working out the matter, how correctly his " feelings " have guided him.

Just as unconscious motives condition conscious activity, the reverse is also true. At every moment we decide on actions which are afterwards carried out quite unconsciously, so whilst without previous practice the adjustment of any kind can be final or persistent. In my school days and up to my fifteenth year I had warts on my left hand with which I was always fidgeting; I used to get blood out of them for writing and such-like things. I was then told that warts were kept up by bestowing attention upon them, whereupon I resolved to ignore mine. Six months later my warts were accidentally brought back to my mind; they had disappeared; in the interval I had not thought once about them nor of my decision. From my youth upwards I used, when I was alone, to spin a fairy-tale of adventures many years ahead. I then read in a grammar-book the sentence, " It is a disease of the soul to think the impossible." My fairy-tale became suspect and from that time disappeared from my involuntary fantasies without any effort of will, without any conscious prohibition. Some ten years ago I had some new shirts made; the buttonholes of the cuffs were in unwonted places, so that in putting on my coat I always used to pull out the studs. I finally succeeded in putting on the coat without dragging out the studs; it was not till a year later that I had the old difficulty again. It was on a walk when under difficult conditions I wanted to put on the coat and the studs slipped out; up till then the adjustment made on a single occasion had sufficed.

In all these cases we are dealing with the conscious influencing of processes usually counted as mental, which, in any case, belong not to the reflex, but to the plastic functions. The transformed motive worked on permanently, although it became quite unconscious for a long time after the new adjustment.

There are similar adjustments towards centripetal processes.

One is looking for a certain plant on a walk; after a while one ceases to think about it, but as soon as the plant comes into view the attention is at once directed to it with an inhibition of all other processes present at the moment in consciousness. You are running through the pages of a book to find a name, get interested in the book; are not thinking, perhaps, for the next hour why you took up the book, but as soon as you come across the name, it is noted and brought into connexion with the original purpose. In such cases the adaptation is directed to what we call, in the conscious, the attention. There is an " unconscious adjustment of attention."

But there is also a continuous unconscious attention, as when in the street traffic I push by or step aside, feeling for the most convenient way, or when I unconsciously search the hedges for some flower.

The equivalency of unconscious presentations is best shown in the course of series of associations which jump from presentation to presentation, quite unconcerned as to whether the individual associations are conscious or not.

Many instances are found in this book ; I mention only three types. Stimulus-word : *mild* ; the reaction *bed* slurs over the words *child — child-bed* conditioned by a constellation which remained unconscious. To *high* a subject was about to answer *deep* ; she corrected it before she had quite uttered the word and said *low*. She did not know why ; analysis shows that *deep* read backwards is the name of a former adorer—a fact about the word of which she was previously not aware. To *despise* there came the reaction *mépriser*, the only reaction in French. The word is given by the stimulus, but the French form is conditioned in the unconscious by the reading of a French novel, which had reminded the subject that she might be herself despised under certain conditions.

Hypnosis gives us the means of experimenting with unconscious processes. Sense-images can be made completely unconscious by suggestion of anæsthesia, of negative hallucination, and they can be nevertheless employed to direct movements, whilst after any desired interval their existence can be established as memory-pictures. In conditions of experimental hyperæsthesia sense-images can be turned to other unconscious uses and even to better uses than the conscious ones.

In mirror-reading by letters reflected from ordinary writing-paper, in the recognition, by the sense of smell, of movements taking place in any object, all the factors are scarcely conscious. (The literature of hypnotism contains numerous other examples of unsuspected finer qualities of sensations which would be quite impossible to " supraconsciousness.")

If during hypnosis I give a command for a visit to be paid one hour after waking, the subject performs the action, in most cases, in his normal consciousness ; but the real motive of his visit remains quite unconscious, he believes he has other grounds for it. If I require the post-hypnotic visit to be made sixteen days later, the days are counted unconsciously, or the mental mechanism is so attuned that the action is carried out on the appointed day. If I say, " When I have clapped hands twenty-seven times you will go to sleep again," sleep takes place even if the subject on awaking has quite forgotten the command, and I take several days over the twenty-seven hand-clappings. The clapping must have been counted unconsciously. If I say, " If a mouse rustles in the wall you will feel an itching in the nose," the unconscious attention is attuned to the rustling of a mouse.

Many inferences made by hypnotized persons are unconscious ; the best known is the clever guessing of the hypnotist's aims, which has so frequently simulated thought transference. The subjects do not always know that they have made a deduction, and scarcely ever know out of what elements they have formed it. If we use the experiments, stupidly forbidden, of thought-reading, of the planchette (unconscious writing), and of table-rapping, we find among hypnotized and unhypnotized, among healthy and unhealthy persons, remarkable unconscious activities. Memory-pictures quite inaccessible to consciousness emerge with wonderful distinctness and are combined in logical ways as well as in fantasies. A girl writes (from left to right) an Arabic dedication which she must have seen at some time without understanding it ; she displays knowledge which she certainly never consciously possessed.

In trance, with automatic writing, she composes stories, the incidents in which she must have stored in her childhood, but which have not left a trace in her consciousness (cryptomnesia).[1]

Automatic writing, in particular, deserves more attention from psychologists than it has received. In so-called mediums it is a very common function. In Mulhouse there is a Nature doctor, without professional qualifications, who successfully trains most of his patients in this automatic activity and gets them to write the diagnosis.

Automatic speaking is found in dementia præcox. The patient hears himself talking (mostly cursing) as if he were a third quite disinterested spectator. In the visionaries of Cevennes, about whom we possess fairly accurate reports, this phenomenon was so developed that they delivered whole sermons without their consciousness taking the slightest part. The study of all forms of " possession " furnishes other examples of this.

In thought-reading, the guide makes unconscious movements of the extremities and muscles which the thought-reader interprets, in many cases quite unconsciously, as I have been able to convince myself from many instances. Here again unconscious sensation and interpretation extend far beyond anything we can accomplish consciously. By a mere touch, direction can be much more accurately determined than might be expected, and the guess is often so extraordinary that at present we can offer no explanation. For instance, whole words or concepts are trans-

[1] Flournoy, *Des Indes à la Planète Mars.*

ferred in this way. Jung placed his hand on the back of the medium and thought of Cæsar, whereupon the medium automatically wrote "Brutus." According to Jung's unpublished experiments numbers can be correctly given if the medium only joins in the first movements of the answering table, and then interrupts all contact with the table and the medium.

These unconscious thoughts have often a tendency to express themselves in quite uncommon ways, e.g. they prefer a symbol which is foreign to the consciousness. If an innocent young girl, much taken up with some strapping youth just introduced to her, makes the table say, "I am hungry and thirsty for human flesh," we easily recognize a disguise. Freud in his work on dreams, which has not met with the recognition it merits, has shown that somewhat similar ideas exist in dreams, and Jung and Riklin have found similar ideas to be the conscious or unconscious core of the bizarreries of dementia præcox.

I came across another instance of this to-day in the sphere of dreams. A girl about whose dreams I inquired on medical grounds, who would be very unhappy if I explained to her the meaning of her dream, told me the following : She was with her former teacher in the garden. He showed her an outline of the map of Switzerland. She showed him the Bernina range. He then wanted her to point out to him something else, the Popocatepetl. She wished to look for the mountain, when he bade her show him the Pacific Ocean ; she had only to go up a step when she would see it. She did so and remarked that it was a beautiful kind of "Pacific Ocean " ; it was most stormy, the foam spurted up to the sky and up to her herself, the sky was quite dark (this repeated with emphasis). Those unpractised in dream interpretation may take as key the clang to Popocatepetl ; with this key the rest, up to and including the black sky, is easily made out (with the exception of the Bernina range).

We notice again in "unconscious cerebration" a tendency to witticisms foreign to our waking state.[1] One of our assistant physicians named Woerlin was selected for a better post and had to leave at once, which put us into great difficulty. In reporting the case to the authorities I left out the "r" in the name (Woe – lin) ; consciously I had never thought of such a pun. Observation has convinced us that Freud is right in claiming that most of these slips have a deeper meaning.

Unconscious feelings often express themselves in snatches of tunes which seem to spring up from nowhere, and their significance is undiscoverable to the subject himself without analysis.

[1] Fundamentally these are not so much witticisms as unexpected associations of ideas which give the impression of wit.

Quotations serve the same end ; in association experiments they very frequently conceal emotional complexes (see chapter v).

Automatic writing and the related expressions of unconscious activity (designation of letters with the planchette, tables, movements, etc.) often conceal a " mood " of the unconscious which so far remains unexplained—words, syllables, and even sentences are misplaced in various ways or even written backwards. An acquaintance experimenting with the planchette (which, it should be noted, succeeds with most people) received words which were quite incomprehensible. To the question, " What language might this be ? " his own unconscious replied to him by the planchette, but with the letters now correctly in place, " Idiot, turn it round." This gave him the key. Jung [1] quotes a case from Myers where the automatic writing furnished complete anagrams.

Such complications are not only foreign to conscious thinking, but they require work of a kind that very few persons could carry out consciously in their heads. In this connexion we must again recall the hypersensitiveness of unconscious sense-perceptions and the hyperintelligence of many unconscious deductions.

And, nevertheless, in all these experimental expressions of the unconscious there is scarcely ever produced any really original piece of work, whatever similarity such play of ideas may have with the creations of genius. Some day we shall certainly succeed in interpreting all these things in the manner of Freud's explanation of dreams, and of the instance given above of hunger and thirst for human flesh.

The same tendency to witticisms and tomfoolery is found, as is well known, among the mediums of the spiritualists and among hysterics, whose symptoms arise to a great extent in the unconscious.

Unconscious feelings are somewhat more difficult to understand. We find their effects in association and we see their influence most markedly in changes of consciousness, in the dissociation of the different personalities, and similar phenomena (see below).

The way in which they first arise in the unconscious, by an unconscious elaboration of the content of experience, and can then be transferred to conscious personality, the following example will show. I once received some unpleasant news when I was very busy. The full extent of the matter had not become quite clear to me whilst listening to the messenger. For an hour or more I gave various instructions and orders. During this time the news had quite vanished from my mind. I had forgotten

---

[1] Jung, *Collected Papers on Analytical Psychology*, chap. i, p. 54.

it and was quite as usual. I then went to the wards, when it seemed to me suddenly as if I felt a heavy weight on my chest, as if I had had some accident. It was only after long reflection that I discovered the cause to be the unpleasant news which was unconsciously at work ; it had linked itself to further associations, and had succeeded in obtaining notice by the conscious self through a movement of the feelings.

Every novelist knows that, besides the feelings, the instincts play a large part in the unconscious. Two examples from real life will suffice. A young man went to a ball fully determined to get engaged to a girl who was, on rational grounds, a good match for him. He there got engaged it is true, but to another lady, who did not correspond so well to his conscious wishes, but, as the sequel showed, was the right woman for him (communicated by Jung). A rather elderly bachelor discovered that he was in love with a girl who did not come up to his former conscious ideal of a " housewife." He first noticed this when stopping at an hotel ; he found himself always asking for letters, even when he knew that none could possibly have arrived. Here again the unconscious instinct had chosen, as against all the fine theories of the conscious.

In the region of psychopathology we also find the unconscious in constant activity.

Hallucinatory paranoiacs complain daily about voices which seem strange to them, but which must undoubtedly have arisen from the unconscious working of the mind. The Maid of Orleans had hallucinations in which the Mother of God told her exactly what to do ; these proved the right things to do until the Maid's mission was accomplished ; they must have arisen from a highly intelligent unconscious mechanism. (The writer has studied the documentary evidence and is convinced that no other explanation is possible.)

Here likewise belong the common teleological hallucinations. For instance, a hebephreniac wanted to throw himself out of the window ; on coming to the window he saw that it was filled up by a flood of light and he felt at the same time that he was knocking against an irresistible obstacle (hallucination of sight and of perception of resistance). In hysteria there are a number of other teleological symptoms which have hitherto been insufficiently observed. For some time past a young lady has always had an attack of aphonia when she goes into a shop to buy something. Previously she had never been able to resist the importunities of the salesman, but had often taken things home which she did not want, and which, moreover, far exceeded her means. The aphonia was a defence of the unconscious which, as a rule, sufficed, but it was a means really unworthy of the lady's highly developed intelligence.

One of my college friends suffers from paranoid dementia præcox which set in late and is of very slow course. He tries to prove to me that the injunctions, voices, etc., have not arisen in his brain. He therefore keeps a very exact account of all events which refer to these things. On one occasion he thought of the word *retour*. Then he heard a voice calling out, " *Retour-chaise.*" He assured me, quite truly, with the greatest conviction, that neither immediately nor long before had he thought of this word; it must have come from another person. He hears on many occasions things of which he would never think : surely he would not insult or threaten himself ? He had been accustomed for a long time to observe himself with hypochondriacal exactitude, and his intelligence is still so good that on this occasion he allowed they were not " outside " influences, but hallucinations.

This is one case among hundreds. Independently of the conscious personality, wishes and fears regulate ideas to their liking and combine them in a compact complex, whose expressions emerge as " hallucinations " ; these appear to be so consequential and deliberate that they simulate a third person. This third person sometimes criticizes the subject, his thoughts and actions (" voice of conscience "). But it is merely a piece of the split-off personality ; it represents aspirations of this personality which would otherwise be suppressed.

We thus find in the unconscious all those activities which we usually ascribe to the conscious mind, sensation, perception, logical thinking, imagination, attention, aspiration, action.

But that is not the end. We have yet to add the chapter of multiple personality, although in these cases both complexes possess a conscious quality. But we shall see that dissociation of personality is fundamentally nothing else than the splitting off of the unconscious ; unconscious complexes can transform themselves into these secondary personalities by taking over so large a part of the original personality that they represent an entirely new personality.

In the dream of the normal individual personality is already changed. The dream shows traits and memories foreign to one when awake. Such dream-personalities are rarely complete ; they sway hither and thither and have but an ephemeral duration. A permanent grouping of experiences in two or more personalities we see in cases of doubled or multiple " consciousness." The most famous of these is Azam's Felida, who is well known to every psychologist. A young girl suddenly forgot most of her former circumstances, and from being a serious person became witty, jolly, almost boisterous ; after a time her normal state returned, and then both states interchanged at irregular intervals throughout life. In her normal state she had no recollection of her experiences in the second state ; in the latter, however, she remembered in later years the events of her normal state.

Thus several distinct personalities (up to a dozen have been observed) can interchange in the same individual.

In these cases memory behaves in various ways. As a rule the abnormal and its experiences are quite unknown to the normal consciousness, whilst the abnormal state can often make use of the memories of the normal—but not invariably ; sometimes the subjects live like two personalities, completely separated in time and content.

Jung [1] has carefully described the case of a girl at puberty who in trance exhibited an idealized personality, together with two groups of persons of another sort. In the former he suspected that he saw the later character of the girl breaking through, whilst the two others personified traits of character which were to be cast off. The patient's subsequent development has shown that he was right.

Such personalities can, however, exist permanently side by side, and not merely in succession ; it seems probably true that in every one groups of psychical elements lead a more or less independent life.

Max Dessoir has brought together in his *Doppel-Ich* [2] (" Double Self ") a number of points in favour of the view that by the side of the conscious ego there is also present a " subconscious." This work, otherwise of great merit, suffers from the mistake of speaking always of one subconscious only. In truth, a practically endless number of different unconscious groupings is possible, and these all occur, although only the one or other complex, as a rule, besides the " supraconscious," seems to reach expression.

Naturally the different complexes representing different types of personalities have much in common. The ordinary acquired capacities such as gait, eating, speech, etc., are generally the same. More than this, the universal concepts, etc., acquired by experience are generally the same in the different complexes. They do not, therefore, lead an absolutely separate life, and activities of the subconscious often interact on the " supra-

[1] Jung, *Collected Papers on Analytical Psychology*, chap. i, " On the Psychology and Pathology of so-called Occult Phenomena."
[2] Leipzig, 1890.

conscious " and conversely in just the same way that we have indicated when speaking of unconscious activity alone.

In many cases the different personalities are only distinguishable by the absence or presence of a few memory complexes. Riklin has related a pretty instance of this (*Psych.-neurol. Wochenschrift*, 1904–1905, No. 22). A prisoner under observation got into a state of hysterical delirium at certain questions ; at one moment he was the father of a family and a driver (as in fact he was), then he became an unmarried servant who did not know his name ; both personalities were for the rest very much alike in this, that neither knew anything about the crime.

The selection and grouping of elementary constituents of the memory in the different personalities always arise under the powerful influence of affects, just as in delirium and dreams.

In the instance just quoted one could, by arousing the complex during examination, produce at will the greater part of the patient's past, and by arousing emotional reminiscences about his family reproduce his whole position in life as the father and the mainstay of the family.

### THE THEORY

The foregoing observations show us indisputably that all conscious psychical functions can occur also in the unconscious, without any change in their character on that account. Sensation, perception, deduction, desire, action, can all take place in us without becoming conscious. In this sense we are obliged to speak of "unconscious sensation, thinking and doing," if we do not wish to make new words for these concepts. The conscious quality, the becoming aware of a psychical process, is therefore something of quite secondary importance in the consideration of our psyche, although the centripetal side of our psyche is only of importance to our ego in so far as it is conscious. (We only suffer from conscious pains, we only rejoice at conscious pleasures.[1])

We must now ascertain under what conditions psychical processes are conscious.

I believe they become so by association with our ego, that is, with the presentations, sensations, desires, which at any given

---

[1] What is to be understood by the word *conscious* is, unfortunately, by no means a uniform concept. There is no definition of this concept and there can scarcely be one. I hope, nevertheless, that I shall be understood here : by this word *conscious* no one must think of conscious reflection, orientation and other equally different things, but of the essential characteristic which distinguishes us from an automaton who might behave like a man, of the common components that are fundamental to the concepts sensation, perception, doing, willing, feeling.

moment compose our personality.[1] Hence it follows that all those processes which are at the moment not in associative connexion with the ego complex are unconscious.

The difference between conscious and unconscious is often presented as essentially a dynamic one. Strong sense-impressions will certainly, *ceteris paribus*, receive attention sooner than weak ones. Probably strong psychical processes correspond to these. I say "probably," because we have no test of the strength of our psychical processes. But if we start with the presumption of such a test the dynamic theory becomes at once impossible. But, assuming that strong stimuli correspond to strong sensations, we see that the strength of a sensation is of very slight importance as regards attaining consciousness ; it is by no means the most striking feature. Amid the loud roar of the railway-train we notice only the interesting conversation, even if it is much softer than the noise around. I had been exactly one year in Rheinau when I first consciously heard the clock strike eleven, and yet the church tower, which contains a very clear-sounding bell, is next to the superintendent's house. I used to wake at any hour of the night at the slightest sigh of a sick member of the family, when the fire-alarm cannon which was quite near my open bedroom window never awakened me. The brightest flashes of lightning are often unobserved, whilst scarcely perceptible changes in the lighting or the tint, for instance in picking out unhealthy plants, may strike us at once. During an attack an officer was shot in the right arm ; but he did not notice this until he wanted to use his sabre. It is a commonplace fact that strong stimuli of one sense-organ do not prevent the weak stimuli of other sense-organs from becoming conscious, unless the question of pain enters, which then, properly, dominates everything. I do not hear a soft sound in bright light any worse than in the dark.

It is not possible to exhaust this theme here, but it can be strongly maintained that in all the differences which we know, "adjustment" alone plays any substantial part. What this is, upon what it rests, we do not yet know, although many scientists write about "attention," which about corresponds to this kind of adjustment, as if it were something known.

What at present can be stated with certainty about adjustment, or attention, is simply that it facilitates certain definite associations and inhibits others. If we may be allowed to employ again the illustration of the railroad used in chapter i, adjustment is a definite points-station, or, to use the popular comparison

[1] The question whence our conscious ego complex derives its consciousness we shall not here discuss. It is quite irrelevant to our purpose.

of an electric storehouse, a definite place of contacts, which only allows connexions to and from definite directions.

Let us test our hypothesis by a few examples.

I go along the street making way for people without being conscious of the fact. At the time I am occupied with some question which entirely absorbs my conscious thinking. This complex of ideas inhibits, according to known laws, other psychical activities which do not pertain to it, including, therefore, this making way. This inhibition is certainly not to be understood as meaning that the making way will not occur at all or only with more difficulty when I am entirely lost in thought than at other times ; on the contrary, such automatic movements generally are made better unconsciously than consciously. The inhibition does not, therefore, in this case concern the function itself but only the connexion with the ego complex—or, in other words, with the becoming conscious. The automatic process of maintaining your direction is, as we have shown, an act solely distinguished from other psychical functions by the absence of the quality of consciousness. The function has in so far made itself independent that, once begun, it can carry on with or without connexion with the ego complex. None the less, the whole content of memory is at the individual's disposal : the dangers from bicycles, motors, electric cars, and, as recent investigations have shown, their rate of travelling and their direction, are better appreciated by this independent complex of ideas than by conscious deliberation. Probably Stern's remark (*Psychologie der Aussage*) applies here : that time is better appreciated when the attention is otherwise occupied, e.g. in reading, than when the interval of time to be estimated is not filled up.

If we observe ourselves whilst learning to ride a bicycle, the whole process of our detachment from the complex of propulsion is very distinctly conscious. At first we set out with conscious effort, sometimes aided by deliberation ; we must now turn the left handle-bar to the left and bend the body to the same side. By and by everything goes smoothly and we begin to look at other things on the road ; finally we learn to think of things quite unconnected with riding—at first timidly, superficially, and at short intervals, then more boldly and connectedly. The thought complex inhibits the development (not the function) of the motor complex more and more ; this complex becomes more hazy to consciousness as the links with the ego decrease, for the ego is now engaged elsewhere and is hence shut off on this side. At the same time the motor complex becomes more " habitual." Through habit there is not merely an easier and safer disposal of nervous activity but also a binding of the psycho-chyme (*sit venia verbo*) to the absolutely essential paths. This we see in the infant's every habit as well as in ourselves. An increasing tendency must exist within the motor complex to limit or to inhibit associations with other complexes. Finally, this tendency of both sides to close leads to both activities, thinking and riding, working independently of each other ; we can then ride for hours together without thinking of the machine or of the road.

The complex which has here become unconscious behaves as a dissociated piece of the mind, gathering experiences and making use of them. Some years ago I had frequently to traverse a much broken up road. The getting out of the way disturbed me exceedingly. Even if the street was only slightly crowded I was obliged to walk much more slowly than I was accustomed to. It was only after some time and after much resolution that I found courage to jostle along somewhat faster. The consequence was that I kept to the tramway lines, the dangers of which my conscious self did not know at all, whilst something within me had carefully calculated how quickly and quietly I could get along the lines without danger. Such instances could be freely multi-plied by the dozen. I will just call attention to the fact that only the unconscious of an asylum officer is perfectly at home with the different locks of his asylum. If for some particular reason he has to open a lock consciously he gets worried, because he does not know how far he should insert the key, upon which side to turn it, how much force is required ; all things which his lock complex knows and carries out accurately.

Unconscious perceptions exist by the myriad, but they would not afford us anything new. Special mention need only be made of those which later arrive at consciousness or of those which influence our conscious feeling or doing.

If I am busy with some mental work I do not, as a rule, hear the clock strike. If a few minutes later I am recalled to the time by some association or other, the memory-picture of the clock's striking is frequently revived—sometimes so accurately that I am able to count the beats up to five. The mind has unconsciously perceived the clock striking, without association with the momentary ego complex ; this association is only restored later by the revived memory-picture. The clock striking has simply become conscious because the thought which had occupied me has now been disposed of. The inhibition which it was exercising upon all other mental processes thus ceases. It should be noted that the memory-picture of the unconscious perception can subsequently become conscious without any conscious association causing a scearh for the memory-picture ; the amnestic after-image of the clock striking can now unite associatively with the personality and is thus consciously perceived.

If I have a nail in my shoe which I have not noticed but which is obviously spoiling my temper the same mechanism comes into play. Every civilized person has become practised in not paying attention to such small inflictions whilst otherwise engaged. Mental occupation also prevents the conscious perception of pain—the associative union of this pain with the self is busied with other matters. But the pain is none the less present in the mind ; it influences the behaviour, the temper, the affect, as if it were conscious. For the total separation of emotional impulses from the conscious part of our mind is much more difficult than that of the purely intellectual processes ; teleologically expressed, it is the purpose of the affects to govern the whole mind.

In the earlier cited cases where my unconscious correctly recognized the servant or her knocking, whilst my conscious thinking was in error, the explanation is likewise easy. Sitting up is automatic as soon as I can decide, from the kind of knocking, perhaps also from the unconsciously perceived steps and the like, that the person approaching is some one with whom I am not quite at home. Lying still, when the opposite decision is arrived at, is likewise automatic, if this expression may be allowed for the non-carrying out of an action. In ordinary cases I feel that the reaction to the knocking of a stranger consists in a movement of the corresponding muscles, or at least in a tension of these muscles ; beyond this no correct knowledge of anything else passes through consciousness, which recognizes at most the knocking and the sitting up. Whether in the unconscious there has really been a recognition of the person, or whether the reaction here is merely *Sit up or lie quiet*, I am unable quite to settle. From the daily occurrence of much more complicated processes in the unconscious it does not seem very likely that the only suggestion from the perception is a knocking, leading one to sit up or lie quiet, and not a knocking of a definite person. But it is certain that an unconscious part of my mind correctly recognized the kind of knocking requiring me to sit up, whilst the conscious mind was at fault.

My unconscious reaction through my feelings to a (false) perception of my fiancée cannot be the result of rapid deduction. We can exclude the view that a sense-impression, e.g. the look of a bit of dress, had aroused the reaction of feeling without the assistance of the (unconscious) concept of the fiancée herself.

The reaction corresponded so exactly to the perception of a person, and not to that of a fetishism—towards which I am, moreover, much less sensitive than most people. The change of mind on seeing my fiancée approaching was so specific that it is not easy to separate it from the concept of the fiancée under normal conditions.

If we have once proved the absence of associative links between the slighter complexes and the ego, the occurrence of more complicated chains of thought and reflections in the unconscious can occasion no surprise. They do not show anything new in principle. When carrying my rabbits to the laboratory I did not notice that I got fatigued, although the fatigue occasioned the unconscious changing of hands : complicated unconscious associations have here nothing surprising. A part of the mind works out a task, under the guidance of some instinct, without union with the ego ; then some mental product, such as the solution of a problem or a poem, emerges suddenly into consciousness as a finished result, or it may be written without full participation of the ego, semi or entirely automatically.

We stand in need of a critique of those cases where but part of an apparently unitary process is unconscious.

Indirect associations come in here. The concept *child-bed*, which served as a bridge between *mild* and *bed*, was associatively linked on one side with the conscious stimulus-word, and on the other with the reaction-word about to be conscious : why did it not become conscious also ? [1]

First of all, it must be said that for anything to become conscious a certain time, a certain direction of the presentation, is necessary. The concept which served as a bridge had a very short life, as the time-measurement of the whole association showed ; no wonder, then, that it was unnoticed. Add to this that it only possessed two links with the conscious processes (with the stimulus-word and the reaction-word) and no direct one with the ego complex. The latter was obviously the essential. Only the presentations directly connected with the ego become conscious, not the indirect ones ; if otherwise, when I consciously turn down a certain street all the requisite movements of the muscles would have to become conscious also.

Such a bridge concept can be both " quite obscure " and transiently conscious, so that one is afterwards not quite clear

---

[1] Wundt, indeed, regards it as remaining " obscurely conscious." But in agreement with our conception, he accepts a whole scale of degrees of consciousness ; may not this extend to 0 or almost to 0, so that for practical purposes our inner perception touches 0 ? Moreover, Wundt's conception of indirect association is a little different from what it is in these papers.

whether it should be ascribed to conscious or unconscious presentations. For a time it was just on the border-line or it contained only one link, or at most few links, with the ego. In observing oneself it will be seen that on arriving at consciousness the time element and the number of links play a great part. A decline of both these factors lowers also the degree of consciousness, which finally sinks to 0. We thus understand that the conscious must be regarded as relative, that there are no clear boundaries between the conscious and the unconscious.

Like the bridge concept of indirect associations, the unconscious motive of a decision or of a reflection has a kind of link with the conscious self, otherwise it could not work towards a decision. Here the brevity of the time plays no part, whilst the boundary of the association connexions becomes more obvious. For the elucidation of these latter we must remember that in reality whole functional complexes are never fully conscious to us. When I write I have no suspicion of the innervation of the muscles, not even of the formation of the letters, and frequently I am so occupied with the content of the writing that probably for relatively long intervals of time I do not know that I am writing. When bicycling, even after many years' practice, certain individual manœuvres which I make in passing others become conscious, but not in all their components. In short, we can prove a thousand times over that individual components of complexes which are proceeding unconsciously can become immediately conscious—that is, can become associated to the conscious thought complex.

A peculiarity of the psyche must here be considered which obviously possesses great importance, but, unfortunately, has not been sufficiently studied. Wundt rightly lays stress upon this : that the psychical complexes do not merely represent the sum of their parts. Every complex has, as a whole, definite qualities which belong only to the whole. An apparently simple concept like that of " water " is composed of a number of sense-presentations ; we operate with it as if it were a unit. Under other circumstances it is decomposed or partially or wholly blended with other concepts to a new unity. If I speak of " water " in chemistry a number of associations are excluded which under different circumstances apparently belong to the concept " water." Nobody then thinks of its importance in navigation, in the landscape, in nourishment, etc. In other words, in ordinary life we never operate with one concept, " water," but with a number of concepts, wider in one direction, narrower in another : " water in the chemical sense," " water in connexion with the land " ; the associations to be linked on to this are not formed, in normal persons, from the partial concept " water " but from the concept " water with a definite connotation." [1]

Every concept, in the usual sense of psychological abstraction, has also a very different value according to the momentary connexions with which, for the time being, it forms a whole. This whole, as a unity, has also its special connexions ; just as the associations which are linked to the concept " rose " are quite other than those of its individual components (form, colour, smell, growth on stalk, etc.). All the complexes, from the simplest presentations of a sensation to the most complicated and elaborate presentation of a scientific theory, behave thus, and the ego complex behaves in like manner. A presentation can be as readily associated to the whole ego complex as to one of its components. But in the former case it is conscious, if our view is correct ; while if it is united with some individual partial presentation it remains unconscious.

When I go into town I often make it consciously clear to myself whether I am going to walk, or bicycle, or take the tram. But not always ; occasionally, I am only thinking of my business there. Then somehow, on the way, I find that the street is really too muddy for bicycling when I am bicycling, or, inversely, that I should have done better to have cycled than to have walked. In the cases which arrive at consciousness when I have made a mistake, that complex of mine which is occupied with the means of transit is associated only with the thought of going to town, but not with my whole ego, to which the settling of the proper way should belong. In those cases where I consciously decide how I shall go to town, the preparations for departure, different according as I walk or cycle, are separated by an (unconscious) adjustment from the concept of the mode selected ; it is unconnected with the aims and thoughts of the ego, it remains unconscious.

In the case of a logical idea controlled by an unconscious motive the activity will usually encounter some affect (wish, fear, instinct) which is more or less conscious, but was liberated by the unconscious motive. From other experiences we are well acquainted with the power the affects possess of inhibiting opposing associations, of expediting others, and controlling logical thought even when all the motives are conscious.

It is unpleasant to the drinker to be disturbed in his habits. He therefore adduces silly reasons to justify drinking, gives them an importance which they do not possess, and suppresses any critical thoughts he may have.

[1] In dementia præcox we find that these complexes lose their unitary value ; the chain of ideas thus becomes ill-regulated—the dement who speaks about " water " often mixes up its different significances.

For centuries great thinkers believed in the sophisms about the proofs for the existence of God ; Kant, who demonstrated their complete futility, shrank before the consequences. So without noticing the weakness of his logic, he reintroduced by another route into his philosophy the idea of the Lord, the freedom of the will, and the other pretty things which he had first rejected.

When we thus learn to recognize the power of the affects, their influence upon the dissociation of personality is more readily understood. These manifestations are not really so very peculiar ; in the healthy mind they have far-reaching prototypes, of which they are only pathological exaggerations. If you test a child's knowledge by questions in a pedagogic manner, he is a very different being from what he is when you are able to test his knowledge accidentally in a tactful conversation. He is shy and inhibited, or he displays the whole school psyche in the deplorable manner and accentuation of the child repeating its lesson ; great effort is often required to make a natural being again out of the child.[1]

We have here a complete analogy to the hysterical delirium of the carter previously described.

What a difference there is between the associations, ideas, aspirations, and character of a young man who has just said "good-bye" to his parents when setting forth into the world, and these mental processes in the same youth when a few days later he is at some jolly party. He is another person just as is the hysteric in delirium, though the change is a slighter one. A whole mass of presentations and motives which were then in the forefront are now inaccessible ; his good resolutions have been blown to the winds, to reappear next day when he is down in the dumps.[2]

In the joyous mood in this case, in depression in another case, a wish or a fear selects those associations which can be immediately formed. The criminal under medical observation

---

[1] It is extremely probable that most of the published cases of extraordinary ignorance among recruits have only been misinterpreted on account of an " emotional stupidity " (Jung) readily to be understood.

[2] One difference between the child and the frivolous youth on the one side, and the hysteric on the other, is that in the latter there is a sharper division of the two states on account of the action of the affects being heightened by disease. The transition from one state to another is a gradual one in normals—in hysteria it often takes place suddenly. But the content is also different: the hysteric as a rule only carries over a small part of his personality into the delirium, just as much as corresponds to the affect ; in healthy persons the greater part of the ego is common to the two states. Amnesias are hence rare in healthy persons, the rule in hysterics.

thinks, more or less consciously, that if he could only pretend to be mad he would get off better. Without any effort on his part—it would be quite impossible for him to interfere voluntarily to the same degree with his psychical mechanisms—his associative inhibitions and paths become set, following his desire, in accordance with his notion of madness. He says and does everything upside down : he gets the Ganser syndrome.

A woman received, just after childbirth, a letter from her husband, full of reproaches and threatening to leave her. If only the letter had not come ! A few moments later and it hasn't come, she knows nothing more about it, and everything has vanished from her mind that was connected with the letter and the bad news ; what does not fit in is altered—the woman has an attack of hysterical delirium. A young woman who had once gone through an attack of dementia præcox falls in love with a young man who one day makes her clearly understand that she is nothing to him. Her wishes now take control of her associations ; she sees only the possibilities of their fulfilment, and soon has hallucinations in this direction ; during the next few months she is convinced that she is married to him and that she is pregnant. An imbecile feels injured by his brothers and generally badly treated by them. He would like to get into a furious temper and do something to the wretches. And then he gets into a rage. His blind impulse of destruction is directed against everything in his reach, without regard even to himself or to the things that belong to him. And when the anniversary of the day returns on which he was injured he recalls it all, and a repetition of the attack is the consequence. A great number of outbursts among imbeciles are due to such a mechanism.

In these cases the mechanisms which have led up to the disease symptom are alone unknown. The dissociated complex of ideas is united with the ego like other real events ; the normal experiences have sunk into the subconscious, that is, their associative links with the ego complex are quite inhibited. In hysterics, portions of the normal personality can at any time be rejoined different ways, but it is not so in hebephreniacs, whose chain of thought we are quite unable to direct.

Sometimes a double personality of this kind is formed entirely in the unconscious. Some wish, some fear, groups the corresponding presentations, as in the instances cited of hysterical delirium, but no direct union with the ego is formed ; in addition to the permanent presentations the complex makes use of indifferent elements of a general nature, such as speech, writing, muscular co-ordinations, etc. These personalities, which can be, perhaps, formed in great numbers, can be manifested through automatic writing and similar procedures without ever arriving at consciousness. In Flournoy's *Hélène* there was a person of this kind who signed herself Marie Antoinette, in whom Hélène's desire for a great position thus became embodied.

Such partial personalities can sometimes become more complete by assimilating some of the most important elements of the ego ; they then arrive at consciousness. They have thus passed from hysterical delirium, from trance conditions, into the "second person" in Azam's sense. There is, therefore, no difference in principle between unconscious complexes and these several personalities endowed with consciousness. When an unconscious complex associates to itself an increasing number of the elements of the ordinary ego, without linking itself with the ego as a whole, it becomes finally a second personality.

The influence of unconscious emotional presentations on experimental associations, as proved in this work, finds ready explanation on our theory. We know that an effect has the tendency to influence the entire psyche. If I have experienced anything sad, I am not only sad when I think of it, the sadness is also shown in all my actions which are not in associative connexion with the cause of it, even in the more automatic actions such as carriage, gait, writing, etc.

Should a stimulus-word arouse an emotional presentation in the unconscious, the affect corresponding to it must exercise its influence upon the associative activity. According to well-known laws every affect has a tendency to inhibit all psychical processes which are foreign to it ; the affect thus disturbs the experimental associative activity, makes it longer or superficial. That the affect itself does not usually reach the conscious is understandable ; it is too weak, lasts only a brief time, is inhibited by the attention paid to the experiment and by the unpleasant feeling of being disturbed (which on its part may likewise inhibit secondarily the associative activity).

The phenomena of hypnosis are too complicated for us to review here. It must suffice to remind the reader who has followed us so far that, bearing our exposition in mind, they can be all explained quite easily as inhibitions and mental paths ; inhibitions which only permit definite complexes of ideas to arrive at function, and which also separate complexes at will, e.g. a pain from the conscious ego, whilst the ready-formed mental paths act in just the reverse way. But nothing new enters the mind ; individual functions in daily use are simply aroused in a one-sided way and exaggerated as regards the relationships of ordinary life. I hope soon to find time to show that suggestion only uses the known mechanisms which hourly set our affects in motion so that I may corroborate the view which has often been expressed, but which is, strangely enough, still often contested— that suggestibility is but a normal and necessary quality of the mind.

In accordance with these views, the phenomena of dreams receive an explanation which suffices to make them lose the odium of obscurity and mystery.

In dreams we see that the rudder which controls the direction of thought whilst awake is absent entirely or in great part.

The associations thus penetrate in directions which they avoid in the waking state. One of the first consequences of this is that the ego becomes composed of other partial presentations and partial complexes ; hence the personality becomes different. That is why we " forget " dreams so easily. There are but few associations formed by the events of the dream which proceed from that other ego, the waking ego ; few associations which the dream could link (consciously) as revivified memory-pictures to the ego. If one awakes slowly, the dream complex has time to join some links with the ego during the act of returning to the normal self, and recollections become easier than on sudden awaking. We see the same thing in the transition from the self, changed by conditions of illness (twilight states, periodic attacks, intoxications) to the normal state. In sudden changes amnesia occurs, *ceteris paribus*, more easily and to a higher degree than in gradual transition.

The altered self must have other desires, a changed aim for the direction of thought, and this increases still more the abnormality of the associations. As a rule, we can say that in dreams a correct idea of purpose, according to the self when awake, is absent, or is at least weak and vacillating. The associations are directed by other motives than in the waking state, when one or two dominant impulses guide conscious reflection in the required direction, using as far as possible the laws of thought. In the dream, logic goes to the wall and the dominant places are taken here, as in children, by the feelings accidentally present and by the affects of the moment. In Freud's sense, the dream associations are governed chiefly by the emotional life.

We have still a few remarks to offer on the relationship which transition into the conscious bears to memory and will, although this is not the place to go into the matter thoroughly.

The revival of memory-traces has been hitherto attributed to the associative paths. Those traces, whose function forms the concept of the " rose," are in close union with those which represented the concept of " thorns." The psychochyme goes from one to the other and thus makes the association real. As we have seen, this process also takes place in the unconscious. The fact that a memory-picture passes again into function thus does not in itself condition the memory-picture's becoming conscious. The aroused memory-picture only becomes conscious when it passes at the same time into associative union with the ego.

The study of conscious psychical phenomena has long since shown that, together with the concepts and other memory-pictures, their associative connexions become fixed at the same time. Psychical elements thus stimulate common associations if at their first occurrence they were associatively united. That is why things we have experienced in the unconscious can only exceptionally be brought to conscious memory. The objects against which I have unconsciously jostled in the streets I can only in rare cases remember again. But these traces remain united with their contemporary unconscious functions, otherwise habit would be impossible to the unconscious. The great number of pictures of movements which make bicycling possible for me have become unconscious ; unconsciously they again become active and control my actions on the bicycle without my having a suspicion of them ; the conscious mental thoughts and the body's balancing go on separately although side by side. In order to bring the co-ordination of movement into consciousness I must direct my attention to them just as if they were something outside me. They then become united associatively to the conscious ego, and can remain so if I do not prefer to render them automatic again.

Should the self change naturally, many of the memory-pictures which are not firmly fixed by practice become inaccessible. What has been experienced in a dream, in a twilight state, in intoxication, is united to an abnormal self. Hence a mass of associative links with these occurrences are absent from the normal self ; consequently one does not remember at all, or but vaguely, the twilight state, whilst during a recurrence of the same condition there may be a very clear recollection of it.

It is perhaps in place here to note that *conscious* and *willed* are by no means synonymous concepts in all cases. In the morning I wish to get up, dress myself, wash myself. Consciously, I only introduce the automatism, whilst my consciousness seems quite separated from these proceedings ; the action has become automatic and goes on without connexion with my ego, which meantime is occupied with other things. The dressing is desired but is not conscious.

Obsessions are not desired, but they are certainly conscious, because they remain in union with the self. In another way many actions are conscious which are not desired, e.g. the automatic actions of the insane, of catatoniacs. In these cases the purely motor act is carried on without any connexion with the conscious ego. The patients see themselves, hear themselves doing something, and thus come to consciousness of an action as if they were perceiving the action of a third person.

The mechanism of attention is too little known to us in the conscious for us to be able to "explain" it in the unconscious. But it is easy for us to imagine that those same dispositions which form conscious attention can exist also without associative connexion with the self. I resolve to pay attention to a certain plant and then think no more about it. If I come across the plant its identity at once occurs to me. I must take it that not only was the latent disposition prepared to form further associations at the sight of the plant, say to gather it, but to establish union with the ego at the same time. That the latter process is no necessary partial manifestation of the adjustment is proved by the daily occurrence of adjustments which do not become conscious to us. Whilst still at home I propose to go to such and such a place. On the way thither I no longer think about it but at every crossing I take the correct turning. This is not an unconscious adjustment of the attention but an unconscious attention, or, to follow the convenient usage of many psychologists in personifying the "unconscious," an attention of the unconscious. The mental complex which unconsciously governs my direction notices all the crossings and chooses the correct ones without uniting itself with the otherwise occupied self.

Association is a process dominating our entire psyche and one we already find in reflexes [1] which are not psychical. Our conception introduces no new element into psychology. That processes can run their course outside the ego complex as well as within, the instances quoted in the first part of this chapter will prove ; that they are not associated with the remaining content of our thought is obvious ; it is equally obvious that everything which proceeds in " our conscious " is associated with the presentations which for the moment form our personality, our ego. What is new in our conception is this : that the presence or absence of consciousness depends upon whether connexion with the ego is present or absent ; this factor can be always made out.

I am not in a position to give a strict proof of the correctness of this hypothesis. It seems to me highly probable because it

---

[1] This and other points pertaining hereto I have examined more thoroughly in the *Allgemeine Zeitschrift für Psychiatrie*, Bd. L (" Versuch einer naturwissenschaftlichen Betrachtung der psychologischen Grundbegriffe ").

fully explains all the facts which I have noticed during twenty-six years' observation both in healthy and in sick people ; nor is anything postulated which is not already known.  Its simplicity is a further recommendation.  Whether it is right or not, it seems to me, anyway, to fulfil a weighty task.  It links the unconscious psychical phenomenon to the rest of our knowledge and removes it from the realm of the mysterious.  I hope, therefore, that it will serve to destroy the current prejudices against an objective investigation of the facts in this sphere, and will thus pave the way for further fruitful studies.

Many have already said something similar, but so far as I know either they have not worked out the idea, or, like Wundt, they have turned aside from the consequences.  Of the former I will only mention Janet, Exner, Löb, who set out from very different points of view.  It must indeed astonish every observer that the consciousness which we observe in ourselves is so closely united with those functions which we term association and connected recollection (associative memory ; Löb).

It is more difficult to understand the position of those who absolutely deny the "unconscious."  So far as I know, the consequential carrying out of their supposition is never made by them, and they are unable to reconcile themselves with many facts.  Just two recent instances.  Raimann [1] says, clearly and definitely, "there is no unconscious knowledge."  Ten pages further we find, "Experience forces us to assume that hysterics do not distinguish between conscious and unconscious."  Hellpach,[2] in his denial of the unconscious, first of all brings to his aid a *petitio principii* : "But the unconscious which lies between *b* and *a* seems to have changed the first presentation within these, and can, naturally, not be the object of psychology, for the psyche has only to do with the conscious " (p. 222). And on pp. 403–406 he begins a really beautiful deduction which is to show that the mechanisms which can condition false connexions do not require any unconscious for their explanation.  At one moment it is said that the hysteric is naturally not conscious of the associations which have developed in him.  But this unconscious is only a subjective essence, for objectively all these phenomena are causally connected quite as well as they are in the normal way.  The last sentence is the coping-stone of the whole edifice and suddenly introduces the concept of causality, which has as much to do with the deduction as a straw hat with the arch of a bridge.  This quite apart from

[1] *Die hysterichen Geisstesstörungen* ("Hysterical Mental Disorders "), p. 232.
[2] *Grundlinien der Psychologie der Hysterie* (" Foundations of the Psychology of Hysteria"), pp. 222, 403–406.

the fact that there is so far no objective consciousness, and thus in what preceded the unconscious psychical mechanism was already granted. On p. 35 again the obscurities of Wundt's concept take revenge on their adept.

That the unconscious mental functions do not fit into most of the theories is certainly not their fault. They are facts to which theories must accommodate themselves, however often the reverse process be tried. The difficulties attending the recognition of the unconscious are truly significant of the power of preconceived opinions and academic speculation.

If we mean not only to prove the existence of the unconscious but to apprehend it in its connexion with other mental happenings, with the reserve which science everywhere enjoins on us, we must accommodate ourselves to the idea that there are a number of functions of the brain of which only a portion becomes conscious. And this becoming conscious is sometimes only a secondary matter and occurs, according to our hypothesis, by association with the ego. The independence of the mind from the function of the brain is about as demonstrable as the dependence of water considered in its aggregate state on warmth and pressure [1]; so far as I know, the heinousness of pressure has not been a reason for denying this dependence. We are therefore not in bad company if we ignore the "psychophysical parallel," which helps us to no understanding but only conceals the renunciation of any understanding by a positive expression ; nor are we in bad company when we do not allow preconceived opinion to brush aside the facts of daily observation.

### SUMMARY

There are effective and numerous processes in us which comport themselves in all respects like conscious processes with the one exception that consciousness is absent.

Psychology cannot ignore them because the processes influence the conscious mind just as well as conscious sensations, thoughts, and wishes.

The study of these unconscious (mental) functions are quite indispensable in psychopathology for they often control its symptoms.

We can best represent such processes to ourselves by imagining that physical processes in the brain, which form the foundation of all psychical happenings, only become conscious when they become functionally linked—associated—with the ego complex.

---

[1] We as little possess an "explanation," like that of the effect of the (hypothetical) phenomena of ether upon the (hypothetical) molecules of water, as we possess any presentation of the transference of the movement of one body to another—or the effect of the physical upon the psychical.

# PSYCHO-ANALYSIS AND ASSOCIATION EXPERIMENTS

## By Dr. C. G. JUNG

IT is not easy to give in a few words the basis of Freud's theory of hysteria and his psycho-analytic method. The nomenclature and Freud's conceptions are still in flux—fortunately, I would add. For despite the extraordinary progress which our knowledge of hysteria has made in the last few years, thanks to Freud's works, neither Freud nor we who follow him have reached finality. No one must be astounded, therefore, if Freud in his most recent work on hysteria [1] has again, to a large extent, abandoned the nomenclature of his *Studies in Hysteria*, and has substituted a series of other and more fitting expressions. Freud's terms should not be always regarded as strictly limited scientific concepts, but rather as occasional expressions of a language rich in new forms. Those who write about Freud should avoid logomachy but should keep in mind the essence of the thing.

Freud traces every hysteria back to a series of psychical traumata, which finally reach their apex in a sexual trauma of prepuberty. Naturally, the so-called psychogenic character of hysteria was known before Freud. (For a precise demarcation of the psychogenic we are particularly indebted to Möbius.) It was known that hysteria arises from presentations which are distinguished by their strength of emotion. But Freud was the first to show us the path traversed by the psychological process. He found that the hysterical symptom is essentially a symbol for presentations (sexual in the ultimate analysis) which are not present in the conscious, but are repressed from the conscious by strong inhibitions. Repression arises from the critical presentations being so charged with pain (unpleasure) as to be insupportable to the conscious self.

Inseparably bound up with this conception is the psycho-

[1] " Bruchstück einer Hysterieanalyse," *Monatsschrift für Psychiatrie u. Neurologie*, 1905. Republished in *Sammlung kleiner Schriften zur Neurosenlehre*, zweite Folge.

analytic method. It provides us with the knowledge of the repressed material of presentation that has become unconscious. If we ask patients directly as to the cause of their illness we always receive incorrect, or at least imperfect, information. If we did receive correct information as in other (physical) illnesses, we should have known long ago about the psychogenic nature of hysteria. But it is just the point of hysteria that it represses the real cause, the psychic trauma, forgets it and replaces it by superficial " cover causes." That is why hysterics ceaselessly tell us that their illness arose from a cold, from over-work, from real organic disorders. And many physicians thus allow themselves again and again to be deceived. Others go to the opposite extreme and maintain that all hysterics lie. But that is because they completely misconceive the psychological conditionings of hysteria, which really consist in this, that presentations insupportable to the conscious ego are repressed and cannot be therefore reproduced. Freud's psycho-analytic methods circumvent the inhibitions which the conscious ego sets up towards the repressed presentations. The essence of the method consists in the patient simply relating everything, without selection, that comes into his mind (Freud called this " free association "). The method is completely presented in Freud's work, *The Interpretation of Dreams* (1900).[1] Although it is theoretically a priori certain that law will control all the thoughts that occur to a person, it is readily understandable that a person without great experience would go astray in this labyrinth of ideas, and would finally get hopelessly stuck. It is, and will remain, one of the chief reasons against the general application of Freud's method that delicate psychological intuition in the doctor is as much a requisite as technique for a psycho-analysis ; the physician must possess individual characteristics which cannot be presupposed to exist in every doctor or psychologist. Then for psycho-analysis one's thoughts must have a particular bent, having in view the understanding of symbols. But this adjustment is only to be gained with industrious practice. It is a tendency of the mind, inborn in a poet, but carefully avoided in scientific thought, the constellation here being towards sharply-cut images. Thinking in symbols requires a new adjustment from us just as if we had to begin to think in flight ideas. It would seem that these are some of the reasons why Freud's methods have only been understood by few, and practised by even fewer ; there are, indeed, but a few workers who value Freud's work theoretically or practically.

Despite the many valuable experiences which Freud has

[1] English translation by Dr. A. A. Brill, 1912.

expounded for us, psycho-analysis is a very difficult art, for every beginner rapidly loses courage and orientation in face of the innumerable obstacles. Safe foundations are wanting from whence to start ; when you have to begin with a patient at haphazard, so to say, you are often at a loss where to begin the attack.

Association experiments have helped us to get over these first and chief difficulties. I have shown in the chapter on time-measurements (chapter v) that the emotionally charged presentation complexes give rise to characteristic disturbances in the experiment ; their presence and probable nature can be recognized from the disturbances themselves. This fact forms the foundation of *The Psychological Diagnosis of Facts* founded by Wertheimer and Klein,[1] Hans Gross,[2] and Alfred Gross.[3] It seems fairly possible by this method to diagnose by the associations the complex of a crime. Every one has naturally one or more complexes which make themselves manifest in some way in the associations. The background of our consciousness (or the unconscious) consists of complexes of this kind. The whole material of memory is grouped around them. They form higher psychical unities analogous to the ego complex (Bleuler,[4] chapter vi). They constellate the whole of our thinking and doing, hence the associations also. We sometimes join a second experiment to that of the association one, *reproduction.*[5] The experiment consists in making the subject repeat his reactions to the stimulus-words in the first experiment. Where memory fails we have generally to do with a constellation due to a complex. Reproduction, therefore, assists in the closer circumscribing of the complex disturbances.

*All psychogenic neuroses contain a complex* which is differentiated from normal complexes by being endowed with extremely strong emotional tones, possessing such constellating power that it brings the whole individual under its influence. The complex is hence the *causa morbi* (given, of course, the predis-

[1] Wertheimer, *Experimentelle Untersuchungen zur Tatbestandsdiagnostik* (Dissert : Würzburg, 1905.)

Wertheimer and Klein, " Psychologische Tatbestandsdiagnostik," *Archiv. für Kriminalanthropologie*, Bd. XV.

[2] Hans Gross, " Zur psychologischen Tatbestandsdiagnostik," *Archiv. für Kriminalanthropologie*, 1905.

[3] Alfred Gross, " Die Associationsmethode im Strafprocess," *Zeitschrift für die gesamte Strafrechtswissenschaft*, Bd. XXVI. Grabowsky, " Psychologische Tatbestandsdiagnostik," 1905.

[4] Bleuler, " Versuch einer naturwissenschaftlichen Betrachtung der psychologischen Grundbegriffe," *Allgemeine Zeitschrift für Psychiatrie*.

[5] Jung, " Experimentelle Beobachtungen über das Erinnerungsvermögen," *Centralb. für Nervenheilk, u. Psych.*, Bd. XXVIII.

position). The associations often enable us to recognize the nature of the complex, thus obtaining valuable clues for causal therapy. A by-product, not to be under-estimated, is the scientific knowledge which we thus gain of the origin and inner construction of the psychogenic neuroses. Freud has assuredly long since given us the substance of this knowledge, but he has anticipated by a long way the understanding of his time. It will not, therefore, be superfluous if I offer some new approach on the experimental plane to the Freudian store of knowledge. In previous chapters Freud's principles have several times been drawn on in explanation. Here I would present the connexion between psycho-analysis and association experiments by some practical examples. I choose an ordinary case of obsessional neurosis which I treated in June 1905.

Miss E. came to me for hypnotic treatment for sleeplessness of four months' duration. Besides the sleeplessness she complained of inner unrest and excitement, irritability towards her family, impatience and quarrelsomeness. She is thirty-seven, a teacher, cultured and intelligent; has always been nervous; has a younger sister feeble-minded; her father was an alcoholic. Condition: well nourished; physically nothing of moment was found. Her agitated and convulsive movements are remarkable. Whilst talking she seldom looks at the doctor, as a rule not addressing him but speaking out at the window. From time to time she turns away still more, is often obliged to laugh involuntarily, frequently shrugs her shoulders as if shaking off something disagreeable, protruding the lower part of her abdomen in a peculiar manner.

The anamnesis which she gives is very incomplete and indefinite. She had formerly been a governess abroad, but had not then been ill. The illness only occurred in recent years and has gradually developed to its present pitch. She says she has been unsuccessfully treated by many doctors. She would now like to try hypnosis, but immediately adds that she is firmly convinced that hypnotism will not succeed. Her disease is incurable and she is sure she will go mad. She has, indeed, often thought that she cannot be normal now and that she is already insane. It here occurred to me that the patient was obviously talking round something that she would not or could not say. On being urged she finally explained, with many gestures of resistance and constant blushing, that she could not sleep because whenever she disposed herself to sleeping the idea came to her that she would not, of course, be able to sleep, that she would never sleep again until she were dead; she would then wake right up and be unable to sleep again the whole night. Whenever she felt worn out and desired to sleep a terrible fear would rouse her up again—she would never sleep again until she were dead or mad. She had to wrench this explanation out of herself in such a way, and with such gestures of aversion, as almost to arouse the impression that she was telling something sexually improper which caused her to be ashamed. Again there were the movements of the abdomen. She frequently laughed as if abashed, which made a peculiar impression of inadequacy. This peculiar state caused me to ask if there were other ideas present which troubled her during the sleeplessness: " No, I can't remember anything—things just pass through me—oh, it's thousands of things that keep running through my head." She was unable to recall anything, made gestures of aversion and said suddenly: She has really such stupid thoughts; these force themselves upon her and she cannot possibly shake herself free from them. She is sorry she cannot communicate these ideas to me for she is afraid I would then get these obsessions. She had once told a doctor and a clergyman about her thoughts and now she is always thinking that she had infected those people and that they also had obsessional ideas. She was sure she had already infected me. I reassured her; I had already heard many ideas of that kind and they had not injured me in the least. Upon this she admitted with the same gestures that, besides the ideas mentioned with which she had infected the doctor and the clergyman, she was chiefly bothered by the thought that a neighbour, a woman, who had recently died, had on her account died unhappy and had had to suffer all the torments of hell. She had only had that idea since her death; previously, she had had for many years the idea that a boy whom she had formerly educated had subsequently died from the punishments she had occasionally imposed upon him. Her anxiety was so great that she had been obliged to write twice to the family for news about his health. She had done it each time in a way that would not arouse suspicion. The good news which she received each time had momentarily quieted her, but a few days later the anxiety was as great as ever. That idea had now ceased, but she had now to reproach herself with the unhappy death of her neighbour. Reason told her that these ideas were nonsense (she said this in a very uncertain voice) or was it perhaps the truth? (she quickly added). Thus she did not entirely correct herself, but was obviously completely mastered by the obsessional ideas.

The anamnesis did not succeed in discovering any sexual abnormalities, that is to say, anything which could in any way refer to sexual matters was denied as a matter of course.

Any attempt at hypnotism was useless because she could not fix her attention in any way. Not to spoil this method at the beginning by useless attempts, I decided first to obtain some certainty about the psychical material which was at the root of the illness. I therefore arranged an association experiment with her.

## I. The Association Experiment

The whole experiment is reproduced here.

| Stimulus-word | Reaction | Reaction-time | Reproduction |
|---|---|---|---|
| 1. *Head* [1] | *thoughts* | : 2·2 seconds | hair |
| 2. Green | grass | : 1·8 ,, | † [2] |
| 3. *Water* | *drinker — drink* | : 2·4 ,, | glass |
| 4. Prick | needle | : 3·6 | † |
| 5. Angel ‡ [3] | heaven | : 2·6 | † |
| 6. Long ‡ | short | : 4 | † |
| 7. Ship | sea | : 1·4 ,, | † |

I note that I am not in a position to give an exhaustive analysis of the associations. The subject met all questions by assuring me that nothing special occurred to her mind at the so-called critical places. In this way it was impossible to discover the determinants of the individual reactions by subjective analysis.

[1] Associations which were absent or incorrect in reproduction are in italics.

[2] † denotes correct reproduction.

[3] ‡ denotes that the patient quickly repeated the stimulus-word. This phenomenon is frequently encountered both with and after complex reactions.

But, after all, the objective result of the experiment suffices for a diagnosis, at least in its outlines, apart from the statements of the subject. I should like to give in as much detail as possible how I arrived at my diagnosis.

The probable mean (Kräpelin) of all the reaction-times of the experiment amounts to 2·4 seconds. This mean is far too high for an intelligent and cultured person. The mean figures I obtained in twelve educated persons are 1·5 second. As the effects of emotion are chiefly responsible for the prolongation of the reaction-time,[1] a marked emotivity of the subject may be concluded from this rather high figure. I beg the reader to keep hold of this figure, 2·4 seconds, during the following consideration of the reactions.

Reaction 1, *head — thoughts*, reproduced incorrectly. The complex of the illness may have been at work here. Reaction 3, *water — drinker — drink*, is verbally disturbed. *Drinker* has been improved to *drink*. Her father was a heavy drinker. The subsequent three reaction-times are all prolonged to over 2·4 seconds ; there are besides two repetitions of the stimulus-word. One may therefore accept a perseveration due to emotion after *drinker*.[2] Reaction 5, *angel — heaven*, may have aroused the obsessional idea of the unhappy death of her neighbour.

| Stimulus-word | Reaction | Reaction-time | Reproduction |
|---|---|---|---|
| 8. Pluck | sow | : 2·2 seconds | † |
| 9. *Wool* | *spin* | : 3·4 ,, | — [3] |
| 10. *Friendly* | *lovable* | : 3·6 | good |
| 11. *Table* | *woman* | : 4·6 | — |
| 12. Ask | answer | : 2·4 | † |
| 13. State | church | : 2·2 | † |
| 14. *Haughty* | *spirited* | : 1·8 | friendly |
| 15. Stalk | flower | : 1·8 ,, | † |

What disturbance caused the prolongation at *wool* I cannot say. Experience has shown that with reaction 10, *friendly*, erotic reminiscences readily occur. The striking reaction 11, *table — woman*, which patient cannot explain, seems to refer to an erotic significance of reaction 10. In sensitive persons, as all neurotics are, stimulus-words are always taken personally. One can easily suppose that the patient would like to be the " lovable, good woman." That the word *friendly* has a certain tendency to reproduction in the patient is seen in its recurrence in reaction 14. (Naturally emotional presentations have a stronger tendency to reproduction than indifferent ones.)

[1] See chapter v.

[2] I cannot here enter into the justification for this deduction and must refer the reader to chapter v.

[3] — means not reproduced.

| Stimulus-word | Reaction | Reaction-time | Reproduction |
|---|---|---|---|
| 16. Dance | jump | : 1·8 seconds | † |
| 17. Sea ‡ | water | : 2·4    ,, | † |
| 18. Ill | healthy | : 2 | † |
| 19. Proud | arrogant | : 5 | † |
| 20. Cook | roast | : 2 | † |
| 21. Ink | barrel | : 2 | † |
| 22. *Wicked* | *good* | : 3 | — |
| 23. Needle | prick | : 2·2 | † |
| 24. Swim | water | : 2 | † |
| 25. Journey | railway | : 2·2 | † |
| 26. Blue | red | : 1·8 | † |
| 27. Bread | knife | : 2    .. | † |
| 28. *Threaten* | *naughty* | : 8    ,, | — |

Reaction 16, *dance*, is prone to arouse erotic reminiscences. This supposition is not unjustified here, for the reaction following is disturbed. Reactions 18 and 19, *ill* and *proud*, may have easily had personal references. With *proud* there are distinct complex signs, likewise *wicked* and *threaten* have obviously aroused feelings. The reaction to *threaten — naughty* sounds like the association to the presentation of a child. Perhaps the reminiscence of her pupil has been aroused ? *Threaten* is capable of arousing many emotional relationships. People with vivid complexes generally have some anxiety about the future. We often see that they refer *threaten* to the threatened uncertainty of their future. Naturally concrete references frequently underlie this emotion. It should not be forgotten that a word like *threaten* is not quite usual, and by its " difficulty " alone has a somewhat exciting effect, without there being necessarily a definite complex beneath. All the same, it seems more prudent to put it down to the influence of a complex than to " difficulty." (I would remind the reader of Freud's analyses.)

| Stimulus-word | Reaction | Reaction-time | Reproduction |
|---|---|---|---|
| 29. Lamp | light | : 1·8 seconds | † |
| 30. Rich | poor | : 1·8    ,, | † |
| 31. Tree | green | : 1·2 | † |
| 32. Sing | dance | : 2 | † |
| 33. Pity | poor | : 2 | † |
| 34. *Yellow* | *flower* | : 4·2 | green |
| 35. Mountain ‡ | mine | : 2·8 | † |
| 36. *Play* | *children* | : 2·2 | dance |
| 37. Salt | bread | : 2·8 | † |
| 38. New | old | : 1·6    ,, | † |

In this series *dance*, which was the stimulus-word of reaction 16, recurs twice, betraying a distinct tendency to reproduction, corresponding to the not inconsiderable emotional tone which obviously clings to it. Frequent repetition can betray a person in this way, as the following case indicates : A gentleman, whom

I asked to take part in an experiment, was convinced that he would disclose no complexes. On his way to me he thought over what words he would answer to my stimulus-words. It at once occurred to him to say *Paris*, a word that seemed to him void of all personal significance. In the experiment he repeated *Paris* several times, explaining that the word was absolutely accidental. Six months later he admitted to me that, at the time of the experiment, he was entirely absorbed by an affair which greatly upset him which was taking place in Paris. But at the time it seemed to him that *Paris* had no significance at all for him. I have no reason to doubt the truthfulness of this person. Reaction 34, *yellow*, certainly had a personal reference, to judge from the surrounding complex disturbances. Patient has a rather yellowish complexion, giving her an elderly appearance. Women are very sensitive to these things, especially when an erotic complex is present.

That *children* (reaction 36) is not reproduced but is replaced by another of erotic nature is worth mentioning.

| Stimulus-word | Reaction | Reaction-time | Reproduction |
|---|---|---|---|
| 39. *Habit* ‡ | *ugly or bad* | : 12·2 seconds | bad manners |
| 40. Ride ‡ | drive | : 2·4 ,, | † |
| 41. *Wall* | *room* | : 3 | — |
| 42. Stupid ‡ | clever | : 2·8 | — |
| 43. Copy-book ‡ | book | : 3 | † |
| 44. *Despise* ‡ | *disesteem* | : 15·2 ,, | to disesteem |
| 45. Tooth | abscess | : 1·4 ,, | † |

In this series we meet various severe complex disturbances. At reaction 39, *habit*, and reaction 44, *despise*, the patient made gestures of aversion and stamped her foot. An " ugly or bad habit " can easily be understood in a sexual sense : onanism, for instance, is a bad habit. People are despised who have such bad habits. Reaction 42, *stupid*, can be personal or can be a perseverating emotional tone extending over from *habit*. The movements accompanying the expressions are certainly not against a sexual complex. *Habit* might also be *drinking habit*, and thus have aroused the complex of her drunken father.

| Stimulus-word | Reaction | Reaction-time | Reproduction |
|---|---|---|---|
| 46. *Right* ‡ | *I always feel like saying exactly the opposite* | : 7·6 seconds | wrong |
| 47. People ‡ | father | : 6 ,, | † |
| 48. Smell | pleasant smell | : 4·8 | † |
| 49. *Book* ‡ | *pen* | : 4·4 | copy-book |
| 50. *Unjust* ‡ | *opinion* | : 3·6 | just |
| 51. Frog | green | : 2·4 | † |
| 52. Divorce | marriage | : 2·2 | † |
| 53. Hunger | thirst | : 1·4 | † |
| 54. White | black | : 1·8 | † |

If, as we presume, the subject takes the stimulus-word personally and has a sexual complex in the direction suggested, it will be readily understood that in reaction 46, *right*, she *always feels like saying the opposite,* for that agrees with her actions ; it is more suitable also in regard to her father's drunkenness. Double or manifold determinations should not be excluded ; according to Freud, they are indeed the rule.

It is noticeable that reaction 47 runs *people — father.* She seems still to be within the region of the emotional tone of *right.* We might conclude that there is some obscure connexion between her self-reproaches and *father.* (This connexion will become clear later.)

What was the nature of the disturbance in *book — pen* is not easy to say. (Book = German *Buch,* and, thus pronounced, means in the Swiss dialect *Bauch* = belly.) An assimilation of this kind could easily occur with a sexual complex. I have often come across it in other persons.

The constant decrease of the reaction-times from *right,* 7·6 seconds, speaks, however, rather in favour of a severe complex disturbance which began at this stimulus-word and gradually decreased in the seven reactions that followed. Reaction 50, *unjust,* seems to be taken personally, which bears out the idea of self-reproach.

| Stimulus-word | Reaction | Reaction-time | Reproduction |
|---|---|---|---|
| 55. Cattle ‡ | cow | : 4·2 seconds | † |
| 56. Take care | disobedient | : 4   „ | † |
| 57. *Pencil* | *sharpen* | : 3   „ | pointed |
| 58. Cloudy | weather | : 1·8 | † |
| 59. Plum | tree | : 3·8 | † |
| 60. Touch | certain | : 1·4 | † |
| 61. Law | state | : 2·8 | † |
| 62. *Dear* | *good* | : 4   „ | child |
| 63. Glass | wa-water | : 1·6 | † |
| 64. *Quarrel* | *dispute* | : 2·2   „ | discord |
| 65. *Goat* | *milk* | : 2   „ | to give milk |

I cannot explain the disturbance at reaction 55, *cattle.* Reaction 56, *disobedient,* recalls the previous *naughty,* which one should probably refer to the pupil. The disturbance in the succeeding reactions speaks for perseveration of the emotion. Reaction 59, *plum — tree,* judging from the length of the reaction-time, does not seem to have gone quite smoothly. Plum is not an everyday word, but it is not likely that an educated person would require so much time for the reaction. (In Wehrlin's idiots the average times varied from 3 to 3·7 seconds ; in an educated person 3·8 seconds thus seems far too long.) *Plum* (like an egg-shaped plum), Swiss *zwetschge*, is a favourite sexual symbol in Swiss colloquial speech.

Reaction 62, *dear*, can be readily claimed as an erotic complex. In reaction 63, *glass*, the complex of the alcoholic father came again to the surface, with the strong emotion bound up with it. (Hence the disturbance of the two subsequent reactions.)

| Stimulus-word | Reaction | Reaction-time | Reproduction |
|---|---|---|---|
| 66. Big | small | : 2·6 seconds | † |
| 67. Potato ‡ | mealy | : 0·6 ,, | † |
| 68. Paint | mill | : 2 ,, | † |
| 69. Part ‡ | small | : 11·6 ,, | † |
| 70. *Old* | *ugly* | : 3 ,, | young, not beautiful |
| 71. *Flower* | *beautiful* | : 2 ,, | scent |
| 72. Hit | cane | : 2·8 ,, | — |
| 73. Chest | table | : 2·8 ,, | — |

Reaction 66, *big*, is usually taken personally. The patient is of very small stature. In an erotic complex there will be, as we have already seen, many references to the body. That must be the explanation of the disturbances in the subsequent reactions. Reaction 69, *part*, has a greatly prolonged reaction-time ; part(s) taken as sexual part(s) is very common. The strong emotional tone of this is characteristic. That among these constellations reaction 70, *old*, is apprehended in the personal erotic sense is not to be wondered at. How strongly marked the question of personal beauty is in the patient is seen from the perseveration *beautiful* (reaction 71). Reaction 72, *hit — cane*, may have been especially constellated by the obsession that she was responsible for the death of her former pupil.

| Stimulus-word | Reaction | Reaction-time | Reproduction |
|---|---|---|---|
| 74. Wild | child | : 2·4 seconds | † |
| 75. Family | big | : 2·4 ,, | † |
| 76. Wash ‡ | clean | : 3 | † |
| 77. Cow | milk | : 1·8 | † |
| 78. Strange ‡ | home-sick | : 14·8 | † |
| 79. Luck ‡ | ill luck | : 3 | † |
| 80. Relate | stories | : 1·6 ,, | † |

The slight disturbance at reaction 76, *wash*, is explicable by the previous erotic associations, *child* and *family*. Reaction 78, *strange*, has obviously awakened a personal reference of which we shall get the explanation later.

| Stimulus-word | Reaction | Reaction-time | Reproduction |
|---|---|---|---|
| 81. Standing | understanding | : 4·6 seconds | † |
| 82. Narrow ‡ | small | : 3·2 ,, | † |
| 83. Brother | sister | : 1 | † |
| 84. Injure ‡ | neighbour | : 4 | † |
| 85. Stork ‡ | church | : 2·4 | † |

| Stimulus-word | Reaction | Reaction-time | Reproduction |
|---|---|---|---|
| 86. False ‡ | faithless | : 3 seconds | † |
| 87. Anxiety | feeling | : 2·4 ,, | † |
| 88. Kiss | mouth | : 2·2 | † |
| 89. Burning | fire | : 1·8 | † |
| 90. Dirty | clammy | : 2·2 | † |
| 91. Door | crease | : 1·6 ,, | † |

The clang-association *standing — understanding* [1] is very striking ; we recall the disturbance evoked by *habit*. We there suspected the *bad habit* of onanism. This complex may have been aroused here also. The popular belief is that onanism destroys the understanding (mind). Remember also the subject's complaint that she feared she would go mad. Reaction 82, *narrow — small*, is under the influence of the previous reaction : *small* probably belongs by analogy with its former occurrence to the bodily complex ; *narrow* can be referred, under the constellation of the previous association, to the introitus vaginæ and thus be linked with the *small*, which hints at her stature ; the suspicious " part(s) " are *small*. (This supposition will be confirmed.) Reaction 84, *injure*, is probably taken personally. *Neighbour* agrees well with this. She caused immeasurable injury to her neighbour by being the cause of her unhappy death. But *injure* can be also taken personally under the sexual constellation ; one causes oneself physical and mental injuries by onanism (as above). The neighbour is thus only a cover person (cp. Freud's similar demonstrations). Her neighbour is an easy means of concealing herself. Subsequent disturbances indicate that an emotional tone set in here.

In reaction 86, *false — faithless,* a definite erotic reminiscence may easily have emerged in an elderly single woman.

| Stimulus-word | Reaction | Reaction-time | Reproduction |
|---|---|---|---|
| 92. Choose ‡ | teacher | : 4·4 seconds | † |
| 93. Hay | straw | : 1·8 ,, | † |
| 94. *Still* ‡ | *stool* | : 13 | child |
| 95. Scorn | derision | : 1·4 | † |
| 96. Sleep ‡ | wake | : 3·4 | † |
| 97. Month | year | : 1·6 | † |
| 98. Tinted | bright | : 2·4 | † |
| 99. Dog | cat | : 1·2 | † |
| 100. Talk | silence | : 1·4 ,, | † |

Reaction 92, *choose*, women are prone to link on to thoughts of marriage. The subject's father was a teacher, she is a teacher. It is a likely supposition that she thinks of marriage with a

[1] This should be understood as *standing in society* : the German is *Anstand* (station, demeanour, etc.), *Verstand* (understanding).—TRANSLATOR.

teacher. Again the father-complex comes up for consideration (see later about this.) Reaction 94, *still — stool*, is a striking clang-association. The explanation is given by the eroticism *child*. A child can be *still*, but the dead are also *still* (obsessional idea— she caused the death of her pupil through ill-treatment). But erotic relationships can be also present ; for *stillen* means in German to *suckle, nurse, hush* an infant. One can " still " a child, " still " the sexual impulses.

Reaction 96, *sleep*, has many sexual references. Patient is unable to sleep. Sleeplessness in younger people is frequently the expression of want of sexual satisfaction (Freud).

Those without experience in the sphere of pathological association-psychology will probably shake their heads at the above suppositions ; perhaps they will not only see herein hypothesis, but also fantasies. Very likely the same criticism will be made here as at Freud's *Dream Interpretation*.

We will first recapitulate the result of the association and reproduction experiment. As already mentioned, the patient gave no explanations ; I am thus thrown entirely upon the objective data of the experiment, and on my experience.

The probable mean of the reaction-times amounts to 2·4 seconds ; 44 per cent. of the reaction-times exceed 2·4 seconds. Among these are figures up to 15·2 seconds, from which we may deduce a considerable emotion, or, in other words, a considerable want of command over the psychical material.

We have pointed to the existence of various complexes during the analysis. The erotic complex seems to play a chief part. It will not be superfluous if I again summarize the individual complex reactions so as to obtain a better perspective.

The following refer to an erotic complex [1] :

| Stimulus-word | Reaction | Reaction-time | Reproduction |
|---|---|---|---|
| 10. *Friendly* | *lovable* | : 3·6 seconds | good |
| 11. *Table* | *woman* | : 4·6 ,, | — |
| 12. | | : 2·4 | |
| 13. | | : 2·2 | |
| 14. | | : 1·8 | |
| 16. Dance | jump | : 1·8 ,, | † |
| 17. Sea ‡ | water | : 2·4 ,, | † |
| 34. *Yellow* | *flower* | : 4·2 ,, | green |
| 35. Mountain ‡ | mine | : 2·8 ,, | † |
| 36. | | : 2·2 | |
| 39. *Habit* | *ugly or bad* | : 12·2 ,, | bad manners |
| 40. Ride ‡ | drive | : 2·4 ,, | † |

---

[1] To emphasize the complex disturbances I add the phenomena of perseveration, especially the gradually decreasing times of the succeeding reactions.

| Stimulus-word | Reaction | Reaction-time | | Reproduction |
|---|---|---|---|---|
| 41. *Wall* | *room* | : 3 | seconds | — |
| 44. *Despise* ‡ | *disesteem* | : 15·2 | ,, | to disesteem |
| 45. | | : 1·4 | | |
| 59. Plum | tree | : 3·8 | ,, | † |
| 62. Dear | good | : 4 | ,, | child |
| 66. Big | small | : 2·6 | ,, | † |
| 67. Potato ‡ | mealy | : 6 | ,, | † |
| 68. | | : 2 | | |
| 69. Part | small | : 11·6 | ,, | † |
| 70. *Old* | *ugly* | : 3 | ,, | young, not beautiful |
| 71. *Flower* | *beautiful* | : 2 | ,, | scent |
| 72. *Hit* | *cane* | : 2·8 | ,, | — |
| 73. | | : 2·4 | | |
| 74. Wild | child | : 2·4 | ,, | † |
| 75. Family | big | : 2·4 | ,, | † |
| 76. Wash ‡ | clean | : 3 | ,, | † |
| 81. Standing | understanding | : 4·6 | ,, | † |
| 82. Narrow ‡ | small | : 3·2 | ,, | † |
| 83. | | : 1 | | |
| 86. False ‡ | faithless | : 3 | ,, | † |
| 87. | | : 2·4 | ,, | † |
| 88. | | : 2·2 | | |
| 89. | | : 1·8 | | |
| 92. Choose ‡ | teacher | : 4·4 | ,, | † |
| 93. | | : 1·8 | | |
| 94. *Still* ‡ | *stool* | : 13 | ,, | child |
| 95. | | : 1·4 | | |
| 96. Sleep ‡ | wake | : 3·4 | ,, | † |
| 97. | | : 1·6 | ,, | |

These reactions, all showing characteristic disturbances which are *ex hypothesi* of a sexual nature, can be linked together into the following story :

The subject feels that she is *old, ugly* ; she finds her *yellowish* complexion very disagreeable and her physique, upon which she bestows anxious attention, displeases her as being too *small*. She has a great longing for *marriage*, she would be a *loving wife* to her husband and would like to have *children*. Beneath these erotic yet quite innocent symptoms there seems to be a sexual complex which the patient has every reason to suppress more strongly. There are hints from which it may be inferred that she bestows unusual attention upon her genitalia ; in a respectable and educated single lady that can only signify *onanism*, of course, in the wider sense of perverse sexual self-satisfaction.

Onanism is one of the most frequent sources of *self-reproach* [1] and self-criticism. We find suggestions of this

---

[1] The reproaches need not, of course, be limited entirely to the sexual complex but are rapidly generalized.

complex, or rather this side of the sexual complex, in the associations :

| Stimulus-word | Reaction | Reaction-time | Reproduction |
|---|---|---|---|
| 14. *Arrogant* | *courageous* | : 1·8 seconds | friendly |
| 19. *Proud* | spirited, stupid | : 5 ,, | † |
| 22. Wicked | good | : 3 ., | — |
| 23. | | : 2·2 | |
| 42. Stupid ‡ | clever | : 2·8 .. | — |
| 43. Copy-book | book | : 3 | † |
| 46. *Right* ‡ | *I always feel like saying exactly the opposite* | : 7·6 ,, | wrong |
| 47. *People* ‡ | *father* | : 6 .. | † |
| 48. Smell | pleasant smell | : 4·8 ., | † |
| 49. *Book* ‡ | *pen* | : 4·4 ,, | copy-book |
| 50. *Unjust* ‡ | *opinion* | : 3·6 ,, | just |
| 51. | | : 2·4 | |
| 52. | | : 2·2 | |
| 53. | | : 1·4 ,, | |

Referable to the complex of the alcoholic father are :

| | | | |
|---|---|---|---|
| 3. *Water* | *drinker — drink* | : 2·4 seconds | *glass* |
| 4. | | : 3·6 ,, | |
| 63. Glass | wa-water | : 1·6 ,, | † |
| 64. *Dispute* | *quarrel* | : 2·4 ,, | *discord* |
| 65. *Goat* | *milk* | : 2 ,, | *to give milk* |

It is obvious from this summary that the sexual complex is very prominent. Although, as has been said, no direct confirmation of this interpretation could be obtained from the subject, I regard the complex diagnosis as certain upon the basis of the considerations I have advanced.

I therefore said to her : " I am certain that your obsessional ideas are merely excuses and screens ; in reality you are tormented by sexual ideas." The subject contested this explanation with affect and sincere conviction. If I had not been persuaded by the association experiment of the existence of a strongly marked sexual complex my conviction would probably have wavered. I made an appeal to her intelligence and her love of truth : she assured me that if she knew of anything of the kind in herself she would say it, for she knew it would be stupid to conceal such thoughts from the doctor. She had thought of marriage " like every one else, but not more." I then ended the interview, and made an appointment for two days later.

## II. The Psycho-analysis

In psycho-analysis the mental condition of the patient is important, but still more important is the mental condition of the doctor. This must assuredly be the reason why Freud's psycho-analysis is treated by science with silence. The analyst who goes into a case without assured conviction is soon lost in the pits and snares which the hysterical complex constructs at every turn. He must know beforehand that everything in the hysteric resists the bringing forth of the complex. When convenient, not only do interest and sympathy for the doctor disappear, but the subject loses the power of thought, the possibility of recollection, and finally even speech. But it is exactly these peculiar measures of defence that serve to betray the complex.

Just as in the association experiment hesitation, prolongation of time, absence of reproduction occur when the complex is aroused, in analysis likewise difficulties occur where the complex is being approached. To circumvent these difficulties Freud insists upon " free association." It is a very simple method which has only to be used a few times to be understood to a certain degree. In this case I undertook the psycho-analysis, following exactly Freud's method. I made the subject sit in a comfortable chair and seated myself behind her so as not to confuse her. I asked her to tell me quietly everything that came into her mind, to be quite indifferent as to what it was. The subject laughed : "One can't tell every bit of nonsense that occurs to one." I stood to my demand. A couple of times she tried to say something, but broke off each time with the excuse that it was silly, that I should be obliged to laugh and would think that she was a stupid or ungrateful person. I confined myself again to urging her to speak out, and finally she brought out these sentences : " I think that I never shall be well—now you'll laugh—but I'm convinced that I shall never be well. You can't hypnotize me, for I'm convinced that nobody can hypnotize me. You'll not be able to cure me any more than any other doctor. It will only be worse for me, for I shall reproach myself for having taken up your time unnecessarily with my rubbish." This idea was not quite unjustifiable, for the patient only threw the sentences out after long pauses, so that we had required almost half an hour to produce this meagre result. She went on : " I am now thinking of the people at home, how they are working and require me whilst I am here for nothing but my own silly thoughts —of course, you'll be infected by them—now I am thinking that I cannot sleep, that last night, despite your order, I took a gramme of veronal—of course I shall never be able to sleep again, how will you cure me then ?—what am I to say to you ? (There was here noticeable a certain restlessness.) I can't tell you all the silly thoughts that come into my head. (Restlessness increases, shrugs her shoulders, stamps up and down, shakes herself as if in great depression.) Now this is rubbish—I don't know anything more—nothing else occurs to me—let me go home now, nothing else comes to me." (Very restless—turns about on the chair, gestures of disgust, shaking the upper part of her body to and fro and her elbows moving as if thrusting aside ; at last she jumps up to leave.) Nothing else comes to her. With gentle force I persuade her to sit down again and point out to her that she has really come to get better, so she must carry out my prescription. After much discussion as to the purpose and meaning of my method she finally agrees to remain and continue. But the same depression and gestures of disgust soon recommence ; she twists about on the chair, from time to time sitting upright with a forced movement as if after a great victory she had come to a determination, and finally says despondingly : " Something silly comes to me—you will certainly laugh—but you must not tell it to anybody else—no, I really can't tell you, never—it is something very simple—it has nothing to do with my illness—I am robbing you of your time—it is nothing important— am I really obliged to tell it you ? It is not easy to say it— here goes : Well, once I was in France—it won't come, not if I sit for a month in this chair—(then with sudden determination) well, once I was a governess in France—no, I really can't tell it— there was a servant there—no, there was a gardener there—my God, what will you think of me !—this is martyrdom—I have never thought of anything like this."

Amid such interjections of distress there came out in the end, with innumerable stoppages and interruptions in which she swore that this would be her last consultation, that to-morrow she would go away, the following story :

There was among the servants a gardener who once said to her he would like to sleep with her. Whilst saying this he tried to kiss her, but she pushed him away. At night on going to bed she listened at the door and imagined what it would be like if he were to come and sleep with her ; she got fearfully excited lest he might come. In bed her thoughts again turned to what it would be like if he were to come, and then she drove these ideas away. But she could not get rid of thinking what it would be like, although she again and again shuddered at the idea that she could be thinking of anything of the sort. In this turmoil of thought she could not get to sleep until the morning.

This first sitting had lasted no less than an hour and a half. The result was a sexual history. Especially interesting was the fact of the disclosure being accompanied by the same mimetic manifestations which I had noticed at the first consultation. These tic-like phenomena were thus in very close and easily explicable connexion with the repressed sexual incidents. I made an appointment for the day after next, which she at once agreed to, seeming much relieved, and saying no more about going away.

At the time of her appointment I was engaged with some urgent work, and therefore requested her to come in the evening. But she sent me a message that it was impossible for her to wait, it was absolutely essential for her to talk to me. I supposed that something special had happened and went to her. I found her greatly excited ; she had not slept at all, not a minute ; she had been obliged to take sleeping medicines. I asked her if she had been again worried about her obsessions : " No, something much worse ; my head is now full of that nonsense about which I spoke to you last time. Now I can only think of these stories and of nothing else ; all night I have been tossing and turning about and cannot banish the thoughts for a minute. I must have a talk with you at once; it gives me no peace." She stated that on the last occasion she had felt much relieved and calmer and had gone home in good spirits, hoping that she would now be able to sleep ; but then she recalled an affair which she ought really to have mentioned last time, but which she thought wasn't worth while. She was now firmly resolved " not to act so stupidly " as last time but to speak out freely whatever came up into her mind. In this way the confessions would soon be ended. I began the analysis again, hoping that it would now go smoothly, without the endless preliminaries of the last time. But I was hopelessly mistaken. The patient went through almost exactly the same interjections as in the first sitting. After an hour and a half of real spiritual torment I had brought out the following history :

In the same house where my patient was a governess there was a servant-girl [1] who had a lover ; the girl had also had sexual intercourse with the gardener. The patient had frequent talks with her about sexual matters, especially about the sexual intercourse of the master and mistress. She and the servant had from time to time even examined the bedding of their master and mistress for spots of semen and other signs of coitus. After these conversations the patient used every time to reproach herself bitterly with her immorality, and passed sleepless nights in which she would be tossed about by painful reproaches and voluptuous fantasies.

When the story was brought to an end after wearisome struggles, the patient said " that was the last, there was nothing more in her mind." If only she could sleep ; repeating these events was no help at all.

---

[1] Cp. the mention of this servant at the first sitting.

Two days later she came for the third sitting and stated : After the last interview she felt fairly calmed, but hardly had she got into bed when another event at once occurred to her which had tormented her ever since, together with the self-reproach of not having told me everything the last time. She was now certain that to-day she would tell me about it quickly, without the constant resistance of the previous occasions. But the third sitting was exactly the same : continuous interjections, excuses, etc. Most remarkable was a tendency to present the affair as a matter of course, as if there were nothing in it. It concerned a second servant-girl in the same house. The master had a page-boy who pursued the girl, but did not succeed in seducing her. Finally, one evening when there was a party going on he managed to seduce the girl in the garden. But the couple were taken unawares by the mistress at the critical moment. The lad is said to have exclaimed, " What a pity ! I was just ready." The governess had been told this story by the servant-girl first mentioned. At first she pretended that the story had no interest at all for her, as if it were disagreeable, but she was lying, for in reality she had the greatest interest in it ; she had tried a couple of times to bring the girl back to the story so as to learn all the details. That night she could scarcely sleep on account of her curiosity and was ceaselessly asking herself " what the couple were doing in the garden, in what position were they when the mistress discovered them, for what was he ready if his mistress had not arrived ? " Although she knew the answers to these questions quite well, she could not rest without putting the questions to herself over and over again. Then she was constantly considering what she would have done in such a position. The excitement lasted several days.

In telling the story her attitude was, as mentioned, that it was a matter of course. For instance, under great resistance she told how the boy had pursued the servant. From the resistances one supposed that something unpleasant was to come ; but then she went on in a tone of indifference : " True, the page-lad was in love with the girl ; there's nothing wonderful in that ; that frequently happens, doesn't it ? Ah ! now something else comes—oh well, that's nothing." During the recital she tried again and again to minimize the importance of the event to herself by throwing in general rhetorical questions of this kind.

From that time on the former obsessional ideas were absent during the whole time of the analysis (three weeks), but the sexual ideas took their place ; as soon as one story was finished another took its place, worrying the patient with a real obsession.

She found no peace again until it had been told. She expressed herself as much astonished at the change; the stories would come up like clockwork, just as if they had been "experienced yesterday." Things came back to her of which she had lost all remembrance, but which she now recognized again (Freud's hypermnesia). These excuses must naturally be accepted with the same reserve as were the common "I don't know." The subject may easily have nourished and jealously cherished all the sexual ideas up to the present moment without on that account being able to recall them when she has to speak of them objectively. Her mimetic expressions during the talks are often in themselves sufficient to let me know what is coming, whilst she assures me a dozen times that she really can remember nothing more. Her ordinary self and her sexual self are really two distinct complexes, two different consciousnesses, which neither desire nor dare to know anything of each other. There is here but a suggestion of the dissociation of personality (as, moreover, in every vivid complex whose peculiarity is a striving after autonomy). But it is only a step to the classical cases of dissociation of personality, which are naturally all conditioned by Freud's mechanisms.[1]

A certain termination had been reached in these three sittings, so far as concerned the obsession that she was responsible for the death of her former pupil and the self-reproaches connected with her sexual stories. The patient felt this obviously, for she stated herself that many years had passed since these affairs, and the idea that she was responsible for her pupil's death had not troubled her for a long time. Probably to circumvent the unbearable sexual ideas she had transferred the reproaches from this sphere and fastened them on to her educational methods, in the well-known way. If one has constantly to reproach oneself about one set of ideas compensation is sought elsewhere as if a similar defect were present there. This is especially noticeable in onanists (hypercriticism, obsessions of cleanliness and tidiness). It does not seem to be mere accident that those incidents were first related which lay at the root of a past obsessional idea. As in her actual consciousness no obsessional ideas were present which could directly support these incidents, no special inhibitions were present. These incidents were therefore relatively indifferent material.

I do not want to describe the succeeding sittings in detail; they all followed the type described. No exhortation, no allusion to the ridiculous nature of her stereotyped resistances, could

---

[1] Cp. Jung, *Collected Papers*, "The Psychology and Pathology of Occult Phenomena" (Baillière, Tindall and Cox; 1916).

induce the subject to a quicker and less embarrassed narrative. Each fresh sitting was a fresh torture, and in nearly every one the subject assured me that it was the last. Usually the night following new material came up which afforded her no rest.

To the governess reminiscences there were appended a series of indecent stories which had served as the themes of talks with her neighbour for whose unhappy death the patient reproached herself. The dubious past of her neighbour was whispered on every hand. The subject, who is a highly respectable person and comes of an honourable family, has in her sense a dubious past also ; she indeed reproached herself about it. It was therefore not psychologically wonderful that she had been immediately attracted by her interesting neighbour. The *chronique scandaleuse* was discussed there, and the patient was obliged to narrate a whole series of highly obscene stories and jokes which I need not repeat here. To this she had again linked a number of self-reproaches. When the neighbour rapidly succumbed to an illness the subject transferred the reproaches, really due to her own sexual curiosity, on to the death of her neighbour, who must have died unblessed since the patient's visits had induced her to sinful talk. The nature of the reminiscences and of the chain of thought seem to be in favour of the view that these obsessional ideas were simply a new edition of her earlier ideas about her pupil's death. She had brought the religious obsessional ideas first to the clergyman and then to the doctor. To both she linked the presentation that she had infected them with her obsessions, to a certain extent in the same way as she had infected her neighbour, and originally her pupil. At the root of all this there is the general idea that she is a terrible creature who infects every one with her own corruption.

In the following sittings the patient chiefly disclosed a number of incidents which she had talked over in earlier years with a friend. This friend had a position in the office of a large business. There she heard all kinds of piquant things from gentlemen, which she brought post-haste from time to time to the patient. One day her friend said she would like to have relations with a man to see what it was like. This idea excited the patient powerfully ; she was obliged to keep saying to herself she would like to do the same. That was reason enough for renewed reproaches. From this narrative onwards the sexual incidents become more distinctly fastened on to her own person, although at nearly every sitting obscene jokes and the like had to be reproduced. Of the stories referring to her own person there were first of all reminiscences of earlier love affairs and expectations. The reproduction of these events, innocent enough on the whole, went pretty smoothly. Only one story had a more marked emotional tone. She had been in love with a young foreigner and believed he wished to marry her. But afterwards he left without a good-bye and she heard no more of him. She waited a long time, always hoping that he would write again to her. Reaction 78, *foreign — home-sick*, 14·8 seconds, refers to this affair. As already mentioned, the subject could not at the time explain the meaning of this reaction. Whilst the old love affairs were related without too great difficulties, there recurred at the end of this phase considerable resistances. The subject wished absolutely to leave ; she had nothing more to tell. I suggested to her that I had heard nothing about her earlier youth. She thought that would soon be got over, for she had not much to say about her youth. Hardly had she spoken this sentence when she was obliged to repeat a couple of times her tic-like gestures of disgust—an infallible sign that some important material was to be expected. Amid inconceivable stoppages and painful twistings she told me, by fits and starts, about a book that at the age of ten she had found at home called *The Way to a Happy Marriage*. She assured me that she had no longer any idea of what was in the book. But as I remained inexorable, memory after a time returned, and it was seen that the patient remembered all the details, frequently indeed the very words. She described the first coitus and its complications ; this academic description seemed to me peculiar and unusual. I suspected that at the back of this general description much must lay concealed. There was not long to wait before the patient related how at the age of fourteen she had found in the pocket of her elder brother a small book in which a letter was pressed. The letter was addressed by a young woman to a bosom friend and treated the secrets of the wedding night in a very obscene and lascivious way. As this showed, I was obviously on the right path. The next thing that came to the patient referred to erotic dreams which she had had in earlier days. The dreams were distinct pollution dreams and represented coitus without disguise. She then confessed to having sometimes tried to retain the dream-picture and to masturbate. Bound up with the onanism was a constant thinking about her own genitalia ; she was concerned as to whether she was " properly formed," if her introitus was not somewhat too narrow, and she felt compelled to investigate this problem with her finger. She was frequently obliged to look at her naked body in the looking-glass, and so on. She felt compelled to make a whole series of imaginary pictures about coitus—how she would behave at the first coitus, etc. Finally she acknowledged feeling violent sexual libido (which she had at first vehemently denied), admitting that she would very much like to marry, and had sexual images about most of the men with whom she had associated. She could not resist putting herself in the leading part in all the sexual events which she had piled up. For instance, she told about a young, naïvely frank acquaintance who in an excursion in an overfilled railway carriage had sat her teacher on her lap. The girl said afterwards, laughingly, that the teacher never failed to play his part, he had even taken a ruler with him in his trousers pocket. The patient was always thinking how pleasant it would be for her also if a teacher sat upon her knees, and she would know then what the ruler in the trousers pocket signified. (The earlier reaction, *choose — teacher*, must have been constellated by this incident.)

Amid great resistance she related how at the age of fourteen she had once lain upon a younger sister " as if she were a man." In one of the last sittings she succeeded in recalling an event which agrees in every way with the importance attributed by Freud to early psychical trauma. At the age of seven or eight she had on several occasions overheard the coitus of her parents. Once she heard her mother preventing it and refusing to give in to her father at all. After that it was a long time before she could look at her parents. Her mother became pregnant and gave birth to the patient's younger sister. She hated her sister from the first moment and was only able much later to overcome a deep antipathy to the child. It is not at all improbable that the subject had imagined herself as the second person in this affair, and she has indeed taken over the rôle of mother. The strong emotional tone which occurred in all the associations to " father " is readily comprehensible from this intimate link.

The psychological trauma of a perception of this kind is naturally preserved in the child's mind as an extremely emotional complex which constellates thinking and doing for years. This was classically the case in this patient. Her sexual function was thus given a very definite direction.[1] The analysis of her repressed presentations shows this; it is chiefly concerned with the grubbing out and picturing of coitus situations. It is remarkable that despite her extraordinarily vivid fantasy, she had never got deeply entangled with men and had rejected all attempts at seduction. On the other hand, she has been attracted by women of dubious character and equivocal conversation with an almost magical compulsion, an unexpected

[1] With this may be compared the fact that many sexual perverts (fetishists) have acquired their abnormality through an accidental sexual event. Cp. v. Krafft-Ebing, *Psychopathia Sexualis*.

tendency in a woman of her education and intelligence. The two last sittings were peculiarly instructive in this respect. She reproduced a cunning accumulation of the most disgusting indecencies which she had occasionally heard in the streets. What was common to all these indecencies, the repetition of which we may be spared, was the different abnormalities of coitus (too wide or too narrow an introitus, coitus of a young man with a big, fat woman, etc.). The amount and the deep vulgarity of these jokes seemed to me almost incomprehensible in so cultured and respectable a lady. The phenomenon is, however, explained by the early perverse direction of the sexual function, which was chiefly concerned 'with the hunting out of sexual filth, that is, the symbolical repetition of the overheard coitus. This complex has therefore affected the whole of her previous life and determined a mass of sexual doings and associations in its particular form. That is, for instance, why the patient carried out a kind of coitus action with her little sister, why her listening at the door to find out whether the gardener is coming is still so impressed upon her, why she engaged in the disgusting business of snuffling in the bed of her master and mistress, why she sought the company of sexually despicable people. Her defensive gestures and the peculiar projection of her abdomen show the effect of the complex at work everywhere. It is also very noticeable that at every sitting she appeared in another dress.

Such a use of the sexual function is bound to be unbearable to an otherwise finely planned character ; a repugnance to and repression of the tendency, as absurd as it is detestable, must arise. It is impossible that an educated and finely sensitive woman could bring these obscenities into union with the rest of her mental content. These things can therefore only exist in repression. But they do exist, they carry on a separate existence, they form a state within a state, they constitute a personality within a personality ; or, otherwise expressed, two consciouses are present which are kept apart by violent emotional inhibitions. One mind can and does know nothing of the other mind. That is the explanation of the remarkable disturbances in reproduction which work against analysis. The ethically higher mind does not deal with the associations of the other mind ; that is why it seems to her that she has forgotten these ideas, as if she had never known about such things. I am inclined to agree with her conviction that she really knew nothing more, that it was not a lie when she assured me with the greatest obstinacy that she had nothing more to say.

But although a complex be repressed ever so much from normal consciousness it must still influence and constellate the content of normal consciousness—for the deepest dissociation of the conscious does not extend to the unitary basis of personality. Repression must therefore leave behind a certain residue in the functions of the conscious ; normal consciousness must in some way direct the state of feeling which a repressed complex leaves behind. What is simpler than for any one of the ideas compatible with normal consciousness to be projected and accepted as the explanation of the constant self-reproaches and discontented mood ? To find a motive for the pangs of conscience attributable to her sins at the time she was a governess, the patient projects her reproaches on to her methods of education. These must have been bad is the view taken by her conscious self, for she would not otherwise have a constant feeling of reproach when she recalls memories of that time. As we have already seen, the origin of this obsession becomes the model of the obsession about her guilt for the unhappy death of her neighbour. The accumulation of obsessional ideas around the doctor and clergyman were well grounded, for, as the subject confessed to me, these persons were not sexually indifferent to her. Inasmuch as they affect her sexually they are quasi-accessories in her depravity ; hence they must also be reproaching themselves.

After this analysis we can understand the part her father played in her erotic complex, a part that was not clear in the associations. The analysis confirms, in the fullest way, the suppositions aroused by the associations. The associations served me as a safe signpost in the maze of moving fantasies which sought to put the analysis at each step on a wrong road.

The analysis was undertaken during three weeks every second day and lasted each time from an hour and a half to two hours. Although at the end of the three weeks there were neither proper sleep nor real quiet, I dismissed the patient from further treatment and did not hear from her till the end of November. In the last days of November 1905 she came to see me unexpectedly and announced that she was cured. After breaking off the analysis she said she was in the most violent, agitated mood, and remained thus for some four weeks. At night she was either tormented by her sexual images or by the re-emergence of her obsessional ideas. The obsessions about her neighbour were particularly frequent and gave her no rest until she had again visited the daughter of the deceased, to be told for the $x$th time about the death scene. When the daughter again assured her that her mother had died quietly, the subject became suddenly convinced that the woman had died at peace. Then at one blow all her obsessions disappeared.    Sleep returned and was only on rare occasions troubled by sexual images.

To what is this fortunate end of the treatment to be attributed ?

Obviously the daughter's version, which the patient had repeatedly heard without result, was only the occasion of the removal of the obsessions.    A real turn for the better took place at the beginning of the treatment, when the sexual images replaced the obsessional ideas.    The confession of her sinful thoughts must have enormously lightened the patient.    But it seems improbable that it was to this speaking out or to the " abreaction " alone that the cure was attributable.    To keep down such fancies permanently great energy is required.    People with obsessions are weak, they are incapable of holding in their images with a tight rein.    Treatment therefore always works best with them. The best treatment is to compel them, with a certain ruthlessness, to reproduce and display all the presentations incompatible with their consciousness.    The energy is thus not only put to a severe test, but the conscious gets accustomed to the existence of images formerly repressed.    The mental separate existences become crushed, since they are dragged by an effort of will from repression into daylight.    In the process they lose considerably in nimbus, and hence in danger ; the subjects receive at the same time the feeling of being masters of their images. I therefore lay stress upon the strengthening of the will, and not upon the mere " abreaction," as Freud did formerly.

It seems from some recent works that Freud's theory of obsessional phenomena is still systematically ignored.    It is hence a great satisfaction to me to be able to recall attention to Freud's theories—even at the risk of falling into the sphere of this systematic amnesia.

### SUMMARY

(1) The complex appearing in the associations of a psychogenic neurosis exhibits the *causa morbi* (excluding the predisposition).

(2) Associations can be a valuable aid for the discovery of the pathogenic complex as well as serving for the shortening and lightening of Freud's psycho-analysis.

(3) Associations give us experimentally an insight into the psychological structure of the neurotic symptoms : Hysteria and obsession phenomena arise from one complex.    The physical and psychical symptoms are but the symbolical pictures of the psychogenic complex.

# CHAPTER VIII

# CASES ILLUSTRATING THE PHENOMENA OF ASSOCIATION IN HYSTERIA

## By Dr. FRANZ RIKLIN

THE following investigations deal with association experiments in eight cases of hysteria.

### FIRST CASE

CATTERINA H. showed signs of hysteria whilst still at school. She studied at a Russian high school and took an active part in the tumults of the last few years. She had a friendship, probably platonic on her side, with a student. The patient has a peculiar sexuality which gives evidence of her hysteria. She is able so to repress all sexual experiences, and that knowledge which every one necessarily acquires in the course of growth, that she was over twenty without having any correct ideas on the subject, although she was a student. She even took part in a discussion on prostitution without really knowing what prostitution was; and she praised an acquaintance who afterwards admitted that he had once taken up with a prostitute. She believed it was a question of a girl despised by society, and considered he had acted meritoriously. Later, when a catastrophe had opened her eyes, she could only think shamefacedly of that " silly " conversation. It was, moreover, obvious how little she recognized her sexuality even later.

Her friend R. loved her, but not merely platonically. He wrote to her from abroad, confessed his love, and wished to marry her. Annoyed by these " bourgeois and conventional outbursts," she wrote him an indignant letter, whereupon he committed suicide. Going one day in high spirits to some compatriots, she saw the news in a Russian paper. She wanted to make herself believe that it must be somebody else with the same name, and did not change her light-hearted mood. Nevertheless the news drove her to the house of a friend who would be likely to know more about it. After a prolonged search she saw her friend in the distance, and when with one word she was told everything the patient collapsed and had her first hysterical attack. (She is said to have once had a slight twilight condition as a school-child, also from some psychical cause.) It was not possible to obtain any more exact account of the fit. Soon afterwards she went to another university. The attacks repeated themselves, especially on certain anniversaries (day of the week, month, year of R.'s death) and on other occasions connected with this event. (I cannot here discuss in more detail the analysis of the attacks and twilight states.) Her condition was made worse by another circumstance. The patient was informed by a woman acquaintance, a midwifery student, about male sexuality and the sexual act, upon which the knowledge on the subject, hitherto repressed, entered completely into consciousness. She felt herself

322

unhappy ; mankind, hitherto idealized, became a beast ; the idea that R. loved her sensually (perhaps also repentance that her ignorance was responsible for his death) troubled her terribly. In slight twilight states she would often say, " I must go to his grave and ask him if he knew it." She hated mankind on account of its sexual function, hated also her doctor, whom she imagined was also like the rest ; she could only esteem him when she saw him in attendance upon his patients and was then able to exclude the sexual image. About two years after R.'s death the patient entered the asylum, after having been treated at different places.

I must mention some of the individual phenomena of the numerous minor twilight states and symptomatic actions (Freud [1]), because they illuminate the fundamental phenomena of hysterical associations and of hysteria in general— the pathological dissociation and the disposal of repressed complexes in the acts and thoughts of the hysteric ; elements which we also find among normals.

The patient often wanted to learn the violin and inquired earnestly about a teacher, especially on days when she was in a minor twilight state. Her sweetheart had played the violin. She cannot look at closed or half-open eyes because she then thinks that a dead person is there. She does not see the flowers on the table because she would then have to see the doctor who is in the room ; she dares not look at him because she thinks blood is flowing from his temples. Apparently as an innocent joke, she placed some crushed rose-leaves on a little pimple on her forehead (gunshot wound). She liked to sing music-hall songs where the name R. occurs (false, inadequate affect). She is frightened at any meeting (first attack). She represents her illness as if she had two souls, a big and a small one ; the small one has been poisoned and has been exchanged with the big one ; when the small one acts upon the big one she is ill. This is a very pretty image of a repressed complex which became noticeable in the reactions.

The five hundred associations employed were made in four tests ; the first and last were carried out with German test-words and with time-measurements, in the second and third experiments Russian words were used without any time-measurements. The first three experiments took place in the early part of her stay in the asylum, on the first, fifth, and eighth day, the last one was made ten weeks later.

Her two complexes—the relationship to R. and her sexuality, both intimately connected—run like a thread through all the reactions—those carried out the first two days as well as those carried out later, i.e. at a time when we had a fairly complete analysis of the case.

Working out the two hundred associations of the first experiment, we find that 15 per cent. refer to the R. complex, about 7 per cent. to the complex " sexual knowledge," and about 12 per cent. to a third, a political complex (Russia, socialism, revolution). This also stands in the closest connexion with the others, as we shall learn in detail ; on the whole, therefore, 35 per cent. of definite complex reactions.

The number of egocentric reactions exceeds that found among

[1] Freud, *The Psychopathology of Everyday Life.*

normals ; in our patient it is 8–9 per cent. (In normal educated women it is, on the average, 2·1 per cent.)

### EXAMPLES OF EGOCENTRIC REACTION

| | | | |
|---|---|---|---|
| Needle | cruel | Frog | brr |
| Needle | fright | Water | fearful |
| Lake | fear | Dance | stupid |
| Mountain | cruel | Cat | pfui |
| Dream | fearful | Bird | darling |
| School | fearful | Now | bad |
| School | hateful | Bad | me |
| Hair | unpleasant | Time | weary |
| Attendant | good | | |

Most of these highly subjective reactions are explained by particular events.

### EXAMPLES OF COMPLEX REACTIONS

R. = Repressed complex ; S. = Sexuality ; P. = Political complex ; D.T. = Delayed reaction-time.

I. *Test :* Table   books        : 7·2 seconds R.
II. „    Table   letter       R.
III. „   Table   dissection-table  : 1·4   „

Patient thought of the table in R.'s room on which lay his revolver ; then of a letter of farewell. Dissection-table signifies the reminiscence of a psychological experiment on a frog, which made a very unpleasant impression upon the patient. All reminiscences of blood are closely connected with R.'s *bloody death* and play a rôle similar to the symptomatic action—as the "representative" of the repressed complex.

I. *Test :* Bread   nourishment : 5 seconds, S.
II. „    Bread   daily

The latter is an abbreviated quotation ("Give us this day our daily bread"), and therefore suspect of being a complex indicator. In the patient's view eating belongs to what is animal in man, like sex (cp. Freud). This idea is also expressed by the fact that she invariably eats *very little,* and will *not eat in company.*

I. *Test :* Hit   cruel      : 3·4 seconds, R.
II. „    Hit   whip, knout, R.

She first saw R. bleeding at a Russian demonstration ; he had been gashed by Cossacks.

I. *Test :* Dark red   "I can think of nothing," R.

A so-called fault, a complex indicator ; nothing comes up to the patient. Dark red is associated with blood, as is seen from many of her expressions ; it is a colour which occupies her a good deal.

I. *Test :* Sweet     fruit, melon : 2·2 seconds, R.
II.   „     Sweet     mankind, R.

In the second experiment patient immediately adds a quotation ; I cannot enter into its accuracy : " Bitter is also the sweet fruit of the sweetest woman ; the warrior may not have it, and so he would have the woman." Surely a symbolism of the conception of her relationship to R.

In the third test she reacts *raspberry — bitter,* 4·6 seconds, founded upon the same ideas.

IV. *Test :* Idle     " Show me the fruit which rots ere it is broken " : 0·8 sec.

It is a quotation (therefore probably a complex indicator) which the patient refers to herself. In this test she explained, when she was less repressed (i.e. less hysterical) after the long treatment, that she referred this association to herself : " When you understand nothing (of sexual matters) you are not spoilt ; now you will be spoilt in time." According to her view she is the early rotting fruit.

I. *Test :* Divorce     woman             : 6 seconds
II.   „     Divorce     dead . . . for ever : 4 seconds, R.

The first reaction, *woman,* is clearly a cover reaction for the idea which emerges clearly in the second experiment.

I. *Test :* Game     children : 2·2 seconds
II.   „     Game     woman, a woman is a toy (quotation)
IV.   „     Game     I am too old to enjoy games, too young to be without desires : 1·6 second (quotation)

The references to the sexual complex seem to me obvious. Here are two quotations, and at the suspect first reaction a prolonged reaction-time.

I. *Test :* Babble     author : 3·6 seconds
II.   „     Babble     go on talking, gossip
III.   „     Babble     impossible ; I will not narrate it : 2·2 seconds
IV.   „     Speak     I would rather not : 3·6 seconds ; " and they speak like our deeds," S.

All the reactions refer, even on the patient's own declaration, to her " secret "—i.e. to the sexual complex ; at the first, apparently unequivocal, reaction there is suspiciously delayed reaction-time, at the last an apparently mutilated quotation ; in the third reaction a sentence which the patient uses in stereotyped fashion in her twilight states, when she speaks of her " secret," the sexual complex.

I. *Test :* Love     father—occurs to me : 2 seconds

The patient laughs loudly hereat, and cannot make out how she arrived at this answer (mimetic reaction !).

III. *Test :* Love　　in order to forget again

The next moment the patient knew nothing about this reaction, she did not even understand what it could mean. She had said it quite unconsciously ! The connexion is obvious to us.[1]

I. *Test :* Love　　I do not know what to say

No reaction. A fault. Patient contorts her face (mimetic reaction).

IV. *Test :* Love　　child : 1 second

Patient uttered this reaction imitating the voice and tone of a patient in the asylum, who constantly used the expression (a kind of quotation therefore).

I. *Test :* Tears　　uneasy : 2·6 seconds
III. „　Tears　　death ; tears are shed at death

The two reactions complete one another, the first by its delayed reaction, the second by its transparency. Reference to death, which occupied her more than anything.

IV. *Test :* Month　　when budded every shrub and tree in the wondrous month of May, love into my heart did steal to make me like them fay

This quotation, again a complex reaction, glosses harmlessly over the memory of R.'s death, *who shot himself in May.*

I. *Test :* Right　　(Shrugs her shoulders, no reaction) " The word doesn't come " ; at last after 11 seconds, " universal "

Patient frequently reacted with " universal vote," but that is only a cover reaction, apparently belonging to the political complex. In reality this hysterical inhibition was caused by the sexual complex, the idea being that nothing was right, that mankind ought not to have sexual feelings. The patient later gave this explanation herself in a series of cases, especially in the later tests ; this holds good of the following reaction :

IV. *Test :* Law　　(Fault—with a gesture of warding off—mimetic reaction)

Patient thinks of the natural laws of sexuality.

II. *Test :* Right　　none, it doesn't exist
I. „　False　　women : 5 seconds
II. „　False　　man, S. (in the sense of man is falsely organized)
II. „　False　　corruption of man, S. (in sexual sense)
III. „　Correct　　not everything, S.
I. „　Unjust　　Russia : 2·8 seconds

Apparently a political complex ; in reality the idea was again present that man was created wrongly ; the sexual complex is

---

[1] Cp. Jung, " Experimentelle Beobachtungen über das Erinnerungsvermögen," *Centralbl. f. Nervenheilk. u. Psychiatrie*, September 1905, for a review of methods of reproduction.

here masked by the political one. (Unjust, wrong, unrighteous are terms more allied in the Russian than in the German language.)

I. *Test :* Revenge     friend, a particular one : 7·6 seconds (R.'s brother)
II.    „    Despise     N. (name of the brother)

" That doesn't tell you anything." She laughed and, whilst laughing, took the portrait of N. from the table ; we have here an inadequate feeling reaction in consequence of repression. The inadequacy is very clear when it is known that revenge, hatred, and scorn of the brother of the dead man, and her fear of him, play an important part in her twilight states. Thus we get the following reaction :

II. *Test :* Threaten     no, he will not do it to me . . .

This is a stereotyped sentence in the attacks : " No, no, he will not kill me," i.e. N. But suddenly she cannot recall her reaction ; she must have been absent-minded. We have here a kind of twilight state, which is dissociated by " amnesia " from consciousness.

This fear of N.'s revenge, which possessed the patient after R.'s death, is quite unfounded. In reality her relationship to him was quite good. She thinks she must worship him as a kind of martyr, as he must have suffered immensely from the same cause.

I. *Test :* Pure     the Germans : 6 seconds, D.R.
II.    „    Pure     life, my ideal ; it is no longer so : 2 seconds, S.

*The Germans* are obviously a cover reaction. The effect of the sexual complex is obvious. Here belong the following reactions :

IV. *Test :* Dirty ·     thoughts : 2 seconds
I.    „    Murderer     minister : 3    „

(Laughed aloud.) " I wanted to say Kaiser." Political complex, R. occurring again (inadequate emotional reaction).

II. *Test :* Murderer     myself ; it is only an accident that this word came out. (Inadequate, apparently indifferent)
IV.    „    Intention     no, without : 14 seconds

" I had no intention to kill him," is one of her constant sayings in the twilight states.

I. *Test :* Suppose     (fault ; patient sighs !)
IV.    „    Suppose     never, nobody would ever have supposed it : 1 sec., S.
I.    „    Soft     quiet : 2·4 seconds
II.    „    Soft     in the churchyard
IV.    „    Quiet     grave : 1 second

(Weeping.) " I was at the cemetery with him."

Here we have, as frequently in the repetition of the same reaction-word, an increase of the cover reaction from Test I to a distinct expansion of the association pertaining to it in Test IV.

I. *Test :* To wipe     goloshes : 7·2 seconds (cover reaction)

Patient laughed, making a grimace, R. (inadequate emotional reaction, mimetic reaction) ; *to wipe* signifies for the patient to wipe the blood away from his face. She remembers a childhood's game with a refrain "To wipe, wipe, wipe!" sings it over and over again, laughing at the same time [1] (complex song with inadequate emotional tone).

I. *Test :* Natural     (fault)

Nothing comes up to the patient ; she turns aside. The natural law of sexuality is again meant.

I. *Test :* Remember    carry on a revolution : 3 seconds
III.    „     Remember    R. That tells you nothing, that is a dead person ;
                               I could have answered anything else

The first reaction seems to belong to the political complex. The second reaction, with its apparently superficial, indifferent tone (inadequate affect) explains itself.

This collection of examples of complex constellations, which could be easily increased, demonstrates its extremely frequent and intense occurrence in hysteria. By means of comparison with other reaction-times in the same patient, apparently indifferent reactions with a delayed reaction-time are discovered to be complex constellations. The so-called faults, the mimetic reactions, quotations, etc., prove to be nearly always complex representatives.

We have even seen phenomena occur, in response to definite stimulus-words, behaving as cheats of consciousness ; we see, moreover, how a complex (the political one) in reality stands for and conceals the sexual complex. We see that *forgetting,* both in Freud's investigations and in Ganser's symptom complex, is a function of repression. *It is not the kind of mechanism but the frequency and intensity of the complex indicators which distinguish hysteria from the normal.*

## SECOND CASE

ANNA L., 20 years, a seamstress. The patient is a poor, simple girl. Her stepfather treats her badly, although she works diligently and contributes towards the household ; her mother is good ; there is thus a mental conflict. She would like to marry in order to avoid this conflict and to assuage her desire for peace, quietness at home, and love. Her first sweetheart was faithless, for he never wrote again after going abroad. She has another now, but is worried as to whether her wish is to be fulfilled. Together with some other hysterical symptoms she is suffering from enuresis nocturna.

---

[1] Cp. *Melody Automatisms,* chapter v.

Two hundred associations were carried out.  I give some of the results, omitting, for the sake of concentration, a small number of indifferent reactions.  Patient had, especially during the first half of the test, a frequent embarrassed laugh.  The predominance of subjective values will be noticed.

| | | |
|---|---|---|
| Prick | needle | : 1·2 seconds |
| State | beautiful | : 6·2   „ (latter in the sense of stately) |
| Angel | beautiful | : 1·6   „ |
| Long | street.  Later: at night-time with my sweetheart in the street | |
| Insolent | hateful | : 3·4 seconds (at home) |
| Stalk | flower | : 1·6   „ |
| Ship | big | : 2   „ (a trip on a gondola when they got acquainted with one another) |
| Plough | field | : 1·6 seconds |
| Wool | sheep | : 1·2   „ |
| Friendly | good | : 2·6   „ |
| Carry | child | : 5·8   „ |
| Dance | jolly | : 3   „ |
| Lake | nice | : 3·8   „ (the gondola trip) |
| Angry | (fault).  After 10 seconds: "Nothing occurs to me." (Laughs.) "Father is angry, very." | |

She then tells the experimenter, who was not previously aware of her circumstances : " My stepfather does not like me, he can't bear me ; he doesn't even like my mother to be good to me." (There is meaningless laughter at this memory.)

| | | | | | |
|---|---|---|---|---|---|
| Needle | prick | : 1·4 seconds | Bread | hard | : 1·8 seconds |
| Swim | not | : 2·6   „ | Threaten | father | : 3   „ |
| Travel | far | : 3   „ | Rich | money | : 1·6   „ |
| Blue | sky | : 1   „ | Tree | green | : 1·6   „ |
| Sing | nice | : 1   „ | Play | children | : 2   „ |
| Mountain | high | : 1·2   „ | Salt | bitter | : 1·2   „ |
| New | clothes | : 3   „ | Ride | horse | : 2   „ |
| Habits | country | : 4·4   „ | Wall | white | : 2·2   „ |
| Stupid | (fault).  "Nothing occurs to me."  Then: "That one should not get the person one likes, and the other one doesn't want it either." | | | | |
| Copy-book | write | : 1·4 seconds | | | |
| To despise | not nice | : 2·2   „ | | | |
| Tooth | painful | | | | |
| Right | (fault).  "Nothing occurs to me."  Then she says, weeping: "It is not right that I was happy with mother and then father is so cross " | | | | |
| Prudent | (fault).  Later: "I am that in choosing " | | | | |
| Forget | (fault).  The unhappy affair with her first sweetheart | | | | |
| Love | Patient laughs for 5 seconds ; after 19·6 seconds she says: " Those belonging to you—and those you like—these are questions " | | | | |
| Understand | to understand one another well : 2·8 seconds (laughing) | | | | |

## THIRD CASE

MATILDE R., hospital nurse, about 25 years. She is full of enthusiasms. Her father, a drunkard, was a riding-master. The patient first worked in a country house and was better treated than a servant-girl. In a gynæcological clinic where she wanted to train as nurse she was seduced, as alleged, through being made drunk. Afterwards she brought an action against the seducer. She wanted to conceal the pregnancy from her people, and by night duty earned a miserable pittance, giving out that all was well with her. She gave birth quite alone, without help, and then took the premature stillborn child (8–9 months) and ran with it to the river, where she placed it in the water. The affair was found out. There was an inquest, but the patient was not arrested, as it was proved that it was not a case of infanticide.

The privation and the court proceedings had strongly affected the girl and brought about a series of hysterical symptoms (shriekings, tremors as if in a rigor). Afterwards she became a hospital nurse and found a refuge and an altruistic aim in life which was of therapeutic value. Besides many other hysterical features and physical symptoms, she is a noctambulist and has remarkable somnambulistic dreams.

The reactions of this patient are distinguished by the preference for the sentence form. But they are quite different from the sentence reaction of imbeciles. Wehrlin has shown (chapter iii) that among imbeciles the tendency to definition in its various forms is the chief characteristic. In hysteria, on the other hand, the occurrence of strong emotional tones seems to be crowded into sentence formation. The sentences often have the character of cover reactions, the form of school answers that apparently tell you nothing.

### I. EXAMPLES OF SENTENCE REACTIONS WHICH EXPRESS EMOTION

| | | | |
|---|---|---|---|
| Tree | the leaves are now falling : | 4 | seconds |
| Flowers | are now all shed | : 2·4 | ,, |
| Bird | are already all away | : 3·6 | ,, |
| Mountain | I should like to climb one : | 3·2 | ,, |
| Book | something delicious for me : | 1·8 | ,, |
| Dance | I like it | : 1 | |
| Swim | I can't | : 1·6 | |
| Proud | I am very | : 4·2 | |
| Flatter | I don't like it | : 2 | |
| Child | I'm no longer one | : 1·4 | ,, |
| Friendly | that I'm not | : 2 | |
| Soldier | oh, how I'd like to be ! | : 1·6 | ,, |
| Rich | unfortunately, I am not | : 2 | ,, |

It will be noticed that the subject soon leaves the objective sentence type and then produces only " I " sentences.

## II. Examples of Cover Reactions

Lake        the lake of Zurich is very beautiful: 7·7 seconds

Patient once thought of jumping into the water, when she was in a very unhappy situation among relatives and was suffering from home-sickness ; she went to the lake but had a fit and was brought back to the house.

Water        is a very useful . . . : 2·2 seconds

Sudden stoppage—betraying much. We think of the foregoing and the event at the river previously mentioned. The stoppage can also stand for the word *drink*, which would complete the sentence. The following reactions favour this view :

Thirst        drunkards have . . . : 10·4 seconds

The subject has never touched alcohol since that one excess with its fatal results ; it makes her sick to think of it. This is behind the affect :

Public-house    is something disgusting: 4·4 seconds

Other examples :

Evil        one must avoid : 18·6 seconds

The subject at first wanted to quote the words " Deliver us from evil." It is thus a cover reaction coupled with a most significant delay in the reaction-time. The reaction refers to the fatal occurrences.

Decorum      one must have : 2·2 seconds

Again refers to her complex.

Suffer       yes . . . our patients do, much : 5·6 seconds

Thought, " I must suffer much."

Despise      everybody sometimes : 2·6 seconds

Spoken with feeling ; thought of her seducer who left her in misery.

Remember    one sometimes thinks of something . . . and forgets it
            again : 7 seconds

Refers again to the events of her life.

Faithfulness  is something beautiful : 7·4 seconds

with a deep sigh, mimetic reaction.

Unjust       are many men : 3·8 seconds

with the same reference (prosecution).

False        snakes are : 2·6 seconds

same reference.

| Sin | every man sins : 6 seconds |

Thinks of the same affair.

| Love | I don't know—is a feeling : 15 seconds |

(Says afterwards, " That is stupid ; there is no real love.")

### III. EXAMPLES OF SENTENCES WHICH EXPRESS WISHES

| Mountain | I should like to climb one |
| Soldier | I wish I were one |
| Bicycle | I should like to be able to ride it |
| Carriage | I should like to drive |

(Partly reminiscences.)

| Ride | a jolly sport : 4·4 seconds |

Her father was a riding-master ; she had a situation in a country house where she often used to ride.

| Dance | I like it |
| Charm | when one's very beautiful : 10·2 seconds |

then adds, " I should like to be very charming ! "

### IV. EXAMPLES OF SENTENCES DEMONSTRATING HER EDUCATIONAL LEVEL

| Faust | Goethe wrote that |
| Arithmetic | I'm pretty fair at it |
| Potatoes | came from America |
| Powder | Gutenberg discovered powder—didn't he ? |

### V. EXAMPLES OF SENTENCES WHICH EXPRESS HER COMPLEX MORE OR LESS DISTINCTLY

| White | innocence is | : 2·4 seconds (quotation) |
| Prison | preserve me from it | : 1·8 ,, (Inquest) |
| Marriage | I shall never marry | : 1·8 |
| Appearance | is oft deceptive | : 1·6 ,, (quotation) |
| Youth | has no virtue | : 2 ,, (quotation) |
| Sorrow | I have had much already | : 2·6 |
| Kiss | is a sign of love | : 6·8 |
| Natural | everything in nature is natural | : 5·6 ,, |
| Bad | many people are | : 3·4 |
| Pool | is a town in D. | : 3·4 ,, |

This is explained by there being a prison in Poole. See the stimulus-word *prison* above.

| Love | I love my patients : 3·8 seconds |
| Tears | I have shed many : 1·6 ,, (quotation) |
| Terrible | murder : 10·6 ,, |

The experimenter repeated the stimulus-word with affect— we recall her anamnesis.

| Hope | if there were no hope | : 2·4 seconds (quotation) |
| Love | so long as you can love | : 3·2 ,, |
| Misery | in London there is the greatest misery : 3·8 ,, |

The reaction refers to her own misery in the big town of X.

| Corner | a life in the corner | : 3·6 seconds (quotation) |
| Hot | love burns hot | : 5 ,, |
| Consciousness | one has not always got it : 3 ,, |

Says she means our patients ; but it refers to her seduction.

| Snare | to put a snare for some one : 3·8 seconds |

Certainly belongs to the same complex.

The two following cases also show sentence reactions. The sentences are here chiefly cover reactions for the complex. I have published the histories of these two patients elsewhere in another connexion.[1]

## FOURTH CASE

MRS. MARIA C. The point about this history is that the patient was in the women's clinic on account of a thrombosis following labour when she received a letter from her husband that excited her. The latter, a labourer (Italian), had made the unpleasant discovery that his wife had incautiously lent a sum of eight hundred francs which he could not recover. Although they loved each other he considered this an unwarrantable folly, for it made his savings illusory, and he threatened that he would have nothing more to do with her. This threw the woman into a hysterical twilight state with the Ganser syndrome complex, and she was taken to the clinic.

One hundred and fifty associations were carried out on the third day of her sojourn in the asylum, when the patient's mind was fairly clear but still troubled as to whether her husband would forgive her. Twenty further associations were made on the next day after a reassuring visit from her husband.

Most of the reactions are in sentence form and are usually cover reactions. The expression *one* is frequently repeated. Generally this means the patient's husband or herself ; a confirmation of the view which we expressed in the work on the associations of normals, that *one* is a cover word for the principal characters in emotionally toned presentation complexes. This view cannot be extended to the associations of imbeciles, when *one* more often appears in the reactions as a tendency to definition.

More than half of the associations are certainly complex reactions and probably a good part of the rest, about which, however, we have no sufficient evidence.

Mimetic reactions are strikingly frequent, e.g. *friendly — one* is at times 3·2 seconds. Patient laughs and explains, "My husband is friendly." Cover reaction in sentence form with mimetic reaction.

---

[1] "Zur Psychologie hysterischer Dämmerzustände und des Ganserschen Symptoms," *Psychiatr. neurol. Wochenschrift*, 1904.

Carry       one carries many things : 3·2 seconds

(What ?  " Water  to  table."  Then  " a  helpless  creature."
(The last child is very weakly.)

Stubborn      one is sometimes : 2·8 seconds

Then " I am like that ; obstinate people are stubborn."

Lake       that is a great mass . . . water : 9 seconds

Note the hesitation.  The patient had intended jumping into
the lake when she was stopped by her husband.

Ill       one is : 3·2 seconds

(Laughs.)  " I and my baby."

Proud       an unfriendly person : 14·4 seconds

At first thinks, *My relatives — aunt.*  Refers to the dissatisfaction
of her relatives on account of her marriage with the Italian.

Angry       I am . . . myself

but adds softly, " but I hope to alter."

Threaten      and if one is disobedient, one is threatened : 4·2 seconds

Under this generalized form of the sentence is to be understood
herself and her husband.

Rich       a man is who has plenty of money : 6 seconds

Patient begins to cry and recalls the story of the eight hundred
francs.

Sing       one does this when glad : 4·4 seconds

Cp. the remark about *one.*  The  patient  means  herself  and
thinks of the contrast with the happy times when she could be
full of joy.

Pity       a fine man has that : 3·6 seconds

Then, " I do not know who has pity for me " (cries).  Does not
mean her man (husband) but her relatives, who were against
her marriage and had a malicious joy in her misfortune.

Mountain      there's many mountains : snow mountains : 16·8 seconds

Cover  sentence  for  the  reminiscence  of  her  joyous  youth
when she lived in F. mountain.  A contrast determined by the
complex between now and then.

New       new, are . . . new buildings, a new building : 7·2 seconds

(Laughs).  Her man is a mason.

Habits       man has good . . . and bad habits : 4 seconds

Again thinks of her story.  Again *man* and a cover sentence in
the most generalized form.

Stupid       that is the insane man, some one who is not quite right in
          the head (*ego reference*) : 4·6 seconds

Despise       the proud man does so : 2·4 seconds

Explains : " My relatives ; perhaps my man."

Tooth      that is man's (3·8 seconds) help . . . for eating, at least
not to control oneself

Patient had the habit of biting something when defending herself in altercation with her husband.

Right      the honourable man is : 4 seconds

A very forced complex reaction.

People      there are many kinds—Italians, Germans, Swiss—oh, many
kinds of people : 4·2 seconds

Patient immediately said, " I would like to see how it finishes between Franz and myself.

Book      library book, novels are also books, also *book-keeping* :
3 seconds

(The eight hundred francs.)

Separate      separate that . . . : 4 seconds; a pause of 4·8 seconds.
Then, " That hurts me " (begins to cry)

Hunger      one must often suffer that (2·2 seconds) . . . animals
sometimes also

The latter sentence in High German—a phrase to complete the cover reaction because the patient always reacts in dialect ; cp. the complaint in her husband's letter that he has to work for the family whilst his wife is so careless of the money.

White      is snow (2·2 seconds) and white clothes . . . linen

(Laughs, and then suddenly cries.) " I thought of burial clothes.' The laughter at the beginning is to be regarded as an expression of affect inadequate to the occasion.

Cloudy      that is . . . (2 seconds) water often is. (After a further
5 seconds) Sometimes one is, first occurred to me
Dear      my man is that      : 3·2 seconds (spoken very softly)
Quarrel      when two persons quarrel : 3·2  ,,

Patient laughs, shrugs her shoulders.

Imbeciles can make answers like this,[1] but the explanation here shows it to be a cover reaction. The mimetic play favours this view ; the reaction is probably evoked by the idea of the present relations between the patient and her husband.

The same holds good of the following reaction :

Family      that is when there are a couple together and they have
children : 5·2 seconds

Patient thinks of her family.

Stranger      the wanderer is a stranger : 3 seconds

Patient thought of herself. She again reacted in High German instead of the usual dialect. To the stimulus-word *happiness* there was no verbal reaction (fault), but after about 15 seconds she began to cry. At the stimulus-word immediately following,

[1] See Wehrlin, chapter iii.

*tell*, the patient was still unable to control her crying, but after 30 seconds reacted somewhat more quietly with *to tell stories*.

We have here a clear perseveration ; the reactions that follow do not, however, seem to be influenced by it.

| | | |
|---|---|---|
| Decency | one should have | : 3·2 seconds |
| Narrow | a small space is narrow | : 4·2  „ |
| Stork | that is . . . (3·2 seconds)—my husband (spoken softly) | |

To the stimulus-word *kiss* patient reacted after 3·8 seconds, "That is a question I cannot answer." She sobbed violently and meant she did not know whether her husband will kiss her again. "He will not forgive me ; and I have little happiness." We see here the stimulus-word apprehended as a question, as among the normal uneducated, and as usually among imbeciles.

> Song    kind-meaning people have songs : 5 seconds

formed after "Where singing is then all is quiet and still ; for wicked people have no songs at will." Patient thought of herself who had lost her joyousness.

> Idle    lazy people are idle : 7·6 seconds

(Refers to herself.) "I do nothing." Her husband had written her he alone must keep the family, he could not count upon her.

References to her husband now become increasingly frequent :

| | | |
|---|---|---|
| Bear | my man must bear heavy sorrows : 14 seconds | |
| Tired | my man is tired in the evening ; he wrote it also in the letter : 3·4 seconds | |
| Intention | my man perhaps means I did it intentionally : 3·6 seconds | |
| Strong | my man is | : 2·2 seconds |
| Modest | my man is | : 1·2  „ |
| Mix | people often mix | : about 50 seconds |

Thinks of her husband being an Italian.

> Blood    that is in man (2·6) . . . and in animals

"Thought of mine and my husband's blood."

After her husband's visit the next day the complex reactions somewhat diminish.

| | | |
|---|---|---|
| Light | (laughs) I am light (= light-minded) | : 11 seconds |
| Wish | I wish that I may be soon home | : 3·6  „ |
| Love | I love my husband | : 2    „ |
| Gentle | my man is that | : 7·4  „ |
| Seek | all seek (6·6 seconds) . . . would most like to seek flowers if I could go home with my man | |
| Good | my husband is that : 3 seconds | |

A number of reactions refer to another presentation complex, which occurred before her marriage, when she participated in jolly club meetings and dances, e.g. :

| | | |
|---|---|---|
| Dance | that is done in the dance, with music : | 2 seconds |
| Play | with music, play music | : 7·6 „ |
| Jolly | I'm no longer that | : 3·8 „ |
| Drum | the gymnasts use that (2·2 seconds) . . . with whom I used to enjoy myself and act before I got married | |

## FIFTH CASE

MRS. VERENA D. This is a case of hysterical twilight state which set in when shortly after her husband's death her only child ("Roseli") got ill. I have published it together with the previous case.[1]

During the twilight state there was amnesia for the child's illness. When she learnt that her child was going on well she became clearer in her mind, and after seeing her child again, a cure rapidly set in. Ten years before she had had her first slight twilight state, when late in the night after the birth of her first child her husband came home drunk.

This is another case of pathological affect. Here likewise at least 50 per cent. of the reactions are complex reactions. Four hundred and twenty-eight associations were taken in all. This person also reacted with a pronounced sentence form, which, however, in the first test (128 associations), before her child's visit, began only at the fifty-third reaction to the stimulus-word.

| | | |
|---|---|---|
| Beat | the mother beats : | 2·8 seconds (patient had beaten her child) |
| Console | children console : 3·4 „ etc. | |

The sentence type remains till the end of the test. In the second test the first sentence form occurred at the seventh reaction :

| | |
|---|---|
| Father | the child obeys her father : 3·4 seconds |

Then a few reactions in one word came in between ; finally after reaction 21, which ran :

| | |
|---|---|
| Copy-book | school-children use copy-books : 3 seconds |

the reactions are almost all sentences ; many are cover sentences, others extremely subjective, dependent upon the "complex." On the whole, however, these sentences are much more school-like and childish than in the last patient. It also seemed as if the imitation of apparently clumsy school sentences was a "symptomatic action." The reactions with *child* and *pupil* refer to her sick child "Roseli." The first fifty-two reactions, not in sentence form, are of a very superficial type, and all belong to the group of the verbal-motor form (chapter ii). The reaction-time does not, as a rule, exceed the probable mean (chapter v), 2·4 seconds.

[1] See foot-note, p. 333.

| Sunday | Monday | : 1 sec. | Hair | hairpin | : 2·4 sec. |
| Father | land | : 1·2 ,, | School | school-house | : 2·2 ,, |
| Table | cloth | : 1·8 ,, | Window | pane | : 0·8 ,, |

A few have a prolonged reaction-time ; some of these are connected with the idea " school " or " pupil."

| Copy-book | copy-books : 17·6 sec. | Asylum | educational asylum | : 3·2 sec. |
| Sing | sing late : 6·4 ,, | Play | evening play : 4·4 ,, |

The last refers to an arrangement made by the school in which her child took part. A delayed reaction-time occurred in *begging— go*, 6·8 seconds ; it clearly arises from an idea which worried the patient very much—the worry and struggle for existence after her husband's death.

Reactions in sentence form :

| Console | children console | : 3·4 seconds |
| Child | children play : 6·4 seconds (thought : " you, my child ") |
| Friendly | children are friendly | : 3 seconds (my child) |
| Thank | the child thanks her mother | : 2·6 ,, |
| Send | the mother sends her child | : 4·6 ,, |
| Well-behaved | children should be well-behaved | : 3·6 ,, |
| Youth | a child plays in his youth | : 5·6 ,, |
| Take care | children take care at school | : 3·2 ,, |
| Arithmetic | children do arithmetic at school | : 2·4 ,, |
| Indulge | the mother indulges her child | : 5·2 ,, |
| Kiss | the mother kisses her child | : 2·6 ,, |
| Play | the children go to evening play | |
| Walk | the children go for a walk | : 3·6 ,, |

In the first test of 128 reactions we find 13, i.e. 10 per cent., of the sentences with the word *child*. We never find such frequency among normals. Nearly all these reactions have delayed reaction-times.

From the second test (after her child's visit) :

| Father | the child obeys her father | : 3·4 seconds |
| School | children go to school | : 1·6 ,, |
| Play | the children play | : 1·8 |
| Stubborn | children are stubborn | : 1·8 |
| Child | the child is good | : 3·4 |
| Amiable | children should be amiable | : 1·4 ,, |
| Thank | children should give thanks | : 2·2 ,, |
| Send | the child is sent by mother | : 6 ,, |
| Naughty | the children are rather naughty adds the patient) | : 4·8 ,, (" Roseli," |
| Threaten | the father threatens the boy | : 2 ,, (laughs) |
| Manners | the children should learn manners | : 1·8 ,, (see above) |
| Joke | children like to joke | : 3 , |
| Small | the child is small | : 1·8 |
| Love | the mother loves her child | : 2·6 ,, |
| Fruit | children like fruit | : 1·4 |
| Run | the child learns to run | : 4·4 |

Out of 200 reactions in the second test there are 20 sentences with the word *child*—again 10 per cent.  In those places in the first test where the sentences contained *child*, it usually occurred again in the second test ; but the reaction-times in the second test tended to become shorter.

Nowhere is it more clearly seen than here that this kind of complex reaction must be placed among Freud's symptomatic actions.

In the third test five days later we find a similar relationship, almost all the reactions were sentences, and among them 9 per cent. had *child*.

The word *schoolboy* plays a similar part ; it stands for *child* and *Roseli*.

In the first test—

| | |
|---|---|
| Schoolboy | schoolgirl : 3·2 seconds |

Then we find :

| | |
|---|---|
| Song | school-children sing songs : 4 seconds |

In the second test—

| | | | |
|---|---|---|---|
| Schoolboy | school . . . slate | :: 4 | seconds |
| Copy-book | school-children use copy-books : 3 | | ,, |
| Book | school-children use books | : 3·8 | ,, |
| Pay attention | school-children pay attention | : 2 | ,, (cp. above :: |
| | children pay attention at school) | | |
| Song | (as in first test) : 2·6 seconds | | |

In the third test—

| | | |
|---|---|---|
| Praise | the teacher praises the school-child : 2·4 seconds | |
| Favour | the schoolboy tries to get the | |
| | master's favour | : 13·4 , |
| Forget | the schoolboy forgets his lessons | : 4   ,, |

With the same chain of thought we have :

| | | |
|---|---|---|
| Correct | the lesson must be done correctly | : 6·2 seconds |

(Her husband often helped Roseli with her preparation.)

Sentences to *schoolboy* are not as frequent as those to *child,* but belong to the same group of symptom reactions.  I must refer to what was said in chapter ii about repetitions.  It is a question of complex action.  To the same category belongs a series of sentences in pedagogic form :

| | | |
|---|---|---|
| Manners | children should have good manners | |
| Thank | children should give thanks | |
| Justice | we should always bestow justice | : 17·4 seconds |
| Self | we should help our neighbours | : 4·4   ,, |
| Proud | we should not be proud | : 5 |
| Clean | we should be clean | : 4·4 |
| Behave | we should be well behaved | : 9·2 |
| Prudent | we should be prudent | : 4·4 |
| Modest | we should be modest | : 2 |

Her way of falling into the child's kind of associations recalls the phenomena of pathological dreamy states as described by Pick among hysterics.

Symptomatic is the frequent emerging of the word *Rose*, conditioned by the image of her child (*Rosa, Ros-eli*).

In the first test the patient reacts

Some people like to gossip (klatschen) : 8·4 seconds

This is a cover reaction and refers to a naughty act which she had to forbid her child.

| I. *Test :* (Klatschen) Gossip | klatsch-rose (corn-poppy) | : 5·2 seconds |
|---|---|---|
| II.  „    Dark red | a dark red rose | : 2      „ |
| III.  „    Smell | the rose smells nice | : 1·4    „ |
|      Yellow | a yellow rose | : 4·8    „ |

We find a mass of associations which refer to her child, to her husband and his agreeable and especially his disagreeable characteristics (drunkard !), his death, the family life, care about the future. Among these we find the best examples of sentences which are actually *cover reactions*. Perhaps it is proper to distinguish between the common *symptom* reaction and the peculiar cover reaction ; both are complex phenomena. The reactions with *child, schoolboy*, and especially the school sentences framed like a child's, are partly only simple symptom reactions (e.g. *yellow — rose*). One gets the impression that instead of a customary reaction (*yellow — green, yellow — colour*) there occurs a reaction dictated by the preference of the complex. In the cover reactions, on the other hand, we get the slurring over of a disagreeable fact, of a reminiscence emotionally toned, by an apparently innocent reaction, by some seemingly indifferent sentence universally valid. As I tried to show before, these cover reactions are by-associations of a complex which arises when the stimulus-word directly encounters the complex ; the complex is then under repression, under the dissociation of what is incompatible with consciousness. Varying with the degree of repression, of the dissociation of the complex, it becomes possible to inquire of the subject as to the motive for the origin of the cover reaction and to bring the repressed complex into consciousness.

In the higher grades of repression (hysteria) the significance of the reaction is inexplicable to the subject herself ; the dissociation is then too strong. Hypnosis, or Freud's method of Free Association, then often discovers the explanation. All degrees of normal concealment and hesitation (delayed reaction-time), from ejaculation to complete repression, and dissociation of consciousness (amnesia) occur objectively ; it makes no difference whether the mechanism occurs in the conscious or the unconscious.

When necessary the explanation is given in the following instances :

I. *Test :* Come    to me (spoken softly) : 12·8 sec. (thought of Rosell)
       Year       yes, I'm coming     : 15·8 ,,    (thought:   I'm
                  going home to my child)

These were two successive reactions in our schedule. With the first there was a mimetic reaction (spoken softly) ; in the second a perseveration of the emotional tone ; in both a marked adaptation of the complex to the stimulus-word.

I. *Test :* Heart     thou my heart : 22·4 seconds
II.   ,,     Bird      the bird      : 5·6   ,,

The reactions were successive. The second reaction, a repetition of the stimulus-word, is, as mentioned in earlier chapters, a phenomenon of perseveration where the attention is riveted to the previous reaction.

II. *Test :* Heart     (fault). After 40 seconds, explanation : " I thought
                  of papa "
I.   ,,     The words are successive
       Rich       there are many rich people : 3 seconds
       Leap       out of my reach

Patient was asked what was the second stimulus-word : answer, *reach.* We here see an assimilation by the apprehension of the second stimulus-word (*reach — rich*) to the awakened complex, which perseverates so that the patient has not taken in the stimulus-word. Economic worry is the complex here (since her husband's death), as expressed in numerous other reactions. We find this phenomenon of the assimilation of the stimulus-word, of which indications are found among normals, very strongly marked in hysteria.

I. *Test :* Sunday    I like Sunday : 2·4 seconds (is expecting her child's
                  visit on Sunday)
II.   ,,     Inn       one gets alcoholic drinks at an inn : 7·4 seconds

(A cover reaction. Hates all inns because her husband used to drink. Much delayed reaction-time.)

I & II. *Test :* Family    family happiness    : 4·8 seconds

Explains : " It was so nice whilst papa was alive."

I. *Test :* Sorrow    cares make sorrow    : 5·6 seconds
II.   ,,     Sorrow    one has some sorrow   : 6    ,,

Explains : " When papa was away." (Cover reaction.)

I. *Test :* Hunger    the poor are hungry    : 10    seconds
II.   ,,     Hunger    poor people are hungry : 7·4    ,,

Explains (superficially) : " They often came to the house and asked for food." The delayed reaction-time refers rather at her own economic troubles.

| I. *Test :* Bad | the apple is rather bad | : 12·6 seconds |
| II. „ Bad | there are bad people | : 15·4 „ |

Explains : " or bad things like vegetables," etc. " Oh, my husband promised me he would get home earlier " (and did not keep it). (Cover reaction.)

| I. *Test :* Rich | riches are not everything | : 15 seconds |
| II. „ Rich | there are many rich people | : 3·8 „ |

(Cover reaction, economic troubles.)

| I. *Test :* Quarrel | nasty people like to quarrel | : 4·2 seconds |
| II. „ Quarrel | people quarrel at times | : 8·2 „ |

Explains : " with her husband on account of his drinking."

| I. *Test :* Beat | the smith hits | : 2·8 seconds |
| II. „ Beat | naughty children hit one another: | 6 seconds ; |
| | " at first I think one beats the tree " | |

" Children hit one another." " Roseli is so wild " (omitted). " I once hit Roseli when we had visitors."

| I. *Test :* Three | the tree is high: 4·6 seconds (stimulus-word misunderstood) |
| II. „ Three | (fault ; after 20 seconds still no reaction) |

" Three is an odd number." (Why so long before reacting ?) " I had first to make sure that it was odd." Then : " We were three—papa, Roseli, and myself."

| I. *Test :* Thirst | water | : 7·2 seconds |
| II. „ Thirst | we are rather thirsty | : 7·4 „ |

Explains : " One drinks when thirsty." Then : " Papa used to be thirsty." (Thinks of her own illness of ten years before.)

We note the successive explanations, which at first are to conceal the explanation and are resistances to the repressed idea ; it is the same resistance with which we meet in Freud's psycho-analysis.

| I & II. *Tests :* Separate | death separates us: 8 seconds ; and 8·6 seconds, thinks of her husband's death |
| I & II. „ Ill | I am ill: 5·6 seconds and 4 seconds |

" Thought of Roseli, but she's all right." We see here the repression which during and directly after the twilight state had led to a full amnesia emotionally grounded for the illness of her child.

| II. *Test :* Faithful | servants should be faithful: 8 seconds |

Explains : " The wife should be faithful to her husband." Then : " I feared when my husband was away so long that he was unfaithful to me." It should be mentioned here that in Test II, after her child's visit, the complex *husband* occurs much more frequently.

| Wreath | my husband got many wreaths : 7·4 seconds (at the funeral) |
| Elect | the boroughs elect . . . (18·2 seconds) mayor |

("At election times her husband was always in the public-house.")

| Law | a vote is taken about a law : 8·4 seconds |

Explains : "Her husband had to vote." Then : "He then came home, but he was drunk."

| Right | we must bestow the right : 17·4 seconds |

Explains : "I was often in the wrong at home."

| Annoying | vermin are annoying (explains : "drinking") |
| Unjust | (20 seconds no reaction ; then at 25·6 seconds, "The unjust must suffer ") |

In her endeavour to form a sentence according to pattern, patient was unable to produce anything. Explains : "I had to suffer much injustice. He believed that I was unkind to him when I warned him against drinking."

| Misery | the poor are in misery : 5·8 seconds (her economic position) |
| Suppose | one rather supposes  : 6·6   ,, |

Explains : "When Roseli had a headache I thought she was going to die."

| Much | I go walking a lot : 18·2 seconds (she was in the park yesterday, looked down into the town and had home-sickness) |

To give an impression of the whole, I append a series of reactions from the first test without further remarks. The beginning of the sentence type is nicely seen at the stimulus-word *beat*.

| Frog | leg | : 1·4 seconds |
| Flower | flower-pot | : 1·6   ,, |
| Cherry | cherry-tree | : 1·6 |
| Asylum | educational asylum | : 3·2 |
| Warder | asylum warder | : 3·6 |
| Piano | piano-stool | : 1·6 |
| Fern | ferns | : 7·2 |
| Oven | door | : 1·6 |
| Walk | go for a walk | : 1·6 |
| Cook | cookery book | : 1·8 |
| Water | water-bottle | : 1·4 |
| Dance | dancing floor | : 2 |
| Cat | cat's paw | : 12 |
| Begging | to go | : 6·8 |
| Dark | darkness | : 1·2   ,, |
| Heart | you, my heart | : 2·8   ,, |
| Swim | swimming-bath | : about 3·8 seconds |
| White | white bread | : 1·6 seconds |
| Play | play evening | : 4·4   ,, |
| 13 | Number 13 | : 2·4 |

| Emperor | empire | : | 2 | seconds |
|---|---|---|---|---|
| Moon | half-moon | : | 2·4 | ,, |
| Beat | the smith beats | : | 2·8 | |
| Console | the children console | : | 3·8 | |
| A fire | the house is on fire | : | 2·4 | |
| Star | the star is beautiful | : | 2·4 | |
| Stroke | the cat is stroked | : | 4 | |
| Wonderful | natural events are wonderful | : | 4 | ,, |
| Child | children play | : | 6·4 | |
| Dark red | the mouth—blood is dark red | : | 4·6 | ,, |
| Ride | the rider rides | : | 7·4 | |
| Sweet | sugar tastes sweet | : | 5·6 | |
| Friendly | children are friendly | : | 3 | |
| Bread | the bread is cut | : | 2·2 | |
| Bronze | in mines there is bronze | : | 3·6 | |
| Crown | the Crown Hotel | : | 5·4 | |
| Thirst | water | : | 7·2 | |
| Greenish | leaves are greenish | : | 2·8 | |
| Thank | the child thanks her mother | : | 2·6 | ,, |
| Raw | potatoes are raw | : | 1 | |
| Stinks | rotten meat stinks | : | 6·2 | |
| Bright | the colours are bright | : | 3·8 | |
| Sends | the mother sends the child | : | 4·6 | |
| Seven | seven o'clock | : | 12·2 | |
| Prison | the thief is in prison | : | 6·2 | |
| Separate | we are separated from the dead | : | 8 | ,, |
| Ill | I am ill | : | 5·6 | |
| Song | pupils sing songs | : | 4 | |
| Potatoes | one eats potatoes | : | 2·2 | |
| Sacrifice | the ancients made sacrifices | : | 5·6 | |
| Wedding | people enjoy a wedding | : | 7 | |
| Now | I am going home | : | 4·8 | |
| Angry | the dog is rather angry | : | 5·4 | |
| Soldier | the soldier obeys the rules | : | 3 | |
| Gossip | many people like to gossip | : | 8·4 | |
| Come | to me (spoken softly) | : | 12·8 | |
| Year | Yes, I'm coming | : | 15·0 | ,, |
| Above | the stars are above | : | 4·4 | ,, |
| Long | the old woman goes slowly | : | 10·4 | ,, (mother) |
| Behave | children should be well behaved | : | 2·6 | ,, |
| Rich | there are many rich people | : | 6 | |
| Sour | the apple tastes sour | : | 2·8 | |
| Suffer | one offers the hand | : | 6·8 | .. |
| | *(stimulus-word heard as " offer ")* | | | |
| Suffer | the sick must suffer | : | 5·2 | |
| Eye | the eye is beautiful | : | 4·4 | |
| Doctor | the doctor prescribes medicine | : | 4·6 | ,, |
| Sunday | I enjoy Sunday | : | 2·4 | ,, (visit) |
| Youth | the child plays in his youth | : | 5·6 | ,, |
| Indulge | the mother indulges the child | : | 5·2 | ,, |
| Inn | alcoholic liquors are drunk in the inn | : | 7·4 | ,, |
| Stupid | the donkey is stupid | : | 13·2 | |
| Family | family fortune | : | 4·8 | |
| Trouble | sorrow produces trouble | : | 5·6 | |

| Pay attention | the children pay attention at school : | 3·2 seconds |
| Fist | the angry man clenches his fist | : 10·6 ,, |
| End | everything comes to an end | : 6·4 ,, |
| Hunger | the poor are hungry | : 10 |

## SIXTH CASE

BERTHA SCH. This patient, 28 years of age, has suffered for the last three years from hystero-epileptic attacks; her sister has suffered likewise for the last seven years. Before her marriage patient had sexual connexion for about a year with her present husband, a drunkard. When a neighbour in a dispute accused her of this she got a brief aphonia—"The words stuck in her mouth." She had her first attack when the marriage was definitely settled. She would rather not have married the drunkard, but dared not go back. During the attack gestures of repugnance and abhorrence played an important rôle. The marriage was unhappy ; the patient separated from her brutal husband and went back with her rather delicate and nervous child to her family. Her husband frequently annoyed her again. Owing to these causes attacks took place from time to time. After hypnotic treatment the woman remained for six months without any attack and was vigorous and able to work. After having been again waylaid by her husband some isolated attacks took place after violent scenes.

In the associations we find at least 35 per cent. that certainly belong to the hysterogenic complex—husband, unhappy marriage and its consequences ; poverty, hard work, worry about the child. The patient is one of those persons who react, on the average, pretty quickly, and not in sentence-form ; with them the accent is on the more or less abrupt, long prolongations of the reaction-time and on the faults. In the latter the stimulus-word strikes the complex and no verbal reaction follows at all. In this case, as in many cases of hysteria, the patient is quite unable to say why she cannot answer, whilst in hypnosis she gives a correct answer. In many normals no verbal reaction is produced in quite analogous places ; we register a fault, and finally we can, in the waking state, get information as to the correct grounds of the fault. There are " faults " of different intensity. In both cases we have a fault, due to the " complex." The mechanism of its occurrence, whether conscious or unconscious, is the same, only the degree of dissociation of the complex is much stronger in the first case ; the complex is removed from consciousness.

Examples :

*Journey* — (fault). Cannot give the reason for the fault. In hypnosis : " Honeymoon journey."

*Proud* — (fault). Subsequently *bag*. In hypnosis : " Purse-proud," thinking of her brother's wife with whom she is now living.

*Strange* — (fault). No reason found in waking state. In hypnosis : " After the separation I wanted at first to go to some strangers, not to my brother's wife, but finally I did so." She complains, however, that she has to eat humble-pie there.

*Mix* — (fault). Cannot state the reason. In hypnosis : "Sexual connexion with her husband." The stimulus-word *mix* is often taken in this sense (cp. the stimulus-words *mix* and *blood* in Case 4—Mrs. M. C.).

*Forget* — (fault). In hypnosis : " Misery, my husband." Her husband worries her all the time.

(*Gleich*) *similar* — (fault). Laughs ; she cannot explain why nothing occurs to her, that she cannot say anything. In hypnosis with a great deal of resistance she thought of a *part of the body*. (The dialect word *gleich* is a slang word for limb or penis.) Her husband is again persecuting her, wishing to renew sexual life.

*Stalk* — (fault). In the waking state patient cannot give the meaning of the fault. In hypnosis she states that her husband is a " withered stalk." Is that the final explanation ? We have seen that in many cases *stalk* arouses the presentation of penis and causes a long reaction-time. Our case is to some extent an answer to the question how far complex reactions influence the succeeding indifferent associations (cp. chapter iv).

The series

| | | | |
|---|---|---|---|
| Disesteem | esteem : 1·6 seconds | Folk | right : 19·6 seconds |
| Tooth | mouth : 3·6 ,, | Stink | smell : 1·4 ,, |
| Just | unjust : 7·2 ,, | | |

shows a gradual increase of the reaction-times up to *folk* — *right*. The next reaction is short and seems to be independent of the previous ones. It could not be definitely proved whether the first ones are independent of one another.

In

| | | |
|---|---|---|
| Just | unjust : 7·2 seconds | Folk | right : 19·6 seconds |

that is certainly not so ; the first influences the second ; we have a kind of perseveration.

In

| | |
|---|---|
| Just | unjust : 7·2 seconds |

we get the explanation in hypnosis, latterly her husband is again pursuing her ; that is *unjust*.

Folk (*Volk*) right (*recht*)

is a form of perseveration to *unjust* ; perhaps there is a slang association to *Volkrecht*, the title of a newspaper which circulates among the patient's friends and neighbours. Hypnosis shows she was thinking about her husband. We find, moreover, in the associations the following :

| | | | |
|---|---|---|---|
| Unjust | treatment : 7 seconds | Frog | toad : 9 seconds |

Both associations refer to her husband. The first obviously, as was confirmed in hypnosis ; to the second the hypnotized patient said *frog* gave her a feeling of nausea ; immediately adding, " so does my husband." We find a similar after-effect in the reactions

| White | black : 3·6 seconds | Ring | finger : 6·8 seconds |

Her husband's name is Black, hence the delayed time. To *ring*, the immediate association was *wedding-ring*.

A few other typical complex reactions require notice. There is a complex *child*, which means an increase of the attacks. The patient complains that she can no longer sleep or rest ; since her separation she must keep herself and look after her restless child.

| Angel | child | : 5 seconds | |
| Quiet | noise | : 2·4 „ | (refers to the child) |
| Sleep | get up | : 3·4 „ | „ „ |
| Tired | courage | : 3·2 „ | |
| Modest | child | : 8·8 „ | |
| Wake | child | — | |
| Bed | sleep | : 1·4 „ | |

The reaction *sleep* is frequently repeated. She generally uses such repetitions when there is a complex, in this case about the child.

| Separate | come | : 1·6 seconds | Certain | come : 9·2 seconds |
| Meet | come | : 1 „ | | |

A repetition of the reaction referring to the last invitations and plottings of her husband. To a reaction *wild — hunter*, 12·2 seconds, patient explains that her brother is a hunter. Then : " I thought of myself ; I'm often wild (with rage) ; my husband often came home wild."

## SEVENTH CASE

JULIUS SCHW., a clerk, 23 years. Many tests were tried with this patient ; on twenty-third, first, seventh, eleventh, fourteenth ; eleven without time-measurements, on fifteenth with time-measurements ; six hundred and ninety associations altogether. The patient had perpetrated eleven arsons within six weeks in a hysterical twilight state with amnesia and under the influence of drink.

We will limit ourselves to repeating peculiar manifestations of perseverations which were strongly marked in this case.

From the first test—

| Light | fire |
| Star | red (thought of fire) |
| Strike | a match |

This short series shows a peculiar form of perseveration of the content in three successive reactions. In the reaction

| Strike | a match |

it comes out very clearly. That this phenomenon of perseveration began at the stimulus-word *light* explains itself.

In the second test we meet this phenomenon more and more ; stimulus-words set up far-reaching series of presentations, the *stimulus-word being forgotten*.   We find a beginning in the following places :

| | |
|---|---|
| Head | red |
| Ink | black |
| Needle | pointed |
| Bread | bath   "What was the stimulus-word ? "   "Ink "—a little later |
| Mountain | book |
| Hair | beard   (" Stimulus-word ? "   Pat bare) |
| Salt | water   (" Stimulus-word ? "   Old ; or was it Old salt ?) |
| Dream | foam |
| Copy-book | skittle   (" Stimulus-word ? "   Patient, dazed and laughing, says : " Here's copy-book "—laughing more and more obviously in hallucination) |

After a while he points with astonishment to the examiner and says, " I thought I saw some one else ; I have—played skittles somewhere in W——, surely ? "   The patient suddenly thinks the examiner has given another stimulus-word.   This dream state was certainly set up by the stimulus-word *dream*.   The patient is frequently concerned with a dream of playing skittles in W—— ; what is connected with this could not, unfortunately, be found out.

The ten reactions that followed had nothing noteworthy ; the patient seemed clear-headed.   Then the following series came (the vertical lines denote the length of the perseveration) :

| | |
|---|---|
| Window | fowl |
| Frog | dog |
| Flower | good.   (Patient gets a staring look, gradually increasing, but still reacts regularly) |
| Cherry | sun (long reaction-time) |
| Asylum | star |
| Warder | flower (long reaction-time) |
| Piano | music (beats with the hand upon the table as if lost in thought) |
| Fern | Mignon |
| Stove | mirror |
| Walk | orange |
| Cook | lemon (the head sinking more and more upon the table) |
| Water | Mozart  (long reaction-time) |
| Dance | Philine      ,,         ,, |
| Cat | Laertes     ,,         ,, |
| Dozen | —   (no answer.   " What word did I say ? "   " Italian ") |
| Dark | light  (Patient awakes) |
| Heart | hand |
| Bird | air |
| Swim | fly (perseveration) |
| White | blue, etc. |

It then occurs to the patient himself that he is always falling asleep ; he often "dreams" in the same way, calling up melodies.

In the second test similar phenomena occur :

| Wonderful | — beautiful |
| Child | blue |
| Dark red | fire |
| Sweet | cry |
| Ride | — jump |

Shortly after—

| Crown | trumpeter |
| You | room (does not know stimulus-word or reaction immediately afterwards) |
| Greenish | red |
| Against | again |
| Raw | brilliance |
| Smell | fortune |
| Bright | Count |
| Sweet | Duke |
| Love | veranda |
| Prison | carpet |
| Separate | Walberg (Walpurg ?) |
| Ill | — orchestra |

We see that states arise set up by certain stimulus-words, when the stimulus-words are not followed by any reaction that make sense, but serve as sparks for a reaction. The reactions that follow correspond to a circle of ideas aroused by the first stimulus-word, remaining active for some time. Careful examination of the patient at such moments shows him to be in temporary twilight states which are produced by the particular stimulus-word. A definite circle of ideas is aroused ; the patient forms it while subject to complete hallucination, ignores the sense-presentations, is untroubled about his surroundings, and lives in a quite other *milieu*. (Passion for fire, skittles, a bit out of *Mignon* at the play.) On the particular day when the above tests were given the patient was much inclined towards twilight states ; but in the other tests much the same thing occurred. The tendency to twilight states was very common, and was so far under control that it was usually determined by some affect— a visit from his parents, moving books, and especially sentimental love scenes in performances given at the asylum, and "lyrical" music.

In the series of perseverations there is some strong emotional situation. Emotions are often the cause of perseveration in association experiments (where it is not a distraction of attention). Attention is concentrated for some time on the critical presentation ; hence the subsequent reactions come up shorn of attention, then the phenomenon of distraction occurs. In well-pronounced cases this expresses itself by no reaction occurring to the stimulus-words, but only to the content of the previous critical reaction. It is in this wise that we are to understand the occurrence of the perseverating series.[1] The situation aroused by the critical stimulus-word is so emotionally powerful that it completely chains the interest, so that the patient quite loses consciousness of his surroundings ; he passes into a twilight state (Pick's dreamy state). These examples are of theoretical interest because they show how the common complex perseverations are only separated by degree from the hysterical twilight state.

## EIGHTH CASE

BETTY SL. This patient, 19 years old, was an illegitimate child brought up by a foster-mother. Her own mother later married somebody else. At the age of fourteen Betty returned to her mother, but was soon badly treated. She was driven, after all kinds of dissensions, to take a place as servant in the same town.

After taking the situation she once unexpectedly met her mother, who looked at her with hatred and scorn. The patient staggered home and had her first hysterical attack. The content of the attack corresponded to this origin. The patient had a hallucination—her mother's face with its expression of hate and scorn. The last attacks occurred when the patient got news from home.

The associations were taken in French. There are markedly long reaction-times.[2]

| Récalcitrant | aimable | : 8 | seconds | |
| Malade | convalescent | : 7·8 | ,, | (refers to herself) |
| Menacer | caresser | : 6 | ,, | |
| Mépriser | agréer | : 6 | ,, | |

Peculiarly remarkable in this case is the frequent distraction from the surroundings, which we have already met with in a more rudimentary form in the associations of normal persons. It is a complex indicator. The correct reaction is blocked ; as a cover reaction some external perception is taken, some object in the room or something similar. We find the same phenomenon in the associations during states of *emotional paralysis* [3] (examination paralysis), showing manifestations similar to affective complexes. In this state faults, repetition of the stimulus-word, etc., occur also. In the case under consideration there are peculiar relationships between the emotional stupidity which expressed itself at the beginning of the experiment, chiefly in her distraction

---

[1] Cp. Stransky, *Ueber Sprachverwirrtheit*, 1905.

[2] The associations have been left in the original French.—TRANSLATOR.

[3] Jung, "Ueber Simulation von Geistesstörung," *Journal für Psych. u. Neur.*, Bd. II, 1903.

to her surroundings, and the complex to which the associations with the delayed reaction-times belong.

| Tête | *rue* (looking through the window) | | | |
|------|------|------|------|------|
| Vert | *lampe* (in the room) | | | |
| Eau | feu | : 2 | seconds | |
| Piquer | *encrier* | : 1·2 | ,, | (in room) |
| Ange | *fenêtre* | : 1·4 | ,, | ,, ,, |
| Long | *lunette* | : 1·2 | ,, | (on the table) |
| Bateau | *arbre* | : 2·2 | ,, | (through windows) |
| Labourer | *feuille* | : 3 | ,, | (looking at a tree) |
| Laine | *pierre* | : 3·4 | ,, | (outside) |
| Aimable | méchant | : 1·8 | ,, | (gives place to laughter; this is an instance of appropriate emotion, to which attention was called in Case 1) |
| Table | *cuiller* | : 3·4 | ,, | (Is the delayed reaction-time an aftermath of the previous complex reaction ?) |
| Porter | *tableau* | : 1·4 | ,, | (in room) |
| État | *volet* | : 2·2 | ,, | (through window) |
| Récalcitrant | aimable | : 8 | ,, | |
| Danser | boire | : 3·2 | ,, | |
| Tige | loup | : 2 | ,, | (Patient can give no explanation at all of these " meaningless " reactions) |
| Lac | rivière | : 1·2 | ,, | |
| Malade | convalescent | : 7·8 | ,, | (reference to her condition) |
| Orgueil | simplicité | : 1·6 | ,, | |
| Cuire | bruler | : 4·8 | ,, | |
| Encre | plume | : 1·6 | ,, | |
| Méchant | sage | : 2·4 | ,, | |
| Aiguille | fil | : 2·6 | | |
| Nager | noyer | : 2 | ,, | |
| Voyage | repos | : 7·2 | ,, | (Journey from her home in Switzerland, away from her mother) |
| Menacer | caresser | : 6·9 | ,, | (complex) |
| Lampe | chapeau | : 2·2 | ,, | (chapeau de lampe) |
| Riche | pauvre | : 0·8 | ,, | |
| Arbre | branche | : 4·8 | ,, | |
| Chanter | pleurer | : 1·6 | ,, | etc. |

The distraction to the surroundings (the corresponding reactions are in italics) as shown at the beginning is an expression of the slight emotional stupidity present in this reserved, somewhat frightened girl. We see that these reactions, with the exception of the superficial reaction *eau — feu*, are only interrupted when complex reactions occur, and that they quite disappear after the second complex reaction:

Récalcitrant     aimable: 8 seconds

In the fifth case (Verena D.) it was a complex which set up the continuous reaction in sentence form ; here the complex breaks down the reactions due to emotional stupidity. We found a similar phenomenon, the liberation, by a definite word, of an almost unbroken series of complex reactions, in the associations of normal persons (Subject No. 7, Educated Men). Emotional stupidity is also seen in the associations of many imbeciles and epileptics. In some cases of hysteria it persists during nearly the entire experiment. These often present a picture similar to certain pictures obtained from persons in a twilight state. In later experiments carried out with the same person it may quite disappear.

## SUMMARY

In the forefront of the hysterical type of reaction we find more or less independent and active presentation complexes with much affect, whose expansion seems to be much more powerful than among normals. The reactions are frequently interrupted by complex disturbances. Together with the usual complex indicators, we occasionally find some with *amnestic manifestations* and *phenomena of consciousness*. The critical stimulus-word is often forgotten and in its place the previous one is named.

The cause of the fault is unknown to the subject ; the " distraction to the surroundings " and the misunderstanding of the stimulus-word are other complex indicators. A further large group of complex indicators is formed by reactions which do not denote the complex by the stimulus-word, but are only associated in the remotest way with the word denoting the complex. This arises in one of two ways : either the complex excited by the stimulus-word is repressed and the reaction is superficially associated with the complex, being so apprehended as not to betray the complex but to call up instead a seemingly indifferent reaction. Take as examples the cover reactions in Cases 4 and 5 (Mrs. M. C. and Verena D.).

Mrs. Verena D. reacts :

Faithful     servants should be faithful

Behind this innocent sentence lies the fear about her husband's infidelity. The *replacement of the complex presentation by a seemingly innocent reaction is a symptom of repression.* I interpreted similarly the " conversion symptoms " of Lina H.[1]

The physical conversion symptom is associated to the complex, but is not noticeable to the observer and to the consciousness of the patient, thus guaranteeing the dissociation between

---

[1] *Analyse der Sympt. und Assoz. eines Falles von Hysterie.*

the complex and the conscious. Or the action of the complex is so powerful that its influence reaches out to a distant series of presentations, determining them likewise. (Cp. a number of the reactions in sentence form in Cases 4 and 5.)

Among the complex indicators, distraction to the surroundings and the non-understanding of the complex excitant stimulus-words play a certain rôle. I have adduced numerous instances. The stimulus-word may be assimilated to the complex. (The stimulus-word is apprehended as best suits the complex or as best conceals it.)

Distraction to surroundings often appears when it is a question of an affect-determined distraction in order to avoid the critical stimulus-word: I once had the following experience : A boy of twelve injured his knee one Sunday from a fall. Numerous stitches were required to close the wound. The anæsthesia was very light, so that the boy still reacted at each stitch, although faintly and with amnesia after the operation. In this light narcosis he carried on a conversation, the whole meaning of which was to distract himself from the operation, to repress all thoughts about it. It partly recalled Ganser's answers, partly wish-fulfilment dreams, which have likewise their roots in repression and distraction from a disagreeable complex. He said sponta-neously and loudly : " To-day's Monday ! Then come along, Tony, we're leaving off and going for a game." Then, as if in scorn of the intense pain of the operation, he told a friend what Christmas presents he had got, and so on. Not infre-quently we find this occurring. Jung [1] quotes the case of a woman who during an operation fell into a twilight state where in hallucination she was walking among flowery fields.

The observations in Ganser's twilight states speak partly in favour of these answers and the formation of wish-fulfilment deliria as semi-complex phenomena of a related nature ; partly, however, the observations speak in favour of an unconscious simulation.

The complex can alter the apprehension, remove the stimulus (or stimulus-word), produce hallucinations favouring the repres-sion or wish fulfilment, so that the contrary of that which is the content of the repressed presentation complex occurs.

So far as my observations permit a conclusion, my view already expressed several times in this work has been confirmed, that *the complex with its activities is the all-important matter in hysterical psychology, and that all the hysterical symptoms can be derived therefrom.*

[1] *Occult Phenomena.*

z

# CHAPTER IX

# ASSOCIATION, DREAM, AND HYSTERICAL SYMPTOMS

## By Dr. C. G. JUNG

### I. The Associations

THE object of this investigation is to support and elucidate the views expressed in chapters vii and viii about the nature of the anomalies of association in hysteria. The following is the case :

A young woman, aged 24, intelligent and of average education, physically healthy. Her mother suffers from osteomalacia, which has entirely crippled her; otherwise there is no demonstrable taint. The patient is the youngest child, the only daughter, and has four elder brothers. She was well until school began; was very sensitive at school, but made good progress. In her second year tremors of the right arm set in, which soon made writing impossible ; the tremors became generalized, till finally a hysterical chorea occurred. The patient became the starting-point of a small school epidemic of St. Vitus's dance. The chorea expressed itself in tic-like attacks which sometimes lasted one to two minutes. In these attacks the patient hit out around her and stamped, occasionally giving vent to a shriek. Consciousness was not disturbed during the attacks. The attacks occurred fifteen to twenty times a day. Menstruation began at the age of fifteen. With the occurrence of the first period the choreiform attacks ceased as by magic. (The patient had two years before consulted a specialist, who said that the attacks would leave off with the periods.) But in the same week the patient experienced one day, towards evening, a dull feeling in her head. The feeling gradually took on the character of heat, which became far worse during the periods. The pain increased as the years went on. From about ten o'clock in the morning these hot feelings increased regularly and gradually until they became "insupportable." For the last three years the pain had been so bad that she was completely prostrated by these hot feelings in the head lasting nearly all day long. Innumerable treatments with all kinds of methods had been unavailingly tried. Sometimes the patient could assist a little with the housework in the morning. From ten o'clock onwards she went about doing nothing, continually complaining about her head. She became gradually misanthropic and withdrew altogether from society. During the summer, on hot days, she remained in the cellar. During the winter she would not be in any heated room. She consulted me in the summer of 1905, when she was getting rapidly worse. She felt she was going out of her mind, and had hallucinations of white and black figures. She begged to be admitted to the local asylum. In the autumn of 1905 she was admitted.

*Condition.*—Well nourished, slender person ; her appearance of suffering seemed to be directed towards obtaining pity; entire absence of energy in her behaviour, this is indicated by her extremely fine, frail handwriting. Constant complaints about feelings of heat in her head. The tone of the complaint is pronouncedly elegiacal. She describes her feelings in the following way: " The whole head is stopped from the neck up and quite hot; I have at least forty degrees of fever in my head—it is quite tense, choking. My neck is strangled, hot, dry, withered up. The feeling of dry heat and warmth is most terrible at the back of my neck, the top part. It's always worse after eating. My body is quite cold and my hands blue-black; my feet are like ice. My idea is that if I could but once have a great bleeding of my nose I would be much better. I am always imagining that I am *bleeding* from the *nose and mouth*, a basinful; I am always imagining *big clots of fresh blood. I am always dreaming of blood.* I often dream that I am wading in blood, that the room is full of blood, or that *blood is spurting out of my nose, mouth, eyes, and ears.* I likewise often dream of *fire*; everything is then in *flames*."

On going to sleep she often has the vision of a black man stretching out his black hand towards her and seizing her arm; occasionally she also sees indistinct white figures of women.

Her *periods have stopped* since February 1905; she is very constipated; *meteorism*, noticeably distending the lower part of the abdomen, has been present for several months. She has great *resistance to sitting down*; generally stands up or walks up and down the room. *Great repugnance to meat;* avoids everything which makes heat. If she but hears the steam ascending in the heater her bad condition increases. She indulges in *cold ablutions* every day and does gymnastics in her room, attaching great importance to these activities. This is in strange contrast with her repugnance to and fear of any continuous work, which she believes is very injurious to her. She has a *morbid love of order and cleanliness* (she states that formerly she had for a time an obsession to touch things, which showed itself in an impulse, whilst walking about the room, to touch any objects). She has no insight into the mental nature of her pain but is firmly convinced that there is an organic change in her head; but she laughs involuntarily when telling us that one of her doctors took it to be a case of Basedow's disease. Naturally she has no more idea what was the cause of her illness than have the doctors who have hitherto treated her.

There can be no question but that this is a case of hysteria. The extraordinary chronic nature of the case and the absence of any change in the chief symptoms, rather unusual in hysteria, speak in favour of a profound paralysis of energy and complete subjugation of the personality to the disease complex. She has been ill seventeen years. In considering the peculiarity of the symptoms it must be remembered that the " St. Vitus's dance " (choreiform tic) developed by continuity into the present condition. We cannot accept the view that the " St. Vitus's dance " was healed ; on the contrary, everything is in favour of the view that the effect of the first menstrual period was simply to change it suddenly into another form of the fundamental disease. Her completely childlike and asthenic personality show all the signs of the infantile, Meige-Feindel type of tiqueur.

To make the description of the case quite clear I will first describe the association experiments which were carried out with the patient, who was under treatment in the asylum from

October 1, 1905, till December 21, 1905. The experiments were spread over this period. The treatment had a certain measure of success, which was not without an important influence on the experiment. The tests were at times carried out in a room only moderately warm (13°), for the patient could not permanently bear more than 11° of heat.

## THE ASSOCIATION TESTS

### First Series

*July 23, 10 a.m., with the Reproduction Test*

| Stimulus-word | Time [1] | Reaction | Reproduction |
|---|---|---|---|
| 1. Head | 6 | -ache | |
| 2. Green | 33 | stone | |
| 3. Water | — | — | |
| 4. Prick | 9 | bee | |
| 5. *Angel* | 105 | hotel | |
| 6. Long | 65 | knife | — |
| 7. *Ship* | 35 | steamship | — |
| 8. *Plough* | 21 | field | garden |
| 9. Wool | 75 | knit | |
| 10. Friendly | 11 | -ness | |
| 11. Table | 30 | cloth | |
| 12. Ask | — | — | |
| 13. State | — | — | |
| 14. Stubborn | 40 | person | |
| 15. Stalk | 11 | of flower | |
| 16. Dance | 10 | dancing floor | |
| 17. Lake | 29 | of Zurich | |
| 18. Ill | — | — | |
| 19. Proud | 19 | haughty | |
| 20. To cook | 13 | cookery school | |
| 21. Ink | 9 | ink-bottle | |
| 22. Wicked | 9 | wickedness | |
| 23. Needle | 10 | pincushion | |
| 24. Swim | 45 | swimming school | |
| 25. *Travel* | 60 | travelling rug | |
| 26. Blue | 35 | Blue-street | |
| 27. Bread | 20 | breadless | |
| 28. *Threaten* | 60 | punishment | punish |
| 29. Lamp | 11 | lamp-shade | |
| 30. Rich | 21 | riches | |
| 31. Tree | 23 | fruit-tree | |
| 32. Sing | 16 | choral society | |
| 33. Pity | 35 | to regret | |
| 34. Yellow | 25 | yolk of egg | |
| 35. Mountain | 23 | Utli mountain | |
| 36. Play | 16 | chess | |
| 37. Salt | 12 | salt-cellar | |

---

[1] These figures give the time in one-fifth seconds.

| Stimulus-word | Time [1] | Reaction | Reproduction |
|---|---|---|---|
| 38. New | 15 | Newbury | |
| 39. Custom | 46 | propriety | |
| 40. Ride | 18 | riding school | |
| 41. *Wall* | 12 | Spanish wall | |
| 42. Stupid | 45 | stupidity | |
| 43. Exercise-book | 15 | school exercise-book | |
| 44. Despise | — | — | |
| 45. *Tooth* | 15 | eye-tooth | |
| 46. *Correct* | 25 | to arrange | |
| 47. People | 23 | people's paper | |
| 48. *Smell* | 50 | sink | |
| 49. Book | 15 | reading book | |
| 50. *Unjust* | — | — | |
| 51. Frog | 25 | tree-frog | |
| 52. Separate | 32 | divorce | |
| 53. Hunger | 19 | eat | |
| 54. White | 18 | snow | |
| 55. Cattle | 32 | herd of cattle | |
| 56. To take care | 30 | esteem | |
| 57. Pencil | 31 | pencil-holder | |
| 58. Cloudy | — | — | |
| 59. Plum | 66 | plum jam | |
| 60. Meet | — | — | |
| 61. Law | — | — | |
| 62. Love | 15 | loveless | |
| 63. Glass | 8 | tumbler | |
| 64. *To quarrel* | 23 | dispute | |
| 65. Goat | 12 | goat's milk | |
| 66. Big | 15 | generous | |
| 67. Potato | 20 | potato-meal | |
| 68. Paint | 21 | oil paintings | |
| 69. Part | 26 | part-payment | |
| 70. Old | 49 | Oldtown | |
| 71. Flower | 51 | nosegay | |
| 72. *Strike* | 30 | stroke with hammer | |
| 73. Basket | 21 | clothes-basket | |
| 74. Wild | 21 | wild duck | |
| 75. Family | 26 | family party | |
| 76. Wash | — | — | |
| 77. Cow | 10 | cow's milk | |
| 78. Foreign | 30 | foreign book | |
| 79. Happiness | 53 | congratulations | |
| 80. To narrate | 15 | stories | |
| 81. Deportment | 55 | lesson in deportment | |
| 82. Narrow | — | — | |
| 83. Brother | — | — | |
| 84. Malice | 10 | malicious joy (*Schadenfreude*) | |
| 85. Stork | 26 | stork's nest | |
| 86. False | 37 | falsity | |
| 87. Dread | 20 | feeling of dread | |
| 88. Kiss | 65 | sisterly kiss | |

[1] These figures give the time in one-fifth seconds.

| Stimulus-word | Time [1] | Reaction | Reproduction |
|---|---|---|---|
| 89. Fire | 28 | huge fire | |
| 90. Dirty | — | — | |
| 91. Doors | 21 | lock of door | |
| 92. Choice | 55 | choice of comradeship | |
| 93. Hay | 19 | hay-wagon | |
| 94. Still | 39 | peace | |
| 95. *Ridicule* | 10 | ridiculous price, ridiculously cheap | |
| 96. Sleep | 17 | sleeplessness | |
| 97. Month | 15 | monthly meeting | |
| 98. Coloured | — | — | |
| 99. Dog | 15 | dog-faithful | |
| 100. Speak | 67 | consultation | |

This test was made at the consultation. Let us first of all consider the associations from the statistical point of view. I content myself with the classification into inner and outer associations, clang-associations, faults, and indirect associations (see chapter ii). This summary classification suffices for our purpose. These are :

| | |
|---|---|
| Inner associations . . . . | 16 per cent. |
| Outer ,, . . . . | 60 ,, |
| Clang-reactions . . . . | 9 ,, |
| Faults . . . . . . | 14 ,, |
| Indirect associations. . . . | 1 ,, |
| Reproduction anomalies . . . | 14 ,, |

The outer associations are the most numerous, predominating in a most unusual degree. The patient is not without intelligence, but she has not been highly educated. (She only went through the elementary schools, and this with many intermissions.) A glance at the reactions shows that the outer associations consist chiefly of verbal-motor connexions, of *word-combinations.* Side by side we find a good many *word-completions* (clang-reactions). The number of faults is striking. Compare the figures with these :

*Average Figures of Educated Women* [2]

| | |
|---|---|
| Inner associations . . . . | 35 per cent. |
| Outer ,, . . . . | 58 ,, |
| Clang-reactions . . . . | 3·3 ,, |
| Faults . . . . . . | 1·4 ,, |

and we see that the figures for this patient show a much more superficial mode of association ; they approach the figures of the distraction test.

[1] These figures give the time in one-fifth seconds.
[2] P. 146.

Average of the distraction test with 100 metronome beats per minute :

*Educated Women, excluding the Predicate Type*

| | | |
|---|---|---|
| Inner associations | . . . . | 20·8 per cent. |
| Outer „ | . . . . | 62·8 „ |
| Clang-reactions | . . . . | 13·2 „ |
| Faults . | . . . . . | 0·4 „ |

One might believe that there had been distraction of attention during the test. The question then arises to what the distraction must be referred or what factor this disturbing influence had upon the attention. There were no external causes, so that we are led to consider some psychological disturbance. We need not seek very far, for the patient is entirely occupied with one thought which extinguishes every kind of interest in her surroundings ; she is absorbed entirely in the *presentation complex of her illness.* Her whole attention is focussed on the symptoms of her illness, so that only a small remainder is left at the disposition of the association test ; hence the superficial reaction type. Her illness makes so great a claim upon her that she scarcely allows the meaning of the stimulus-word to reach her. As a general rule she contents herself simply with apprehending the outer form of the words ; and her intellectual work is limited to finding some ready-made connexion to the stimulus-word. Hence she only listens with " half an ear " and allows the stimulus-words almost to slip off of themselves. She cannot rouse herself to direct her attention to the experiment ; obviously this is far too unimportant to her compared with her disease complex. Her slight degree of self-control sinks from time to time to zero (fault), not infrequently just where some ready-made verbal connexion is not at hand ; this also occurs frequently when the stimulus-word has aroused emotionally toned connotations, as we shall see later. As soon as she noticed that the reaction was not immediately at hand she abstained entirely from enforcing one. We have here an experimental expression of the clinically remarkable abulia, which, as usual, consists in the surrender of the entire interest to the disease complex, the hysterogenic complex which is at the root of her symptoms ; hence nothing remains over for what is going on around. (A similar case of distraction phenomena is referred to on p. 69, where, however, the cause of the disturbance was a quite recent affect).

The probable mean time of this test was 5·2 seconds, a very high figure. We believe that such prolongations rest upon certain emotional inhibitions.

Just as in the case reported in chapter vii, an analysis of the patient was impossible for she was utterly indifferent, and would not enter into any questions which did not refer to her symptoms. The repression or the inhibition arising from the pathogenic complex was obviously too strong at that time.

After the consultation when this test was made the patient returned home, and, as mentioned, her illness rapidly got worse. Three months later she was admitted to the asylum.

TEST II

*October 5, 5 p.m.*

| Stimulus-word | Reaction | Time |
|---|---|---|
| 1. Head | headache | 1·6 |
| 2. Green | — | — |
| 3. Water | water-carriage | 2·8 |
| 4. Prick | thorn-apple | 2·7 |
| 5. Angel | — | — |
| 6. Long | longing | 2·2 |
| 7. Ship | — | — |
| 8. Plough | — | — |
| 9. Wool | cotton-wool | 2·2 |
| 10. Friendly | friendliness | 3 |
| 11. Table | table companion | 2·2 |
| 12. Ask | note of interrogation | 6·6 |
| 13. State | — | — |
| 14. Stubborn | person | 3·2 |
| 15. Stalk | flower-stalk | 6 |
| 16. Dance | dancing floor | 4 |
| 17. Water | water-lily | 9 |
| 18. Ill | illness | 3·4 |
| 19. Proud | — | — |
| 20. To cook | — | — |
| 21. Ink | ink-eraser | 4·6 |
| 22. Wicked | wickedness | — |
| 23. Needle | pincushion | 2·4 |
| 24. Swim | swimming pool | 4 |
| 25. Travel | — | — |
| 26. Blue | | |
| 27. Bread | | |
| 28. Threaten | — | — |

At reaction 28 the patient refused to proceed, declaring that she could not hold out any longer. She could not be persuaded to remain any longer in the examination room. It was also impossible to add a reproduction test or any analysis. Nevertheless certain results may be noticed. First of all, there is the strikingly peculiar character of the associations; they are mainly word-combinations and there are numerous faults. Comparing the two tests we find:

| Test | | | I | II |
|---|---|---|---|---|
| | | | Per cent. | Per cent. |
| Inner associations | . | . | 16 | — |
| Outer      ,, | | . | 60 | 46·4 |
| Clang-reactions . | . | . | 9 | 14·2 |
| Faults      . | . | . | 14 | 39·2 |
| Indirect associations | . | . | 1 | — |

This is a most unusual record. The patient's behaviour during the examination was characteristic ; she supported her head with both hands and sighed from time to time about the unbearable heat in her head which the heated room caused her (13° ! It did not trouble her in the least that in summer she found a temperature of 13° pleasantly cool whilst the same temperature in winter was unbearable. The part played by the temperature of the air was therefore only due to imagination !) She was obviously quite obsessed by her disease complex during the test. It is not surprising that she had no attention left for the dull experiment. We have again an experiment in distraction, but in a much higher degree than in Test I. The decline in her condition had increased the distraction of attention ; that is, attention is now more than before directed to the disease complex, so that there is less attention to give to the experiment. It clearly cost her enormous trouble to direct her attention to the tests ; she is worn out after twenty-eight reactions and is obliged to relinquish the experiment. The energy at her disposal is reduced to a minimum. The enormous increase in faults is an expression of this fact, they are almost threefold those of the first test. She rejects all stimulus-words which do not lend themselves to ready word-connexions. But all the faults are not absolutely referable to the absence of a ready-made word-connexion (e.g. to *cook*, there are such common combinations as cookery, cooking ; to *State*, state affairs ; to *travel*, travelling bag, etc.). Nor are all the long reaction-times attributable to verbal difficulties (e.g. *water* with 9 seconds, to which there are numerous combinations). We are obliged to think of some affective causes for these disturbances, which may be conditioned by unconscious inhibitions arising from the pathogenic complex which is at the root of the disease complex.

The probable mean time of the test was 5·2 seconds (taking the faults at 20 seconds, although one usually waited up to thirty seconds). The probable mean is, therefore, very high.

TEST III

*October 9, 5 p.m. With Reproduction Test*

| Stimulus-word | Reaction | Time | Reproduction |
|---|---|---|---|
| 1. Lamp | lamp-glass | 1·8 | — |
| 2. Rich | riches | 1·8 | |
| 3. Tree | tree-trunk | 1·4 | — |
| 4. *Sing* | *choral society* | 5·2 | sing-song |
| 5. Pity | — | — | pitiful |
| 6. Yellow | golden yellow | 3·2 | — |
| 7. Mountain | mountain chain | 4·8 | — |
| 8. *Play* | sing-song | 6·6 | play at ball |

| Stimulus-word | Reaction | Time | Reproduction |
|---|---|---|---|
| 9. Salt | salt-cellar | 6·8 | — |
| 10. New | new moon | 3 | — |
| 11. *Habits* | — | — | customary |
| 12. Ride | riding school | 3 | — |
| 13. Wall | wall paintings | 4·6 | |
| 14. Stupid | stupidity | 4 | — |
| 15. Copy-book | school copy-book | 2·2 | — |
| 16. *To despise* | — | — | despicable |
| 17. Tooth | toothache | 2 | — |
| 18. Right | — | — | |
| 19. People | people's holiday | 2 | |
| 20. Smell | — | — | |
| 21. Book | reading book | 3·8 | |
| 22. Unjust | — | — | |
| 23. Frog | tree-frog | 2·4 | — |
| 24. *Separate* | — | — | conjugal separation |
| 25. Hunger | heat hunger | 5 | — |
| 26. White | snow-white | 2 | — |
| 27. Cattle | drove of cattle | 4·1 | |
| 28. To take care | caution | 2·4 | |
| 29. Pencil | pencil-holder | 6·6 | |
| 30. Cloudy | — | — | |
| 31. Plum | | | |
| 32. Meet | — | — | — |

This test shows some changes as compared with the earlier ones. The results expressed in percentages are :

| Test | II | III |
|---|---|---|
| | Per cent. | Per cent. |
| Inner associations . . | — | 3·1 |
| Outer      „      . . | 46·4 | 59·3 |
| Clang-reactions . . . | 14·2 | 6·2 |
| Faults . . . . | 39·2 | 31·2 |
| Anomalies in reproduction . | — | 18·7 |

This is therefore another experiment in distraction. The probable mean time is :

| *First Test* | *Second Test* | *Third Test* |
|---|---|---|
| 5·2 | 5·2 | 4·6 |

There is a certain diminution of the reaction-time, which must be chiefly attributed to the relative decrease of the " faults." It may perhaps be inferred from this result that the patient has pulled herself together a little. This seems also to be expressed by the fact that despite her early abandonment of the experiment, she allowed herself to be persuaded into the reproduction test. This test also went four reactions further than the first one (28, 32). The number of clang-reactions has considerably diminished in favour of the outer and inner associations. This must be also regarded as a certain improvement in attention.

TEST IV

*October 17, 5 p.m.  With Reproduction Test*

| Stimulus-word | Reaction | Time |
|---|---|---|
| 1. Law | lawless | 5 |
| 2. Love | loveless | 3 |
| 3. Glass | glass chest | 2 |
| 4. Quarrel | — | — |
| 5. Goat | goat milk | 2·8 |
| 6. Big | big city | 4·8 |
| 7. Potato | potato patch | 5·6 |
| 8. Pain | painting studio | 5·4 |
| 9. Part | parties | 3 |
| 10. Old | Old-town | 9·6 |
| 11. Flower | calyx | 2·4 |
| 12. Hit | — | — |
| 13. Basket | clothes-basket | 5·6 |
| 14. Wild | — | — |
| 15. Family | family party | 4 |
| 16. Wash | — | — |
| 17. Cow | cow milk | 3·2 |
| 18. Foreign | foreign book | 3·4 |
| 19. Luck | lucky wish | 2·8 |
| 20. Narrate | — | — |
| 21. Deportment | teaching deportment | 2·8 |
| 22. Narrow | — | — |
| 23. Brother | — | — |
| 24. Malice | malicious joy | 3·6 |
| 25. Stork (stimulus-word at first misunderstood, then fault) | | |
| 26. False | falsity | 8·2 |
| 27. Anxiety | anxious feeling | 3 |
| 28. Kiss | sisterly kiss | 4 |
| 29. Flame | black flames | 6·8 |
| 30. Dirty | dirty speck | 7 |
| 31. Door | door-trap | 4·8 |
| 32. Vote | — | — |
| 33. Hay | | |
| 34. Quiet | | |

This test was carried out at a time when the patient was not feeling so well (one of those variations which are not uncommon in the course of hysteria). This test looks, likewise, as if it were a distraction test. With the exception of a few individual reactions (*kiss — sisterly kiss*) the patient never enters into the meaning of the stimulus-words, but contents herself with apprehending the outer form of the word. There were no disturbances in reproduction. The test went two reactions further than the previous one (32, 34).   Expressed in percentages :

| Test | II | III | IV |
|---|---|---|---|
|  | Per cent. | Per cent. | Per cent. |
| Inner associations . . | — | 3·1 | 2·9 |
| Outer ,, . . | 46·4 | 59·3 | 58·8 |
| Clang-reactions . . | 14·2 | 6·2 | 5·8 |
| Faults . . . . | 39·2 | 31·2 | 32·3 |
| Reproductive anomalies | — | 18·7 | — |

The probable mean time is

| Test | II | III | IV |
|---|---|---|---|
|  | 5·2 seconds | 4·6 seconds | 5·4 seconds |

There is an increase of the reaction-time referable to the temporary unfavourable condition of the patient.   The absence of reproductive anomalies may be accidental in such a small series of reactions, but may be also attributed to the fact that the patient did notice the reactions this time so as to make no mistakes in the reproduction.

## TEST V

*October 9, 5 p.m.   With Reproduction Test*

| Stimulus-word | Reaction | Time | Reproduction |
|---|---|---|---|
| 1. Scorn | — | — | |
| 2. *Sleep* | rest | 1·8 | tired |
| 3. *Month* | — | — | time |
| 4. Coloured | painter | 6·8 | |
| 5. Dog | domestic animal | 3·4 | |
| 6. Talk | narrate | 4·8 | |
| 7. Coal | to iron | 4 | |
| 8. Moderate | — | — | |
| 9. Song | singing | 3·6 | |
| 10. Suppose | facts | 10 | |
| 11. *Pain* | *ill* | 5·2 | *illness* |
| 12. Lazy | work | 5·4 | |
| 13. Moon | — | — | |
| 14. Laugh | jolly | — | |
| 15. Coffee | breakfast | 2·2 | |
| 16. Broad | measure | 3·6 | |
| 17. Air | warm | 5 | |
| 18. Frighten | dread | 7·6 | |
| 19. Plate | cat | 7 | |
| 20. *Tired* | *sleep* | 4·4 | *bed* |
| 21. *Aim* | *injure* | 7·4 | ? |
| 22. Fly | — | — | |
| 23. Eye | — | — | |
| 24. Strong | powerful | 2·6 | |
| 25. Fruit | — | — | |
| 26. *Create* | *industrious* | 3 | *work* |
| 27. Sail | ship | 7 | |
| 28. Modest | content | 6·4 | |

| Stimulus-word | Reaction | Time | Reproduction |
|---|---|---|---|
| 29. Floor (does not under-<br>stand the stimulus-<br>word at first) | land | 10 | |
| 30. Whistle | tune | 6·4 | |
| 31. Purpose | cause | 3·4 | |
| 32. *Hot* | yes, yes, in there | 4 | *light* |
| 33. Hand | limb | 3 | |
| 34. *Wake* | *awake* | 3 | *get up* |
| 35. Apple | don't know | 15·6 | |
| 36. Bad | — | — | |
| 37. Mouth | teeth | 7·2 | |
| 38. Drink | fluid | 4·4 | |
| 39. *Bed* | *tired* | 7·2 | *sleep* |
| 40. *Beautiful* | *pretty* | 4 | ? |
| 41. *Danger* | — | — | *terrible* |
| 42. Visit | — | — | |
| 43. *Artisan* | *occupation* | 6·4 | *make* |
| 44. High | mountain | 4·6 | |
| 45. Axe | wood | 9·4 | |
| 46. Notice | take care | 2 | |
| 47. Way | walk | 5 | |
| 48. Round | ball | 2·4 | |
| 49. *Blood* | — | — | *red* |
| 50. To yield | — | — | |
| 51. Caution | take care | — | |
| 52. *Jolly* | *stories* | 4·8 | *laugh* |
| 53. Market | buy | 3·6 | |
| 54. *Forget* | *thoughts* | 5·4 | *stories* |
| 55. Thunder | noise | 5 | |
| 56. Free | outspoken | 6·6 | |
| 57. Carriage | drive | 3·2 | |
| 58. Eat | appetite | 5 | |
| 59. Impudence | — | — | |
| 60. Quick | go | 2·4 | |
| 61. Chimney | smoke | 2·6 | |
| 62. Enjoy | pleasure | 3·2 | |
| 63. Vicar | preach | 2·4 | |
| 64. Light | weight | 3·6 | |
| 65. Neck | slender | 7 | |
| 66. Wish | present | 5·6 | |
| 67. Stone | hard | 8·8 | |
| 68. Superior | rich | 1·4 | |
| 69. Tube | rubber | 2·6 | |
| 70. *Love* | *beautiful* | 9·4 | |
| 71. Slate | roof | 3·4 | |
| 72. Mild | temperature | 4·8 | |
| 73. Avarice | miser | 6·4 | |
| 74. Seek | — | — | |
| 75. Cover | | | |
| 76. Good | | — | |
| 77. Leaf | — | — | |
| 78. Complain | illness | 6 | |
| 79. Railway | travel | 4·8 | |

This test presents a very different association type from the others. It is as if the patient had suddenly found another adaptation.[1]

The percentage relationships are :

| Test | II | III | IV | V |
|---|---|---|---|---|
| | Per cent. | Per cent. | Per cent. | Per cent. |
| Inner associations . . | — | 3·1 | 2·9 | 56·9 |
| Outer ,, . . | 46·4 | 59·3 | 58·8 | 18·9 |
| Clang-reactions . . . | 14·2 | 6·2 | 5·8 | 1·2 |
| Faults . . . . | 39·2 | 31·2 | 32·3 | 21·5 |
| Indirect associations . . | — | — | — | 1·2 |
| Anomalies in reproduction . | — | 18·7 | — | 21·5 |

We see from these figures that the patient has now achieved a normal type. She now enters into the meaning of the reaction-word, linking with it a preponderating number of inner associations.[2] The abnormal components have been pretty well abandoned, so that, e.g., the clang-reactions do not exceed the normal mean. The number of faults remains high, but has also considerably decreased. The patient is now able to hold out much longer, for this test exceeds the others by forty-five reactions. The mean time is 5·4 seconds, as in the previous tests ; it thus remains very long.

This test was made three weeks after the previous one. Meanwhile treatment had much improved the patient's condition. In the earlier tests we pointed out the *absence of entering into the meaning of the stimulus-word*, the *dominance of outer associations*, the enormous *number of faults*, and the rapid fatigue as pathological signs showing her extreme subjection to the disease complex. The improvement of the condition is psychologically shown, particularly by the patient's having acquired an interest in objective processes, although her interest was quickly exhausted ; the treatment had assuaged the tyranny of the complex. Her personality gradually became free from the tyranny of her illness and able to assimilate objective facts ; in other words, she could now adapt herself to her environment. Certain hysterical stigmata were maintained : the enormous number of faults, the long reaction-times, and other signs of a complex—signs of pathological emotivity which, as we know, is the psychological foundation of hysteria.

---

[1] But in fact this is not the case, for in Test I the patient had shown tendencies to a less superficial association type.

[2] This patient now exhibits a type which we not infrequently see amongst the uneducated : very many inner associations, few outer, and very few clang-reactions.

TEST VI

*December 1, 5 p.m. With Reproduction Test*

This test consisted of 100 reactions, concluded at this number not on account of the patient's exhaustion, but because 100 reactions seemed to me sufficient for analysis. I will therefore give a critical review of the test in sections. The probable mean time of this test, I will begin by remarking, was 5·2 seconds— not longer, therefore, than the previous tests. Despite this apparent agreement the time relationships are, on the whole, quite different from the earlier attempts. To bring out these relationships I have split each test up into series of six to ten reactions and calculated the arithmetical mean time of each series.[1]

The results of the six tests would show curves of the following nature:

*Test I.*—The curve shows a strong fluctuation. At first a level of relatively " short times " is soon reached, which after various fluctuations keeps ascending higher. Towards the end very strong prolongations of time occur, which to some extent are again made up for but never quite reach the first level. The curve gives one the impression that the patient had noticed the long times and had in consequence pulled herself together during a few reactions. Test I was carried out at the first consultation. As already mentioned, her condition afterwards got worse. This aggravation is seen in the curve of

*Test II*, where the curve begins pretty high and, after a brief recovery, is rapidly followed by a collapse.

In *Test III* the curves begin low: the patient had (as she then said) made the good resolution to take every pains to react quickly. But the energy so painfully aroused is not long maintained; the times become progressively longer until very high figures are reached. The perception of this weakness probably determined in the patient a slight final effort, which, however, exhausts her last trace of energy.

*Test IV.*—The curve begins rather higher than last time (as stated, the patient was having a bad turn at the time of the experiment). There occurred here also an uninterrupted rise in the reaction-times.

Tests I–IV had furnished predominantly *outer associations and faults.* We see from the curves that this mode of assimilation is linked with rapidly rising reaction-times.

*Test V.*—The curve begins very high (perhaps because the patient had been greatly discouraged by the previous tests and had thus resistances towards the experiment). The curve rapidly falls, and after one strong variation is maintained at a moderate level, which, however, slowly ascends. There follows a strong and a final effort maintained for a long time, which ends in a rapid and uninterrupted ascent of the " times." The final effort had entirely exhausted her energy.

*Test VI.*—In this last test (after two months' treatment) the curve begins at a moderate height and then rapidly sinks to a very low level, which is maintained more or less during the whole experiment without noteworthy fluctuations,

---

[1] The faults have been each reckoned as 20 seconds.

only towards the end showing a tendency to rise. Test V shows, at least in its middle parts, a tendency towards stability, which is fully expressed in Test VI. But Tests V and VI are those which exhibit a normal mode of association. The normal type occurs here with the tendency to stability in the reaction-times. At the same time a very low level is reached and maintained in Test VI. The one hundred stimulus-words which are the basis of Test I were employed also in Tests II and IV and in Test VI. As the curves show, we cannot perceive any shortening of the reaction-times from the repetition of the same stimulus-words. From Tests II to IV we might rather suppose the opposite. According to Kräpelin's investigations we should rather expect a fixation of the reactions to produce a relatively rapid abbreviation of the time. In Test VI there are, however, not only no fixations but quite other reactions (corresponding to the new adaptation whose beginning was seen in Test V).

The prolongation of the reaction-times is seen to be connected with a great loss of energy, i.e. with an entire inability to withdraw attention from the disease complex. It cost the patient great trouble to direct her attention for any length of time upon anything else than her illness, her fatigue corresponding with her endeavour. The curves which exhibit the prolongation of time are therefore *curves of want of energy.* This becomes clear if we turn them round and read them from right to left. Then they look rather like the work curves of a very exhausted neurotic (exhaustion of will!). In curves I, V, and VI we notice the *increase due to practice,* and the reactive rises in curves I, III, and V, which is the final effort. In curves I and VI this progressive fatigue is clearly marked. Thus the association experiment gives us information in certain cases about energy and fatigue.

### Analysis of the Associations in Test VI

I place the associations of Test VI parallel with those of I–VI for analytical comparison.

| Tests | | | sec. | II, IV (V) | sec. | VI | | sec. |
|---|---|---|---|---|---|---|---|---|
| 1. Head | -ache | : | 1·2 | headache | : 1·6 | pain — pains in the head | : | 1·8 |
| 2. Green | corn | : | 6·6 | — | | forest | : | 5·2 |
| 3. Water | - | | | water-carriage | : 2·8 | deep | : | 1·4 |
| 4. Prick | bee | : | 1·8 | thorn-apple | : 2·4 | bee | : | 2·8 |
| 5. *Angel* | hotel | : | 2·1 [?][1] | — | | — | | |
| 6. *Long* | knife | : | 9 [?] | longing | : 2·2 | street | : | 5 |
| 7. Ship | steamship | : | 7 [?] | — | | sea | : | 4 |
| 8. Plough | field (garden) | : | 4·2 | — | | demand—give | | 7·4 |
| 9. Wool | knit | : | 1·5 | cotton-wool | | (stimulus-word not understood) knit | : | 10·2 |

[1] Absence of reproduction is shown by the brackets.

| Tests | I | | II, IV (V) | | VI | |
|---|---|---|---|---|---|---|
| | | sec. | | sec. | | sec. |
| 10. Friendly | -ness | : 2·2 | friendliness | : 3 | — (men) | |
| 11. Table | (does not un-<br>derstand<br>stimulus-<br>word at first)<br>-cloth | : 6 | table com-<br>panion | : 2·2 | room | : 9 |

Reaction 1, *head*, naturally arouses the disease complex, for the patient has localized her chief symptoms in her head. The times are not long, but we find in Test VI a disturbance through a slip of speech. The two earlier reactions have the superficial character which is not infrequently seen in complex reactions, which the patient would like to slide over lightly.

Reaction 3, *water*, seems to have the well-known signs of perseveration of an emotional tone.

Reaction 5, *angel*, has complex signs. The patient is not religious but is still very childish. In the last few months she had frequent thoughts of death, she had hallucinations in the evenings of a " black skeleton " stretching out his hand to her. That is reason enough for a complex disturbance ; but we must go deeper. The patient has an inner and intimate relationship to her mother. The two women have another link in common through illness. Her mother suffers from osteomalacia and is a complete cripple. Her daughter takes her mother as her pattern not only from a moral point of view, but perhaps also as presaging her own fate. The fear of a fate similar to that of her mother is never very distant. Finally, it must be remembered that young girls and hysterics talk of death when they wish to have love. Disturbances proceed from *angel* to reaction 8. In Test I there even occurred a slight amnesia here.[1]

At reaction 8 in Test VI another stimulus-word was inserted in order to bring out the complex—*demand* ; it requires 7·4 seconds for the reaction, and the succeeding stimulus-word, *wool*, is at first not understood and requires 10·2 seconds. To *demand* I obtained some further thoughts. In her own words, " I thought that you demand too much of me ; it is *too much* when you always want me to be well." It seemed to me that the patient was here rather sliding lightly over something—although thoughts about the doctor who is treating her seem to be accompanied in hysterics by a strong emotional tone (transference to the doctor ; see Freud). I therefore simply said, " The demand." The patient jerked herself slightly together and said : " I don't know what you mean—I can't make out what you are now wanting of me." Then she suddenly broke out into loud laughter, flushed, and said nothing more. The course of this bit of analysis is as follows : At first the patient complains that I am demanding too much from her, then the well-known negative subterfuges appear, and finally a strongly emotional thought with laughter, the cause of which is not difficult to guess. Laughter is of diagnostic importance ; in psycho-analysis it often shows that one has struck a complex. It is clear that it is not any one but the patient herself who is demanding too much. Freud [2] says : " Many of my neurotic patients are during psycho-analysis regularly wont to show by a laugh that one has succeeded in correctly showing to their conscious perception what the unconscious had concealed ; they even laugh when the content of what has been concealed has nothing in it to justify their laughter.

---

[1] Cp. " Experimentelle Beobachtungen über das Erinnerungsvermögen," *Zentralblatt für Nervenheilkunde und Psychiatrie*, 1905.

[2] *Der Witz* (" Wit and its Relation to the Unconscious "), by Professor Sigmund Freud. (London : Fisher Unwin.)

2 A

This happens when the physician having recognized the condition has prepared the way for the patient to recognize himself this bit of his unconscious when it looms up."

Reaction 10, *friendly*, seems to be critical in Test II but not in Tests I and VI.

*Analysis.*—At first strong resistances ("I don't know anything," etc.); then: "I thought of you, doctor. Recently you were not very friendly to me." This reminiscence refers to a definite event when the patient transferred her ill-humour to me and afterwards maintained that it was I who was in a bad temper (transference of affect). This reminiscence seems sufficient to explain the disturbance. I have already pointed out that the patient transferred the "demanding too much" to me; she also endows me with her own ill-humour and complains that I am not friendly to her. Her "demand" is therefore that I should be friendly with her, and as I always am, then that I am not friendly enough, for she still complains of my unfriendliness. She is ever wanting greater friendship from me—which means that I am indifferent to the patient in an erotic sense. Naturally I cannot agree to this demand. Thus the *patient is demanding too much*. This piece of complex she only acquired here, and so the complex disturbances were bound to increase at *friendly*.

| Test | I | | II-IV | | VI | |
|---|---|---|---|---|---|---|
| | | sec. | | sec. | | sec. |
| 12. Ask | | | note of interrogation | : 6·6 | answer | : 5·8 |
| 13. State | | | — | | state buildings | : 11·6 |
| 14. Stubborn | stubborn person | : 8 | stubborn person | : 3·2 | character | : 6 |
| 15. Stalk | flower-stalk | : 2·2 | flower-stalk | : 6 | flower-stalk | : 10·6 |
| 16. Dance | dancing floor | : 2 | dancing floor | : 4 | ball | : 5·4 |
| 17. Water | Zurich | : 5·8 | water-lily | : 9 | deep | : 7·2 |
| 18. Ill | — | | sickly | : 3·4 | hospital | : 6·2 |
| 19. Proud | haughty | : 3·8 | | | longing— home-sick | : 7·4 |
| 20. Cook | cookery school | : 2·6 | | | kitchen | : 3·6 |
| 21. Ink | ink-bottle | : 1·8 | ink-eraser | : 4·6 | write | : 2 |

Reaction 12: at *ask* there were obvious complex disturbances which affect the subsequent reactions also.

*Analysis.*—"I thought that you asked me a lot, but I know absolutely nothing—I certainly know nothing more." The patient says this with emphasis, and with a nasty ill-tempered expression contrasting strikingly with her usual good-nature and submissiveness. She then broke out into loud laughter, which she tried to suppress by the expression of her ill-humour. "Oh, what a nuisance —that won't do—I never thought of that at all." At the moment of the reaction she had not thought of the peculiar meaning of the word *ask*, so fraught with meaning to any young woman. She believes that this meaning has only just occurred to her; "she really never thinks about anything of the kind." We have here another hint of the presence of an erotic complex.

Reaction 16, *stubborn*, is well adapted for ego relationships. If the reaction is *character* or *trait* or *bad habit*, reference may be suspected to the patient under examination. The ego relationship occurs clearly in *character*. and thus we get stronger disturbances than in the earlier reactions.

*Analysis.*—" People are often stubborn—I was as a child—once I was awfully stubborn and wouldn't go to school at all—I think I was about twelve then—after that I did not go to school again."

It will be remembered that the patient attributed her inability to go to school to the St. Vitus's dance ; now she is regarding this illness as naughtiness, and even says it was from stubbornness that she stopped going to school. But if during the course of another conversation she is asked why she stopped going to school she says that she was then very ill. We can be content with this explanation. But her twelfth year has another significance of much greater import, as we shall see later.

Reaction 16, *dance — dancing floor*, also gets away from the deeper meaning. It is only with the reaction *ball*, which shows a deeper penetration into the meaning of the stimulus-word, that we rouse the complex. *Dancing — saloon* is something that horrifies the circle in which the patient lives, whilst *ball* is quite a legitimate occasion for erotic relationships. The patient was obliged to laugh directly she was asked what came into her mind about *ball*. Erotic thoughts were again to the fore.

To reaction 19 the stimulus-word in Test VI was *longing*.

*Analysis.*—Patient declared obstinately and with obvious resistance that nothing except *home-sickness* occurred to her at *longing*. I maintained that something would occur to her. There was then suddenly loud laughter, which was at once angrily suppressed. " No, no, this disgusts me ; it's a bore." We had the same reaction as at *demand*. There was certainly some strongly repressed erotic desire.

| Test | I | | II-IV | | VI | |
|---|---|---|---|---|---|---|
| | | sec. | | sec. | | sec. |
| 22. Wicked | wickedness | : 7·8 | wickedness | : 3·8 | disobedient (child) | : 7·6 |
| 23. Needle | pincushion | : 2 | pincushion | : 2·4 | child; work (love) | : 7·8 |
| 24. Swim | swimming school | : 9 | swimming pool | : 4 | bathing-place | : 6·4 |
| 25. Travel | travelling rug 12 ? | | — | | railway | : 4·8 |
| 26. Blue | Blue-street | : 7 | | | colour | : 1·8 |
| 27. Bread | breadless | : 4 | | | baker | : 2 |
| 28. Threaten | (does not understand the stimulus-word) punishment 12 (punish) | | | | expect—visit | : 3·6 |

This was the end of Test II

Test III

| | | sec. | | sec. | | sec. |
|---|---|---|---|---|---|---|
| 29. Lamp | lamp-shade | : 2·2 | lamp-shade | : 1·8 | light | : 4 |
| 30. Rich | riches | : 4·2 | riches | : 1·8 | money | : 6·8 |
| 31. Tree | fruit-tree | : 4·6 | tree-stem | : 1·4 | garden | : 3·6 |
| 32. Sing | choral society | : 3·2 | choral society | : 5·2 | concert | : 5·2 |

Reaction 22, *wicked*, is taken personally ; *disobedient* seems to express the complex most clearly.

*Analysis.*—" Recently I was angry with you—formerly I was often wicked and disobedient • school " etc. Association 23, *child — work*, is peculiar and could not be explained by the patient.  In reproduction came the more appro-priate association *love*.  The school complex comes first, which is most deeply bound up with the idea of " work."  Remember that the stimulus-words *create* and *artisan* in Test V caused complex disturbances.  Moreover, the patient is always insisting that she is not " lazy " ; she would like to find some real work ; she also complained about certain relatives who said she was only suffering from laziness.  The stimulus-word *child* is a word which as a rule has a critical effect in erotic complexes among women.

Reaction 25 : at *travel* there are complex indicators.

*Analysis.*—" I am thinking of a beautiful journey to Italy which I should so much like to make one day "—a long pause, then with great embarrassment, " honeymoon journeys are made to Italy."

Reaction 28, Test VI, *expect*.

*Analysis.*—" I am expecting nothing, absolutely nothing, health and "—again loud laughter, which the patient, annoyed, tries to suppress.  The same reaction again as at *demand* and *longing*.

Reaction 30, *rich*.

*Analysis.*—" I should like to be rich, then I could remain longer here under treatment " ; then a block occurred which stopped all further flow of thought. " Longer under treatment " means " remain longer in the present relationship to the doctor."

| Test | I | | II-IV | | VI | |
|---|---|---|---|---|---|---|
| | | sec. | | sec. | | sec. |
| 33. Pity | regret | : 7 | (full of pity) | | — | |
| 34. Yellow | yolk of egg | : 4·8 | golden yellow: | 3·2 | canary bird | : 5 |
| 35. Mountain | Utli moun-tain | : 4·6 | mountain chain | : 4·8 | mountain chain | 10·8 |
| 36. Game | chess | : 3·2 | singing (game of ball) | : 6·6 | game of ball | : 6·8 |
| 37. Salt | salt-cellar | : 2·4 | salt-cellar | : 6·8 | cook | : 2·2 |
| 38. New | Newbury | : 3 | new moon | : 3·8 | house | : 7 |
| 39. Custom | propriety | : 9·2 | — (decorum) | | expect happy (joy) | : 8·2 |
| 40. Ride | riding school | : 33 | riding school | : 3 | path | : 1·8 |
| 41. Wall | Spanish wall | : 2·4 (?) | wall paint-ings | : 4·6 | room | : 5·2 |
| 42. Stupid | stupidity | : 9 (?) | stupidity | : 4 | un—derstand | : 7·2 |
| 43. Exercise-book | school exer-cise-book | : 3 | school exer-cise-book | : 2·2 | exercise-book | : 5·2 |

Reaction 33, *pity*.

*Analysis.*—" I can't think what pity has to do with me—oh, perhaps with my illness—people ought to have pity on me."

I have only given a sample of the resistance the patient had at this word ; in reality the resistance lasted much longer and was expressed also mimetically in her sorrowful face.  The tendency to evoke pity has great significance in the history of the patient's illness.  Through her illness she managed not to go to school any more.  Later she is the central figure for the pity of the whole family.  The patient must have some consciousness of this even if obscurely ; the strong inhibition is probably referable to this.

Reaction 35, *mountain*.

*Analysis.*—Refuses to acknowledge anything.  She has had nothing to do with mountains, the word doesn't concern her at all ; she has never been on a mountain.  Certainly she would enjoy a tour in the Alps, but that's been impossible on account of her illness ; besides, she could not travel by railway, she could not bear that.  The patient speaks here in negations as if a mountain tour had no meaning for her.  A few days before this test I had been away on an excursion to the mountains ; the patient was afterwards unhappy because I had not taken her—she had never seen the mountains in the neighbourhood, etc.  She suppresses this circumstance altogether, for which there was no obvious ground if *travel* had not some complex import.  She has all kinds of imaginary relationships to the doctor ; a journey with the erotic " symptomatic figure " is a metaphor for " honeymoon journey."  This is certainly the reason why this event takes part in the sexual repression.

Reaction 38, *new*.

*Analysis.*—The patient has been intimate with a lady who has moved into a *new* house for which the patient exhibits an extraordinary liking.  She envies the lady her whole household : " I should like to have something of the sort." The interest appears to be symptomatic.  The analysis discovers great resistances (" people often move into a new house—we have also got a new room at home," etc.).  I now ask pointedly, " When does one move into a new house ? "  This apparently most general question causes the patient great confusion ; she blushes and admits, " When they marry."  She had assimilated the " *new house* to her erotic complex.

Reaction 39, Test VI, *expect*.

The analysis arouses at once laughter—which says enough.  The laughter is here quite appropriate.

Reaction 23, *child*, likewise caused a disturbance.  We shall return to this complex at reaction 69.

Reaction 42, *stupid*.

Analysis brings out self-reproaches relating to the time when she left school (aged twelve).  She reproaches herself that from want of energy she learnt too little and is therefore *stupid*.

| Test | I | | II-IV | | VI | |
|---|---|---|---|---|---|---|
| | | sec. | | sec. | | sec. |
| 44. Despise | — | | — (despicable) | | people | : 7·2 |
| 45. Tooth | eye-tooth | : 3 (?) | toothache | : 2 | mouth | : 3·6 |
| 46. Correct | arrange | : 5 | — | | control | : 6·6 |
| 47. People | people's paper | : 4·6 | people's holiday | : 2 | crowd | : 5 |
| 48. Smell | sink | : 10 | — | | die—cemetery | : 3·4 |
| 49. Book | reading book | : 3 | reading book | : 3·8 | read | : 2·2 |
| 50. Unjust | — | | — | | marriage : church | : 3·2 |
| 51. Frog | tree-frog | : 5 | tree-frog | : 2·4 | green | : 2 |
| 52. Separate | divorce | : 6·4 | — (divorce) | | divorce | : 4 |
| 53. Hunger | eat | : 3·8 | violent hunger | : 5·6 | dog—bark | : 6·8 |
| 54. White | snow | : 3·6 | snow-white | : 2 | snow | : 3·2 |
| 55. Cattle | herd of cattle | : 6·4 | herd of cattle | : 4·2 | herd of cattle | : 9·4 |

Reaction 44, *despise*.

Patient feels herself always at a disadvantage ; her want of education she regards as something for which people must despise her ; people also despised her on account of her illness, which they regarded as laziness. Perhaps there is something else in the illness which makes her peculiarly despicable ? We know that sexual self-reproaches are readily made here.

Reaction 46, *correct*, also shows disturbances. The analysis gave nothing but generalities, which are difficult to interpret. Perhaps there is something in her actions which is, or was not, *correct* ?

Reaction 53, *dog* (Test VI) has a very long reaction-time—6·8 seconds.

*Analysis.*—Patient dreamt about two dogs which probably have an erotic meaning (see below).

| Test | I | | II-IV | | VI | |
|---|---|---|---|---|---|---|
| | | sec. | | sec. | | sec. |
| 56. Take care | esteem | : 6 | esteem | : 2·4 | esteem | : 2·8 |
| 57. Pencil | pencil-holder | : 6·2 | pencil-holder | : 6·6 | black | : 5 |
| 58. Cloudy | — | | — | | weather | : 2 |
| 59. Plum | plum jam | | | | cat—domestic animal | : 8 |
| 60. Meet | | | | | protection | : 3·6 |

This is the end of Test III

Test IV

| | | sec. | | sec. | | sec. |
|---|---|---|---|---|---|---|
| 61. Law | — | | illegal | : 5 | illegal | : 5·4 |
| 62. Love | loveless | : 3 | loveless | : 3 | child | : 2 |
| 63. Glass | tumbler | : 1·6 | glass-cupboard | : 2 | bottle | : 8 |
| 64. To quarrel | dispute | : 4·6 | — | | want of peace | : 7·8 |
| 65. Goat | goat's milk | : 2·4 | goat's milk | : 2·8 | fire : house | : 3·8 |
| 66. Big | generous | : 3 | big town | : 4·8 | sea | : 11 |
| 67. Potato | potato-meal | : 4 | potato patch | : 5·6 | food | : 6·8 |

Reaction 57, *pencil*.

*Analysis.*—The patient thinks of the attempts at work when I sat opposite to her, and from time to time during the additions marked her copy-book with a blue pencil. Nothing else occurred to her. These attempts took place shortly before beginning Test VI. It may, however, only have to do with some past memory which must be constellated somewhere. There is perhaps some mastur- bation complex or some other sexual fantasy. I avoided the sexual theme as far as possible during the whole time of her treatment and only got her to speak about it at the end. If there was some masturbation or other physical sexual complex, this was not aroused during the treatment (i.e. before Test VI) but was more or less dormant, especially if it was not actual at the moment.

Tests I-IV took place at the beginning of the treatment, when the complexes were more strongly stimulated ; Test VI only occurred in the third month. This perhaps explains the absence of complex indicators at this point in Test VI. In Test I the after-effects could be seen up to reaction 61.

In reaction 62, *love*, the more obvious *child* has stronger perseveration than the earlier and more superficial reaction *loveless*.

| Test | I | sec. | II-IV | sec. | VI | sec. |
|---|---|---|---|---|---|---|
| 68. Paint | oil paintings | : 4·2 | studio | : 5·4 | picture | : 2·4 |
| 69. Part | part payment | : 5·2 | participate | : 3 | birth—diffi-cult | : 4 |
| 70. Old | old town | | old town | : 6·6 | greybeard | : 3 |
| 71. Flower | nosegay | : 10·2 | calyx | | garden | : 5·4 |
| 72. Strike | stroke with hammer | : 6 (?) | — | | sit : tired | : 2·2 |
| 73. Basket | clothes-basket | : 4·2 | clothes-basket | : 5·6 | room | : 7 |
| 74. Wild | wild duck | : 4·2 | — | | lion | : 3·4 |
| 75. Family | family party | : 5·2 | family party | : 4 | big | : 5·2 |
| 76. Wash | — | | — | | kitchen | : 6 |
| 77. Cow | cow milk | : 2 | cow milk | : 3·2 | man—father | : 8·8 |
| 78. Foreign | foreign book | : 6 | strange book | : 3·4 | guest-room | : 5 |
| 79. Happiness | congratu-lations | : 10·6 | congratu-lations | : 2·8 | joy | : 5·2 |
| 80. Narrate | stories | | — | | stories | : 3 |

Reaction 69, Test VI, *birth — difficult.*

*Analysis.*—" My mother had difficult childbirths ; she told me her illness came from these." (Recall reaction 23, *child — love* ; reaction 39, *expectat — happy.*) Reaction 69 does not show any outer complex indicators at all striking but it contains a definite designation of the complex. Her mother's fate was a warning example to the daughter, and she may readily fear that she may also suffer from osteomalacia if she were to marry. It is not to be wondered at if her sexual ideas are accompanied by very gloomy emotions and can only be dwelt upon with a certain *reservatio mentalis,* i.e. with repression, for they were not linked with any joyous expectation but, on the contrary, with a strong feeling of unpleasantness. This knowledge came, perhaps, very early in life and had a share in the formation of the illness.

Reaction 76, *wash,* may have been constellated by the obvious disturbance from *family,* or by her obsesssion of cleanliness (see the dream analysis).

Reaction 77 : that it is somewhat connected with family is seen by *man — father of family :* 8·8 seconds.

| Test | I | sec. | II-IV | sec. | VI | sec. |
|---|---|---|---|---|---|---|
| 81. Deport-ment | lesson in deportment | : 11 | teaching of deportment | : 2·8 | habits | : 2·4 |
| 82. Narrow | — | | — | | place | : 3·6 |
| 83. Brother | | | | | brothers and sisters | : 7·8 |
| 84. Malice | malicious joy | : 2 | malicious joy | : 3·6 | loss | : 8·2 |
| 85. Stork | stork's nest | : 5·2 | (does not catch the stimulus-word) | | fly | : 7·4 |
| 86. False | falsity | : 7·4 | falsity | : 8·2 | men | : 3·2 |
| 87. Dread | feeling of dread | : 4 | feeling of dread | : 3 | trembling | : 3·8 |
| 88. Kiss | sisterly kiss | : 13 | sisterly kiss | : 4 | sisterly kiss | : 3·8 |
| 89. Fire | huge fire | : 5·6 | cinders | : 6·5 | house | : 8·8 |
| 90. Dirty | — | | dirty speck | | street | : 1·8 |
| 91. Door | lock of door | : 4·2 | door-latch | : 4·8 | door-lock | : 2 |

| Test | I | | II-IV | | VI | |
|---|---|---|---|---|---|---|
| | | sec. | | sec. | | sec. |
| 92. Choice | choice of comrade | : 11 | | | | |
| 93. Hay | hay waggon | : 3·8 | | | barn | : 2·2 |
| 94. Still | peace | : 7·8 | — | | peaceful | : 6·8 |

End of Test IV

Test V

| 95. Ridicule | ridiculous price | : 2 | — | | laugh | : 2·8 |
|---|---|---|---|---|---|---|
| 96. Sleep | sleeplessness | : 3·4 | peace (tired) | : 1·8 | night | : 6·8 |
| 97. Month | monthly meeting | : 3 | — (time) | | long | : 6·4 |
| 98. Coloured | — | | Moor | : 6·8 | painter | : 2·6 |
| 99. Dog | dog faithful | : 3 | domestic animal | : 3·4 | river : broad | : 3 |
| 100. Speak | consultation | : 13·4 | narrate | : 4·8 | people | : 6·2 |

Reaction 81, *deportment*, readily arouses sexual complexes.

Reaction 85, at *stork* there are obvious disturbances which may refer to this stimulus-word (whose erotic significance is well known) or to the previous *malice*.

Reaction 88, *kiss*, is covered by the innocent *sisterly kiss* and clearly shows the naïve impulse at repression (similarly *stork — fly*). But perhaps *sisterly kiss* had a deeper meaning, one could not suspect at the time (cf. the dream analyses).

Reaction 89, *fire*, shows long reaction-times throughout. It is one of the expressions that the patient uses for her headaches. The reaction *house* is constellated by the dreams of fire, where she often saw houses burning.

Reaction 92, *choice*, arouses the far-off reaction *choice of comrade*.

*Analysis.*—" Many things can be chosen, e.g. a town councillor or anybody else." (Block—then laughter and confusion.) We know very well what a young woman associates with *choice*; it is indeed an election of membership—for life partnership. This explains the subsequent reactions, for that is the burning question *par excellence*.

Reaction 97, *month*, frequently arouses in women the idea of the periods, and this has a special significance in this case; hence the complex disturbances.

### SUMMARY OF THE ANALYSIS

The association experiment and its analysis have given us some impressions about a number of processes, which are, however, very obscure as a whole. The analysis was carried out under peculiar difficulties, for very few reactions in the three series presented normal relationships.

Complex signs abound, and this is further evidence of how greatly the patient is under the yoke of her complexes; it might be almost said that it is not she, but her complexes, which carry out the reactions. Great as are the difficulties of analysis from the unwonted extent of the complex signs, the task is even more difficult when it seemed necessary to get further help from the patient as to what was going on within. The patient frequently stops short after a few generalities and her laughter alone betrays the idea that is coming up. There are rarely any suggestions which the patient can confirm. She is so greatly under the influence of her complex that where she should be able to appraise its emotional value she is unable to form any judgment about it and does not know whether it is important or not. We are therefore driven to suppositions, which, however, do allow of certain conclusions. It has been probably noticed that I have only seized upon certain complex constellations, although a good many others were present. These relationships are, however, only of secondary importance, so that for the sake of brevity I leave aside their analysis.

There are a whole series of associations which show complex signs in all the tests, and these may therefore be regarded as constant complex constellations. A fairly thorough · interpretation is possible in the majority of these cases. For instance, it cannot be doubted that erotic ideas play a great part ; here and there they can be recognized in relationship to the physician. The disease complex comes next. These two complexes, apparently independent of one another, have side chains which are connected.

Analogous to the patient's illness is that of her mother's, which in its turn touches the daughter's sexual complex (*birth — difficult*, etc.). There are also certain signs of a possible *physical sexual complex*. Finally there is a school complex.

These are the threads which can conduct us through the patient's labyrinth of thoughts. The patient, however, raises barriers ; by her want of self-control, by her impotency towards these complexes, she makes it difficult for us to find the confirmation of our suppositions, and we must discover other help for this.

Nature has a mechanism which works up the complexes into a concentrated essence and brings them into consciousness in an unrecognizable and therefore non-dangerous form : this mechanism is the dream. As I thought I had only discovered general ideas from the association experiment, I collected the patient's dreams. Earlier ones that could be remembered were only the stereotyped dreams of blood and fire, and these were very indistinct. Naturally, one could not rely on obtaining from the past anything but a carefully selected material, from which the strong inhibition would have blotted out everything at all obvious. The patient dreamt very little during the treatment, that is, she remembered very few dreams. The material is therefore less voluminous than might be wished.

## THE DREAMS

In the first months of her treatment I frequently asked for dreams. Apparently there were few ; now and then the patient said that she had again dreamt of *fire*, or of *blood* : " the whole room was full of fire or blood." Occasionally she dreamt that blood was spurting out of all the orifices of her head, or she dreamt this about another patient whom she saw in a dream in her room. She did not mention any other dreams. These dreams of fire and blood seemed to me to be stereotyped expressions for the dream, like the feelings of heat in her waking life— mainly a symbolical expression of her way of speaking (that she had too much blood in her head, the blood was too hot, it was 40°, she wished she could have a good flow of blood, her whole head was on fire, everything was withered up and burnt out, etc.). In the second place, these stereotyped dreams are, as usual, symbolical expressions of the complex which we have not yet clearly described. To mitigate these dreams, which were often attended with anxious dread, was my therapeutic aim, and to see whether she could forgo these stereotyped dreams, replacing them by something else, was my theoretical aim. I therefore determined to experiment, and said to the patient : " Blood is red, red signifies love ; fire is red and hot ; you know the verse, ' No fire, no coal can burn so hot,' etc. Fire also signifies love."

This explanation made a strong impression on the patient. She could not control her laughter and was extremely embarrassed. My explanation had, therefore, found a re-echo. The simplicity of my dream interpretation was based on the supposition that the dream symbolism of any one with the mentality of the patient would be simple and childish. The explanation was given in the middle of November. The following dreams occurred in the latter half of November

FIRST DREAM, *Nov. 27.*—" *The room is full of cats, which are making a horrible noise.*" During the dream great dread and anger. Further details were denied ; there remained but this rather general setting. The analysis was conducted in the same way as the associations : avoiding all suggestive remarks, I obtained the first ideas that came up and only urged the patient when she seemed to be labouring under some stronger inhibition. (The decline of energy before a complex thought is just the same as the absence of any reaction at critical places.) In the following analysis the conclusion is placed first, and the material afterwards in small print. Any one only interested in the conclusions can omit the material.

*Result of the Analysis.*—She lived for eleven years at a place where she was frequently disturbed by the noise of cats. The noise arose from the combats of the animals when pairing. Ideas of pairing are concealed in the dream-picture.

*Material.*—Cats: " The last few nights cats were in the garden in front of my room. Otherwise I can't think of anything, absolutely nothing." (Note the strong negations, which are preparatory to intense resistance. I insist.) " Nothing at all occurs to me—oh, yes, once we had a fine Angora cat which, unfortunately, was stolen from us." It is odd why such a simple reminiscence is subject to such strong inhibitions ; one supposes that this reminiscence has another side of some more personal significance. I beg her to go on with her ideas. (In a tone of annoyance) " There are lots of cats which run about in our garden, yellow, black, white. I can't make out what you want " (becomes very indignant, as if one were forcing her to something repugnant)—" well, nothing more occurs to me." This decided refusal had to be parried ; I therefore asked her, " Were you ever disturbed at night by cats ? " " No, that was impossible, for where I slept at home we could not hear the cats ; as I've said, I was never disturbed by them." (Then in a superficial tone, as if by the way) " Oh, yes, I do remember that when I was about ten or eleven—oh, no, nine years (!) old—we were living at a place where there were always such lots of cats making such a noise at night-time we thought the house would tumble down. Sometimes there were about sixteen cats together that made this horrible noise at night."

I then asked, " How long did you remain in that place ? " " Eleven years, from my twelfth to my twenty-third year." The patient was now twenty-four. So for eleven years until last year she was living in a place where she was disturbed by the noise of cats. The inhibition at the reminiscences of the cats is so extremely strong that it leads her to the most obvious contradictions. It is to be noted that the patient's voice, usually so amiable and unassuming, became irritable and aggressive during the analysis, At the same time her face grew more and more mournful, until it was one of extreme suffering ; it took on the mask which belonged to her disease complex. I next asked her if she knew the meaning of the nightly noise of the cats ; this she indignantly denied ; I insisted, but there was only instant refusal. A normally intelligent young woman of twenty-six who has herself kept cats and, moreover, has had plenty of opportunity of learning all about their habits does certainly know the meaning of these meetings. If she is a hysteric her ego complex may not know it, but her sexual complex certainly does.[1] I thereupon explained to the patient that the noise meant *pairing.* Visible excitation followed this explanation ; she did not answer, blushed, and looked out of the window. So far as concerned the dream, I said to her the cats were really symbols, she would discover the explanation later. Dreams about cats or dogs always mean something definite. The next few days the patient frequently asked about the meaning of the dream as it interested her.

SECOND DREAM, *Nov. 30.*—" *The whole room is full of mice, which are running about everywhere, making a great noise. The mice look very peculiar ; their heads are bigger than ordinary mice, more like rats, but they have great black ears, and they also have remarkably brilliant hot eyes.*"

[1] Cp. Bleuler, chapter vi.

*Result of the Analysis.*—The mice covered reminiscences about two dogs (a male and a female) which the patient has often seen playing together. She has noticed how dogs jump upon one another. She had also seen a dog standing up on a maid-servant. It is again a question of *pairing*.

*Material.*—This dream repeats the general situation of the last one, the cats being replaced by mice, which, however, do not appear to be ordinary mice. The " brilliant hot eyes " seem to be part of the fire dream. I make the patient review the text of the dream ; she has nothing to add.

Thoughts about the mice : " It struck me that the mice all ran out of small wooden houses." (This essential modification was obviously dependent upon some inhibition, and therefore could not be reproduced beforehand.) " The little houses looked like dog-kennels." This is a new track, for dogs do not occur in the dream. But in the last dream I called the patient's attention to dogs. The idea of " dog " seemed to be hinted at indirectly (i.e. repressed) in the dream. So I made " dog-kennels " the starting-point of the analysis.

Ideas called up by " dog-kennels " : " There are lots of dog-kennels " (annoyed). " I don't know what you mean ; no one in our neighbourhood had a dog. You can see dog-kennels anywhere—in gardens and in yards ; I can't understand what you can imagine about that—what could be behind that ? For instance, a garden was just at the back of our house where there was a dog-kennel. There were two dogs, two black ones ; I think they were setters— perhaps a male and a female, but the female was soon got rid of ; they used to play together—they used to tear up paper or wood, or they barked." Then came a complete block with extreme ill-humour ; she does not want to speak any more about dogs. After much resistance it at last comes out that she often saw how the dog jumped upon the maid-servant when she went into the garden ; she vehemently denies that the male dog ever jumped upon the female. But we know that it is impossible for the patient to say certain things because the inhibitions are too strong. It is extremely probable that she did see it ; that may be concluded not only from the way in which the thing was said, but from the situation as a whole. I said, " But one often sees a dog jumping on the back of another." " Yes, I've often seen that in the street, but the two dogs did not do it." I asked her what this jumping meant ; she said it was a kind of play, she did not know any other meaning. The last was said in a tone of irritation. As of the last dream, so of this we may remark that it is inconceivable that she did not know the meaning ; at all events we are obliged to consider the influence of the sexual complex upon perceptions of the ego complex. In this wise the dream may be reconstructed somewhat as follows : The mice are cover figures which at various places are broken into by the elements of the cat dream. Mouse is a ready association to cat ; the two words can replace one another in dreams (in a condition of diminished attention).[1]

The mice, like the cats, make a noise in a room and are very numerous. The mice have big heads, so they are not really mice but bigger animals. They have great black ears like the black setters. The mice jumped out of dog-kennels. The analysis leads to a very ambiguous situation, the interpretation of which is not difficult ; it is pairing again as in the former dream. That the dog jumps

---

[1] We have proved that in conditions of distraction the indirect associations are increased and that some very ready or current association replaces either the stimulus-word or the reaction ; so that it often seems as if the stimulus-word had been misheard or the reaction misspoken (see chapter ii).

up on a maid-servant seems to be a delicate hint as to the person to whom these thoughts of pairing refer. There was no such hint in the first dream. It is not unreasonable to suppose that the patient's sexual complex was aroused by the first analysis, so that she herself was more markedly dragged into the next dream. Note also that, just as in the earlier blood and fire dreams the whole room was full of blood and fire, so here the whole room was full of cats and mice. The analysis took place on December 1, after the third dream, which I now give. I did not inform the patient about the result of the second dream, so that at her third dream she had received no explanation about the content of dream two.

THIRD DREAM, Dec. 1.—" *She goes into town to a shop to buy something. A great black dog comes in which is fearfully hungry and jumps up on her as if she might be giving him something to eat.*"

*Result of the Analysis.*—In this dream the patient takes the place of the servant in the previous dream, thus expressing the idea that the pairing concerns herself.

*Material.*—After the analysis of the previous dream the form of the dream is enough to betray its meaning. The patient is now in the servant's position, so that the critical point which remained unexplained in yesterday's dream is cleared up, and exactly in the form which the patient could not understand the day before. Had she understood this symbol it would probably not have been used, like the cats, the significance of which had been brought home to her.

Thoughts about " the dog jumping up." At first, as usual, we get generalities, evasions, and blockages, which, in order to save time, I will not repeat. Finally, the scene between the dog and the servant occurs to her. Naturally this was the first scene that occurred to us in considering the dream ; with the patient it was different. She was seeking for a long time as if for some memory which had been long forgotten and buried. She had first to overcome all the resistances which gathered round this reminiscence. We had not these resistances. Her dream analysis is just like the association experiment, where at critical places exactly the same hindrances occur at a second or repeated repetition, although one would really think that a reaction obtained at such great pains would remain more fixed than an indifferent one.

The same night I carried out the analysis of her chief symptoms (see below). That night she had the following dream :

FOURTH DREAM, Dec. 2.—*She is standing in the corridor of her section and sees a great black man coming ; he is leading somebody through the corridor, but she does not see whether the person led is a man or a woman.*

*Result of the Analysis.*—The black dog becomes a black man, the scene is shifted into the asylum. The black man is the sexual complex which had formed her illness and has led the patient into the asylum. It is to no purpose that she seeks to still her craving for love by falling in love with her doctor, for he is already married.

*Material.*—In form the dream recalls the dog scene, only the big black dog is now changed into a big black man. The servant from the dog scene (the patient herself) has become indistinct (she does not know whether it is a man or a woman).

The patient does not seem to participate further in the dream ; we must look for her, therefore, in some dream figure, and are probably correct in supposing that she is this vague figure.

Thoughts in regard to the " black man " : " The man is coming from the entrance door as if leading some one to the section. He is dressed like a *vehm-richter* (whom she had once seen on the stage) ; he looks like a ghost, " like the black man whom I once saw as I fell asleep." I asked her if she was afraid then. " No, I was not afraid at that—oh, yes, I wanted to flee into a room through fear. A nurse called out, ' Stop, that's not allowed ; the room is occupied.' " There was obviously an inhibition at " fear." We have now led the " black man " of the dream back to the " black man " of her vision. In the vision the black man was stretching out his hand towards her and wanting to take her, and she experienced great fear. The vision was a stereotyped complex expression like the blood and fire dreams ; it is a stable psychical formation which it is not very easy for analysis to overcome. The analysis does now really impinge upon powerful obstacles which the patient cannot break through. Hence we find the way out in some combination. The black man who approaches wants to seize her, and is analogous to the black hungry dog which jumps upon her. The dog had a strong sexual background, which must apply also to the black man. The vision arose at the crisis of her illness, when the patient had frequent thoughts of death, and feared that she would die from her illness. As was hinted in the analysis of the associations, thoughts of death by no means exclude the sexual background—on the contrary, they can stand for sexuality. As we have seen from the analysis of the associations and the previous dreams, the patient is utterly possessed by a sexual complex. It is therefore highly probable that in this dream also there are thoughts about pairing. But we will leave this aside for the moment and consider the action of the black man more closely. At the height of her illness she feared she would die, and expressed this belief symbolically : the hand of Death is stretched towards her—that is, the illness will carry her off into the grave. The black man in the dream is leading a shadowy figure into the asylum and to that section where the patient really is herself ; the illness, it is true, has not brought the patient to the grave, but it has led her to the asylum.

The black man arises from the sexual dog, and the disease from the sexual complex.

For the understanding of this sentence we must recall all that has been established up till now. In the associations the distinct and intense reality of her sexual complex was brought out ; in the dreams we have hitherto found nothing but metaphors for this sex complex. At first we have the stereotyped dreams of blood and fire, which are naïvely symbolic ; they say, " My blood is hot ; I have strong sex feelings of love." The dreams speak of pairing. Her illness is obviously connected with the monthly periods. The patient recognizes herself that the illness is connected with the first period. Thus everything that we have hitherto been able to establish speaks in favour of the sexual origin of the illness. *What the patient is longing for is obviously the man.* She would like a husband, but has an illness instead, and as long as she is ill she cannot marry. Does she want to be ill ? We know the will to be ill of the hysterics. From some ground or other they take refuge in illness, they wish to be ill. That is a truth which is forced upon the observer in many cases of hysteria. From the asthenic nature of the patient, who for no obvious reason broke down in a simple and non-fatiguing association experiment, I could not help inclining to the view that she was at no pains to react normally or to be healthy. On the contrary, she behaved in such a way as to make one bound to see how ill she was and how slight was her interest to be well. The illness must stand for her as a hindrance to marriage. Her choice is therefore between illness and a husband so far as her relationship to her surroundings is concerned ; a choice, then, between the joy of sexual love and the protected mothering of a sick child, which to a naïvely feminine disposition is not without its advantages. Some days before I had explained to her that she wanted to be ill because she dreaded marriage and health. Her dream is the answer. Scores of times I had said to her, " You are again fleeing into your illness ; you mustn't, that's forbidden." I said this whenever she wished to keep back something that was unpleasant to her, hiding it away behind a headache or feelings of heat. What does the dream say ?

" A nurse called out, ' Stop, that's forbidden.' " The nurse (therefore my representative) called this out when the patient wanted to rush into a room from fear of the black man. (This part of the dream, as was obvious from its telling, is fraught with peculiar obstacles ; it was only reproduced whilst the analysis was going on.) Fear of her sex future and of all its consequences is too great to enable the patient to decide on abandoning her illness. As hitherto, she prefers to be ill—that is to say, in practice, to be nursed and cosseted by her mother.

But this is not the whole of the chain of thoughts in the dream ; she cannot flee into the room, it is occupied. As our analysis shows, we take it that " to flee into the room " is a symbol for flight into the illness, therefore " room " equals " illness." But the patient is occupied by her illness, so that it cannot be occupied by some one else. But we must remember that the " illness " has a double meaning. Her illness is the sex complex—the repressed sex feelings. The prohibition, therefore, runs : It is forbidden to have sex feelings because something has already " taken possession " of sexuality. From want of time I was obliged to break off the analysis here, postponing it to the next day. I had intended her to tell me what room it was in the dream. The next day I at once asked the patient which room it was. She promptly answered, " No. 7." So as not to spoil anything, I asked the patient before beginning the analysis about her dreams of the previous night. She had had dreams again.

FIFTH DREAM, *Dec. 3.*—" *I was outside standing next to Miss L. We both saw that a house was in a blaze. Suddenly a white figure came behind the house ; we were both afraid and exclaimed as with one voice, ' Lord Jesus ! '* "

*Result of the Analysis.*—The black man is changed into a white figure, the burning house is the sex complex. Miss L. is a patient who gushes about the writer. Like the patient, she had become ill through an erotic complex. Miss L. is used by the patient to express her having fallen in love with the writer. The patient has now replaced the too affectionate relationship to her mother, so harmful to her will-power, by the erotic relationship to the doctor.

*Material.*—The form of the dream shows us that by reason of our earlier explanations the black man must now assume another garb ; he is changed into a white figure, who, however, plays the same terrifying rôle as before. The situation is somewhat the same, since the patient is suddenly prevented from doing something which she had begun. It may be presumed that in the burning house we get the ardour of her sex feelings. As a guide to the analysis we make use of the bit of the former dream which was not concluded yesterday—the room No. 7. In this room Miss L. lives, who is of the same age as the patient. This is a new starting-point for the earlier dream, the dream idea running like this :

" I go into Miss L.'s room, I am doing the same as Miss L." A marked feature of Miss L. is that she is in love with the writer, and that it is hopeless, since he is already married. Thus in a double sense the patient finds the room is occupied : (1) Miss L. is already in love with the writer, so that there is nothing left for the patient; (2) the writer is married, so that any tender feelings are out of question. In to-day's dream this idea of yesterday's dream is carried further. Throughout the dream the patient is doing exactly the same as Miss L. She sees the burning house. She has, therefore, red-hot desires or burning love. The patient knows that Miss L. became ill through an unhappy love affair. Here is a further and alluring analogy : that is why they both see the white figure, *alias* the black man, *alias* the illness, suddenly emerging behind the fire, *alias* love, and they are both frightened, for both have become ill through love. Miss L. suffers from sudden attacks of depression, when she behaves quite confusedly and senselessly. The patient was often struck by this, and often maintained with joy that she was not so ill as to behave like that. I had often told her (our patient) that if she had allowed herself to go on much longer she would have become much worse. In her wild jealousy of Miss L. it was easy for her to think that Miss L. had allowed herself to go further and that was why she became so ill. This would be a further reason for " room No. 7." This point was not settled at the time; therefore, we meet it again later on.

The content of this dream throws light upon the former ones in the same kind of way : fear of the black man (the sex future) drove her to flight in her illness, but that is forbidden ; therefore, seeking some fresh outlet, she finds it with Miss L. ; she falls in love with the doctor, who knows what estimate to place upon the illness ; he is a man not sexually dangerous, so the dream finds a lucky compromise. It replaces her mother, who gives her tenderness but causes her illness, by a man who can cure her and is also of sexual significance. But there is a difficulty ; the patient is poor and will not be able to remain much longer here because she has not enough money. Miss L., however, is very rich, and can remain a long while if she wants to. So she takes Miss L.'s place and occupies the " room."

This rendering remained unsolved also, and therefore usable. When I discussed the content of the dream in cautious terms she made a *disappointed and sad face*—the explanation was obviously too crude—and said in a tone of suffering : " Oh, if my mother knew what things are being brought out of me ! "

This reaction was noticeable, for these fine shades of feeling on the daughter's part were hardly noticed by her mother. But the answer portrays the cooling off and turning away of her infantile sexual need for affection from her doctor, and her return for security to her mother's love ; a sure sign that the compromise was untenable, and that the patient could not rid herself of her infantile relationship to her mother.

SIXTH DREAM, *Dec.* 6.—" *My father is here and I am showing him the asylum, and am going through all the sections with him.*"

*Result of the Analysis.*—This satisfies her wish to be able to remain longer under the treatment of the writer, whom she hopes will cure her.

*Material.*—The patient states that this is only a fragment of a much longer dream, of which she can remember no more. The dream is not difficult to understand, it represents an unfinished piece of yesterday's dream. In this dream she behaves as if she were more or less at home in the asylum. I had occasionally asked her if her father was not going to visit her, whereupon she would suggest that since she would be only here for a short time it would not be worth while for her father to travel so far. In the dream a situation is accepted which has made the visit worth while. She can therefore remain longer here (which she also wished). The dream also shows the patient in an unexpected position of trust; she has the master-key by which she can open all the sections; from which we must conclude that she enjoys the full, special confidence of the doctors. It is not difficult to guess the meaning of this position of trust in regard to the doctor.

SEVENTH DREAM, *Dec.* 6 (the same night as the last one).— "*I am at home. My mother is at table ; you, doctor, are opposite to her and are eating. There is an empty chair between you and mother. I want to sit on this empty chair and eat also. Whereupon my mother has a hot flat-iron which she pushes towards me so that I get hot in the head. I tell mother she ought to put the flat-iron away, it makes me hot so that I can't eat ; I wanted to eat with you. You, doctor, then stand up and shriek at me that I need not eat now at all, I can very well eat later.*"

*Result of the Analysis.*—The patient is desiring a sexual affair with the doctor, hoping by this to rid herself of her mother's influence, which induces her illness. But since the doctor is married the wish cannot be fulfilled. Therefore she must remain ill.

*Material.*—The symbolism of this dream is very obvious; through the indications obtained from Dream IV we can solve it without difficulty. In that dream we saw that she had begun to make a compromise between her infantile relationship to her mother and her sex relationship to a husband, the doctor appearing clearly in the rôle of husband. The animal symbolism was dropped in the latter dreams because it had been explained and had become too obvious. She must, therefore, create other coitus symbols. So the dream begins by the patient being at home. That is the main question which she places before me every day : " How will it be when I get home ? I'm afraid it will all go wrong again at home." At home the danger means, of course, her mother, who as the too tender guardian and pattern of her early childhood had brought the patient to hysteria. The question, therefore, again arises concerning her life at home : " Am I to play again the rôle of the sick child who needs a nurse, or shall I, following the doctor's advice, courageously trust myself to a sex future ? " She is therefore between doctor and mother. The doctor is eating; she would like to join him. But how far can she do the same as the doctor ? There is only one possibility, and that is the one so frequently considered—marriage. She would like to sit on the chair next to me, that is, to sit at my side, which is again nothing but assimilating me in the sense of " husband." Does eating stand for the conjugal function ? We know the Freudian basic principle of *displacement from below upwards.* What takes place in the mouth (in dream, in hysteria, in dementia præcox) is taking place at the genitalia. In the act of eating, something is placed in the mouth.

(An early case of dementia once expressed this idea in her delirium when she asked that the man she wanted as her bridegroom should give her something to eat with a spoon so that she might become pregnant and beget a child.) She would like to enter into sexual relationship with the doctor. Whereupon her mother makes her so hot with the flat-iron so that she cannot sit down at table ; her mother

2 B

again calls up her illness (feelings of heat in her head) and so prevents her marriage. The fear that she will get worse when she goes home here plays its part. Up till now the doctor had only played a passive part; it was only her mother who was preventing her carrying out her inclination towards the doctor. But now he stands up and repulses her rudely, forbidding her to eat with him, i.e. to have sexual thoughts about him, and consoles her at the same time by telling her she will be able to marry later. This passage refers to a conversation that I had with her a few days before, when I cautiously hinted that later, when she was quite well, the question of marriage would not be so difficult. We see that the patient deals again in the dream with the scene of the occupied room, plus a few variants; to this is added the deep impression which the earlier analysis had made when I pitilessly disturbed her illusions. By this refusal she finds herself thrown back upon her mother; and in the company of her mother she becomes ill because her mother does not wish her to marry (see below). Hardly had I finished this analysis when she said, quite unprompted: " I just recall a dream that I often used to have; I used always to dream about worms, red and white ones—the floor and the whole room was full of them (like the blood, the fire, cats, etc.). It seemed, also often, as if some one was pulling an enormous worm out of my mouth." The dream in this connexion can hardly be anything else than one of those penis dreams as frequent among normals as among the sick (early dements often have particular neologisms for this, such as snakes, stalks of a lily, etc.). The mouth is again the displacement from below upwards.

It is improbable that her mother's objection to marriage was the fundamental hysterogenic event. With the patient's vivid eroticism one would rather expect some sexual trauma. I explained to the patient that I was not yet satisfied; there was some event which she had not yet told me, which must have been of great importance. Perhaps she would disclose it in her dreams. Perhaps the event was connected with her obsession about cleanliness. During the next eight days she could not remember a single dream, although she was aware that she had dreamt. During this time I tried, as always, to get her to take an interest in some occupation, and was planning with her to find some way by which she could earn something. At the end of eight days she remembered a dream.

EIGHTH DREAM.—" *I am at home and am gathering up small gold coins on the floor ; I also find some beautiful stones, which I wash. I then place the money and stones on the kitchen table and show them to my brothers.*"

*Result of the Analysis.*—The patient is thinking about returning home ; she has various good resolutions, and is thinking that she may find in her family, particularly among her brothers, compensation for her impossible relationship to the doctor. But the background of the dream remained unexplained.

*Material.*—In this dream she realizes that she will be earning money in the future. The " beautiful stones " are a new factor ; she washes them (a cleanliness obsession ?) and shows her brothers what she has washed, on the kitchen table (this perhaps is called up by the dining-table ?). The analysis only resulted in generalities ; the strongest obstacles prevented any deeper penetration into this dream. What are the brothers doing at the kitchen table ? Do they, perhaps, stand for the doctor at the dining-table of the earlier dream ? I could not solve the question.

ELEVENTH DREAM, *Dec. 12.*—"*I go for a walk in Zurich, but suddenly it is my home. In front of my house I see standing a rural policeman who is speaking to some shadowy-looking man. The policeman has a fearfully sad expression and goes into the house. Then Miss L. suddenly goes along the street, also with a fearfully sad expression. Then we are together in a room and sitting at a dining-table. Suddenly we know there is a fire. Miss L. says, ' I'm going to bed now.' I can't make that out at all, rush into the corridor, but then it appears nothing is the matter ; it was only a false alarm. I now go in again and find myself at home with mother, and my two brothers are also there. A basket with splendid apples is there. One brother says, ' That's something else for me.' "*

*Result of the Analysis.*—Like Miss L., the patient is disappointed in her expectation about love ; she understands this in Miss L., whose minor defects she mockingly emphasizes. Therefore she goes home, where she enters into a suspiciously intimate relationship with one of her brothers.

*Material.*—The general situation of the dream resembles that of Dream VII. There is again the appearance of the dining or kitchen table. In the first part of the dream there is a " policeman " with a fearfully sad expression. Immediately, thereupon, Miss L. appears with the same traits. The policeman goes into a house, whereupon the patient is eating together with Miss L. in a room. Obviously Miss L. and the policeman stand for one another.

Why and how is it that Miss L. is changed into a policeman ? I ask her about any striking characteristics of Miss L. She replies that Miss L. has such peculiar ways, she is only half a woman ; besides, she is very thin. In Switzerland we have a long thin sausage which we call a " dried-up policeman " [1] (*dürren Landjäger*). This word is also used as a nickname for thin people. The patient has symbolized the less striking sides of Miss L. The reason for her doing this is seen in the fact that the policeman is speaking to a shadowy man ; when Miss L. is speaking to a man in a dream that man is certain to be the writer. Probably the patient is therefore jealously emphasizing Miss L.'s feelings for the writer and depreciating Miss L. Then she sits down at table with Miss L. ; that is, she enters into some sexual situation with her. We are not to think, however, of anything homosexual, for the sexual significance of " dining-table " has already been exploited for the doctor ; thus it would be too obvious. Here it merely means, " I have sexual feelings like Miss L." The alarm of fire which follows has the same meaning.

The patient goes out to see what is happening ; but Miss L. goes to bed, i.e. becomes ill from love. To understand this it must be known that whenever Miss L. gets excited she goes to bed. At the beginning of the dream the patient depreciates her rival, and as soon as the sexual situation (the fire alarm) develops, Miss L. even becomes ill, and hence quite innocuous. So the rival is overcome. But the patient now finds that it is only a false alarm ; that is the disappointment (" the room is occupied," " she cannot join in eating "). The writer has destroyed her illusions, the transference of her need for affection towards a man has not succeeded ; so she must go back to her mother, where at least she will find an

---

[1] Cp. our English term " soldier " for a red herring.

equivalent for her need of love. So the scene changes in the second part of the dream. She is suddenly at home; instead of at the dining-table she is in the kitchen with her mother. Were it only a question of her relationship to her mother, her brothers would be superfluous. But two brothers are here as in Dream VIII, at the kitchen table; instead of the " beautiful stones " there is only a basket with " beautiful apples " ; one brother says, " That's something else for me." The scene of the dining-table in Dream VII, like the one in this dream with Miss L., is scarcely susceptible of other than a sexual meaning ; and immediately following the sexual scene we get a very similarly constructed picture, " dining-table " being replaced by " kitchen." First of all, the beautiful apples look like the " beautiful stones " which lay on the kitchen table, and secondly, they are also something edible (cp. Eve's apple); that is, something for the brother, he gets something. We must realize this picture. In the first part of the dream a sexual wish is destroyed ; the second part can hardly refer to her mother only, some sexual element plays a part somewhere. I asked for her thoughts about the " apples." " I thought about the apples which I saw yesterday in a shop where they sell Southern fruits. I was there with your wife." This opens up a track. The analysis now stops and cannot be further followed up. So I go to the brother : " It was my brother who lives in Italy ; he has often invited me to make a journey to Italy and pay him a visit."

Recall here reaction 25, Test VI.

Travel : Patient supposed *a nice journey to Italy — honeymoon journey.* Her brother had no share in that and yet the apples are intended for him. Here I must add a dream which the patient had right at the beginning of her treatment. She dreamt that I came into the room and she said to me : " It's a pity we can't gather the nuts yet, but at home there is a whole basketful." In this dream she offers me the fruit, nuts. Nuts are hard stones, they have to be opened to be eaten. We recall the " beautiful stones," the " splendid apples " which are now intended for her brother. What her erotic hopes at first promised me is now given to her brother after she has turned away from me. Here I think there is obviously something connected with the brother which proceeds from some brother-sister relationship. The importance of the brother to his sister seems suspicious (cp. *kiss — sisterly kiss*), and we cannot forbear the suspicion that here is something we have long sought which might explain much if it could be known.[1] Some adventure of childhood where her brother played some rôle which left a deep impression seems to lie at the root of this—a Freudian trauma. The secret was, however, well guarded and the analysis brought out nothing.

I only communicated the results of the analysis very superficially to the patient so as to avoid giving any hints of a sexual nature. I wished to prevent an explanation of the symbolism leading to greater concealment in the next dream. The inner development of the patient which this dream suggested, i.e. the alienation from the writer, the renunciation of his standpoint and the invalidation of his advice and teaching, manifested itself (apart from any objective set-back) in the important fact that she now again began dreaming of fire and blood, she " heard the fire-horn every night, the alarm was raised."

[1] We may also recall that in the dream of the occupied room it is said, " Stop, that's forbidden." Perhaps this expression became fixed because it aroused a complex, and expressed something of great significance to the patient.

The time for her departure was now fast approaching, and I was hoping for some decisive dream, but she did not remember any more dreams with the exception of the fire dreams, save for a small fragment, which said nothing, on the morning of the day she was to leave. I asked her, as usual, if she had dreamt. She said " Yes," but quickly added : " But I know already what the dream means, I saw it at once. But I couldn't tell it you ; it is something about earlier times which I can, perhaps, only tell mother." All my requests were fruitless ; she maintained it was something of a kind that she could only tell her mother. Finally I said to her, " Then it's a very unpleasant sexual matter." She did not answer, but stared out of the window. More I dared not.

So, unfortunately, our dream analysis and the analysis of the illness as a whole remained incomplete at this point, which seems, however, narrowly circumscribed.

*Summary of the Dream Analysis.*—Although none of the dreams reached the complete understanding that was wished, and the last broke off at an important point, we have obtained a series of valuable suggestions. We see that the dreams fully confirm the complex of the association tests. The associations exhibited an intense sexual complex, and the dreams, it may be said, treat only of the theme of pairing. We recognize that the complexes which constellate the associations of her waking life constellate likewise her dreams. The dream analysis presents the same obstacles that occurred in the association experiment. By the analysis of the dreams the sex complex was made clear— its displacement to the writer, the disappointment and the falling back of the patient upon her mother, and, again, the resumption of some mysterious childhood relationship to her brother. The next section shows the sex complex in the hysterical symptom as the cause of her illness.

### III. THE HYSTERICAL SYMPTOM

It remains to turn the knowledge gleaned in the two previous sections as to the form and content of her sex complex to the symptoms of her illness. We will begin with the " St. Vitus's dance."

According to the anamnesis as given by the patient, this simply began from reasons unknown. She answered all questions as to its origin in the negative, and it seemed as if it were impossible to arrive at the cause because this was unknown to the patient. But we know fully the resistances which are put forth to the reproduction of all complex ideas. Hysterics are only able to

carry out mental introspection in so far as indifferent matters
are dealt with ; where it is the question of a complex they are
powerless.   The complex does not belong entirely to the hierarchy
of the ego (conscious) ideas ; by reason of its powerful emotional
tone it is (like, moreover, every strong affect) more or less autonomous, and drives the association in its direction even when the
ego complex strives to think and to act in its own way.   For
this reason we cannot reproduce "intimate" things with the
same certainty and quietness that we can objective things.
The impetus to the concealment of "intimate" things can
amount to an almost total incapability of reproduction, as we
saw in the case given in chapter vii.   To obtain information from
a hysteric about "intimate" things, about a complex, we must
make a flank attack.   Freud has built this into a method—it is
psycho-analysis.   First of all we liberate all the general cover
ideas which stand in any kind of associated (often symbolical)
relationship to the complex ideas, and then we gradually approach
the complex from different sides.   At bottom the method is
the same as used by a clever examiner towards some shy candidate.   The candidate cannot answer specific and direct questions,
he is too excited ; so the examiner first gets answers to a series
of general and easy questions where the emotional feeling is not
so great, and then the desired answer comes of itself.   Were I to
ask the patient directly as to the cause of her St. Vitus's dance,
I should get nothing ; I therefore first obtain her answers to
simple indifferent questions, and arrive at the following :

> She liked going to school and liked her teachers.   She did not like all the
> lessons, although she does not recollect that there were any which she especially
> disliked, or that there were any teachers she especially disliked.   She did not
> like the writing lesson, indeed she disliked going to these.   It was during a
> writing lesson (her second school year) that her (right) hand first began to tremble.
> The trembling grew gradually stronger, so that she was unable to write ; so she
> had to miss the writing lesson.   Then the tremors began in her right leg, so that
> very shortly she could not go to school at all.   Thus the St. Vitus's dance gradually
> arose.   She remembered also that she could not help crying fearfully and was
> afraid to go into the streets when it rained, so that she often missed school on
> this account.   The attacks were sometimes stronger, sometimes weaker, so
> that some days she could go to school, sometimes she couldn't.   In her twelfth
> year the illness became so extreme that she had to give up school altogether.

I think that this narrative brings out clearly enough that the
patient was an extremely pampered child who used every opportunity to stop away from school ; as if on purpose to cut out
the hated writing lesson, the tremors began in the right arm, and
finally these served to keep the child away altogether.   The
patient admits that when she took the trouble she could suppress
the tremor.   *But it suited her to be ill.*   It seemed to me instructive

that at the beginning of the analysis she spoke with uncertainty of her feelings about her school recollections. At first it seemed to her that she liked going to school, then we got the feeling expressed that it was not quite so, and then we got the exact contrary, which corresponds to the facts. This inconsequential way of revealing herself points to method in her (cp. the earlier analyses). There is nothing to show that the patient was conscious of this inconsistency ; on the contrary, it seemed that she believed everything she said at the time of saying it. The school complex, the well-known phenomenon in all asthenic children, led to the formation of a hysterical symptom. It is understandable that the success of an automatism affords a suitable *locus minoris resistensiœ* out of which other automatisms can be developed.

The day after this analysis her tone had again changed. She maintained that she could not say she disliked going to school, she quite liked going. School never made any special impression upon her. Other events occupied her much more, e.g. that once a teacher (female) violently quarrelled with her. Here again we get the same uncertainty and inconsequence.

The St. Vitus's dance got worse in her twelfth year. This was the year when (according to the analysis) the recollections of the sexual cat dreams were produced. In the twelfth year the first feelings of puberty become distinct in many girls, and they begin to be interested in sexual matters. But her twelfth year had still another significance for the patient. In reference to the mother complex the following was obtained :

It occurred to her (after a long pause) her mother was so ill, and still so contented and jolly; if she could only be like that. Her mother always used to say that her osteomalacia came from being married. But she had become ill twenty-eight years ago, and the doctors say the disease is now curable.

These remarks caused me to ask: " Has that any meaning for you ? " "None; I can't think of any meaning it would have for me—I have never thought about it." I threw out that it was just possible she had the idea that she might inherit such a disease. " She had never feared that ; in spite of that she could have married." I remarked that some kind of fear like that had perhaps arisen at the time of her first period. " That's impossible, for my mother had said to me long before I was twelve years old that I ought not to marry or I might get the same illness."

We may conclude from this remark that in her twelfth year there were conversations of far-reaching sexual significance, which must have made a strong impression upon the patient to judge from the strength of the resistance with which she sought to hide the explanation of this point. At any rate, we find in her twelfth year one of the first components of her sex complex. The first period had two complexes before it, one having a fully developed automatism, the other one associated with sex feelings.

The possibility of the transposition of this decisive event into a hysterical symptom is given, but not the necessity for it, for the non-ability to marry seems insufficient. One requires the existence of some event which would prepare the way for the repression of the sex complex, some sexual event of childhood. This would be the right place for a sexual trauma, at which the dream seems to hint.

With her menstrual period a new phase in her existence begins—the sexual. It is not surprising that the school complex gives place to the sex complex, although only apparently so. As we have seen, it is still present in the associations, forming a wound which is still scarred and kept up by self-reproaches. That her school complex, the St. Vitus's dance, is still potentially present is seen from the following. One day she felt particularly bad. She described the feelings of heat as unendurable ; whilst speaking, her right arm twitched from time to time, then her left arm. I drew her attention to these movements ; then her legs began slowly to tremble and she said, " It is only with great trouble that I pull myself together, that I am not hitting all round me like before ; I've the greatest desire to do it." We see that at a moment when her energy is quite slackened the old automatisms are again ready to break forth (a confirmation of Janet's theory that every *abaissement du niveau mental* is accompanied by a flaring up of the automatism).

Her first period supplied the provocation for the origin of her present difficulties—feelings of heat in the head and neck, feelings as if there was nothing but blood in the head, that her blood was 40°. Her hands, feet, and body are cold. With these feelings there are always the same obsessional ideas : she is compelled to imagine that she is bleeding from the nose, from all the orifices of her head ; she imagines that clots of the blood which came at her first period are in her head, she is always wanting a whole basin of blood to come away from her head.

This peculiar symptom complex is undoubtedly referable to her period ; it is nothing else than " a displacement from below upwards " (Freud). The mechanism for this displacement is present in the patient ; we have already seen it unmistakably in her dreams. The heat (blood and fire in the dream) is certainly the sexual heat which occurs at the period. The periods have stopped for some months after having been previously very irregular ; distinct meteorism arose and a posture which made the lower half of the abdomen more prominent. For Freud these are imaginary symptoms of pregnancy. Psychological experience speaks to the same effect ; in any erotic expectation complex in a young woman the child plays a definite part in the associations and dreams.[1] It will be recalled that this takes place also in the associations of our patient. Pregnancy has, moreover, for the patient the particular significance of the danger of osteomalacia—a significance that must be repressed. But I cannot adduce any positive evidence from this case in favour of Freud's views.

The following symptomatic actions are probably dependent upon sex feelings :

(1) The constant seeking for cooling.

(2) The cold ablutions.

(3) The repugnance to meat in any form.

(4) The inability to sit down.

(5) The predilection for gymnastic exercises in her room, accompanied by aversion from all other physical exercises.

These symptomatic actions correspond exactly to the popular hygienic ideas for decreasing sexual excitement.

Positive evidence of the repression of sexual feelings is found in her consequent and obstinate circumlocution in all sex questions. As soon as the examination touched anything relating to sex a full stop was reached, and we were generally left with invincible resistances. On theoretical grounds I was able to be convinced by careful questioning that the patient was correctly informed about sex matters ; but she could not tell me whence came her knowledge, and stubbornly denied ever having read anything on the subject or hearing anything from anybody. She simply knew it. Just before the conclusion of the treatment she admitted, after long hesitancies, that once a girl friend had explained things to her when she was twelve years old. This only serves to show again how strong were the barriers which guarded her sex secrets.

I need not go any further into the visions, they have been explained through the analysis of the dreams.

The course of improvement was tedious, with frequent relapses. Her energy visibly improved, so that her ability to work gradually extended to four or five o'clock in the afternoon (previously she was exhausted by ten o'clock in the morning). She was again able to read and do normal work. But the feelings of heat remained, although they seemed less intense ; in the third month of her treatment she began not to speak about them any more to me ; she expressed surprise that latterly she had had such frequent depressions, the cause of which she could not under-

---

[1] E.g., cp. the somnambulic fantasies of the case described in the " Psychology and Pathology of so-called Occult Phenomena " in *Collected Papers on Analytical Psychology*, by C. G. Jung. Authorized translation edited by Dr. Constance C. Long. (London : Bail'ière, Tindall and Cox.)

stand. (Formerly if anything unpleasant happened she had no depression but increased feelings of heat.) But the patient still spoke about her feelings of heat to my assistant (a lady doctor). After the dream about the dining-table where I had cleared up her relationship towards me, the earlier nomenclature returned with me also ; she heard the fire-alarm in the dreams and several times, especially in the last week of her sojourn here, the black man returned ; he had disappeared after her first analysis. The dream-analysis explains these recrudescences. The patient could not give vent to her inmost secret ; the sexual compromise as regards myself had failed (in me she could obviously find nothing beyond the sexual as to make it worth while to depart from her rôle of invalid). Unable to tear herself away from her secret, she was obliged to remain with the repressed meaning of the feelings of heat ; she was thus driven back to her earlier symptoms, and to the corresponding terminology, thus assuring herself that my explanations were all lies ; for she could not acknowledge that I was right—this would have jeopardized the apparent genuineness of her illness.

About a month after her departure her doctor wrote to me that she was as bad as before, and that she was full of abuse of the asylum and the doctor, with hints that the doctor had only sought opportunities to have immoral conversations with her. Her morbid personality, i.e. her sexual complex, thus entrenched itself behind an aggressive defence ; the complex discredited the doctor's morality as far as possible in order to obtain the normal mental equilibrium.

The automatism of the disease creates in this wise a free path for its unimpeded development, for every complex has the urge to live itself out unrestrained.

## Summary

The complex discovered in the associations is the root of the dreams and of the hysterical symptoms.

The disturbances caused by the complex in the association experiment are but the resistances found by Freud in psycho-analysis.

The mechanisms of repression are the same in the association experiment as in dreams and hysterical symptoms.

In hysteria the complex has an abnormal autonomy, and leads to an active separate existence which progressively degrades and destroys the constellating power of the ego complex. A new morbid personality is then gradually created whose tendencies, judgments, and resolutions proceed entirely in the direction of the will to disease.   The remainder of the normal ego is absorbed by the second personality and forced into the rôle of a secondary dominated complex.

A practical treatment of hysteria must endeavour to strengthen the normal rest of the ego, which is best done by introducing a new complex which shall free the ego from the dominance of the morbid complex.

# ON DISTURBANCES IN REPRODUCTION IN ASSOCIATION EXPERIMENTS

## By C. G. JUNG

THE reproduction method which I first described in a short communication in 1905 in the *Centralblatt für Nervenheilkunde und Psychiatrie,* has been recently subjected to frequent criticism (A. Gross,[1] Heilbronner,[2] Isserlin[3]).

Being overwhelmed with other work, I was unfortunately unable till now to supplement my former incomplete communication by means of the statistical results. In 1905 I maintained : If after completing about one hundred word-associations the subject is requested to repeat the answers to each stimulus-word separately and any of the following conditions occur : (1) memory fails at certain places, (2) the former reaction-word is not given at all, (3) it is given incorrectly, (4) there is silence, (5) it is reproduced with great hesitation—the analysis of the associations distorted in any of these ways in reproduction proved that in most cases this failure was constellated by a " complex." As most investigators in this branch seem disinclined to recognize the slightest heuristic value in Freud's psycho-analytic method, I am, unfortunately, debarred from taking the shortest way, which would simply be to give the analyses in support of that statement. In order to exclude that subjective factor in analysis which is so much feared, there remains no course other than to separate out the objective signs of the complex constellations, the " complex indicators," and their relation to the failure in reproduction ; this will be untainted evidence. I discovered the complex indicators empirically in the analysis ; I saw that in the associations which were distinguished by certain indications a complex was, as a rule, constellating with particular strength and had sometimes led to a " disturbing " interference. If these indicators are

[1] A. Gross, " Kriminalpsychologische Tatbestandsforschung," *Jurist.-psychiat. Grenzfragen,* Bd. V, H. 7. (Marhold : Halle, 1907.)

[2] Heilbronner, " Die Grundlagen der psychologischen Tatbestandsdiagnostik," *Zeitschrift für die gesamte Strafrechtswissenschaft,* Bd. XXVII, p 601.

[3] Isserlin, " Ueber Jung's ' Psychologie der Dementia Præcox,' etc.," *Centralblatt für Nervenheilkunde und Psychiatrie,* Bd. XXIX, p. 329.

really characteristic, i.e. if the analytic method has led to a correct result which will stand proof, the indicators must be in close relation to one another. They will recur preferably at certain associations—for instance, at failures in reproduction and at delayed reactions. If that is not the case, and if the complex indicators are distributed without any selection over the whole test, analysis will have led us to a false conclusion. In my former communication I mentioned, further, that :

(1) The failures in reproduction have occasionally an arithmetical mean time which exceeds the general arithmetical mean (one example).

(2) The failures in reproduction are apparently as frequent at the critical as at the post-critical reactions.

(3) Occasionally there is a tendency to disturbances in reproduction, which may be serial or isolated.

(4) The theory of this phenomenon was sought in the general characteristics of the complex. I there emphasized one characteristic—repression (Freud), because this seemed to me peculiarly well fitted to explain the inhibition to correct reproduction. The chief characteristic of the complex is, at all events, its relative autonomy, which may find expression in two directions : by increased emphasis and stability in consciousness, and by repression—that is, resistance to reproduction in the unconscious. Hence the associations which belong to the complex lack the " flexibility " of the remaining and more indifferent psychic material. (This only holds good of the case when the special complex is inhibited and cannot reach reproduction. The complex itself naturally has complete command of its material, it is even hypermnestic.) This reference of the disturbance in reproduction to a more general psychological peculiarity seems to me a helpful explanation. Obviously the hypothesis is not true of all cases, for one must be first sure that all external sources of disturbance (accidental) have been entirely excluded. My hypothesis is only true for the majority of cases, and, speaking generally, for the majority of complex indicators also.

(5) The complexes exhibited in the association experiment have usually a tone of unpleasure, so that the exceptional condition in which the complex stands during the test may be well qualified as " repression."

I must now prove in detail the fundamental principles of this conception ; that is, that the disturbances in reproduction are complex indicators and agree, as a whole, with the other complex indicators. The method adopted for obtaining this proof is not quite simple, for we must remember that the disturbance in reproduction, like all complex indicators, is no necessary accompaniment of the complex ; furthermore, like the other complex indicators, it is not exclusively linked to the critical places but can arise also in the subsequent reactions. The commonest complex indicator is the reaction-time.

### DISTURBANCE IN REPRODUCTION AND REACTION-TIME

The readiest method of comparison would be simply to compare the arithmetical mean time of the failures in reproduction with the arithmetical mean of all times or all the rest of the times. But this method would be only adequate if the disturbances in reproduction agreed with the " too long " times. But that is not the case at all ; the relationships are much more complicated.

The following very different cases occur :

(1) Critical reaction with $<$ too long time. disturbance in reproduction.

(2) Critical reaction with too long time.
    Post-critical reaction with disturbance in reproduction.

(3) Critical reaction with disturbance in reproduction.
    Post-critical reaction with too long time.

(4) Post-critical reaction with $<$ too long time. disturbance in reaction.

(5) Disturbance in reaction at a critical and post-critical reaction (two-limbed series of disturbances).

(6) Disturbance in reproduction at a critical reaction and at three or more subsequent reactions (three- or four-limbed series of disturbances).

The method has to take account of these complicated relationships. In chapter v I made use of the probable mean for the definition of the " too long " reaction-time, with due regard to the fact that the arithmetical mean, as a rule, is disproportionately high in consequence of the influence of the exceedingly long times ; these cannot be compensated by exceedingly short times, for the reaction-time is only infinitely variable at the top. The probable mean, therefore, gives, on the whole, a far better picture of the average rapidity of the reaction. Whatever exceeds this average should be regarded, as a rule, as not quite normal. But the probable mean should be only used for large series of figures ; it becomes too inexact otherwise, for it is considerably affected by slight accidents. In small series of numbers we must use the arithmetical mean. I start, therefore, from the probable mean of the whole test, and first of all count how many reaction-times with absence of reproduction exceed, how many agree with, and how many are below the probable mean. If my previous suppositions are correct we should expect to find that the majority of disturbances in reproduction exceed the probable mean. Those disturbances in reproduction which exceed or are below the probable mean may be perseverations and may directly follow a too long time ; in these cases the reaction - time immediately preceding cannot be examined. Properly speaking, the reaction - time immediately following should be investigated, because the prolongation of time might only follow afterwards. But that would take us very far. I have hitherto not attempted this examination because it seemed to me that such cases are not very frequent. We will first see how far we get with the above two methods. Be it noted that in these methods my subjectivity is entirely excluded. This makes any re-examination perfectly safe.

The material selected as the basis of my investigation consists of twenty-eight cases which were all picked out considerably earlier and for a purpose quite other than the examination of this particular question. Rather less than a third were selected by myself ; the other two-thirds were selected by various assistants, some of them many years previously. Among the persons tested there were only three mentally healthy, the others were nervous and mental patients of different kinds and of the most diverse reaction type. The material is thus as varied as could be desired, presenting the fewest possible chances of any uniformity in the results. I summarize the results in the following table :

|  |  |  | Association reproductions with absence of reproduction. | | | | |
|---|---|---|---|---|---|---|---|
|  |  |  | Above the probable mean. | At the probable mean. | Under the probable mean. | I.[1] | II.[1] |
| G. | Hebephrenia . | 100 associations Probable mean (P.M.)= 8·5 Arithmetical mean (A.M.) = 9 35 per cent. failures in reproduction (F.R.) | 22 | 5 | 8 | 10·6 | 12·5 |
| A. | Moral insanity | 100 ass., P.M. 12·30 A.M. 15·2 45 per cent. F.R. | — | 6 | 9 | 14·1 | 10·2 |
| R. ♀ | Hebephrenia . | 100 ass., P.M. 13·5 A.M. 20·6 15 per cent. F.R. | 11 | — | 4 | — | 11·7 |

[1] The figures in these two columns give the arithmetical mean of the reaction-times of the associations immediately preceding the reproductions that failed : (I, the associations in reproduction absent at the probable mean ; II, for those that were absent below the probable mean.

| | | | Association reproductions with absence of reproduction. | | | | |
|---|---|---|---|---|---|---|---|
| | | | Above the probable mean. | At | Under | I. | II. |
| P. | Paranoia | 100 ass., P.M. 11<br>A.M. 12·9<br>22 per cent. F.R. | 13 | 2 | 7 | 13 | 13·2 |
| H. | Catatonia | 100 ass., P.M. 22<br>A.M. 30·3<br>53 per cent. F.R. | 33 | 1 | 19 | 25 | 31 |
| G. ♀ | Hysteria and imbecility | 50 ass., P.M. 14<br>A.M. 17<br>16 per cent. F.R. | 6 | — | 2 | — | 16 |
| W. ♀ | Dementia præcox | 100 ass., P.M. 10·5<br>A.M. 11·3<br>53 per cent. F.R. | 29 | — | 24 | — | 10·2 |
| G. | Organic feeble-mindedness | 100 ass., P.M. 47<br>A.M. 57<br>67 per cent. F.R. | 34 | 2 | 31 | 165 | 67·4 |
| Z. ♀ | Dementia præcox | 100 ass., P.M. 10<br>A.M. 14·4<br>51 per cent. F.R. | 32 | 6 | 13 | 14 | 16·7 |
| H. ♀ | Dementia præcox | 100 ass., P.M. 10<br>A.M. 11·5<br>41 per cent. F.R. | 22 | 5 | 14 | 9 | 10·3 |
| V. | Imbecility | 100 ass., P.M. 11<br>A.M. 11·1<br>28 per cent. F.R. | 16 | 5 | 7 | 10·2 | 16·1 |
| E | Moral insanity | 100 ass., P.M. 15<br>A.M. 18·1<br>30 per cent. F.R. | 21 | 5 | 4 | 17·8 | 18 |
| K. ♀ | Dementia præcox | 100 ass., P.M. 17<br>A.M. 21·8<br>38 per cent. F.R. | 23 | — | 15 | — | 24·4 |
| K. ♀ | Dementia præcox | 100 ass., P.M. 5<br>A.M. 7·1<br>25 per cent. F.R. | 18 | 4 | 3 | 4·7 | 9·6 |
| A. | Paranoia | 100 ass., P.M. 13·5<br>A.M. 13·9<br>14 per cent. F.R. | 7 | — | 7 | — | 10·4 |
| B. | Psychopathia | 113 ass., P.M. 18<br>A.M. 19·5<br>27·4 per cent. F.R. | 16 | 2 | 13 | 19 | 17·6 |
| S. | Catatonia | 100 ass., P.M. 11<br>A.M. 14·3<br>32 per cent. F.R. | 24 | 3 | 5 | 11·6 | 16·6 |
| H. | Imbecility | 104 ass., P.M. 18<br>A.M. 30·4<br>27·8 per cent. F.R. | 14 | 4 | 11 | 56·7 | 24·4 |

| | | | | Association reproductions with absence of reproduction. | | | | |
|---|---|---|---|---|---|---|---|---|
| | | | | Above the probable mean. | At | Under | I. | II. |
| S. | Psychopathia . | 100 ass., P.M. | 12 | 26 | 4 | 7 | 19 | 16·4 |
| | | A.M. | 17·4 | | | | | |
| | | 37 per cent. F.R. | | | | | | |
| R. | Dementia | 50 ass., P.M. | 32 | 14 | 2 | 2 | 12·5 | 33·5 |
| | præcox . | A.M. | 38·3 | | | | | |
| | | 36 per cent. F.R. | | | | | | |
| R. ♀ | Cerebral syphilis | 100 ass., P.M. | 14 | 23 | 3 | 20 | 12·6 | 15·3 |
| | | A.M. | 17·3 | | | | | |
| | | 46 per cent. F.R. | | | | | | |
| S. | Imbecility . | 100 ass., P.M. | 26 | 13 | — | 8 | — | 55·8 |
| | | A.M. | 37·5 | | | | | |
| | | 21 per cent. F.R. | | | | | | |
| J. ♀ | Normal . . | 100 ass., P.M. | 7 | 8 | — | — | — | — |
| | | A.M. | 7·9 | | | | | |
| | | 8 per cent. F.R. | | | | | | |
| H. | Alcoholism and | 100 ass., P.M. | 10·5 | 28 | — | 9 | — | 13·3 |
| | imbecility . | A.M. | 13·5 | | | | | |
| | | 37 per cent. F.R. | | | | | | |
| P. | Normal . . | 100 ass., P.M. | 7 | 20 | 6 | 7 | 7·7 | 8·6 |
| | | A.M. | 7·9 | | | | | |
| | | 33 per cent. F.R. | | | | | | |
| A. | Normal . . | 100 ass., P.M. | 7 | 11 | — | 4 | — | 8·1 |
| | | A.M. | 7·8 | | | | | |
| | | 15 per cent. F.R. | | | | | | |
| S. | Moral insanity | 100 ass., P.M. | 12 | 27 | 2 | 11 | 9 | 13·3 |
| | | A.M. | 13·9 | | | | | |
| | | 40 per cent. F.R. | | | | | | |
| W. | Neurasthenia . | 100 ass., P.M. | 15 | 21 | 1 | 9 | 9 | 16·8 |
| | | A.M. | 17·2 | | | | | |
| | | 31 per cent. F.R. | | | | | | |

We may conclude from these figures that, on the average, 62·2 per cent. of the absent reproductions lie, as regards the reaction-times, above the probable mean, 7·5 per cent. coincide with it, and 30·2 per cent. are below it. This agrees with expectation. On the average, 33 per cent. of the associations were not reproduced. The mean time of the two last columns must be considered with the critique mentioned above. They contain cases of very different import. As we have said, we have only taken note of the reaction-time which immediately preceded the disturbance in reproduction, and that, moreover, only in those cases where the disturbed reproduction itself was below the general mean time. But it is quite possible that the disturbance in reproduction is itself no perseveration, but takes place at the critical reaction with a short reaction-time, and that the long reaction-time only follows subsequently. This occurrence would make the result much worse.   So we must here work with minimal figures.   Still the time of the disturbed reproductions here under review exceeds, on the average, the common probable mean by 7·8 and the common arithmetical mean by 4·1.   The values which form the basis of this calculation vary extraordinarily.   The series of figures of the last column are more uniform and yield richer material, but are subject to the same consideration as the figures of the last column but one.   We find here also that, on the average, the reaction-time which precedes this disturbance in reproduction exceeds by 4·2 the probable mean, and by 0·4 the arithmetical mean.   We must remember that the arithmetical mean tends to be displaced upwards, out of all proportion, as our figures sufficiently demonstrate.   In my opinion these figures also speak in favour of, not against, expectation.   If it be remembered how infinitely complicated psychical processes are and how difficult to control, especially in the region of associa-tion, we cannot help being astonished at the relative regularity of the results, which are not to be impugned by an incomplete scheme.

### DISTURBANCES IN SERIES AND REACTION-TIME

In my material 63·9 per cent. of all failures in reproduction are arranged in series.   This fact shows that there is every reason to relate the failure to the complex, for the complex with its perseveration is in the association experiment a factor *par excellence* for the formation of series, just as it is in ordinary psychological life (which according to the opinion of some ought not to be brought into connexion with psychology at all).   If this deduction from analogy is correct the serial disturbances should exhibit the same complex indicators as the series of complexes—that is, before all, delayed time.   Not to accumu-late tables unnecessarily, I omit the tables of the individual series.   The percentage numbers already furnished show that the material is large enough for statistical averages.   The number of disturbances in reproduction which serve as the foundation of these statistics amounts to rather over six hundred.   We calculate the arithmetical mean of all failures in reproduction associations which follow directly on one another, and we compare the mean figure with the individual probable mean and arithmetical mean of the subject in question.

| 2-limbed series of disturbances are, on the average, | | | | | 7·7 above the P.M. |
|---|---|---|---|---|---|
| 2- | ,, | ,, | ,, | ,, | ,, | 3·6 ,, A.M. |
| 3- | ,, | .. | | ., | 9·6 ,, P.M. |
| 3- | .. | ,. | | ,, | 6·3 ,, A.M. |
| 4- | ,. | . | | ., | 11·6 ., P.M. |

4-limbed series of disturbances are, on the average, 6·4 above the A.M.
5·  „ & over „        „        „        „   6·7   „   P.M.
5·  „  „  „        „        „        „   2·4   „   A.M.

There is a rise of the time values up to the series of four. Series of five and over are again lower. This result does not agree badly with the analytical considerations. We not infrequently find a strong complex perseverating over three or more terms with a final step-ladderlike decrease of the reaction-times. The stronger the complex that is aroused the stronger become, *cum grano salis*, the disturbances proceeding from it. In longer series, however (which are also much rarer), other kinds of experimental disturbances often enter into play.

We can summarize the foregoing by saying : The main disturbance in reproduction occurs at a too long reaction-time ; if it does not coincide with this the previous reaction-time is wont to be too long in the majority of cases. (The question as to the subsequent reaction-time we leave unsolved, as it is of slighter importance.)

Another method, perhaps even more instructive, can be used to demonstrate the higher time values of the series of disturbances. Taking the twenty-four cases with well-developed series, I arrange them in two classes, one upon another, in the following way : First I take those series which begin with a reaction-time longer than the association immediately preceding, e.g. :

| Association correctly reproduced | 1st disturbance | 2nd disturbance | 3rd disturbance | 4th disturbance | Association correctly reproduced at the end of the series |
|---|---|---|---|---|---|
| 9 | 10 | 8 | 6 | 6 | 7 |
| 10 | 82 | 15 | — | — | 11 |
| 6 | 92 | 15 | 8 | — | 8 |
| 12 | 35 | 16 | 16 | — | 14 |
|  |  | and | so on |  |  |

In this way I arranged 119 series of this class, one upon another, added together the individual columns, and divided by the number of the terms of the sum.

The second class relates to those series where the disturbance first set in with a reaction-time that is shorter than the association correctly reproduced that immediately preceded. For comparison I take the reaction-time of the two previous associations (it is a matter of indifference whether this is correctly or incorrectly reproduced). I have excluded from the calculation all those complicated by " faults," although such series would have supported my results much more strongly.

This class can be thus summarized :

| Previous association | Correct reproduction with increased time | 1st disturbance | 2nd disturbance | 3rd disturbance | Correct reproductions at end of series |
|---|---|---|---|---|---|
| 14 | 17 | 8 | 21 | — | 10 |
| 12 | 15 | 13 | 55 | 12 | 13 |
| 8 | 40 | 12 | 20 | — | 9 |
| | | and | so on | | |

There were fifty-six series in this category. A few series where the correct reproduction and the first disturbance in the series had the same reaction-time I have divided equally among the two classes. The results are as follows (given in the arithmetical mean and in one-fifth seconds).

CLASS I

| Correct reproduction | 1st disturbance | 2nd disturbance | 3rd disturbance | 4th disturbance | 5th disturbance | Correct reproduction at end of series |
|---|---|---|---|---|---|---|
| 14·8 | 37·2 | 22·8 | 23·9 | 33 | 27 | 17·9 |

CLASS II

| Previous association | Correct reproduction with long R.T. | 1st disturbance | 2nd disturbance | 3rd disturbance[1] | Correct reproduction at end of series |
|---|---|---|---|---|---|
| 18·3 | 22·5 | 13·3 | 22·7 | 30 | 17·6 |

The average arithmetical mean time of the twenty-four cases made use of here amounts to 19·8. We thus see that with one exception all the times considerably exceed this mean. The exception is in those disturbances in reproduction (Class II) which immediately follow on a longer time.

[1] I omit the fourth and subsequent disturbances, because they are based upon too small a series of figures (under 20)   But they are all considerably above the general arithmetical mean—for this reason alone, that the number and the series of disturbances in reproduction frequently increase with the length of the reaction-time.

## DISTURBANCES IN REPRODUCTION AND PROBABLE MEAN TIME

If, as seems proved by this investigation, the disturbance in reproduction occurs chiefly in connexion with the too long times, we may venture to suppose that the number of disturbances increases with the longer individual mean times. That seems, at least, to be the fact in my (limited) material.

With a P.M. time of 5–10 there are, on the average, Dist. Reprod. 29·7
,,          ,,     10·5–15      ,,              ,,              ,,     31·8
,,          ,,     15·5–20      ,,              ,,              ,,     31·8
,,          ,,     20·5 and over ,,      ,,              ,,     44·2

But for the elucidation of this question a far larger material is required.

## DISTURBANCES IN REPRODUCTION AND COMPLEX INDICATORS WITH THE EXCLUSION OF THE TOO LONG REACTION-TIMES

Besides the too long reaction-times I have found as complex indicators : a reaction with two or more words where the subject usually reacts with one word, repetition of the stimulus-word, misunderstanding of the stimulus-word, faults, slips of speech, translation into a foreign language, reaction with an otherwise unusual foreign word, interpolation of " Yes " or some other exclamation before or after the reaction, unusual content of the reaction, perseveration in essence and in form. Estimation of the unusual nature of the content and judgment as to perseveration is open to subjective influences. I have, therefore, omitted these two criteria in the investigation. I only except obvious perseveration of a reaction-word when it appears identically the same in the reaction following. I have selected out of the material the nineteen cases characterized by their generally reacting with one word. I count off how many of the complex indicators are present in the whole test and how many of these correspond to the association which failed in reproduction.

The following table presents the results of this investigation in individual figures :

| | Correctly reproduced associations. | Absence of reproduced associations. |
|---|---|---|
| | Complex signs | Complex signs |
| 1 . . . . . | 0·08 | 0·16 |
| 2 . . . . . | 0·11 | 0·31 |
| 3 . . . . . | 0·03 | 0·27 |
| 4 . . . . . | 0·03 | 0·11 |
| 5 . . . . . | 0·15 | 0·20 |

|  | | | | | Correctly reproduced associations. | Absence of reproduced associations. |
|---|---|---|---|---|---|---|
|  | | | | | Complex signs | Complex signs |
| 6 | . | . | . | . | 0·11 | 0·28 |
| 7 | . | . | . | . | 0·37 | 0·40 |
| 8 | . | . | . | . | 0·08 | 0·26 |
| 9 | . | . | . | . | 0·06 | 0·16 |
| 10 | . | . | . | . | 0·12 | 0·42 |
| 11 | . | . | . | . | 0·27 | 0·39 |
| 12 | . | . | . | . | 0·03 | 0·18 |
| 13 | . | . | . | . | 0·06 | 0·15 |
| 14 | . | . | . | . | 0·01 | 0·02 |
| 15 | . | . | . | . | 0·06 | 0·33 |
| 16 | . | . | . | . | 0·23 | 0·29 |
| 17 | . | . | . | . | 0·04 | 0·15 |
| 18 | . | . | . | . | 0·31 | 0·54 |
| 19 | . | . | . | . | 0·18 | 0·29 |

If it be remembered that all complex reactions do not necessarily lead to absence of reproduction, and that the absent reproductions only occur in one-third of all the associations, the result shown by the above table is sufficiently striking. We see that, without exception, in every case more complex indicators occur at the associations with absence of reproduction ; so that as a rule they are signalled out beforehand. Those associations with absent reproduction exhibit, on the average, rather more than twice as many complex indicators as those which are correctly reproduced.

### SUMMARY

There is in my very diverse material an undoubted connexion between absence of reproduction and too long reaction-time ; the main disturbances in reproduction occur when the reaction-time has been too long, and sometimes partly also subsequent to too long reaction-times. Moreover, the association which afterwards fails to be reproduced has, on the average, double as many complex indicators as those correctly reproduced. We have excluded complex indicators which depend upon a subjective estimation of the content of the reaction and the corresponding perseveration. We learn from this that the complex indicators have a tendency to group themselves round certain definite associations ; without analysis we cannot, of course, perceive what is the origin of the relationship between these very diverse complex indicators.

CHAPTER XI

# STATISTICAL INVESTIGATIONS ON WORD-ASSO-
# CIATIONS AND ON FAMILIAL AGREEMENT
# IN REACTION TYPE AMONG UNEDUCATED
# PERSONS

By Dr. EMMA FÜRST

At the instigation of Professor Bleuler and Dr. Jung I undertook
a statistical investigation of the associations that chiefly occur
among normal persons, and as to modifications in these associations due to age, education, and family.

For practical reasons the work divides itself into two parts ;
the first part deals with the results obtained among the uneducated.

## I. Arrangement of the Experiment

Associations were obtained in twenty-four families comprising
one hundred subjects, forty-two males and fifty-eight females,
aged between nine and eighty-one years.

Those taking part in these tests were :

> 4 families each consisting of 2 subjects
> 6    ,,    ,,    ,,    ,,   3   ,,
> 3    ,,    ,,    ,,    ,,   4   ,,
> 4    ,    ,,    ,,    ,,   5   ,,
> 3    ,    ,,    ,,    ,,   6   ,,
> 2    :    ,,    ,,    ,,   7   ,,
> 1 family       ,,    ,, 10   ,,

So far as language is concerned the material is very much
the same, only the last family of ten being of Austrian nationality ;
all the other subjects are Eastern Swiss with dialect as their
usual speech. But so far as regards intelligence and education
the material is very unequal. The subjects were of all degrees
of intelligence and class, from the quite unintelligent class up
to highly intelligent and educated persons. Twenty-nine of the
subjects had only an elementary, and thirty-five a secondary
schooling ; fourteen had gone through an intermediate school,
and eight had an education corresponding to this ; fourteen of
the subjects had had a university career.

Out of the twenty-four families all the subjects in thirteen of these families had about the same degree of education ; in eleven families it was pretty equal as to some members, very diverse as to others. In eleven families all the members lived together. The experiment was carried out among normals. Nevertheless among these persons there were some of a very low degree of intellect, with imbecile traits ; a few others, especially women, showed slight hysterical symptoms, whilst among the older subjects were some with the physiological changes of age. But all were capable of living in society.

Care was taken not to carry out the tests in conditions of fatigue, after a heavy meal, or late in the evening. In two cases where the tests could only be carried out late at night quite abnormal results were obtained. One subject always saw the stimulus-word as if written before her, but could find no associations. With another the experiment was made at ten o'clock at night after a heavy day's work and moderate indulgence in alcohol. For external reasons no second test could be made. Naturally these two results are not included in the statistical averages. A man of eighty-one had also to be excluded because he proved to be suffering from dementia senilis, with hallucinations of persecution and gave 61 per cent. clang-reactions. These three cases were all men ; so that the number of men was reduced to thirty-nine, and the total number of subjects to ninety-seven.

Before beginning the tests an explanation was given by means of a few examples of the various possibilities of association, and the subject was enjoined to react with the first word that occurred. With ninety persons two hundred, with ten persons four hundred associations were made. As a rule two hundred associations were carried out at a session. In two cases with high definition figures and very long reaction-times the test had to be carried out in two sessions both on the same day. The tests were carried out with each individual quite alone, that is, not in the presence of any other member of the family. The stimulus-word was called out in literary German. Jung's list of words was used, the peculiarities of which have been described in chapter ii. The total number of associations carried out and used amounts to twenty-two thousand in round numbers. With eighty-one persons I carried out the tests personally ; another nineteen were investigated by four colleagues (men or women) ; they were their nearest relatives. Unfortunately, time measurements were not made ; the experiments began in 1903, when the importance of time in the reaction was not so well known. That my investigations are but little, sometimes not at all, concerned with the effects of the complexes, although these are of chief importance as regards the constellation, be attributed to this circumstance.

## II. Classification

I have classified the material according to the Kräpelin-Aschaffenburg [1] method as improved by Jung.

The same criticism has been made against Jung's classification as was formerly made against the Kräpelin-Aschaffenburg classification. Despite Jung's express warning, some critics, e.g. Watt, made the mistake of thinking that Jung claimed to have found, by his classification, the intrapsychical association. There is no suggestion of this anywhere, as any attentive reader of the second chapter in this book can convince himself. Jung's classification is entirely logical-verbal and in no wise prejudges the intrapsychical association. Nevertheless, taking the result as a whole, some conclusions can be drawn as to the general intrapsychical process ; thus in chapter ii a conclusion was made as to attention. The outer classification cannot of itself settle anything about the inner conditions of the association ; it does not, indeed, deal with the question. That belongs to the psychoanalytic method as demonstrated in chapters vii and ix.

That a classification based upon logical points of view does not afford merely accidental and arbitrary results is best seen by the changes of the reactions in disturbed attention, changes which follow certain laws and can be expressed in figures. Naturally the classification does not bring out everything ; still it brings out a great deal which makes the investigation valuable. In spite of the many difficulties of this classification, I decided on it because no better one is known to me ; for its principles I refer the reader to chapter ii.

## III. Results of the Tests

As the following investigations show, the subjects showed a preference for certain association forms. This is particularly true of the predicative relationship, substantive-adjective, and inversely (predicate type). According to the frequency of the different kinds of associations in a subject, five types of association may be distinguished, among which there are transition types. In fifty subjects we found two or more kinds of associations about equally represented, e.g. co-ordinations and motor reactions, or co-ordinations and predicates, or predicates and motor reactions. These I grouped as *mixed types*. In the rest of the subjects one definite kind of association predominated over the others, amounting, approximately, to more than 40 per cent. of all the associations.

[1] Aschaffenburg, " Experimentelle Studien über Assoziationen " (Kräpelin's *Psychologische Arbeiten*). *Investigations on the Associations of Normal Persons*, chapter ii. Certain changes were made in Jung's list, as will be seen.

In nearly every subject I came across more or less well-marked complex phenomena. A detailed investigation of these was not possible in all cases on account of the amount of the material, the absence of time measurements and the absence of analyses. In the following descriptions of individual families a particular description of the individual subject is often necessary. I have begun with those families standing lowest in the scale as regards intelligence and education, in order to show the change in association type with increasing education. This procedure is justified by the fact that education is one of the factors which most seriously influences the nature of the reactions. All the figures in the tables are given in percentages.

In several families a striking agreement was found between the members of the family as regards the nature of the associations. To express this agreement or this difference, as the case might be, by a simple figure, Dr. Jung devised the following calculation :

The individual figures of any two members of a family who are to be compared are placed together, the differences are written out, these differences are added together, and the sum is divided by the number of classes in the classification.

*Example*

| Kind of association | Husband | Wife | Difference |
|---|---|---|---|
| 1. Co-ordination | 6·5 | 0·5 | 6 |
| 2. Sub- and supra-ordination | 7 | — | 7 |
| 3. Contrast association | — | — | — |
| 4. Predicates as to value | 8·5 | 95 | 86·5 |
| 5. Other predicates | 21 | 3·5 | 17·5 |
| 6. Relationship of subject and object | 15·5 | 0·5 | 15 |
| 7. Designation of time, place, means, etc. | 11 | — | 11 |
| 8. Definition | 11 | — | 11 |
| 9. Coexistence | 1·5 | — | 1·5 |
| 10. Identity | 0·5 | 0·5 | — |
| 11. Verbal-motor connexion | 12 | — | 12 |
| 12. Word-formation | 6 | — | 6 |
| 13. Word-completion | — | — | — |
| 14. Clang-association | — | — | — |
| 15. Remainder group (faults, meaningless, indirect associations) | — | — | — |
| Total | | = | 173·5 |

$$\text{Average difference, D} = \frac{173 \cdot 5}{15} = 11 \cdot 5$$

$$D = 11 \cdot 5$$

D gives, not perhaps in the most ideal way, the typical measure of the difference ; in practice it is a very useful figure, considerably abbreviating the exhibition of the differences and avoiding much repetition. As the above table shows, the calculation of this difference was not based upon Jung's detailed classification ; first, on account of greater simplicity, and secondly, because a nicer classification increases the number of unavoidable vagaries. Therefore all divisions which seemed uncertain or were infrequent were grouped in one class. All coadjuncts with the same supraconcept, similarity, inner and outer relationship, by example, and causal dependence were included in the class of co-ordination ; similarly, the verbal-motor connexions and quotations were put together. The inclusion of indirect associations, faults, and meaningless reactions in one class is justified by the fact that these are, as a rule, all to be regarded as disturbances ; their individual estimation is unimportant in this inquiry. The distribution of the associations among these fifteen groups is, on the whole, very simple if one keeps to certain logical norms, and it should lead to approximately satisfactory conclusions. The following results seem to justify this view :

### Description of the Individual Test Families

#### Family I

*Daughter, 16 years, polisher; mother, 45 years, laundress; father, 47 years, tailor. All three test persons are very unintelligent and very badly educated.*

| Test persons | Value predicates | Other predicates | Other inner associations | Outer associations | Clang-reactions | Sentence reactions | Type |
|---|---|---|---|---|---|---|---|
| Father, 47 years. | 8·5 | 21 | 51 | 19·5 | — | 9 | mixed |
| Mother, 45 ,, . | 95 | 3·5 | 1 | 0·5 | — | 63 | predicate |
| Daughter, 16 ,, . | 98 | 0·5 | — | 1·5 | — | 95 | predicate |

| Stimulus-word | Father | Mother | Daughter |
|---|---|---|---|
| 1. Green | colour | joy | is nice |
| 2. Water | bluish | good | is useful |
| 3. Prick | with a knife | disagreeable | is not good |
| 4. Angel | appearance | good, always good | nice |
| 5. Long | measure | correct | it's long |
| 6. Table | furniture | is nice | is useful |

| Stimulus-word | Father | Mother | Daughter |
|---|---|---|---|
| 7. Haughty | question of the heart | unpleasant | is not nice |
| 8. Proud | vulgar | bad sign | is also not nice |
| 9. Wicked | not good | disgusting | is wicked |
| 10. Friendly | good feeling | is pleasant | is nice |
| 11. Bear | a burden | is good, is pleasant | is nice |
| 12. State | the people's laws | is proper | useful |
| 13. Stalk | liquorice root | must be so | is nice |
| 14. Ink | black | good, useful | also useful |
| 15. Rich | private income | good in all cases | is also nice |
| 16. Mountain | high | O, beautiful | nice |
| 17. Salt | marriage | very good | useful |
| 18. Habits | of the people | very good, good habits | nice |
| 19. Stupid | silly | it's stupid | it's stupid |
| 20. Tooth | in the mouth | is good, is useful | is nice |

The daughter is an extreme predicate type. Throughout the whole experiment she makes use almost exclusively of the same reactions—*good, nice, useful,* and their negatives.

In many places the form of the reaction is quite unsuitable and without meaning, as, e.g. *bear — is nice ; part — is nice ; month — is nice ; broad — is nice.* Very characteristic of her limitations are the identities she makes which vividly recall imbecility. She even notices herself her frequent repetitions, and tries to find another association ; finds none, and simply repeats the stimulus-word in sentence form : *long — is long.* Probably a slight emotional stupor had a share in this, although at the time of the tests she did not seem embarrassed.

Still the general impression is that of embarrassment ; we may recall the difficulties of adjustment that Wehrlin's imbeciles had (chapter iii) ; there seems to be something of the sort here. Comparing the examples we have given, a high degree of resemblance between daughter and mother will be noticed.

The mother shows the same disposition towards the finer peculiarities of the reactions as her daughter, but she has a freer choice of predicates, which is further expressed by the existence of a few objective predicates ; still, she also has a very limited vocabulary.[1] Thus we find *good, is good, very good, always good, is not good,* 54 times ; *beautiful, is beautiful,* 17 times ; *useful,* 10 times ; *necessary,* 7 times ; *must be,* 5 times ; *also right,* twice.

In contrast with the daughter, in whom we find, it is true, judgments as to value, but without strongly pronounced subjective

---

[1] This remark is, of course, only made as regards her mental condition during the experiment.

valuations, her mother does show rather more distinct traces of her own personality.

### Examples

| Stimulus-word | Daughter | Mother |
|---|---|---|
| Yellow | not nice | no, delicate colour |
| New | nice | much better than old |
| Book | useful | I like a good one |
| Frog | not nice | I don't like |
| Plum | good | I like |
| Coffee | useful | I love my coffee |

This rather freer way of reaction suggests a lesser degree of embarrassment. Many awkward reactions (*is nice, pleasant, unpleasant,* etc.) point to her very low intellectual level.

The father belongs to the mixed type, deviating in behaviour both from his wife and his daughter. We get, nevertheless 29·5 per cent. of predicates, which show, however, but slight agreement in kind with those of the other two persons.

His intellectual and educational level is well expressed in the following figures :

Designation of place, time, etc.     .   11 per cent.

Definition   .   .   .   .   .   11   ,,

As is well known, imbeciles prefer the use of these forms. There are, besides, many awkward and affected reactions.

### Examples

| | |
|---|---|
| Fear | pressure over the heart |
| Kiss | delivery of love |
| Family | consists of parents and children |
| Cow | does chew the cud |
| Sofa | pleasant piece of furniture |
| Understanding | lies in the brain |

This kind of reaction is very similar to that found by Wehrlin (chapter iii) in slight degrees of imbecility. In this case, as in his, the adjustment is towards the meaning of the stimulus-words, with a tendency to explain the meaning of the stimulus-word and to give the reaction in sentence form. But there are essential differences ; we have a greater wealth of ideas, better powers of abstraction, greater verbal facility—all shown by the quite appropriate predicates, which are external and rather objective, and by verbal reminiscences, quotations, and word-formations, which are almost entirely absent in imbeciles.

*Examples*

| | |
|---|---|
| Soldier | servant of the State |
| Love | affection |
| Eye | of the law |
| Book | of life |
| Laugh | in one's sleeve |
| Prudence | is the mother of wisdom |
| Folk | crowd of people |
| Moon | a heavenly body |

This family shows various types. The two females belong to one type with a difference between them in the subjective and egocentric apprehension of the stimulus-word. The husband belongs to an objective type. So far as age is concerned the relationship of inner to outer associations discloses no laws ; in mother and daughter the classification is almost the same ; the father, as the oldest test person of the family, has fewest inner associations. Common to all three is a verbal want of facility corresponding to their low level of intellect and education. This is noticed in the frequent sentence form, the many repetitions and the clumsy reactions, partly in dialect, partly new formations.

Average difference of the reaction type [1] :

$$\left.\begin{array}{l} \text{Father} \\ \text{Mother} \end{array}\right\} 11\cdot5 \qquad \left.\begin{array}{l} \text{Mother} \\ \text{Daughter} \end{array}\right\} 0\cdot5 \qquad \left.\begin{array}{l} \text{Father} \\ \text{Daughter} \end{array}\right\} 12\cdot1$$

Agreement between father and mother is extremely slight (be it remembered that by the method of calculation used the greatest difference could only be 13·3) ; it is still less between father and daughter. On the other hand, there is an extraordinary agreement between mother and daughter, the daughter proceeding still further in the direction of the maternal reaction type, withdrawing still more from the father. It is difficult to say on what the difference, on the one hand, between father and mother, and the agreement, on the other hand, between mother and daughter are founded. One is inclined to think first of all that the female sex of the experimenter has an effect upon the adjustment of the subject. We need only think here, of course, of a phenomenon of adjustment, for the type of reaction is not necessarily constant, as Jung and Riklin have already proved. It is conceivable that the subject would have had a different attitude towards another experimenter. Again, the fact that the experimenter (a woman) is of higher intellectual and social grade than the subject may influence the result. Experience shows that such factors are of great importance in the reaction type. We must, above all, realize that we are here only dealing with relative

---

[1] The figures are from calculations made by Dr. Jung.

values which are in no wise chiefly connected with the intellectual qualities of the subject, but mainly with the emotions. Jung and Riklin have shown that, influenced by relaxation of attention, the reaction type can undergo considerable changes in the same experiment. But attention is after all but a fragment of affectivity [1] (Bleuler). We must consider the possibility that the experimenter, by reason of her sex, her intellectual and social class, touched specific complexes in the subjects which condition the peculiar phenomena of the adaptation. Finally, the striking differences between husband and wife would also find its explanation in factors concerned with the test persons themselves ; such an explanation would require information about the " spiritual bond " between the couple, and about their complexes, obviously a very delicate and complicated investigation. That perhaps some repelling complex was here in question seems suggested by the fact that in other married couples there is a striking agreement in type between husband and wife. That many other complicated mental factors do enter into consideration is, of course, perfectly obvious ; but these are beyond our present knowledge. The explanation of the agreement between mother and daughter we are disposed to find in their common life and *milieu*, as well as in the mental dependence of the child upon her mother. But it is questionable whether the matter is quite so simple for there are cases where this assumption does not hold. It would rather seem as if greater importance must be attributed to the individual complexes and their more or less accidental agreements.

### FAMILY II

*The associations were carried out in two sisters and three brothers aged 31–43 years, and for comparison in the wife of the youngest brother. All belong to the artisan class and are uneducated ; their intelligence varied from weak to moderate.*

| Test persons | Value predicates | Other predicates | Other inner associations | Outer associations | Clang-reactions | Sentence form | Type |
|---|---|---|---|---|---|---|---|
| 1. Brother, 34 years | 20 | 47·5 | 25·5 | 6·5 | — | 11 | predicate |
| 2. His wife, 32 ,, | 29 | 40 | 20 | 7·5 | — | 8 | ,, |
| 3. Brother, 41 ,, | 17 | 35·5 | 28·5 | 19·5 | 0·5 | 22 | ,, |
| 4. ,, 39 ,, | 12 | 12·5 | 35·5 | 39·5 | 0·5 | — | mixed |
| 5. Sister, 43 ,, | 7 | 16·5 | 26 | 45 | 1 | 13 | superficial |
| 6. ,, 31 ,, | 12·5 | 3 | 33·5 | 49 | 0·5 | 2 | ,, |

[1] *Affektivität, Suggestibilität u. Paranoia.* (Halle: Marhold, 1906.)

| Stimulus-word | No. 1 | No. 2 | No. 3 | No. 4 | No. 5 | No. 6 |
|---|---|---|---|---|---|---|
| Head | big | hard | hair | brain | hair | neck |
| Green | grass | grass | carpet | blue | field | red |
| Water | cold | thin | to wash | wine | cold | cloud |
| Prick | needle | pain | needle | to lighten | holly | sensitive |
| Long | short | short | meter measure | short | — | short |
| Ship | big | round | sail | anchor | sea-ship | water |
| Plough | nice | nice | lie | field | hero | field |
| Bear | heavy | heavy | children | lie | ill | lift |
| State | big | big | hat | Swiss | taxes | republic |
| Haughty | wild | not | when angry | soft-hearted | Anna | soft-hearted |
| To dance | difficult | jolly | schottische | jollity | — | jump |
| Lake | big | big | Vevey | sea | Zurich lake | river |
| Ill | heavy | heavy | nose-bleeding | healthy | Mrs. X. | healthy |
| Proud | wild | not nice | calling | unpleasant | M. | high-spirited |
| Wicked | peaceful | not nice | often | good | Anne | good |
| Swim | difficult | jolly | water-bird | sing | not I | water |
| Travel | nice | nice | often | pleasant | I should like to, to Italy | nice |
| Blue | green | colour | nice | green | lake | red |
| Threaten | danger | not nice | often | obedient | — | punish |

*Subjects Nos. 1 and 2. Both very unintelligent and uneducated ; artisans.*—The similarity between these two, husband and wife, is very striking both in the chief and in the sub-classes. In both the predicates are high (67·5 and 69 per cent.); there are very few motor reactions, co-ordinations, and coexistences. The agreement extends to the more subtle peculiarities of individual reactions. Both react to the same stimulus-word thirty times with the same reaction. The associations are very simple and obvious and refer, especially in the wife, to their immediate surroundings. The predicates mainly give colour, form, and size, or some very general estimate of the stimulus content such as *good, nice*, without subjective estimate ; they are frequently repeated. The wife more especially reacts to verbs by general concepts, as *mankind, child*.

The agreement is seen not only in the general quantitative relationships, but also in both persons having a strong tendency to repeat certain words. The husband reacts with the word *big* 23 times, his wife 15 times (in the other members only, on the average, 0·7 times). *Beautiful* is repeated by the husband 11 times, by the wife 25 times (by the other members, on the average, thrice). The word *difficult* is repeated 9 times by the husband, 4 times by his wife ; it does not occur at all among the others.

In both subjects there are distinct complex constellations, which are rather more numerous in the wife. To stimulus-words suggesting a certain agility, the man who is physically weak and clumsy reacts several times by *difficult* (*dance, swim, take care, meet, sing*). A few other reactions are constellations from the family and household life of the subjects, worried by economic troubles.

The wife's complexes are mainly economic worries, a great number of children, and quarrels with her husband's relatives. She feels herself despised and unjustly treated. The complex reactions are sometimes expressed very openly, sometimes by motor and meaningless reactions and particularly by general concepts. The latter are found exclusively in response to stimulus-words with an emotional tone (as *unjust, despise, stranger*, etc.) to which *mankind* is always the reaction. But we cannot hold the complexes altogether responsible for the frequency of these general concepts in the uneducated as contrasted with the educated. The verbal want of facility among the uneducated is partly responsible. Whilst educated persons are usually able to find a motor reaction when there is a momentary blockade to the activity of association evoked by some emotionally toned stimulus-word, no such motor reaction occurs to the uneducated and unintelligent, who then employ some general concept which means nothing.

The want of education in these two subjects is again shown : by reactions that are inappropriate or make no sense ; by taking the stimulus-words in their dialect sense and by reactions in clumsy or dialect forms ; by the use of numerous designations of place, time, purpose, and means with the preposition ; by the small number of motor reactions. The wife shows this, furthermore, by her numerous, though extremely simple, general concepts and her difficulty in reacting to rarer words, especially abstracts.

| | |
|---|---|
| A fire | difficult (thick smoke) |
| Colour | wild |
| Deaf | bull (*taub* (deaf) in dialect = mad) |
| Hatchet | cutting |
| Dog | free (dialect = good-natured) |
| View | of the dog |

*Subject No. 3. Elder brother of No. 1, of medium intelligence and slight education ; holds a responsible position as warder in a house of correction.*—Quantitatively there is great resemblance to No. 1. But there is a very essential difference ; in his reactions

No. 3 shows himself influenced to a large extent by indifferent recollections and by emotionally toned events of the past and present. The associations thus receive an extremely individual turn ; i.e. were we to reckon up with how many other ideas this subject makes the like reaction to the same reaction-word we should obtain a great number of associations which were entirely individual. Thus this subject was the only one out of one hundred subjects who reacted *proud — occupation*. We shall be certainly right in assuming that by this reaction he expresses joy at his present position, which means an advance for him which he made great efforts to obtain. A few other emotionally toned chains of thought may be gathered from the associations. In the following associations he touches upon the relationship to his superiors.

| | |
|---|---|
| Modest | question of occupation |
| Trust | with a certain treatment |
| People | civil servant |
| Choose | authority |
| Honour | yes |
| Haughty | when angry |
| Seek | large orders |

The strongest emotional tone is found in his feeling of responsibility for the criminals, in his fear of their attempts at escape, and especially in his apprehension of the danger of his being attacked. The latter very intensive affect constellated a whole series of associations :

| | |
|---|---|
| Wild | interned |
| To take care | of the interned |
| Danger | every day |
| Meet | unfavourable |
| Fear | little |
| Blood | human blood |
| Door | open |
| Caution | master |
| Locksmith | proper guard |
| Pipe | weapon |

Besides these there are a number of more or less emotionally toned reactions, part of them arising from his former occupation of tailor, part from narrower or wider surroundings.

| | | | |
|---|---|---|---|
| Bring | on requisition | Public-house | little |
| Paper | examine | Write | much |
| Wagon | three pieces | Travel | often |
| Forget | what, already | Angry | often |
| Free | a little | Pity | may be |
| Soldier | none | Luck | seldom |
| Smell | air of cells | Family | three in family |

| Pencil | pocket-shaped | Lake | Vevey |
|---|---|---|---|
| Copy-book | examine | Full | anger |
| Punish | often | Threaten | often |
| Railway-station | best when near | Brother | two |

His want of education is documented by some awkward, coarse expressions, with formation of new words or word combinations, e.g. *purpose* — *family-purpose*, by dialect expressions and by the wrong use of words, e.g. :

| Eat | with good taste (in the sense of enjoyment) |
|---|---|
| Neck | formerly tainted (had a goitre) |
| Fireplace | necessity for a Russian |

He belongs to the complex-constellation type described by Jung and Riklin, in whom a stimulus idea arouses a whole memory complex. We recognize in this case that the feeling of responsibility and fear of his own life, perhaps also the thought that he is not quite adequate to his position, determine the subjective constellation of the associations.

The divergence from these two subjects, 4 and 6, is clearly seen in the eldest brother and the youngest sister, who both belong to the mixed type and agree with each other in many respects ; for instance, in the classes supraconcept, similarity, contrast, coexistence, and motor reactions, as also in their common tendency towards reaction with the same grammatical form (the sister 54·5 per cent. and the brother 66·5 per cent., corresponding with the greater number of co-ordinations). Whilst both subjects had to the same stimulus-word the same reaction in twenty-eight cases and a very similar reaction in thirty-eight cases, the brother has the following reactions in common with the rest of his family :

| With subject No. 1 | . | . | . | 11 reactions |
|---|---|---|---|---|
| ,, ,, ,, 2 | . | . | . | 7 ,, |
| ,, ,, ,, 3 | . | . | . | 1 reaction |
| ,, ,, ,, 5 | . | . | . | 3 reactions |

The number of predicates is considerably less in both these subjects, the number of coexistences and motor reactions much greater than in subjects 1 and 3. Still there are considerable differences between subjects 4 and 6. The brother, who is the most uneducated and rather imbecile, gives a very objective and but slightly individual impression quite unaffected by personal memories, and this despite the many value predicates. Beyond the predicates *big, beautiful, good, friendly, pleasant,* and *unpleasant,* the associations are mainly coexistences, slang phrases, and contrasts. There is very little that is individual.

*Subject No. 6. Unmarried sister, 32 years old ; no better educated but rather more intelligent.*—Her reactions are rather

more superficial than her brother's ; she has far fewer co-ordinations and objective predicates but more verbal reminiscences.
In contrast with her brother, she shows more complex indicators,
which are sometimes quite open and expressed by very frank
subjective judgments, whilst sometimes they are concealed in
faults and very long reaction-times at emotionally toned stimulus-
words :

| | | | |
|---|---|---|---|
| Beloved | grand | Suppose | one can |
| Make | I like | Kiss | nice |
| False | hateful | Quarrel | hateful |
| Decency | one must have | Love | nice |
| Beat | hateful | Dirty | hateful |
| Stupid | — | Wild | hateful |
| Right | — | Choose | — |
| Pain | suffer | View | to have |
| Modest | be | Fear | to have |
| Visit | we can | Understand | understood |
| Worthy | be | Separate | hurts |
| Caution | to have | Hunger | hurts[1] |
| Forget | we can | | |

The reactions are likewise very simple, with many familiar
phrases ; there were no affected or meaningless reactions.

*Subject No. 5. Elder sister, unmarried,* 43 *years old ; of medium
intelligence, secondary education ; fairly read, vivacious and
energetic, with many interests.*—The relationship of inner to outer
associations is the same as her sister's, with whom she has most
similarity—especially seen in the complex phenomena as faults
and delayed reaction-times. But the association type is much
more superficial. Despite the large number of predicates there
are very few value predicates. On the other hand, there were
30 per cent. word-formations, some very simple, taken from
her immediate surroundings, her housekeeping and occupation ;
others were more unusual, showing fair reading. The rest of
the associations are also simple and appropriate. There were no
meaningless, affected, cumbersome reactions. There were 4·5
per cent. of faults. It is not impossible that this is connected
with the motor type. Faults are chiefly found in persons with a
lively complex. But a strong complex demands much psychical
energy, leaving less power of concentration at the disposal of
indifferent matters ; this results in decrease of attention and a
superficial type. She is chiefly differentiated from her sister by
a greater number of individual associations. The faults are all
found at emotionally toned stimulus-words : *friendly, dance,
manners, threaten, despise, take care, worthy, impudence.*

---

[1] Perseveration from the previous reaction.

As will be seen from the tables, the ratio of inner to outer associations shows no relationship to age reducible to rule.   There is no great similarity in type between the brothers and sisters ; they were separated in early youth and only lived together for a time.   Although the ratio of the figures is relatively similar, the qualitative relationships are most diverse, dependent principally upon difference in the complex constellation.

In one subject the complex constellation is chiefly expressed by a freer occurrence of individual associations exhibiting the chief complex without disguise ; in another subject it was chiefly shown by its effects in causing disturbances in attention and inhibitions to associations ; this naturally conditions a great difference in the reactions.   According to Dr. Jung's calculations on my material $D = 5·9$ for all uneducated men who are not related, for women it is 6.   The relationship of the husband and wife, 1·8, is considerably below these figures ; that of the husband and his eldest brother is 2·7 ; the intermediate brother and younger sister is 2·8 ; all the other differences exceed 5·9, sometimes even 6.   The familial similarity is thus very limited.   But, in contrast with the previous family, there is very considerable agreement between husband and wife.

## FAMILIES III AND IV

*Six subjects.   The associations were taken in three brothers aged 74, 71, and 63 years ; a sister aged 67 and her children, a son of 31 years, and a daughter aged 27.   The intelligence in all was but medium ; all were uneducated, peasants or artisans.*

| Test persons | Value predica es | O her predica es | Definitions | O her inner a otia ion | Ou er as otia ism | Clang-reaction s | Remainder group | Predicate |
|---|---|---|---|---|---|---|---|---|
| 1. Brother, 74 years | 40 | 21·5 | 11 | 17 | 10·5 | — | — | predicate |
| 2. „ 71 „ | 10 | 14·5 | 34·5 | 30 | 11 | — | — | predicate definition |
| 3. „ 63 „ | 31 | 27 | 1·5 | 27·5 | 13 | — | — | predicate |
| 4. Sister, 67 „ | 24·5 | 14·5 | — | 36·5 | 24 | — | 0·5 | predicate co-ordination |
| 5. Her son, 31 „ | 6·5 | 22 | — | 32 | 39 | — | 0·5 | mixed predicate |
| 6. Her daughter, 27 „ | 18 | 30·5 | — | 33 | 17·5 | — | 1·5 | predicate |

We must divide this family into two groups : Group I with subjects Nos. 1–3 ; Group 2 with subjects Nos. 4–6.

Group I have all considerably more inner associations and

are strongly differentiated from Group II in the finer relationships also. They are very similar among themselves; all three have relatively few outer associations. The eldest and the youngest of the brothers are pronounced predicate types with many value predicates; the intermediate brother is a mixed type in whom definitions predominate; the eldest has also 11 per cent. definitions. All three react extremely slowly, with great attention and reflection; this is especially true of subjects 1 and 2, who usually suppressed or did not speak out the first unconscious association in order to give a "better answer" (e.g. *head — green — who is unskilled*).

*Subject No. 1. Eldest brother, 74 years old, uneducated.*— Together with 11 per cent. of definitions, there are 40 per cent. value and 17 per cent. objective predicates; some of them such as occur in many uneducated or. elderly persons.

The intense striving to produce something "good, clever," leads to a series of affected, studied, awkward reactions, to dialect forms and neologisms.

*Examples of Ordinary Value Predicates*

| | | | |
|---|---|---|---|
| State | good | Way | wearisome |
| Rich | pleasant | Salt | indispensable |
| Quarrel | unpleasant | Air | blows away (i.e. violent wind) |
| Hay | nice smell | Wood | agreeable |
| Bread | tastes good | Hit | objectionable |
| Sail | indispensable | Deaf | objectionable |
| Dog | pleasant | Good | encouraging |
| Unjust | insulting | Fear | fatiguing |
| Law | orderly | Seek | deceiving |
| Beloved | uniting | Tired | uneasy |
| Brother | amiable | Family | widespread |
| Long | sadly | Great | remarkable |
| Ill | pitiable | Ring | holding together |
| Haughty | disapproving | Proud | fatiguing |
| Flower | nice smell | | |

Although many of these reactions belong to the predicate type, it can be seen that there is an easy transition to the definition type; the predicate, which is largely charged with emotion, gradually assumes an explanatory character. The subject endeavours to make some intellectual addition to his personal estimation of the object designated by the stimulus-word; this quite corresponds to the tendency to react as "cleverly" as possible. The following associations show a further stage of this tendency; they consist essentially of combinations of value predicates with subordinations, some of which are appropriate, some of which are too general; these lead again to true explanatory reactions such as are found among imbeciles:

| | | | |
|---|---|---|---|
| Blue | beautiful colour | Month | part of the year |
| Stork | clever animal | Resin | preparatory substance |
| Coffee | valuable drink | Neck | part of the body |
| Ask | valuable answer | Sleeper | part of the railway |
| Laugh | comfortable frame of mind | Looking-glass | reflection |
| Market | old custom | Moon | heavenly body |
| Chimney | heavy work (building) | Bed | household furniture |
| Hatchet | dangerous object | Stone | material |
| Goat | useful animal | Railway-station | halt for travellers |
| Potato | pleasant food | Sofa | pause for a rest |
| Clergyman | indispensable teacher | Write | business matters |
| Coal | useful substance | Bone | substance |
| Kiss | recognition of friendship | To make | industry |
| Locksmith | fatiguing work | Angel | life |
| Plate | necessary object | Portfolio | writing stuff |
| Pipe | dangerous substance | Play | for pleasure |

In the stress upon the meaning of the word, the far-fetched association, and especially in the tendency to explanation these reactions resemble those found among imbeciles. The tendency to explanation is particularly expressed by the universal concepts, which are either too narrow or too broad and by the true explanations. The difference consists in the large number of predicates, which are to a large extent subjective, in the far bigger vocabulary, in the appropriate concepts, and in the rarer use of the sentence form.

The reactions of this subject, who is by no means an imbecile and is not a senile dement, are theoretically very remarkable ; the question therefore arises : Why does this subject react as if he were an imbecile ?

We have seen that not only does he belong to a family where predicates predominate, but he himself shows an unmistakable tendency to predicates. As Jung and Riklin have shown, in the predicate type the stimulus idea is very plastic, and thus arouses associations that are very rich in their content. The plasticity of the stimulus presentation depends in the first place upon the adjustment, i.e. upon the question whether the reaction carries with it great strain of attention or not. This increased attention can arise from different emotional considerations. In the first place, the unusual and exciting situation which recalls a school examination plays a part. People mostly conceive the experiment as an examination of intelligence, and so endeavour to react as " cleverly " as possible, so as not to appear " stupid." This feeling is, furthermore, aroused by the fact that many uneducated persons feel themselves mentally inferior to the educated even if they do not always openly admit it. Many people are, indeed, very sensitive in this respect. We may, then, really speak of an " intelligence complex." The like holds true of imbeciles (who, moreover, do not all exhibit the typical definition), who frequently have an insight into their own intellectual defects and have therefore a certain ambition not to appear so " stupid."

Our subject is an old man who obviously fears that he will be regarded as stupid and therefore takes the experiment very seriously. Hence the amount of thought and reflection given to the reactions. This emotional constellation is, moreover, easily read in the associations (e.g. *knowledge — to wish*). This case throws a certain light on the imbecile way of reacting and illuminates something fundamental in the predicate type. We see that between the definition and the predicate type there is a transition ; in the predicate type it is not a question of an entirely new attitude but only of something that has been changed in form. The extreme predicate types really at bottom also make " explanations " ; their predication reaction, *pleasant, beautiful, to be recommended*, always means *that is something pleasant, beautiful*, etc. These are emotional explanations without any intellectual addition.

Subject No. 2 reacted very slowly ; the experiment lasted four hours. Despite a quantitative difference, No. 2 has qualitatively a fair resemblance with No. 1. The attitude is likewise explanatory, the intellectual factor overcoming the more moderate emotional predicates. We therefore find here an increased number of definitions and co-ordinations, whilst the value predicates decrease considerably. The following examples show the similarity of the attitude with that of No. 1.

| | | | |
|---|---|---|---|
| Air | necessary for life | Pay | a duty |
| Give | good deed | Swim | great advantage |
| Bring | kindness | Tooth | advantage for the stomach |
| Proud | improper | Hit | necessity |
| Needle | of good steel | Head | of man |
| Mug | beautiful gift | Basket | for clothes |
| Ride | better than running | Mock | improper behaviour |
| Ring | is not square | Speak | fortunate gift |
| Big | certain States | Laugh | jolly mood |
| Part | of a piece of land | Hot | means of warming |
| Table | in the room | Market | place for sale |
| Sleep | for strengthening | Wagon | transport |
| Month | a part of the year | Chimney | smoke conductor |
| Moon | part of the world | Portfolio | paper-holder |
| Plate | kitchen utensil | Forget | neglect |
| Pain | interrupts sleep | Eat | necessary for stomach |
| Fruit | healthy food | | |

Subject No. 3. Here the tendency to definition and explanation recedes somewhat and is chiefly replaced by predicates ; among these are many value predicates and co-ordinate relationships in which the tendency to explanation can be indistinctly recognized. As compared with the two previous subjects these reactions leave a much more natural and less forced impression ; they are not so affected and far-fetched ; the individual reactions also show a freer treatment of the stimulus-word and much less limitation to the meaning of the stimulus-word.

| | | | |
|---|---|---|---|
| Month | to record | Air | necessary |
| Purpose | carry out | Wicked | dangerous |
| Floor | good, guaranteed | Ask | adverse |
| Bear | powerful | Flower | costly |
| Haughty | nervous | Ring | fits |
| Husband | intoxication | Ink | brilliant |
| Fear | unavoidable | Salt | necessary |
| Hot | pleasant | Hatchet | dangerous |
| Plough | uneven | To cook | troublesome |
| Lake | melancholy | Narrate | difficult |
| Play | quarrel | Law | acceptable |
| Strong | overspirited | Pride | imperious |
| Needle | useful | Soldier | necessary exercise |
| Tooth | serviceable | Family | comfortable |
| Stupid | insufficient | Hunger | devouring |
| Useful | pleasant | White | soilable |
| Song | unschooled | Intention | accident |
| Work | difficulties—in writing | Pipe | transport |
| Coffee | shortly | Duty | responsible |
| Broad | spread out | Give | charitable |

Subject No. 4 is the married sister of these persons. As the tables show, she does not differ greatly from her brothers' type ; she is relatively most like her youngest brother but shows rather more tendency to value predicates. These consist in numerous repetitions of *beautiful, useful, painful*, etc. There is also a certain tendency to explanation, which is, however, only hinted at in the rather numerous supraordinations and frequently partakes rather of the nature of value predicates.

### Examples

| | | | |
|---|---|---|---|
| Moderate | virtue | Clergyman | learned man |
| Coffee | plant | Deaf | illness |
| Modest | virtue | Sing | virtue |
| Floor | wood | Folk | mankind |
| Apple | fruit | | |

There is a distinct tendency to give the " material " of the object called up by the stimulus-word, e.g. :

| | | | |
|---|---|---|---|
| Wall | iron | Ship | wood |
| Cover | iron | Copy-book | paper |
| Needle | steel | Portfolio | leather |
| Floor | wood | | |

A like tendency is often very pronounced in imbeciles.

Subject No. 5 (the son of No. 4) deviates somewhat from his mother, for the number of value predicates is considerably less, whilst the outer associations increase. He approaches his mother's type, for description of the material of the object plays a part and predicates are rather numerous ; but, in contra-distinction to his mother, the predicates are less emotional relationships than some external or objective quality. That his attitude towards the meaning of the stimulus-word is less intensive is seen also by the increased coexistences and frequent colloquial phrases. He is an artisan and relatively intelligent ; hence his somewhat greater adaptability to the new position. The following comparative list shows how much more objective and unrestrained his reactions are.

| Stimulus-word | No. 1 | No. 2 | No. 3 | No. 4 | No. 5 |
|---|---|---|---|---|---|
| Goat | useful animal | small milch animal | useful | useful | milk |
| Potato | pleasant food | food | indispensable | food | earth |
| Old | troublesome | buildings | different | weak | young |
| Hit | reprehensible | necessity | powerful | painful | hammer |
| Family | widespread | parents and children | agreeable | beautiful | members |
| Narrow | unpleasant | difficult to breathe | objectionable | painful | broad |
| False | unpleasant | unfaithful | quarrelsome | vice | understood |
| Quiet | pleasant in old age | lonely | lonely | wild | the lake is quiet |
| Speak | with caution | happy gift | naughty | lovable | tongue |
| Rich | pleasant | who has much knowledge | tempting | beautiful | money |
| Mountain | extensive view | view-point | great strength to climb | high | stone |
| Stupid | not clever | weak-minded | insufficient | pity | clever |
| Unjust | injurious | innocent | shame | punishable | affair |

Subject No. 6 approximates more closely to her mother's type both quantitatively as well as in the finer relationships of the reactions. The tendency frequently to repeat certain predicates is even more pronounced. Such words as *big, beautiful, high, naughty*, are repeated. The following list shows this similarity between mother and daughter.

| Stimulus-word | Mother | Daughter |
|---|---|---|
| Prick | to pain | painful |
| Angel | lovable | lovely |
| Wool | warm | dyed |
| Dance | beautiful | jollity |

| Stimulus-word | Mother | Daughter |
|---|---|---|
| To cook | good | art |
| Ink | black | black |
| Wicked | silly | naughty |
| Swim | drown | dangerous |
| Travel | beautiful | pleasure |
| Mountain | high | high |
| Play | joy | jollity |
| Habits | virtuous | beautiful |
| Ride | art | pleasure |

In 11·5 per cent. of like stimulus-words mother and daughter react with the same word. This is a very high concordance in association. The difference between mother and daughter is only 2·5, whilst between mother and son it is 4·2 ; between son and daughter it is a little higher, 4·4. The mother is differentiated from her brothers by, on the average, 4·4.

## FAMILY V

*Husband, wife, son, and sister of the husband who, however, was not living with the family. Their intelligence is medium ; they are all uneducated—an artisan family.*

| Subjects | Value predicates | Other predicates | Co-ordinates | Relationship of subject and object | Other associations | Clangs | Type |
|---|---|---|---|---|---|---|---|
| Father, 42 years . | 14 | 39·5 | 14·5 | 12·5 | 19·5 | — | predicate |
| Mother, 42 ,, . | 18 | 22·5 | 15 | 13·5 | 30 | 1 | predicate (superficial) |
| Son, 12 ,, . | 7·5 | 17·5 | 19 | 17 | 29 | — | mixed |
| Sister of father, 41 ,, . | 14 | 22·5 | 9·5 | 23 | 31 | — | predicate (superficial) |

Subject No. 1 has a large number of predicates (in this family the predicates increase with age), which, however, disclose the emotional factor far less than, e.g., certain subjects in the last family. Subject No. 2 shows more emotionally toned reactions and value predicates than the others. As the table shows, the relationships of the reactions are very uniform in this family, although there are great differences of age, and the single sister does not live with the family. The average difference of all the members of the family among themselves amounts to 3·1 ; subjects No. 3 and 4, nephew and aunt, approach nearest to one another (D = 2·1).

*Examples*

| Stimulus-word | Father | Mother | Son | Sister of Father |
|---|---|---|---|---|
| Prick | pain | poisonous | hurts | needle |
| Angel | pure | heaven | beautiful | innocent |
| Bear | heavy | child | heavy | child |
| State | kingdom | greater | great | America |
| Ill | difficult | old | difficult | mother |
| To cook | good | good | good | kitchen |
| Ink | black | black | black | teacher |
| To threaten | ambush | bad luck | insult | storm |
| Rich | proud | men | poor | health |
| Separate | distance | hurts | parents | sad |
| Quarrel | like to | not nice | naughty | men |
| Old | grandmother | people | young | grey-headed |
| Memory | dance lesson | good | duty | nice |
| Dog | angry | nicer | St. Bernard dog | faithful |
| Choose | people | people | President | walk |
| Kiss | girl | love | mother | mother |
| Laugh | joyous | jolly | about nonsense | gay |
| Air | cold | good | good | clear |
| Intention | wicked | good | closed windows | useless |

This family has no other peculiarities worth mentioning.

## FAMILY VI

*Husband, wife, three daughters, and two sons (twins). Uneducated but relatively intelligent people. The husband is a merchant in a small way.*

| Subject | Value predicates | Other predicates | Other inner associations | Relationship of object and subject | Outer associations | Clangs | Type |
|---|---|---|---|---|---|---|---|
| Father, 60 years . . | 17 | 28·5 | 17 | 14·5 | 23 | — | predicate |
| Mother, 53 ,, . . | 40 | 28 | 11·5 | 11 | 9·5 | — | ,, |
| Daughter, 30 ,, . . | 23 | 20 | 27·5 | 12 | 17·5 | — | ,, |
| ,, 20 ,, . . | 14 | 32 | 16·5 | 18·5 | 19 | — | ,, |
| ,, 13 ,, . . | 11·5 | 38·5 | 18·5 | 23·5 | 8 | — | ,, |
| Son I, 17 ,, . . | 12·5 | 29 | 24 | 15·5 | 18 | — | ,, |
| ,, II, 17 ,, . . | 8 | 23 | 17·5 | 19 | 32·5 | — | mixed |

The female members of this family show an increase in their value predicates with increasing age ; with the exception of the mother, however, these value predicates are not strongly marked, although in most cases a pronounced predicate type is present. The more objective type, the opposite of the predicate type, is stronger in the males and in the youngest daughter than in the mother and the two elder daughters.   The relationship of the twin brothers should be the most interesting because the conditions are here favourable, one would expect, for a high measure of agreement.   But their average difference amounts to 3·7, which is not an especially low figure, and the figures given above suggest a divergent behaviour.   Son No. 1 approximates most closely to his sister, who is nearest to his age ; the difference is here only 1·9—the agreement is thus very great.   Son No. 2 approximates more nearly to his father's type, the difference being 2·3 (son No. 2 differs from his father by 2·8).

The following examples illustrate these relationships :

| Stimulus-word | Son No. 1 | Daughter No. 2 | Son No. 2 | Father |
|---|---|---|---|---|
| Head | part of body | part of man | man | round |
| Green | grass | grass | forest | frog |
| Water | clear | wet | lake | sugar-water |
| Angel | in heaven | gracious | heaven | heaven |
| Ship | warship | on the lake | sea | big |
| Plough | peasant | peasant | field | field |
| Wool | soft | soft | sheep | sheep |
| To bear | a soldier the gun | commission-aire | burden | hat |
| Haughty | naughty child | pupil | child | child |
| Proud | high-spirited | vice | horse | fool |
| To cook | the cook | the cook | mother | coffee |
| Ink | for writing | fluid | write | copying-ink |
| Needle | pointed | fine | sew | dull |
| Journey | pleasure | beautiful | business | honeymoon |
| Bread | food | food | eat | black |
| To threaten | enemy | enemy | war | teacher |
| Tree | green | tall | forest | cherry |
| Ride | cavalry | on horseback | horse | horse |
| Wall | part of a room | part of a room | room | carpet |
| Tooth | should be white | hard | mouth | contagion |
| Book | means of learning | square | read | Bible |
| Hunger | unpleasant | the best cook | bread | hurts |
| Pencil | writing material | long | write | ink |
| Big | house | buildings | land | tree |
| Luck | gracious | beautiful | in games | advantageous |
| Manners | necessary | necessary | man | beautiful |
| Kiss | the beloved | the loved one | love | bride |
| Door | for opening | for opening | wide | imperfect |
| Hay | dry | brittle | barn | tastes good |
| Month | period of year | part of the year | February | year |
| Surprise | mistake | event | something | stolen |
| Moon | heavenly body | part of the world | night | full |

This comparative table shows pretty clearly the similarity between son No. 1 and the second daughter. They have not only several associations verbally alike but there is a striking harmony in the tendency of their reactions. Their predicate attitude is also shown in the reactions which are not counted among the predicates; there is attention to the meaning of the stimulus-word, whilst son No. 2 and his father show a somewhat more objective and superficial adjustment. These examples seem to show that the difference in reaction type does not correspond with any merely intellectual difference but rather with peculiarity of affect. This probably consists in the two first subjects (son No. 1 and the second daughter) having a particular emotional relationship towards the experimenter, which accidentally (?) is the same in both; it is absent in the other two.

Whilst the eldest daughter has but few more value predicates than other predicates, her mother has a preponderance of value predicates. In this family she exhibits the highest number of predicates; the youngest daughter comes next to her, but her predicates are chiefly objective.

| Stimulus-word | Mother | Daughter |
| --- | --- | --- |
| Dance | pleasure | in ball-room |
| Swim | healthy | child |
| Journey | pleasure | the traveller |
| Bread | healthy | we eat |
| To sing | beautiful | loud |
| Habits | good | old habits |
| Ride | healthy | rider |
| Tooth | intolerable | white |
| Book | useful | rectangular |
| Plum | good | blue |
| Potato | useful | round |
| Cow | useful | gives milk |
| Hay | smells nice | light |

We see that the daughter, with her definite tendency to predicates, expresses these chiefly as positive attributes; her mother seems to put much more personal feeling into her reactions. The father with his moderate predicate type is, on the whole, much nearer the type of the children than the mother. Jung's calculations make the average difference between father and children = 2·8, between mother and children = 4·2. The relationship between father and sons = 2·5, between father and daughters = 3. The relationship of the mother shows corresponding but higher figures: between mother and daughters = 3·9, between mother and sons = 4·7. These figures prove the fact, confirmed by the nature of the associations, that in this family the sons approximate to the father's type and the daughters to the mother's.  This would have been even greater in the case of the eldest daughter if a particular cause of disturbance had not arisen in the second hundred test words.  In the second hundred there was an increase of the motor reactions, especially of the word completions and definitions, to the prejudice of the predicates and co-ordinations.  The cause was as follows : The experiment took place on a day when she was expecting to meet her betrothed at a party in the evening.  She was able to keep her attention directed to the experiment during the first hundred, showing no distraction.  Her attention wandered in the second hundred and she reacted very slowly.  Being repeatedly requested to take notice of what she was doing, she reacted for a little while with supraordinations and definitions, again slacking off into verbal reactions.

Family VII

*Very unintelligent and quite uneducated artisan family.*

| Subject | Value predicates | Other predicates | Relationship of subject to object | Definitions | Other inner associations | Other outer associations | Types |
|---|---|---|---|---|---|---|---|
| Father,      46 years | 3·5 | 1 | 2·5 | 60 | 26·5 | 6·5 | definition |
| Mother,     44   ,, | 5·5 | 30·5 | 18·5 | 8 | 24 | 13 | mixed predicate |
| Daughter, 14 years | 7 | 32·5 | 22·5 | 3·5 | 24 | 6 | ,,      ,, |
| Son,          9   ,, | 2 | 15 | 6·5 | 55·5 | 15·5 | 5·5 | definition |

The peculiarity of this family which at once strikes the eye is the sharp division into two different types—the father and son having a definition type, the mother and daughter a mixed type leaning towards the predicate.  The associations of father and son, the ratio of whose figures shows such close agreement, have a very different appearance on the surface, and deserve therefore special review.

The son's associations :

| Water | clear and cold | Potato | grows in the field |
|---|---|---|---|
| Lake | deep and much water | Plate | what's flat |
| Resin | what's sticky | Smooth | feather |
| Stories | to tell | Narrow | clothes |
| Understand | arithmetic | Stone | hard |
| Apple | what one eats | Steeple | what's high |
| Book | what one reads | Cart | where sacks are loaded |
| Visit | to friends | Station | where trains go |

| | | | |
|---|---|---|---|
| Coffee | people can drink | Goat | what has horns |
| Tree | what bears fruit | Public-house | where you drink beer |
| Hay | what the cow eats | Lamp | to make it light |
| Angel | is not seen | Friendly | to greet relatives |
| Buy | cow | Rich | when you get lots of money |
| Needle | which pricks | | |
| Clergyman | who preaches | Mountain | where you must climb up |
| Punish | if you gossip | | |
| Satchel | where you put your exercise-books | Quarrel | when one person says another thing than the other |
| Bed | when you sleep | | |
| Stork | what has a great beak | Impudence | to take something right away from somebody |
| Cupboard | where you put clothes | | |
| Pipe | where water goes through | Quick | when you run |
| | | Sleep | when the eyes are closed |
| Sheet | what you write upon | Strong | when you can lift something heavy |
| House | where people live in | | |
| Sofa | what you sit upon | Modest | when you don't say much |
| Soldier | who is in military service | | |
| | | Locksmith | who works with iron |
| Air | what floats about the earth | Free | after being shut in |

The form of the association with its numerous sentences, 70 per cent. beginning with *what the*, etc., conditions a reaction type which is deceptively similar, on a cursory examination, to the method of associations Wehrlin found in high-grade feeble-minded.

A more thorough examination shows that the similarity is only superficial and that the associations go far beyond that kind.

In comparison with the associations of imbeciles and idiots we have :

*Points in Common*

(1) In the majority of the associations the meaning of the stimulus-word is apprehended as if it were a question.

(2) The reaction is not automatic but is thought out with great attention and straining ; it has a tendency to explanation. The subject became emotional and reacted very slowly. (The experiment lasted three hours.)

(3) The reaction is in many words or whole sentences (70 per cent. with *where you, when you*).

(4) The formation of school sentences.

(5) The circumlocutions.

(6) The large number of associations of purpose and example.

(7) Many definitions (55 per cent.) and many tautologies.

(8) Many associations of activities.

*Points not in Common*

(1) The relatively large number (35 per cent.) of normal non-explanatory reactions in a single word, or with selected, appropriate, changing, objective, outer and value predicates, which show very few repetitions.

These reactions alone show that this subject stands above imbeciles in regard to wealth of words and understanding; for imbeciles when they use predicates do so monotonously, using very few words, perhaps *black* and *white*, throughout the whole experiment and using them most inappropriately.

(2) The ordinary coexistences and associations of activities.

(3) The almost complete absence of far-reaching and specialized general concepts (such as *tree — portion of; cherry — thing in the garden*), of superordinations, simple tautologies where the stimulus-word is explained by a synonym, diminutive, attribute, or by the opposite with the negative, such as: *mountain — a high mountain; flower — a mayflower; flower — a little flower; light — is not dark.*

(4) The greater developed power of abstraction. The examples and true definitions are more general and abstract, and generally explain the meaning of the stimulus-word neatly and sufficiently by bringing out the essential. We do not find here instances as we do in Wehrlin's idiots, where the subject explains the stimulus-word by some quite secondary, external and visible attribute, nor do we find the specially concrete examples of the idiot such as *prison — that's got a little window; father — he once threw me downstairs; hair — what gets cut; mountain — there's a tree upon which cherries grow.*

Although the father's associations are very near the son's qualitatively, externally they differ considerably; but the same tendency is present, as the following instances from the father's list show:

| | | | |
|---|---|---|---|
| Head | part of body | Stalk | part of plant |
| Wool | factory | Resin | sap of tree |
| Snake | reptile | Soldier | liable to service |
| Ink | liquid | State | corporation |
| Ship | means of transport | Table | furniture of room |
| Decency | human nature | Wall | part of house |
| Coal | stuff for burning | New | thing just made |
| Ill | natural thing | Goat | domestic animal |
| Hay | part of plant | Sail | part of ship's body |
| Coloured | colour combination | Plum | stone fruit |
| Talk | human need | Axe | tool |
| Despise | human vice | Tree | plant class |
| Clergyman | personality | Threaten | human wickedness |
| Book | reading matter | Copy-book | mass of paper |

2 E

| Angel | unseen being | Write | work |
|-------|--------------|-------|------|
| Bread | daily food | Mountain | a massive |
| Quick | rapid movement | Swim | bodily exercise |
| Folk | community | Month | calculation of time |
| Law | is caution | Hunger | bodily feeling |
| Quiet | human nature | | |

The subject is an extreme definition type. 85·5 per cent. of the associations have a defining quality, 60 per cent. of these being direct definitions. The subject showed strong emotion during the tests and endeavoured earnestly to give correct answers. The reaction-times were very long ; the experiment lasted two and a half hours. After repeated reminders to give the first reaction he could not be turned away from his association type.

In contrast with the son, the similarity of the associations with those of imbeciles are here rather in content than in form, whilst many of the associations sound like those of an affected hebephreniac. Here again we find the apprehension of the stimulus-word in the sense of a question and the tendency to explain or to define it. But the associations differ from those of the imbecile in many respects ; the superordinations are generally more appropriate and sufficiently characteristic of the content of the stimulus-word. Only occasionally do we come across general concepts used too specifically, and subordinations used too broadly, giving a very imperfect characteristic of the stimulus-word.

In contradistinction to the imbecile, the true definitions are more general and more abstract and really explain the stimulus-word. Associations such as *family — corporation ; fire — mass of heat ; song — combination of tunes ; sail — part of ship's body*, make a curious impression, scarcely explicable by want of intelligence. Such reactions, which one must regard as affected or extravagant, speak in favour of a lively impulse to react in " as educated " a way as possible. In this wise he seeks to compensate for a vivid feeling of inferiority (cp. Jung's *Psychology of Dementia Præcox*, p. 74). I have seen the same thing among intelligent people, e.g. in a student who was also a pronounced definition type but naturally expressed himself in a more educated way. The young man was somewhat embarrassed and obviously endeavoured not to display his intellectual nakedness before me. He could not have found any better way of demonstrating his embarrassment.

The comparison of father and son shows much similarity in their tendency of reaction, although the reactions appear outwardly very different ; this is again evidence that emotional factors play the chief part in the difference of reaction type.

The associations of mother and daughter also show an extreme adaptation to the meaning of the stimulus-word, but there was less embarrassment ; there was no special emphasis on the intellectual factor so distinctly found in father and son.   There is great agreement both in type and in individual reactions, as the following examples show :

| Stimulus-word | Mother | Daughter |
| --- | --- | --- |
| Angel | innocent | innocent |
| Haughty | bad boy | bad boy |
| Stalk | leek's stalk | stalks for soup |
| Dance | couple | gentleman and lady |
| Lake | much water | great |
| Threaten | father | father |
| Lamp | burns bright | gives light |
| Rich | king | king |
| New | dress | dress |
| Tooth | biting | pains |
| Take care | industrious pupil | pupil |
| Pencil | long | black |
| Law | God's command | Moses |
| Love | child | father and mother |
| Glass | light | breakable |
| Great | God | father |
| Potato | bulb | bulb |
| Hit | father | bad boy |
| Family | several persons | of five persons |
| Strange | traveller (male) | traveller (female) |
| Brother | loves me | love |
| Kiss | mother | mother |
| Fire | great pain | painful |
| Door | wide | big |
| Hay | dry | dry |
| Mock | shame | stupidity |
| Month | many days | thirty-one days |
| Air | cool | moist |
| Coal | sooty | black |
| Fruit | sweet | sweet |
| Make | father | parents |
| Jolly | happy child | little children |

These examples, which show a far-reaching similarity between mother and daughter, are still more striking on comparing the reactions of father and son.   According to Jung's calculations the difference between father and mother is 9·4, between mother and daughter 2, between father and son 4, between mother and son 7.   The son therefore is more like his father than is his mother by 2·4.

## FAMILY VIII

*An artisan family with the usual schooling and of medium in-telligence; it includes a sister of the mother who lives with the family.*

| Subjects | | Value predicates | Other predicates | Relationship of subject and object | Other inner associations | Outer associations | Clangs | Type |
|---|---|---|---|---|---|---|---|---|
| Father, | 37 years | 20 | 37·5 | 12 | 10·5 | 20 | — | predicate |
| Mother, | 35 ,, | 19 | 28·5 | 7·5 | 12·5 | 32·5 | — | ,, |
| Mother's sister, | 29 ,, | 12·5 | 35 | 17 | 13·5 | 18 | 3 | ,, |
| Daughter, | 15 ,, | 21·5 | 38 | 13 | 16·5 | 11 | — | ,, |
| ,, | 12 ,, | 22 | 44 | 14·5 | 7·5 | 12 | — | ,, |

The whole family present a definite predicate type. Like Families VI and VII with their twelve- and thirteen-year-old daughters, the twelve- and fifteen-year-old daughters have a more pronounced predicate type than the mother. The greatest agreement is found between father and the two daughters (D = 1·2 and 1·65), then between the two daughters (D = 1·8).

| Stimulus-word | Father | 1st daughter | 2nd daughter |
|---|---|---|---|
| Family | large | large | large |
| Time | perishes | short | long |
| Ground | deep | deep | firm |
| Sleeve | long | long | wide |
| Thousand | number | big number | big number |
| Smart | beautiful | new | big |
| Slate-pencil | short | pointed | black |
| Raspberry | sweet | good | sweet |
| Hedge | thorny | thick | long |
| Vinegar | sharp | sharp | bitter |
| To crack | glasses | egg | egg |

These examples will serve as illustrations of their common predicative adaptation. The mother's associations do not differ considerably from these. Her difference from the father is 2·6. Her type is rather more superficial than her husband's (12·5 more outer associations). Otherwise we find in her, as in her husband, a preponderance of indirect predicates as compared with value predicates (she belongs to the " reserved " predicate type). It is chiefly in consequence of her more superficial type that she differs by 3·6 from her daughters, who, as mentioned, present an intense predicate type.

The mother's sister, living with the family, likewise shows a similar predicate type, which approximates rather to the type of the daughters (her nieces) than to that of her sister (difference from her nieces 3, from her sister 4·4).   The cause of this difference is partly to be found in the fact that she, like her nieces, produces considerably more inner associations than their mother.   We shall investigate this relationship more closely in the following family.

FAMILY IX

*Artisan family.   Husband and wife of medium intelligence, unedu-cated.   The wife is the third sister of the wife in foregoing family ; has been married several years and lives in another milieu.*

| Subjects | Value predicates | Other predicates | Relationship of subject and object | Contrasts | Inner associations | Outer associations | Clangs | Type |
|---|---|---|---|---|---|---|---|---|
| Husband, 33 years . | 1 | 3·5 | 2·5 | 23·5 | 20·5 | 47 | 1·5 | Co-ordination |
| Wife,      34   „   . | 1·5 | 0·5 | 0·5 | 21·5 | 36 | 38·5 | 0·5 | „ |

This family exhibits a type diametrically opposed to the last one.   Only traces of predicates are present, whilst we find a surprising number of inner associations, especially of contrasts.

Whilst there were practically no contrasts in the last family (0·4 per subject), here they average 22·5.   There is an unusual agreement between husband and wife in their associations ($D = 1·4$), which seems the more remarkable for there is an appearance of the wife having possibly had another type formerly. We may perhaps venture to suppose, from the facts hitherto observed, that members of the same family approximate in type to one another, especially if they are of the same sex.   It is likely, therefore, that the wife did belong rather more to the type of her two sisters ; it was only subsequently, after her joint life with her husband, that she took on his type (i.e. acquired the same affective factors which produce the type).

By the following comparative results of this family and the two sisters of Family VIII the reader can judge of the differences in attitude, uninfluenced by any differences of views as to classification.

| Stimulus-word | 1st sister, mother in Family VIII | 2nd sister, Family VIII | 3rd sister, wife in Family IX | Her husband, Family IX |
|---|---|---|---|---|
| Ink | black | black | water | Indian ink |
| Bread | fresh | white | sweet | potatoes |
| Lamp | light | light | flower-vase | umbrella |

| Stimulus-word | 1st sister, mother in Family VIII | 2nd sister, Family VIII | 3rd sister, wife in Family IX | Her husband, Family IX |
|---|---|---|---|---|
| Tree | leafless | tall | shrub | root |
| Copy-book | dirty | thick | book | book |
| Book | thick | learned | album | copy-book |
| Pencil | black | short | penholder | ink |
| Sing | nice | entertaining | jump | laugh |
| Tooth | white | false | tongue | -ache |
| Flower | scent | red | bushes | grass |
| Water | cool | clear | milk | cold water |
| Dance | joy | waltz | jump | drink |
| Haughty | naughty child | little children | friendly | soft-hearted |
| Song | nice | hymn | music | zither |
| Potato | good | frozen | bean | carrots |
| Threaten | wicked | stupid | complain | to adjust |
| Manners | nice | in company | and customs | no manners |
| Family | big | widespread | congregation | sex |
| People | big | warlike | town | country |
| Foreign | wander | foreigner | home | liveable |
| False | bad | snake | friendly | like a cat |
| Fruit | good | dear | wine | vegetables |
| Public-house | great | frequented | shop | restaurant |
| Kiss | child | fiancé | cuddle | love |
| Blood | red | red | water | frog's blood |
| Love | love God | parents | praise | hate |

These examples will suffice to show the similarity between the first two sisters and the dissimilarity of the third. Jung's calculations show that the first and second sisters differ from the third by 8–8·8, whilst their difference from each other is only 4·4. Our classification may have its own defects and vagaries but such cases teach us that, at least, they suffice to express statistically such differences. Thus we have an instrument which enables us to reap the firstfruits in these still uncultivated fields.

## SUMMARY OF THE RESULTS

The material here reviewed consists of nine families with thirty-seven subjects aged from nine to seventy-four years. With the exception of one person who is rather more highly educated, all the subjects are quite uncultured. Only ten had attended the secondary schools for two years; the remaining twenty-six had only an elementary schooling; the persons all lived in an uncultured *milieu*. We were able to examine the relationship of inner to outer associations in regard to parents and children in six cases. In five families we experimented with both parents, in one family with the mother only. Let us first of all consider the relationship of mother and child and compare it with the results of Jung and Riklin.[1]

In three families all the children had more inner associations than the mother. The children were between nine and fifteen. In two families the youngest child (a thirteen- and a twenty-seven-year-old daughter respectively) had more inner, all the others more outer, associations than the mother. We can express these results in a formula : all children under sixteen have *more inner associations than the mother and (with one exception) all children over sixteen have more outer associations than the mother.*

The relationship of children to father is somewhat different. Eight children had more inner, and three more outer, associations than the father. No rule can be laid down as regards the age of the child. Hence Jung and Riklin's statement is only confirmed conditionally. A further result is that *the husbands tend to have more outer associations than their wives and, in general, the sons more than the daughters.* From this we may conclude that in my investigations the attention of the female subjects was less inhibited towards the experiment.

A comparison of brothers and sisters shows that in youth the sisters have a greater tendency towards inner associations, in the intermediate and later years the brothers have the greater tendency.

We are unable, so far as these tests are concerned, to draw any definite conclusions as to the effect of age ; we have considered the sisters and brothers, all the male and all the female subjects, and all the subjects in general, and we find enormous individual differences ; the conclusion of Ranschburg and Balint seem therefore to require revision. The examination of this question in married couples gave no results. In seven families the husband had more inner associations (the wives were aged between thirty-two and forty-four, the husbands aged between thirty-four and forty-six). In three cases the wives (aged between thirty-four and forty-six) had more inner associations than their husbands (aged from thirty-three to sixty). On the other hand, the more intelligent and better educated or better read individual of a married couple seems to have more outer associations.

The predicate type preponderates among these uneducated persons. The following table shows in individual figures

---

[1] Jung and Riklin, chapter ii, pp. 50–57, point out that there is not only a familial type relationship between mother and daughters, but apparently a regularly quantitative behaviour of the individual associations. This behaviour is such that as we proceed from the mother towards the youngest daughter the type become increasingly more superficial. They bring forward two cases of this, although with certain reservations.

and percentages the frequency of the individual types of associations :

Predicate type, 21 subjects = 54 % $\begin{cases}\text{Men} & \quad 8 \\ \text{Women} & : \quad 13\end{cases}$

Mixed type, 11 ,, = 29 % $\begin{cases}\text{Men} & \quad 6 \\ \text{Women} & : \quad 5\end{cases}$

Definition type, 2 ,, = 5 % (father and son)
Co-ordination type, 2 ,, = 5 % (husband and wife)
Superficial type, 2 ,, = 5 % (women)

Besides the twenty-one persons of the predicate type having more than 40 per cent. predicates, there were six persons in the mixed type with a great number of predicates ; in them the number of predicates exceeded the numbers of all the other chief groups, such as co-ordination, coexistences, and motor-speech reactions. If we add these six of the mixed type with their predicative tendency to the predicate type we have twenty-seven persons of the predicate type = 72 per cent. of all the subjects.

The frequency of the predicate type is rather greater in women (seventeen women to ten men), which corresponds with the findings of Jung and Riklin.

The remaining types are so poorly represented in this material that nothing definite or characteristic can be said about them, with the exception of the *definition type*, which was seen exclusively in males, both in its pure form and in a mixed form (three cases). Jung and Riklin have put forward the hypothesis that the predicate type corresponds to a psychological peculiarity, which is even preserved during artificial distraction (chapter ii, p. 160). They hold that the mechanism of the predicate type consists in the primary appearance of vivid pictures which by reason of their powerful emotional tone give rise to a corresponding subjectively coloured, predicative, verbal reaction. From my tests I can but confirm their view of a marked emotional factor. But it is difficult to say upon what psychological factor this predicate attitude rests. An accidental individual complex can hardly be the cause ; the type is too common and likewise too familial for that. The most probable supposition seems to me to be that this arises out of a general emotional attitude towards the experimenter. The frequency of the predicate type makes it worth while to study its occurrence more accurately ; let us first of all consider its quantitative behaviour in males and females.

The ratio of value predicates to other predicates is, in males,

1 : 1·55 ; in females, 1 : 0·84. That means that among men the positive predicate predominates as against the subjectively toned value predicates ; in women it is the reverse.

How does the predicate type behave as regards different age periods ?

We will first investigate the ages between ten and forty and then between forty-one and eighty ; we get these results :

*In men :*

Years 10–40, value predicates : objective predicates = 1 : 2·17
,,   41–80,  ,,       ,,        ,,        ,,     = 1 : 1·27

*In women :*

Years 10–40, value predicates : objective predicates = 1 : 1·14
,,   41–80,  ,,       ,,        ,,        ,,     = 1 : 0·38

In both groups there is seen a greater tendency to value predicates in age than in youth ; greater in women than in men. In women the preponderance of value predicates begins at forty-one years, in men only at sixty-one years (from sixty-one to eighty years the ratio among men is 1 : 0·68 ; from forty-one to sixty years it is 1 : 2·14).

Should these figures be confirmed we should be able to say that in these experiments the disposition peculiar to the predicate type, i.e. an increase of the subjective tendency, undergoes a considerable increase in women about the fortieth year, but in men much later, about the sixtieth year. If we venture to regard this tendency as an inflow of more personal emotions, it must be accepted that about this period of life there are important changes in the affective disposition.

We can give the main classes in the following percentages so far as regards the general figures of the individual groups :

|  | Male subjects | Female subjects |
|---|---|---|
|  | Per cent. | Per cent. |
| Inner associations   .   .   . | 76·9 (40·5) | 78·9 (46·6) |
| Outer   ,,   .   .   .   . | 21   (55·6) | 19·7 (49·4) |
| Clang-reactions   .   .   .   . | 0·1 (0·6) | 0·2 (0·7) |
| Remainder group .   .   .   . | 0·1 (2·4) | 0·7 (2·3) |

The figures in parentheses are the corresponding ones from the work of Jung and Riklin (chapter ii). In contrast to theirs, my figures show a considerable preponderance of inner associations. This difference cannot be due to classification, for Dr. Jung confirmed my conclusions and compared my material with his earlier one. Besides, the important differences in those reactions where abnormalities are easily recognized (clang-reactions and remainder group) show that it is not a question of classification. The difference must be in the material. Jung and Riklin took as their uneducated subjects the male and female attendants of the asylum, whilst my material was gathered from persons less intellectual and of a lower social grade. Another circumstance is probably not without importance : in Jung and Riklin's experiments the persons were in the service of the experimenters ; this influences the affectivity. The increase of inner associations as the intelligence and social scale decreases, as shown by the figures, is the expression of a well-known fact, which has been fully explained in earlier chapters. The finding of Jung and Riklin corresponds to the rather more superficial type of reaction in men as compared with women. The details of the individual classes are shown in the following table.

| Kind of association | Males | Females |
|---|---|---|
| Co-ordination . . . . . . | 10·1 | 9 |
| Sub- and supra-ordination . . . . | 6·4 | 5 |
| Contrast . . . . . . . | 2·6 | 1·7 |
| Value predicates . . . . . . | 12·9 | 24·6 |
| Objective and outer predicates . . . | 23·2 | 24 |
| Subject and object relationship . . . | 9·7 | 12·1 |
| Definition of place, time, means, purpose, etc.. | 1·8 | 1·5 |
| Definition . . . . . . . | 10·2 | 1 |
| Coexistence . . . . . . . | 9·2 | 6·2 |
| Identity . . . . . . . | 1·7 | 1·6 |
| Verbal-motor connexion . . . . | 7·1 | 7·7 |
| Neologisms . . . . . . . | 3 | 4·2 |
| Word-completion . . . . . . | — | 0·2 |
| Clang-association . . . . . . | 0·1 | — |
| Remainder group (fault, meaningless, indirect). | 0·1 | 0·7 |

Among the inner associations the greatest difference is in the number of value predicates. Jung and Riklin pointed out a preference among women, especially among the uneducated, for the predicate type. The difference ought to come out markedly here, because I have separated the individual predicates as far as practicable, whilst they were all reckoned together by Jung and Riklin. The difference lies, we find, chiefly in the value predicates. Another prominent difference is the *preference of the definition* type by men. The above figures show that the female subjects have a subjective " personal " attitude, whilst the men have generally an objective intellectual attitude. Whilst in Jung and Riklin's figures the remainder group, which chiefly contains the results of disturbance, shows higher figures, on the average, among men, here the women have the higher figure. Whether this is related to the sex of the experimenter or is a merely accidental difference is hard to say.

The familial agreements in the tendency of the reaction, which I found to be qualitative and pointed out in the individual cases, have been worked out by Jung statistically. Based upon 268 comparisons of unrelated men and women in my material, requiring 8000 single comparisons, the mean difference of non-related men is 5·9 and of non-related women is 6. These mean figures are valuable because they give a measure for the estimation of the intrafamilial differences, clearly shown in the following figures.

The mean difference of related men is 4·1, that of women 3·8. These figures are considerably lower than the difference of non-related persons, and we may conclude that relations have, on the whole, a tendency to agree in their reaction type. The mean deviation [1] of the series of figures lying at the base of the first figures amounts to 1·2, that of the latter is 1·5. The difference among the men rests, therefore, upon a series of fairly uniform composition, whilst the mean difference among the women is composed of an unequal series. Verbally expressed : Some related women differ very strongly, whilst others agree in their reaction type much more than do related men.

Mean difference between fathers and children  : 4·2 (2·4)
,,          ,,          ,,    mothers and children : 3·5 (1·0)

(The figure in brackets is the mean deviation of the mean.)

Mothers and children present a relatively strong and uniform agreement, whilst fathers and children, on the whole, agree less, although there are some exceptions where there is close agreement, as the high figure for mean deviation shows.

Mean difference between fathers and sons       : 3·1 (0·6)
,,          ,,          ,,    mothers and daughters : 3   (1·0)
,,    fathers and daughters  : 4·9 (3·5)
,,    mothers and sons       : 4·7 (1·2)

[1] The mean deviation is calculated in this way : first calculate how much each figure of the whole series differs from the arithmetical mean of the series, add the difference figures, and divide the sum by their amount. The quotient gives the mean deviation of the mean.

The agreement between fathers and sons is almost uniformly even, likewise that between mothers and daughters. The crossed relationships show the same thing by their relatively high differential values :

Mean difference of brothers among themselves   : 4·7 (14)
    ,,     ,,   ,, sisters    ,,     ,,     : 5·1 (2·4)

Brothers show a relatively slight agreement, that of the sisters is still less ; but the figure for the mean deviation of the mean shows that there are exceptions. This is at once seen when one excludes the married sisters from the comparison :

Mean difference of unmarried brothers among themselves : 4·8 (1·0)
   ,,    ,,    ,,    ,,   sisters    ,,     ,,    : 3·4 (1·7)

Whilst the difference among brothers does not alter essentially, the difference among sisters sinks considerably. This signifies that the married sisters differ considerably among themselves but not the single ones. It would seem that marriage disturbs the agreement in reaction type (in so far as the husband may belong to another type ?).

Mean difference of brothers and sisters : 4·4 (1·5)

In this relationship a relatively uniform, slight agreement seems to prevail.

Mean difference of husband and wife : 4·7 (3·2)

Here we note a fairly slight average agreement, which, however, varies very greatly, i.e. there are cases of higher agreement, and others of the greatest divergence. This was already brought out in the presentation of the individual families.

The best and most uniform agreement is found among parents and their children of the same sex. The children differ more among themselves than from their parents ; they differ more from the father than from the mother ; the daughters approximate more to their mothers than do sons to their fathers. Unmarried daughters agree in their reactions among themselves more than do unmarried sons, just as related women in general agree more among themselves than do related men. Marriage seems only exceptionally to lead to a greater agreement of the pair.

*Tabular Summary of some Cases of Familial Agreement and Difference*

| Kind of association | Husband | His wife | Father | Mother | Daughter | Father | 1st daughter | 2nd daughter | Father | Son | Mother | Daughter |
|---|---|---|---|---|---|---|---|---|---|---|---|---|
| Co-ordination | 16·5 | 33·5 | 6·5 | 0·5 | — | 7 | 7 | 4 | 3 | 8·5 | 17·5 | 13·5 |
| Sub- and supra-ordination | 4 | 2·5 | 7 | — | — | 3·5 | 9 | 2·5 | 23·5 | 3 | 5·5 | 7 |
| Contrast | 23·5 | 21·5 | — | — | — | — | — | — | — | — | 0·5 | 0·5 |
| Value predicates | 1 | 1·5 | 8·5 | 95 | 98 | 20 | 21·5 | 22 | 3·5 | 2 | 5·5 | 7 |
| Objective and outer predicates | 3·5 | 0·5 | 21 | 3·5 | 0·5 | 37·5 | 38 | 44 | 1 | 15 | 30·5 | 32·5 |
| Subject and object relationship | 2·5 | 0·5 | 15·5 | 0·5 | — | 12 | 13 | 14·5 | 2·5 | 6·5 | 18·5 | 22·5 |
| Definition of place, time, etc. | 0·5 | — | 11 | — | — | — | — | 0·5 | — | 4 | 0·5 | 3 |
| Definition | — | — | 11 | — | — | — | 0·5 | 0·5 | 60 | 55·5 | 8 | 3·5 |
| Co-existence | 20·5 | 20 | 1·5 | — | — | 6·5 | 5 | 1·5 | 0·5 | 2 | 1 | 4·5 |
| Identity | 2 | 2 | 0·5 | 0·5 | 1·5 | 1·5 | 1 | — | 4·5 | 0·5 | 4 | — |
| Verbal-motor connexion | 16 | 14·5 | 12 | — | — | 9·5 | 4·5 | 7·5 | 1 | 2 | 6·5 | 4 |
| Neologisms | 8·5 | 2 | 6 | — | — | 2·5 | 0·5 | 3 | 0·5 | 1 | 1·5 | 2 |
| Word-completion | 0·5 | — | — | — | — | — | — | — | — | — | — | — |
| Clang-association | 1 | 0·5 | — | — | — | — | — | — | — | — | — | — |
| Remainder group | — | 1 | — | — | — | — | — | — | — | — | 0·5 | — |

The whole material is too limited for these figures to be regarded as authoritative and final ; they should be merely considered as indications.

Finally, let me express my best thanks to Professor Bleuler for his stimulus in this work, and especially to Dr. Jung for his kind co-operation and valuable advice when carrying it out.

CHAPTER XII

# ON THE PSYCHOGALVANIC PHENOMENON IN ASSOCIATION EXPERIMENTS

By Dr. L. BINSWANGER

## PART I

INTRODUCTION : HISTORICAL SURVEY : TECHNIQUE OF THE
EXPERIMENTS

At the instance of Dr. Jung I have carried out association
experiments as modified at the Zurich psychiatric clinic on
twenty-three healthy persons, who during the entire experiment
were subjected to a very feeble electric current.

The source was in most cases one Bunsen cell of not more than 15 volts
tension ; the electrodes were made of thin brass plates which were placed on
the hands. In the current there was inserted a sensitive Deprez-d'Arsonvals
mirror-galvanometer (constants : $5100 = 10^{.10}$ amperes : $0.08$ mm. in dia-
meter), which registered the fluctuations of the current during the experiment ; there was also a shunt which reduced the oscillations of the current
upon the galvanometer and quickly brought the excursions of the mirror
to rest again.[1] A celluloid scale divided into millimetres and centimetres, with
a lamp upon it, was placed one metre from the galvanometer, the lamp throwing
a perpendicular beam of light upon the galvanometer mirror. The variations
of the mirror and the variations in the strength of the current are measured by
the excursions of the beam of light upon the scale.[2]

When associations are carried out with this arrangement
it is noticed that in almost any reaction under normal conditions
the beam of light undergoes a greater or lesser excursion on the
scale ; at first this is in the direction of the conducting current
(in our tests always from left to right) ; it then halts a moment,
thereupon returning again to the proximity of its first position.
This excursion of the beam of light, which corresponds to a change
in the strength of the current in our circuit, is called the galvanic

[1] S. Veraguth, " Das psychogalvanische Reflexphänomen," I. Bericht,
*Monatsschrift für Psych. und Neurol.*, Bd. XXI, Heft 5, p. 387. We always
placed the stopper contact at 1/1.

[2] Cp. Jung, " On Psychophysical Relations of the Association Experiment,"
*Journal of Abnormal Psychology*, vol. i, p. 247. The entire arrangement of the
tests is given there in detail with a figure of the apparatus.

deviation. As psychical processes in the subject influence the changes in the strength of the current, we designate the whole phenomenon, after Veraguth, as the psychogalvanic phenomenon.

Attempts to connect galvanic changes with psychical processes are not new. The history of these attempts shows two widely separated movements which originally were quite distinct. In these movements (Tarchanoff,[1] Sticker [2]) the reactions of the subject towards a current were not investigated, but the currents which occur on the superficies of the skin of the subject during psychical processes were directly measured. For this purpose unpolarized electrodes were used, by means of which the current is led through the galvanometer. I agree with Tarchanoff, despite Sticker's objection, that this is essentially a measurement of the secretory current of the skin (sweat glandular system). The experiments of Sommer and Fürstenau [3] form a transition from the first method to the second, to which latter we adhere. They used zinc and charcoal plates as electrodes but without using any galvanic cell as the source of the current. I speak of this method as a transition because it is still partly a question of " secretory currents " [4] ; to this, however, a second factor is added, which probably plays the chief part : changes in the resistance of the subject to electrical conduction. This method can be combined with the second method by using a galvanic cell as well as electrodes of zinc and charcoal.[5]

Féré [6] was the first to make investigations of the effect of psychical processes upon the changes in resistance to electrical conduction ; he applied sensory stimuli to his subjects.

From a certain point of view one might include here the investigations begun in 1878 by Romain Vigouroux [7] on hysterics

[1] Tarchanoff, " Ueber die galvanischen Erscheinungen in der Haut des Menschen bei Reizungen der Sinnesorgane und bei verschiedenen Formen der psychischen Tätigkeit," *Pflüger's Archiv.*, 1890, Bd. XLVI.

[2] Sticker, " Ueber Versuche einer objectiven Darstellung von Sensibilitäts-störungen," *Wiener klin. Rundschau*, 1897, Nos. 30 and 31.

[3] Sommer und Fürstenau, " Die elektrische Vorgänge an der menschlichen Haut," *Klinik für psychische und nervöse Krankheiten*, Bd. I, Heft 3, 1906.

[4] It should not, however, be forgotten that we are dealing here with currents which owe their origin to the potential difference between skin and electrodes, whilst the true secretory currents arise entirely in the living body.

[5] The latter must then, of course, be placed in the direction of the circulating current.

[6] Féré, " Note sur des modifications de la résistance électrique sous l'influence des excitations sensorielles et des émotions," *Comptes rendus hebdomadaires des Séances et Mémoires de la Société de Biologie*, 1888, p. 217 ff. Féré remarks that the resistance diminishes " sous l'influence d'émotions sthéniques " and increases under " l'absence d'excitations," p. 218.

[7] R. Vigouroux, " Sur la résistance électrique considérée comme signe clinique," *Le Progrès medical*, 1888, Semestre I, pp. 45 and 86.

and Graves's disease and those made by his nephew, A. Vigouroux,[1] on melancholics. These works show us clearly the effect of psychic factors upon the electrical resistance of the human body. In 1904 the engineer E. K. Müller made experiments in Zurich upon " the changes in physical resistance to the galvanic current "; Veraguth[2] learnt the phenomena from these experiments, to which Jung[3] then drew attention.

I cannot enter here into the physical and physiological sides of the phenomenon. So far it seems to me that even with the tests in a conducting current the sweat-glandular system plays a great part. That does not mean that we only deal with sweat perceptible to our senses, but rather that it is a question " of the secretory process brought about by stimulation of the nerves." I am here in agreement with the views expressed by Biedermann[4] in his *Electrical Physiology* (" On the Electro-motor Effects of Epithelial and Sweat Cells "). That the secretion of sweat is intimately bound up with psychical processes is current knowledge, experimentally proved by Adamkiewicz[5] in 1878. Nevertheless, despite numerous experiments we are still in the region of hypothesis, and do not even know if we really measure the same physiological processes under different arrangements of the experiments.

All these investigators noticed the influence of psychical action upon the galvanic processes. Tarchanoff,[6] who seems to have been the first to confirm the connexion of sweating with psychical activity, concludes : " Nearly every kind of nerve action, although there may be a time limit, from the simplest impressions and sensations to the highest mental activity and spontaneous motor expression, is accompanied by increased activity of the sweat glands." He regards this increased activity of the sweat glands as the cause of the variation in the electric current, shown by the galvanometer. Sticker[7] writes : " I have repeatedly convinced myself that the origin of the galvanic skin phenomenon is under the influence of exciting mental impressions, and that the will has no effect upon it ; this reflex could be used with great advantage for the discovery of words and pictures

[1] A. Vigouroux, *Étude sur la résistance électrique chez les mélancoliques.* Thèse de Paris, 1890.

[2] Veraguth, loc. cit., p. 387.

[3] Jung, loc. cit.

[4] Biedermann, *Elektrophysiologie* (Jena, 1895). See also Hermann, *Lehrbuch der Physiologie*, 12th edition, p. 145 ff.

[5] Adamkiewicz, *Die Sekretion des Schweisses : Eine bilateralsymmetrische Nervenfunktion.* (Berlin : Hirschwald, 1878.)

[6] Tarchanoff, loc. cit., p. 53.

[7] Sticker, loc. cit., p. 518.

that influence the emotions.  In a word—which will be listened to by many without any reaction—whoever takes the meaning of something to heart will react with a strong galvanic skin phenomenon.  Whoever is from any cause emotionally roused on looking at a picture will react with a definite increase of the current ; whilst whoever is unmoved by the picture, or in whom it arouses no memory, will have no skin excitation." Sticker calls attention to the forensic importance of the phenomenon.

Sommer, on the other hand, writes :  " We have not observed with any certainty that psychical processes have any influence, such as Tarchanoff has noticed, upon the current, apart from the reaction phenomena after tickling."  When some psychical influence does occur, as after fright, it is conditioned, according to Sommer and Fürstenau, by the muscular contractions that arise and the contact changes thus caused in the electrodes. We shall see later that such muscular contractions do now and then play a part in the psychogalvanic experiment, but they do not explain the whole phenomenon.

A. Vigouroux, referring to Féré on this point, says :  " Ce dernier observe que la résistance électrique de ces sujets (he is dealing with hysterics) est diminué par le fait d'excitations sensorielles diverses, visuelles (verres colorés), auditives (diapason à poids), gustatives, olfactives, etc." ;  and adds :  " On pourrait également rapprocher de ces faits la diminution de la résistance chez les malades atteints de la maladie de Basedow : une émotivité extrême est, en effet, la caractéristique de l'état mental de ces malades." [1]

Müller [2] writes :  " Toute influence psychique, propre ou étrangère, a pour effet immédiat, les cas échéants, une énorme différence dans les résultats de mesurage (diminution de la résistance jusqu'à $\frac{1}{3}-\frac{1}{5}$)."

Veraguth insists as clearly as possible upon the effect of psychical factors, especially of the emotions, in sensory and psychical stimuli causing changes in the current. [3]  But when he says (p. 420), " It is not the emotional tone alone which conditions the strength of the galvanic reaction ; in higher psychical stimuli further factors to be considered are their actuality," I must submit that the division of these two factors does not seem necessary.  The only concept we can frame about *actuality* is surely its increased emotional tone in regard to non-present things.

---

[1] A. Vigouroux, loc. cit., 46 ; Féré, loc. cit., p. 218.

[2] *Conférence expérimentale de M. le directeur E. K. Müller à Zurich à la Société suisse des Sciences naturelles (Section médicale)*.  I am indebted for this quotation to Dr. Veraguth.

[3] Veraguth, loc. cit., p. 420 ff.

It is noticed that stronger deviations occur when a stimulus-word arouses a presentation which is "actual" for the subject, i.e. one which occupied him just before or during the test; it is stronger than when a complex is touched which years ago played some part. But "actuality" is not an addition to the emotional tone, the actuality is the emotional tone; it is only another expression for "increased emotional tone."

I have myself avoided the word "actual" because we can always replace it by the less dubious expression "emotionally toned." In many cases, moreover, it is difficult to say whether a complex is really actual for the subject in Veraguth's sense. The analysis in many cases discloses undoubted relationships of an "old" complex to the present; in the same way an apparently "actual" complex, which momentarily seems very much to occupy the subject, may derive its essential affect from events of long ago. Both will come to light quite clearly in Test I. For this reason also I have avoided the designation "actual."

This survey of the views of other authors shows us that they nearly all have observed deviations at emotionally toned psychical processes only. Tarchanoff alone claims to have found galvanometric changes in "every kind of nerve action." At all events, in our experiments with the conducted current we could only perceive that the psychogalvanic phenomenon occurred in affective processes. With associations indifferent to the subject, which aroused no emotion, there was no deviation, any more than when reading something indifferent (an observation that Veraguth had already made) or on adding up easy figures, which entail no effort. In the same way purely intellectual sensations produce no deviation when their emotional tone is lowered (e.g. by repetition); this we shall call attention to in the section on physical movements and deep inspiration. Naturally the expressions "not emotionally toned," "purely intellectual," must be taken *cum grano salis*. They are entirely relative to the order of the research as a whole, and particularly to the sensitiveness of the galvanometer used. Reactions which evoke no response in one galvanometer, which are for us therefore "not emotionally toned," may evoke response in a more sensitive instrument. Hence it is very important to consider the sensitiveness of the galvanometer. With an extremely sensitive instrument we could receive responses during an indifferent reading, addition, etc., for we are never in a state completely devoid of emotion—free from innervations altogether.

To Veraguth are due our thanks for having been the first to take associations with the galvanometer: he noticed that the association curve moved in an ascending line, in contradistinction to the "rest curve" (which is obtained when the subject sits quietly, taking as little part as possible) ; that in the same person different words evoke extremely different changes in the curves, that those stimulus-words which touch an "actual emotional complex" produce stronger fluctuations than indifferent words. He also observed that the excursions are stronger when the subject reacts by words than when he does not, and that the first (indifferent) stimulus-words usually evoke stronger fluctuations than the later indifferent ones. Tarchanoff had previously determined the influence of expectation upon the galvanic phenomenon ; Veraguth noticed its occurrence in association experiments (fluctuation from expectation).[1]

Besides these psychological effects upon the galvanic phenomenon there are a great number of physiological and physical effects which we cannot here consider. In so far as they influence the experiment they will be discussed later. We shall just mention the enormous effect of cold and warmth and the degree of moisture of the epidermis upon the conducting powers of the skin.[2] If despite these effects we still regard the psychogalvanic phenomenon as an invaluable instrument in the analysis of the emotions, it is because we were able to convince ourselves in the course of months of investigations that the psychological factors can generally be separated pretty easily from the others ; when the former are at all pronounced we may disregard the physical and physiological influences. Of course these psychological factors, in order to be noted by the galvanometer, must of themselves produce physiological and physical changes, which will be of an extremely fine kind. In the striking promptness and exactitude found in the connexion between the galvanic phenomenon and the psychical processes there can be no question of gross physical (or chemical) processes interpolated between the two. Above all, it is no question of processes which, once aroused, pursue their path independently of psychical events ; rather are we constrained to admit processes whose course is continually controlled, furthered, or stayed by the central organ.

The experiments demand no further detailed description. Of the thirty subjects, tests in twenty-three were undertaken with the conducted circuit and brass or nickel electrodes, in two with the conducted circuit and "water contact," in five with the Sommer-Fürstenau arrangement (zinc and charcoal

---

[1] Cp. Veraguth, "Der psychophysische galvanische Reflex," *Bericht über den II. Kongress für experimentelle Psychologie*, pp. 219–224. (Barth: Leipzig, 1907.)

[2] Hermann, loc. cit., pp. 303, 305, especially E. du Bois-Reymond, *Untersuchungen über tierische Elektrizität*, Bd. II, chapter viii, section 4. (Berlin, 1849.)

electrodes or galvanic cell). We shall return to this in reviewing the single groups.

### *Reading off and Registering the Galvanometer Deviations : Determining and Marking the Reaction-time*

The subject is instructed, as usual, how to react and is requested to avoid all movement as far as possible ; this is not asking too much, for the sitting only lasts thirty to forty minutes, and the patient can rest quite comfortably. The test is then begun. Before calling out the stimulus-word a glance is given at the scale and the place noted where the beam of light (its right margin) persists. The stimulus-word is called out, and as a rule a galvanometer deviation follows at once. The deviation is taken to be the greatest excursion which the beam of light makes in a positive direction on the scale. As soon as the positive fluctuation returns again, i.e. becomes negative, the beginning and end of the excursion are written down.[1] The reaction-word is then noted, and then, last of all, the reaction-time ; the latter is fixed by the one-fifth second watch, whilst the two former data must be kept in the memory. The reaction-time is determined by pressing on the button of the watch held in the left hand at the moment the stimulus- and reaction-words are pronounced. At first it is easy to forget this because the experimenter's attention is taken up with observing the beam of light. But it soon becomes automatic. At the reproduction test it is best to calculate the difference in the figures noted for the deviation and to write it down. For each reaction there is the following schedule :

| Stimulus-word | Deviation | Reaction-word | Time in $\frac{1}{5}$ sec. | Deviation absolute in mm. | Reproduction[2] |
|---|---|---|---|---|---|
| Head . | 12·5–14 | nice | 9 | 15 | ± |

At the conclusion of the test the *reproduction* test is at once carried out. When the subject does not remember the reaction-word or states it incorrectly, or when he has to reflect about it a long time, it is nearly always a question of disturbance from some emotionally toned presentation complex. We then speak of

---

[1] It not infrequently occurs that whilst writing it down the negative deviation again changes into a positive one ; this arises from perseveration or from fresh emotional tone, and would in any case be noticed in the subsequent reactions since these would begin with a higher figure. If the subsequent positive fluctuation is again followed by a negative one, it is best to correct the lower figure that has been written down by adding the second positive movement to the first.

[2] Here we only give the absolute value of the deviation. Its height on the scale can be read off on the accompanying curves, at least for the big analyses. In the reproduction test the — sign will be given or the incorrect reaction. No sign means that the reproductions are correct.

disturbances of reproduction.[1] It may be here said that the complex which causes the disturbance in reproduction need not necessarily be contained in the particular reaction, it may have been incited in one of the previous reactions. It must not be, therefore, assumed that in the reaction where there is disturbance in reproduction there is a complex. To which reaction the disturbance in reproduction is due must be cleared up by other means.

The analysis is then added after the reproduction test. These can be combined. The figures of the movements and the reaction-times are exhibited graphically by the " bar " method, as seen in the illustration. The original curves are shown on 2 mm. paper, 1 mm. of the paper corresponding to 1 mm. of the scale, and each one-fifth second is expressed by 1 mm. In the reproduction of the curves in this work the relationships have all been reduced by one-half. In the presentation of the galvanometer deviations it was found necessary, instead of placing the absolute values on an abscissa side by side, to express also their position to one another ; this was done by placing the deviations on the paper directly after their course on the scale. It is only in this way that we get a curve of any real use. The reaction-times are shown by the " bars " placed next one another on the abscissa. The deviation and the time pertaining to it are placed exactly on top of each other. Faults in this method are easily recognized. But it had the great advantage of showing the individual deviations directly and clearly, and that is the chief thing.

Jung [2] devised a very beautiful method for registering the movements but it was less useful for our purpose ; he devised a movable slide which follows the beam of light on the side. A pulley transfers the movements of the slide to a kymograph. This method is indispensable for finer investigations, but it had the disadvantage for us that it requires two experimenters, and that it does not give a good general view (100 associations may take up a roll of paper of almost 2 metres).

*The Tempo of the Test : Latent Time : Oscillations due to Expectation*

The *tempo* in which the words are called out deserves a few remarks. The pauses should not be too long between the individual reactions, so as to avoid the interpolation of too many

[1] Jung, " Experimentelle Beobachtungen über das Erinnerungsvermögen," *Centralblatt für Nervenheilkunde und Psychiatrie*, Bd. XXVIII; also chapter 10.

[2] " On Psychophysical Relations of the Association Experiment," *Journal of Abnormal Psychology*, vol. i, No. 6.

fresh ideas which are not directly conditioned by the reactions, but sufficient time must be allowed for the positive oscillation which sometimes follows the negative one to come to rest ; this takes longer with strong than with weak deviations. I took a middle course by only slightly varying the pauses, waiting rather longer when the movements were strong but not for the negative oscillation to cease entirely, if it did not last too long. In time one learns fairly well to estimate how far a deviation will follow from the *tempo*. If the stimulus-word is pronounced whilst there is still a negative oscillation this will continue for a time until it changes into a new positive one. The time spent between the occurrence of the psychical process and its galvanic expression is the *latent time*.[1]

A further reason for not waiting too long between the single reactions is the occurrence of oscillations due to *expectation*. If there is no stimulus-word for a longish time there suddenly occurs, quite regularly with some subjects, an oscillation when the subject believes the next stimulus-word is about to be given. These expectation oscillations can be beautifully exhibited on the kymograph, and they show that these occur as a rule just before pronouncing the new stimulus-word. Several such expectation-waves can be obtained one after another if one waits long enough. Raising one's eyes from the association formula and looking at the scale often suffices to obtain an expectation oscillation. For the experimenter to look at the scale generally means calling out a new stimulus-word, and the subject then becomes disposed to concentrate his attention on the coming stimulus-word. In other words, he is in a state of " strained expectancy "—a concentration of the attention upon what is to come (Lehmann).[2] It is better, therefore, for the subject not to observe the experimenter. By an approximately uniform *tempo* the expectation oscillations are for the most part excluded. When they do occur they can generally be separated from the fluctuations due to the stimulus-word itself, for there is a slight pause between the two ; the expectation oscillation often falls a little so that an interval may be noticed between the two on the kymograph curve. It is then that we must separate this expectation oscillation from that due to the stimulus which follows, for it has nothing to do with the stimulus-word in question. It only gives us

[1] The latent time can be always observed whether the mirror is at rest or in movement. According to our observations it varies between 1·5 and 5 seconds if the electrodes are placed on the hands.

[2] We shall often have occasion to consider the influence of attention upon the psychogalvanic phenomenon. I refer the reader to the section upon attention in Bleuler's book, *Affektivität, Suggestibilität, Paranoia* (Halle, 1906), p. 31, where Bleuler is very insistent that attention is nothing but a " special case of affect."

information about the degree of attention which the subject is
giving to the experiment.

### CONCERNING THE EFFECT OF BODILY MOVEMENTS AND DEEP INSPIRATION ON THE PSYCHOGALVANIC PHENOMENON

We shall here only consider such movements as change the
contact between the subject's hands and the electrodes ; chiefly,
then, movements of the hands and arms, but of the legs also
if these are of such a nature as to affect the subject's position as
a whole.  Such fluctuations in the current caused by contact
alterations to the electrodes are readily recognized, for they are
much more brusque than those psychically determined, and display
no temporal or psychological connexion with the particular reactions.  It is often a question of negative oscillations.  If a disturbing oscillation of this kind arises one must wait before going on until
it has spent itself.  For later orientation I marked at the appropriate place in the list of words, " Moved." With strong disturbances the experiment is interrupted.  Not to exaggerate the
contact changes, it may be added that within narrow limits their
effect is very slight as compared with that due to psychological
causes.  On pressing voluntarily a little harder on the electrodes
so that a distinct movement of the hand is just noticed, one
occasionally obtains slighter galvanometer movements than with
emotional reactions when the hand is quite at rest.  To produce
such strong galvanometer deviations as many persons make at
strong complexes one would have to press with a good deal of
force upon the electrodes.  Besides these voluntary movements,
which occur when the subject finds his position uncomfortable
and wants to change it, involuntary movements may also have
a share.  Many subjects themselves admit that they had felt
that they had pressed now and then more strongly upon the
electrodes at complex than at indifferent reactions.  We must
not regard this kind of " movements " as faults, for they take
place quite regularly at any increased stimulus of affectivity [1]
and increase the fluctuation set up by other processes of innervation.  We here quite agree with Sommer [2] when he says that
involuntary movements affect in a remarkable degree the strength
of the circuit.  But since we know that in the use of water
contact, when the hands and electrodes do not touch, the psychogalvanic phenomenon likewise occurs, we cannot regard the

[1] We use the term affectivity in Bleuler's sense.  He understands thereby
not only affects in the ordinary sense, but also slight feelings or tones of pleasure
and unpleasure at every possible kind of experience.

[2] Sommer and Fürstenau, loc. cit., p. 202.  Cp. E. du Bois-Reymond, loc.
cit., Bd. II, p. 321 ff.

changes in contact of the electrodes as the essential condition for the occurrence of the phenomenon.[1] Besides increased pressure on the electrodes the movements of the muscles may also increase the galvanometer movements by exciting the activity of the sweat glands (cp. du Bois-Reymond's experiment and its interpretation by Hermann [2]).

We are not always justified in regarding what occurs at deep inspirations (laughter and coughing) as *faults*. We must distinguish between those which are entirely accidental, caused by fatigue, and those which we must regard as "complex indicators," standing in close relationship to the affectivity, like the involuntary increased pressure on the electrodes. This occurred very noticeably in a young lady who, whenever she could not find the reaction-word (and Jung has shown that this is almost invariably due to emotion), heaved a deep sigh. The complex reactions in question are strongly shown on the galvanometer curve. Very deep inspirations can so affect the strength of the current that as the whole thorax rises, contact with the electrodes becomes loosened. There is then a brusque negative oscillation. That seldom occurs. Much more frequently the deep inspiration, sighing, works by and through the emotional tone only which produces it. The emotional tone connected with the sigh can act more powerfully upon the physical expression of that feeling than the sigh by itself would have evoked. But if the sigh is rather accidental, due, say, to fatigue, it can itself produce a strong emotional tone by reason of its associative connexion with ideas of grief, anxiety, worry, etc. That a sigh does not affect the strength of the current apart from its accompanying emotional tone follows from the experiments of Jung and Peterson,[3] who often caused their subjects to make deep inspirations in quick succession. The first inspirations produced strong deviations, the succeeding ones were smaller and smaller, the last of all again became large as the business began to be disagreeable and wearisome to the subject. Vasometer changes evoked by inspirations are therefore no criterion for the occurrence of oscillations. The deep inspiration behaves exactly like a psychological stimulus. In one of Jung and Peterson's cases the excessively large deviations in deep inspiration were caused by the reawakening of the subject's fear that he was consumptive.

The systematic repetition of one and the same stimulus shows very neatly that it is not the perception of the stimulus itself, but the emotional tone connected with it which affects the psycho-

[1] Water contact was first used in these tests by the engineer E. K. Müller.
[2] Hermann, *Lehrbuch der Physiol.*, 12th edition, p. 146.
[3] Jung and Peterson, *Brain*, July 1907, p. 153.

galvanic phenomenon.   If the emotional tone of a sensation, e.g. pricking with a needle, can be reduced by frequent repetition, there is no oscillation of the current.   What is true of sensations is also true of presentations, as shown in the work of Veraguth, and in the experiments made by Jung and Peterson and by the present writer.

## The Material

Our subjects were educated and uneducated men and women : doctors, students, male and female asylum nurses, and three male patients, two of whom were found to be mentally sound and discharged ; the third did not show any disturbing deviation from the normal in those experiments.   One female subject was an obvious hysteric.   There were in all 23 subjects with 2160 reactions.   The smallest number of reactions in one subject was 20, the largest 200 ; as a rule between 50 and 100 associations were carried out.   With some subjects second experiments were carried out on different days.

## PART II

### Report on some Experiments and their Results

I will begin with an experiment on a subject remarkable for penetrating and reliable self-observation.

### Experiment I

A married doctor well acquainted with the association experiment.

The probable mean (P.M.) of the reaction-time (R.T.) in these tests was 9/5 or 1·8 second, that of the galvanometer deviation was 8 mm.   Times or deviations (so-called " too large values ") above the average are to be regarded, therefore, as disturbances due to emotionally toned complex (see chapter v). The average values or reaction-times which I obtained cannot be directly compared with Jung's, for my personal equation is greater and the conditions of the order of my research are also different from his.   The lowest probable mean that I obtained, and that was only in one normal experiment, was 8/5 = 1·6 second ; so that 1·8 second is a low average value.

Curve 1 shows the experiment graphically :

| Stimulus-word | Reaction-word | Reaction-time in one-fifth sec. | Galvan. deviation in mm. |
|---|---|---|---|
| 1. Head | hand | 7 | 16 |
| 2. Blue | sea | 9 | 6 |

These times disclose no particular emotional tone.   A deviation of 16 in Test I demands an explanation.   Veraguth had already pointed out that the first deviations in an experiment are usually greater than the subsequent ones.   Besides complicated physical causes, it depends also on the fact that most persons are somewhat embarrassed and excited at the beginning and their attention is stretched. So that, quite apart from its content, the first word will discover a complex connected with ideas of the experiment itself, such as : " What will my reactions be like—long or short ? Shall I be able to find a reaction-word at all ? Will any of my secret thoughts and wishes come out ? What will the experimenter think about them ? " These are all ideas which strongly excite the ego complex, and are hence emotionally toned in a striking degree.[1] The relationship of the subject to the experimenter has a particular influence which produces its effect throughout the whole experiment. Jung has brought this out very clearly (see chapter v) and Veraguth likewise (loc. cit., p. 35). In this case, where the subject is relatively unembarrassed as regards the experimenter and has often had the tests carried out on himself, the second deviation already falls below the mean.

|  |  | R.T. | G.D. |
|---|---|---|---|
| 3. Wall | star | 9 | 14 |

Whilst the time is average, the deviation as compared with the previous one exhibits a considerable difference. *Wall — star* is an unusual association requiring explanation. Asked what had here occurred to him, he explains that he really wished to say *stone*.[2] I got his free associations to *stone* and we obtained the following series : *stone — stone-blue* (blue sky) ; *star — sister-in-law* (who when engaged often reacted with the word *star*) ; *brother-in-law — wife*—a Mr. St. No. 1 and another Mr. St. No. 2. He now recollected that the word *wall* sounded for a moment like *will*, and the connexion became clear to him. He has been waiting for some time for a work from Mr. St. No. 1 which he very much wants. He had often said to himself, " *Will* the work ever appear and has Mr. St. finished it ? " He had exactly the opposite feeling about the second Mr. St., about whose power of working he was astonished. (Both names have a close clang-relationship to the above series of associations.)

The reaction could be therefore expressed somewhat as follows : " When will Mr. St.'s work appear ? If only Mr. St. No. 1 were as energetic as Mr. St. No. 2 ! " The determination of the reaction *wall — star* is thus disclosed ; we see the way in which, through the complex of Mr. St.'s work and its emotional tone the word *wall* gets the clang of *will*. But from *wall* to *star* there are chains of thought which pass alongside the former, although more " superficially." [3] The *over-determination* which Freud has shown to take place in dreams is also true of association tests. The subject states that at *wall* he had thought of the walls of the asylum, and had thereat the feeling of something severing, inhibiting, insurmountable. In seeking an explanation of these determinants for *star*, the (English) word *stone* given in the above scenes occurred to me, and I noticed that the previous reaction-word was *sea*, which with *star* was the title of a well-known book in which England played a great share. The subject affirmed that

---

[1] Naturally such thoughts need not be clearly conscious although the affect be present. Cp. Jung, " Affects have as a rule an intellectual content, which need not always be conscious." (*The Psychology of Dementia Præcox*, by Dr. C. G. Jung. Translated by Peterson and Brill. New York : The Journal of Nervous and Mental Diseases Publishing Coy., 1909, p. 34.)

[2] The word *stone* was said by the subject in English.—TRANSLATOR.

[3] Freud's *Interpretation of Dreams*.

he had read *Star of the Sea*, 1906, with great interest, and it at once occurred to him that on the title-page of the book there was a blue flag with a *white star*. He further explains that he had described a great star in a poem just as it was illustrated in the *Star of the Sea*, 1906. In reality there is no star on the title-page of the book, as he thought. It was, as the subject himself recognized, a paramnesia by assimilation. A third reference to England is the association *brother-in-law*, who had frequent opportunities of travelling to England and was not so fixed to one place as the subject himself. He was also recently trying to arrange with a colleague for a journey to England which was of some importance to him, but his work at the asylum stood in the way, hindered him. (The subject is, be it remarked by the way, passionately fond of travelling.) *Wall* thus seems to signify a hindrance to this journey through his work in the asylum. Finally it occurred to him that his colleague had advised him to combine with the voyage to England one to America, and not to take the Norddeutscher Lloyd but to travel by the White *Star* Line. We shall find a third determinant for this reaction in reaction 59, where I purposely interpolated the word *star* as a stimulus-word during the test so as to obtain further evidence about the curious reaction 3. Although this analysis is incomplete, it does show the wide ramifications and chains of ideas leading up to two strong complexes; it is enough to show us why the deviation was so extensive here. We also learn at the same time that the complexes need not be conscious, at the moment of the reaction, to obtain such large deviations. The subject had only a "vague feeling of hindrance." The intellectual content of the "feeling" was quite concealed from him.

|  |  | R.T. | G.D. |
|---|---|---|---|
| 4. Prick | knife | 6 | 6 |

The subject had carried out several association tests with the same stimulus-word; this reaction, which is one frequently heard, is for him merely verbal, without emotional tone.

| 5. Devil | angel | 7 | 9 |
|---|---|---|---|

He knew that the stimulus-word *angel* followed *prick*, and was therefore surprised when *devil* was pronounced. (We changed the stimulus-words of our usual list at several places because he knew the list.)

| 6. Lame | ill | 7 |  |
|---|---|---|---|

*Lame* is again my stimulus-word; subject is surprised.

| 7. Boat | row | 9 | 8 |
|---|---|---|---|

The day before he had passed by a Mr. Boat without seeing him and so had not saluted him, which made him feel uncomfortable. No distinct influence upon the two values could be recognized.

| 8. Plough | field | 1 | 1 |
|---|---|---|---|

As in reaction 4, this has become through usage a purely verbal-motor reaction. The low deviation clearly shows the difference in the emotional tone between this indifferent reaction and the above reactions.

| 9. Will | strive | 7 | 12 |
|---|---|---|---|

The subject has a strongly pronounced striving for knowledge, work, and recognition. The long deviation accords with this strong complex.

| 10. Friendly | hateful | 7 | 5 |
|---|---|---|---|

Wanted to say *to hate*. Constellated by a dream of the previous night which referred to an old complex not recently revised and which will be dealt with later.   So far there had been a rapid rise of the whole curve,[1] as is usually observed in normal tests.   The more rapid or slower rise of the curve at the beginning has become for me a valuable criterion of the (psychical) sensibility.   The more finely organized the subject, the more labile his affectivity, and the greater the consequent excitation through the experiment, the more rapidly does the curve rise.   Physiological and physical influences also have a share in this, but the psychological peculiarities of the subject still seem to me the most important.   There is no doubt as to the effect of psychical factors at the beginnings of the curves in Tests II (c), III, and IV.

|            |        | R.T. | G.D. |
|------------|--------|------|------|
| 11. Fish   | water  | 9    | 7    |

*Fish* was put in by me ; it therefore seemed " strange " to the subject.

|             |        |   |   |
|-------------|--------|---|---|
| 12. Ask     | answer | 7 | 4 |
| 13. State   | law    | 7 | 3 |
| 14. Haughty | hateful| 6 | 5 |

In reactions 12 and 13 the same holds good as for 4 and 8.   Reaction 14 is constellated by the same dream as reaction 10.   Note that the complex shows no signs in reactions 10 and 14 except the rather indirect content of the reaction.

|            |       |   |    |
|------------|-------|---|----|
| 15. Thorn  | flesh | 7 | 10 |

It at once occurs to him that *thorn* signifies a sexual symbol and has replaced the similar *stalk*.   During the reaction he is thinking that Paul says of himself he has a thorn in the flesh.

|              |        |    |    |
|--------------|--------|----|----|
| 16. To dance | joyous | 12 | 12 |

Time and deviation obviously increased.   The subject is annoyed at having to go to a ball next day ; thereat a mass of strongly toned reminiscences.

|          |      |   |   |
|----------|------|---|---|
| 17. Sea  | lake | 6 | 5 |

Lower values for time and deviation, but the curve nevertheless rises.   Possibly reactions 15 and 16 are here at work, but there is an emotional tone at reaction 17, for he formerly had great longings for the sea which were again aroused by the promised journey to England.   The emotional tone is not expressed in the deviation itself but by a positive fluctuation which is not followed by any negative, as usual, but by a second strong positive fluctuation.   The emotional tone does not diminish but is strengthened after saying the reaction-word (see curve).

 · The flat course of the curve from reactions 10–17 is explained by the low emotional tone of most of these reactions.   It is only after reaction 15 that stronger fluctuations arise, and at reaction 17 cause a rise in the level.

|           |         |   |    |
|-----------|---------|---|----|
| 18. Ill   | poor    | 6 | 6  |
| 19. Proud | eminent | 9 | 15 |

He is often reproached by his family with being too proud !   He has, in general, a strongly developed conscience.

|             |        |   |    |
|-------------|--------|---|----|
| 20. England | France | 9 | 14 |

(See reaction 3.)

---

  [1] By " curve " I designate the whole graphic course of the experiment, whilst the expression " complex wave " is only used for the individual undulations interposed in the total curve, and which are again composed of individual deviations.

| | | R.T. | G.D. | Reproduction |
|---|---|---|---|---|
| 21. Ink | drink | 7 | 10 | |

He meant to say *drinker*. On his last journey to England he had charge of a female patient, a "drinker." The reaction belongs to the strong complex of the journey planned to England.

| | | | | |
|---|---|---|---|---|
| 22. All | ton | *i* | 14 | |

Alton is the name of the estate where his wife's parents live and where his wife grew up. The size of the deviations and the rise of the curve show that complexes were met with in reactions 19–22.

| | | | | |
|---|---|---|---|---|
| 23. Nidel | bath | ī | 10 | |

Was surprised at the dialect word *nidel*. Nidelbad is a sanatorium near Zurich. The deviation = 10 is partly related to surprise at the stimulus-word—it was inserted instead of *needle*. He subsequently recalled " Cleopatra's Needle " in London and the Needles at Southampton. England is here again.

| | | | | |
|---|---|---|---|---|
| 24. Swim | water | 7 | 7 | |
| 25. Leave | take | 11 | 12 | have |

Three complex signs in this reaction : prolonged time, increased deviation, and disturbance in reproduction. *Leave* is a strong complex for, as mentioned, he is very fond of travelling, but as physician to a State asylum only receives short leave. The journey to England is again involved.

| | | | | |
|---|---|---|---|---|
| 26. Rude | gruff | 11 | 8 | |

The reaction-time 11 is due to the perseveration of the reaction 25 (see later about the influence of perseveration on time and deviation).

| | | | | |
|---|---|---|---|---|
| 27. Red (rot) | blue | 9 | 10 | |

Apparently a purely verbal reaction. But the deviation points to a complex. He thinks of the pathologist Rot, who did a post-mortem on his father, and of the proverb " To-day red, to-morrow dead." He can think of nothing further. For the analysis see reaction 63.

| | | | | |
|---|---|---|---|---|
| 28. Threaten | hit | 9 | 11 | lengthy reflection |

The complex aroused in reactions 10 and 14 occurs to him on account of which he was for a time "threatened." Whilst there were no complex signs there, here we get two.

| | | | | |
|---|---|---|---|---|
| 29. Asylum | have | 11 | 8 | |

Believed he had answered too soon, before the stimulus-word was quite spoken.

The reaction-time 11 shows that he deceived himself. He at first thought it was *manners*. *Manners* is connected with the complex in reaction 28, and was heard in the sense of the complex.[1] Asylum at the same time was repressed.[2]

---

[1] These cases are spoken of as assimilation of the stimulus-word to the complex. See Riklin, chapter viii.

[2] For repression consult Freud's works, and Jung, chapter v.

Analysis 3 showed us that in *asylum* there is a tone of unpleasure.

| | | R.T. | G.D. | Reproduction |
|---|---|---|---|---|
| 30. Rich | poor | 8 | 20 | |

Twenty is the biggest deviation so far.  Money complex plays a large part in this subject and is closely connected with his love of travelling, his salary at the asylum, and his future way of living.

| 31. Place | time | 7 | 13 | |

Place is apprehended in its philosophic sense.  He asked himself whether I had inserted the word to arouse his " philosophic complex."  Was, then, the emotional tone, which the galvanometer showed, not to be brought into connexion with a complex already present and only conditioned through the person of the experimenter ?  Not at all, for the transference of the emotional tone to the experimenter points to a definite source of affect, which has, however, another origin.  The period when he was much engaged with philosophy is emotionally toned to an extreme degree for him.

| 32. Ring | swing | 7 | 6 | |
| 33. Pain | heavy | 14 | 14 | |

The rhyme in reaction 32 accords with the weak deviation.  It is a purely verbal mechanism which in a subject so practised in language as himself demands the minimum of attention.  But we may note that the clang-association, with its slight deviation, follows directly after a reaction with distinct emotional tone.

Reaction 33 was heard as *rain,* a good example of repression and of the assimilation of the stimulus-word to the sense of a complex.  That *pain* should be repressed is not astonishing ; he would like to enjoy life but has a slight disposition to hypochondriacal ideas (as we shall see later).

| 34. Money | have | 9 | 24 | |

The deviation exceeded No. 30, *rich — poor,* by 4 mm.  We see how strongly developed is the money complex with all that pertains to it.

| 35. Mountain | climb. | 9 | 12 | |

He regrets that in consequence of his asylum work he has little time for mountaineering.

| 36. Play | cards | 11 | 5 | (reflects) |

Here he thought of his wife and children.

| 37. Speck | neck | 9 | 6 | |
| 38. Repent | spent | 11 | 7 | |

The time is prolonged but not the deviation.  But the rise of the curve afterwards denotes a rising emotional tone.  Reaction 38 is connected with the complex (not gone into) which he had in mind in reaction 10, without its becoming objective there (analysis showed that he wanted to say *to hate* and substituted the more harmless *hateful*).  In reaction 14, *haughty — hateful,* the complex was not yet recognizable, but it came out in reactions 28, *threaten — hit* and 29, *asylum — have.*  The complex is objectively evident in reactions 38 and 39.  It would seem that the complex became more and more autonomous, coming more to the surface with the addition of the stimuli.  The " autonomy " of the complex is seen also in the curve, which in the section 34–38 presents for the first time the picture of a distinct complex curve (long deviation with a subsequent fall of the curve and smaller deviations).

|  | | R.T. | G.D. | Reproduction |
|---|---|---|---|---|
| 39. Custom | manners | 9 | 10 | (reflects) |
| 40. Ride | drive | 7 | 11 | |

Regrets he has now no time for riding.

| 41. Sand | sea | 9 | 10 | |
|---|---|---|---|---|

Thinks of the journey to England and of a friend's dream where the word santonin played a part.   It was this friend who suggested the journey to England.

| 42. Stupid | donkey (Dubel) | 9 | 18 | |
|---|---|---|---|---|

The reaction was the dialect word *dubel* (a fool—donkey).   He explains that this reaction was emotionally toned ; he was thinking of a particular person.

| 43. Sap | rap | 7 | 6 | |
|---|---|---|---|---|
| 44. Despise | esteem | 9 | 6 | |
| 45. Tame | wild | 11 | 5 | (reflects) |

At first he understood *tooth* (instead of *tame*), the word used in the ordinary schedule.

| 46. Important | unimportant | 7 | 1 | |
|---|---|---|---|---|
| 47. People | ruler | 9 | 10 | (reflects) |

Here Napoleon occurred to him, and a dream analysis where Napoleon came in. But the emotional tone is derived from the " will to power " which is strongly marked in him.   The experiment was here interrupted by a message, and his hands were removed from the electrodes ; after a few minutes the experiment was continued.   We now observed a very rapid rise of the curve, which in four reactions reached the same height which it took sixteen reactions to reach in the first part. In general the second part of the curve shows a much more "nervous," labile character than the first.   On close investigation the same kind of change is seen between the end of the first part of the curve and its beginning and middle ; a more distinct effect of the complexes on the curve is noticeable.

| 48. Drown | swim | 17 | 14 | |
|---|---|---|---|---|

As this is the first reaction in the second part of the curve, the great deviation must not be regarded as a complex sign without investigation ; but the long reaction-time, 17 seconds, points to one.   The subject apprehended the reaction-word as *Aprilchen* (this has rather more clang-association to the German than to the English reaction-word), and at once thought of a journey to England which was to take place next April—another good instance of assimilation to the complex.

| 49. Belly | lie | 8 | 18 | |
|---|---|---|---|---|

Apprehended sexually and in the sense of " crawling on one's belly " to some one ; something very antagonistic to the subject, especially in scientific matters.

| 50. Wrong | right | 9 | 3 | |
|---|---|---|---|---|
| 51. Kröte | spöte | 16 | 40 ! | |

He thought of the well-known verse with these rhymes to the name of Goethe. Goethe sets up through a particular constellation, which cannot be here gone into, a strong emotional tone.

The subject admits that from this time on he experienced distinct excitation. We shall deal with this section of the curve 51–58 again.

| | | R.T. | G.D. | Reproduction |
|---|---|---|---|---|
| 52. Divorce | force | 9 | 5 | |
| 53. Hunger | thirst | 6 | 6 | |
| 54. Knowledge | thirst | 9 | 8 | |

As thirst for knowledge.

| | | | | |
|---|---|---|---|---|
| 55. Child | have | 10 | 5 | |

He thinks that his youngest child is slightly unwell. But there seems to be some stronger complex behind this apparently "innocent" reaction. The reaction-word *have* suggests this, for this word only occurs in definite complex places: see *manners — have; money — have;* and later, *fame — have; salary — have.* Jung calls such stereotyped reaction-words complex representatives (chapter v). The complex is quite unconscious here. Besides the stereotyped reaction-word the complex is betrayed by prolongation of the reaction-time— one-fifth of a second above the mean; we shall meet the complex again in reaction 59.

| | | | | |
|---|---|---|---|---|
| 56. Hat | put on | 11 | 6 | |
| 57. Pencil | write | 11 | 5 | |

Remembers that *pencil* is occasionally apprehended as a sexual symbol.

| | | | | |
|---|---|---|---|---|
| 58. Carrot | sugar | 7 | 2 | (reflects) |

Again a sexual symbol.

| | | | | |
|---|---|---|---|---|
| 59. Star | house | 12 | 20 | (reflects) |

This reaction enabled us to penetrate into the deepest layers of the reaction, *wall — star.* The subject has the feeling that it was the same thing here as in reaction 3; he really wanted to say *wall.* The wish which accompanied the reaction was, "May a lucky star shine over our house." That refers to the future of his family in general but also to its past (see the poem mentioned in reaction 3 where he described his lucky star). To *star* the subject next thought of *Star of Bethlehem;* and, recalling the associations *sister-in-law* (now pregnant) and *wife* from the series of associations in reaction 3, reaction 35, *child — have,* and also reaction 75, *family — have,* we easily recognize the wish concealed behind all these reactions. But the association *Star of Bethlehem* ("Unto us a son is born") first gives us the correct clue. He has now two daughters. The wish for a son is easily understandable. We can summarize the analysis of reactions 3 and 59 (although it is far from exhausted, as the expert will quickly see):

> 1st layer: When will Mr. St. No. 1's work appear? If only he were as energetic as Mr. St. No. 2. What was the wall (= hindrance) here was not mentioned.
>
> 2nd layer: When *shall* I travel to England? Shall I go on to America with the White Star Line? If only the asylum were not such a wall (brick wall = hindrance).
>
> 3rd layer: When shall I have a son? May a lucky star grant him to me. The wall (= hindrance) is fate in general, which has hitherto opposed his desire.

| | | | | |
|---|---|---|---|---|
| 60. Cellar | excellent | 9 | 1 | |

A very superficial reaction. The very slight deviation is explained by the previous reaction. The deviation of reaction 60 is at the short, descending limb of a complex wave which here consists of two reactions only. We shall see later why the deviations found at the down-stroke of a complex wave are particularly short, and the corresponding reactions particularly superficial.

|  |  | R.T. | G.D. |
|---|---|---|---|
| 61. Light | beat | 13 | 10 |

Patient heard the stimulus-word as *fight* and at once thought of an opponent; it is the same complex as in reaction 42.

|  |  |  |  |
|---|---|---|---|
| 62. Love | dear | 6 | 7 |

Note the subsequent rise of the curve; *love* has in itself a strong emotional valuation.

|  |  |  |  |
|---|---|---|---|
| 63. Grass | herb | 12 | 7 |

The reaction-time is prolonged; the deviation indifferent. Biblical sayings are at the base of the reaction : " For all flesh is grass." Again : " Let the earth bring forth grass, the herb yielding seed, and the fruit-tree yielding fruit after his kind, whose seed is in itself, upon the earth."

The second saying was not verbally remembered by the subject during the analysis but its content was present ; moreover, during the reaction he saw the picture illustrating it in the Carolsfeld Bible ; especially vivid was the rain which is so closely connected with the passage. We have already, during the test, come across one saying expressing a similar idea : " To-day red, to-morrow dead." It was at reaction 27, *red — blue* (R.T. 9, G.D. 10), when he at the same time thought of the pathologist Rot, who performed an autopsy on his father. Here again *father* at once occurred to him. The association of *father* was aroused in both reactions by ideas of death, which the sayings " To-day red," etc., and " All flesh " contain. The *father* can be here but a cover figure concealing some other person. We shall not go far astray in suspecting it is the subject himself ; for Freud's remark about dreams—that the chief actor is always the dreamer himself—is equally true here. After much reflection he remembered his father used to say that the L.'s (his surname) never lived long, and it was at the age of thirty that he had expressed these hypochondriacal thoughts most frequently. We know now that, although he does not want to admit it, similar thoughts are passing in his own mind. He is now thirty-one years old. The saying " Let the earth," etc., is a turning away from himself to his successor (son) ; in the two reactions 27 and 63 we thus find the instincts of self-preservation and of the preservation of the species (which are in other ways well marked in him). The saying also leads to our understanding reaction 59 (" May a lucky star "). Very remarkable is the Biblical colouring in which all these complexes are arrayed. The subject was very religious in childhood. Thus past, present, and future combine in the short analysis. One might expect that to the words *red* and *grass* we should get *dead* and *flesh* ; whilst the reactions are *blue* and *herb*— most innocent reactions. This brings out very clearly the censure in Freud's[1] sense. These two sayings containing thoughts of death touch him painfully ; he thus seeks to elude them and succeeds. To put it in Jung's language : the " ego complex " has overcome the very unpleasantly toned death complex and has " assimilated the stimulus-word in a sense appropriate to the ego complex," thus concealing the painful thoughts, or hiding them from himself.

And, as so frequently happens, in the repression of one complex another suppressed complex, that of propagation, found a means to make itself evident. We shall return later to the relationship between deviation and time in this reaction.

---

[1] Freud, *Interpretation of Dreams and Psychology of Everyday Life.*

|  |  | R.T. | G.D. |
|---|---|---|---|
| 64. To yield | yield up | 11 | 3 |

The disproportion between R.T. and G.D. is explained by perseveration from the previous reaction.

| 65. Goat | buck | 7 | 14 |
|---|---|---|---|

He thought of a gentleman whom a colleague had called a goat the day before. At the same time the thought arose: "The experimenter will draw analogous conclusions about me." The curve now rose rapidly. One gets the impression that the complexes force themselves more to the front, withdrawing from the force of the ego complex. The ego complex has lost its inhibitory action, and so the remaining complexes gain in autonomy. Thus, instead of the fairly regular first half of the curve we find extreme fluctuations in the second half where the individual complexes gain expression.

| 66. Big | little | 6 | 8 |
|---|---|---|---|
| 67. Potato | new | 5 | 5 |
| 68. Tired | I am | 7 | 5 |

Reaction 68 is the beginning of the well-known child's prayer. The reaction is constellated by the subject's momentary condition. The fatigue helps in the complex becoming autonomous.

After this reaction the curve shows a tendency to fall, and one might expect that there would be peace again. But a critical stimulus-word followed in which the subject feels that he now has exposed his complexes. He acknowledges in analysis that after reaction 69 he became more excited and had the feeling, "Now everything will come out." The curve shows the excitation at reaction 65. The test is more subtle than conscious perception. The feeling of fear that now everything will come out must attain a certain threshold value in order to reach consciousness.

| 69. Sex | determination | 9 | 25 |
|---|---|---|---|

Thinks of Schenk's method of determining sex before birth. We know that he has two daughters and would like a son. Besides, the word *sex* is itself very "complex-rousing" (see the connexion with reaction 65, when the excitation not yet conscious had begun).

| 70. Young | old | 7 | 16 |
|---|---|---|---|

The subject admits that the death complex reverberated here.

| 71. Fame | have | 7 | 15 |
|---|---|---|---|

We have mentioned *have* as a complex representative. We are here dealing with the complex of ambition, thirst for knowledge, "will to power," which we have frequently met. The section of the curve 65–71 can be regarded as an up stroke of a complex curve.[1] On closer examination it can be split into two halves belonging to two complexes which are not entirely separated from one another. The first complex (65–68) was aroused by the reaction *goat — buck*, and was fading when the new complex (*sex — determination*) arose, causing a further rise of the curve (together with the subsequent reactions). It is only in reaction 73 that the down stroke of this composite complex curve

---

[1] Hitherto we have only spoken of complex curves when a down stroke with slight deviations followed a long deviation. But in place of one long deviation we can get several deviations, which are then usually found upon the up stroke.

begins; the reactions 74–76, which have but little emotional tone, belong to this down stroke.

|  |  | R.T. | G.D. | Reproduction |
|---|---|---|---|---|
| 72. Bear | heavy | 11 | 12 | |

Thinks of reaction 33; also of pregnancy and his wife (son).

| 73. Box | bed | 11 | 12 |
|---|---|---|---|

Perseveration of thoughts about his wife, for *box — bed* is an association due to her former pregnancy.

Notice how the complexes increase and that they are not new ones. They now extend because the inhibition on the part of the ego complex is absent.

| 74. Coarse | se-sex | 8 | 0 |
|---|---|---|---|

The hesitation at the reaction-word points to the commencing "emptiness of association" caused by the complexes. No deviation at all; the reaction only detained the descent of the curve for a moment.

| 75. Family | have | 6 | 4 |
|---|---|---|---|

*Have* alone betrays the complex.

| 76. Wash | pure | 8 | 3 |
|---|---|---|---|

To the last three associations a minimum of attention was given. The complexes aroused at reactions 69–73 are still at work. In a subject less fluent in speech we might here expect clang or verbal-motor reactions. But for this subject a mere trace of attention is sufficient to find a word that makes sense.

| 77. Ambition | to be | 7 | 15 |
|---|---|---|---|

The complex again breaks through without bothering about the verbal form of the stimulus-word. The reaction is very superficial, verbal-motor, which probably accounts for absence of any prolongation of time.

| 78. Foreign | far | 12 | 7' | wide |
|---|---|---|---|---|

Foreign is taken in the geographical sense; the incorrect reproduction *wide* points to the love of travelling.

| 79. Back | rack | 7 | 9 |
|---|---|---|---|

A verbal reaction, hence the short time; constellated by a reminiscence of a patient.

| 80. To count | count out | 9 | 8 |
|---|---|---|---|
| 81. State | état | 12 | 23 |

Three complex indicators: translation of the stimulus-word and the prolongation of both time and deviation. The reaction refers both to the sexual and to the social spheres. Its emotional tone must be very strong for the curve scarcely descends between reactions 81 and 82.

| 82. Narrow | broad | 7 | 8 |
|---|---|---|---|

The curve now begins to fall. If we are to regard reactions 81 and 82 as the beginning of a complex wave, reactions 83–87 are its descending limb.

| 83. Brother | sister | 7 | 3 |
|---|---|---|---|
| 84. Harmful | useful | 7 | 2 |

The superficial verbal apprehension of these two reactions accords with the lower figures for time and deviation.

|  |  | R.T. | G.D. |
|---|---|---|---|
| 85. Birth | accoucheur | 8 | 13 |

Thought of his sister-in-law and his wife. We recognize the old complexes, but they no longer exercise the same effect upon the curve for they cannot restrain its descent. It is probable they have been somewhat "abreacted" by now through their frequent expression in so many reactions.

| 86. Falsify | deceive | 11 | 10 |
|---|---|---|---|

relates to the "opponent" whom we have already encountered.

| 87. Regret | lively | 8 | 8 |
|---|---|---|---|

Seems a superficial verbal reaction. Still the curve ascends; he regrets having insufficient time for the execution of his scientific and travel plans.

| 88. Kiss | beloved | 9 | 10 |
|---|---|---|---|

Probably a reminiscence from the subjects with whom he has himself conducted experiments; this is a common reaction on their part.

| 89. Toy | play | 9 | 25 |
|---|---|---|---|

Was confused by the stimulus-word; thinks of children's toys, but the long reaction can scarcely be accounted for by this confusion alone. *Toy* leads to toying, *play* to his children and his wife.

| 90. Foul | useful | 14 | 14 |
|---|---|---|---|

Death complex. But there is an additional complex referring to himself whose existence seems to him at times quite useless.

| 91. Doors | open | 7 | 6 |
|---|---|---|---|
| 92. Choice | trouble | 9 | 18 |

The question of the future here rose up.

| 93. Repentance | fast | 11 | 20 |
|---|---|---|---|

See reaction 87.

| 94. Suckle | suck | 11 | 7 |
|---|---|---|---|
| 95. Mockery | scorn | 3 | 6 |
| 96. Sleep | at night | 11 | 17 |
| 97. Salary | have | 7 | 17 |
| 98. Vienna | Paris | 7 | 23 |

Reactions 94–97 require no further explanation now. Reaction 98: he is contemplating a journey to Vienna as soon as the vacation begins; he can hardly wait.

| 99. Round | earth | 7 | 6 |
|---|---|---|---|
| 100. Soon | yes | 13 | 33 |

Is again thinking of the vacation and the Vienna journey. Has a general feeling "something is soon going to happen." The strong deviation points to the subject's great need of new "sensations."

The analysis shows that we are dealing with a sensitive, emotivated subject. This is proved by the great number of complexes (eleven different complexes, which constellate more than one reaction, and many lesser ones) and the frequency with which they give rise to strong physical innervations. The strong emotional nature comes to light also in the increase of the complex waves in the second half of the curve, where we notice a "penetration" of the complexes, i.e. a retrogression of the inhibiting influence of the ego complex.[1]

The reaction-times seem to contradict the results of the psychogalvanic phenomenon. The former are nearly always short, and would often have failed us as complex indicators, whilst the galvanometer behaved with much greater certainty. The comparison of the probable and arithmetical mean more especially eludes us, since the former does not take very long times into account whilst the latter does ; and since there is a certain ratio between length of reaction-time and the intensity of the feelings, Jung thought that he found in the difference of the two means a starting-point whence one could draw certain conclusions as to the intensity of the feelings. In this case the probable mean is 9 seconds and the arithmetical mean, usually greater than the other, is here 8·8 seconds, which is another proof that there are no very long times. But it would be a fundamental error to conclude that there was no intense emotion. We see that in experimental psychology there are, owing to idiosyncrasies, many individual exceptions to conclusions that are correct for most cases. The idiosyncrasies in this case are those to which we have frequently alluded ; the subject is very fluent in speech both by disposition and from usage, and can thus dispose of emotional inhibitions with great facility. The verbal mechanism has attained great autonomy. The numerous rhymes are evidence of this ; they amount to 7 per cent. of the reactions, whilst among educated men Jung found only 0·6 per cent. The verbal-motor reactions are about 30 per cent., a figure which according to my experience is very high, whilst Jung gives them as 34·2 per cent. for educated men. This seems to me extremely high and rests upon a too narrow selection of his "Educated Men."

The galvanometer deviations show a distinct difference between probable and arithmetical mean : P.M. of the deviations, 8 mm. ; A.M. of the deviations, 10 mm.—a difference of 2 mm. ( = 25 per cent. of the P.M.), which shows that there were a considerable number of very marked deviations. As a general rule we may infer that, like the very long times, these denote intense emotion.

[1] In phlegmatic subjects the whole curve runs a regular course as this one did at the beginning, without distinct complex waves. The curve then presents almost a line without breaks. In hysterically disposed persons the curve is very different ; it is quite bizarre, interrupted by sudden ascents and as rapid descents. The course of the galvanometer curve has become for me a reliable criterion of the affectivity of the subject.

Much is learned also from the comparison of the mean of those deviations which followed "too long times"[1] with the mean of the galvanometric deviations of the whole test. The deviations occurring with times above the P.M. were therefore written out and their P.M. determined. Since we regard the prolonged times as well as the increased deviation as of intense emotional tone, we must take it that there is a certain agreement between the two. In our case it is seen that though the "too long" times exceed the P.M. by very little, the "too long" deviations do correspond to them :

P.M. of all the deviations : 8.

P.M. of deviations where there are too long times : 10.

The difference in many cases is the same as that between P.M. and A.M. of all the deviations together.

The "clang" associations demand notice ; in our experiment they were in the form of rhymes. Jung and Riklin consider that clangs appear when there is a decline of attention. In their view "clang" associations are the most primitive phenomena of similarity, being but little above simple repetition. Distraction acts in the first place as a bar to inner ("higher") associations and favours the appearance of the outer associations—these being more mechanical and therefore predominantly clang-associations (chapter ii, p. 42). In order to understand the behaviour of the psychogalvanic phenomenon in clang-reactions we must distinguish carefully whether the distraction which favours the occurrence of clang-reactions is conditioned by one or more previous complex reactions, or is conditioned entirely by the stimulus-word itself, i.e. by a new complex. In the former case the deviation is usually below the norm, in the second case generally above it. The examples in this test help to elucidate this question. We shall later on return to this. We will first set out the instances where distraction was consequent upon a previous complex (remember that the P.M. of the deviations amounts to 9).

|  |  |  |  | R.T. | G.D. |  |
|---|---|---|---|---|---|---|
| 1. Previous complex | 30. | Rich | poor | 8 | 30 | |
| | 31. | Place | time | 7 | 13 | |
| Clang-reaction | 32. | Ring | swing | 7 | 6 | |
| 2. Previous complex | 42. | Stupid | donkey (dubel) | 9 | 18 | |
| Clang-reaction | 43. | Sap | rap | 7 | 6 | |
| 3. Previous complex | 34. | Money | have | 9 | 24 | |
| | 35. | Mountain | climb | 9 | 12 | |
| | 36. | Play | cards | 11 | 5 | (reflects) |
| Clang-reaction | 37. | Speck | neck | 9 | 6 | |
| | 38. | Repent | spent | 11 | 7 | |

[1] "Too long" times or deviations always signify those above the P.M. in question.

In the analysis we have already referred to the interesting section of the curve 34-38 and termed it a *complex wave*. The name seemed to me justifiable for these sections of the curve, because it clearly shows how a complex is expressed on the galvanometer curve. (In subjects with fewer complexes the behaviour is much more obvious than here where there are such numerous complexes affecting one another—both in the psyche and in the curve.)

The complex causes first of all, at the reaction where it is aroused, a long deviation, which exceeds by more or less the mean of the deviations of the whole test. But this does not exhaust its effect upon the curve. For we are able to notice in the curve not only the excitation of the complex but its reverberation, its longer or shorter mastery of the psyche. To the great positive deviation there is a corresponding negative one, and the succeeding deviation begins at the same height as that of the complex reaction. Should the emotional tone conditioned by the complex persist, only a slight negative follows the positive deviation, or if the emotional tone is very strong there is a further ascent of the curve. If the subsequent reactions are also strongly toned by emotion, i.e. if new complexes are added, we may find a long ascending wave as we found in the section 65-71. But after a shorter or longer interval we always find a down-stroke, unless an excitation is added which is in some way conditioned by the test. The wave begins to fall if the subject is no longer susceptible to new stimuli, because he is completely mastered by the complex or complexes.

The attention is completely distracted from the external world by the complex to which it becomes wholly attached. That is why complex reactions so frequently give superficial, verbal-motor or clang associations.[1] Distraction acts similarly as a check upon physical innervations, as we shall have occasion to see. The curve consequently falls and the deviations following immediately become smaller (unless a new complex again rivets attention). This is the origin of the down stroke of the complex wave. We can therefore say : The longer the down stroke of a complex wave, and the shorter the deviations belonging thereto, the stronger is the complex and the longer it perseverates. So that besides the deviation in the complex reaction we have another essential sign wherewith to estimate the strength of the complex in the down stroke of the complex wave. The behaviour of the complex wave in different individuals gives us a criterion of the type of their affectivity. We can notice in a labile character that the wave is like a bonfire that is soon extinct, or in a tenacious

---

[1] Jung, *The Psychology of Dementia Praecox*, p. 50.

resistant character that it preserves for a long time what has once aroused it. We can only just indicate these relationships here, and refer the reader to Curve II *c*.

Let us return to our examples (R. 34–38). Since the subject reacts very superficially, we must not lay much weight upon the verbal-motor reactions. But the two clang-associations *speck — neck, repent — spent*, point to the strong distraction which is evidenced by the descending limb of the complex curve. Reaction 38, *repent — spent*, requires attention for itself. It forms the end of the down stroke and the beginning of the ascending limb of a complex wave. This is expressed by the clang-association and the short deviation, both indicating the distraction of attention by the previous complex. The prolonged time, 11 seconds, and its part as the beginning of a new complex curve, shows it to be a new " entrenchment of attention " (Freud), a new complex, the repentance complex already mentioned.[1] In this reaction we had to do with a clang-association of that second kind which owes its origin to the appearance of a new complex and determines a deviation above the mean. The deviation is here also above the mean if we reckon the rise of the curve that follows as belonging to it, a rise that corresponded to a subsequent positive deviation. As we know, a subsequent positive deviation of this kind generally corresponds to a new emotional tone occurring after the reaction-word has been called out; here this is conditioned by the repentance complex. For this complex developed its effect upon the physical innervation only after the clang-association had been produced. But that it exercised its effect upon the reaction before it entered consciousness we recognize by the prolonged reaction-time. It is for this reason that I would make it, together with the effect of the previous complex, responsible for the clang-association. Freud has discovered in his *Interpretation of Dreams* the mechanism by which a complex leads to the occurrence of clang-associations and of superficial associations in general. In this book, to which we owe an overwhelming fund of new points of view for psychology and psychopathology, he says [2] : " Whenever a psychical element is connected with another by some superficial association there is a real and deeper link between the two which is subject to the resistance of the censure. If the censure makes this normal way of linkage inaccessible, the superficial replace the deeper associations in the presentation. It is as if some barricade, e.g. an inundation in the mountains, had made the

---

[1] For personal reasons this complex was not analysed more thoroughly.

[2] Freud in this book does not make use of the term " complex " but the idea is implied in his conclusions.

large and best roads impassable; transport then becomes restricted to the inconvenient and steep bridle-paths, which are otherwise only used by the hunter " (*Interpretation of Dreams*, p. 310).

The obstacle to transport is the complex which interposed between stimulus- and reaction-word ; the censure is shown by the repressing action of the ego complex upon this complex. The inconvenient, steep bridle-paths are in our case the clang-associations of which Jung and Riklin speak (chapter ii, p. 42). What Freud says of the dream is only true in the association experiment of the clang-associations of the second kind. In those of the first kind which owe their origin to distraction from a previous complex, a " more real and deeper " link cannot be proved in analysis. This is also seen by the striking character of the psychogalvanic phenomenon, for this generally shows a diminution in the first kind and an increase in the second kind.

The reaction *repent — spent* led up to the clang-association of the second kind. The deeper connexion between the two associations is obvious. We have had further instances in our experiment of clang-associations with increased deviation.

*First Example*

|  |  | R.T. | G.D. |
|---|---|---|---|
| 51. Kröte | spöte | 16 | 40 |
| (52. Divorce | force | 9 | 5) |

Despite the clang-association both time and deviation are enormously increased in reaction 51. The deeper connexion between these associations, namely, that both occur in a poem of Goethe's, was the cause of the pronounced effect. But Goethe is an extremely powerful complex for this subject, into which, as already mentioned, we are, unfortunately, unable to enter further.

It is also noteworthy that Goethe was not associated, an association which lay at the root of the whole reaction and which would also have rhymed to *kröte* ; instead we get the less " indiscreet " word *spöte*, which the censure can more easily allow to pass. What the censure was particularly careful about was the great embarrassment of the subject at revealing this complex to the experimenter. The complex became at once conscious.

(The reaction 52 that follows, *divorce —force*, with its slight deviation, is clearly a clang-association of the first kind which arose through the strong influence of the previous reaction and had no complex of its own.[1])

*Second Example*

|  |  | R.T. | G.D. |
|---|---|---|---|
| 92. Choice | pain | 9 | 18 |

[1] See p. 474.

An indifferent reaction preceded this; clearly it contains the complex in itself. The deep connexion between the two associations is clear (" who has the choice has also the pain "). It refers to the strong complex of the " question of a future." Here the complex was conscious also.

### Reactions with " Too Long " Reaction-time and " Too Short " a Deviation

In the one hundred associations we were struck by eleven where the time exceeded the probable mean whilst the deviation was less than the probable mean (P.M. of reaction-time, 9 ; P.M. of deviation, 8). The reactions in question are 26 ; 36 ; 38 ; 45 ; 55, 56, 57 ; 63, 64 ; 78 and 94.

In looking at the curve we notice that four of these deviations, 26, 36, 78, and 94, follow directly a too long deviation, whilst 38 and 45, the groups 55–57 and 63–64, are separated from " too long " deviations by two, or at most three short deviations. It would seem that here, as with clang-associations of the first kind, distraction has a share through a complex which had acted upon the previous strong deviation. Let us now denote the after-effect of a complex by the term perseveration. Jung has proved so abundantly that the perseveration can prolong the times of those reactions within its sphere of influence that it is unnecessary for us to set forth the proofs of this.[1]

That the perseveration can also diminish the deviation we have just seen (see the down stroke of the complex wave). We shall later return to a detailed instance of this kind (II c) ; we here want to clear up the disproportion between deviation and time when it arises in the sphere of perseveration.[2]

Whilst in the measurement of the psychogalvanic phenomenon we have to do with a quite involuntary, automatic innervation process, in which the subject does not actually participate, but is merely a spectator, the measurement of the reaction-time is a process which demands the active co-operation of his personality. In order to find an appropriate reaction-word he must now turn part of his attention directed towards the previous complex to the reaction itself. To overcome the resistance that proceeds

[1] Jung, chapter v.

[2] Jung and Riklin understand by perseveration " the continuance of the previous idea so far as it becomes manifest in the nature of the reaction following." The designation is purely " formal " and has nothing to do with " perseveration in organic cerebral processes." Jung and Riklin only consider the effect upon the reaction that follows and " leave aside the effect of a reaction that has been itself influenced " ; there they speak of " constellation." I do not draw this distinction, but believe I am justified by the behaviour of the galvanometer curve in speaking of " perseveration " in both cases.

from the complex takes up time, so that the reaction-time is longer than in a reaction where the whole attention is at disposal. But the innervation process (the deviation) measured by the galvanometer gives us information about this residue of attention which is to be turned to the new stimulus-word. The portion of the attention linked to the complex acts, as shown above, upon the whole curve upon which the deviations arise. This is the origin of the down stroke of the complex waves. It can be pertinently expressed in this way : In the galvanometer curve we exhibit complex and new reaction, separated, the former by the course of the curve, the latter by the deviation. In the reaction-time, on the contrary (of course, only in perseveration) we perceive a sign of the intensity of the conflict between the two. The greater this conflict is, the longer is the reaction-time. But this law is only true of the deviation in which we see only one of the parties in the struggle, not the struggle itself. According to whether the complex or the subsequent reaction remains victorious (in the struggle for the possession of the attention) so will the deviation be above or below the mean. The reaction-time thus tells us how " warm " the struggle was, but the deviation tells us which was victorious. Since we measure by these two estimates entirely different things (in cases of perseveration), we must not demand any ratio between them. At the most we can say that when the perseveration is very strong and the new reaction in itself very strongly toned by emotion, the reaction-time tends to be long, the deviation tends to be short.

The following example, a section of which was dealt with in the clang-associations, may clear up this discussion.

In the curve section 51–58 we notice a complex wave which begins with the long deviation at 51, followed by a series of seven short deviations. But we never obtain here, remarkably enough, any down stroke of a complex curve. That obviously depends upon the fact that we are still at the beginning of the second section of the curve. The tendency of the wave to descend, which follows a long deviation, is opposed by the tendency to rise which we encounter at the beginning of almost every normal curve. This wave contains three of the eleven reactions (55, 56, 57).

|  |  | R.T. | G.D. |
|---|---|---|---|
| 51. Kröte | spöte | 16 | 40 |

contains the very powerful Goethe complex.

| 52. Divorce | force | 9 | 5 |
|---|---|---|---|
| 53. Hunger | thirst | 6 | 6 |
| 54. Knowledge | thirst | 8 | 9 |
| 55. Child | have · | 10 | 5 |

| | | R.T. | G.D. |
|---|---|---|---|
| 56. Hat | put on | 11 | 6 |
| 57. Pencil | write | 11 | 5 |
| 58. Carrot | sugar | 7 | 2 |

The perseveration proceeding from reaction 51 is expressed in the associations, which are very superficial even for this patient : one rhyme, five verbal-motor associations, one coexistence. Moreover, in reaction 54 the reaction-word of 53 is reproduced, which again distinctly points to perseveration. The effects of the perseverating emotional tone upon the reaction-time and deviation above described give us an easy explanation of the striking differences of the two values in reactions 55, 56, and 57. Reaction 55 contains the *son* complex and the *propagation* complex in general, reaction 56 contains the latter. Reaction 57 is erotically constellated by reminiscences of association tests he has himself carried out, and at the same time by the sense of the relation to the ego. The rhyme and the slight deviation show that only slight attention was given to reaction 52, which is the first after the critical reaction. The time shows that in consequence of this there was no great " conflict."

Reaction 53 : The dissociation of association which this reaction demanded must have been even easier than in 52, for the reaction-time is very low.

Reaction 54 : A strong " conflict," for *knowledge* is emotionally toned and demands a greater " entrenchment of attention " (R.T. = 9). The deviation (= 8) shows that in fact the reaction did try to enchain the attention. We next get the three emotional-toned reactions 55–57. A violent " conflict " is renewed (R.T. = 10 and 11). The perseverating emotional tone, which is probably strengthened by reaction 54, retains, in contradistinction to reaction 54, the greatest part of the entrenched attention and has but little left for the new reaction (deviations 5, 6, 5). At reaction 58 the reaction-time, as well as the deviation, show that there was no distinct dissociation of attention, but the reaction became very superficial, purely verbal-motor.

I hope I have shown that, in reactions which occur at a perseverating emotional tone, there cannot be expected the slightest ratio between reaction-time and deviation—that we might, indeed, easily get an inversed ratio between the two. When we find such an inversed ratio we must consider the possibility of a perseveration.

It would not take us any further were we to apply these deductions to the other instances (R. 63–64 ; 26 ; 36 ; 78 and 98). I will here only refer to another factor which may also produce a disproportion between the two values ; I refer to indistinct apprehension of the stimulus-word.

| | | R.T. | G.D. | Reproduction |
|---|---|---|---|---|
| 45. Tame | wild | 11 | 5 | (reflects) |

The subject at first understood *tooth*. This indistinct apprehension is more easily understood because the original list contained the word *tooth*, which I changed into *tame*.

In such cases the time is prolonged by " the feeling of uncertainty " as to whether the word has been correctly heard or not ; an intellectual feeling in Nahlowsky's sense.   Bleuler [1] has shown that such " intellectual feelings, which are memory processes, are utterly different from affectivity."   We see here how important this sharp distinction is.   According to Bleuler it is only " affectivity in the strictest sense " that has definite effects upon body and mind.   Since we only register affective processes by the psychogalvanic reflex when the reaction - time registers both memory or intellectual processes as well, the disproportion is explicable in such cases.   But there need by no means always be this disproportion in reactions where the word has been indistinctly understood.   First, the indistinct apprehension may be a complex sign when the deviation is increased by the complex ; secondly, a real affect in the strictest sense may be added to the " intellectual feeling "—for instance, when the subject is endeavouring to react quickly and feels himself inhibited by his indistinct apprehension so that he is not sure to what he is to react.   Then annoyance, confusion, or some similar affect steps in.   This is noticed in subjects who stand in any kind of affective relationship to the experimenter, e.g. in attendants, who are often unable to forget that the experimenter is their chief, and sometimes in female nurses, where there is in addition the sex difference. With close acquaintances—especially if they happen to be women—this relationship to the experimenter can act both as to time and deviation upon apparently most innocent reactions.

### SUMMARY OF EXPERIMENT I

Both halves of the association curves show a rapid rise at the beginning ; but the second half rises much more rapidly than the first, due chiefly to the increased excitation of the subject. The second half is marked by numerous and very pronounced complex waves, which point to the complexes becoming autonomous and to the growing excitation.   The typical complex wave consists of a very long deviation, followed by a down stroke with deviations that are " too short."   The down stroke of the

[1] Bleuler, loc. cit., p. 10 ff.

complex curve and the too short deviations are explained by the distraction of the attention, which is still fettered to the complex reaction (perseveration). In this experiment, where the complexes were so numerous, there were few favourable opportunities for pure complex waves.

" Too long " deviations correspond in most cases to complex reactions, short deviations to non-emotionally toned reactions. Exceptions are seen when a perseveration makes itself felt.

Perseveration acts partly by decreasing the corresponding deviation, partly by prolonging the corresponding time. The explanation is this : the reaction - time gives us information about the intensity of the conflict between perseveration and the new reaction, whilst the deviation informs us about the result of this conflict—that is, about the entrenched attention which the new reaction contains. Having regard to the difference expressed by these two values as regards perseveration we conclude there cannot be any direct ratio between time and deviation ; on the contrary, when perseveration is strong we should rather expect an indirect ratio. That the complexes in our test are indicated with greater certainty by the deviations than by the reaction-times is found in the verbal fluency of this particular patient.

The clang-associations in our experiment exhibit prolonged deviations when caused by a complex, abbreviated deviations when caused by a perseveration.

## EXPERIMENT II

The subject is about forty years old, an intelligent mechanic, who rose from being a simple journeyman in a machine manufactory to a position of respectability and wealth. An ineradicable tendency to fraud by the use of his own half-perfected discoveries soon brought him to prison. In the summer of 1906 he was sent to us from prison, where he was undergoing his third term of punishment, as doubt was entertained about his sanity. After three months' observation we were obliged to send him back to the prison as " mentally sound in a legal sense." There was nothing abnormal to be found in him save a very strong emotivity, a disposition to quarrel, and a certain want of clarity in his thoughts. As I had to form an opinion about the man, and therefore spent much time with him, I obtained in the three months a good insight into his mind. After association tests had been repeatedly made with him I made the first galvanometer test on July 21, 1906. (The analysis of the three following tests remained very incomplete because at the time when I did them I was insufficiently at home in psycho-analysis. If, nevertheless, I cite these tests here it is because the Curve II c in and for itself, and compared with Curves II a and II b, seems to be to be particularly interesting.)

Test (a) (July 21, 1906).—The subject was greatly interested in the experiment, especially from the technical side, and he had prepared himself for it by various curves which he had drawn for me.

The P.M. of the reaction-times is 11, the A.M. 13·1. The P.M. of the galvanometer deviations is 30, the A.M. 37.   The P.M. of the deviations which coincide with too long time is 35.[1]

From the distinct difference between the P.M. and the A.M. of the times we infer that we are dealing with an emotional personality.

The arrangement of the experiment in all three tests differed from the previous one because two galvanic cells were employed instead of one.   The deviations cannot be compared off-hand with the former because, through the use of a stronger current, the deviations were made stronger.   For this reason the difference between the deviations obtained in the third test with this subject, and the results from Tests I and II become the more evident.[2]

|        |        | R.T. | G.D. |
|--------|--------|------|------|
| 1. Head | round | 10 | 15 |
| 2. Green | tree | 16 | 16 |

No explanation could be given for the prolongation of the time.

| 3. Water | thin | 9 | 10 |
|----------|------|---|----|
| 4. Prick | heart | 11 | 25 |

He has a pricking pain in the region of the heart and fears he may have heart disease.   There have been several cases of death from heart disease in his family. The complex increases the deviation but it is still under the P.M.

| 5. Angel | fantasy | 16 | 17 |
|----------|---------|----|----|

A rather curious association.   In a test carried out three weeks earlier, without the galvanometer, he had used the same reaction-word at this place with obvious complex disturbances.   The reaction-time was then 20.   The time is here increased but not the deviation.   Inasmuch as the subject has already reacted to the same stimulus-words, the conditions are peculiarly complicated.   We as yet know too little about the effect of repetitions of the same stimulus-words on the psychogalvanic phenomenon to be able to give an explanation of the disproportion between reaction-time and deflection.   The reaction is partly rooted in the subject's position towards religion (angels are only imaginary figures), but partly also in his everyday life (it would be imaginary to think one could find " an angel in life ").   He is divorced from his wife and often speaks of her in abusive terms.   He granted the truth of the first statement but could neither affirm nor deny the second.   But it is pretty certainly near the truth to any one who knows the psychology of this subject.

| 6. Long | fir-tree | 25 | 40 |
|---------|----------|----|----|

In the first experiment, three weeks earlier, the reaction-time was 37 with the same reaction-word.   Between the associations *angel — fantasy* on the one side and *long — fir-tree* on the other a pathway had been made by the first test, and they have now shorter reaction-times.   But the strength of the complex is still very strong, as is seen by the very long time and the long deviation.

---

[1] At those places where the times are not indicated the deviations have also not been used for calculating the mean, otherwise the comparison between the two means would not be accurate.

[2] I emphasize again the statement that even with the case of the same strength of current the deviations vary in their average size according to the individual tested.   This is somewhat dependent upon physical and physiological conditions (thickness of epidermis, temperature of the skin and of the whole surroundings, more or less pressure upon the electrodes), but predominantly it depends upon the psychological character of the subject.   It is this which stamps the whole curve.

In *long — fir-tree* he had thought of the expression *rolling-pin* used in his occupation, and this was repressed in favour of the word *fir-tree* that got dragged in. The complex which in our experience usually occurs here among patients is the length of the detention. This complex was particularly strong in this subject.

|  |  | R.T. | G.D. |
|---|---|---|---|
| 7. Ship | sailing ship | 7 | 10 |
| 8. Plough | field | 7 | 12 |
| 9. Wool | cotton-wool | 8 | 3 |

Three indifferent associations taken from his first experiment.

| 10. Friendly | friendly face | 16 | 27 |
|---|---|---|---|

Explains he prefers that people should be friendly to him; refers to doctors, especially to the experimenter. It matters a good deal to the subject whether the experimenter is friendly to him or not.

| 11. Table | square | 9 | 14 |
|---|---|---|---|
| 12. Ask | ask ? words | 28 | 45 |

That the repetition of the stimulus-word is due to a complex is clear from the very prolonged reaction-time. The complex is the experimenter himself. In the first experiment he associated to *ask — we did!* Since he is the subject of a medico-judicial inquiry we understand the great importance that he attaches to the course of the experiment.

| 13. State | Federal State | 15 | 35 |
|---|---|---|---|

In his view he cannot help his misfortune, it is the fault of society, of the State.

| 14. Proud | mankind | 8 | 25 |
|---|---|---|---|

Slipped in and somewhat " abreacted " through the first experiment. *Mankind* almost always represents a complex. Who is here meant (himself ? his wife ?) remains unexplained.

| 15. Stalk | hempstalks | — | 23 |
|---|---|---|---|
| 16. Dance | little couple | 15 | 35 |

He was a good dancer and great gourmand.

| 17. Lake | Lake Zurich | 22 | 25 |
|---|---|---|---|

" Sunday excursions on the lake are very pleasant memories," he said in analysis (contrast with his present life).

| 18. Disease | heart disease | 15 | 58 |
|---|---|---|---|

The complex of reaction 4 is here fully revealed. This is another instance of how a complex at first appears indistinctly, and by repeated " echoings " shows the complex signs distinctly.

| 19. Proud | old maid | 8 | 30 |
|---|---|---|---|

Dragged in from the former experiment. The reaction-word may be conditioned by the separation from his wife.

| 20. Cook | electric cooking | 16 | 50 |
|---|---|---|---|

" He had recently read about it." Cooking reminds him of his wife and his former housekeeping (very extravagant for his means). In the first test he associated to *cooking : housekeeping, household, kitchen.*

|  |  | R.T. | G.D. |
|---|---|---|---|
| 21. Ink | black | 10 | 45 |

Not explained.

| 22. Wicked | mankind | 16 | 35 |
|---|---|---|---|

He thinks he has been wickedly treated by several people, especially by the Public Prosecutor, as whose victim he regards himself. But it remained unexplained whether this was concealed beneath the innocent *mankind*.

| 23. Needle | pointed | 10 | 75 |
|---|---|---|---|

Wanted to say *needle prick*—unexplained.

| 24. Swim | lake | 11 | 17 |
|---|---|---|---|
| 25. Travel | round the world | 15 | 70 |

This stimulus-word frequently acts very strongly upon prisoners, as contrasting with their confinement and as expressing a flight of ideas. A reaction in more than one word points, moreover, to the influence of a complex.

| 26. Blue | sky-blue | 8 | 45 |
|---|---|---|---|

He here noticed that the experimenter looked for a moment out of the window, and asked himself, " Is he looking at the weather ? " It is significant how closely he watches the experimenter (see also R. 54). The curve rises still higher after reaction 26, a sign of the presence of some excitation.

| 27. Bread | daily | 10 | 95 |
|---|---|---|---|

He here thought of " Our Father," etc., and that next day he was to go to the asylum church. He has no religious beliefs. He only went to church as a distraction.

The strong deviation remained for a long time unexplained until I learnt that he only went to church because he saw a female patient there with whom he had fallen in love at a dance in the asylum. At the time he could hardly wait for the day of divine service. But this does not sufficiently explain the strong deviation.

| 28. Threaten | laws | 15 | 80 |
|---|---|---|---|

The complex is clear.

| 29. Lamp | table-lamp | 11 | 55 |
|---|---|---|---|

" He would like to have the nice lamps he had at home." Unexplained.

| 30. Rich | poor | — | 85 |
|---|---|---|---|

He had himself gone from poverty to wealth and from wealth back to poverty. He had learnt both to know the luxury of a Parisian *salon* and the misery of the prison-house. Day and night he is thinking of regaining his freedom and of acquiring wealth by his inventions.

The curve rapidly rises from the end of the first half, after reaction 13. A glance shows that the deviations are, in general, considerably greater in the second half of the curve. The arithmetical mean of the reaction-time of the second half of the experiment (13) is greater than that of the first half (11·7). We may conclude from the rapid rise of the curve, the increase in the deviations, and in the arithmetical mean of the times in the second half of the test that the subject has been somewhat stimulated by the experiment. We also saw that the individual reactions gave opportunity enough to stimulate a very emotional subject. The fact that the experimenter is likewise the medical judge of the patient, this creating in the latter a marked condition of dependence, also contributes somewhat to increasing the excitation. The latter fact must be added to the general experimental excitation, which experience shows influences the action of complexes.

*Test* (*b*) (July 24, 1906).—P.M. of reaction-times, 11 ; P.M. of deflections, 23 ; A.M. of reaction-times, 11·5 ; A.M. of deflections, 30 ; P.M. of the deviations which coincide with the " too long " times, 30.

The " emotive inhibitions " are seen more distinctly in this test in the relationship of the deviations than in those of the reaction-times ; the difference between the P.M. and A.M. of the latter is slight (0·5 as against 2 in Test (*a*)), whilst the difference of the former (7) is almost as great as in Test (*a*). That the deviations are, on the average, shorter (P.M. 23 against 30, and A.M. 30 against 38) was due chiefly to a physical cause. The experiment was twice interrupted by making the subject wash his hands in cold water. I tried to prevent the beam of light from overstepping the scale, as this had nearly happened in Test (*a*), and I also wanted to study the effect of washing hands, for I then ascribed great influence to the amount of perspiration produced.[1]

It is easy to see how slight is the influence of this strong physical interference upon the character of the curve. It cuts the curve into three parts, but each of these parts shows the picture that we have already seen in Test (*a*)—an almost uninterrupted rapid rise showing no distinct complex waves. The curve of Test (*c*), where we caused a *psychological* interruption, is quite different, as we shall see.

The same list of words was continued ; we keep to the same numbers for the reactions.

|  |  | R.T. | G.D. | Reproduction |
|---|---|---|---|---|
| 31. Tree | green | 9 | 10 | |
| 32. Sing | tenor | 9 | 25 | |

He sang in a small asylum choir which I was conducting. One sees that in some way his " ego complex " must have become more stirred so as to receive a strong deviation. In excitable persons it is a regular rule for a strong deviation to follow any reaction that touches the " ego complex." These reactions need not be strongly emotionally toned ; quite indifferent reminiscences of the long past will produce it. Beyond a certain degree of emotionalness the subject has a definite affect to the experimenter, as was the case here. We see that in everyday life the more we like a person the more emotionally toned becomes every kind of relationship. It is the same with other affects.

| 33. Pity | mankind | 12 | 18 | |
| 34. Yellow | golden yellow | 10 | 13 | |
| 35. Mountain | high mountain | 9 | 12 | high mountains |
| 36. Play | child's play | 13 | 20 | |

The subject here thought, " It would be child's play to make a new apparatus " (for galvanometric measurements). His grandiose complex is here distinctly

---

[1] Washing the hands in cold water increases the resistance to conduction of the skin. Moreover, the drying of the previously moist hands diminishes the contact at the electrodes. The curve, therefore, begins each time lower than it was before.

seen. He had, in fact, made me a sketch of a contrivance for transferring the galvanometer fluctuations directly on to the kymograph. On paper this looked, like all his drawings, very neat and serviceable, but there were fundamental difficulties in its execution.

|  |  | R.T. | G.D. | Reproduction |
|---|---|---|---|---|
| 37. Salt | race | 14 | 22 | |

Unexplained.

|  |  | R.T. | G.D. | Reproduction |
|---|---|---|---|---|
| 38. New | clothes | 12 | 25 | — |

He thinks much of his appearance. He would like to produce the impression of a person of distinction.

|  |  | R.T. | G.D. |
|---|---|---|---|
| 39. Customs | country customs | 10 | 15 |
| 40. Ride | horse-ride | 10 | 38 |

He had served in the artillery. That the memory is emotionally toned is seen by the reactions 48, *smell — horse-dung*, and 72, *beat — beat horses*. He then had charge of a " kicker " in the stable, and the smell of the manure disturbed his sleep when he was on stable duty. The distinct recollection, in the association test, of his military service, although it was twenty-one years ago, was due to the fact that he did not become an officer. After going through the officers' school he did no more service because he went abroad, where, nevertheless, he gave himself out as a Swiss officer. We had brought that home to him here and it annoyed him.

|  |  | R.T. | G.D. |
|---|---|---|---|
| 41. Wall | vertical | 11 | 43 |
| 42. Stupid | hoggishly stupid | — | 110 |

" It is hoggishly stupid the kind of talk sometimes in the section." A very strong expression indicating strong feeling. As he laughed during the reaction the deviation became peculiarly strong (see R. 55).

|  |  | R.T. | G.D. |
|---|---|---|---|
| 43. Copy-book | exercise-book | — | 40 |

He has a great number of exercise-books in which he made notes of everything he read. The books were clasified into divisions : Philosophy, Art, Crafts, etc. He is very proud of all this.

|  |  | R.T. | G.D. |
|---|---|---|---|
| 44. Despise | despise men | 12 | 90 |

" Men have a tendency to despise one another." He has often had to suffer from having been in prison. Once he was expelled from a church society when his past became known. When he speaks about this he is seized by strong affect.

|  |  | R.T. | G.D. |
|---|---|---|---|
| 45. Tooth | ache | 8 | 53 |

At the reaction it came over him that he " got no tooth-powder here " ; again the complex of his present position, which receives its increase of affect from a number of sources. The short time is explained by the speech-motor form of the reaction. In such verbal reactions the speech mechanism, as previously remarked, reacts almost automatically without becoming influenced by the " emotive inhibition."

|  |  | R.T. | G.D. |
|---|---|---|---|
| 46. Correct | logical | 25 | 50 |

(Did not understand.)

|  |  | R.T. | G.D. |
|---|---|---|---|
| 47. People | Swiss people | 11 | 10 |
| 48. Smell | horse-dung | 17 | 22 |
| 49. Book | good book | 10 | 20 |
| 50. Unjust | punishment | 12 | 35 |

One cannot say exactly to what extent he himself believes in his innocence : certainly to a very large extent. He overwhelmed the judges and the governor of the prison, the Public Prosecutor and the Chief Superintendent of the Asylum, with endless communications in which he tried to prove his innocence.

|   |   | R.T. | G.D. |
|---|---|---|---|
| 51. Frog | tree-frog | 7 | 25 |

Since a strong complex was aroused at reaction 50 we must regard perseveration as acting here. Reaction 51 was a purely verbal reaction without any particular emotion. There can be, therefore, no strong conflict for the possession of attention here. Hence time is very short. In this case we should expect the same of the deviation, but it is here rather above the probable mean. The reaction did, therefore, contain a perceptible measure of attention; in other words, there occurred a distinct splitting of the attention. This happened so easily in this case (R.T. = 7) because the subject endeavoured in Tests (a) and (b) to concentrate himself as far as possible upon the experiment itself, which interested him, in order to be ready for each new stimulus-word. The rapid rise of the curve (a) and (b) accords well with this great straining of his attention to the experiment, and the complete absence of pronounced complex waves (for these are conditioned by the attention being chained to the complex and its distraction from the experiment). In this test we can demonstrate a general experimental excitation.

|   |   |   |   |
|---|---|---|---|
| 52. To divorce | marriage, divorce | — | 25 |

The divorce occurred under very unpleasant circumstances.

|   |   |   |   |
|---|---|---|---|
| 53. Hunger | heat hunger | 7 | 30 |

Unexplained.

|   |   |   |   |
|---|---|---|---|
| 54. White | snow-white | 11 | 30 |

The experimenter's collar was meant by this. The experimenter belongs, in a large measure, to the test complex. We saw in reaction 26 how the subject watched the experimenter. Here is a second proof. When reactions occur which refer to the appearance of the experimenter we can be sure that there is an inner bond between the subject and the experimenter. That is why such reactions are much more frequently found in persons of the other sex.

|   |   |   |   |
|---|---|---|---|
| 55. Ox | cattle | 11 | 60 |

He recalled the manager of a factory where he was an apprentice, who often used this word to his workpeople. Reactions which are insults or the like are usually accompanied by a strong deviation. This is because whilst pronouncing the word the feeling usually comes up that the experimenter might regard it as referring to him; for in ordinary life such words are usually addressed to some one else, more rarely to oneself. Nevertheless the latter case does now and then play a part in the experiment. Thus with Subject No. 1 at the reaction *stupid — fool* " he thought that I might think he meant himself." Such delicate shades give us sign-posts for estimating the subject's character. In No. 1, together with the degree of self-consciousness there is a suggestion of " tendency to self-depreciation "; the two very often go together.[1]

---

[1] As a rule strong deviations also occur, as with insults, when the subject is made to hold his tongue out. As most people only do this in their childhood, it is inseparably connected with a strong emotional tone. If we put out the tongue in the presence of some one else and not for a doctor, that affect (anger, contradiction, mockery) is again aroused. But as there is nobody present except the experimenter, we quite unconsciously transfer that affect to the experimenter. It takes much to make it quite clear that this is only an experiment. The unconscious is stronger than our conscious reflections; it is only after frequent repeti-

| | R.T. | G.D. | Reproduction |
|---|---|---|---|
| 56. To take care  look out | 13 | 50 | |

He thought of electric circuits.  *Look out* is a warning which is in itself emotionally toned.

| | | | |
|---|---|---|---|
| 57. Pencil | sharpen | — | 40 |

The patient is a distinguished technical draughtsman, a fact upon which he plumes himself not a little.

Interruption by washing hands.

| | | | |
|---|---|---|---|
| 58. Cloudy | weather | 11 | 10 |
| 59. Plum | sweet | 10 | 7 |

The deviations are very small in consequence of the hand-washing. But the succeeding reaction showed that a strong centrifugal excitation is but slightly influenced by such physical conditions.

| | | | |
|---|---|---|---|
| 60. Meet | shoot | — | 30 |

Recalls the shooting competitions in which he used to take part in his good days. Besides that, he has occupied himself very much with artillery problems and claims to have invented a shrapnel bomb.

| | | | |
|---|---|---|---|
| 61. Law | people's law | — | 23 |
| 62. Love | have | 10 | 35 |

Completes it in analysis with "my children." He is much attached to his children. It is a thorn in his flesh that they live with his wife.

| | | | | |
|---|---|---|---|---|
| 63. Glass | brittle | — | 23 | |
| 64. Quarrel | parties | 14 | 40 | the parties quarrel |

He was in constant warfare with his wife and her parents. Whenever he speaks about it he explodes with visible excitement (see also R. 75).

*Test* (*c*).  *July* 25, 1906.—For easier survey I place the average figures of Tests (*a*) and (*b*) by the side of (*c*).

| | I. P.M. of R.T. | II. A.M. of R.T. | Difference | III. P.M. of Dev. | A.M. of Dev. | Difference | P.M. of deviations which follow "too short" times |
|---|---|---|---|---|---|---|---|
| Test (*a*) . | 11 | 13 | 2 | 30 | 38 | 8 | 35 |
| Test (*b*) . | 11 | 11·5 | 0·5 | 23 | 30 | 7 | 30 |
| Test (*c*) . | 14 | 14·9 | 0·9 | 5 | 9 | 4 | 3 |

Disturbances in reproduction : (*a*) 0 ; (*b*) 4 ; (*c*) 8.

This comparative table shows us (1) that the P.M. of the reaction-times in Test (*c*) amounts to 14, as against 11 in the other two tests ; (2) that against this the P.M. of the deviations is only 5—much lower than in Tests (*a*) and (*b*) ; (3) that in Test (*c*) the P.M. of those deviations which occur at too long times is shorter ; (3) that the P.M. of all the deviations together = 5, so that the average " too long " times are simultaneous with " too short " deviations ; (4) that the disturbances of

tions, when it has become purely automatic, that the process loses its affective components and therewith its effect upon the psychogalvanic phenomenon. (Cp. the remarks on repetition tests with deep inspiration.)

reproduction have considerably increased. The remarkable disproportion between reaction-times and the deviations in this test itself, and as against Tests (*a*) and (*b*), must be regarded (after what was found in Experiment I) as due to a strong perseveration. The increased errors in reproduction point also to the distraction of attention.

If we look at the curves we realize at once that Curve *c* has a very different character from Curves *a* and *b*. There is no steep ascent to a summit with big deviations, but, on the contrary, a steep descent with remarkably small deviations. The beginning of the curve recalls the down stroke of a complex wave, again the perseveration of a complex. The riddle is solved when we learn that a strong complex was aroused shortly before the beginning of the experiment. When his hands were just laid on the electrodes, but the galvanometer was not yet interpolated, I purposely declared to him that we had come to the opinion that he was just an ordinary swindler, that his discoveries were valueless because they could not be carried out. This declaration affected him greatly, for he saw the sudden destruction of his hope of winning us on his side, and thus his prospects here were as bad as previously in prison. We have learnt in Tests (*a*) and (*b*) his strong emotionalness ; we understand how he would be bound to react to this communication. Had he not possessed a considerable degree of good nature he might well have refused all further experiments. But he kept his hands quietly upon the electrodes and turned to the experiment, which after the intercalation of the galvanometer I began.

| | | R.T. | G.D. | Reproduction |
|---|---|---|---|---|
| 65. Goat | animal | 14 | 0 | — |

The time of the P.M. is maintained but the absence of deviation and of reproduction points to the aroused complex.

| | | | | |
|---|---|---|---|---|
| 66. Big | men | — | —1 | (long reflection) |

The word *men* (a word of embarrassment for him) shows the " blankness of association " conditioned by the complex. The reaction could not prevent the fall of the wave for one moment, much less bring about any positive deviation. Only the subsequent rise of the wave shows some slight action. The — sign in front of the deviation shows that despite the reaction the curve sank 1 mm. This is not here a negative deviation conditioned by the reaction, but simply an absence of any effect of the new reaction upon the descending complex wave. This behaviour is only seen when there is strong perseveration, i.e. a complete blockade of the subject against new impressions in consequence of a previous complex action. In the calculation such negative values are reckoned as 0. In the curves the negative deviations are marked by a *.

| | | | | |
|---|---|---|---|---|
| 67. Potato | field | 10 | 0 | |

The superficial reaction and 0 for the deviation point to the perseveration.

|     |     | R.T. | G.D. | Reproduction |
|-----|-----|------|------|--------------|
| 68. Paint | faint ? fate | — | 3 | |

The disturbance of attention is shown by the non-understanding of the stimulus-word.

|     |     |     |     |     |
|-----|-----|-----|-----|-----|
| 69. Portion | inheritance | 13 | 2 | |
| 70. Old | men | — | — 2 | (reflects) |
| 71. Flower | red flowers | 14 | 4 | red |

Constellated by the flowers which one of his fellow-patients had placed in front of the windows.

|     |     |     |     |
|-----|-----|-----|-----|
| 72. Hit | hit horses | 16 | 2 |

See R. 40.

|     |     |     |     |
|-----|-----|-----|-----|
| 73. Box | clothes-box | — | 5 |
| 74. Pick | good picture | 10 | 8 |

Understood picture. In a short time there were two misunderstandings of the reaction-word, which never occurred in Tests (a) and (b).

This reaction was the first to claim any large measure of attention. The subject thought of Napoleon I, his hero, of whom he possessed several portraits.

|     |     |     |     |
|-----|-----|-----|-----|
| 75. Family | nice family | 18 | 15 |

Means his wife's family. There was a strong complex. The sarcastic expression *nice family* points to a strong emotional content. Nevertheless perseveration acts very powerfully, for in comparison with the deviations (a) and (b) this is still very low.

|     |     |     |     |     |
|-----|-----|-----|-----|-----|
| 76. Wash | face | 14 | — 2 | (face-washing) |
| 77. Cow | milch-cow | 12 | — 2 | |
| 78. Foreign | workman | 25 | 2 | (reflects) |

Explains that he was here thinking of a strike near Zurich in which many of his friends participated, and to which the military were called out. The Public Prosecutor, as whose victim he regarded himself, commanded the regiment in question. He afterwards said that this was the cause of the military handling the strikers so badly ; grounds enough to produce a vivid emotional tone at the memory of the strike.

|     |     |     |     |
|-----|-----|-----|-----|
| 79. Fortune | domestic fortune | 15 | 0 |

Said he was longing for this. See reactions 19 and 20.

|     |     |     |     |
|-----|-----|-----|-----|
| 80. Narrate | stories | 13 | 2 |
| 81. Manners | asylum-manners | — | 15 |

A curious composite word. He said he was thinking of the bad manners of the patients in his section. Despite perseveration, a perceptible deviation. We saw that nearly all the reactions which recall his life in the asylum are accompanied by strong deviations.

|     |     |     |     |     |
|-----|-----|-----|-----|-----|
| 82. Narrow | pass | 35 | 2 | room |

He said that he here thought his sentence would be due to narrow-mindedness if it were such as my remarks seemed to indicate. We notice that the conversation has undoubtedly an after-effect during the test. It is remarkable how low the deviation is (see R. 66).

|     |     |     |     |
|-----|-----|-----|-----|
| 83. Brother | younger | 15 | 3 |

Thinks of his brother who died young.

|   |   | R.T. | G.D. | Reproduction |
|---|---|---|---|---|
| 84. Damage | damage by hail | 15 | 5 | |

Unexplained.

| 85. Stork | children | 25 | 28 | |
|---|---|---|---|---|

It came to him that his little daughter liked to tell "stories about storks." We noticed in reaction 62 that the reminiscences of his children are strongly emotionally toned. Reaction 88 points to the same.

From here to reaction 89 there is an "island" where the curve takes on the character of (a) and (b). As strong complexes were aroused it is understandable that the influence of that perseverating affect is momentarily interrupted.[1]

| 86. False | mankind | 10 | 12 | |
|---|---|---|---|---|

It would not be going far astray to suppose that the experimeter himself is intended by this reaction.

| 87. Dread | never | 25 | 60 | |
|---|---|---|---|---|

The reaction-word arises from the subject's personal disposition. From the foregoing there must be many emotional-toned associations linked to *dread*.

| 88. Kiss | children | 15 | 30 | |
|---|---|---|---|---|

Although he is fairly amorously disposed, I do not think that children is here only a "cover association." He was always a loving, anxious father towards his children. Nevertheless amorous ideas may play a part.

| 89. Fire | -like | 10 | 30 | |
|---|---|---|---|---|

Unexplained.

| 90. Dirty | street | 7 | — 2 | |
|---|---|---|---|---|
| 91. Doors | great | 10 | 7 | |
| 92. Vote | people | 13 | 3 | |
| 93. Hay | parched | 15 | 3 | |
| 94. Quiet | room | 10 | 5 | |
| 95. Sarcasm | men | 20 | 17 | |

He is extremely susceptible to sarcasm, as he is to disesteem (see R. 44, where men is also associated).

| 96. Sleep | go | 15 | 3 | room |
|---|---|---|---|---|
| 97. Month | ten | 10 | 16 | |

Says he has now done ten months of his punishment. The short reaction-time betrays how intense is his occupation with the question of finishing his time. Otherwise the reaction *ten* could not so promptly follow *month*. The deviation corresponds to the strength of the complex, which even conquers the perseveration (see the subsequent rise of the curve).

| 98. Coloured | nature | 15 | 18 | |
|---|---|---|---|---|

After the foregoing reaction has broken the ban of the perseveration it can more easily succeed with a marked deviation. He was not able to give any explanation in answer to simple questioning.

| 99. Dog | yard dog | 10 | 5 | |
|---|---|---|---|---|
| 100. Speak | little | 7 | 5 | |

---

[1] This "island" shows clearly that it is no physical cause that is responsible for the peculiar course of Curve c. We see that as soon as the psychological constellation approximates to the Tests (a) and (b) the character of the curve becomes the same.

SUMMARY OF EXPERIMENT II (a), (b), AND (c)

Curves a and b rise very rapidly ; the deviations are very strong.  There are no obvious complex waves.  He gives great attention to both tests.

Curve c exhibits the up stroke of a complex curve ; the deviations are very slight, they are entirely absent at places.  The complex was aroused before beginning the experiment, hence the absence of the long deviation that precedes the up stroke.

Test (c) shows clearly the effect of inner distraction from an affect upon the psychological phenomenon and confirms what was said about perseveration in Test I.

In other words :

A strong affect, independent of the experiment, conditions the decline of the association curve and the diminution or absence of the deviations.  It is only in those places where stimulus-words interrupted the action of the affect and a new condition of affect was created that the deviations become greater again and the curve rises (curve section 85–89).  The affect perseverates so strongly during the test that the P.M. of the reaction-times is increased from 11 (Tests (a) and (b)) to 14, and the P.M. of the deviations is lowered from 30 (Test (a)), 23 (Test (b)), to 5.  With "too long" times we get "too short" deviations, whilst in Tests (a) and (b) the prolonged times are, on the average, accompanied by longer deviations.

## EXPERIMENT III

The subject is a young married doctor who has carried out association tests with others very often but has never had one carried out on himself. This in itself shows a certain disinclination towards the psychological investigation of himself.  He is also reserved in ordinary conversation.  This reserve is a defence measure against his extreme sensibility, but it is not so much inherited as acquired from various events which have acted upon him as boy and youth, and which even to-day are still to some extent active.  Since the affect bound up with it cannot be yet "abreacted," the complex in question produces much dissociation.  It has taken him very far.  The consequences of these disinclinations, partly conscious, partly unconscious, directed against those events are making themselves felt in the whole of his being.  The bright, careless boy early became a very serious man who has developed, as compensation, a most unusual zeal for duty, and anxiety about his work.

The arrangement of the experiment was the same as in Test I (one cell, brass electrodes).

The average values are as follows :

| P.M. of R.T. | A.M. of R.T. | P.M. of deviation | A.M. of deviation | P.M. of deviations with "too long" times | Disturbances in reproduction |
|---|---|---|---|---|---|
| 8 | 8·7 | 0 | 4 | 0 | 33·3 per cent. |

The P.M. of the reaction-times is very short, and the difference from A.M. slight. This shows us that he reacted very nimbly. These two values tell us nothing about emotional inhibitions. The value 0 for the P.M. of the deviations is striking. In no " normal test " with any kind of arrangement of the test have I found 0 as P.M. We must look to some complication. The A.M. of the deviations (4) tells us that there must have been deviations. From the P.M. of these deviations which arise at " too long " times (0) we learn that the prolongation of the reaction-time is accompanied by no average prolongation of the deviations. 33·3 per cent. of disturbances in reproduction is a high figure for an educated man. We must conclude that either very strong complexes were aroused in the experiment or that from some other ground there was present a disturbance of attention. The behaviour of the reaction-time and the deviations favour the latter.

If we look at the curve we shall be struck by the similarity to Curve II c. The curve falls instead of rising as in the normal association curve. But whilst in Curve II c the steepest ascent and the slightest deviations are found at the beginning, in Curve III we have at first moderate deviations, and it is only later that the curve falls and the deviations are absent. We may, therefore, conclude that the disturbance of attention only made itself felt little by little.

The behaviour of the average values and of the curve is explained by the subject's psychological constellation. He afterwards told me that he began the experiment with a certain distrust as to the worth of the galvanometric method of investigation. He thought that the deviations were caused by a certain auto-suggestion, and wanted to find out whether deflections would occur if one did not wish them. Secondly, he felt sure that he, the subject, could control the association experiment and that he would be able to conceal his complexes. He therefore purposely reacted as quickly as possible and took care that no prolongation of time should occur. He succeeded herein to a considerable extent. But the complexes only came out the more clearly in the reaction-words.

He would have been very pleased, as he afterwards admitted, if the deviations as complex signs had left me in the lurch ; this was to a certain extent out of envy that I had time to give myself up to the galvanometric investigations, whilst he himself, overwhelmed with practical work, had no leisure for scientific activities. (The experiment will show how strong was the complex of this hindrance to scientific work.) Then the test took place after dinner, when he was somewhat sleepy. We have, therefore, two motives for a conscious and active barrier to attention, and the fatigue is a further reason towards making concentration of attention difficult.

But by far the most important condition for the successful barring of his attention seems to me the unconscious complexes of which we have spoken ; he afterwards said he could not and did not wish to inform me about one of his main complexes. The inhibition arising from that complex seems to me to have been chiefly responsible for the absence of the deviations. It is as if in this case the stimulus-words were, in consequence of this barrier, generally not apprehended in their full significance, and hence could not evoke any development of affect. The short reaction-times speak also for this view. The reason why I ascribe little value to his conscious barrier is due to the fact that in a second test, upon which he had concentrated his good-will, the curve showed exactly the same course. On this second occasion he was also slightly tired. But fatigue does not of itself suffice to lower the curve, as was shown by a test on a female nurse, taken the day after night duty. That the barrier did not succeed at the beginning is plain from the first part of the curve. According to his own account the test did at first somewhat excite him (easily to be understood). But from about reaction 26 he felt " his complexes were now set aside," and he felt safe after that.

The curve sinks distinctly after reaction 26, although we notice before this a tendency to fall. Whilst in Experiment I the rise sets in before the subject had the feeling of excitation, here the ease of mind was shown by the curve, before the subject himself perceived it. Whilst in Test I the ego complex lost more and more its mastery over the other complexes, here the ego complex grew ever stronger. If we calculate the average values of the section of the curve 1–26 we recognize how much more strongly the attention is claimed, as contrasted with the succeeding section of the test.

| P.M. of R.T. | A.M. of R.T. | P.M. of deviations | A.M. of deviations | P.M. of deviations with " too long " time | Disturbances in reproduction |
|---|---|---|---|---|---|
| 7 | 8·1 | 5 | 8 | 11 | 23 per cent. |

That the P.M. of the reaction-times is shorter than in the test as a whole shows that the subject's intention to react as quickly as possible succeeded better at first than later. That there was much more affect at the beginning of the experiment is shown by —(1) the great differences between P.M. and A.M. of the times ; (2) the increased values for the deviations (note the P.M. of the deflections which are simultaneous with too long times) ; (3) the decrease of disturbances in reproduction.

| | | R.T. | G.D. | Reproduction |
|---|---|---|---|---|
| 1. Head | beautiful | 9 | 16 | |

Believed I thought that he was thinking about his wife. Naturally this is an immediate association to his wife, at least unconsciously ; the thoughts are only subsequently clad in this form. It vividly recalls to me a case of dementia præcox where the patient explained in katamnesis that whenever he was in the presence of ladies he always thought that the lady would think he was in love with her.

| | | | | |
|---|---|---|---|---|
| 2. Green | fields | 7 | 10 | |
| 3. Water | blue | 6 | 15 | |

Unexplained.

| | | | | |
|---|---|---|---|---|
| 4. Prick | deep | 7 | 12 | |

Here thinks that this reaction is apt to arouse sexual associations in other subjects.

| | | | | |
|---|---|---|---|---|
| 5. Angel | angel ? high | 14 | 18 | |

At first misunderstood *angle*. The cause of the misunderstanding is the perseveration (cp. reaction 4, *deep*, reaction 5, *high*, and the analysis). Why *angel* was understood is unexplained. The reaction *high* he analysed himself, "He did not want to prick the angel deep." The repetition of the stimulus-word, the reaction-time, and the deviation are objective evidence of the complex, not the least being the reaction-word itself. The symbolism is obvious.

| | | | | |
|---|---|---|---|---|
| 6. Long | deep | 8 | 11 | big |

He knows that the stimulus-word *long* often arouses sexual complexes. He therefore reacts with what, as we shall see, is his " complex representative "— *deep*. The wrongly reproducted *big* is only a replacement for *long*. That a personal sexual complex was here aroused and that the disturbance was not merely conditioned by his experiences with other subjects seems fairly plain. Reactions 4, 5, and 6 are closely connected.

| | | | | |
|---|---|---|---|---|
| 7. Ship | sail | 8 | 8 | big |

The incorrect reproduction and the deviation (the P.M. of the first twenty-five reactions is 5) again point to a complex. *Big* is suspicious ; the matter only got cleared up when in the test carried out four weeks later he reacted *ship — mast*. He then also had an incorrect reproduction—*water*. I have often received elucidation, in later tests, of apparently innocent reactions of earlier tests which showed distinct complex signs. If we remember that months later an extraordinary percentage of reactions will be exactly the same as in the first test, we shall understand how firmly, as a rule, the associations are held. It does not therefore seem overbold to draw conclusions from a test made four months later, even though I assume that the complex in the meantime has not changed.[1]

| | | | | |
|---|---|---|---|---|
| 8. Plough | field | 6 | 1 | |

This reaction has an emotional tone for only a few people ; we can see how dependent the psychogalvanic reflex is upon the emotional tone of ideas.

| | | | | |
|---|---|---|---|---|
| 9. Wool | cotton-wool | 7 | 13 | |

The reaction reminded him that some of his subjects had understood the word as *well*, and that in a sexual sense.

---

[1] Cp. "The Experiments in Reproduction," by Peterson and Jung, *Brain*, 1907, p. 187.

|  |  | R.T. | G.D. | Reproduction |
|---|---|---|---|---|
| 10. Friendly | beloved | 8 | 13 | |

He said that *beloved* was always, in the experiment, a word that stood for his wife.

| 11. Table | chair | 6 | 5 | |
| 12. Ask | answer | 6 | 5 | |

He moved his hands between reactions 12 and 13. But I cannot therefore say the strong fall of the curve was the result of the movement; the strong deviation, however, may have been. For as a rule one finds a rise of the curve after movements, probably because the hands then generally press more strongly upon the electrodes. It was the contrary here; his hands were removed from the electrodes. This might be due to a decrease of interest, and, inversely, a stronger pressure of his hands might be ascribed to the occurrence of a stronger complex which evoked motor innervations.

| 13. State | land | 9 | 2 | people |

The stimulus-word was misunderstood. He possesses a strong social complex; has a pronounced social vein but regrets that he has too little time and knowledge to busy himself with politics or economics. *State*, moreover, reminds him of State service and the personal want of liberty it occasions.

| 14. Haughty | friendly | 7 | 3 | |
| 15. Stalk | high | 11 | 17 | long |

(See R. 6.)

| 16. Dance | much | 11 | 10 | |

Thinks of his wife.

| 17. Lake | blue | 6 | 0 | |
| 18. Ill | healthy | 9 | 4 | |
| 19. Proud | polite | 11 | 2 | |

The reaction is constellated by an incident when he was reproached with being too proud.

| 20. Cook | much | 9 | 0 | |
| 21. Housekeeping | wife | 7 | 4 | |

The thought about his wife's housekeeping is strongly emotionally toned. The reaction influences the next one.

| 22. Wicked | good | 6 | 12 | |

Explains he referred to his wife and the housekeeping. The strong deviation is not to be interpreted by the emotional tone of reaction 21 first making itself felt at reaction 22; it was only at reaction 22 that the complex aroused distinct feeling.

| 23. Needle | scissors | 7 | 0 | |
| 24. Swim | deep | 6 | 1 | |

The association omitted is *water*; hence the complex representative *deep*. Cp. reaction 3, when the deviation was so strong at the association *water*. The complex did not become distinct there either.

| 25. Furlough | long | 14 | 16 | |

*Furlough* is for this subject, as for No. 1, a strong complex with a wealth of emotionally toned associations.

|           |         | R.T. | G.D. | Reproduction |
|-----------|---------|------|------|--------------|
| 26. Blue  | green   | 7    | 3    | water        |

The disturbance in reproduction is obviously conditioned by perseveration. As reaction 3 was *water — blue* too much stress must not be laid upon this.

| 27. Dead | life | 9 | 0 | — |

From here on the first series of absent deviations began.

| 28. Threaten | much | 8 | 0 | — |

It was after about reaction 26 (as we said) that he had the feeling "the sexual complex was now out" and he felt at peace. Note that at this place we get three disturbances in reproduction following one another. It is the expression of an inner distraction at this place.

| 29. Lamp | wick  | 6 | 0 |      |
| 30. Rich | poor  | 6 | 0 |      |
| 31. Earn | money | 7 | 0 | rich |

To earn money plays a share in the subject's psyche, although there is no deviation. One had the impression that he was thinking, "Now it's all the same to me; I need not get excited; the worst is over." Only the disturbances in reproduction point to a complex.

| 32. To care | much | 9  | 0 | beautiful |
| 33. Pity    | good | 11 | 0 |           |

He remarked during the analysis: "I ought to have an occupation complex here, seeing that I'm a doctor."

| 34. Yellow   | blue     | 9  | 0 |      |
| 35. Mountain | valley   | 8  | 0 |      |
| 36. Play     | children | 8  | 0 |      |
| 37. Eager    | much     | 16 | 0 | work |
| 38. New      | old      | 6  | 3 |      |

At reaction 37 his occupation complex was aroused and he felt distinct excitation (he feels himself hindered in his scientific activity by his profession of doctor). The strikingly long reaction-time accords with this. But there is no deviation. This only occurs at the next reaction—one quite indifferent and with a very short time.

It is not unusual to observe such delayed effects upon the galvanometer. a real delay in the action of affect upon the galvanometer can only be accepted with caution (cp. reactions 21 and 22). One does not know whether the affect was not clearly perceived at the particular reaction. or whether it was not a new complex that produced the apparently delayed deviation. Self-observation left the subject this time in the lurch.

| 39. Customs | old | 9 | 0 | manners |

*Old* perseveration from reaction 38; a hint that there is a certain emotional tone at *old*—which seems to me very probable for reasons which cannot be gone into (reference to the subject's most important complexes). In the reproduction, when the perseveration is removed the very usual reaction-word *manners* was given—a good example of one of the conditions leading to disturbances in reproduction.

| 40. Ride | well | 9 | 9 | |

During his military service he would like to have learnt to ride well, but an illness prevented his riding. He admits that this worried him afterwards.

We see that everything that hinders him in his ambition provokes vivid emotional expressions.

|  |  | R.T. | G.D. | Reproduction |
|---|---|---|---|---|
| 41. Wall | room | 11 | 0 |  |
| 42. Stupid | clever | 7 | 0 |  |
| 43. Copy-book | book | 8 | 0 |  |
| 44. Despise |  | 14 | 0 | deep |

The reaction reminds him of one of the events of his youth which have so perma-nently affected him.

|  |  |  |  |
|---|---|---|---|
| 45. Tooth | mouth | 14 | 0 |

Thinks of his dentist's account and a "tooth extraction" dream of his wife. Both are emotionally toned.

|  |  |  |  |
|---|---|---|---|
| 46. Right | false | 7 | 0 |
| 47. People | State | 9 | 9 |

The social complex of reaction 13 again. One of the components of it is that the State makes such demands upon him that he has little time to devote to his wife. Therefore the wife and social complexes are often mixed. This is seen by comparing this with Test II.

|  | 1st Test | Reproduction | 2nd Test | Reproduction |
|---|---|---|---|---|
| 47. People | State | + | love | state |
| 50. Unjust | just | + | state | love |
| 92. Vote | love | yes | town council | + |

|  |  | R.T. | G.D. | Reproduction |
|---|---|---|---|---|
| 48. Smell | bad odour | 7 | 1 |  |
| 49. Book | exercise-book | 8 | 0 |  |
| 50. Unjust | just | 7 | 20 |  |

See R. 47.

|  |  |  |  |
|---|---|---|---|
| 51. Child | mother | 12 | 0 |

At this reaction he thinks of his wife. The reaction ought not, in his view, to be very emotionally toned, for he "split off" the complex it contained.

I omit for the sake of brevity some reactions which proved nothing.

|  |  |  |  |
|---|---|---|---|
| 61. Law | State | 7 | 0 |

Despite the complex, no further disturbance.

|  |  |  |  |  |
|---|---|---|---|---|
| 62. Love | faithful | 9 | 11 |  |
| 63. glass |  | 29 | 6 | drink |

*Glass* reminds him of *drink* (afterwards reproduced) and of the teetotal movement, of which he is a fervid partisan. The strong emotional tone rests upon the fact that this propaganda takes away very much of his time from scientific work.

|  |  |  |  |  |
|---|---|---|---|---|
| 64. Fight | to like | 11 | 1 | quarrel |
| 65. Worm | soup | 7 | 3 |  |

constellated by a term used among his colleagues. The section of the curve 62–68 presents a distinct complex wave. The fall of the curve is again inter-rupted by the different complexes in reactions 62–65 and he is shaken out of his calm.

|  |  |  | R.T. | G.D. | Reproduction |
|---|---|---|---|---|---|
| Down stroke | 66. Big | little | 6 | 0 | |
| of the com- | 67. Potato | earth-apple | 6 | 0 | |
| plex wave | 68. Paint | picture | 7 | 0 | much |

At reaction 68 he thought of his wife, which at once produced a disturbance in reproduction.

| 69. Parts | sex | 9 | 5 | |
|---|---|---|---|---|
| 70. Old | young | 6 | 0 | |
| 71. Flower | through the flowers | 11 | 0 | |

Constellated by a comical use of the word *flower*.

| 72. Pit | deep | 7 | 0 | |
|---|---|---|---|---|
| 73. Box | high | 8 | 0 | wall |

*Pit* reminds him of *prick*, hence the reaction-word *deep*, and this perseverates, as in reaction 4, in the subsequent reaction (cp. reaction 5, *high = not deep*).

The perseveration is probably the cause of the disturbance in reproduction.

| 74. Wild | very | 9 | 0 | |
|---|---|---|---|---|

Refers to a patient.

| 75. Family | child | 7 | 0 | |
|---|---|---|---|---|

As in reaction 51, we note that the content of this reaction plays no great part with him.

| 80. Narrate | report | 10 | 0 | much |
|---|---|---|---|---|

That he is thinking about his wife is betrayed by the incorrect reproduction (see reactions 16, 68, 88, 101, etc.). "He ought to tell his wife a lot about his work."

| 81. Manners | customs | 7 | 2 | |
|---|---|---|---|---|

Here movement of his hands and rise of the curve. The movement seems to have been due to a complex that cannot be gone into.

| 82. Narrow | broad | 7 | 1 | |
|---|---|---|---|---|
| 83. Brother | sister | 6 | 0 | |
| 84. Injure | unfaithful | 7 | 0 | |
| 85. Stork | child | 7 | 0 | |

See reactions 51 and 75.

| 86. False | good | 8 | 0 | faithful |
|---|---|---|---|---|

In the second experiment *women* was the association here

| 87. Fear | yes | 11 | 0 | |
|---|---|---|---|---|
| 88. Kiss | much | 12 | 2 | |

Cp. reaction 80.

| 89. Fire | fire-brigade | 9 | 0 | |
|---|---|---|---|---|
| 90. Dirty | clean | 8 | 0 | |
| 91. Door | gate | 8 | 0 | |

He was aware of the symbolism, as he was in reaction 82.

| 92. Vote | love | 12 | 0 | yes |
|---|---|---|---|---|

See reaction 47.

| | | R.T. | G.D. | Reproduction |
|---|---|---|---|---|
| 93. Marriage | faithful | 11 | 0 | |

From about now on he closed his eyes, whilst before he had been drowsily looking about him.

| | | R.T. | G.D. | Reproduction |
|---|---|---|---|---|
| 94. Still | soft | 7 | 0 | good |
| 95. Mockery | yes | 9 | 0 | |

Social constellation—recalls an event of his youth.

| | | R.T. | G.D. | |
|---|---|---|---|---|
| 96. Sleep | together | 9 | 104 | |

The enormous deviations occurred because the complex was brought out quite unconcealed. He had reacted " as if asleep " ; the reaction was driven out before he knew it and could stop it. He could not help laughing to himself, and his hands trembled so that the deviation became stronger. The most important thing about this reaction is that the curve now remains at the summit—i.e. the excitation is maintained. This proves clearly that the curve is by no means bound to sink (say from physical causes) after every long deviation, but that its behaviour is conditioned by the momentary psychological constellation of the subject. In this case there was a sudden transition from the somnolent to the waking state. The stimulus is so strong that it not only aroused him but evoked an excitation with numerous innervations. So no fall of the complex wave occurred (if the experiment had not been soon after broken off we should, of course, have had a fall).

| | | R.T. | G.D. | |
|---|---|---|---|---|
| 97. Month | year | 12 | 1 | |
| 98. Coloured | green | 9 | 0 | blue |
| 99. Dog | hog | 9 | 6 | |

Unexplained.

| | | R.T. | G.D. | |
|---|---|---|---|---|
| 100. To talk | much | 8 | 0 | entertain |
| 101. Night | much | 17 | 27 | — |

This complex sensitiveness is well seen here.[1]

| | | R.T. | G.D. | |
|---|---|---|---|---|
| 102. Sew | grass | 9 | 8 | field |

Misunderstood stimulus-word. Unexplained.

| | | R.T. | G.D. | |
|---|---|---|---|---|
| 103. Wine | glass | 12 | 8 | |

See reaction 63.

| | | R.T. | G.D. | |
|---|---|---|---|---|
| 104. Beautiful | good | 8 | 0 | |
| 105. Watch | -works | 8 | 5 | |

Unexplained.

The strong deviations that appeared in reactions 99–105 show the action of reaction 96 upon the subject's consciousness. The barrier and the drowsiness were overcome, a state of increased irritability arose.


SUMMARY OF EXPERIMENT III

The experiment shows the influence of the distraction of attention, partly purposely determined, partly determined by the subject's psychological constellation.

He was in a state of " active opposition " to the analysis.

[1] By complex sensitiveness Jung understands "the readiness to react to similar but much weaker stimuli with approximately the same force" after a complex idea has once been aroused. (*Psychology of Dementia Præcox*, p. 40.)

This active opposition causes the "association curve" to fall. A certain time (to R. 26) elapses before this opposition succeeds in making itself felt. Up till then the curve sinks but little. This opposition is responsible for the frequent absence of the deviation, an absence which begins after reaction 26.

In contradistinction to Test II c, the reaction-times are very short; the P.M. of the reaction-times for the whole test is 8, for those of reactions 1–26 it is only 7. This shortness of the reaction-times again shows the influence of activity, of an endeavour to react as quickly as possible so as to avoid tell-tale reaction-times. Active opposition works, therefore, contrary to passive distraction of attention (by a perseverating complex) by shortening the deviations as well as the reaction-times.

The reason for this difference as against Test II c can easily be recognized, in that the whole attention was directed towards one end—to react quickly. The "emotive inhibition" comes into conflict with another much stronger intention working in the opposite direction.

This endeavour to react as quickly as possible, to abolish as far as possible the psychological results of the experiment, causes the stimulus-words in many cases to be apprehended quite superficially; the complexes are not touched, so that no development of the affect arises. The deviations are consequently omitted.


EXPERIMENT IV

After I had recognized the effect of distraction of the attention upon the galvanometer curve in two different ways, viz. by the perseveration of a complex (Test II c) and by active opposition (Test III), I tried to attain by a third experimental method the distraction of attention. I used Jung and Riklin's method of outer distraction (see chapter ii). In order to observe at the same time the behaviour of the psychogalvanic curve, I placed the electrodes on the (naked) soles of the feet so that the subject had his feet resting on the electrodes instead of on the ground. I had previously convinced myself by repeated experiments that this method gave the same results as when the electrodes were placed on the hands. The deviations are even stronger because the area of contact is larger and the contact is closer. In the "normal experiment" the curve rises more quickly than when the electrodes are placed on the hands.

In order to bring out clearly the difference between the normal association curve and the "distraction curve" I will describe a distraction test on the subject of Test I. As he was a highly educated man the *tempo* of the metronome beats had to be as rapid as possible in order to reach any dissociation of attention at all. The metronome was placed at 94, i.e. 94 straight beats, each exactly 1 cm. long (the lengths being assigned by horizontal lines), were executed per minute. The stimulus-words only began to be called out when everything was in order. A comparison of Curve 4 with Curve 1 shows the extreme differ-ence. Curve 1 rises rapidly at the beginning, as it did after the interruption (after R. 47). Curve 4 falls rapidly at the beginning, as it does after the interruption (R. 26). It recalls both the small size and the complete absence, at times, of the deviations at the beginnings of Curve 2 c and Curve 3 ; it shows in large what we found as the down stroke of a complex wave in the "normal" experiment. The curve begins very high (between 37 and 38 mm.), partly because the soles of the feet form a better circuit for the electric current. But there is also a psychological factor. For if under the same condition the experiment is at one time made with "distraction" and then for a time without "distraction," it is found that those parts of the curve where there was "distraction" begin higher than the other. The psychological factor is conditioned by a certain degree of excitement which is of different strength in different individuals, consequent upon the complicated demands which the distraction experiment imposes. Now compare the average values of the normal Test I and of the distraction Test IV, and remember that in Test IV the deviations are, as a rule, greater and the rise of the curve is more rapid with the use of the soles of the feet. When we find that despite this the deviations are less than in hand contact, we get an estimate of the great influence of the psychical process of distraction upon the psychogalvanic phenomenon.

| | P.M. of R.T. | A.M. of R.T. | Dif-ference | P.M. of deviations | A.M. of deviations | Dif-ference | Disturbances of repro-duction |
|---|---|---|---|---|---|---|---|
| Test I . | 9 | 8·8 | − 0·2 | 8 | 10 | + 2 | 10 % |
| Test II . | 7 | 8·4 | + 1·4 | 0 | 2·5 | + 2·5 | 21 % |

Both the P.M. and the A.M. of the reaction-times is less than in the normal test. This is another distinct difference as against inner distraction from the perseveration of a complex (II c). There the reaction-time was increased, on the average, against the normal test of the same person. We there regarded the prolongation of the time as due to an increased dissociation of attention, which was claimed by the complex, thus leaving only a residue for the reactions themselves. Remember that the quality of the associations was not remarkably superficial because the subject, despite the complex, endeavoured to react according to the sense of the words. In this test (IV) the abbreviation of time is due simply to the dissociation of attention being much more complete, for the patient's reactions are almost entirely verbal. By reason of his great verbal fluency he was able to give his whole attention to making the strokes and allowed the verbal mechanism to work almost automatically. The more autonomically the verbal mechanism worked the shorter became the reaction-times. The conditions are very similar to those in the last test (III). In that case the attention was almost wholly occupied by the endeavour to act quickly, here by making the strokes. The difference between the P.M. and the A.M. of the reaction-time in the test shows that there must have also occurred a series of " too long " times ; that emotive disturbances must have crept into the purely verbal course of the reactions. The P.M. of the tests is 0, as in Test III ; but the A.M. of these shows that deviations must have occurred. The frequent absence of deviation is explained on the same grounds as in Test III. The distraction of attention is proved also by the fact that disturbances in reproduction are almost twice as frequent in this test as in the normal test. In communicating the associations in this test I chiefly desire to show the extremely superficial type of the associations.

|  |  | R.T. | G.D. | Reproduction |
|---|---|---|---|---|
| 1. Head | face | 7 | 16 | |
| 2. Green | grass | 7 | 2 | |
| 3. Water | water | 6 | 11 | |
| 4. Prick | pain | 7 | 14 | knife |
| 5. Angel | angle | 7 | 6 | |
| 6. Long | gong | 6 | 2 | |

The four first reaction-words contain the vowel a, and reactions 5 and 6 are entirely clang-associations.

| 7. Ship | ship | 6 | 8 | (reflects) |
|---|---|---|---|---|

The repetition of the stimulus-words at reactions 3 and 7 shows most distinctly how strongly the attention has been distracted.

| 8. Plough | f-fly | 14 | 25 | |
|---|---|---|---|---|

The long time was caused by the stuttering in pronouncing the reaction-word ; the long deviation was certainly caused by the disturbance which occurred whenever he began marking a new line ; this occasioned a movement of the whole of the upper part of the body and of the legs also. This disturbance is seen in reactions 8 and 16 and at regular intervals after reactions 34, 49, and 62.

On the first two occasions, when the subject was not quite accustomed to the experiment and was still a little excited, the disturbance was expressed by a stronger deviation than later, when it is only shown by a slight rise of the curve.

| 9. Wool | m-knit | 11 | 4 | |
|---|---|---|---|---|

He wanted to say *mull*. Notice the endeavour to react with clangs.

| 10. Friendly | hateful | 7 | 2 | |
|---|---|---|---|---|
| 11. Table | able | · 6 | 0 | |

This is the first time there is no deviation.  As in the normal experiment, the deviations are at first bigger than afterwards.

| | | R.T. | G.D. | Reproduction |
|---|---|---|---|---|
| 12. Ask | answer | 7 | 0 | task ? |
| 13. State | courage | 11 | 4 | Switzerland |

At first thought of a " deed " where courage was required.  *Courage* is an indirect association.

| | | | | |
|---|---|---|---|---|
| 14. Haughty | friendly | 16 | 0 | violent |

See reaction 32.

| | | | |
|---|---|---|---|
| 15. Stalk | baulk | 6 | 4 |
| 16. Dance | to idle | 9 | 24 |

The intermediate term was *waltz*.

| | | | |
|---|---|---|---|
| 17. Lake | sea | 6 | 7 |
| 18. Ill | weak | 6 | 0 |
| 19. Proud | loud | 6 | 0 |
| 20. Locks | sock—rocks | 9 | 2 |

He explained that the stimulus-word had at first evoked the visual picture of a sea grotto, and this again the word *rock*, which gave *rocks*.  *Sock* was arrived at by amalgamation of the clang pictures *sea* and *rocks*.  It seems more probable that *locks* just evoked the clang-picture *rocks*.  Let us remember that in earlier reactions we had the reaction *lake — sea* with a strong deviation.  We know from Test I that *sea* is very emotionally toned for this subject.  We can understand why it is so suppressed.

| | | | |
|---|---|---|---|
| 21. Ink | to sink | 6 | 0 |

He wanted to say *fish*.  Cp. this reaction in Test I.

| | | | |
|---|---|---|---|
| 22. Wicked | sc—false | 14 | 4 |

He intended to say *scoff*, which is a dialect expression (*höhn sein*) for *angry*.

| | | | |
|---|---|---|---|
| 23. Needle | pin-prick | 11 | 0 |

Wanted to say *navel*.

| | | | |
|---|---|---|---|
| 24. Swim | fish | 7 | 0 |
| 25. Journey | make | 9 | 0 |
| 26. Blue | lake | 9 | 0 |

Wanted to say *mew ;* a perseveration of the *m* in *make*.
The test had to be interrupted here because the strip of paper was finished.  The curve at once rose again to 33·6 ; the electric resistance improved in the pause.  With the beginning of distraction the curve at once fell ; the electric resistance rapidly increased.

| | | | |
|---|---|---|---|
| 27. Bread | h'm red | 12 | 9 |

Wanted to say *cut*.

| | | | |
|---|---|---|---|
| 28. Threaten | hit | 7 | 4 |
| 29. Lamp | shine | 7 | 6 |
| 30. Rich | poor | 6 | 0 |
| 31. Tree | stem | 6 | 0 |
| 32. To sing | { sting [1] ding | 7 | 9 |

---

[1] Again two reaction-words.  That two words, even if they are often truncated words, are so frequently associated shows that the attention is withheld from the associations, that none has sufficient stress of attention to triumph over the rival associations.

We notice that certain sounds are much to the fore in this experiment. I knew that shortly before the experiment the patient had been informed that a former female patient, whose name begins with this sound, had slandered him. At the end of the experiment I made him rest in order to notice the curves at rest  He went to sleep and had a dream in which this lady played the chief part. I thus discovered that his thoughts about her were unconsciously perseverating during the experiment. I am strongly inclined, and the subject agreed with me, to see in the prominence of these sounds a "symptomatic action." [1]

It is also possible that the complex signs in the reactions 14, 22, 28, and 64 refer to this unpleasant complex.

|  |  | R.T. | G.D. | Reproduction |
|---|---|---|---|---|
| 33. Pity | the poor | 6 | 0 | poor |

This reaction, like *friendly — hateful*, *ask — answer*, are stereotyped replies he gets in his experiments with others and therefore trips off his tongue like rhymes and clangs.

| 34. Yellow | poor | 9 | 0 |
|---|---|---|---|

*Poor*, perseveration from reaction 33. See reaction 8.

| 35. Mountain | climb | 7 | 0 |
|---|---|---|---|
| 36. Play | children | 8 | 0 |
| 37. Salt | paint | 9 | 0 |

Wanted to say *pot*.

| 38. New | old | 6 | 12 |
|---|---|---|---|

We must not pay too much attention to the occurrence of too long deviations (unaccompanied by other complex signs) in this test, where movements play a disturbing part.

| 39. Customs | bad customs | 8 | 1 |
|---|---|---|---|
| 40. Ride | horse | 6 | 5 |
| 41. Wall | stall [2] | 7 | 2 |

As in Test I, an English word (*wall*) occurred to him (reaction 3 in Test I). Test IV took place seven weeks after Test I. Then *star* was reacted. The word *stall* occurred in the analysis (*Star of Bethlehem*). Despite the distraction the complex can still be recognized.

| 42. Silly | billy | 7 | 7 |
|---|---|---|---|
| 43. Copy-book | knife | 9 | 0 |
| 44. Despise | esteem | 7 | 0 |
| 45. Tooth | time | 7 | 0 |
| 46. Right | wrong | 7 | 4 |
| 47. People | full | 6 | 0 |
| 48. Smell | cattle | 9 | 0 |
| 49. Book | Huch | 12 | 0 |

Thinks of Ricarda Huch.

| 50. Unjust | just | 7 | 0 |
|---|---|---|---|
| 51. Frog | h'm—brooch | 14 | — |

---

[1] Freud, P*sychopathology of Everyday Life.*

[2] *Stall* is also the German word and has the same meaning—it is not a rhyme in the original but a clang (*Wand — Stall*).—TRANSLATOR.

*Brooch* (a clang in the original *Frosch — Brosche*) may be constellated by his intention to give his wife a present.

|  |  | R.T. | G.D. | Reproduction |
|---|---|---|---|---|
| 52. Divorce | avoid | 7 | 0 | |
| 53. Hunger | thirst | 6 | 0 | |
| 54. White | black | 6 | 0 | |
| 55. Cattle | herd | 6 | 0 | |
| 56. To take over | h'm, to observe | 12 | 0 | |
| 57. Pencil | point | 6 | 0 | |
| 58. Cloudy | h'm, water | 9 | 0 | |
| 59. Plum | sweet | 7 | 0 | |
| 60. Meet | greet | 7 | 0 | |
| 61. Law | book | 9 | 0 | |
| 62. Loving | dear | 7 | 0 | |
| 63. Glass | clear | 6 | 0 | |
| 64. Strife | str-uggle | 12 | 0 | { strig striggle |

See reaction 32.

|  |  |  |  |  |
|---|---|---|---|---|
| 65. Goat | h'm, animal | 11 | 0 | |
| 66. Big | heavy | 9 | 0 | |
| 67. Carrot | capital | 9 | 0 | |

A very superficial clang-association; *capital* is of momentary importance, for he had just bought some bonds.

|  |  |  |  |  |
|---|---|---|---|---|
| 68. Panel | picture | 7 | 0 | |
| 69. Part | have | 7 | 0 | inheritance |

See reaction 67.   He has a share (part) in a manufactory.

|  |  |  |  |
|---|---|---|---|
| 70. Old | to be | 7 | 0 |
| 71. Bloom | lumen | 11 | 0 |

*Becoming old* and *lumen* both play a rôle.

|  |  |  |  |  |
|---|---|---|---|---|
| 72. Beat | watch | 9 | 0 | (reflects) |

Constellated from the metronome beats.

|  |  |  |  |  |
|---|---|---|---|---|
| 73. Chest | cash | 7 | 0 | |
| 74. Wild | mild | 7 | 0 | wild |
| 75. Family | have | 6 | 0 | |
| 76. Wash | water | 6 | 0 | |
| 77. Cow (*Kuh*) | high (*hoch*) | 9 | 0 | |

Understood as *book*.   Reaction 49 was *book — huch*.

At the end of the test the beam of light went again to 42, i.e. he passed in a few seconds the distance from 13·6–42.  I therefore made the subject rest quite quietly; whereupon he fell asleep and had the dream.  During this time (5 m.) the beam of light went down from 45 to 25, and after he awoke it again rose.  The sleep wave, therefore, behaved like a distraction wave.

## Summary of Experiment IV

The test shows the action of " outer distraction " upon the galvanometer curve. The action is here like that of active opposition in Test III : fall of the curve, decrease or absence of the deviations, strikingly small reaction-times. In Test IV the P.M. of the reaction-times is 7, against 9 in the normal experiment on the same subject. Tests III and IV are the opposite of Test II (c) in respect to their short reaction-times. The difference in the behaviour of the reaction-times is to be explained by the fact that in the former tests the attention was actively directed to a definite process, whilst in Test II (c) it was passively fettered by the complex previously aroused. The dissociation of attention is therefore much more complete in Tests III and IV ; the reactions occur without arousing many associations—in Test III through active opposition, in Test IV by the purely verbal-motor attitude. In Test II (c), on the other hand, the subject endeavoured to direct his attention away from the complex towards the single reactions ; hence conflict and prolongation of times.

At the conclusion of the experiment the beam of light ascended very quickly (not shown), whilst usually it falls at the end of the normal test.

Whilst he was asleep (5 min.) the beam of light fell on the scale (about 17 mm.). The sleep-wave thus behaved in this case like waves in distraction, or as if the subject were at rest.

## Conclusions derived from Experiments II–IV

In the selection of these three cases from my total cases I had three different aims in mind.

First, I wanted to show what real service the psychogalvanic phenomenon in association tests can render us in psychological investigation, for it enlarges our knowledge by an objective complex sign and gives us more direct information about the affective reactions than other complex signs.

Secondly, I wished to draw the attention of those unacquainted with the association tests to the results, however small they be, of their general experimental-psychological nature—of those, especially, who regard the phenomenon as " an arbitrary means of expression " in experimental psychology.

Thirdly, I selected these tests because one could study in them the physical expression of one and the same psychological process, the distraction of attention. The investigations into the influence of attention in the experiment, when compared with other investigations, give us some indications as to the essential meaning of the psychogalvanic phenomenon.

We must remember, in the first place, that in the tests as carried out we have to do, chiefly or exclusively, with changes of the electrical resistance of the skin—this, in its turn, causing fluctuations in the intensity of the current ; the galvanometer marks these fluctuations. We must accept this, at least until more exact electro-physiological investigations have been made on the subject.

The earlier French scientists to whom we have referred accept, without more ado, these changes of electrical resistance in their tests. We know nothing at all about changes of electro-motor power in the experiments. Therefore we are compelled to regard the rise of the galvanometer curve (i.e. the increase in the strength of the current) as expressing the decrease of the electrical resistance of the skin, and the fall of this curve as expressing an increase of its resistance.

Féré proved that there was a decrease of electric resistance on the application of sensory stimuli. E. Müller, Veraguth, Jung, and myself have made the same observations. With the exception of Féré (who only used sensory stimuli), these workers find that this resistance decreases also with the higher psychical stimuli. (Veraguth only speaks of a decrease or increase of the strength of the current measured directly by the galvanometer, without saying what conditions it.) On the other hand, the resistance increases when at rest and, as we have seen, in sleep. The resistance also increases in quiet mental work, e.g. in adding up, or in uninteresting reading (Veraguth). We will place these observations alongside those found in our experiments.

I. *Decrease of the Electrical Resistance to Conduction :*
(a) In sensory stimuli ;
(b) In higher mental stimuli ;
(c) In the course of an association test accompanied by attention, which is nothing more than a combination of (a) and (b).

II. *Increase of the Electric Resistance to Conduction :*
(a) At rest ;
(b) In sleep ;
(c) In quiet (not exciting) mental work ;
(d) When the attention is fettered by a complex (down stroke of the complex wave, Test II (c)).
(e) When the attention is distracted by voluntary opposition to the experiment (Test III).
(f) By outer distraction (Test IV).

As we have seen, it is sensory and psychical stimuli that produce the emotional tone which causes the psychogalvanic phenomenon. It is upon this that the usefulness of the phenomenon in association tests is based. The tests have shown us sufficiently the close connexion between the strength of the deviation and the emotional tone which the individual reactions arouse. The psychogalvanic phenomenon owes its origin to purely affective processes, i.e. those which we know are the only ones which act upon the functions of the body.[1] But this action consists of changes in innervation. What the kinds of innervation (secretory ?) in our experiment are we cannot say as yet with certainty ; we only know their specific effect, which is the lowering of the electric resistance of the skin. The deduction, therefore, is that whenever the resistance of the skin to conduction decreases we have an increase, and whenever the resistance increases we have a decrease of innervation.

How is this deduction borne out by the results of Test II ?

It is readily understood that the innervation should decrease at rest, when asleep, and with quiet mental work. For here we get no affective processes. But the explanation is more difficult in cases (d), (e) and (f), for here affective processes have a great share, and we have more or less strong affects. In (e) and (f) the attention is directed towards a certain aim—again an affective process. If, then, we get here a decrease of innervation it can be only the result of inhibition.

Consider, first, case (d).

This is the case Test II (c) with down stroke of the complex wave. May we here speak of an inhibition of innervation ? Certainly. For it is not a question of the galvanometric registration of just that movement when an affect is aroused (this movement is shown by the deviations which occur at the complex reactions) ; what we find is the subsequent manifestations of the affect in the falling of the complex wave and in Test II (c). It is an old and well-known fact that an affect does not only act as a barrier to the associations to which it belongs but is inhibitory to all others. Thus the stimulus-words following the complex reactions or the affect aroused become inhibited in their action upon the flow of ideas and upon the physical functions. This is the explanation of distraction upon a complex and its effect upon the galvanometer curve.

In cases (e) and (f) the distraction follows from the attention being diverted to a particular end. Why does not this tension of the attention, which must be an affective process, produce any innervation ? But this, again, is a wrong way of putting

[1] Bleuler, loc. cit., p. 14.

the problem, for here again we are concerned with the effects of an already existent concentration of the attention. At the moment when the attention is turned towards a definite point a deviation is obtained, as I have often been able to observe. But in Test II (c) such moments occurred before the experiment.

The effect of distraction of attention turned towards a definite process and away from the experiment is just the same as that of an existing affect. Bleuler says of attention : "It is a side of affectivity which does nothing but what we already know about it, for it paves the way for some associations and obstructs others. To these paths (and obstacles), naturally, not only do the intracentral and the centripetal connexions belong, but also a number of centrifugal connexions." Lehmann comes to the same conclusion : "Attention is a pathway to some single point whereby the energy streaming in at the particular point acts at the same time as an inhibition to other simultaneous processes in the central organ." [1]

To sum up :

Whenever the attention is distracted, either through an affect, or through voluntary opposition or through outer distraction, the stimulus-words provoke weakened physical expressions or none at all.

This result is closely related to the findings of Lehmann and of Zoneff and Meumann,[2] who likewise proved that there was a diminution or cessation of physical expression when the stimulus was applied in states of distracted attention. The observations or distraction of attention also lead us to the galvanometric investigations on the insane.

A. Vigouroux [3] found in melancholics an increased electric resistance to conduction which we can thus interpret : the melancholic is in a permanent state of distracted attention. His complexes occupy him permanently, like the affect which, purposely introduced, occupied Subject 2 temporarily.

There is in both cases a hindrance to centrifugal innervation and thus an increased resistance to conduction.

Jung and Ricksher [4] found in catatoniacs and organic dements an increased resistance to conduction and an absence of deviation to stimuli of various kinds. This must be due chiefly to primary disorders of perception rather than to inhibition from

[1] Lehmann, *Elemente der Psychodynamik : übersetzt von Bendixen*, 1905, p. 362.

[2] Zoneff and Meumann, "Ueber die Begleiterscheinungen psychischer Vorgänge in Atem und Puls," Wundt's *Phil. Studien*, 1901, Bd. XVIII, p. 1.

[3] A. Vigouroux, loc. cit.

[4] *Journal of Abnormal Psychology*, vol. ii, 1907–1908, p. 189.

" inner distraction." The observation made by R. Vigouroux [1] that in hysterics the electric resistance is increased on the hemi- anæsthetic side as compared with the sound side seems to me now understandable. If we regard the hysterical hemianæsthesia as occurring when this side is functionally split off from conscious- ness, then we see that the innervation flowing towards that side will be slighter. And we have hitherto always found that this decrease of innervation is accompanied by increased resistance.

In conclusion, I would like to point out the difference the " at rest " wave shows according to whether the current used is of lesser or greater strength. In the latter case we always find that the resistance of the skin decreases with the length of the current. Veraguth proved this contradiction in the rest curve with slight currents. The resistance then increases the longer the circuit lasts. The explanation of this contradiction must be that by the use of a considerable strength of current (I cannot give the limits) one is not dealing with a rest wave but always with a stimulus wave, i.e. that we here get physiological and finally psychological effects. We need but recall the stimulus action of the electrodes upon the skin with a strong galvanic current. [2] Moreover, purely physical conditions may have a share in this. A permanent complex (permanent affect, permanent concentra- tion of attention upon something other than the experimental stimuli) hinders the psychical working up of the stimulus, which remains poor in association and feeling. The absence of new innervations, and therefore the disappearance of the deviations, is the result of the absence of new affects. The gradual sinking of the curve is explained by the gradual wearing off of the affect, whilst the intellectual attitude of inhibition created by the affect is maintained for a longer period.


PART III

EXTENSION OF THE POINTS OF VIEW OBTAINED IN PART II
TO THE MATERIAL AS A WHOLE

*Reaction-time and Galvanic Deviation*

We shall review in this section the mutual behaviour of these two complex indicators in their connexion with one another, and shall refer to further conditions which lead to a disproportion of these two values. From the experiments we have learnt that, as a rule, a " too long " reaction-time corresponds with a " too long "

---

[1] R. Vigouroux, loc. cit.
[2] Cp. Erb, *Handbuch der Elektrotherapie*, 1882, p. 116.

deviation.  It has also been shown that, as a rule,[1] with a prolongation of the reaction-time there goes an affective process ; we shall
not be in error if, with Jung, we make this affective process
responsible for the prolongation of the time.   But we have given
sufficient instances of exceptions to the ratio between reaction-
time  and  deviation,  which  are  largely  due  to  the  influence
of  a  perseverating  emotional  tone.   We  have  seen  that  in
cases  where  an  emotional  tone  was  handed  on  from  an  earlier
reaction  there  was  no  question  of  any  direct  ratio  between
these  two  factors  in  the  following  or  next  following  reaction ;
that,  on  the  contrary,  when  the  perseverating  complex  is  very
strong the ratio is inverse—the time is prolonged and the deviation
shortened.   I have sufficiently explained the reason for this.

We  saw  a  second  cause  for  this  prolongation  of  the  reaction-
time  without  a  simultaneous  increase  of  the  deviation  in  the
occurrence  of  an  " intellectual  feeling "  in  Nahlowsky's  sense ;
this  is  of  no  practical  importance  but  is  of  theoretical  interest.
It  was  due  to  a  " feeling  of  uncertainty "  when  the  stimulus-word
was  not  clearly  understood.   It  was  shown  that  these  cases  are
extremely  rare  because  the  conditions  for  the  occurrence  of
purely  " intellectual  feelings "  only  arise  exceptionally  in  the
association  test.   To  the  example  *tame — wild,*  when  *tooth*  was
understood,  I  will  add  another  that  seems  to  me  beyond
criticism :

| *Subject No.* 16, *Physician :* | | R.T. | G.D. |
|---|---|---|---|
| R. 14. Craft | boat | 21 | 7 |
| | | (9) | (19) [2] |

He  hesitated  whether  I  had  said  *craft*  or  *crafty* ;  finally  he
decided  for  the  former.   It  is  easy  to  see  that  when  two  words
which  clang  emerge,  neither  of  which  has  any  particular  emotional
tone  for  the  patient,  a  certain  time  is  spent  till  the  subject  decides
on  one.   We  might  speak  of  a  " selection-time "  which  is  added
to  the  reaction-time  in  the  strict  sense.   This  hesitation  did  not
here produce any affect, for the deviation is still below the probable
mean.   The  indistinct  apprehension  of  the  stimulus-word  is  often
followed  by  its  repetition  or  by  a  *what ?*   In  such  cases  the
reaction-time  is  particularly  long,  because  I  only  let  go  the  watch-
spring  of  the  hand  when  the  real  reaction-word  is  pronounced.
The  size  of  the  deviation  in  such  cases  depends  upon  whether  an
intellectual feeling or an affective process is connected with the

---

[1] We shall find there are exceptions, to which we shall refer later.
[2] The figures in parentheses give the probable means of the two values for
the whole test.   The values only have a meaning when compared with these
probable means.

repetition of the stimulus-word. The latter is commonly the case, but I have some distinct examples of the former.

| Subject No. 13, Female Attendant : | R.T. | G.D. | | |
|---|---|---|---|---|
| 82. Bend | end ? beginning | 12 | 1 | |
| | | (9) | (2) | |

| Subject No. 12, Female Student : | | | | |
|---|---|---|---|---|
| 4. Prick | what ? pain | 18 | 3 | |
| | | (11) | (5) | |
| 6. Long | what ? many | 26 | 3 | |
| 15. Stalk | what ? flowers | 27 | 5 | |

The following case of disproportion between reaction-time and deviation seems due to the difficulty of the word.

| Subject No. 11, Uneducated Man : | | | |
|---|---|---|---|
| Salt | mineral | 18 | 2 |
| | | (9) | (2) |

Delayed reaction-times are often seen at the word *salt*. At present I can only find the cause in a certain difficulty in finding appropriate associations (*pepper* and *bitter* are the commonest). The subject had, like many uneducated persons, taken the stimulus-word as a question—*What is salt ?* The correct answer gave him intellectual difficulties without his getting " excited " about it. The following delayed time seems partly due to special intellectual effort, The reaction occurred in Test II (c) :

| 82. Narrow | pass | 35 | 2 |
|---|---|---|---|
| | | (14) | (5) |

We saw that the reaction took place under the influence of a perseverating emotional tone ; but the excessive prolongation of the time seems to require explanation. He wanted to say *narrow-hearted*, which is extremely emotionally toned for him. In order to suppress *narrow-hearted* and to find the harmless *narrow — pass* required severe intellectual effort, made still more difficult by the perseveration.

It was remarkable that despite this repression and affect the deviation was so slight. I cannot avoid the impression that we had here an inhibition of innervation by the intellectual effort which made such demands upon the subject's attention.

Whilst we can show that, besides perseveration, intellectual difficulties may lead to a prolongation of the time without pro-longation of the deviation, those cases where the deviation, but not the time, is prolonged are found chiefly when there are verbal reasons. These are generally cases of complexes which pass unnoticed in the reaction-time because the subject was able to slip in a verbal association.   We have seen that emotive inhibitions are manifested with difficulty in such associations.   This may be due to the strong pathway between the associations which then rapidly follow each other, although other associations also become aroused.   Very often, however, the reason is that the verbal association that slipped in was already formed before the complex became generally aroused and could make its whole inhibitory action felt.   I have often observed this in myself. The deviation, which follows much more slowly, has time to come under the influence of the complex.

Other examples :

| Subject No. 22, Male Attendant : | | R.T. | G.D. |
|---|---|---|---|
| 61. Law | opposed | 8 | 24 |
| | | (10) | (14) |
| 69. Part | have | 8 | 20 |
| 75. Family | relations | 8 | 25 |
| 82. Narrow | -hearted | 8 | 17 |
| 83. Brother | love | 8 | 17 |
| 84. Injure | joy | 7 | 46 |
| 89. Fire | cause | 6 | 25 |
| Subject No. 12, Female Student : | | | |
| 62. Love | have | 11 | 9 |
| | | (11) | (5) |
| Subject No. 19, Doctor : | | | |
| 79. Book | have | 8 | 16 |
| | | (9) | (5) |
| 88. Kiss | like | 8 | 12 |

(He had heard this reaction in a great many subjects.)

| Subject No. 2 : | | | |
|---|---|---|---|
| 45. Tooth | -ache | 8 | 53 |
| | | (14) | (5) |
| Subject No. 18, Attendant : | | | |
| 68. Paint | painter | 9 | 7 |
| | | (14) | (2) |

## CLANG-ASSOCIATIONS AND GALVANOMETER DEFLECTIONS

### Action of " Unconscious " Complexes upon the Galvanic Deflection

Before leaving the individual analyses and proceeding to the purely statistical working out of our material I must again refer to the clang-associations, which will give an opportunity to study the action of " unconscious " [1] complexes upon the psychogalvanic phenomenon.

In the analysis of Test I we were able to prove that the clang-reactions which arose from distraction of attention due to a previous complex showed a " too small " deviation, whilst those which themselves awoke a complex had a " too long " one.

We also saw in the examples *kröte — spöte* (R. 51) and reactions 92 and 38 that beyond the " contact " connexion by the clang-association there was a deeper link between stimulus- and reaction-word. In all three reactions the clang-association was determined by a complex which the stimulus-word aroused ; in reaction 38, *repent — spent*, perseveration also took part, so that the deviation itself did not exceed the probable mean. The complex participating in the disturbance was indicated on the galvanometer by the subsequent rise of the curve. When a perseverating emotional tone had caused both the deviation and the clang-association no deeper connexion could be demonstrated (R. 32, *ring — swing ;* R. 37, *speck — neck ;* and R. 52, *divorce — force*). What we had been able to prove in Test I was also found in the clang-associations of the other tests. The grouping together of cases like *divorce — avoid* is very informative ; of fourteen subjects to whom the word *divorce* was called out five reacted with *avoid*.[2]

We will first give two cases where there was also perseveration, and then three where complexes were at work.

| *Subject No. 1 :* | | R.T. | G.D. |
|---|---|---|---|
| 52. Avoid | divorce | 9 | 8 |
| | | (9) | (8) |
| *Subject No. 23, Doctor :* | | | |
| 52. Avoid | divorce | 11 | 6 |
| | | (11) | (7) |

In both these cases there was the perseveration of an emotional tone. In Subject No. 1 this came at the preceding reaction, which, as we saw, aroused a very strong complex. In Subject No. 23 perseveration is also observed. It is due to

| 50. Unjust | just | 11 | 13 |
|---|---|---|---|
| | | (11) | (7) |

---

[1] We shall see that these are not " unconscious " complexes in Freud's sense but only suppressed complexes ; that is, they were once in consciousness and can reappear there at any time (Freud's foreconscious). Freud understands by unconscious complexes in the strict sense complexes which have never become conscious to the person and which can only be brought into the conscious by psycho-analysis.

[2] In English *divorce — avoid* is a clang-association ; in the German it is a rhyme—*scheiden — meiden.*—TRANSLATOR.

Upon which follow :

|          |       | R.T. | G.D. |
|----------|-------|------|------|
| 51. Frog | water | 12   | 5    |
| 52. Divorce | avoid | 11 | 6   |

The complex in reaction 50, perseverating in reactions 51 and 52, is objectively shown by the long deviation.  The reaction-time is, as so often, only prolonged in the next reaction, 51.  Subjectively the complex was fully confirmed, for the subject acknowledged that he had had to fight a great deal against injustice and possessed a strong *justice* complex.  In the three other cases where there was a complex, the deviations were very prolonged, whilst the time was only prolonged in one case.

*Subject No. 12, Female Student :*

|             |       |      |      |
|-------------|-------|------|------|
| 52. Divorce | avoid | 19   | 12   |
|             |       | (11) | (5)  |

Both words show the complex.  She explained at once that the reaction made her think of a much-loved girl friend who had lately married and left Zürich.  This friend, or rather her marriage, plays a great rôle in the experiment.

*Subject No. 4, Educated Woman :*

|             |       |      |      |
|-------------|-------|------|------|
| 52. Divorce | avoid | 11   | 15   |
|             |       | (11) | (5)  |

One of the rare cases where the clang-association caused by a complex has, for no obvious reason, no time-prolongation.  But the deviation, which is thrice the probable mean, is enough.  The emotional tone is here on *avoid*.

*Subject No. 19, the Writer :*

|             |       |      |      |
|-------------|-------|------|------|
| 52. Divorce | avoid | 8    | 8    |
|             |       | (9)  | (5)  |

The short reaction-time is explained by the reaction having slipped in from tests carried out on others.  Still the complex comes out and is recognizable by the galvanometer.  The emotional tone was on *avoid*.

I group these reactions together :

|                          |       | R.T. | G.D. |                      |
|--------------------------|-------|------|------|----------------------|
| Subject No. 1.  Divorce  | avoid | 9    | 5    |                      |
|                          |       | (9)  | 8    | clang-association    |
| 22.                      |       | 11   | 6    | due to perseveration |
|                          |       | (12) | (7)  |                      |
| 12.                      |       | 19   | 12   |                      |
|                          |       | (11) | (5)  |                      |
| 4.                       |       | 11   | 15   | clang-association    |
|                          |       | (11) | (5)  | due to complex.      |
| 19.                      |       | 8    | 8    |                      |
|                          |       | (9)  | (5)  |                      |

Twice I found the rhyme *to prick — brick*, but on both occasions neither complex nor perseveration could be discovered.  But the stimulus-word *to prick* is the fourth one in our list, i.e. it comes quite early, when there is still some excitation about the experiment and the attitude towards the meaning of the stimulus-word is still laboured.  It might be said that the distraction of attention

2 K

is here due to the perseveration of a complex, the complex which refers to ideas about the test itself.

The following is another instance of the effect of perseveration upon clang associations.

The probable means are 17 and 10.

| Subject No. 15, Female Student : | | R.T. | G.D. |
|---|---|---|---|
| 11. Young | old | 24 | 28 |
| | | (17) | (10) |
| 12. Ask | answer | 23 | 29 |
| 13. State | Russia | 12 | 7 |
| 14. Stubborn | -minded | 14 | 10 |
| 15. Stalk | talk | 13 | 5 |

Two strong complexes were aroused at reaction 11 which were and are still important to her. Reaction 12 brought up thoughts of her approaching examination for the doctorate—quite enough to provoke an affect. Reaction 13 shows nothing special. Reaction 14 is verbal-motor. The superficiality of this association points clearly to the distraction of attention shown again in the clang-association 15. It is in consequence of this that the deviation reduced the probable mean by a half.

In the clang-associations mentioned so far with " too long " a deviation, the complex became known to the subject during the reaction (see *divorce — avoid*). But I have a number of striking clang-associations showing distinct lengthening of the deviation where the subject was quite unable to assert that the reaction in question was connected with any emotional event, with any complex at all

As, apart from No. 1, I did not obtain many clang-associations in my tests, I have only a few examples to quote, but each one seems to me worth study. They again show what great importance the unconscious has in association activity. The importance of the unconscious in association activity is most clearly seen in Freud's works : *Interpretation of Dreams ; Psychopathology of Everyday Life ; Wit*, etc.[1]

We shall here venture on a proof of the influence of an unconscious or, as we prefer to say, of a repressed complex upon the development of affect, i.e. upon the physical innervations. Here

[1] See also Bleuler, chapter vi, Jung and Riklin, chapter ii, and Jung, chapter iv. In his *Psychology of Dementia Præcox* Jung says, after having spoken of the influence of the complex upon association : " It is of theoretical importance that the complex need not be conscious. By repression it can cause an inhibition of attention in the conscious ; in other words, it can suspend for a time the intellectual activity of consciousness (delayed reaction-time !), or suspend it totally (fault) or diminish its worth (clang-associations)." See also " The Theory of Association," by Münsterberg, *Beiträge zur experimentellen Psychologie*, Heft 4, p. 1 (Freiburg i. B., 1892), and Scripture's penetrating work " Ueber den assoziativen Verlauf der Vorstellungen " (Wundt's *Phil. Studien*, Bd. VII, p. 50). As to the justification for speaking about unconscious psychical processes and as to the part they play in mental life see Lippe, *Leitfaden der Psychologie* (Leipzig, 1903), p. 37 ; Ebbinghaus, *Grundzüge der Psychologie*, Bd. I (Leipzig, 1905), p. 54 ff. ; Höffding, *Psychologie in Umrissen auf Grundlage der Erfahrung*, p. 99 ff.

again Freud has laid down the theoretical principles.  In *The Interpretation of Dreams* he says : " This (i.e. the development of the affect) is regarded as a motor activity or as one of secretion ; the key to its innervation is placed in the unconscious."

Before dealing more closely with our examples I should like to add some remarks about the method.  It deviates in many respects from that hitherto customary in experimental psychology. In his *Principles of Physiological Psychology*, Wundt, when discussing the analysis of the emotions, says : " It must, moreover, be noticed in all cases that the vasomotor, like the respiratory symptoms, are in themselves only signs of alterations of innervation in the respiratory, cardiac, and circulatory nerve centres. They convey nothing of themselves either about the causes of these symptoms, which are grounded in the mechanism of the nerve centres or about the remoter physiological connexion of the innervations in question.  The chief psychological value of these symptoms is rather that they are phenomena which are demonstrated objectively in so far as they regularly accompany emotional ideas ; and by their differences we are enabled to obtain indications of the corresponding psychical differences. But it should never be forgotten that these are only indications and never proofs.  If subjective observation does not discover the presence of a definite emotion no amount of objective phenomena can establish it.  Experience teaches us, nevertheless, that traces of feelings can escape subjective observation if there is not some special motive for the attention being directed to them."

What is here said of the vasomotor and respiratory symptoms must also refer to the galvanometric phenomena, about whose physiological foundation we have no absolutely certain knowledge.  If we were to follow Wundt it would be an error to attempt to discover the relationship of unconscious complexes, which introspection cannot detect, to physical symptoms.  But it must have occurred to readers that we have not posited, as the final authority for the connexion of galvanometric with psychical differences, any subjectively demonstrated emotion. In the association test, where the various emotions interchange so rapidly with one another, either increasing or hindering one another, subjective statements as to the nature or form of these feelings are quite unreliable.  It is only gross differences of feeling, qualitative and quantitative, that are differentiated by introspection.  Wundt agrees that traces of feeling can escape introspection. I believe that the galvanometer, although the shunt does considerably deaden the oscillations of the current, is a far finer reagent for quantitative differences of emotion.  As subjective control we found, as we have sufficiently demonstrated, that a reaction which was accompanied by a too long deviation belonged to an emotionally toned complex. In the majority of cases the subject feels the constellation, is often quick to recognize it, although sometimes only after reflection. But when the subjective proof of this connexion is unobtainable we have another means of discovering it. It is the method of psycho-analysis which psychology owes to Freud. It is to be used whenever the information given by a subject about a reaction is unsatisfactory (see, e.g., the reaction 3, *wall — star*, in No. 1), and especially when repression influences the association so that its working is unknown to the subject. Taking the view that unconscious psychic processes can provoke physical changes of innervation, Lehmann's remark will not lead us astray : an outer stimulus must enter consciousness in order to produce organic reactions.[1] He makes Consciousness = Psyche. Naturally, from this point of view he is bound to conclude that if a definite external stimulus creates no definite state of consciousness the organic reactions must be also absent.[2] The contradiction between our view and Lehmann's statement is that Lehmann obviously recognizes only one mental process for the origin of organic reactions, whilst we also recognize unconscious mental processes.[3]

The first example is from a doctor (No. 16), who was kind enough to give me all the information possible. He himself succeeded in discovering the complex repressed during and for a few hours after the experiment.

|  |  | R.T. | G.D. |
|---|---|---|---|
| Worry | source | 9 | 15 |
|  |  | (9) | (9) |

The reaction-time is the same; the probable mean of the deviation is, however, much increased. He felt at once impelled to seek some deeper connexion between *worry* and *source* (a clang-reaction in German, *quälen — Quelle*). It occurred to him in analysis that he was recently in the town of B. with a female patient who was to be operated upon there. As this particular patient often comes into his associations at other places without giving rise to any increase of deviation, no significance could be attached to this idea. But, as will be seen, the

---

[1] Lehmann, *Die körperlichen Ausserungen psychischer Zustände*, translated by Bendixen, vol. i, p. 158. (Leipzig, 1899.)

[2] See vol. ii, p. 313 ff.

[3] In a certain sense the stimulus, here the stimulus-word, did reach the conscious in the cases now to be related. The subjects reacted to it with one word, afterwards remembering the stimulus-word, and so on. What did not reach consciousness was the relationship of the stimulus to a definite group of ideas. And even here we must put a further limit. A reference to some complex or other is often more or less conscious to the subjects as a " feeling of constraint," some uncertainty, " the reaction might refer to a complex," etc. But what is not conscious to them at all is the complex itself.

town of B. does point to the complex.   At any rate, he did not know how he came to this association, and introspection failed to notice any distinct feeling during the reaction.   There was no time for a thorough psycho-analysis.   I was therefore greatly pleased when my colleague gave me the solution next day in writing.   During the course of the evening it came back to him that *source* = *fons amoris* (*sempiterni fons amoris*) was formerly one of his " complex symbols." It was a question of a strong "bachelor complex" which, when he lived in the town of B., was the *source* of much *worry*.   The words " sempiterni fons amoris " had become for both the symbol of friendship and service, being used as a formula in greeting.   The matter becomes quite clear when we recall the whole strophe of Scheffel's student's song, of which this was the first line :

> Sempiterni fons amoris,
> Consolatrix tristium,
> Pia mater Salvatoris
> Ave virgo virginum.

That *fons amoris* has also a concrete meaning need be merely indicated. It is interesting that for years he had not thought of this episode in his life and that it was only again noticed in his dreams after he had married (about six months before the test).   By his marriage the complex had at first increased the associations in the unconscious, thus allowing it to overcome the " censure," first in his dreams and then in the waking consciousness.

The next two examples are from myself.

|              |       | R.T. | G.D. |
|--------------|-------|------|------|
| 28. Threaten | drone | 14   | 19   |
|              |       | (9)  | (5)  |

The reaction-time and the deviation are markedly prolonged.   I was not aware of any complex during the reaction, nor had I any particular feeling after I had uttered the reaction-word.   I felt some surprise about it—it seemed to me so remote and I hardly felt that I myself had pronounced it.   Nor could I link, at first, any further associations to it, and gave up trying to find any meaning to this reaction.   It was only two months later, after returning from a fortnight's journey and looking over my associations again, that its meaning became clear (without my then seeking it) ; it occurred just as my eyes fell on the reaction *the drone*, that's me !   My colleagues had often twitted me with my infrequent appearance in the wards and my not relieving them of some of the work.   For bit by bit I had limited myself entirely to the scientific work.   A little of their banter had taken effect.   Beyond the complete inner certainty that I felt as to the correctness of this interpretation there is in its favour that I only found it after a journey during which I had received many new impressions ; my psychological constellation had become different and so the inner resistances had become displaced.   Furthermore, during the journey my real interest in the part I played in the asylum had receded (cp. Freud, P*sychopathology of Every-day Life*).   On the first day of my return the complex had acquired an additional affect when I compared the strenuous work of my colleagues with my own life during the journey.

My complex had perceived the opportunity for the application of the stimulus-word to myself by a process of assimilation in the same way as in the other cases of misreading, misunderstanding, etc., which Freud has described in so masterly a way.

▸ To *threaten* is an unpleasurably toned word and at the same time one rather difficult to respond to.   There was thus sufficient cause for inhibitory factors.

The complex may have used this moment of hesitation. One of my subjects reacted by *to dry* to this reaction. In that case the time, but not the deviation, was increased ; no reason for the occurrence of the word *to dry* could be found (there must certainly have been one); but, on the other hand, *threaten* was energetically parried, for the patient was a female nurse threatened with a crisis in a love-affair which for many reasons caused much excitement.

It was likewise after that journey that I solved the following clang-association :

|  |  | R.T. | G.D. | Reproduction |
|---|---|---|---|---|
| 73. Bös (angry) | öl (oil) | 9 | 13 | (reflects) |
|  |  | (9) | (15) |  |

The series of associations was :

| | | | | |
|---|---|---|---|---|
| 71. To cook | kitchen | 7 | 3 | |
| 72. Ink | fish | 9 | 3 | write |
| 73. Bös | öl | 9 | 13 | (reflects) |
| 74. Needle | ear | 9 | 4 | prick |
| 75. To swim | prick | 9 | 10 | |

The many disturbances in reproduction, the meaningless clang-associations *bös* (angry) — *öl* (oil), the perseveration of the association *prick* — *to swim*, indicate a great disturbance of attention. This was partly conditioned by a certain degree of momentary fatigue at the time, but chiefly by several complexes. During this section of the experiment I was at the same time the observer who went through the associations almost automatically. It was at the reaction *to swim* — *prick*, which seemed to me absurd, that I had a distinct feeling of unpleasure. The deviation is here increased. The clang-association *bös* — *öl* is the centre of interest [1]; this followed as automatically as the others (the reaction-times nowhere exceed the mean). My interest in it only arose later, when my attention had been turned to the action of repressed complexes upon physical innervations. Despite many attempts I could get nothing out of it at first. It was only after my return, when I again took up the forgotten associations, that I distinctly felt that to find the solution I must *translate* something. But the resistance was still so great that the right thing did not occur to me. I was still hitting away in the dark and translating *oil, oleum, œil, oil* (an attempt to get away from the *ö*) ; then I placed *bös* and *öl* together and wrote in French orthography *beuseul, seul, beul* and similar words, most of them absurd. We shall presently see that the proceeding was correct, but that I went astray in the choice of what to translate. It is remarkable that in my attempts I did hit upon the word *Vesoul*, a station between Basle and Paris. But as there were other resistances to overcome, I was unable to make anything out of Paris. I gave it up, opining that there really was no solution here. Five days later I was drawn back to this association. A thought occurred to me which enabled me to penetrate into the unconscious and break up the chief resistance. At *bös*, which I had entirely neglected, putting all the weight on *öl*, which I had not tried to translate, the proper name, *Böss*, came up to me (it had taken me two months). At once an event which had taken place a year and a half before came up to me very clearly—how I had bought a trunk at Mr. Böss's, a leather merchant in X., and how at the last moment he had painted my monogram with a *black fluid* (see reaction *ink* — *fish* ; reproduction, *write*) in Latin characters on the brown trunk. At the same time I became aware that I had always connected a *yellow* colour with the sound *ö*. (The day after the purchase I went to Paris ;

---

[1] In uttering the word *öl* I had no image of it in consciousness but merely the clang-picture.

this only came up to me later). But it became already clear that *öl* meant simply *el* (L), which was by clang assimilated to *bös*. The complex was not cleared up. Trying to call up the monogram L.B. on the trunk, I had a feeling that the word *trunk* had to be translated. I did this step consciously, asking myself what was the French for trunk—*malle*. The solution became instantly clear to me and was also shown involuntarily by a sigh. The *m* in *malle* led to a monogram M. L. B. that I had often seen in Latin letters (like my own L. B.) on a trunk. It is the monogram of that lady who had in the first place suggested my buying the trunk, and who in the second place had intended travelling to Paris with me—an intention which, however, was not carried out. I had been very put out by this. Only in this roundabout way did it become clear who was meant by *angry* (*bös*). (It must be added that this complex is only the portion of a much bigger one which is still present.) *Bös* (angry) thus led to *angry — trunk — L. B. — malle*, and thus to *M. L. B.* There is also a more direct way from *bös* to *M. L. B.* by the translation into *mal*. But here the Latin seems to take part, as indicated by my first association to *öl — oleum*. *Mala* would be the exact Latin equivalent for *bös* (angry) in this case; the French *mal* is only a hint. *Mal* also allowed me to understand when I wrote down the analysis why to the following stimulus-word *needle — ear* was reacted. In the reproduction I thought I had said *prick*. It seems highly probable that *malheur* had determined *ear* (*öhr*) both by its clang and its meaning; it was also now clear why at the beginning I felt compelled to connect the words *bös* and *öl* and write them in French. It was just as if some one had said to me. "Translate into French, combine them, and write down a German clang in French letters—that will give you the answer." We see that the unconscious prescribes the way that psycho-analysis must follow. We know now that a translation had to be made : *bös* into *mal*, written in French ; *öhr* (*heur*) ; *mal* and *heur* combined into *malheur*. The word *malheur* was the summit of the analysis.

At *bös* the clang-picture *ör* had become aroused together with the clang-picture *öl* (for from *bös* to *mal* and from *mal* to *malheur* is but a short step). This must, however, have been the stronger for it provoked the corresponding innervation of the speech musculature, whilst *ör* remained unsaid and unconscious. It was only when the word *needle* followed that the clang-picture *ör*, which lay ready waiting, received a stronger impulse and repressed the reaction-word *prick*, which was for me a more labile one. This again appears in the following reaction. Only the chief stages of the analysis can be given here, whilst the psychical impulses of the whole mechanism can only be hinted at. But I hope that I have shown through my trial and error how the psychical course of such an introspection proceeds. The inner feeling of certainty which accompanies such a task can naturally not be communicated to others. Those who attempt analysis on themselves will be the first to adopt our methods.

It is not to be wondered at that a repressed complex which, despite repression, causes physical reactions expresses itself preferentially in clang-associations. It would seem that the common occurrence of clang-associations and physical reactions are an indication of the strength of a repressed complex, or rather of the resistance which a repressed complex has to overcome in order to become conscious. This resistance was striking in all three cases, especially in my own. The occurrence of clang-associations is only a sign that the complex is held back by the " censure " and, just as in dreams, dare only manifest itself in innocent shape. It is a fair conclusion that a repressed complex evokes physical reactions, or in other words affects, when there is strong resistance to its becoming conscious.

I have one other example in which I can prove by the galvanometer the working of a repressed complex.  It manifested itself in an educated lady and was as follows:

| Subject No. 19 : | | R.T. | G.D. | Reproduction |
|---|---|---|---|---|
| 20. Eat | eat ? dinner | 18 | 18 | long reflection |
| | | (16) | (16) | |

Four complex signs: repetition of the stimulus-word, disturbance in reproduction, prolonged reaction-time, and prolonged deviation.  She is surprised at the stimulus-word: that in itself points to a complex.  Obviously the word itself cannot cause surprise, but the surprise is a hint that something strange, i.e. unconscious, is going on within her.  She had great resistance for a long time, maintaining that nothing occurred to her.  Finally, a smile heralded the solution: she does not like eating with her relations before strangers and does not like visitors at her table, because people would then see that she does not like one of her relations (an aunt).  The reason of this antipathy was not communicated, nor did I press for it.  It is very probable that this antipathy to the aunt exhibits the complex concealed here.

A very pretty example of the influence of a repressed complex on the psycho-galvanic complex is given by Jung and Peterson (*Brain*, 1907).

It occurred in a male nurse who was very emotional.  The same series of stimulus-words was used three times in succession—a method which brings out the working of a repressed complex particularly well.  The greatest deviation occurred with the association *the sun — burns*.  Other strong deviations were at the associations *floor — parquet ; pay — write ; warm — the stove*.  In the last three reactions there were constant disturbances ; all the reproductions were altered.  With one exception, all the deflections exceeded the arithmetical mean of each of the series.  Of the nine reactions four were above, and two coincided with, the probable mean.  The patient said he had no particular thoughts in connexion with these reactions and was not himself aware of anything.  But when asked what personal significance *floor* had for him, he suddenly answered, with surprise and embarrassment, that recently a stove had become defective and burned the floor to such an extent that not only the stove but the greater part of the floor had to be renewed.  He had to pay for this himself, which meant great expense.  Besides, there had been great danger from fire.  Thus all the disturbances above recorded were completely explained, including the strong emotional tone of *sun — burns*.  The strong resistance on the part of the conscious shows that the patient had not become aware of the complex in the three tests, despite the numerous stimulus-words and its recent occurrence.

# PART IV

## STATISTICS OF THE NORMAL TESTS

In this last part of the work I shall show from the statistics of the whole material what are the laws between reaction-time and deviation, and between complex signs and deviation.  We shall find that the relationships are constant between the factors mentioned and the deviations, and disregard the differences in the methods of the tests, sex, and the educational status of the test persons.  We shall review these relationships in the four groups of the educated and uneducated men and women separately, so as to show that they are present in all groups.   I must warn the student against comparing the deviation values of one group with those of another, and against drawing conclusions as to the influence of emotionalness, education, or sex.   To do this we must be certain that the same experimental methods have been used, and even then regard must be had to the condition of the skin in men and women, in hand or brain workers.   It is only the values of the reaction-time that can be properly compared with one another.   I shall not, therefore, take notice of the absolute values of the mean of the deviation in the individual groups, and shall limit myself to describing the differences between the probable and arithmetical means.   Since these differences are entirely due to psychological processes (for the physical conditions remain exactly the same during the experiment, as a rule, or if there is any change, it is directed equally to those two values) we can compare these group differences.

We have four groups :

### 1. *Educated Women*

Five tests on five different persons ; 304 associations.   In all the tests a current was led through the person tested, brass electrodes were used four times and nickel electrodes once.   The number of galvanic cells was once three, twice two, thrice one.

### 2. *Educated Men*

Twelve tests on eight different persons ;   830 associations. Sommer's method was used once (zinc and charcoal electrodes without any current) ;   eleven times we used brass electrodes and a galvanic cell (thrice two, eight times one).   We have not included Test II (c) in the statistics.

### 3. *Uneducated Women*

Five tests on four different persons ;   491 associations. Sommer's method was used once, brass electrodes with one galvanic cell twice, twice water-contact and two galvanic cells. In the two experiments with water-contact two nickel electrodes were placed each in a glass vessel and the subject required to dip the second and third finger of each hand in one of the vessels without touching the electrodes.   The test does not differ essentially from the others, only the deviation is lower on account of the slight surface contact (two fingers).   The probable mean of the deviations was 2 in both tests carried out on the same subject ; the arithmetical mean of one test was 1·5, of the second test 2·6 (when the experimenter knew the subject's complexes).

#### 4. *Uneducated Men*

Seven tests on six different persons; 535 associations. Sommer's method was used three times; three times brass electrodes, once nickel electrodes with conducted current (twice two cells, once one cell).

In all, twenty-nine tests on twenty-three persons with 2160 associations. A comparison of the mean of the reaction-time of the different groups follows. (The figures are here given in seconds, not in one-fifth seconds).

TABLE I

|  | P.M. | A.M. | Difference | Too long times in percentage |
|---|---|---|---|---|
| Uneducated men . . . | 2·94 | 3·51 | 0·57 | 39·8 |
| Educated women . . . | 2·9 | 3·3 | 0·4 | 32·2 |
| Uneducated women . . . | 2·5 | 2·7 | 0·2 | 33·4 |
| Educated men . . . . | 2 | 2·2 | 0·2 | 32·2 |

Compared with Jung's results (chapter v) my results here seem to be, on the average, higher. These depend, as already stated, upon the personal factor, and also to some extent on the very complicated test methods in my experiments. Uneducated women (all nurses) occupy the first place in Jung's work, the third in mine; the other series agree. This is due to the fact that two of the uneducated women (both Swabians!), who took up two-thirds of the associations, were both remarkably fluent in speech. The A.M. of their time is scarcely greater than the P.M. In one of them the association type is remarkably superficial. Only one Swiss brought up in the country showed the type of uneducated women dealt with in former experiments. I am disposed to attribute the great differences of the two means in my uneducated men as much to want of fluency in speech as to lively emotivity. But the great difference in the educated women is a clear sign of emotionalness, as can be proved from the following comparison (see Table II).

Let me first point out that in all groups we find a prolongation of the A.M. of the deviations as against their P.M. In the reaction-time intellectual and verbal conditions share, but this is not the case in the deviations, so that the difference of the two means enables us to draw conclusions as to emotivity. For when the A.M. is very great as compared with the P.M. the deviations must have been very large, and these are caused by affects. The

TABLE II

| | Difference between P.M. and A.M. of deflection | Difference between P.M. of time and A.M. of time | Too long devia-tions in percentage |
|---|---|---|---|
| | mm. | second [1] | |
| Educated women    .    .    . | 7·6 | 0·4 │ | 45·9 |
| Educated men    .    .    .    . | 2·8 | 0·2, | 43·8 |
| Uneducated men    .    .    . | 2·5 | 0·57 | 49·9 |
| Uneducated women    .    .    . | 1·1 | 0·2 | 40·0 |

figure for the difference among educated women is surprising. We see clearly that in this group there was great emotionalness, so that we are justified in referring the great difference between P.M. and A.M. of the reaction-time simply to emotional causes. From the contradictory values between the differences of time and deviation means among uneducated men I feel justified in concluding that the great difference in time is not solely conditioned here by their emotivity, but through their unreadiness in speech and their inferior degree of intelligence.    For if the time differences were due entirely to emotional conditions the differences in de-viation caused by the emotionalness should be correspondingly greater than in the other groups.    The low difference in de-viation among the uneducated women corresponds with the low difference in time.    This led me to deduce a low emotionalness for this group.    As a matter of fact, the two subjects mentioned were not greatly excited by the experiment.    But as two tests were made with water-contact, which conditions a low amount for deviation and therefore a low difference for both means, I shall draw no conclusions from these values.    From a comparison of the values of the educated men one could deduce great verbal fluency (low difference in time) together with highly developed emotionalness, which agrees with the behaviour of these persons as otherwise known to me.

The most important factor for a comparison of the reaction-time and deviations is the measure which tells us how much greater is the P.M. of those deviations which coincide with " too long " times than the P.M. of the deviations of the whole experi-ment.    To obtain this result these deviations are written out and their P.M. calculated.    If the P.M. of these deviations is greater than that of the whole deviation it means : in this test " too long " times correspond with " too long " deviations.    The following table shows us that this is the case in all four groups.

I will not repeat the values for the deviations which coincide

---

[1] I add the differences of the mean time for the sake of clearness.

with the " too long " times, but take the differences of these with the P.M. of the whole experiment. For comparison I again include the differences of times and deviations.

TABLE III

| | Differences between the deflections occurring at too long times and all the deflections of a test | Difference between P.M. of deviations and A.M. of deflections | Differences between P.M. of R. time and A.M. of R. time in seconds |
|---|---|---|---|
| Educated women . . . | + 5·3 | 7·6 | 0·4 |
| Uneducated women . . . | + 2·8 | 1·1 | 0·2 |
| Educated men . . . . | + 2·8 | 2·8 | 0·2 |
| Uneducated men . . . | + 1·0 | 2·5 | 0·57 |

Again the educated women exhibit the highest average value, i.e. among educated women the deviations which coincide with " too long " times are most distinctly prolonged. This is a further proof that the prolonged times are of emotional origin in this class. Among uneducated women the difference is strikingly greater than the difference between the P.M. of the deviations and the A.M. of the reaction-times. We can express these relationships by saying : Among uneducated women there are few long deviations and few very long times, but when the latter do occur there is a definitely prolonged deviation (viz. 6·8 against P.M. of deviations for the whole = 4). As the uneducated women in our test are fluent talkers and hence only show a low difference between P.M. and A.M. of reaction - times, their " too long " times are clearly due to emotion (as shown by the great increase of the deviations which coincide with too long times). Among educated men, who, as we have seen, are equally fluent in speech, the prolongation of time is again of emotional origin. The fact that the difference between the A.M. of the deviations and their P.M. is the same as the difference here reviewed indicates that the prolongation of the deviations, coinciding with " too long " times, is less pronounced than among uneducated women. The low difference (+ 1) of the uneducated men confirms the view that the times are only to a small extent prolonged by emotional inhibitions (since the corresponding deviations are so slightly increased) ; for the most part it is a question of speech or intellectual difficulties which, as non-affective processes, are unaccompanied by any prolongation of the deviation.

We see that the comparison of the three differences allows us to draw more accurate conclusions about the emotionalness during the test than the difference between the arithmetical and probable mean times alone.

Besides the relationship between reaction-time and deviation, that between the deviation and the total complex signs was also calculated.  Though a definite ratio seemed probable between the length of the reaction-time and the deviation, no constant ratio could be at first discovered between deviation and complex signs.  At Jung's suggestion I therefore wrote out all the " too long " deviations which were the only complex indicator ; next, those which occurred together with one complex indicator, quite irrespective of its kind ; and finally, all those which occurred together with two or more complex indicators.  We regarded as complex indicators too long reaction-times, all kinds of reproduction disturbances, repetition and misunderstanding of the stimulus-word, stereotyped repetition of the same reaction-word (complex representative), translation into a foreign language, slips of speech, " peculiar reactions," and clang-associations which were afterwards shown to be conditioned by a complex.  There were no " faults " in my tests.  It will be seen that sometimes complex indicators need not be conditioned by the particular reaction with whose deviation they are compared, e.g. reproduction disturbances due to perseveration.  If, nevertheless, the size of the deviation increases with the number of complex indicators, it shows that these exceptions (which are wont to occur with too small a deviation) need not enter into the final result.

I will again place in juxtaposition the individual groups and give (1) the A.M. of the whole test for each group ; (2) that of the deviations which are the only single complex indicator ; (3) the deviations which occur with one other complex indicator ; (4) the A.M. of those deviations which are connected with two or more complex indicators :

TABLE IV

| | A.M. of total deviations (1) | A.M. of deviations forming the only complex indicator (2) | Deviation + one complex indicator A.M. (3) | Deviation + two or more complex indicators A.M. (4) |
|---|---|---|---|---|
| Educated women    .    .    . | 13·7 | 18·2 | 24·9 | 29·2 |
| Educated men    .    .    .    . | 13·1 | 18·3 | 19·9 | 21·8 |
| Uneducated women    .    .    . | 6·8 | 7·8 | 8·8 | 10·3 |
| Educated men    .    .    .    . | 10 | 15·5 | 15·9 | 17·7 |

We notice that in all the groups the average length of the

deviation increases with the number of complex indicators.  This coincidence is a meaningless and incomprehensible fact without the theory of complexes (and without psycho-analysis).  The complex theory shows us the necessary inner connexion of this phenomenon.  As far as the individual groups are concerned, I would only point out that again the educated women show·the most distinct increase of the single values.  In column (4) the value is more than double that of column (1) ; this is not attained in any other group.

The following table shows in percentages, and in regard to the total number of associations, how often the deviation formed (1) the only complex indicator, (2) how often it occurred with one complex indicator, and (3) how often with two or more complex indicators.

TABLE V

|  | Deviation the only complex indicator | Deviation + one complex indicator | Deviation + two or more complex indicators |
|---|---|---|---|
| Educated women . . . | 13·3 | 17·5 | 13·2 |
| Educated men . . . . | 19·1 | 15·7 | 7·5 |
| Uneducated women . . . | 15·5 | 14·3 | 10·2 |
| Uneducated men . . . | 17·1 | 18·2 | 10·2 |

The table speaks for itself.  It is too soon to draw any particular conclusions from it.  The fact that the educated women show such remarkably large values where emotional factors are concerned may have a common cause apart from any accidental causes.  The emotionalness is directed in this group chiefly towards the experimenter ; it is only to a small extent conscious or conditioned by external circumstances.  It is here a question of " transference to the physician " (Freud),[1] the factor so important in psycho-analysis ; in this case it is transference to the experimenter.

SUMMARY

*Part I*

(1) There are three methods of investigating psychical processes by the galvanometer :

(a) The application of unpolarizable electrodes to unsymmetrical parts of the skin (Tarchanoff, Sticker).

(b) Use of small metal electrodes having a considerable difference of tension (zinc and charcoal : Sommer and Fürstenau).

[1] Freud, *Bruchstück einer Hysterieanalyse.*

    (c) Use of electrodes of the same material and conduction of an electric current through the person tested (R. Vigouroux, Féré, A. Vigouroux, E. H. Müller, Veraguth).

(2) There is still uncertainty about the physiological and physical principles of the psycho-galvanic phenomenon. It would seem that in all three methods the sweat-glands play a prominent part, either (1) by producing the so-called secretory current or (2) by alterations in the resistance to conduction of the skin as against the conducted current. Method (b) seems to be the more complicated as regards a physiological and physical explanation.

(3) Although there are changes in the sweat-glands in all methods of experimenting, we do not yet know whether these changes are absolutely necessary for the occurrence of the psychogalvanic phenomenon, and we do not know whether we are really measuring the same physiological changes in the three methods.

(4) We can only express ourselves in general terms about the final physical changes. In any case, " in view of the extreme promptitude and accuracy which can be observed in the connexion between the galvanic phenomenon and the psychical processes, it cannot be merely a question of gross physical (or chemical) processes which are interpolated between the two. Above all, it can be no question of processes which, once stimulated, pursue their path independently of psychical events ; we are rather constrained to regard these processes as being continuously controlled, furthered, or inhibited by the central organ."

(5) Contact changes of the electrodes cannot be an essential condition for the occurrence of the psychogalvanic phenomenon (in methods (b) and (c)) for it occurs likewise when using water-contact. But involuntary pressure on the electrodes can influence to a remarkable extent the size of the deviation.

(6) Deep inspirations (sighing) act in general just as a psychological stimulus, i.e. on the emotional tone, and not directly by the vasomotor changes which they produce.

(7) In the experimental methods (b) and (c) we have seen that in psychical processes only affective processes (in Bleuler's sense) act upon the psycho-galvanic phenomenon. In pure intellectual work (e.g. adding up figures, the reading of indifferent matter) and in the occurrence of sensations unaccompanied by any distinct emotional tone no deviations occur.

## Part II

(8) Too long deviations (i.e. those above the probable mean of the total test) correspond in most cases with complex reactions ; short deviations, with non-emotionally toned reactions. The too long deviation is therefore a new and valuable complex indicator.

(9) We must differentiate between the association curve (Veraguth), which contains the basis of the total deviations of an experiment, and the complex wave, which refers only to that section of the association curve where secondary waves occur.

(10) The typical complex wave consists of a very long deviation followed by a fall of the curve with short deviations. There are frequent deviations from this norm. In the down stroke of the complex wave we find the opposite condition to the whole course of the normal association curve, which always exhibits a tendency to rise.

(11) A picture similar to the down stroke of the complex wave is obtained—

  (a) By a strong affect which is independent of the experiment (Curve II c) ;
  (b) By active distraction of the attention from the experiment (Curve III) ;
  (c) By outer distraction (Curve IV).

(12) The observations contained in 10 and 11 may be thus expressed : A constant complex (permanent affect, permanent concentration of the attention upon something other than the experimental stimulus) inhibits the psychical preparation of the stimulus. It remains poor in associations and emotions. The absence of new affects gives rise to an absence of new innervations, and thus also to the disappearance of the deviations. The explanation of the gradual fall of the curve is that the acute affect gradually fades, whilst the mental attitude of inhibition created by the affect is maintained for a long time.

(13) Assuming that we are right in regarding the fall of the galvanometer curve as due to an increase of the electrical resistance, and the rise of the curve to a decrease thereof, we may say : Whenever an increase in innervation occurs (from the application of sensory and psychical stimuli in the normal state, from increased emotivity, or from sudden tension of the attention) the resistance to conduction decreases ; wherever there is inhibition to, or decrease of, innervations, the resistance increases (therefore in the cases given in 10 and 11, also in times of rest, in sleep, and in pure intellectual work).

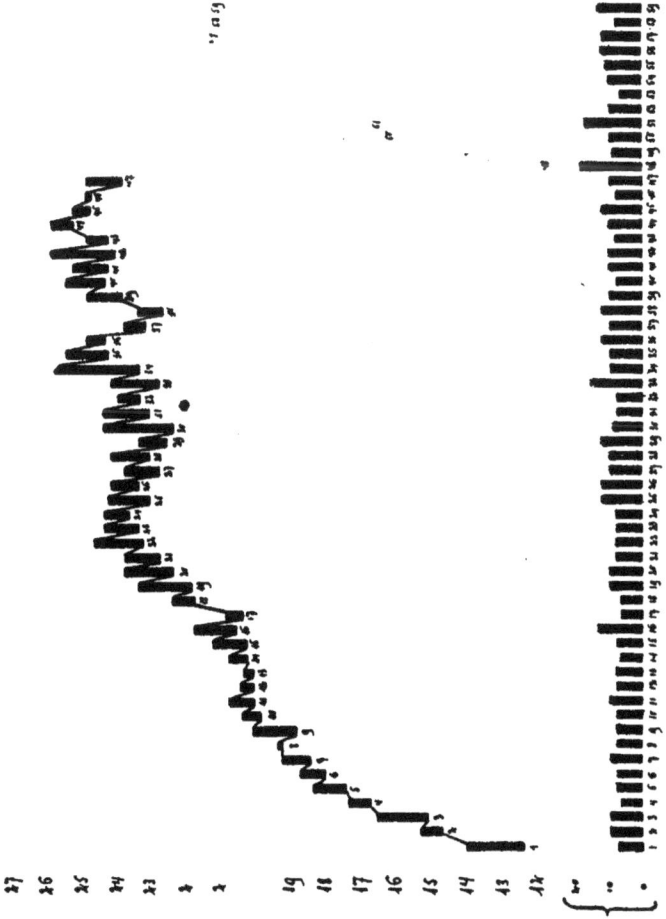

FIG. 1 (CURVE I)

*To face p. 528*

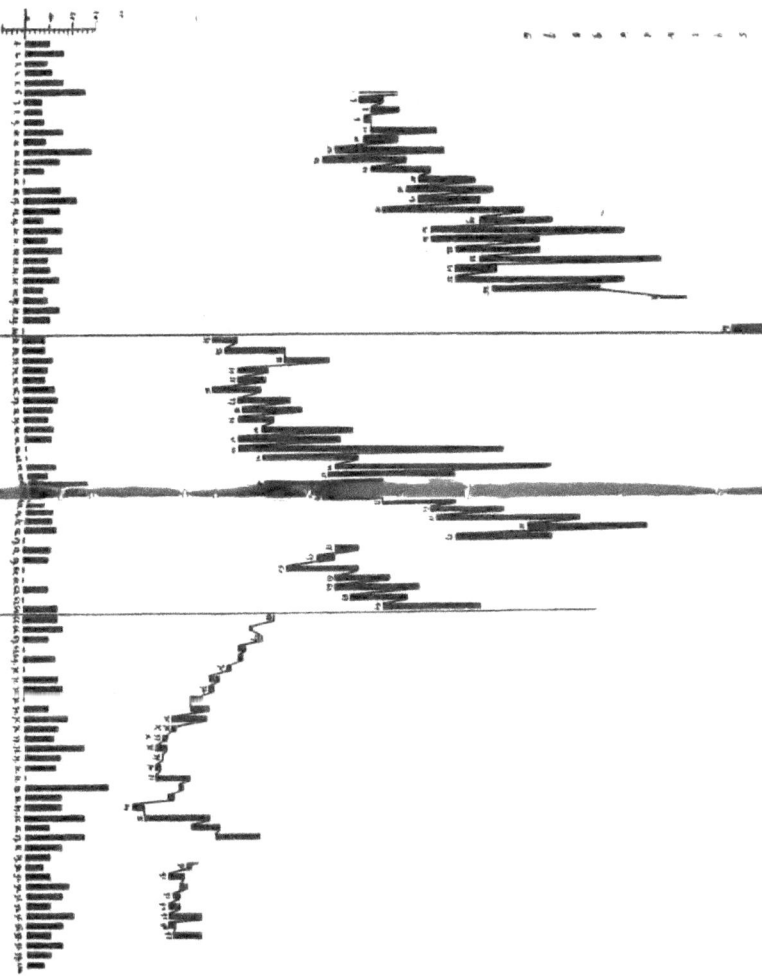

FIG. 3 (II)

To face p. 638

EXPERIMENT III

FIG. 3 (CURVE III)

To face p. 528

FIG. 4 (CURVE IV)

*To face p.* 528

.

## Part III

(14) Prolongation of the reaction-time without simultaneous prolongation of the deviation can occur :

    (a) from intellectual difficulties, such as imperfect grasp of the stimulus-word, its repetition, a rare word given as the stimulus-word ;

    (b) from the influence of perseveration—a much more frequent cause.

When a complex perseverates, the times within the sphere of influence of the perseveration can be distinctly prolonged, the deviations distinctly shortened.  An explanation of this is found in the difference in a perseveration of what we measure by these two values.  The reaction-time gives us the measure of the conflict between the perseverating emotional tone and the new reaction, whilst the deviation gives us the result of the conflict— in other words, the quantity of attention which the new reaction receives.  When the perseverating emotional tone is very strong the reaction-time becomes very long, but the deviation will be very short, since the reaction receives but little attention and therefore has only a slight emotional tone.

(15) Prolongation of the deviation without simultaneous prolongation of the reaction-time can arise from purely verbal reasons.  The complex, betrayed by the prolonged deviation, may not prolong the reaction-time if the subject has at hand a verbal association he can slip in ; the emotional inhibitions arising from the complex can with difficulty be recognized in such verbally fluent associations.

(16) Clang-associations exhibit generally a too long deviation when they are provoked by a complex contained in the reaction itself ; they exhibit a too short deviation when provoked by the perseveration of a previous complex.  In the former case one can usually discover more accurate and deeper connexion between the clang-associations ; in the latter case, usually not.  A deviation which is too long, occurring with a clang-reaction, indicates, therefore, some deeper connexion which often lies in the unconscious, and must find its explanation by psycho-analysis.

(17) It seems that complexes repressed from the conscious are able to influence the psycho-galvanic phenomenon.

## Part IV

(18) The difference between the probable mean and the arithmetical mean of the deviations is a surer criterion for the emotion of a subject than the difference between the two means

of the reaction-times ; for in the latter intellectual and verbal factors may participate, whilst the deviations are conditioned by affective processes only.

(19) In all four groups of the persons tested (educated and uneducated men and women) the mean of those deviations which coincide with " too long " times is greater than the mean of the total deviations. In all four groups there is an average correspondence between " too long " times and " too long " deviations.

(20) In all four groups the size of the deviations increases with the number of complex indicators. The theory of the complex, which ascribes the occurrence of a complex indicator to the presence of an emotionally toned group of ideas, alone enables us to understand this observation.

### EXPLANATION OF FIGURES 1–4

The marks placed next to one another on the horizontal line represent the reaction-times. The (small) figures found at the foot of the ordinate serve as the measure of the length of the reaction-time and refer to one-fifth seconds.

The marks placed on the rising or falling line represent the galvanometer deviations.

The (big) numbers of the ordinates permit their place to be read off upon the scale in centimetres and millimetres.

The reaction-time and deviation of one and the same reaction are placed over one another.

CHAPTER XIII

# ON THE PHYSICAL ACCOMPANIMENTS OF ASSOCIATION PROCESSES

## By Dr. H. NUNBERG [1]

At the suggestion of Dr. Jung I have carried out association tests on a number of persons, investigating at the same time some of the psychophysiological changes that occur during the experiments.

Definite changes in the physical sphere accompany the emotions. Bleuler,[2] e.g., says of affectivity, " Certain affects extend our muscles, others relax them or they produce some other distribution of the muscular tension." When a sudden change takes place in any one—say he gets pale or flushes, sighs, fidgets— we presume that some definite affective process is going on in him. According to Bleuler (p. 15) the affect is a generalized reaction ; according to Breuer and Freud this reaction exhibits a " whole series of voluntary and involuntary reflexes through which, as experience teaches us, the affects become discharged." [3] A reaction of this kind can apparently occur spontaneously, or it may be provoked by a conversation or by some word ; it can take place consciously if the emerging images are associatively connected with the ego complex,[4] or remain unconscious if they do not enter into this connexion. Since a " complex " represents the " total number of ideas which relate to some definite emotionally toned event " (chapter ii), and the emotional tone is nothing but " an affective condition which is accompanied by physical innervation," [5] such reactions must especially arise after complexes.

Two methods require consideration in investigating the physical

---

[1] 1909.

[2] *Affektivität, Suggestibilität, Paranoia*, pp. 7 and 15.

[3] *Studien über Hysterie*, p. 5. (Leipzig and Vienna, 1895; new edition 1908.)

[4] Jung understands by the ego complex "the ideational mass of the ego which we believe to be accompanied by the potent and ever-living feeling tone of our own body." (*The Psychology of Dementia Præcox*, 1909, translated by Peterson and Brill.)

[5] Jung, *The Psychology of Dementia Præcox*, p. 38.

accompaniments of complexes : the one is the subjective method, the other the objective or method through expression.[1]

Now, the persons tested are not always able to talk about their deepest emotions or to remember emotionally toned events. We are thus dependent upon the method through expression, " which comprises all physical symptoms through which the feelings are outwardly displayed, as well as the movements brought about by the feelings." [2]   This objective method can be joined to the association test as elaborated by Jung.

When complexes are present certain disturbances occur in the association experiment—" complex indicators." They are external manifestations of the complex, and conditioned by the emotional tone accompanying it.   In our tests we differentiate in this way the indifferent from the complex associations, placing the reactions which show objective disturbances in a special group.   We next differentiate between unconscious and conscious complex associations.   Our investigations were directed towards finding out whether in the association experiment there are external changes peculiar to each group.

For this purpose we used Sommer's apparatus for the three dimensional determination of tremors, Marey's pneumograph, and the galvanometer.

PART I

TESTS WITH SOMMER'S APPARATUS FOR RECORDING MOVEMENTS IN THREE DIMENSIONS

Freud says [3] : " All our activities proceed from psychic stimuli (inner or outer) and terminate in innervations."   Martius writes [4] that " when a person at rest is submitted to psychological experiments, involuntary movements are not the exception but the rule. They do not only occur with strong and sudden stimuli, or with feelings of fear and expectancy ; they are also connected with every observation, with every effort of attention."   Preyer [5] showed that the hand can write down automatically figures which have been vividly present as ideas.   These movements are to some extent made accessible to experimental observation by

---

[1] Wundt, *Physiologische Psychologie*, Bd. II, 5th edition, 1903.
[2] Wundt, op. cit p. 267.
[3] *Interpretation of Dreams*, p. 426.
[4] *Beiträge zur Psychologie und Philosophie*, Bd. I, Heft 4 (Leipzig, 1905); *Ueber die Lehre von der Beeinflussung des Pulses und Atmung durch psychische Reize*, p. 431.
[5] *Die Erklärung des Gedankenlesens.* (Leipzig, 1886.)

Sommer's [1] apparatus. Sommer writes [2] : " If physiognomy is
(on the other hand) regarded as a factor in the general theory of
expression we try, in place of the old-fashioned physiognomy,
to apprehend the movements of expression just where they are
most readily accessible to presentation and measurement. The
human hand seems most clearly to express these movements for,
like the face, it expresses mental states through these movements ;
for experimental purposes the hand has the advantage over the
face of relatively greater simplicity." A detailed description of
the apparatus will be found in Sommer's book, together with an
illustration. [3]

The principle of the apparatus is the decomposition, by means
of a system of levers and apparatus for equilibrization, of the
movements of the hands into the three dimensions of space
and their transference to a kymograph. Three curves are described on the kymograph, of which the upper corresponds to to-
and-fro or push movements, the middle to lateral, and the lower
to vertical or pressure movements. The subject's hand is fixed
to the apparatus as described by Sommer. The index and middle
fingers are fastened to a plate attached to the equilibrization
apparatus, and the arm is supported in an elbow-socket.

The first test showed at once that the apparatus had some
undesirable secondary effects. First, the pressure and push
movements were very inconstant ; they bent upwards or down-
wards, backwards and forwards, very considerably. The subject
had to be constantly on the watch to maintain the hand in the
same position. This caused very great muscular tension, and
so a large part of the finer involuntary movements were lost.
(One subject, indeed, got cramp by endeavouring throughout the
experiment to keep the hand in one position.) Moreover, the
position of the hand was very largely dependent on the voluntary effort of the subject. The lateral curve was the most
constant, and so in this work we deal only with observations
about changes of lateral movements.

The association test was carried out in the usual way. The
moment of the stimulus and reaction were marked by means of
a Morse-key on the kymograph. The distance of both strokes
was measured at the completion of the test in seconds. A respiratory curve was also traced on the kymograph because, according
to Martius, [4] the arm movements are influenced by the movements
of the chest. The respiratory waves and the individual fluctua-

---

[1] Sommer, *Lehrbuch der psychopathologischen Untersuchungsmethoden.* (Berlin
and Vienna, 1899.)

[2] *Ibid.,* p. 95.                    [3] *Ibid.,* p. 97.

[4] *Beiträge zur Psychologie und Philosophie,* loc. cit.

tions of the lateral curve were measured by means of a nonius. Before beginning the experiment all the starting parts of the single curves must be brought into a vertical line with a plummet, for any slight displacement of the curves would affect the results considerably.

Curves at rest were first taken, the subject being placed in a position where he was subjected to no stimulus. The fluctuations in the lateral curves were then found to run parallel with the respiratory waves, each respiratory curve corresponding to one fluctuation of the lateral curve, except at several places where a sudden quivering movement was observed. At rest the movements of the arm coincide to a certain extent with the fluctuations of the thorax. Our results agree with those of Martius,[1] who found the same relationship in his investigations with the plethysmograph.

The question now arises whether this relationship holds good in association experiments.

We must mention, however, that we had great technical difficulties in working up the curves, for many of the fluctuations in the lateral curve were so small that they could only be measured with great difficulty. The figures so obtained only approximately express the actual values, and this indirectly influences the results. The results given by Sommer's apparatus, therefore, must be received with caution.

Twenty-five associations were taken on six subjects and the size of the respiratory waves compared with the waves of the lateral curve. The tests were (excepting with two persons) carried out twice, at intervals of two to three days. This plan was adopted in all the tests referred to in this work. One could thus see if the phenomenon was constant in the same person, and whether the experimental excitation was lessened or altogether absent at the second test. Jung and Peterson [2] point out that in consequence of the unusual situation (the submission to experiment) the excitation was so great that the stimulus-words could not be apperceived in their full meaning ; this gave rise to incomplete assimilation and to imperfect preparation for the stimulus-word. Thus the whole experiment was disturbed, whilst in the second experiment, when the subject was more accustomed to the conditions, the changes were much more typical. A decline of the experimental excitation could be proved at the second test, unless, of course, there accidentally arose some cause of disturbance independent of the experiment.

Before reviewing the tests we must briefly explain the figures given. The amplitudes of the single respiratory waves and

[1] Loc. cit.          [2] *Brain*, vol. xxx, 1907, p. 199.

fluctuations of the transverse curves were measured directly after each stimulus of the series, separated into complex and indifferent associations,[1] added together, and their arithmetical mean calculated. The figures in the tables are the arithmetical mean of the amplitudes in millimetres, the Latin numerals indicating the serial number of the amplitudes after an association. These numbers are represented graphically in the figures. Each number, which expresses the size of the amplitude of the representation as well as the transverse waves, was entered in single (millimetre) squares of a millimetre paper, the columns thus formed showing the size of the amplitudes. But since some of our numbers are not absolute, but only comparative, values, only as many of the numbers were entered in the millimetre squares as would make the comparison of the different amplitudes visible.

The most general numbers taken from the six subjects tested will be first given ; these refer to the respiratory and lateral curves which were obtained by adding together the indifferent and the complicated.

|  | I | II | III | IV | V | VI | VII |
|---|---|---|---|---|---|---|---|
| Respiratory waves . . | 8·7 | 8·6 | 8·8 | 8·8 | 8·9 | 8·7 | 8·6 |
| Lateral oscillations . . | 0·6 | 0·8 | 0·8 | 0·8 | 0·9 | 0·8 | 0·8 |

As the table shows, the two series run parallel, except for the first and last waves ; a deeper inspiration follows stronger movement of the arm. To a certain extent the strength of the arm movements depends upon the depth of respiration.

FIG. 1

FIG. 2

There are naturally individual deviations from the averages, but among the individual numbers are some which conform to this rule in a very high degree :

|  | I | II | III | IV | V | VI | VII |
|---|---|---|---|---|---|---|---|
| Respiratory curve . . | 13·2 | 14·1 | 13·4 | 13·6 | 13·9 | 15·3 | 12·1 |
| Lateral oscillations . . | 0·8 | 1·1 | 0·6 | 0·6 | 1·0 | 0·3 | 0·5 |

[1] The absence or presence of " complex indicators " distinguishes indifferent from complex reactions.

Here all the waves agree except the sixth, whose amplitude is very small in contrast with a very large amplitude of respiration.

How do the motor experiments of expression behave with indifferent and complicated associations respectively ?

The following are the changes in the curves with indifferent stimuli :

| | I | II | III | IV | V | VI | VII | |
|---|---|---|---|---|---|---|---|---|
| Respiratory waves | 8·1 | 8·5 | 8·5 | 8·6 | 8·5 | 8·3 | 8·6 | Fig. 1 |
| Lateral oscillations | 0·5 | 0·5 | 0·8 | 0·8 | 1·0 | 0·8 | 0·7 | |

The parallelism is here very slight (Fig. 1), although the figures show at the levels of both curves a certain similarity. After complex stimuli we get the following curves :

| | I | II | III | IV | V | VI | VII | |
|---|---|---|---|---|---|---|---|---|
| Respiratory waves | 8·6 | 8·6 | 9·4 | 8·7 | 8·8 | 8·9 | 8·3 | Fig. 2 |
| Lateral oscillations | 0·8 | 0·8 | 0·8 | 0·9 | 0·8 | 0·8 | 0·9 | |

Although a certain similarity can be noticed after indifferent stimuli, in some places there is, except for the two first waves, which are without significance, not merely no agreement but a marked dissimilarity.

The arm movements and respiration correspond most closely in conditions of rest, least of all with complexes. The deviations shown by the indifferent curve are also probably referable to the fact that the association experiment is a psychical activity. The indifferent stimulus-words may be regarded as small and transitory stimuli which effect changes in the mental state; " mental processes of the simplest kind exhibit phenomena of activity." [1] These phenomena are naturally expressed by altered innervation. There is, besides, another factor of perhaps greater importance ; among the indifferent reactions there are probably many complexes. The stimulus-words followed in our tests after relatively long pauses, for we had to wait to note the changes in the curves. The subject could consequently recover himself during the pause and compose himself for the new stimulus-word. The influence of perseveration is thus lost, so that probably a few critical reactions are to be found among the indifferent ones. We have seen that after complexes the agreement between the respiratory and lateral curve is removed, so it is possible that some few complexes influenced the indifferent curves.

We are justified in concluding, therefore, that the movements of the hand behave differently with complexes from what they do with indifferent stimuli ; that is to say, with complexes the

[1] Martius, loc cit., p. 512.

arm movements are less dependent upon oscillations of the chest than when at a state of rest.

A few single curves will be now given.

(1) With indifferent stimuli :

|  | I | II | III | IV | V | VI | VII |
|---|---|---|---|---|---|---|---|
| Respiratory curves . . | 3·0 | 3·5 | 3·5 | 3·2 | 3·5 | 3·4 | 3·7 |
| Lateral oscillations . . | 0·9 | 1·6 | 2·6 | 2·7 | 2·7 | 2·4 | 2·9 |

(2) With complex associations ·

|  | I | II | III | IV | V | VI | VII |
|---|---|---|---|---|---|---|---|
| Respiratory curves . . | 4·5 | 4·5 | 4·5 | 4·7 | 3·3 | 4·0 | 3·4 |
| Lateral oscillations . . | 1·5 | 0·8 | 1·6 | 1·6 | 0·8 | 1·1 | 2·4 |

The parallelism is present with indifferent stimuli, almost entirely absent with complexes.

We have seen that there is in general a difference between indifferent associations and complexes as regards the kind of movement by which they are expressed. Let us next see if this difference extends to the intensity of these movements.

We shall here compare the oscillations of the lateral curves with indifferent stimuli and with complex associations.

Again we proceed from the most general figures ; they represent the arithmetical mean of the amplitudes obtained by adding all the curves together.

The A.M. of the amplitudes of the lateral curves is :

(1) Indifferent stimuli, 0·5 mm. per association.
(2) Complex    ,,     0·7 mm. ,,    ,,

This ratio was found in five subjects. In three persons with whom the tests were being carried out it occurred in both tests.

Only one subject shows an exception :

(1) Indifferent stimuli, 2·2 mm. per association.
(2) Complex    ,,     1·6 mm. ,,    ,,

Unfortunately, this contradictory behaviour could not be more closely examined owing to lack of material. Whether this was an affect type or only an exception conditioned by the experimental method remains uncertain. It is, however, remarkable that this phenomenon occurred in both experiments with this subject.

Of the six subjects, five showed stronger movements of the hands with the complex associations, whilst one showed weaker movements.

The best single curve of the first group shows the same behaviour (i.e. stronger innervations).

|  | I | II | III | IV | V | VI | VII |
|---|---|---|---|---|---|---|---|
| (1) Indifferent stimuli . | 0·5 | 0·3 | 0·4 | 0·6 | 0·4 | 0·3 | 0·3 |
| Complex stimuli . | 1·3 | 1·8 | 1·4 | 1·1 | 1·5 | 0·6 | 1·4 |

With complexes, therefore, the involuntary movements of the arm are other than with indifferent stimuli.  This points to a condition of altered innervation.

Binswanger has shown in the last chapter that involuntary movements often occur in the association experiment, provoking large galvanic deviations because they are for the most part accompanied by strong emotional tones.  Even in a state of rest we noticed an oscillation, and during the association test we also found such isolated oscillations on the curves.  These oscillations occurred quite involuntarily, and were apparently quite irregular in their course.

The question arises as to whether the same law may be discovered here likewise.

For this purpose, these isolated oscillations were counted off after each association and the average of these numbers calculated. An endeavour was made to measure the intensity of the thrust, but no general laws could be made out.

The average of these isolated oscillations among six subjects was :

(1) Indifferent stimuli, 1·9 oscillations to an association.
(2) Complex        ,,      2·2        ,,        ,,        ,,

Among three other subjects :

(1) Indifferent stimuli, 2·2 oscillations to an association.
(2) Complex        ,,      1·1        ,,        ,,        ,,

It is noticeable in the case of every subject that when only two tests were made the same phenomenon occurred in both, except in one of the first six subjects tested.  In this person there were fewer oscillations after complexes in the first test, but in the second test there were more than after indifferent stimuli.

An example will best illustrate these relationships :

(1) Test I—
    With indifferent stimuli, 1 oscillation ;  with complexes, 2 oscillations.

(2) Test II—
    With indifferent stimuli, 1·7 oscillations ;  with complexes, 2·8 oscillations.

There are two types that react differently with complexes.  The one shows increased excitability under affect ;  the other is inhibited by affect.  Bleuler says of these types [1] :

---

[1] Loc cit., p. 25.

"Many people who correspond fairly well to the classical 'sanguinary' temperament react quickly and intensively to emotional impressions, but the affect soon wears off. When the storm is over they are as before. It is as if the acute reaction, the shouting, abusing, hitting out, had 'abreacted' the affect. But if, on the other hand, temperament leads people to suppress the affect, this probably conduces, under conditions not yet ascertained, to displacements and conversions in Freud's sense of pathological reaction. Subsequent abreacting may, under certain conditions, cure the symptoms of the disease which has consisted in a 'converted' affect."

Summarizing our results, we see in the association experiment a series of changes of the psychomotor innervation which deviates from the state of rest :

(1) The relationship between arm movements and the thoracic oscillations is increased with complexes.

(2) The movements of the hand are stronger (with one exception) with complex than with indifferent stimuli.

(3) The frequency of the individual involuntary oscillations is sometimes less with complexes, sometimes greater. This peculiar behaviour leads us to think of the existence of two types.

## PART II

### RESPIRATION

Affects scarcely ever occur without changes in respiration.[1] Respiration is partly under control of the voluntary nervous system, though under ordinary conditions it proceeds involuntarily. Wundt [2] says of the physical accompaniments of the feelings that they only have value as objective signs of emotional processes when subjective observation confirms the presence of the emotion. But in the next sentence he says : "Experience nevertheless tells us that traces of emotion may escape subjective observation." The association experiment enables us to diagnose emotionally toned complexes, and this means the diagnosis of the emotion that accompanies it.

Let us consider the behaviour of respiration in the association experiment.

It may be premised that the actual pronouncing of the reaction-

[1] Wundt, *Physiolog. Psychologie*, Bd. II, p. 271, 5th edition, 1903.
[2] Loc. cit., p. 271.

word influences respiration very slightly,[1] probably because of the close connexion between respiration and speech.[2] The tension of the laryngeal muscles and the vocal cords is different in expiration and respiration. These changes are not passive but arise from active innervation.[3]

Before proceeding to our own tests we will first deal with the results of previous workers :

Mosso [4] obtained no conclusive results in regard to changes in respiration from stimulation of the sense organs.

Delabarre [5] found that during attention respiration increased in depth and frequency, but decreased during intellectual effort.

Lehmann [6] says that concentration of the attention causes irregular breathing. Strongly unpleasant sensations are accompanied by stopping of the breathing, succeeded by a few short and irregular respirations. Pleasant stimuli cause an increased depth of breathing.

Mentz states [7] that with acoustic stimuli there is generally a simultaneous prolongation of respiration, which, however, decreases if the stimulus is maintained. In involuntary attention there is generally a prolongation of the respiration, in voluntary attention the respiration is much diminished. With affects he found there generally occurred a prolongation of respiration. With increasing strength of the affect there is increasing height or depth of the respiration. He also found changes in the form of respiration with different affects.

Zoneff and Meumann [8] are of opinion that with " sensual " attention the respiration is almost entirely inhibited, with " intellectual " attention it is only partially so or not at all. Directly after the stimulus the breathing increases in depth. With increase of respiration it becomes more superficial. In involuntary concentration of the attention inhibition of respiration occurs. Changes in breathing are, moreover, dependent upon the attention's capacity of adaptation. In pleasurable states there is

[1] Minnemann, *Beiträge zur Psychologie und Philosophie*, Bd. I, Heft 4 ; *Atmung u. Puls bei aktuellen Affekten.*

[2] Jung and Peterson, *Brain*, vol. xxx, 1907.

[3] Tigerstedt, *Lehrbuch der Physiologie des Menschen.* (Leipzig, 1905.)

[4] *Diagnostik des Pulses in bezug auf die lokalen Veränderungen desselben.* (Leipzig, 1879.) *Ueber den Kreislauf des Blutes im menschlichen Gehirn.* (Leipzig, 1881.)

[5] *Revue Philosophique*, vol. xxxiii, 1892.

[6] *Die körperlichen Aeusserungen psychischer Zustände*, translated by F. Bendixen, Pt. I. (Leipzig, 1899.)

[7] Wundt, " Ueber die Wirkung akusticher Sinnesreize auf Puls und Atmung," *Phil. Studien*, Bd. XI, 1895.

[8] Wundt, " Ueber Begleiterscheinungen psychischer Vorgänge bei Atem und Puls," *Phil. Studien*, Bd. XVIII, 1902.

acceleration and superficiality of the respiration ; in painful states it is slower and deeper. All emotional reactions provoke more changes in the thoracic than in abdominal breathing.

Gent [1] says that in transitory conditions of tension the respiratory curve is scarcely changed ; the same is true of permanent emotional tension. During mental work the curve is somewhat flatter and more extended, but reaches its former height or exceeds it after completion of the work. In emotional excitement the respiration is more superficial, accelerated, and irregular. Gent also investigated various affects, using the reproduction method. He found that under a stimulating affect the respiration becomes irregular, distinctly deeper, and accelerated as compared with the normal curve. With pleasant affects the respiration is more frequent, often more superficial, and the size of the respiration changes considerably. In unpleasant affects which cause excitement and depression respiration becomes irregular, generally flatter and slower.

Martius [2] writes that in mental activity respiration is accelerated as compared with respiration in a state of rest, whilst the fluctuations decreased in height. Neither pleasure nor pain shows anything characteristic in the symptoms which might enable these to be differentiated from one another. There is a type of affect which is marked by a greater slowing down of the pulse and respiration as compared with rest.

Minnemann [3] says : In strong excitement respiration is accelerated and deepened. It becomes irregular under strong affects. It is most regular in the condition of rest of the norm. But a normal curve is only a relative term. There are great differences in the behaviour of different subjects towards affective stimuli. Speaking influences respiration but little.

Now as to our own experiments. The method was the same as that used by Jung with Peterson and Ricksher.[4]

A Marey pneumograph was fastened round the thorax, and the respiratory movements were recorded on a smoothly running kymograph. The amplitudes were measured and calculated as already described.

The tests were carried out on fourteen subjects, twice with each person, and about twenty-five associations were done each time. If we consider the respiratory curve with indifferent

[1] Wundt, "Volumpulskurven bei Gefühlen und Affekten," *Phil. Studien,* Bd. XVIII, 1902.
[2] Loc. cit.          [3] Loc. cit.
[4] Jung and Peterson, loc. cit. ; Jung and Ricksher, "Further Investigations on the Galvanic Phenomenon and Respiration in Normal and Insane Individuals," *Journal of Abnormal Psychology,* vol. ii, No. 5.

associations, the arithmetical mean of the amplitudes of all the respiratory waves in both tests amounted to :

| I | II | III | IV | V | VI | VII |
|------|------|------|------|------|------|------|
| 11·4 | 11·7 | 12·1 | 12·2 | 12·4 | 12·2 | 12·3 [1] (cp. Fig. 3) |

The first respiration after the stimulus-word is very small in comparison with all the others. The amplitudes that follow increase up to the sixth, when the amplitude becomes suddenly smaller and increases again after the next deep breath. Respiration increases in depth after the stimulus.[2] The irregularity in the curve after the fifth respiration is probably referable to the fact that some complex associations were included among the indifferent ones. Other factors may also have a share.

FIG. 3

What is the respiration like with complex associations ? The A.M. of the amplitudes in both series of tests is :

|  | I | II | III | IV | V | VI | VII |  |
|-----------|------|------|------|------|------|------|------|------|
| Complex | 11 | 11·2 | 11·3 | 11·4 | 11·4 | 11·7 | 11·9 | see |
| Indifferent | 11·4 | 11·7 | 12·1 | 12·2 | 12·4 | 12·2 | 12·3 | Fig. 3 |

A comparison of the two curves shows that the respiratory curve is almost the same ; the amplitude is smallest directly after the stimulus-word, subsequently the respiration increases in depth. But alongside this there is one remarkable difference : the respiratory curve is distinctly lowered with complex as compared with indifferent associations. The average of the seven amplitudes after indifferent stimuli is 12 mm., and after complexes it is 11·4 mm. In consequence of the more superficial and strained respiration with complexes, the average volume of the inspiratory and expiratory air is less.

Almost all authorities agree that with mental activity breathing

---

[1] That the figures do not agree with those on p. 537 is due to our having had more subjects, none of whom were the same persons. Since the size of respiration fluctuates considerably in individuals, the average with different subjects is very different.

[2] Zoneff and Meumann, loc. cit.

becomes more superficial. Zoneff and Meumann [1] regard this as due to the action of attention, Gent [2] to the action of tension. But attention is accompanied by conditions of tension. According to Bleuler [3] attention is nothing but one aspect of affectivity. In our association experiment we have to deal with complexes, i.e. with ideas which are held together by their affect. (See chapter ii.)

Going somewhat further, we shall now inquire whether the behaviour of the respiratory curve with the complex associations remains the same in both series of tests as against the curve of the indifferent associations. The arithmetical mean of the amplitude with (a) indifferent stimuli:

|          | I    | II   | III  | IV   | V    | VI   | VII  |
|----------|------|------|------|------|------|------|------|
| 1st test . | 12·2 | 12·2 | 12·8 | 13·1 | 13·1 | 12·7 | 12·8 |
| 2nd test . | 10·7 | 11·3 | 11·4 | 11·3 | 11·7 | 11·7 | 11·9 |

(b) complex stimuli:

|          | I    | II   | III  | IV   | V    | VI   | VII  |
|----------|------|------|------|------|------|------|------|
| 1st test . | 11·4 | 11·8 | 12·1 | 12·0 | 11·8 | 12·2 | 12·4 |
| 2nd test . | 10·7 | 10·6 | 10·6 | 10·8 | 11·0 | 11·3 | 11·5 |

The course of the respiratory curve is similar in the second test to the first, as is the behaviour of the respiratory curve with indifferent and complex associations. In the second test the respiration is not as deep as in the first test with either indifferent or complex associations.

Our subjects were not used to the experiment, and as a rule they did not like it very much, consequently there was more excitement at the first test than at the second. Gent [4] came to the conclusion that with exciting stimuli the respiration was distinctly deeper compared with the normal. Minnemann [5] found the same and says that under constant strong excitation the respiration is deeper. With constant excitation the respiration becomes stronger and the complexes cause a flattening of respiration; this latter quality of the complex does not seem to be suspended under excitement. We shall discuss an exception to this rule later.

The rule is, accordingly, that with complexes respiration becomes more superficial. As mentioned above, there are exceptions; five subjects showed at the first test a deepened respiration at complexes. The A.M. of the amplitudes in these cases was:

|                        | I    | II   | III  | IV   | V    | VI   | VII  |
|------------------------|------|------|------|------|------|------|------|
| (a) Indifferent stimuli | 10·5 | 10·7 | 11·4 | 11·5 | 11·5 | 11·4 | 11·4 |
| (b) Complexes .         | 11·0 | 12·2 | 12·2 | 11·7 | 11·9 | 11·9 | 12·2 |

---

[1] Loc. cit.          [2] Loc. cit.          [3] Loc. cit.
[4] Loc. cit.                                 [5] Loc. cit.

These five subjects showed strong complex constellations, for on the average there were nineteen complexes to ten indifferent associations.  In the second test they had thirteen complexes to twelve indifferent associations.  In the remaining subjects there were fourteen complexes to ten indifferent associations in the first test, whilst in the second test there were thirteen to eleven. These strong complex constellations in the first five subjects point to great excitation (see p. 555).

The transition from " conscious ' to " unconscious " is really fluid,[1] and it must be admitted that many complexes, for the most part actual complexes, can under certain conditions assume such strength and clearness that they can be easily denoted as conscious.  For the purpose of marking off the conscious from the unconscious complexes we proceeded as follows : At the end of the experiment the subject was asked if anything definite had come into his mind at the complex association, or if it recalled any event important to him.  Those reactions, which showed complex indications and to which an affirmative answer was given, we counted among the conscious complexes. All the others, including those where the statement was not quite certain, were reckoned to the unconscious complexes. There is no doubt as to the conscious complexes, the subject was clearly aware of them ; whilst among the unconscious complexes there may be some which were more or less conscious, as well as perseverations.

The respiratory curve is characteristic for both conscious and unconscious complex associations.  The A.M. of the amplitudes for unconscious complexes is :

|  | I | II | III | IV | V | VI | VII |
|---|---|---|---|---|---|---|---|
|  | 10·5 | 11·2 | 11·4 | 11·4 | 11·2 | 11·7 | 11·7 Fig. 4 |
| (Indifferent  . | . 11·4 | 11·7 | 12·1 | 12·2 | 12·4 | 12·2 | 12·3 Fig. 3) |

This curve (Fig. 4) is somewhat similar to that of the joint common complex curve.  This is explained by the fact that the unconscious complexes can influence the curve more strongly than the conscious complexes, for there were 239 unconscious to 111 conscious complexes.  It, moreover, resembles the indifferent curve.  But there is one considerable difference—the size of the respiration.  Almost all the amplitudes are smaller than in Fig. 3, and, moreover, the curve is more irregular than the previous curves.  The first respiration is much compressed ; the tension of respiration is more intensive in its after-effect at the end of the respiratory period, i.e. the depth of respiration increases relatively towards the end of respiration.  The difference between

[1] Freud, *The Interpretation of Dreams.*

the first and last respirations in the size of the amplitude amounts to 1·2 with unconscious complexes, whilst with indifferent associations it is only 0·9 mm.   The after-effect is, therefore, stronger with unconscious complexes.   The arithmetical mean of all seven

Unconscious                    Conscious
FIG. 4

amplitudes amounts to 12 with indifferent associations, and to 11·3 with unconscious complexes.

When these tests are considered separately the unconscious complexes find expression in the same way in the respiration. The A.M. of the amplitudes is :

|          |   | I    | II   | III  | IV   | V    | VI   | VII  |
|----------|---|------|------|------|------|------|------|------|
| 1st test | . | 10·8 | 11·8 | 12·0 | 11·7 | 11·1 | 12·3 | 12·1 |
| 2nd test | . | 10·2 | 10·7 | 10·8 | 11·2 | 11·3 | 11·2 | 11·3 |

So far as curves and size of respiration go these are like Fig. 4. But the second test series shows smaller amplitudes than the first.   This must be connected with the greater experimental excitation of the first test.   The curve also, especially in Test I, is very irregular.   Two factors may here take part : first, the strong experimental excitation in Test I ; secondly, the inclusion of some conscious complexes among the unconscious complexes. This supposition is supported by the fact that in the second test the curve is more regular, and the two respiratory curves with conscious complex association are almost parallel (see below).

One subject who had only three conscious complexes, although there were several doubtful ones which were accordingly ascribed to the unconscious, shows the same respiratory course with unconscious complexes.   In this subject the A.M. of the amplitude with unconscious complexes is :

|                |   | I    | II   | III  | IV   | V    | VI   | VII   |
|----------------|---|------|------|------|------|------|------|-------|
|                |   | 9·7  | 15·0 | 15·3 | 15·7 | 14·2 | 15·2 | 15·8  |
| (Indifferents  | . | 11·8 | 14·6 | 16·9 | 16·4 | 17·5 | 16·7 | 18·4) |

These tests show that unconscious complexes inhibit respiration.

We now come to the conscious complexes. The A.M. of the amplitudes for both tests is :

|  | I | II | III | IV | V | VI | VII | |
|---|---|---|---|---|---|---|---|---|
|  | 11·8 | 11·3 | 11·1 | 11·4 | 11·5 | 11·9 | 12·2 | Fig. 4 |
| (1. Indifferents . | 11·4 | 11·7 | 12·1 | 12·2 | 12·4 | 12·2 | 12·3 | Fig. 3) |
| (2. Unconscious com- |  |  |  |  |  |  |  |  |
| complexes . | 10·5 | 11·2 | 11·4 | 11·4 | 11·2 | 11·7 | 11·7 | Fig. 4) |

The first respiration is very deep, then there is inhibition, which becomes even stronger at the third respiration than that at the unconscious complex at the same place ; this occasions a greater release of tension ; at the end the respiration is as deep as with indifferent associations. In the first half the curve with conscious complexes is quite different from that of the unconscious complex, for in the former the inhibition is preceded by deep breathing, whilst in the latter inhibition follows directly upon the stimulus-word. We have seen that under strong excitement respiration is deepened. According to Zoneff and Meumann [1] pain strengthens the activity of respiration. When a conscious complex is met, excitation follows accompanied by pain ; this can be occasionally confirmed by subjective observation. The emotional tone of such complexes is very strong ; the emerging mass of ideas engross the attention and this finds expression in the form of subsequent inhibition, while the condition provoked by the attention forms " the psychological background for the emotional toned complex." [2] The curve of respiration is therefore different with conscious complexes from what it is with unconscious complexes, and we can say with Freud [3] "that excitations whose ideas are incapable of reaching consciousness act upon one another differently, proceed differently, and are led to other modes of expression than those we call ' normal,' when we are aware of the content of ideas."

With unconscious complexes the respiratory curve is inhibited as compared with indifferent associations, as it is also with conscious complexes, for the average of the seven amplitudes amounts to 11·7 in the latter (indifferents 12, unconscious complexes 11·3). The fact that this inhibition is less than with unconscious complexes depends, perhaps, upon the excitation occurring at the beginning with the conscious complexes, the after-effect of which does not permit the inhibition to develop completely. With affects which are composed of isolated kinds of emotion, these

[1] Loc. cit.
[2] Jung, loc. cit.
[3] *Bruchstück einer Hysterieanalyse*, p. 102.

emotions influence each other, cross each other, and may even cancel the action of each other.[1]

Do these phenomena occur with conscious complexes in both tests ?

The A.M. of the amplitudes is :

|  | I | II | III | IV | V | VI | VII |  |
|---|---|---|---|---|---|---|---|---|
| Test I . . . | 12·5 | 11·9 | 11·7 | 12·0 | 12·0 | 12·4 | 12·8 | Fig. 5 |
| Test II . . . | 11·2 | 10·7 | 10·5 | 10·9 | 11·0 | 11·5 | 11·7 | |

These curves show not only the same characteristics as the curve in Fig. 4, but are almost the same. The reason for this must be that here we have only selected associations, i.e.

FIG. 5

only purely conscious ones. The second curve is flatter than the first, but that is nothing new.

We gave five tests on p. 543 having deeper respiration with complex associations, which we left over for later discussion. These respiration curves will be decomposed into their components, i.e. into conscious and unconscious complexes.

The A.M. of the amplitudes is :

|  | I | II | III | IV | V | VI | VII |  |
|---|---|---|---|---|---|---|---|---|
| (a) Unconscious complexes . . | 9·9 | 11·8 | 11·6 | 11·0 | 11·6 | 11·5 | 11·6 | Fig. 6 |
| (b) Conscious complexes . . | 12·4 | 12·7 | 12·5 | 12·3 | 11·6 | 12·4 | 13·0 | |
| (c) Indifferents . | 10·5 | 10·7 | 11·4 | 11·5 | 11·5 | 11·4 | 11·4 | |

The curve agrees but little with the former curves save with that found in indifferent associations. The curve with conscious complexes has the greatest amplitudes ; with unconscious complexes it oscillates towards the limit of the respiratory curve of indifferent associations. The respiratory curve of unconscious complexes is less like that of the indifferents than the conscious complex ; as compared with the latter it is but slightly deepened. The A.M. of all the amplitudes is 11·2 indif-

[1] Wundt, *Physiolog. Psychologie*, Bde. II and III.

ferents, 11·3 unconscious complexes, and 12·3 conscious complexes. The respiratory volume is therefore greatest in the latter. The difference in the indifferent reactions and unconscious complexes is a minimum. So far as the course of the curve is concerned, the curve of conscious complexes approximates most nearly to the average type, i.e. it shows at the beginning a deepened

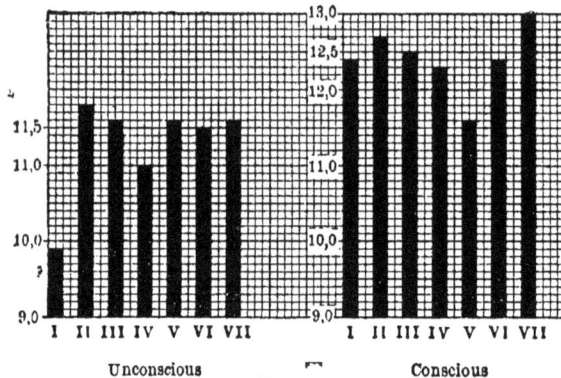

Unconscious     Conscious

FIG. 6

respiration with inhibition occurring later. The respiration with unconscious complexes deviates most of all from the average ; it is the most irregular. Perhaps this curve is caused by a few conscious complexes which are included among the unconscious on account of the subject's faulty introspection. We have already mentioned that these curves occurred with the first test when the subject was excited, and we must add that these experiments had frequently to be interrupted. It would seem that when an affect exists external to the experiment, only the conscious complexes obtain expression in the form of increased respiration, whilst with unconscious complexes this deviates but slightly from that of indifferent associations.

SUMMARY

(1) With complexes the respiration is inhibited as compared with the respiration with indifferent associations.

(2) Unconscious and conscious complexes differ from one another in their type of respiration ; unconscious complexes show strong inhibition of respiration, whilst with conscious complexes there is excitation in addition to the inhibition.

(3) In an affect not directly related to the experiment the conscious complexes seem only to be able to gain expression through increase in the respiration.

(4) Respiration becomes deeper under strong experimental excitation.

(5) There are two types of complex respiration. The one shows itself by laboured breathing. The inspiration is more difficult, there is a kind of dyspnœa, and a feeling of oppression which is probably a partial manifestation of the feeling of anxious dread. The causes of this oppression are not known. Such respiration almost corresponds to the respiration type of unconscious complex associations. In the other type the respiration is irregular, alternately deep and superficial, quasi-sighing. The sighs either occur spontaneously or when a complex is aroused during conversation. When asked the reason for the sighing one is often told that an emotional-toned event has been stirred up. This second kind of breathing corresponds to our respiratory type with conscious complexes. Further investigation must be made to decide the question whether these two types can be separated in practice.

## PART III

### RESPIRATION AND THE PSYCHOGALVANIC PHENOMENON

We have seen that respiration is influenced in typical ways by conscious and unconscious complexes. As Veraguth's work [1] and Binswanger's (chapter xii) have shown, the psychogalvanic reflex has a relationship of its own to these conditions.

The experiment was so arranged that changes in the galvanometer and in respiration were simultaneously recorded on a revolving drum. The method was one which was used and described by Jung and his collaborators, to whose works the reader should refer. [2]

Twenty tests were carried out on ten persons. Binswanger has shown in the last chapter the meaning of the psychogalvanic phenomena. A change in innervation is expressed by a decrease of the electrical resistance, as shown by fluctuations of the current. The deviations are stronger with complexes than with indifferent associations. The length of the deviations increases with the number of complex indicators. Unconscious complexes are also shown by the galvanometer. In distraction of the attention the stimulus provokes slight or no deviations, and the resistance of the body increases.

Veraguth [3] has demonstrated the same results. The psycho-

[1] *Das psychogalvanische Reflexphänomen.* (Karger: Berlin, 1909.)

[2] *Journal of Abnormal Psychology*, vol. i, No. 6, and vol. ii, No. 5; *Brain*, vol. xxx, 1907; also Binswanger, chapter xii.

[3] Op. cit.

galvanic reflect consists in a fluctuation in intensity of the electric current. The current decreases when at rest, increases under stimulus. With acoustic stimuli fluctuations only arise when the stimulus excites the attention of the subject. With the strength of the emotional tone the size of the deviation increases. Veraguth maintains, against Binswanger, that besides the strength of the emotional tone actuality plays a part ; but this is only an apparent contradiction, for actuality is included in the concept of emotional tone.

In certain circumstances all objective complex signs may be absent and the complex is only betrayed by the large galvanic deviation. We have found this often in our tests. Morton Prince and Peterson [1] showed in a person with treble dissociation that the ideas split off from consciousness gave galvanic deviations.

If the galvanometer is an indicator of affective processes, all physical manifestations of affectivity should run parallel with the fluctuations of the galvanometer, at least to a certain extent. Veraguth [2] made such tests in a person with injury of the skull, but obtained no definite results. Jung and Peterson [3] took pneumographic and galvanometer curves and came to the following conclusions.

Fluctuations in respiration often coincide in time with galvano-metric fluctuations, but often they do not. It may happen that the galvanometer curve shows distinct fluctuations whilst the respiratory curve is quite steady, and conversely (in a case of dementia præcox). Disturbances in respiration come to rest less quickly than the galvanometer. They are influenced by conscious affects, if these are strong ; they are dependent upon the will, while the psychogalvanic phenomena is not ; and they are also dependent upon other intellectual processes.

In a subsequent investigation Jung and Ricksher [4] found that the size of the respiration varies ; that during the rise of the galvanometer curve the respirations become smaller, whilst they become larger during its fall. There is no relationship between diminution of the amplitude and the height of the galvanic curve ; here all kinds of individual variations occur. In dementia præcox no changes may occur in the galvanometer curve, whilst they can be found in the respiratory curve. No rules could be determined as to the rapidity of respiration.

The working out and measurement of our curves was done in

---

[1] " Experimentelle Untersuchungen über psychogalvanische Reaktionen von mitbewussten (unterbewussten) Vorstellungen in einem Falle von vielfacher Persönlichkeit," *Journal für Psychologie und Neurologie*, Bd. XIII, 1908.

[2] Loc. cit.        [3] Loc. cit.

[4] *Journal of Abnormal Psychology*, vol. ii.

the following way : A straight line was drawn from the apex of the galvanic curve through the synchronic moment of the respiratory curve, and then the respiratory amplitudes were measured forwards and backwards and written down as follows :

| Before the galvanic apex : | After the galvanic apex : |
|---|---|
| First respiration wave | First respiration wave |
| Second ,, ,, | Second ,, ,, |
| Third ,, ,, | Third ,, ,, |

etc.

The apex corresponds to the strongest galvanic deviation, i.e. to the space between the highest point of the galvanic wave and its base.

I should like to mention here that there are really two kinds of courses for the galvanic deviation. The one shows a rapid rise and fall with great deviations, so that the curve presents more or less of an acute angled apex. The other, with the same base, rises more slowly, the deviation is maintained rather longer at the maximum height, and then again falls slowly ; the apex is flat and the curve looks like a flattened cone. To measure such an apex it must be bisected, but this rather alters the relation of the respiratory amplitudes to the acute-angled apices. This behaviour, however, only slightly influenced the results.

In working out psychological material, where we have but few objective points to which to cling, and more especially in an experimental method which puts very little obstacle to the freedom of the psychological process, it is impossible to eliminate all sources of error. It is, e.g., easily possible that a complex assimilates to a stimulus-word to which it is related without further disturbance, but that nevertheless there is a considerable galvanic deviation. In this case the association would be counted among the so-called indifferents simply from want of objective signs. This occurs somewhat often. Again, since the distinction between " conscious " and " unconscious " is really very gradual, certain complexes of strong emotional tone may be unconscious in one person with bad introspection which would be long since conscious in another person with a good insight into himself. In this way it may easily happen that occasionally complexes, whose quantum of excitation really depends upon consciousness, do still remain in the class of the unconscious. The class of conscious complexes, as may be readily understood, is the purest and least disturbed. Still, all the irregularities to which attention has been drawn form the exception and not the rule.

The next question is whether the maximal deviations correspond with the alteration in respiration. The A.M.'s of the respiratory amplitudes of both series of tests amount to, with indifferent associations :

|  | Before |  | Apex of G.D. |  | After |  |  |
|---|---|---|---|---|---|---|---|
| III | II | I |  | I | II | III | IV |
| 11·8 | 13·0 | 13·0 | 6·08 | 13·0 | 13·4 | 13·2 | 13·1 Fig. 7 |

The apex corresponds to the height of the deviation, its size is given in the figures under apex of galvanometer

Indifferent        Complexes

Fig. 7

deviations. The figures before and after the apex, given serially in Latin numerals, signify the size of the respiratory amplitudes.

There is nothing of special interest about this curve except that the respiration seems to be somewhat checked near the apex ; after the apex it increases in depth.

Complex associations :

|  | Before |  | Apex of G.D. |  | After |  |  |
|---|---|---|---|---|---|---|---|
| III | II | I |  | I | II | III | IV |
| 11·8 | 12·7 | 12·1 | 7·78 | 12·2 | 12·7 | 12·3 | 13·4 Fig. 7 |

The smallest respiratory curves coincide with the height of the galvanic deviation. After the apex the amplitudes are larger than before the apex. The same phenomenon occurs with indifferent associations. Our results agree with those of Jung and Ricksher[1] ; with the up stroke of the galvanometer curve respiration is smaller ; with the down stroke it is greater.

This behaviour occurred in both tests.

(a) Indifferent associations :

|  |  | Before |  | Apex of G.D. |  | After |  |  |
|---|---|---|---|---|---|---|---|---|
|  | III | II | I |  | I | II | III | IV |
| 1st test . | 12·7 | 13·6 | 13·7 | 6·21 | 13·8 | 14·5 | 14·0 | 13·9 |
| 2nd test . | 11·0 | 12·5 | 12·3 | 5·95 | 12·2 | 12·3 | 12·4 | 12·3 |

[1] Loc. cit.

(b) Complex associations :

| | Before | | | Apex of G.D. | After | | | |
|---|---|---|---|---|---|---|---|---|
| | III | II | I | | I | II | III | IV |
| 1st test . | 12·7 | 13·0 | 12·5 | 7·38 | 12·4 | 12·9 | 12·8 | 14·5 |
| 2nd test . | 11·0 | 12·4 | 11·8 | 8·15 | 12·0 | 12·5 | 11·9 | 12·4 |

Except with the indifferent associations of the first test the smallest respiratory amplitudes coincide with the apex of the galvanometer deviation. In all the curves respiration is deeper after the apex than before. With indifferent and complex associations respiration is deeper in the first test than in the second. The galvanometer deviations are likewise greater in the first than in the second series of the indifferent associations. The difference of the deviation with indifferent and complex associations amounts to 1·17 in the first, 2·20 in the second tests. The greater deviations with indifferent associations, and the weaker differentiation of these in the first test when respiration is also deeper as compared with Test II, suggest a certain experimental excitation (see p. 534). The contention previously advanced, that under permanent excitation respiration becomes deeper, is supported by these figures.

Now as to the behaviour of conscious and unconscious complexes. The A.M. of the respiratory amplitudes of the two tests with unconscious complexes is :

| | Before | | | Apex of G.D. | After | | | |
|---|---|---|---|---|---|---|---|---|
| | III | II | I | | I | II | III | IV |
| | 11·8 | 12·6 | 12·1 | 7·57 | 12·3 | 12·6 | 12·1 | 12·7 Fig. 8 |

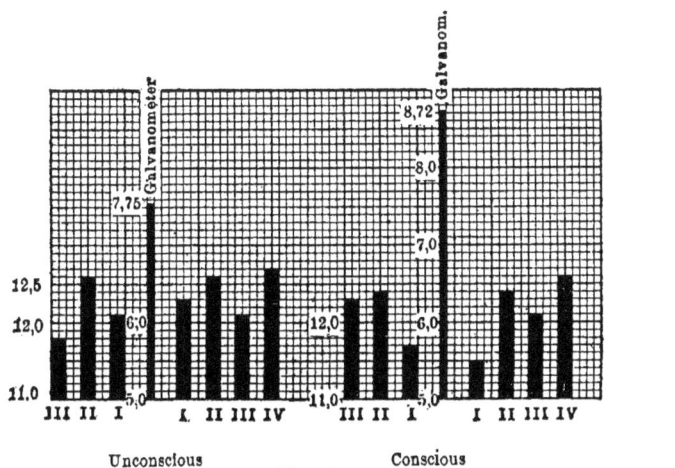

Fig. 8

The A.M. of the respiratory amplitudes with conscious complexes is :

| | Before | | Apex of G.D. | After | | | |
|---|---|---|---|---|---|---|---|
| III | II | I | | I | II | III | IV |
| 12·3 | 12·4 | 11·7 | 8·72 | 11·5 | 12·4 | 12·1 | 12·6 Fig. 8 |

The largest deviations coincide with the smallest respiratory amplitudes. This relationship is seen most distinctly by comparing the above figures and tables. The greater the deviations the smaller the amplitudes of respiration grouped in the immediate proximity of the apex. The greatest galvanic deviation and the strongest inhibition of respiration arise at the height of the development of affect. These great changes in innervation occur with conscious complexes. (In the previous section, in conscious complexes the third inspiration was the most superficial; this corresponds here to the first one before the apex. But this will be shown to be no contradiction.)

The same behaviour is observed when the two series of tests are considered apart.

The A.M. of the amplitude of respiration is :

(a) Unconscious complex associations :

| | | Before | | | Apex of G.D. | After | | | |
|---|---|---|---|---|---|---|---|---|---|
| | III | II | I | | | I | II | III | IV |
| 1st test | 12·7 | 12·5 | 12·2 | | 7·95 | 12·1 | 12·6 | 12·4 | 13·0 |
| 2nd test | 11·0 | 12·7 | 12·0 | | 7·20 | 12·5 | 12·6 | 11·8 | 12·5 |

(b) Conscious complexes :

| | | Before | | | Apex of G.D. | After | | | |
|---|---|---|---|---|---|---|---|---|---|
| | III | II | I | | | I | II | III | IV |
| 1st test | 12·3 | 13·0 | 12·3 | | 8·29 | 12·1 | 12·8 | 12·9 | 14·3 |
| 2nd test | 12·3 | 11·9 | 11·1 | | 9·50 | 10·9 | 12·1 | 11·3 | 10·9 |

If we place together the galvanic deviations, apart from respiration :

With indifferent associations the G. deviation is 6·08
,, unconscious complexes ,, G. ,, ,, 7·57
,, conscious ,, ,, G. ,, ,, 8·72

Conscious complexes therefore form the largest deviations. There is a difference in the strength of the deflections between conscious and unconscious complexes of 0·86, and between unconscious complexes and the indifferents of 1·78.

The ratios are exactly similar in the tests taken separately.

Test  I : Indifferent associations, G. deviation, 6·21
    Unconscious complexes, G.   ,,   7·95
    Conscious complexes,  G.   ,,   8·29

Test II : Indifferent associations, G.   ,,   5·95
    Unconscious complexes, G.   ,,   7·20
    Conscious complexes,  G.   ,,   9·50

In the second test the deviations are more differentiated in consequence of the diminution of experimental excitation. The individual figures of the separate tests behave exactly the same as the average figures, with one exception.

On the average, complex associations are accompanied by greater galvanic deviations than are indifferent associations. The conscious especially are more intensive than the unconscious complexes. This fact says that, *ceteris paribus*, the maximum of changes in innervation coincides with consciousness. The action of consciousness seems, as a rule, to belong to complexes of the strongest psychophysical influence. I express this view with diffidence because there are exceptions to this rule, as we shall see below.

We have now learnt that conscious complexes show greater galvanic deviation than unconscious ones. We have already mentioned that in our experiments the effect of perseveration was often unable to find expression. But perseveration can be so strong that after a reaction, apparently innocent, disturbances suddenly occur in the next reaction, such as false reproduction, prolonged reaction, times becoming gradually shorter, etc. Such associations, which only look like complexes because of the perseverating emotional tone, generally appear to be accompanied by smaller galvanic deviations. Sometimes the emotional tone of a complex is so strong that, despite the long pauses in our experiment, perseverations are seen in the reactions following. For this reason it has happened that associations have been sometimes included in the class of the unconscious complex association which were not really complexes, and this naturally has altered the total results. To obviate to some extent this source of error we proceeded as follows : with every subject we first took the total number of conscious complexes and selected from them the largest galvanic deviations (50 per cent. of the total), and then calculated the mean ; the same was done with the unconscious complexes.

This procedure was based upon the following reasoning : if we count among the unconscious complexes all the associations with complex signs when a complex is not conscious, we should certainly have among these no inconsiderable number of pure perseverations. In such cases, according to all previous experience, the galvanic deviation seldom reaches the size of the greatest deviation with true complexes. Thus with perseverations the deviations tend to be relatively low. This method of the greatest galvanic deviations eliminates the perseverations as far as possible.

We had ten subjects for the experiments with the galvanometer. We will first give the average figures of both tests according to the above method of calculation.

A.M. of the greatest galvanometer deviations with

| Conscious complexes | Unconscious complexes |
| --- | --- |
| 11·0 | 9·0 |

The average figures of the two tests separately are :

| | Conscious complexes | Unconscious complexes |
| --- | --- | --- |
| Test I  . | 10·5 | 8·7 |
| Test II  . | 11·5 | 9·4 |

On the average, therefore, the greatest (selected) deviations in both tests are stronger with conscious than with unconscious complexes. They are, as we have seen elsewhere, stronger and more differentiated in the second test than in the first.

These are the universal relationships. But if we proceed to the individual figures of the subjects separately the relationships become rather different. There are exceptions, so that individual deviations as well as their total average are in some test cases greater with unconscious than with conscious complexes.

*Subject No. 1 : Doctor, 28 years old.*—In the first test the deviations are, on the average, greater with unconscious complexes than with conscious ones :

| Conscious complexes | Unconscious complexes |
| --- | --- |
| 9·0 | 9·3 |

Twenty associations were taken, eleven of which were complexes and four of these eleven were conscious. The A.M. of their reaction-times amounts to 1·8 second, the P.M. 1·7 second. No disturbances of reproduction ; no faults. The complexes are recognized chiefly by too long reaction-times. The subject was acquainted with the association experiment. The second test showed nothing special as regards the galvanometer deviations.

*Subject No. 2 : Medical Student, 24 years old, rather emotional.*—At the first test the average of the galvanic deviations was :

| Conscious complexes | Unconscious complexes |
| --- | --- |
| 9·4 | 9·8 |

Altogether thirty associations, among these twenty-two complexes, of which seven were conscious, five reproduction disturbances, one fault. A.M. = 2 seconds ; P.M. = 1·8 second. The subject was acquainted with the association experiment. The second test went quite smoothly and showed nothing special.

*Subject No. 3: Student of Chemistry, 20 years old.*—In the first test there were eighteen associations, including eight complexes, of which three were conscious; four disturbances in reproduction, no faults. A.M. = 1·6 second; P.M. = 1·4 second. The average size of the galvanometer deviations is smaller with unconscious complexes than with conscious (unconscious 3·9; conscious 4·3), the biggest deviation with the former being, however, just as big as with the latter. The association to this deviation was:

| Stimulus-word | Reaction | R.T. | Reproduction G. | Deviations |
|---|---|---|---|---|
| Water | lake | 2 seconds | (fault) | 4·3 |

At the end of the test the subject was unable to suggest anything definite about this reaction. Subsequently he remembered a dangerous incident which had happened to him on a glacier. In the second test with twenty-three associations, there were fifteen complexes (three unconscious) and four disturbances in reproduction; the deviations were, on the average, greater with unconscious than with conscious complexes. The greatest deviation with the latter was 4·2; with the former, 6·4. The individual associations did not explain much about this behaviour. The A.M. and P.M. of the reaction-times is the same as in the first test.

*Subject No. 5: Student of Philosophy, 25 years old.*—First test shows nothing remarkable as to the deviations. In the second test the average of the galvanometer deviations is 14·5 with conscious complexes and 14·5 with unconscious complexes. Twenty-eight associations, among these being fifteen complexes, five of which were conscious. No disturbances in reproduction. Pronounced predicate type indicating a rather stronger emotional expression (Jung). Very emotional. A.M. = 2 seconds; P.M. = 1·9 seconds. The greatest galvanometer deviation :

| | | | R.T. |
|---|---|---|---|
| Conscious complexes | 15·3 | (journey — long) | 2·7 |
| Unconscious „ | 16 | (window — in the garden) | 3·0 |

*Subject No. 7: Medical Student, 23 years old.*—First test: twenty-seven associations, eighteen of which were complexes, two of these unconscious; nine disturbances in reproduction. The average of the galvanometer deviation with unconscious complexes was 3·9; with conscious, 4·3. The greatest galvanometer deviation :

| | | | R.T. | Reproduction |
|---|---|---|---|---|
| Conscious complexes | 4·3 | (frog — jump) | 1·9 | |
| Unconscious „ | 4·4 | (to aim — good) | 1·8 | (incorrect) |

Second test: twenty-nine associations, eighteen of these complexes, of which two were conscious; nine disturbed reproductions. Average of galvanometer deviations with conscious complexes = 9·5; unconscious = 8·9. Greatest galvanic deviation:

| | | | R.T. | Reproduction |
|---|---|---|---|---|
| Conscious complexes | 9·5 | (box — sand) | 1·8 | |
| Unconscious „ | 10·6 | (love — boy) | 1·6 | (incorrect) |

The reactions in both tests are predominantly predicates.

*Subject No. 8: Student of Philosophy, 25 years old.*—Nothing special with first test. In the second test twenty-six associations, of which seventeen were complexes and five of these conscious; three disturbances in reproduction; overwhelming number of reactions are predicates. A.M. = 1·7 second; P.M. =

1·6 second. Average of galvanic deviations with conscious complexes = 20·2 ; with unconscious = 14·4. The greatest galvanometer deviation :

|  |  |  |  | R.T. |
|---|---|---|---|---|
| Conscious complexes | 21·8 | (marriage | — once) | 2·8 |
| Unconscious „ | 26 | (paint | — faint) | 2·1 |

The association immediately preceding this unconscious one was a conscious association :

|  |  | G.D. | R.T. |
|---|---|---|---|
| Beet | big | 20·6 | 2·0 |

We may, perhaps, have a perseveration here.

*Subject No. 9 : Lady, Ph.D., 35 years old.*—First test : twenty-six associations, fifteen of which were complexes, four being conscious ; one disturbance in reproduction. Average. of the galvanic deviations with conscious complexes is 10·9, with unconscious = 10·2.
The greatest galvanometer deviation :

|  |  |  |  | R.T. | Reproduction |
|---|---|---|---|---|---|
| With conscious complexes | 11·4 | (tired | — jolly) | 2·1 | (incorrect) |
| With unconscious „ | 11·5 | (to whistle — whistle) | | 1·9 | |

It is possible that this was a perseveration, for the associations immediately preceding this association were :

|  |  | R.T. | G.D. | Ref. |  |  |
|---|---|---|---|---|---|---|
| 22. Modest | small | 2·0 | 9·3 | Uncertain | said to be conscious |  |
| 23. Floor | door | 1·9 | 11·1 | + | „ | unconscious |
| 24. To whistle | whistle | 1·9 | 11·5 | + | „ | unconscious |

In almost all the subjects there was a deviation which was greater with unconscious complexes than with conscious. Without a thorough psycho-analysis we cannot go more deeply into the individual associations. It must, however, be said that in many cases the deviations with conscious complexes can be very great in comparison with the unconscious ones, e.g. :

*Subject No. 6 : Medical Student, 23 years old, extremely emotional.*—A.M. = 2·1 seconds; P.M. = 1·8 second. Twenty-three associations, of which ten were complexes, five being conscious ; four disturbances in reproduction. The average of the galvanic deviation with conscious complexes = 32 ; with unconscious = 17·1. The greatest galvanic deviation was :

|  |  |  |  | R.T. | Reproduction |
|---|---|---|---|---|---|
| Conscious complexes | 42·0 | (month | — spring) | 4·7 | (incorrect) |
| Unconscious „ | 19·9 | (bride | — old maid) | 2·5 | |

This short list suffices to prove that our rule holds good that conscious complexes express themselves more strongly than unconscious ones, but that occasionally this rule has an exception —the unconscious complex producing a stronger deviation than the conscious. Whether this inversion of the law is to be apprehended in the sense of Freud's pathological reaction can be only determined by further experiments.

I would draw attention to the example given in Subject No. 3, where an association capable of existing in the conscious, but not conscious during the experiment, gave a deviation quite as large as the size of the deviation which corresponded to a conscious association.

It will be noted that the criterion of consciousness is based upon a subjective statement which may be often incorrect. But, as psycho-analysis teaches us, this is not of primary importance, for between conscious concealment and unconscious repression is but a step ; the difference is not one of kind, but only of degree.

## SUMMARY

### Part I.   Experiment with Sommer's Apparatus

Sommer's apparatus is, for various reasons, not an instrument adapted for the recording of the finer movements of expression. But by it we were able to prove that the movements of the arm or of the hand are stronger with complexes than with indifferent associations.

The respiratory movement of the thorax communicated to the arm in a state of rest and with indifferent associations seems to be so inhibited with complex associations that it is no longer communicated to the arm.

All the other movements of the curves are of external origin and have nothing to do with movement of expression, with the exception of certain involuntary tremors, which seem to conform to a rule which is not yet precisely determined.

### Part II.   Respiration

As contrasted with respiration during indifferent associations the size of respiration shows distinct diminution with complexes. This inhibition is found chiefly with unconscious complexes ; with conscious complexes a type of respiration occurs which is alternately compressed and deepened through excitation.

### Part III.   Respiration and Psychogalvanic Phenomena

The comparison of the psychogalvanic with the respiratory curves shows (in agreement with the results obtained by Jung and Ricksher) a diminution of the amplitude of respiration with the up stroke, and an increase with the down stroke, of the galvanic curve. The highest point of the galvanic curve coincides with the minimum of the amplitude of respiration. Conscious complex associations result as a rule in a greater galvanic deviation than do unconscious complex associations.

# BIBLIOGRAPHY

APTEKMANN, ESTHER. ' Expefimentelle Beiträge zur Psychologie des psychogalvanischen Phänomens," *Jahrb. f. psychoanalyt. u. psychopatholog.
Forschung.*, III (1913), 591–620.

ASCHAFFENBURG, GUSTAV. " Experimentelle Studien über Assoziationen,"
Kräpelin—*Psycholog. Arbeiten*, I (1896), 209–299 ; II (1899), 1–83 ; IV
(1904), 235–373.

ATHERTON, M. VALERIS, and WASHBURN, M.F. " Mediate Associations studied
by the Method of Inhibiting Associations : An Instance of the Effect
of 'Aufgabe,' " *Amer. J. Psychol.*, XXIII (1912), 101–109.

BAWDEN, H. " A Study of Lapses," *Psychol. Rev. Mon. Supp.*, III, 4 (1900), 122.

BECHTEREW. (a) " Ueber zeitliche Verhältnisse der psychischen Prozesse bei in
Hypnose befindlichen Personen," *Neurol. Zentralbl.* (1893).

 (b) "Ueber die Geschwindigkeitsveränderungen der psychischen Prozesse zu verschiedenen Tageszeiten," *Neurol. Zentralbl.* (1893).

BINET, ALFRED. " Le Diagnostique judiciaire par le méthode des Associations,"
*Année psychol.*, XVI (1910), 372–383.

BIRNBAUM, KARL. "Ueber den Einfluss von Gefühlsfaktoren auf die Assoziationen," *Monatsschr. f. Psychiat. u. Neurol.*, XXXII (1912), 95–123,
194–220.

BOLTE. " Assoziationsversuche als diagnostisches Hilfsmittel," *Allg. Zeitschr.
f. Psychiat.*, LXIV (1907), 619–630.

BURR, EMILY T., and GEISSLER, L. R. " An Introspective Analysis of the
Association-Reaction Consciousness," *Amer. J. Psychol.*, XXIV (1913),
564–569.

CLAPARÈDE, ED. *L'Association des Idées* (Paris : 1903), 426.

—— " La psychologie judiciaire," *Année psychol.*, XII (1905), 295–302.

CLAPARÈDE, ED., et ISRAÏLOVITCH. " Influence du Tabac sur l'Association des
Idées," *Compt. rend. Soc. biol.* (1902).

CORDES, G. " Experimentelle Untersuchungen über Assoziationen," *Philos.
Stud.*, XVII (1901), 30–77.

EASTMAN, F. C., and ROSANOFF. " Association in Feeble-minded and Delinquent
Children," *Am. J. of Insanity* (July 1912).

EBERSCHWELLER. *Untersuchungen über die sprachliche Komponente der Assoziation* (Zurich, 1908).

FÉRÉ, CHARLES. *The Pathology of the Emotions* (London : University Press,
1899), 525.

FRANZ, S. J., and WHITE, W. A. " The Use of Association Test in Determining
Mental Contents," *U. S. Gov. Hos. for the Insane*, Bull. I (1909), 55–71.

FREUD, SIGMUND. *The Psychopathology of Everyday Life* (Fisher Unwin, 1914).

—— *The Interpretation of Dreams* (Allen and Unwin, 1913).

GALLUS, KURT. "Ueber Assoziationsprüfung," *Zeitschr. f. psychother. u. mediz. Psychol.*, II (1910), 106–127.

GALTON, FRANCIS. "Psychometric Experiments," *Brain*, II (1879), 149–162.
—— *Inquiries into Human Faculty and its Development* (London: Macmillan and Co., 1883), 182–203.

GEISSLER, L. K. "A Preliminary Introspective Study of the Association-Reaction Consciousness," *Am. J. Psychol.*, XXI (1910), 597–602.
—— "Analysis of Consciousness under Negative Instruction," *Am. J. Psychol.*, XXIII (1912), 183–213.

GIESE, FRITZ. "Das Ich als Komplex in der Psychologie," *Arch. f. d. ges. Psychol.*, XXXII (1914), 120–165.

GRABOWSKY, ADOLF. "Die Anwendung der psychologische Tatbestands-diagnostik in der Strafrechtspraxis," *Monatsschr. f. Kriminalpsychol. u. Strafrechtsref.*, III, 163.
—— "Zur Frage der psychologische Tatbestandsdiagnostik," *Zeitschr. f. d. ges. Strafrechtswiss.*, XVI.

GROSS, A. "Zur psychologischen Tatbestandsdiagnostik als kriminalistisches Hilfsmittel," *Beitr. zur Psychol. der Aussage*, II (1904–1906), 436–439.
—— "Zur psychologische Tatbestandsdiagnostik," *Monatsschr. f. Kriminal-psychol. u. Strafrechtsref.*, II (1905), 182–184.
—— "Die Assoziationsmethode in Strafprozess," *Zeitschr. f. d. ges. Straf-rechtswiss.*, XXVI (1905), 19–40.
—— "Kriminalpsychologische Tatbestandsforschung," *Jurist.-psychiat. Grenz-fragen*, VII (1907).
—— "Zur Frage des Wahrnehmungsproblems," *Ref. in Beitr. zur Psychol. der Aussage*, II (1904–1906), 258–264.

GROSS, H. "Zur psychologische Tatbestandsdiagnostik," *Arch. f. Kriminal-anthrop. u. Kriminalistik*, XIX (1905), 49–59.


HAGGERTY, M. E., and KEMPF, E. J. "Suppression and Substitution as a Factor in Sex Differences," *Am. S. Psychol.*, XXIV (1913), 414–425.

HEILBRONNER, KARL. "Die Grundlagen der psychologischen Tatbestands-diagnostik," *Zeitschr. f. d. ges. Strafrechtswiss.*, XXVII, 601.

HENKE, F. G., and EDDY, M. W. "Mental Diagnosis by the Association-Reaction Method," *Psychol. Rev.*, XVI (1909), 399–409.

HUBER, EDWIN. "Assoziationsversuche an Soldaten," *Zeitschr. f. Psychol. u. Physiol. d. Sinnesorgans*, LIX (1911), 241–272.


ISSERLIN. "Die diagnostische Bedeutung der Assoziationsversuche," *Mün-chener Med. Wochenschr.*, No. 27 (1907).


JONES, ERNEST. "The Practical Value of the Word-Association Method in the Treatment of the Psycho-Neuroses," *Rev. of Neurol. and Psychiat.*, VIII (1910), 641–672.
—— *Papers on Psychoanalysis* (London: Baillière, 1913), 206–240.

JUNG, CARL G. "Ueber Simulation von Geistesstörung," *J. f. Psychol. u. Neurol.*, II (1903), 181–201.
—— "Zur psychologischen Tatbestandsdiagnostik," *Centralbl. f. Nervenheilk. u. Psychiat.*, XXVIII (n.s. XVI), (1905), 813–815.
—— "Die psychologische Diagnose des Tatbestandes," *Jurist.-psychiat. Grenzfr.*, IV (1906).
—— "On Psychophysical Relations of the Association Experiment," *Abnorm. Psychol.*, I (1906–1907), 247–255.
—— "The Association Method," *Am. J. Psychol.*, XXI (1910), 219–269.

KAKISE, HIKOZO. "A Preliminary Experimental Study of the Conscious Concomitants of Understanding," *Am. J. Psychol.*, XXII (1911), 14-46.

KENT, GRACE HELEN, and ROSANOFF. "A Study of Association in Insanity," *Am. J. of Insanity*, LXVII (1910), 317-377.

KOHS, SAMUEL C. "The Association Method in its Relation to the Complex and Complex Indicators," *Am. J. of Psychol.*, XXV (1914), 544-594.

KRÄPELIN, E. *Ueber die Beeinflussung einfacher psychischer Vorgänge* (Jena: Fischer, 1892), 258.

—— "Der psychologische Versuch in der Psychiatrie," Kräpelin—*Psycholog. Arbeiten*, I (1896), 1-91.

KRAMER, F. "Literaturbericht," *Beitr. zur Psychol. der Aussage*, II (1904-1906), 580-586.

KRAMER, F., und STERN, W. "Selbstverrat durch Assoziation," *Beitr. zur. Psychol. der Aussage*, II (1904-1906), 457-488.

KRAUS, O. "Psychologische Tatbestandsdiagnostik," *Monatsschr. f. Kriminalpsychol. u. Strafrechtsref.*, II (1905), 58-61.

KUTZINSKI, ARNOLD. "Ueber die Beeinflussung des Vorstellungsablaufes durch Geschichtskomplexe bei Geisteskranken," *Monatsschr. f. Psychiat. u. Neurol.*, XXXIII (1913), 78-109, 159-178, 254-279.

LADAME. "L'Association des Idées et son Utilisation comme Méthode d'examiner dans les Maladies mentales," *L'Eucéphale*, No. 8 (1908).

LANG, JOSEF B. "Ueber Assoziationsversuche bei Schizophrenen und den Mitgliedern ihrer Familien," *Jahrb. f. Psychoan. u. psychopat. Forsch.*, III (1913).

—— "Zur Bestimmung des psychoanalytischen Widerstandes," *Psychologische Abhandlungen* (edited by Dr. C. G. Jung), No. 1 (1914), 1-35.

—— "Eine Hypothese zur psychologischen Bedeutung der Verfolgungsidee," *idem.*, 35-52.

LANGFIELD, HERBERT SIDNEY. "Suppression with Negative Instruction," *Psychol. Bull.*, VII (1910), 200-208.

—— "Suppression with Negative Instruction," *Psychol. Rev.*, XVIII (1911), 411-424.

LEACH, HAZEL M., and WASHBURN, M. F. "Some Tests by the Association-Reaction Method of Mental Diagnosis," *Am. J. Psychol.*, XXI (1910), 162-167.

LEDERER, MAX. "Psychologische Tatbestandsdiagnostik," *Zschr. f. d. ges. Strafrechtswiss.*, XXVI (1906), 488-506.

LEVY-SUHL, MAX. "Ueber experimentelle Beeinflussung des Vorstellungsverlaufs bei Geisteskranken," *Zschr. f. Psychol. u. Physiol. d. Sinnesorgans*, XLII (1906), 128-161; XLV (1907), 321-340; LIX (1911), 1-90; also Leipzig: Barth (1911), 142.

—— "Ueber Einstellungsvorgänge in normalen und anormalen Seelenzuständen," *Zschr. f. psychother. u. mediz. Psychol.*, II (1910), 141-164.

LEY, AUG., et MENZERATH, PAUL. *L'Etude expérimentale de l'Assoc. des Idées dans les Maladies mentales* (Gand: Van der Häghen, 1911), 199.

LIPMANN, OTTO. "Sammelberichte: Neuere Arbeiten zur Psychologie der Aussage" (Wertheimer und Klein—"Psychologische Tatbestandsdiagnostik"), *Journal f. Psychologie u. Neurologie*, III (1904), 249.

—— "Literaturbericht," *Zschr. f. Psychol. u. Physiol. d. Sinnesorgane*, XLIII (1906), 157-158; XLVI (1907-1908), 306-307.

—— *Grundriss der Psychologie für Juristen* (Leipzig: Barth, 1908), 70-78 (2nd ed. 1914).

LIPMANN, OTTO. "Analyses bibliographiques: Psychologie judiciaire" (Otto Lipmann et M. Wertheimer: "Tatbestandsdiagnostische Kombinationsversuche), *Année Psychol.*, XIV (1908), 493–494.

—— "Die Spuren interessebetonter Erlebnisse und ihre Symptome" (Theorie, Methoden und Ergebrisse der "Tatbestandsdiagnostik"), *Beihefte, Zeitsch. f. angew. Psychol.*, I (1911), 1–96.

LIPMANN, OTTO, und WERTHEIMER, MAX. "Tatbestandsdiagnostische Kombinationsversuche," *Zschr. f. angew. Psychol.*, I (1907–1908), 119–128.

LÖFFLER. "Zur psychologische Tatbestandsdiagnostik," *Monatssch. f. Kriminalpsychol. u. Strafrechtsref.*, III, 449.


MARKUS, O. "Ueber Assoziationen bei Dementia Praecox," *Archiv. f. Psychiatrie*, XLVIII, I.

MAYER, A., und ORTH, J. "Zur qualitativen Untersuchung der Assoziation," *Zschr. f. Psychol.*, XXVI (1901), 1–13.

MENZERATH, PAUL. "Die sogenannten Komplexmerkmale beim Assoziationsexperiment" (Discussion by Sommer, Weygandt, Stern, Wertheimer, Dittrich), *Bericht 5. Kongress f. experim. Psychol.* (Leipzig: Barth, 1912), 170–175.

MEYER, A. "Normal and Abnormal Associations," *Psychol. Bull.*, II (1905), 242–259.

—— "The Problems of Mental Reaction Types, Mental Causes and Diseases," *Psychol. Bull.* (Aug. 1908).

MOLL, ALBERT. "Die Behandlung sexueller Perversionen mit besonderer Berücksichtigung der Assoziationstherapie," *Zeitschr. f. Psychother. u. mediz. Psychol.*, III (1911), 1–29.

MOORE, JARED S. "The Articulation of the Concepts of Normal and Abnormal Psychology," *Am. J. Psychol.*, XXV (1914), 283-287.

MORAVCSIK, E. "Experimente über das psychogalvanische Reflexphänomen," *J. f. Psychol. u. Neurol.*, XVIII (1911), 186–199.

MORAVCSIK, ERNST EMIL. "Diagnostische Assoziationsuntersuchungen," *Allg. Zschr. f. Psychiat.*, LXVIII (1911), 626–673.

MÜLLER, VICTOR J. "Zur Kenntnis der Leitungsbahnen des psychogalvanischen Reflexphänomens," *Monatsschr. f. Psychiat. u. Neurol.*, XXXIII (1913), 235–253.

MÜLLER und PILZECKER. *Experimentelle Beiträge zur Lehre vom Gedächtnis* (Leipzig, 1900).

MÜNSTERBERG. (a) "Die Assoziation sukzessiver Vorstellungen," *Zeitschr. f. Psychol.* (1890).

(b) *Beiträge zur experimentellen Psychologie* (1889–1893).


OTIS, MARGARET. "A Study of Association in Defectives," *Journal of Educational Psychology*, VI, 5 (1915), 271–288.


PELLETIER, M. *Les Lois morbides des Associations des Idées* (Paris: Rousset, 1904), 151.

PETERSON, FREDERICK. "The Galvanometer as a Measurer of Emotions," *Brit. Med. Journ.* (Sept. 1907).

PETERSON, FREDERICK, und JUNG, CARL G. "Psycho-physical Investigations with the Galvanometer and Pneumograph in Normal and Insane Individuals," *Brain*, XXX (1907), 153–218.

PETERSON, FREDERICK, and SCRIPTURE. "Psycho-physical Investigations with the Galvanometer," *Journ. of Nervous and Mental Diseases* (July 1907).

PFENNINGER, W. "Untersuchungen über die Konstanz und den Wechsel der psychologischen Konstellation bei Normalen und Frühdementen (Schizophrenen)," *Jahrb. f. psychoanalyt. u. psychopatholog. Forschung.*, III (1912), 481–524.

POTOTZKY, C. "Die Verwertbarkeit des Assoziationsversuchs für die Beurteilung der traumatischen Neurosen," *Monatsschr. f. Psychiat. u. Neurol.*, XXV (1909), 521–529.

RANSCHBURG, PAUL, und BALINT, EMERICH. "Ueber quantitative und qualitative Veränderungen geistiger Vorgänge im hohen Greisenalter," *Allg. Zschr. f. Psychiat.*, LVII (1900), 689–718.

READ, CHARLES F. "Application of the Word-Association Method to an Acute Psychosis," *Am. J. of Insanity*, LXVIII (1911–1912), 671–681.

RIKLIN, FR. (*a*) "Zur Psychologie hysterischer Dämmerzustände und des ganserschen Symptoms," *Psychol.-neurol. Wochenschr.* (1904).

—— (*b*) "Analytische Untersuchungen der Symptome und Assoziationen eines Falles von Hysterie," *Psychiat.-neurol. Wochenschr.* (1905), 449.

RING. "The Association Test and Psycho-Analysis," *Boston Med. and Surg. Jour.* (Jan. 7, 1909).

RITTERSHAUS, ERNST. "Ueber Tatbestandsdiagnostik," Vereinsbericht (Vorläufige Mitteilung), *Centralbl. f. Nervenheilk. u. Psychiat.*, XXXI (1908), 877–878.

—— "Die Komplexforschung," *J. f. Psychol. u. Neurol.*, XV (1909–1910), 61–83, 184–220; XVI (1910), 1–43.

—— "Zur psychologischen Differentialdiagnose der einzelnen Epilepsieformen," *Arch. f. Psychiat. u. Nervenkrankh*, XLVI (1910), 1–93, 464–545.

—— "Die Spuren interessebetonter Erlebrisse" und die "Komplexforschung," *Zeitschr. f. d. ges. Neurol. u. Psychiat.*, VIII (1911–1912), 273–283.

ROSANOFF, ISABEL R., and ROSANOFF, A. J. "A Study of Association in Children," *Psychol. Bulletin* (Jan. 1913).

RUSK, ROBERT R. "Experiments on Mental Association in School Children," *Brit. J. Psychol.*, III (1909–1910), 349–385.

SCHNITZLER, JOHANN GUSTAV. "Experimentelle Beiträge zur Tatbestandsdiagnostik," *Zeitschr. f. angew. Psychol.*, II (1908–1909), 51–91.

SCHOLL. "Versuche über die Einführung von Komplexen in die Assoziationen von Gesunden und Geisteskranken," Sommer: *Klinik für psychische u. nervose Krankh.*, III (1908), 197.

SCRIPTURE, E. W. "Experiments on Subconscious Ideas." *J. Amer. Med. Assoc.*, L. (1908), 521–523.

—— Reaction-Time in Nervous and Mental Diseases, *J. Ment. Sci.* (October 1916).

SIDIS, BORIS, and KALMUS, H. T. "The Study of Galvanometric Deflections due to Psycho-physiological Processes," *Psychol. Rev.*, XV (1908), 391–396; XVI (1909), 1–35.

SOMMER, R. *Lehrbuch der psychopathologischen Untersuchungsmethoden* (Berlin, Wien: Urban und Schwartzenberg, 1899), 326–388.

STEIN, PHILIPP, "Tatbestandsdiagnostische Versuche bei Untersuchungsgefangenen," *Zeitschr. f. Psychol. u. Physiol. d. Sinnesorgane*, LII (1909), 161–237.

STERN, WILLIAM. "Mitteilungen," *Beitr. z. Psychol. der Aussage*, II (1904–1906), 275–277, 440–441.

SUTHERLAND, ARTHUR H., *Critique of Word-Association Reactions: An Experimental Study*, Dissertation, Univ. of Chicago (1913), 46.

SWOBODA, HERMANN. *Die Perioden des menschlichen Organismus* (Leipzig: Deuticke, 1904), 135.

THUMB und MARBE. *Exper. Untersuchungen über die psychologischen Grundlagen der sprachlichen Analogiebildung* (Leipzig, 1901).

TOWN. "Associations in Practical Work for the Insane," *The Psychol. Clinic.* (1906).

TRAUTSCHOLDT, MARTIN. "Experimentelle Untersuchungen über die Assoziationen der Vorstellungen," Wundt's *Philos. Stud.*, I (1883), 213–250.

UMPFENBACH. "Literaturbericht," *Zschr. f. Psychol. u. Physiol. d. Sinnesorgane*, XXXIX (1905), 222–3, XL (1906), 69; XLIV (1907), 142–143; XLV (1907), 298–299.

VERAGUTH, OTTO. "Das psychogalvanische Reflexphänomen," *Monatsschr. f. Psychiat. u. Neurol.*, XXI (1907), 387; also Berlin: Karger (1909), 187.

WALITZKI. "Contrib. à l'Etude des Mensurations psychometr. d. aliénés," *Rev. phil.*, XXVIII.

WEBER, ERNST. *Der Einfluss psychischer Vorgänge auf den Körper* (Berlin: Springer, 1910), 426.

WELLS, FREDERICK LYMAN. "Some Properties of the Free Association Time," *Psychol. Rev.*, XVIII (1911), 1–23.

—— "A Preliminary Note on the Categories of Association Reactions," *Psychol. Rev.*, XVIII (1911), 229–233.

—— "Practice Effects in Free Association," *Am. J. Psychol.*, XXII (1911), 1–13.

—— "The Question of Association Types," *Psychol. Rev.*, XIX (1912), 253-270.

WELLS, FREDERIC LYMAN, and CADY, FREDERIC B. "A Critique of the Psycho-Galvanic Reflex, with Some Experiments" (Abstract of the Paper read at a Meeting of the New England Society of Psychiatry), *Amer. J. of Insanity*, LXV (1908–1909), 164–166.

WELLS, FREDERIC LYMAN, and FORBES, ALEXANDER. "On Certain Electrical Processes in the Human Body and their Relation to Emotional Reactions," *Arch. of Psychol.*, II, No. 16 (1908–1911, Mar. 1911), 39.

WERTHEIMER, MAX. "Experimentelle Untersuchungen zur Tatbestandsdiagnostik," *Arch. f. d. ges. Psychol.*, VI (1906), 59–131.

—— "Literaturbericht: Zur Tatbestandsdiagnostik," *Arch. f. d. ges. Psychol.*, VII (1906), 139–140.

—— "Tatbestandsdiagnostische Reproduktionsversuche," *Arch. f. Kriminalanthropol. u. Kriminalistik* (1906), 293.

WERTHEIMER, MAX, und KLEIN, JULIUS. "Psychologische Tatbestandsdiagnostik," *Arch. f. Kriminalanthropol. u. Kriminalistik*, XV (1904), 72–113.

WEYGANDT, WILHELM. "Zur psychologischen Tatsbestandsdiagnostik," *Monatsschr. f. Kriminalpsychol. u. Strafrechtsref.*, II (1905), 435-438.

WRESCHNER, ARTHUR. "Eine experimentelle Studie über die Assoziation in einem Falle von Idiotie," *Allg. Zeitschr. f. Psychiat.*, LVII (1900), 241–339.

—— "Die Reproduktion und Assoziation von Vorstellungen," *Zeitschr. f. Psychol. u. Physiol. d. Sinnesorgane*, Ergängungsband 3, Teil I (1907), 328; Teil II (1909), 599.

WUNDT, WILHELM. *Grundzüge der physiologischen Psychologie* (Leipzig: Engelmann, 1911), III, 436–450, 519–543.

YERKES, ROBERT M., and BERRY, CHARLES S. "The Association Reaction Method of Mental Diagnosis (Tatbestandsdiagnostik)," *Am. J. Psychol.*, XX (1909), 22-37.

ZIEHEN, TH. *Die Ideenassoziation des Kindes.*
—— *Sammlung von Abhandlungen aus dem Gebiete der pädagogischen Psychologie und Physiologie*, Bd. I, Heft. 6, 1898, 1-66 ; Bd. III, Heft 4, 1900, 1-59.
—— *Leitfaden der physiologischen Psychologie* (Jena : G. Fischer, 1906), 176-204.

# INDEX

www.ingramcontent.com/pod-product-compliance
Lightning Source LLC
Chambersburg PA
CBHW041254040426
42334CB00028BA/3005